Fodor's

UTAH

Welcome to Utah

From mountain-biking on slickrock to hiking past dinosaur fossils, Utah has thrilling adventures for everyone. World-class ski resorts are a haven for those seeking perfect powder, and national parks offer colorful geology lessons with natural arches, hoodoos, and mesas in brilliant ocher and red. History lovers can ponder petroglyphs made by the earliest inhabitants or explore the Mormons' pioneer past in Salt Lake City. At the end of the day, a hot tub and plush bed await. As you plan your trip to Utah, please confirm that places are still open and let us know when we need to make updates by writing to us at editors@fodors.com.

TOP REASONS TO GO

★ **National parks:** Spectacular Zion, Bryce Canyon, Arches, Capitol Reef, and Canyonlands.

★ **Outdoor fun:** Rafting the Colorado River, fishing at Flaming Gorge, and more.

★ **Sundance:** The resort is an artist's dream, the indie film festival a must-do.

★ **Skiing:** Superb snow, varied runs, and swanky resorts like Deer Valley and Snowbird.

★ **Frontier history:** The Pony Express Trail, Wild West towns, and the Golden Spike.

★ **Salt Lake City:** Remarkable Temple Square, plus renowned museums and gorgeous vistas.

Contents

MAPS

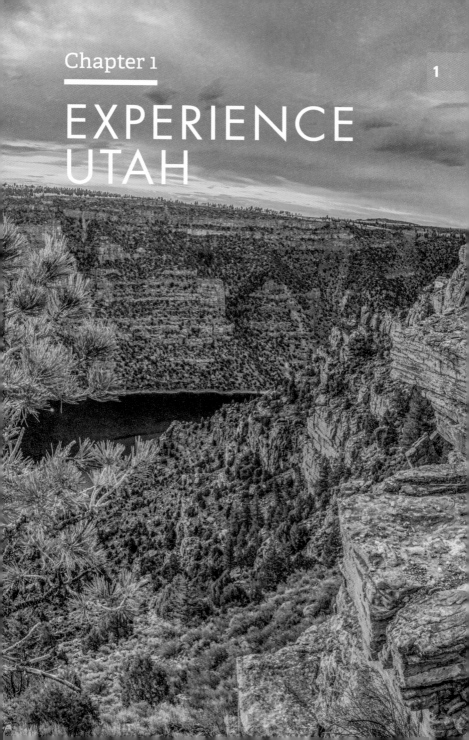

Chapter 1

EXPERIENCE UTAH

20 ULTIMATE EXPERIENCES

Utah offers terrific experiences that should be on every traveler's list. Here are Fodor's top picks for a memorable trip.

1 Winter sports

The "greatest snow on Earth," plentiful sunshine, and beautiful panoramas make Utah an incomparable winter playground. You'll find legendary resorts in and around Ogden, Salt Lake City, and Park City, such as Deer Valley (above). (Ch. 3, 4, 5)

2 Mirror Lake Scenic Byway

This stunning drive from just outside Park City up through the jagged Uinta Mountains is one of the state's unforgettable drives. (Ch. 6)

3 Bryce Canyon National Park

Drive the main park road for breathtaking views into the brilliant-hue natural amphitheater. Hiking trails let you scamper amid the hoodoos and rock formations. (Ch. 9)

4 Sundance

A ski resort and year-round artistic retreat, Sundance is best known for the annual independent film festival founded by Robert Redford and based in nearby Park City. (Ch. 4)

5 Dinosaur tracking

Utah is a treasure chest of dinosaur remains. See fascinating footprints at the Natural History Museum of Utah (above) in Salt Lake City and at Dinosaur National Monument. (Ch. 3, 6)

6 Delicate Arch

Recognize this arch? Utah's calling card is one of several incredible ones in Arches National Park. Enjoy the view on a 3-mile hike, and marvel at its scale. (Ch. 11)

7 Temple Square

Salt Lake City's 35-acre Temple Square hosts musical performances and other cultural events and is decked with amazing light displays during the holidays. (Ch. 3)

8 Two-wheeled fun

Mountain biking trails, such as the world-famous Slickrock Trail near Moab and the White Rim Trail (above), are unparalleled, and there are great trails in many ski areas, too. (Ch. 3, 4, 5, 6, 10, 12, 13)

9 Lake Powell

This stunning reservoir and vacation spot provides boat access to Rainbow Bridge National Monument. (Ch. 13)

10 Scenic Highway 12

Drive this remarkable 123-mile route from Red Canyon to the edge of Grand Staircase–Escalante National Monument en route to Capitol Reef. It's a thrilling series of curves and dips. (Ch. 6, 10)

11 Utah Olympic Park

Built for the 2002 Winter Olympic Games, this world-class recreational facility offers fun activities year-round, like tubing, ziplining, and more. (Ch. 4)

12 Farmers' markets

For amazing people-watching and to sample the state's bounty of produce, baked goods, craft beverages, and more, check out popular markets in Salt Lake City, Park City, and Ogden. (Ch. 3, 4, 5)

13 Logan Canyon Scenic Byway

Stretching 41 miles from Logan to the turquoise waters of Bear Lake, this curving ribbon of blacktop offers eye-popping scenery at every turn. (Ch. 5)

14 Capitol Reef National Park

Abundant with colorful arches, domes, and canyons and bisected by a dramatic 100-mile rift in the earth's crust, Capitol Reef is an underrated gem and less crowded than Utah's other parks. (Ch. 7)

15 Monument Valley

You may recognize this sweeping valley of mammoth sandstone monoliths from countless movies. Take the 17-mile self-guided driving tour for the most amazing views. (Ch. 13)

16 Moab

This outdoorsy gateway town to Arches and Canyonlands National Parks is a hub of artsy activity and a must for biking, hiking, rock climbing, and rafting. (Ch. 13)

17 Great Salt Lake

The best place to explore one of the earth's saltiest locales is Antelope Island, home to scores of bison and a pit stop for migrating birds. (Ch. 3)

18 Water sports

Skiing grabs the headlines, but fly-fishing, boating, and rafting, especially on the mighty Colorado River (above), make Utah a year-round river- and lake lover's destination. (Ch. 6, 13)

19 Salt Lake City

At the foot of the Wasatch Mountains, Utah's fast-growing capital has a stellar culinary, craft-beer, and cocktail scene, along with outdoor activities. (Ch. 3)

20 Zion National Park

The Angels Landing Trail (below), with its exhilarating overlooks, and the Narrows Trail are iconic experiences in this popular park. (Ch. 8)

WHAT'S WHERE

1 Salt Lake City. Home of the Church of Jesus Christ of Latter-day Saints, Utah's fast-growing capital city is a surprisingly progressive place.

2 Park City and the Southern Wasatch. Miners built this region, but these days powdery winter snow and ample summer sunshine draw visitors.

3 Northern Utah. Much of northern Utah lies within the Uinta-Wasatch-Cache National Forest, with breathtaking landscapes, miles of trails, and the turquoise waters of Bear Lake.

4 Dinosaurland and Eastern Utah. Imagine high Western skies and an endless range. Mirror Lake, Flaming Gorge, and Dinosaur National Monument deliver entirely unique experiences.

5 Capitol Reef National Park. Formed by cataclysmic forces that have pushed and compressed the earth, this otherworldly landscape is best known for the 100-mile-long Water-pocket Fold.

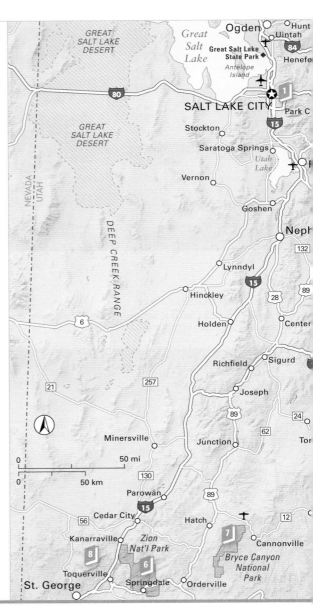

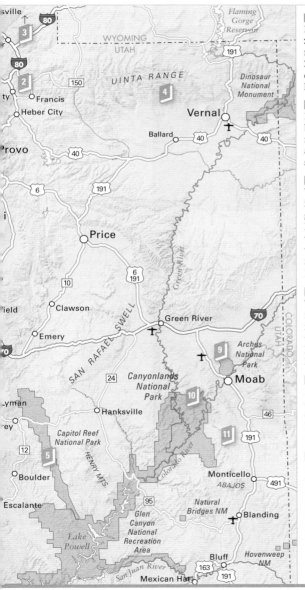

6 Zion National Park. Known for its sheer 2,000-foot cliffs and river-carved canyons, Zion is a must for anyone exploring the southern half of the state.

7 Bryce Canyon National Park. The bizarrely shaped, bright red-orange rocks known as hoodoos are this park's signature feature.

8 Southwestern Utah. Venture onto mesmerizing trails, stay in unique glamping resorts and laid-back lodges, and lose yourself in the expansive wilderness of Grand Staircase–Escalante National Monument.

9 Arches National Park. The largest collection of natural sandstone arches in the world are within this park, but the vast landscapes leave just as lasting an impression.

10 Canyonlands National Park. This sprawling expanse of gorges and cliffs is best enjoyed on a hike, mountain bike, or raft.

11 Moab and Southeastern Utah. Home to the world-famous Slickrock mountain biking trail, Moab is a countercultural retreat, and Lake Powell and Monument Valley offer stunning scenery.

The Best Ski Resort Lodges in Utah

MONTAGE, DEER VALLEY

The ultimate getaway in arguably America's best ski town, Montage Deer Valley sits in the heart of gorgeous Empire Pass and boasts a chic chalet vibe, incomparable service, a state-of-the-art 35,000-square-foot spa, and access to the country's most vaunted slopes.

ALTA'S RUSTLER LODGE, ALTA

A strikingly modern midrise resort in Little Cottonwood Canyon, Alta's Rustler Lodge contains spacious rooms with balconies overlooking the mountains while offering quick access to the resort's Transfer Tow and an impressive spa.

STEIN ERIKSEN LODGE, DEER VALLEY

Built in 1982 and impressively upgraded in recent years through millions of dollars of room and amenity upgrades, the venerable Stein Eriksen Lodge was a pioneer in bringing opulence to Utah's ski slopes.

SNOWPINE LODGE, ALTA

Built in 2019 on the site of the Alta's original 1938 hotel and incorporating some of that structure's original beams and stonework, the Snowpine Lodge has brought an unprecedented level of luxury and newness to this legendary ski area in Little Cottonwood Canyon. Downy duvets and tasteful throws cover the plush beds in the lodge's dapper rooms, which are outfitted with soft robes and slippers and L'Occitane bath products. There's a gastropub on the property as well as a full-service restaurant with tall windows that afford sweeping views of the slopes, which you can get to from the hotel in a snap via a new quad chairlift.

WALDORF ASTORIA, PARK CITY

Fans of old-world refinement and glamour favor the Waldorf Astoria Park City, with its lobby fit for royalty—guests are greeted by a grand staircase, Baccarat crystal chandelier, and centuries-old marble fireplace. A gondola whisks guests up to Canyons Village, which merged with neighboring Park City in 2005 to become the nation's largest ski area. Stylish rooms with fireplaces, balconies, and big jetted tubs provide an idyllic retreat from the elements.

SUNDANCE RESORT, SUNDANCE

Forever associated with founder Robert Redford and the prestigious film festival named for it, the lovely 95-room Sundance Resort hotel lies northeast of Provo—in the shadows

The St. Regis, Deer Valley

of 11,750-foot Mount Timpanogos, on the breathtaking Alpine Loop scenic byway. The 5,000-acre resort surrounding the hotel enjoys nearly 500 feet of snow annually, making it a favorite hideaway among ardent skiers who are happy without the buzzy scene of Park City (which is a 45-minute drive north). The convivial Owl Bar and Tree Room offer après-ski hobnobbing and first-rate dining, and the wood-panel rooms range from cozy standards to roomy high-ceiling lofts.

THE ST. REGIS, DEER VALLEY

The supremely sumptuous St. Regis, which lies at the base of Deer Valley, a short drive from downtown Park City, offers some of the most inviting accommodations in the state.

MARRIOTT'S MOUNTAINSIDE, PARK CITY

A huge perk that comes with staying at Marriott's MountainSide is the opportunity to stay right in the heart of historic downtown Park City, steps from the dozens of bars, restaurants, and shops.

THE CLIFF LODGE, SNOWBIRD

The Cliff Lodge is a mammoth, modern 10-story haven at the base of Little Cottonwood Canyon's Snowbird ski area, offering dozens of activities and amenities, from several bars and restaurants to a huge spa and a rooftop lap pool.

THE INN AT SOLITUDE, SOLITUDE

One of Big Cottonwood Canyon's only ski-in, ski-out lodgings, the upscale if not over-the-top fancy Inn at Solitude stands out for its friendly employees, warmly appointed slope-side rooms, and utter tranquillity. This resort is about resting and relaxing.

The Best Natural Wonders of Utah

FLAMING GORGE, NORTHEASTERN UTAH
Named by explorer John Wesley Powell in 1869 for the brilliant red-rock cliffs, this 91-mile gorge stretches from Wyoming into remote northeastern Utah. A popular reservoir was created via a massive 500-foot-tall dam in 1964.

CAPITOL GORGE, CAPITOL REEF NATIONAL PARK
Best explored from the 8-mile twisting and turning scenic drive that winds through it, this spectacular gorge was traversed by trains of pioneer wagons in the 1860s. Early travelers carved their names into the canyon walls.

HELL'S BACKBONE, GRAND STAIRCASE–ESCALANTE NATIONAL MONUMENT
The name of both a spectacularly scenic 38-mile gravel road and the rugged tract of dramatic canyons for which it's named, Hell's Backbone is one of the most Instagram-worthy drives or bike rides in the state.

THE NARROWS, ZION NATIONAL PARK
When it comes to amazing scenery, It's difficult to settle on one specific section of this beguiling park, but this 16-mile trail that actually requires wading—and sometimes swimming—through the Virgin River will take your breath away. Sheer orange and tan 2,000-foot walls soar above this improbably steep slot canyon.

DELICATE ARCH, ARCHES NATIONAL PARK
An hour or two before the sun sets, legions of park visitors make the steady 1½-mile uphill hike to view this iconic 52-foot-tall arch—it's depicted in everything from dazzling landscape photos to Utah's license plate—in the most alluring light. Part of the fun is that the hike begins at a 1906 cabin and involves crossing a scenic footbridge over a serene river.

GRAND VIEW POINT, CANYONLANDS NATIONAL PARK
Among the seemingly endless array of overlooks in 527-square-mile Canyonlands National Park, Grand View Point rewards visitors with perhaps the most eye-popping imagery. From this promontory at the end of Island in the Sky scenic drive, you can see for 100 miles up and down the Green and Colorado Rivers, toward the rugged rock formations of the park's Needles District, and out toward the jagged peaks of the Henry, Abajo, and La Sal mountain ranges.

The Narrows, Zion National Park

GREAT SALT LAKE, SALT LAKE CITY

Best experienced from the shores of Antelope Island State Park, which you reach via a 7-mile-long causeway north of Salt Lake City, this 1,700-square-mile inland sea is eight times saltier than the ocean—you can float in this buoyant water with the certainty that you will not sink. The island is traversed by hiking and bike trails and is home to a herd of around 600 to 700 bison.

SUNSET PEAK, BIG COTTONWOOD CANYON

Hikeable via the well-marked trails to Catherine Pass from both Brighton ski area in Big Cottonwood Canyon and Alta ski area in Little Cottonwood Canyon, this 10,648-foot summit rewards those who make the strenuous but manageable trek with 360-degree views of Heber Valley, Park City, Mount Timpanogos, and parts of metro Salt Lake City.

BEAR LAKE, NORTH-CENTRAL UTAH

The remarkable azure-blue waters of this 109-square-mile lake on the Utah–Idaho border look like they could be the Mediterranean or even some parts of the Caribbean, and the relative lack of commercialism along the shore results in stunning vistas unspoiled by tourist development. On hot summer days, it's one of the most beautiful places to swim and beachcomb in the state.

BRYCE CANYON, BRYCE CANYON NATIONAL PARK

Although actually a natural amphitheater rather than a canyon, this enormous expanse of fanciful hoodoos and spires seems to stretch as far as the eye can see and is accessible from numerous viewpoints and trails along the 19-mile park road.

What to Eat and Drink in Utah

SMALL-BATCH SPIRITS
It started with High West, which began producing Rendezvous Rye from a copper-pot still in Park City in 2007 and continues to serve it at the world's only ski-in, ski-out distillery and bar. Now Utah has more than 20 craft distilleries.

STEAKS AND BURGERS
Ranching has deep roots in Utah, and from the tony ski resorts up north to the solitary red rock canyons down south, the state abounds with great places to enjoy a dry-aged, locally raised steak or juicy burger—and that's to say nothing of the many establishments that serve bison, elk, venison, and other wild game meats.

CRAFT BEER
Although Utah has some strict liquor laws (which have continued to loosen in recent years), the state's craft brewing scene is booming, and it actually dates back many years. Venerable long-time favorites like Squatters Pub in Salt Lake City, Wasatch Brew Pub in Park City, and Zion Brewery in Springdale continue to impress, but newcomers keep opening, and there are now more than 40 craft brewers—as well as a few cideries— around the state.

LOCAL HONEY
Raw honey has been a sweet treat in these parts since the arrival of the region's earliest pioneer homesteaders, and these days you'll find it on ricotta toast in hip breakfast spots, in teas and lattes at cozy coffeehouses, and on plenty of desserts. But the best way to savor the fragrant, distinctive qualities of the local bees is to pick up a bottle at one of the many excellent farmers' markets around the state, including the Downtown Farmers Market in Salt Lake's Pioneer Park, the Park Silly Sunday Market in Park City, and the Farmers Market on Historic 25th Street in Ogden.

ARTISAN CHEESE
Especially in the north-central region, dairy farming is a big part of Utah's economy, and a natural byproduct of the state's nearly 100,000 dairy cows is cheese. Chefs at many locavore-driven restaurants use local products in their salads, sandwiches, and cheese-boards. Two makers of particular note, which you can also visit, are Beehive Cheese, just outside Ogden, which has earned national acclaim for its espresso-and lavender-rubbed Barely Buzzed cheddar, and Rockhill Creamery, known for its nutty raw-milk Wasatch Mountain Reserve alpine cheese.

HOUSE-ROASTED COFFEE
Utah's embrace of single-origin, house-roasted coffees has become ever stronger in recent years, and it's now easy to find first-rate coffeehouses throughout Utah, but Salt Lake City is the undisputed hub of java love. From longtime favorite Salt Lake Roasting to snazzy spots like Blue Copper Coffee and Publik Coffee Roasters, the state's largest city is rife with terrific places to sample a refreshing cold brew or a decadent Belgian-chocolate mocha.

Authentic Mexican food

TREE FRUIT

From the moment summer arrives until the cooler nights of autumn, Utahns rejoice at the opportunity to enjoy fresh fruit grown in the state's acres upon acres of peach, apple, cherry, apricot, and pear orchards. Farmers' markets are again a good bet, as are famous farms like the U-pick orchards in the Fruita Rural Historic District in Capitol Reef National Park and Rowley's Red Barn outside St. George. Maddox Ranch House restaurant outside Brigham City (aka "Peach" City) is famous for its peach pies, while Bryce Canyon Pines Restaurant serves heavenly apple and cherry pies.

AUTHENTIC MEXICAN FOOD

Immigrants from Mexico have long played a vital role in Utah's workforce, and as the state's percentage of residents who identify as Hispanic has increased from around 8% in 2000 to nearly 20% in 2020, the appetite for and availability of legit Mexican fare has increased. In Salt Lake City, you'll find one of the most celebrated Mexican restaurants in the West, Red Iguana, which specializes in several varieties of complex mole sauce. Plaza Mexicana in Vernal is beloved for its 22 kinds of burritos, while Miguel's Baja Grill in Moab turns out delicious ceviche and other seafood dishes.

ICE CREAM, FROZEN CUSTARD, AND SHAKES

Another reason to appreciate Utah's impressive tradition of dairy farming: it gives locals and visitors the excuse to sample luscious, locally made ice cream all year long, and especially during the state's hot and sunny summers. Traditional go-to's include LaBeau's Drive-in up by Bear Lake, which is famous for its raspberry shakes, and Aggie's Ice Cream, on the campus of Utah State University in Logan— regulars swear by the blue-mint flavor. Also keep an eye out for the many fine farm-to-table restaurants that churn out their own small-batch ice cream and sorbet, often with daily-rotating flavors, including Blacksmith Ice Cream north of Salt Lake City and Color Ridge Farm & Creamery in Torrey.

FRY SAUCE

Given the devotion with which Utahns seem to worship it, you might think this pink condiment available at virtually every burger-and-fry joint in the state contains some hard-to-procure ingredient. In fact, it's just a blend of ketchup and mayo, developed in the 1940s by the regional fast-food chain Arctic Circle.

What to Read and Watch

READ: *DESERT SOLITAIRE*
Ardent environmentalist and provocative essayist Edward Abbey based much of his first—and some say greatest—nonfiction memoir on the time he spent in the late 1950s as a ranger in Arches National Park.

WATCH: *BUTCH CASSIDY AND THE SUNDANCE KID*
George Roy Hill's splendid 1969 western was filmed significantly around Zion National Park, St. George's Snow Canyon, and other parts of southwestern Utah. Robert Redford—who played the Sundance Kid—fell in love with the landscape and went on to establish Sundance Resort and the Sundance Film Festival.

READ AND WATCH: *UNDER THE BANNER OF HEAVEN*
Jon Krakauer's 2003 book shines a light on the renegade fundamentalist outsider communities that exist in defiance not only of the mainstream LDS Church but government authorities as well. It was made into a 2022 Hulu miniseries.

WATCH: *FOOTLOOSE*
Few can forget Kevin Bacon's electrifying performance as a rebellious midwestern teen transplanted to a small western town with a conservative minister (John Lithgow). This rom-com musical from 1984 was shot entirely around Provo and Orem.

READ AND WATCH: *127 HOURS*
Aron Ralston's gripping, autobiographical book *Between a Rock and a Hard Place* is a riveting account of being trapped in Bluejohn Canyon (and ultimately forced to amputate his own right arm)—near Canyonlands National Park. The 2010 movie stars James Franco.

WATCH: *THE SEARCHERS*
Among the dozens of celebrated movies filmed in and around Monument Valley, John Ford's 1956 western about a troubled Civil War Veteran portrayed by John Wayne captures the region's breathtaking terrain as marvelously as any.

READ AND WATCH: *RIDERS OF THE PURPLE SAGE*
Published in 1912, this richly rendered yarn by the Western novelist Zane Grey is set in a fictional Mormon community in southern Utah and still ranks among the most popular works of the genre. The most recent movie adaptation, from 1996, stars Ed Harris and was shot partly in Utah.

WATCH: *THELMA AND LOUISE*
The most iconic landscape scenes in the 1991 drama were filmed in southern Utah in and around Moab, including the most memorable scene, where they drive their 1966 Ford Thunderbird over what's said to be the edge of the Grand Canyon.

READ: *MORMON COUNTRY*
Part of the acclaimed American Folkways series, this early work by the great American novelist Wallace Stegner—who spent part of his formative years in Salt Lake City—describes the migration of Mormon settlers to Utah, where they transformed an unforgiving, parched land.

WATCH: *SLC PUNK!*
Director James Merendino based his depiction of Salt Lake City in this 1998 comedy-drama starring Matthew Lillard on his experiences growing up in what was then a far more conservative environment. The film was shot on location around the city.

WATCH: *HEREDITARY*
The gripping, dread-inducing, and completely bonkers debut film of emerging director Ari Aster was shot entirely in Utah, largely in Park City, the surrounding Heber Valley, and metro Salt Lake City.

A Brief History of Mormonism

From its beginnings in 1830 with just six members, the Church of Jesus Christ of Latter-day Saints has evolved into one of the fastest growing religions in the world. There are more than 16.6 million members, found in nearly every country. The faith drew increased attention with the presidential candidacy of Mitt Romney, and Utah has seen a huge increase in tourism since the 2002 Winter Olympics and the 2006–11 HBO show *Big Love*.

IN THE BEGINNING
The church is considered a uniquely American faith as it was conceived and founded in New York by Joseph Smith, who said God the Father and his son, Jesus Christ, came to him in a vision when he was a young boy. Smith said he also saw a resurrected entity named Moroni, who led him to metal plates that were engraved with the religious history of an ancient American civilization. In 1827, Smith began translating this record into the Book of Mormon, published in 1830.

PERSECUTION AND SETTLEMENT IN UTAH
Not long after the creation of the church, religious persecution forced Smith and his followers to flee New York, and they traveled first to Ohio and then to Missouri before settling in Nauvoo, Illinois, in 1839. But even here the fledgling faith was ostracized. Smith was killed by a mob in June 1844 in Carthage, Illinois. To escape the oppression, Brigham Young, who ascended to the church's leadership following Smith's death, led a pilgrimage to Utah, the first group arriving in the Salt Lake Valley on July 24, 1847. Here, under Young's guidance, Mormonism quickly grew and flourished.

In keeping with the church's emphasis on proselytizing, Young laid plans to both colonize Utah and spread the church's word farther afield. This work led to the founding of small towns not only throughout the territory but also from southern Canada to Mexico. Today, the Church of Jesus Christ of Latter-day Saints continues that work through its young people, many of whom take time out from college or careers to spend two years on a mission at home or abroad.

BELIEFS
Members of the Church of Jesus Christ of Latter-day Saints believe that they are guided by divine revelations received from God by the religion's president, who is viewed as a modern-day prophet in the same sense as other biblical leaders. The Book of Mormon is viewed as divinely inspired scripture and is used side-by-side with the Holy Bible. Families are highly valued in the faith, and marriages performed in Mormon temples are believed to continue through eternity.

With the exceptions of quite progressive and liberal-leaning Salt Lake City along with Park City and Moab, Utah is a conservative state. Utah's civic bodies are overwhelmingly filled by church members, who often simultaneously hold leadership positions in their local church units (called wards).

Utah with Kids

It's hard to think of a part of the country that's more embracing of families and kids than Utah. Indoor and outdoor recreation opportunities abound in the Beehive State, touching upon perennial kid delights such as dinosaurs, trains, planes, sports, and camping. It's easy to find well-designed kids' menus at even many sophisticated restaurants around the state, and even Utah's luxury resorts and ski areas go to great lengths to make young guests feel right at home.

CITY DIVERSIONS

In and around **Salt Lake City,** start with two very kid-friendly museums in **The Gateway** shopping center. **Discovery Gateway Children's Museum** has a Life Flight helicopter, pinewood derby racing, a construction site, and much more—best suited to children up to the age of 10. **Clark Planetarium** opens kids' eyes to the universe and natural phenomena through its interactive exhibits and full-dome and IMAX theaters. **The Leonardo,** an inspirational museum combining science, art, and technology, is on its own a good reason to bring kids to Utah, and the **Natural History Museum of Utah, Red Butte Garden, Tracy Aviary,** and **Hogle Zoo** are also year-round destinations within the city limits. South of the city, **Wheeler Historic Farm** in Murray is a wonderfully engaging living history museum where kids can get an up-close look at farm animals. And on **Antelope Island,** you can see bison in a natural setting (if visiting in late October, don't miss the annual bison roundup).

In **Ogden,** you can fly like a bird in the wind tunnel, learn to surf, or rock climb indoors at the state-of-the-art **Salomon Center.** Young children enjoy the models and playground at the **George S. Eccles Dinosaur Park.** Older kids can catch the Raptors, who are, along with Salt Lake's Bees and Orem's Owlz, a fun, inexpensive, entertaining minor-league baseball team.

Southern Utah's urban hub, **St. George** has several attractions popular with younger visitors, including the excellent **St. George Children's Museum,** the fascinating **St. George Dinosaur Discovery Site,** and **Red Hills Desert Garden,** with its easily strolled trails and interpretive signs.

NATURAL WONDERS

Hikes offer larger-than-life rewards that can even lure kids away from their iPads. Each of Utah's five national parks has special youth-oriented programming and a **Junior Ranger program** that provides them with an interactive booklet of activities and tasks to complete.

In **Arches,** hardy kids over around the age of 6 can likely make the 3-mile round-trip hike to **Delicate Arch.** Make **Sand Arch** a destination for littler ones—it's right off the road and offers a massive "sandbox" of soft red sand. In **Zion ,** kids 10 and up can trek up the Virgin River at least part of the way toward **The Narrows.** At **Bryce** or Zion, you can go **horseback riding** to places that might be tough for little legs.

There are **dinosaur excavation** sites near **Vernal, St. George,** and **Price.** Moonlit hikes and telescope tours are nighttime programs offered by park rangers at **Goblin Valley State Park. Moab** has kid-friendly bike trails, and you might find that your BMX-riding teen is more comfortable on the **Slickrock Trail** than you are.

Finally, if you have swimmers in your party, great places to cool off in hot summers include **Lake Powell, Bear Lake,** and the buoyant waters of the **Great Salt Lake**.

TRAVEL SMART

Updated by
Stina Sieg

★ **STATE CAPITAL:**
Salt Lake City

👫 **POPULATION:**
3.3 million

💬 **LANGUAGE:**
English

$ **CURRENCY:**
U.S. Dollar

☎ **AREA CODES:**
385, 435, 801

⚠ **EMERGENCIES:**
911

🚗 **DRIVING:**
On the right

⚡ **ELECTRICITY:**
120–220 v/60 cycles; plugs have two or three rectangular prongs

🕓 **TIME:**
Mountain time

🌐 **WEBSITES:**
www.visitutah.com,
www.utah.com,
www.skiutah.com

✈ **AIRPORTS:**
Salt Lake City International Airport (SLC), St. George Regional Airport (SGU)

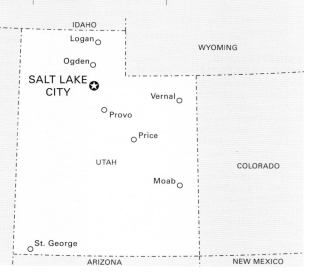

Know Before You Go

Utah is best known for its Mormon roots and the stunning geography. Although a large majority of the state's residents are Mormon, that drops to less than half in Salt Lake City, and some of the strong Mormon influence over laws and traditions has lessened in recent years.

ALWAYS WEAR SUNSCREEN

Like the other southwestern states, the sun shines hot and long in Utah. In fact, it's regularly named one of the top 10 sunniest states. Make sure you have and use sunscreen every day. Wearing a wide-brimmed hat helps, too. UV exposure increases at high altitudes and Utah's average elevation is 6,100 feet, the third-highest in the country. If you're thinking you'll take your chances for a great tan, consider the sobering statistic that the state also has one of the highest rates of skin cancer in the nation.

UNDERSTANDING ALTITUDE SICKNESS

Altitude sickness can be a real downer on vacation (and even dangerous). Breathtaking views and outdoor recreation lose appeal fast when you have trouble getting enough oxygen to breathe normally and feel dizzy, nauseous, or weak, or get a headache. It happens because the level of oxygen gets lower the higher you go. Most of the ski resorts and many mountain trails are above the 8,000 feet in altitude where the sickness begins to affect people. So it's best to take it slow and easy to get used to the mountain air and descend if you feel any symptoms rather than pushing on, as that can cause more severe problems. Stay well hydrated, too, and always carry water with you.

WHAT'S LEGAL AND WHAT'S NOT

With the long-standing influence of the LDS religion, which forbids the consumption of alcohol, Utah has been known for its strict liquor laws. One of those laws changed in 2020, when the maximum 4% ABV limit for beer available at grocery stores and beer bars was increased to 5% ABV, but only a restaurant or state-run liquor store sells anything stronger. Don't drink and drive though—Utah has the lowest allowable blood alcohol level in the nation (.05%). Recreational marijuana is not legal in Utah. And (in case you're curious!), while polygamy is considered a crime in all other 49 states, in Utah it was decriminalized in 2020 and is now an infraction similar to a traffic ticket.

GETTING AROUND SAFELY BY CAR

Utah has some incredible scenic drives and you'll cover a lot of miles exploring the state. When driving long stretches, keep an eye on the gas gauge, as gas stations may be few and far between and hours may be limited. Keep your gas tank at least half full; it's also a good idea to bring an emergency kit and water. Note that cell service can be spotty, so it's wise to bring a map or take screenshots of GPS directions before going off main routes. For winter travel, check road reports and weather forecasts and carry chains if you're not driving a four-wheel drive. Even summer driving can pose challenges, including closed roads due to flash floods from monsoons. Stay alert.

DON'T MISS THE NATIONAL PARKS

Utah is richly blessed with national parks; only California and Alaska have more. Its five parks, all in the southern part of the state, have been nicknamed the "Mighty Five." With canyons, hoodoos, arches and other rock formations, mountains, rivers, wildlife, and exotic flora and fauna, the parks are a delight for outdoor adventurers and photographers. Plan at least a week if you want to see them all, and be prepared for crowds. If you want to stay in the historic national park lodges at Zion or Bryce, you'll need to book far in advance. In 2022, Arches National Park began a pilot timed-entry reservation system from May to October (reservations can be booked three months in advance). It's not clear if this will continue, but it's best to check with *all* national parks about entry requirements before arriving.

UTAH IN THE MOVIES

With its vast expanse of wide-open desert and towering rock formations, Utah has been a go-to spot for Westerns since the beginning of film. Its rugged landscape can be seen in nearly a dozen John Wayne movies, as well as *Butch Cassidy and the Sundance Kid* (1969) starring Robert Redford and Paul Newman. Decades later, Utah was the backdrop for unforgettable scenes in *Thelma and Louise* (1991). In more recent years, the docu-drama *127 Hours* (2010) told the story of a real hiker who was trapped by a boulder against a canyon wall in Canyonlands National Park. The Utah Office of Tourism (⊕ visitutah.com) has suggested tours of film locations with an interactive map.

MORMON ORIGINS

In 1847, a group of Church of Jesus Christ of Latter-day Saints members, led by Brigham Young, came west to settle in the Salt Lake Valley. Young named the settlement "Deseret" (which means "honeybee" in the *Book of Mormon*) to promote the idea of bees working cooperatively for the good of the hive. While the name wasn't adopted for the state, the honeybee symbolism remains with its "Beehive State" nickname (and you'll notice the state highway signs include the image of a beehive). The honeybee is also the state insect. The early settlers were accompanied by African American enslaved people—the first enslaved people brought to the west. Slavery continued until the end of the Civil War. As the only state with a majority religion, Mormonism plays a big role in its culture and laws. Temple Square in Salt Lake City is a must-see to learn more about the Mormon history in the area.

CAN YOU SWIM IN THE GREAT SALT LAKE?

Locals don't have much interest in swimming in Utah's largest lake; they mention how shallow it is and how smelly from the brine shrimp that live there. Gnats can also be a problem. It's been called "America's Dead Sea," though it lacks the tourist appeal of the real Dead Sea. Still, if you have the time and like to do novel things, it's an interesting experience. The best place to go in is at Antelope Island State Park. You'll wade awhile before reaching the deeper water, where you can float effortlessly, buoyed by the heavy salt. Be careful if you have any cuts, scrapes or recently shaved skin; the salt will sting. Fortunately, you can shower off all the salt right at the park when you're done.

STAYING SAFE OUTDOORS

There are endless ways to explore the outdoors here—like hiking, biking, climbing, horseback riding, and rafting—but there are definitely risks. The National Park Service recommends outdoor explorers eat well and drink at least a gallon of water a day while in the hot sun, avoid strenuous activities in the middle of the day, and wear sturdy shoes. Always explore with a buddy if you can, and if you get lost, just wait where you are for rescue. Buying a personal locator beacon, which allows you to request a rescue even without cell service, is a wise purchase. When venturing out alone, let someone know where you're going and when you'll be back. Be prepared for sudden weather changes, including flash floods, and stay low if there's lightning.

WHEN TO VISIT

With its legendary powdery snow, many people come in winter to enjoy snow sports at the state's world-class ski resorts. The Sundance Film Festival is another reason to visit during the chilly season. Summer is hot and dry but attracts many visitors for the abundant outdoor recreation. There are more programs at national parks during the summer, and it's a popular time for families on vacation. If you'd like to avoid crowds and weather extremes, consider the early spring and late fall. Be aware, however, that during "off season," fewer amenities may be available.

Getting Here and Around

Salt Lake City is Utah's major air gateway, although if southern Utah is your primary destination, traveling there from Las Vegas is a convenient and often less expensive alternative.

 ## Air

Salt Lake City has a reputation for having one of the nation's easiest airports for travelers—with a low rate of delayed or canceled flights. Plus, it's a western hub for Delta, so your Utah explorations should get off to a timely start. Nonstop flights are available from larger U.S. cities as well as Europe, Mexico, and Canada.

Salt Lake City is about 12 hours from London, 5 hours from New York, 4 hours from Chicago and D.C., 3 hours from Dallas, 2 hours from Los Angeles, and an hour from Las Vegas.

If you're traveling during snow season, allow extra time to get to the airport, as weather conditions can slow you down. If you'll be checking skis, arrive even earlier.

AIRPORTS

The major gateway to Utah is Salt Lake City International Airport. If you're staying in Salt Lake City, you'll appreciate that it's one of the closest airports to downtown of any American city, and security wait times are minimal. The entire airport is being rebuilt in two phases, with a new terminal and parking garage having opened in 2020 and the second phase due to be completed by 2025.

Flights to smaller, regional, or resort-town airports generally connect through Salt Lake. Provo, Cedar City, Logan, Ogden, and Moab all have small airports.

A convenient gateway to southern Utah, particularly Zion and Bryce Canyon national parks, is Harry Reid International Airport in Las Vegas. More and more visitors to southern Utah are using St. George Regional Airport, which has daily flights to Salt Lake City, Phoenix, and Denver. There are limited services, but you can rent cars here, and it's less than an hour's drive to Zion National Park once you're on the road.

GROUND TRANSPORTATION

You can get to and from the Salt Lake City Airport by light-rail, taxi, bus, rideshare, independent shuttle, or hotel shuttle. A light-rail line called TRAX connects you in less than 30 minutes (and for just $2.50) to downtown Salt Lake City and the rest of the rapid-transit network. It runs every 15 minutes on weekdays and every 20 minutes on weekends. Taxis, though, are faster (15 minutes); the trip to downtown costs around $26. If you're in downtown Salt Lake City, your best bet is to call ahead for a taxi rather than hope to flag one down. Shared-ride shuttle services from the airport are similarly priced to taxis, but can take longer. Lyft and Uber also pick up at the Salt Lake City airport and can cost around half the price of a taxi.

FLIGHTS

Delta and its affiliates offer almost 250 daily departures to destinations around the country. Southwest ranks second in terms of daily flights, with roughly 30 daily departures. Alaska, American, JetBlue, United, and Frontier also have flights each day.

If you're flying in from somewhere other than the United States, you'll likely connect in Los Angeles or San Francisco if you're coming from Asia, or a major airport in the East, such as Detroit, Atlanta, or New York, if you're traveling from Europe. Occasionally you may be delayed by a major snowstorm, but these generally affect the mountain areas, not the airport.

If you're heading to southern Utah, it may be more convenient to fly into Las Vegas, which has more flights and is often cheaper. Be advised that the 120-mile drive from Las Vegas to St. George passes through extremely remote country, and the Virgin River Canyon near the Arizona/Utah border can make for treacherous driving, especially at night.

If your destination is the Moab area, your closest airport of any size is Grand Junction Regional Airport, located about 115 miles east, in Colorado. It serves several nonstop destinations in the West, though you often trade less driving time for steeper fares.

Car

Once on the ground in Utah, a car is your best bet for getting around, and in most of the state it's a necessity. Outside the urban corridor from Provo to Ogden (including Salt Lake City), much of the state's interest lies in natural attractions, including five national parks and terrain that ranges from sun-baked desert to mountain peaks that soar above 10,000 feet. Be prepared for wide-open vistas, extreme temperature variations, and long stretches of road between remote communities. Car rentals may be cheaper in Las Vegas than in Salt Lake City depending on when you arrive.

Train

Amtrak connects Utah to Chicago and the San Francisco Bay Area daily via the *California Zephyr*, which stops in Salt Lake City, Provo, Helper, and Green River. However, long-distance Amtrak routes are notorious for delays. If you happen to be traveling between Denver and Moab, the luxurious *Rocky Mountaineer* uses many of the same tracks, but offers a much more high-end experience (with a vastly higher price tag).

SCENIC TRAIN TRIPS

On the historic Heber Valley Railroad, you can catch the heritage locomotive nicknamed the *Heber Creeper*, a turn-of-the-20th-century train that runs from Heber City across the Heber Valley and alongside Deer Creek Reservoir. Depending on the length of the trip (they can be as short as 40 minutes or as long as 3 hours) you can chug down Provo Canyon to Vivian Park. The railroad offers many specialty trips, as well. Depending on the time of year, you can catch the North Pole Express, the Wild West Train, or an Adventure Train that includes a stop for rafting, plus many more options.

Essentials

🍴 Dining

Dining in Utah is generally casual. Menus are becoming more varied, but you can nearly always order a hamburger or a steak. There are a growing number of fine restaurants in Salt Lake City and Park City, and good places are cropping up even in remote areas. Also look for varied, inventive dining in Springdale, Moab, and Torrey. Seek out colorful diners along the secondary highways like U.S. 89; they usually serve up meat and potatoes along with the local flavor of each community. Authentic international cuisines are easy to find in Salt Lake City but generally not available elsewhere. The restaurants we list are the cream of the crop in each price category.

MEALS AND MEALTIMES

Although you can find all types of cuisine in the major cities and resort towns of Utah, be sure to try native dishes like trout, elk, and buffalo (the latter two have less fat than beef and are just as tasty); organic fruits and vegetables are also readily available, especially in finer establishments in Salt Lake City and Park City. Southwestern food is popular, and you'll find several restaurants that specialize in it or show Southwestern influences in menu selections. Asian and Latin American cuisines are both gaining in popularity (and quality) in the Salt Lake area.

Unless otherwise noted, the restaurants listed in this guide are open daily for lunch and dinner. Dinner hours are usually from 6 to 9 pm. Outside of the large cities and resort towns in the high seasons, many restaurants close by 10 and are closed on Sunday.

RESERVATIONS AND DRESS

Reservations are relatively rare outside of the top restaurants in the urban and resort areas. It's a good idea to call ahead if you can. We only mention them specifically when reservations are essential (there's no other way you'll ever get a table) or when they are not accepted. Large parties should always call ahead to check the reservations policy. We mention dress only when men are required to wear a jacket or a jacket and tie—which is almost never in casual Utah. Even at nice resorts dress is usually casual, and in summer you're welcome nearly everywhere in your shorts, T-shirt, and hiking shoes.

WINES, BEER, AND SPIRITS

Despite what you've heard, it's not hard to get a drink in Utah, though you must be 21 to purchase or consume alcohol. The state overhauled liquor laws in 2009 to bring it more in line with the rest of the United States. The state abolished the "private club" system, which required that each patron have an annual or short-term membership in order to enter the premises. Many restaurants have licenses, which allow them to serve you wine and beer—and occasionally liquor—with a meal. At restaurants, you will have to order food in addition to alcohol. Some restaurants—generally those that cater to families—opt not to carry a liquor license. If you're set on having a drink with your meal, check before you go. Some restaurants will allow you to bring your own wine but may charge a corkage fee. Call ahead if you want to take your own wine or other liquor to a restaurant—lots of regulations cover brown bagging.

Utah has a thriving microbrewery scene, with local lagers produced in Salt Lake City, Park City, Moab, Springdale, Vernal, Ogden, and beyond. There are several brewpubs with their own beers on tap—try Latter Day Stout at Desert Edge Brewery in Salt Lake City and Polygamy Porter at Wasatch brew pubs in Park City and Salt Lake City to get a taste of the local drinking culture. Some brewpubs also have a liquor license that allows the sale of wine and spirits.

Most hotel restaurants carry a liquor license, and you'll be able to get your own drinks from the minibar in your room.

Beer with 5% alcohol by volume is available in grocery stores and some convenience stores. For anything else, you'll have to go to a state liquor store. There are more than 20 liquor stores throughout the Salt Lake City area and still more across the state. They are closed on Sunday, Election Day, and holidays.

Note that Utah has lowered the maximum legal blood alcohol level in drivers from .08% to .05%, giving it one of the lowest and strictest DUI thresholds in the country.

⊕ Health

Salt Lake City and Logan are surrounded by mountains, which can trap pollution and create some of the worst air quality in the nation, particularly in winter. Red Alert action days happen several times a year (often for more than a week at a time), when strenuous activity, particularly by young and elderly people, is discouraged. Visit the Utah Department of Environmental Quality website (⊕ *air.utah.gov*) to find out about air quality if you have asthma, allergies, or other breathing sensitivities.

COVID-19

Most travel restrictions, including vaccination and masking requirements, have been lifted across the United States except in health-care facilities and nursing homes. Some travelers may still wish to wear a mask in confined spaces, including on airplanes, on public transportation, and at large indoor gatherings, but that is increasingly a personal choice. Be aware that some local mandates still exist and should be followed.

Lodging

Utah is home to the founders of the Marriott chain of hotels, whose brands can be found throughout the state. Chain motels are everywhere. The ski resorts along the Wasatch Front—especially in Park City—cater to the wealthy jet set, and there are posh resorts, such as Deer Valley and the Waldorf Astoria Park City, and pampering at Red Mountain Resort. Salt Lake City has hotels in every price range. National chains like Holiday Inn, Marriott, Hilton, Best Western, Super 8, and Motel 6 are dependable in Utah and are occasionally the best beds in town. The gateway towns to the national parks usually have a large range of accommodations. Independent motels can also be found all over the state. Look for guest ranches if you're trying to find an authentic Western experience. They often require a one-week stay, and the cost is all-inclusive. During the busy summer season, from Memorial Day to Labor Day, it's a good idea to book your lodging in advance. Most motels and resorts have off-season rates. Take advantage of these because hiking is best in the south in cool weather and the mountains are beautiful even without snow.

▤ TIP → **Assume that hotels do not include any meals in their room rates, unless we specify otherwise.**

APARTMENT AND HOUSE RENTALS

Increasingly, condos and private homes are available for rent, with more and more options on websites such as Airbnb, Homeaway, and VRBO. Rentals

Essentials

range from one-night to month-long stays. Enjoy slope-side accommodations with all the amenities of home, such as multiple bathrooms and full kitchens, at most ski resorts. Condo and home rentals are also available outside Zion, Bryce, Arches, and Canyonlands national parks.

HOTELS

Most Salt Lake City hotels cater to business travelers with such facilities as restaurants, cocktail lounges, swimming pools, exercise equipment, and meeting rooms. Most other Utah towns and cities have less expensive hotels that are clean and comfortable but have fewer facilities. Wi-Fi is pretty much standard no matter where you're staying in the state.

Many properties in Utah's larger cities have special weekend rates, sometimes up to 50% off regular prices. However, these deals are usually not extended during peak months (summer near the national parks and winter in the ski resorts), when hotels are normally full. Salt Lake City hotels are generally full only during major conventions.

All hotels listed have a private bath unless otherwise noted.

RESORTS

Ski towns throughout Utah, such as Park City, Sundance, and Brian Head, are home to resorts in all price ranges (but primarily high-end); any activities lacking in any individual property are usually available in the town itself—in summer as well as winter. Off the slopes, there are wonderful both rustic and luxurious resorts in the southern part of the state: Red Mountain Resort in St. George, Zion Ponderosa Ranch Resort near Zion, Sorrel River Ranch near Arches, and Amangiri near Lake Powell and Four Corners.

Packing

Informality reigns here; jeans, sport shirts, and T-shirts fit in almost everywhere. The few restaurants and performing-arts events where dressier outfits are required, usually in resorts and larger cities, are the exception.

If you plan to spend much time outdoors, and certainly if you go in winter, choose clothing that will keep you dry and warm. Cotton, including denim—although fine on warm, dry days—can be uncomfortable and even dangerous in cold and/or wet weather. A better choice is clothing made of wool or any of a number of new synthetics that provide warmth without bulk and maintain their insulating properties even when wet.

In summer you'll want shorts during the day. But because early morning and night can be cold and high passes windy, pack a sweater and a light jacket and perhaps also a wool cap and gloves. Try layering—a T-shirt under another shirt under a jacket—and peel off layers as you go. For walks and hikes, you'll need sturdy footwear. To take you into the wilds, boots should have thick soles and plenty of ankle support; if your shoes are new and you plan to spend much time on the trail, break them in at home. Bring a day pack for short hikes, along with a canteen or water bottle, and don't forget rain gear, a hat, sunscreen, and insect repellent.

In winter, prepare for subfreezing temperatures with good boots, warm socks and liners, thermal underwear, a well-insulated jacket, and a warm hat and mittens.

If you attend dances and other events at Native American reservations, dress conservatively—skirts or long pants—or you may be asked to leave.

When traveling to mountain areas, remember that sunglasses and a sun hat are essential at high altitudes, even in winter; the thinner atmosphere requires sunscreen with a greater SPF than you might need at lower elevations. Bring moisturizer even if you don't normally use it. Utah's dry climate can be hard on your skin.

⊕ Safety

Parts of Utah are remote and have poor mobile phone service. It's always best to tell someone—the hotel desk clerk, the ski-rental person—where you're going. If you plan to do more extensive backcountry exploring, you may also want to invest in a personal locator beacon, which pinpoints your location and allows you to request help even in areas with no cell signal.

Many trails are at high altitudes, where oxygen is thinner. They're also frequently desolate. Hikers and bikers should carry basic survival gear, including a flashlight, a compass, waterproof matches, a first-aid kit, a knife, and a light plastic tarp for shelter. Backcountry skiers should add a repair kit, a blanket, an avalanche beacon, a probe, and a lightweight shovel to their lists. Always bring extra food and a canteen of water. Never drink from streams or lakes, unless you boil the water first or purify it with tablets.

Always check the condition of roads and trails, and get the latest weather reports before setting out. In summer take precautions against heat stroke or exhaustion by resting frequently in shaded areas; in winter take precautions against hypothermia by layering clothing.

You may feel dizzy and weak and find yourself breathing heavily—signs that the thin mountain air isn't giving you your accustomed dose of oxygen. Take it easy and rest often for a few days until you're acclimatized. Throughout your stay, drink plenty of water and watch your alcohol consumption as dehydration is a common occurrence at high altitudes. If you experience severe headaches and nausea, see a doctor. It is easy to go too high too fast. The remedy for altitude-related discomfort is to go down quickly into heavier air.

Flash floods can strike at any time and any place with little or no warning. The danger in mountainous terrain intensifies when distant rains are channeled into gullies and ravines, turning a quiet stream-side campsite or wash into a rampaging torrent in seconds; similarly, desert terrain can become dangerous when heavy rains fall on land that is unable to absorb the water and thus floods quickly. Be prepared to head for higher ground if the weather turns severe.

One of the most wonderful features of Utah is its abundant wildlife. To avoid an unpleasant situation while hiking, make plenty of noise and keep dogs on a leash and small children between adults. While camping, be sure to store all food, utensils, and clothing with food odors far away from your tent, preferably high in a tree or in a bear box. If you do come across a bear or big cat, do not run. For bears or moose, back away while talking calmly; for mountain lions, make yourself look as big as possible. In either case, be prepared to fend off the animal with loud noises, rocks, sticks, and so on. And, as the saying goes, do not feed the bears— or any wild animals, whether they're dangerous or not.

When in any park, give all animals their space. If you want to take a photograph, use a long lens and keep your distance. This is particularly important for winter visitors. Approaching an animal can

Essentials

cause stress and affect its ability to survive the sometimes brutal climate. In all cases, remember that the animals have the right-of-way; this is their home, and you are the visitor.

Taxes

State sales tax is 4.85% in Utah. Most areas have additional local sales and lodging taxes, which can be quite significant. For example, in Salt Lake City the combined sales tax is 7.75%; the highest rates are in Alta (8.75%) and Park City (9.05%). Utah sales tax is reduced for some items, such as groceries.

Tipping

It is customary to tip at least 15% at restaurants, though 20% or more is increasingly the norm. For coat checks and bellhops, $1 per coat or bag is the minimum. Taxi drivers expect 15% to 20%, depending on where you are. In resort towns, ski technicians, sandwich makers, baristas, and the like also appreciate tips. For ski instructors, a 10%–15% tip is standard.

⦿ Visitor Information

The Utah Office of Tourism has an excellent website (⊕ www.visitutah.com), and its office (across the street from the state capitol) is open weekdays. Its gift shop, which also includes some travel information, is open daily.

Tipping Guidelines for Utah	
Bartender	$1–$5 per round of drinks, depending on the number of drinks and type of drinks (tip more for a craft cocktail than bottled beer, for example)
Bellhop	$1–$5 per bag, depending on the level of the hotel
Hotel Concierge	$5 or more, if they perform a service for you
Hotel Doorman	$1–$2 if they help you get a cab
Hotel Housekeeper	$2–$5 a day (tip daily since staff may vary)
Hotel Room-Service Waiter	15%–20% unless gratuity has been added
Skycap at Airport	$1–$2 per bag checked
Taxi Driver	15%–20%, but round up the fare to the next dollar amount
Tour Guide	10% of the cost of the tour
Valet Parking Attendant	$1–$2, but only when you get your car
Waiter	15%–20%, with 20% or more being the norm at high-end restaurants; nothing additional if gratuity is added to the bill

On the Calendar

January

Sundance Film Festival. Presented by Robert Redford's Sundance Institute since 1985, this famed festival is on par with international film fests like Cannes and Toronto and attracts serious movie buffs, locals, international media, and plenty of celebrities. It takes place over 11 days at the end of January, primarily in Park City, but also in Salt Lake City and at Redford's Sundance Resort. The festival features both independent filmmakers and major studios, and the best go home with the coveted Sundance Awards. ⊕ www.sundance.org

May

Great Salt Lake Bird Festival. In mid-May, the Salt Lake City area welcomes more than 250 species of migrating birds—and countless bird lovers—to this popular festival just north of the city. While there are always plenty of workshops and a keynote speaker, some of the best times at this festival are had on field trips where attendees are guided through surrounding shores, foothills, and forests in search of these feathered creatures. Some spots aren't normally accessible to the public. The event is held over four days, based at Farmington's George S. and Dolores Doré Eccles Wildlife Education Center. ⊕ www.daviscountyutah.gov/greatsaltlakebirdfest

June

Bryce Canyon Astronomy Festival. Held around the time of the new moon each June at Bryce Canyon National Park, the four-day festival has plenty of activities for the whole family, including model rocket building and launching, solar scope viewings, stories and talks on astronomy by park rangers and scientists—and, of course, stargazing. Admission is free, but you still must pay to enter the park (or use your park pass). ⊕ www.nps.gov/brca/planyourvisit/astrofest.htm

Panguitch Valley Balloon Rally. For three days in late June, the skies over tiny Panguitch fill with dozens of colorful hot air balloons. Get there early to cheer on the balloons as they ascend and then stay to explore the food and craft vendors. Saturday is especially popular, with a 5K run in the morning and a "balloon glow" in the evening, when the balloons are lit up while parked downtown. Live music plays as tons of families saunter past, enjoying the warm night air. ⊕ panguitch.com/panguitch-valley-balloon-rally/

Utah Arts Festival. Salt Lake City's Library Square fills with art booths, music and literary performers, interactive art, kids' activities, and tasty food for Utah's largest outdoor festival. The award-winning celebration of the arts primarily highlights regional artists and is a wonderful opportunity to catch local performances and bring home locally made pieces to remember your visit to Utah. The festival happens the last weekend of June, Thursday through Sunday. ⊕ uaf.org

July

Pioneer Day. On this state holiday every July 24, community celebrations mark the 1847 arrival of Brigham Young and the first Mormons that settled the area. Statewide, you will find fireworks, historical reenactments, rodeos, parades, and fairs. Though meant to be inclusive of all pioneer history from the era, not just the Mormons, the holiday has inspired a smaller alternative celebration called "Pie & Beer Day" for the non-LDS folks.

On the Calendar

August

Craft Lake City DIY Fest. Local, local, local. That's the vibe of this Salt Lake City festival, centered on makers selling all different types of handcrafted goods, including art, jewelry, clothing, and even baby items and Utah-made food. In all, expect 350 booths, as well as performances by Utah-based musicians, multicultural dancers, roving buskers, and one headlining national act. Very family-friendly, it also features make-and-take crafts and a science and technology area—including bottle rocket demos—for the kiddos. ⊕ craftlakecity.com

Helper Arts Festival. Helper is a tiny, off-beat town that can easily steal your heart, and this festival is one of the best introductions to its vibrant arts community. Held since 1994, it offers three days of live music and art demonstrations, as well as food, a car show, and activities for kids. The festival shuts down Helper's main drag, which makes it easy to wander from booth to booth, gallery to gallery. The festival prides itself on being free and accepting of all. ⊕ www.helper-artsfestival.com

September

Great Salt Lake Bird Festival. In mid-September, the Salt Lake City area welcomes more than 250 species of migrating birds—and countless bird lovers—to this popular festival just north of the city. While there are always plenty of workshops and a keynote speaker, some of the best times at this festival are had at field trips where attendees are guided through surrounding shores, foothills, and forests in search of these feathered creatures. Some spots aren't normally accessible to the public. The event is held over four days, based at Farmington's George S. and Dolores Doré Eccles Wildlife Education Center. ⊕ www.daviscountyutah.gov/greatsaltlakebirdfest

Melon Days. Locally grown melons are little Green River's claim to fame, and this two-day festival celebrates all the area's delicious varieties, from watermelons to cantaloupes, canaries to honeydew. Some of the highlights include a 5K run, parade, melon-carving contest, and live music from a nationally known artist. Definitely make sure to pick up some melons from one of the roadside stands while you're in town. The celebration is always held the third weekend in September, and dates back to the early 1900s. ⊕ www.melon-days.com

Midway Swiss Days. Filling the quaint community of Midway the Friday and Saturday before Labor Day, this small-town celebration is actually one of the largest festivals in the entire state. It honors Midway's Swiss forebears: immigrants who settled in the area long ago, happy to have found a spot that reminded them of their alpine home. The biggest draws include Swiss food vendors, artisans selling their wares (with an emphasis on home decor), live music, and a parade that winds through the town, famous for its distinctive Swiss architecture. ⊕ midwayswissdays.org

Moab Music Festival. This three-week festival in late August and early September highlights chamber, jazz, and global traditional music played in stunning outdoor settings around Moab. The unique venues include a grotto that's accessed by jet boat and surrounded by red rock, secluded canyons that you hike to, and multiday luxury adventure experiences that add on rafting, swimming, floating, and hiking, with a plane ride back to the start. A few venues are indoors in Moab, and there's a free concert in the city park, too. ⊕ moabmusicfest.org

Soldier Hollow Classic Sheepdog Championship & Festival. Handlers from all over the world gather in the little town of Midway for four days over Labor Day weekend to see whose pup is top dog. These sheep dogs are incredibly well-trained and are tasked with guiding often unruly sheep through a series of prescribed maneuvers before the clock runs out. While the competitions are fun to watch, they can also be incredibly tense. It's not uncommon for everyone in the bleachers to be absolutely silent, as if they're collectively holding their breath, before letting out joyful cheers and applause when a dog is finally triumphant. Beyond the vast competition field is a festival area with food vendors, a beer garden, and artisan booths. ⊕ soldierhollowclassic.com

October

Snowbird's Oktoberfest. For more than 50 years, Snowbird ski resort has paid homage to Germany's famous celebration of all things beer with its own, family-friendly version of the festival. It takes place on weekends from mid-August through mid-October and is busting at the seams with lederhosen-clad performers, German food, and more than 50 varieties of beer from Utah breweries. You can hike or bike through the resort's snowless slopes, and for the kids there are inflatables and the resort's famed Alpine Slide, which allows riders to rush down a track on a ski run on a little cart. ⊕ www.snowbird.com/oktoberfest/

December

Christkindlmarkt SLC. Named after the German term for a Christmas market, this is a magical way to get into the spirit of the season for four days, starting the Wednesday after Thanksgiving, at Salt Lake City's This Is The Place Heritage Park. Festivalgoers can peruse the nearly 100 booths selling both gifts and food. Other big draws include a live nativity and a lantern parade, in which the public is invited to walk, provided they perform an "act of service" beforehand. That could be anything from checking in on an elderly neighbor to volunteering with a local nonprofit; as long as it's an act of kindness, it counts. ⊕ www.christkindl-markt-slc.com

Great Itineraries

Utah's Five Glorious National Parks, 7 Days

This itinerary will help you see the highlights of Utah's desert parks in a single week.

DAYS 1 AND 2: ZION NATIONAL PARK
(3 hours from McCarran Airport in Las Vegas)

Start early from Las Vegas, and within three hours you'll be across the most barren stretches of desert and marveling at the bends in the Virgin River Gorge. Just past St. George, Utah, on I-15, take the Route 9 exit to **Zion National Park.** Spend your afternoon in the park. Note that in the busiest season (typically May through September), personal vehicles are banned on Zion Canyon Scenic Drive.

For a nice introductory walk, try the short and easy **Weeping Rock Trail.** Follow it along the **Emerald Pools Trail** in Zion Canyon itself, where you might come across wild turkeys and ravens. Before leaving the park, ask the rangers to decide which of Zion's two iconic hikes is right for you the next day—the 1,488-foot elevation gain to **Angels Landing** or river wading along the improbably steep canyon called **The Narrows.** Overnight at **Zion Lodge** inside the park (book well in advance or call for last-minute cancellations), but venture into the bustling gateway town of **Springdale** for dinner.

Start at dawn the next day to beat the crowds and heat if you're ascending Angels Landing (allow three to four hours).

If you're headed up The Narrows, you'll be walking in the river; rent your gear and wait until sunup. Either way, pack a lunch and take your time—there's no sense

rushing one of the highlights of the U.S. National Park system. Work your way back to your hotel and set a date with your hot tub.

DAY 3: BRYCE CANYON NATIONAL PARK
(2 hours from Zion)

It's a long 85 miles from Zion to Bryce via Route 9 (the scenic Zion–Mount Carmel Highway), particularly as traffic must pass through a narrow 1.1-mile-long tunnel. Canyon Overlook is a great stopping point, providing views of massive rock formations such as The East and West Temples. When you emerge, you are in slickrock country, where huge petrified sandstone dunes have been etched by ancient waters. Stay on Route 9 for 23 miles and then turn north onto U.S. 89 and follow the signs to the entrance of **Bryce Canyon National Park.**

Start at **Sunrise Point.** Check out the **Bristlecone Loop Trail** and the **Navajo Loop Trail,** both of which you can easily fit into a day trip and will get you into the heart of the park. Listen for peregrine falcons deep in the side canyons, and keep an eye out for a species of prairie dog that only lives in these parts. If you can't stay in the park (camping or **The Lodge at Bryce Canyon** are your options), overnight at **Ruby's Inn,** near the junction of routes 12 and 63, or the full-featured **Bryce Canyon Grand Hotel** across the street; both are on the park's free shuttle route.

DAY 4: CAPITOL REEF NATIONAL PARK
(2½ hours from Bryce Canyon)

If you can, get up early to see sunrise paint Bryce's hoodoos, then head out on the spectacular Utah Scenic Byway–Route 12. Route 12 winds over and through **Grand Staircase–Escalante National Monument.** Boulder's **Hell's Backbone Grill,** for example, is a highlight, and you don't want

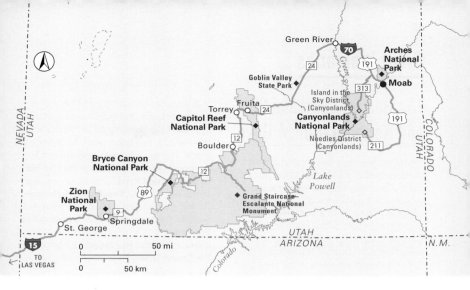

to bypass **Fruita's** petroglyphs and bountiful orchards in the late summer and fall.

At the intersection of routes 12 and 24, turn east onto Route 24 toward **Capitol Reef National Park.** The crowds are smaller here than at other national parks in the state, and the scenery is just as stunning. If it's still daylight when you arrive, hike the 1-mile **Hickman Bridge Trail,** stop in at the visitor center, open until 4:30 (later in the spring through fall), and view the exhibits, talk with rangers, or watch a film. Nearby **Torrey** is your best bet for dining and lodging.

DAYS 5–7: MOAB, ARCHES, AND CANYONLANDS NATIONAL PARKS
(2½ hours from Capitol Reef to Canyonlands)

Explore Capitol Reef more the next morning. An easy way to do this is to drive the 10-mile **Capitol Reef Scenic Drive,** which starts at the park visitor center. When you leave, travel east and north for 75 miles on Route 24. If you want a break after about an hour, stop at the small **Goblin Valley State Park ,** full of otherworldly, mushroom-like rock formations. Continue on Route 24 to I–70 and turn east toward Colorado.

Take Exit 182 south onto U.S. 191, proceeding about 19 miles to Island in the Sky Road. Make sure you have water, food, and gas as **Canyonlands National Park** offers no services, with the exception of water at The Needles visitor center year-round and the Island in the Sky visitor center seasonally. Be sure to follow the drive out to **Grand View Point** to look down on the convergence of the Colorado and Green Rivers. Along the way, **Mesa Arch** is a half-mile walk and offers a sneak preview of what to expect at Arches. More ambitious individuals should hike the mysterious crater at **Upheaval Dome,** a steep 1-mile round-trip hike. Finally, backtrack to U.S. 191 and turn right for the final 12-mile drive into **Moab,** a good base camp for both parks.

Build your Arches itinerary around hikes to the iconic **Delicate Arch** (best seen at sunrise to avoid the crowds) or **Landscape Arch** or a guided hike in **The Fiery Furnace.**

You can raft the Colorado River from Moab or bike the **Slickrock Trail .** Or, explore the **Needles District** of Canyonlands (about 90 minutes south), viewing petroglyphs on Route 279 (Potash Road) and driving along the Colorado River north of town to **The Fisher Towers.**

Great Itineraries

The Best of Salt Lake City and Northern Utah, 4 Days

Utah's increasingly cosmopolitan and diverse capital is the main entry point for most visitors to Utah (at least for those who are not just coming for the southern national parks). With a central location, the northern part of the state and Park City and the Wasatch Range are within easy reach. A summer trip will give you the opportunity to see a wider variety of scenery and participate in a wider variety of outdoor activities, but if you are a skier, then you'll want to visit during the winter season. Utah has some of the best ski slopes in the west.

DAY 1: SALT LAKE CITY

Many people begin their explorations of northern Utah from the comfortable hospitality of downtown **Salt Lake City.** Grab the TRAX light rail from Salt Lake City Airport to **Temple Square** and begin a walking tour of the city. The temple itself is off limits unless you belong to the Church of Jesus Christ of Latter-day Saints, but its grounds and the rest of the complex make for interesting wandering. Immediately south is **City Creek Center,** the city's first upscale shopping district. **Discovery Gateway Children's Museum** and **Clark Planetarium** are your best bets here, as well as **Olympic Legacy Plaza.** Complete your walk by crossing Pioneer Park, heading east through Gallivan Plaza (you may catch live music midday or evenings) as far as the **Salt Lake City Main Library**—a modern architectural gem

that includes a soaring roof that you can ascend for one of the best views of the city. **Salt Lake Roasting Co.,** in the library promenade, is a good place for a drink or snack. There's ample downtown lodging to choose from. Pamper yourself at **The Gr and America Hotel,** or bring your pooch to the pet-friendly **Kimpton Hotel Monaco.** Dining and drinking options are varied. Sample the microbrews at **Squatters Pub Brewery,** then fill up on America's best Mexican food at **Red Iguana** or check out **The Copper Onion** for Continental cuisine.

DAYS 2 AND 3: PARK CITY
(40-minute drive from Salt Lake City)

Salt Lake's majesty lies in the hills surrounding it, so tackle them today. **Park City** is 25 miles to the east along I–80, and you can easily spend the entire day wandering its historic Main Street, where the discovery of silver in 1868 led to a boom era of prospectors, mine workers, and schemers. You can still see in the storefronts that dozens of saloons and a red-light district once flourished here in defiance of the Mormon Church. The **Park City Museum** is the perfect place to discover the town's colorful history, and the **Park Silly Sunday Market** (June to September) portrays its modern-day fun side. For lunch or dinner, **Wasatch Brew Pub** is at the top of Main Street, and **Handle** and **High West Distillery** are just off Main on Heber Avenue and Park Avenue, respectively. You can't go wrong with any of them for a meal. If it's winter, hit the slopes; if it's summer hit the trails, where you might just encounter a moose. Either season, stop at **Utah Olympic Park,**

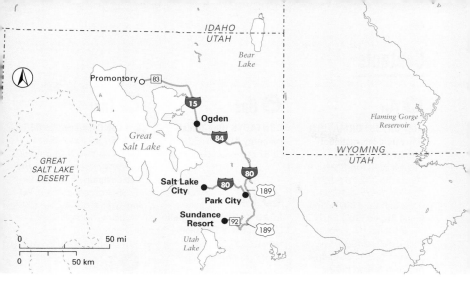

where you will often glimpse America's next gold-medal hopefuls training in any of a half-dozen disciplines, including ski jumping, bobsled, and luge. If you have time and love roller-coaster thrills, ride the bobsled course from top to bottom with a trained driver. Indulge in the spa, lounge, or restaurant at Deer Valley's **Stein Ericksen Lodge,** or opt for the equally refined (but no less expensive) **Waldorf Astoria Park City.** The **Newpark Resort** is a more affordable option near the outlet mall.

DAY 4: SUNDANCE RESORT OR OGDEN

(45-minute drive from Park City to Sundance; or 1 hour 10 minute drive to Ogden)

You can easily spend several more days in Park City, but its environs are beckoning. There's fly-fishing and rafting on the Provo River, balloon rides, and hot springs. Robert Redford's **Sundance Resort** is a year-round destination for artists, filmmakers, and musicians—not just tourists and skiers. It's about 45 minutes south of Park City through the gorgeous Provo River canyon. Dine at the **Foundry Grill** or **Tree Room** and keep your eyes open for Mr. Redford. Railroad buffs may prefer to make the hour drive north to **Ogden,** where **Union Station** has welcomed trains on the transcontinental route since it opened in 1924. Historic 25th Street has a multitude of restaurants. From there, head west to **Promontory,** Utah, to see where the golden spike was hammered in to connect East and West in 1869.

Contacts

Air

AIRPORT INFORMATION Harry Reid International Airport (LAS). ✉ *5757 Wayne Newton Blvd., Airport* ☎ *702/261–5211* ⊕ *www.harryreidairport. com.* **Salt Lake City International Airport (SLC).** ✉ *3920 W. Terminal Dr., Airport* ☎ *801/575–2400* ⊕ *www. slcairport.com.* **St. George Regional Airport (SGU).** ✉ *4550 S. Airport Pkwy., St. George* ☎ *435/627– 4080* ⊕ *www.flysgu.com.*

AIRLINE CONTACTS Alaska Airlines. ☎ *800/252– 7522* ⊕ *www.alaskaair. com.* **American Airlines.** ☎ *800/433–7300* ⊕ *www. aa.com.* **Delta Airlines.** ☎ *800/221–1212 for U.S. reservations, 800/241– 4141 for international reservations* ⊕ *www. delta.com.* **Frontier.** ☎ *801/401–9000* ⊕ *www. flyfrontier.com.* **JetBlue.** ☎ *800/538–2583* ⊕ *www. jetblue.com.* **Southwest Airlines.** ☎ *800/435–9792* ⊕ *www.southwest.com.* **United Airlines.** ☎ *800/864– 8331 U.S. and Canada reservations* ⊕ *www. united.com.*

Bus

CONTACTS Utah Transit Authority (UTA). ☎ *801/743– 3882* ⊕ *www.rideuta.com.*

Car

ROAD CONDITIONS Utah Department of Transportation. ☎ *511* ⊕ *www. commuterlink.utah.gov.*

LOCAL AGENCIES Rugged Rental. ✉ *2740 W. California Ave., Suite 2, Salt Lake City* ☎ *801/977–9111, 800/977–9111* ⊕ *www. ruggedrental.com.*

MAJOR RENTAL AGENCIES Advantage. ☎ *800/777–5500* ⊕ *www. advantage.com.* **Alamo.** ☎ *844/354–6962* ⊕ *www.alamo.com.* **Avis.** ☎ *800/633–3469* ⊕ *www.avis.com.* **Budget.** ☎ *800/218–7992* ⊕ *www. budget.com.* **Hertz.** ☎ *800/654–3131* ⊕ *www. hertz.com.* **National Car Rental.** ☎ *844/382–6875* ⊕ *www.nationalcar.com.*

Health

INFORMATION Utah Department of Environmental Quality. ☎ *801/536–4000* ⊕ *deq.utah.gov.*

Taxi

City Cab Company. ✉ *2880 S. Main St. #212, Salt Lake City* ☎ *801/363–5550* ⊕ *www.citycabut.com.* **Ute Cab Company.** ☎ *801/359– 7788* ⊕ *utecabco.com.* **Yellow Cab.** ☎ *801/521–2100* ⊕ *yellowcabutah.com.*

🚆 Train

TRAIN INFORMATION Amtrak. ☎ *800/872–7245* ⊕ *www.amtrak.com.* **Heber Valley Railroad.** ✉ *450 S. 600 W, Heber* ☎ *435/654–5601* ⊕ *www. hebervalleyrr.org.*

📍 Visitor Information

CONTACTS Utah Office of Tourism. ✉ *Council Hall, Capitol Hill, 300 N. State St., Salt Lake City* ☎ *801/538–1900, 800/200–1160* ⊕ *www. visitutah.com.*

Chapter 3

SALT LAKE CITY

3

Updated by
Andrew Collins

 Sights
★★★☆☆

 Restaurants
★★★★★

 Hotels
★★★☆☆

 Shopping
★★★★☆

 Nightlife
★★★★☆

WELCOME TO SALT LAKE CITY

TOP REASONS TO GO

★ **A downtown renaissance:** Venture into Salt Lake's vibrant downtown, with its respected theater scene, farm-to-table restaurants, craft breweries and coffeehouses, and the impressive City Creek Center retail plaza.

★ **Wander the Wasatch Front:** Lace up your hiking boots and enjoy the dramatic canyons on the city's east side.

★ **Catch the indie spirit:** This region, which has historically embraced chain franchises, has in recent years blossomed with hip independently owned shops, galleries, and cafés.

★ **Shore adventures:** Explore the city's namesake, the Great Salt Lake, by car, on foot, or by bicycle. If you're here in the summer, try floating off the beaches at Antelope Island—the water is so salty it's impossible to sink.

★ **Pow-pow-powder:** Experience the "greatest snow on earth" within an hour's drive of the airport at one of nine renowned ski resorts.

1 Downtown and Central City. Salt Lake City's core is Downtown, a quadrant containing most of the city's top hotels and a slew of theaters, restaurants, and bars, as well as Temple Square, the hub of the Church of Jesus Christ of Latter-day Saints.

2 Capitol Hill and the Avenues. Surrounding the capitol on all sides are residential areas known for historic houses.

3 East Side and Sugar House. This scenic area of the city hugs up against the dramatic Wasatch Range.

4 The North and West Sides. The suburbs of Layton and Bountiful are handy to the city as well as Antelope Island and the city of Ogden. You can also access the Great Salt Lake at the eponymous state park. A bit closer in lies Salt Lake City International Airport.

5 Midvalley and South Valley. The Midvalley and South Valley suburbs contain mostly bedroom communities but also a growing number of notable restaurants—on the eastern side, these towns are also good bases for spending time in Big Cottonwood and Little Cottonwood Canyons.

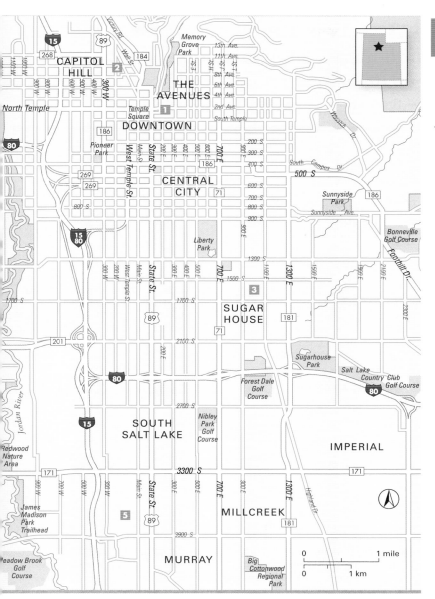

Nestled at the foot of the rugged Wasatch Mountains and extending to the south shore of the Great Salt Lake, Salt Lake City is a relatively small, navigable, and increasingly diverse and vibrant city at the heart of a metropolitan area with more than 1.25 million residents.

Both downtown and many outlying neighborhoods have become hot beds of acclaimed dining, artisan brewing and coffee-roasting, and trendy retail. The city core is in the midst of a stunning housing and commercial boom that's helped turn Salt Lake City into one of the most dynamic smaller cities in the West.

The surrounding Salt Lake Valley offers striking landscapes and accessible outdoor adventures. Canyon breezes turn hot summer afternoons into enjoyable evenings, and snowy winter days are moderated with temperatures warmer than those at most ski destinations, making Salt Lake City an ideal destination year-round.

Salt Lake City's history was built on the shoulders of its Mormon founders, but today its culture draws equally on contemporary events and influences, such as hosting the Winter Olympics in 2002 (and quite possibly again in 2030 or, more likely, 2034) and becoming a preeminent destination for technological or innovative pursuits, earning it the nickname "Silicon Slopes." The city has emerged as the economic and cultural center of the vast Great Basin, between the Rocky Mountains and California's Sierra Nevada range. And its growing population of young outdoorsy types, artists, makers, foodies, and entrepreneurs has infused it

with a progressive sensibility that surprises many first-time visitors. Every mayor of Salt Lake City since 1976 has been a Democrat, and Salt Lake City County has voted Democrat more often than not in the last few presidential elections. Furthermore, the city has a sizable and visible LGBTQ+ community.

Tourists come here to hike and ski, and they stay for Salt Lake City's charm. As seen in other growing metropolitan areas, as the population increases, so does its pollution. Smog can be a serious problem, but Salt Lake City is working hard to shift to greener initiatives that will help alleviate these impacts. However, those susceptible to respiratory infections or allergies might wish to avoid visiting from January to March, as this is when inversion is most likely to occur.

Despite recent demographic changes, including the percentage of Mormon-identifying residents of Salt Lake County falling below 50% as of 2018 (it's far lower than that in Salt Lake City proper), since Brigham Young led his first party of pioneers here in 1847, Salt Lake City has been synonymous with the Mormon Church, formally called the Church of Jesus Christ of Latter-day Saints. The valley appealed to Young because, at the time, it was under the control of Mexico rather than the U.S. government, which the Mormons believed was responsible for much of their persecution. Within days of his arrival, Young drew up plans for Salt Lake City, which was to be the hub of the Mormons' promised land, a vast empire stretching from the Rockies to the Southern California coast. Although the area that eventually became the state of Utah was smaller than Young planned, Salt Lake City quickly outstripped his original vision. Missionaries throughout Scandinavia and the British Isles converted thousands, who flocked to the city to live near their church president—a living prophet, according to Church of Jesus Christ of Latter-day Saints doctrine—and worship in the newly built temple.

The area had few permanent settlements, an adequate supply of water and building materials, and a protected location, with the Wasatch Mountains to the east and a vast desert to the west. Still, on July 24, 1847, when Young gazed across the somewhat desolate valley and reportedly announced, "This is the right place," his followers understandably had mixed feelings. They saw no familiar forests or lush pasture, just a dry valley and a salty lake. Within hours of arriving, Young and his followers got to work, planting crops and diverting water for irrigation.

In the 1860s, income from railroads and mines created a class of industrialists who built mansions near downtown and whose businesses brought thousands of workers—mainly from Europe and few of whom were Mormon—to Utah Territory. By the time Utah became a state in 1896, Salt Lake was a thriving city. Although the majority of the city was members of the Church of Jesus Christ of Latter-day Saints, it claimed a sizable mix of Protestant, Catholic, and Jewish citizens. The Church of Jesus Christ of Latter-day Saints's presence is still evident, as both its headquarters and the Tabernacle, home to the world-famous Tabernacle Choir, call Temple Square home.

A rapidly growing number of high-rise hotels, office buildings, and downtown condominiums mark the skyline. And since the early 2010s, Salt Lake City has developed a respected culinary reputation that reflects both an influx of international eateries and a growing appreciation for farm-to-table cuisine. Increasingly less strict liquor laws have also helped turn the city into a bona fide hub of craft brewers and trendy cocktail lounges.

The city has also become an important center for business, medicine, education, and technology, and it's a major worldwide hub of Delta Airlines. A growing commitment to the arts from both the public and the private sectors has led to a booming cultural scene, and sports fans appreciate the presence of two major-league franchises—basketball's Utah Jazz and soccer's Real Salt Lake.

Although the former mining town and now ritzy getaway of Park City—just a 40-minute drive up the hill—receives the lion's share of Utah's skiing acclaim, Salt Lake County is home to four world-class resorts: Alta, Brighton, Snowbird, and Solitude. And the foothills just north and east of the city teem with amazingly scenic hiking and mountain-biking trails and myriad opportunities for wildlife viewing, as does Antelope Island, at the eastern end of the Great Salt Lake.

MAJOR REGIONS

Salt Lake City proper lies at the northern center of the greater Salt Lake Valley, at the confluence of two huge freeways that cross the country, east–west I-80 (which connects the city with nearby Park City) and north–south I-15, which runs north to the suburbs of Ogden and south into Utah County and Provo. Apart from Great Salt Lake and Antelope State Park, which are 15 miles west and 40 miles north of the city, respectively, most of the side trips you're likely to make from town are to the south and east. Immediately south, in the Midvalley and South Valley regions, you'll find the sometimes sprawling (especially as you head farther west from the Wasatch Range) suburbs of Millcreek, West Valley City, Murray, Sandy, Draper, and others. Heading due east of these suburbs, Big Cottonwood Canyon and Little Cottonwood Canyon are home to the county's four renowned ski areas.

Planning

Getting Here and Around

AIR

For a relatively small city, Salt Lake is served by a large airport—one that's in the midst of a major rebuild and expansion, with the first of two new terminals having opened in 2020 and a second expected to be completed by 2025. The airport is one of the major hubs of Delta Airlines, which offers direct flights to most major U.S. cities and a number of international ones. Additionally, most other U.S. airlines and a few international ones (Aeroméxico, Air Canada, Eurowings Discover, KLM) fly to Salt Lake.

CONTACTS Salt Lake City International Airport. ⊠ *3920 W. Terminal Dr., Salt Lake City* ☎ *801/575–2400, 800/595–2442* ⊕ *www.slcairport.com.*

AIRPORT TRANSFERS

Salt Lake City International Airport is just 6 miles west of downtown via I–80, or you can take North Temple, which leads to the city center. A taxi or rideshare, such as Uber or Lyft, from the airport to town costs about $20–$25. The Utah Transit Authority (UTA) operates TRAX light-rail to and from the airport; the ride takes less than 30 minutes, for $2.50 each way.

TAXI CONTACTS City Cab Company. ☎ *801/363–5550* ⊕ *www.citycabut.com.* **Yellow Cab.** ☎ *801/521–2100* ⊕ *www. yellowcabutah.com.*

CAR

Although traffic has increased as Salt Lake continues to grow, it's still comparatively less daunting than in most U.S. cities. On the whole, it's an easy city to explore by car. Free or inexpensive parking is easy to find in most neighborhoods, and even downtown garages charge a fraction of what you'll pay in many large cities. Finding your way around Salt Lake City is easy as the city is laid out on an orthogonal grid, but keep in mind that city blocks are longer than in many other cities.

PUBLIC TRANSPORTATION

Salt Lake has an efficient public transportation system, although it's used more by locals than visitors. One feature that even tourists rely heavily on is the Free Fare Zone for travel by bus within a roughly 36-square-block area downtown and on Capitol Hill. The TRAX light-rail system moves passengers quickly around the city and to the suburbs south of Salt Lake. There are 50 stations, originating from Salt Lake Central Station, where you can connect to FrontRunner (inter-county light rail), Amtrak, and buses.

The Blue Line runs north–south from Downtown to the suburb of Draper, serving the Downtown landmarks and America First Field (formerly Rio Tinto Stadium) in Sandy, home of Real Salt Lake soccer. The Red line extends eastward to the University of Utah and southwest to the suburb of South Jordan. The Green line originates at the airport and loops into Downtown before heading west to the suburb of West Valley. More than 20 stations have free park-and-ride lots. One-way tickets cost $2.50 and can be purchased from platform vending machines, online, or using the UTA mobile app called Transit.

BUS AND RAIL INFORMATION Utah Transit Authority (UTA). ☎ *801/743–3882* ⊕ *www.rideuta.com.*

Hotels

Although relatively standard chain hotels in every price range have long dominated the lodging landscape throughout Salt Lake, and especially in the suburbs beyond, several more stylish boutique properties have opened in recent years. Other notable exceptions to the many cookie-cutter chains include the historic Peery and Kimpton Monaco hotels, the mammoth and ultra-opulent Grand America, a smattering of B&Bs, and some distinctive properties out in the ski areas. Hotels here cater to skiers in winter months, and many offer packages that include tickets, transportation, and rentals, as well as knowledgeable staff who often head to the slopes when they're not at work. Most of the hotels are concentrated in the downtown area and near the airport, but a growing number of properties have opened on the East Side, and you'll find dozens of options, many of them built since the early 2010s building boom, in the suburbs.

Hotel reviews have been shortened. For full information, visit Fodors.com.

What It Costs			
$	$$	$$$	$$$$
HOTELS			
under $125	$125–$200	$201–$300	over $300

Restaurants

Ever since the 2002 Winter Olympics cast Salt Lake City in a new, contemporary, more diverse light, growing numbers of hip chef-driven eateries specializing in seasonal, locally sourced fare and myriad varieties of international fare have opened, many of these in the downtown core but increasingly in neighborhoods like 9th and 9th, Sugar House, and the Granary District. A number of old-school establishments—places like Ruth's Diner—still thrive and enjoy a loyal following among long-time locals, but for the most part, creativity and locavorism rule the scene. Many chefs focus heavily on seasonal, often organic produce as well as local game and fish, like rainbow trout, elk, and bison. And despite Salt Lake's infamously complicated history with drinking laws, the city has come around in recent years, with most newer restaurants offering carefully curated wine lists and a great selection of craft beers and spirits (many of these produced in Utah).

Restaurant reviews have been shortened. For full information, visit Fodors.com.

What It Costs			
$	$$	$$$	$$$$
RESTAURANTS			
under $16	$16–$22	$23–$30	over $30

Tours

Most excursions run by City Sights include lunch at Brigham Young's historic living quarters. Preservation Utah offers the most authoritative tours of Salt Lake's historic sights—the Kearns (Governor's) Mansion, the McCune Mansion, and the Union Pacific Depot—and their regularly scheduled public tours are free. They also offer downloadable self-guided tours on their website.

City Sights (aka Salt Lake City Tours)

BUS TOURS | A four-hour, 20-mile bus tour of the city includes dozens of major sights and many interesting lesser known places you wouldn't necessarily find on your own, with a 30-minute organ recital at the Tabernacle and a stop for lunch in Brigham Young's Lion House. A 4½-hour tour also includes a Tabernacle Choir at Temple Square concert or rehearsal, and the 1½-hour trolley tour is a nice way to get to know the city if time is a bit limited. The company also offers tours out to Great Salt Lake. ☎ *801/531–1001* ⊕ *www.saltlakecitytours.org* ✉ *From $49.*

Pitta Nature Tours

SPECIAL-INTEREST TOURS | Run by incredibly knowledgeable birder Tim Avery, this tour formerly known as Mountain West Tours is located just outside Salt Lake City and can show you all the best places to see the nearly 500 year-round and migratory birds that frequent this part of the world, including flammulated owls, gray partridges, Himalayan snowcocks, Cassia crossbills, and more. Half-, full-, and multiday tours are available, and Pitta also offers birding tours to other parts of the world, from Mexico to the Himalayas. ⊕ *www.pittatours.com* ✉ *From $150.*

★ Preservation Utah

WALKING TOURS | Tours led by knowledgeable guides from nonprofit Preservation Utah include a walking tour of Memory Grove park, the Kearns Mansion, the McCune Mansion, and the City and County Building. It's a good idea to book several days in advance. You can also explore on your own using the organization's app, "Utah Heritage Walks." Kearns Mansion tours are free, and others start at $12 per person. ✉ *Memory Grove Park, 375 N. Canyon Rd., Capitol Hill* ☎ *801/533–0858* ⊕ *www.preservationutah.org.*

Visitor Information

CONTACTS Salt Lake Convention and Visitors Bureau. ✉ *90 S. West Temple, Downtown* ☎ *801/534–4900, 800/541–4955* ⊕ *www.visitsaltlake.com.* **Utah Office of Tourism.** ✉ *300 N. State St., Capitol Hill* ☎ *800/200–1160, 801/538–1900* ⊕ *www.visitutah.com.*

When to Go

Spring and fall are the best times to visit, as cooler afternoons give way to idyllic breezy evenings. Summertime high temperatures average more than 90° (June–August), with several days above 100° each month. Winters bring snow, but abundant sunshine melts it quickly in the valley. If your plans include trips to Park City or the Cottonwood Canyons, follow weather forecasts closely because a fluffy 6-inch snowfall in the city will often be accompanied by 3 to 5 feet "up the hill." Extreme heat or cold without any wind often brings about "inversions" of polluted air that sometimes linger for longer than a week and prompt red alert warnings against activity in the valley, especially for people who suffer from respiratory issues. Locals often escape to the mountains on these days to get some fresh air above the clouds. Most years, ski season kicks off by mid-November and ends in early April. (During a heavy snow year, Snowbird ski resort will stay open on weekends as late as early July.) Expect larger crowds at the airport and higher rates at hotels and resorts near the ski slopes on winter weekends, particularly around holidays such as Christmas, Martin Luther King Jr. Day, and Presidents' Day, as well as during the Sundance Film Festival, based in nearby Park City but with some screenings in Salt Lake. Most of the rest of the year, city accommodations are cheaper than in other big cities across the country, but occasional large conventions sometimes drive up prices. Utahns reserve much of their patriotism for July 24, rather than July 4, as it's a recognized statewide holiday known as Pioneer Day, celebrated with a parade, a marathon, and fireworks; expect road and business closures.

FESTIVALS AND EVENTS

Gallery Stroll

ARTS FESTIVALS | Mingle with local artists and view their work at various art galleries throughout the city—but especially downtown and in Central City—on the third Friday of the month (or the first Friday of December). Participating galleries change monthly, so it's best to visit the website for each month's current roster. Artists and art lovers chat over wine and snacks at each stop. ✉ *Salt Lake City* ☎ *801/870–0956* ⊕ *www.gallerystroll.org.*

★ Utah Arts Festival

ARTS FESTIVALS | FAMILY | Over the fourth weekend in June, Salt Lake City's premier art event takes place over two full blocks downtown surrounding both Library and Washington Squares. Browse original art at the Marketplace, create your own masterpiece at the Art Yard, treat your taste buds to a food truck–sponsored feast, and get down to live music on multiple stages. ✉ *Library Square, 200 E. 400 S, Downtown* ☎ *801/322–2428* ⊕ *uaf.org.*

Downtown and Central City

With dozens of new mixed-use and residential developments in the works and a population that's expected to double by 2025, Downtown Salt Lake City is one of the most dynamic urban cores in the country. It's also the city's—and the state's—historic heart, as it's home to Temple Square, which continues to serve as the headquarters of the Church of Jesus Christ of Latter-day Saints. Although Downtown has always been important—it's always held the city's greatest concentration of offices, hotels, arts venues, restaurants, and bars—it was until relatively recently a neighborhood that felt eerily quiet on nights and weekends. With its residential population booming, it's finally becoming a lively place to stroll, walk, and

dine around the clock. This is especially evident during Open Streets nights. On Friday through Sunday evenings, late May through early September, Downtown's bar- and restaurant-lined Main Street morphs into a bustling pedestrian promenade. Musicians and artists perform, and businesses extend their outdoor seating along the sidewalk.

Downtown comprises a relatively compact area that extends several blocks west, east, and south of Temple Square (to the north lies Capitol Hill). The area to the west, around Pioneer Park and the Gateway, has undergone the greatest change of late, with its spate of new residential and commercial projects, some of them newly built and others fashioned out of the area's many handsome old warehouse buildings.

Although it sounds as though it might just be another name for downtown, Central City is a larger quadrant that extends east and south from Downtown, as far as 1300 East and 1300 South. This area contains a mix of residential and commercial pockets and some charming shopping and eating districts, such as Trolley Square, 9th and 9th, and gracious Liberty Park. Extending south from Downtown along the Main Street and State Street corridor, you'll find some of the city's most exciting and up-and-coming blocks in the Granary District and along the adjacent Central 9th strip, and farther south in the Ballpark and Liberty Wells areas. This region is where many of the city's swanky new apartment buildings are going up, most of them with trendy bars, eateries, and shops at street level.

◎ Sights

Church History Museum

HISTORY MUSEUM | In this angular 1980s building just west of Temple Square, you can view artifacts and works of art relating to the history and doctrine of the Mormon faith, including personal

The Salt Lake City Public Library was inspired by the Roman Colosseum.

belongings of church leaders Joseph Smith and Brigham Young. There are also samples of Mormon coins and scrip used as standard currency in Utah during the 1800s and beautiful examples of quilting, embroidery, and other handicrafts. Upstairs galleries exhibit religious and secular works by Mormon artists from all over the world. In the courtyard out front, you can visit the Deuel Cabin, an 1847 pine structure that's one of two surviving homes built by Salt Lake City's earliest pioneers. The courtyard also has access to the church's Family History Library, where anyone is welcome to research their genealogy. ⊠ *45 N. West Temple, Temple Square* ☎ *801/240–3310* ⊕ *history.churchofjesuschrist.org/landing/ museum?lang=eng* ☾ *Closed Sun.*

Church of Jesus Christ of Latter-day Saints Conference Center

CONVENTION CENTER | Completed in 2000, this massive center features a 21,000-seat auditorium with a 7,000-pipe organ and a 850-seat theater. Equally impressive are the rooftop gardens landscaped with native plants and streams to mirror the surrounding mountains. Visitors can see the center on 45-minute tours; all guests must be accompanied by a guide. The Center is home to the biannual General Conference and regular concerts by the Tabernacle Choir at Temple Square. ⊠ *60 W. North Temple, Temple Square* ☎ *801/240–0075* ⊕ *www.churchofjesuschrist.org/learn/ conference-center-temple-square.*

★ Clark Planetarium

OBSERVATORY | **FAMILY** | With an array of free hands-on exhibits and state-of-the-art full-dome and IMAX theaters, Clark Planetarium is a great family attraction, and it's reasonably priced, too. Traipse across a moonscape and learn about Utah's contributions to spaceflight, but save a few minutes for the Planet Fun Store. ⊠ *110 S. 400 W, Downtown* ☎ *385/468–7827* ⊕ *www.slco.org/ clark-planetarium* ☒ *Exhibits free; movies from $7.*

Discovery Gateway Children's Museum

CHILDREN'S MUSEUM | FAMILY | The region's premier children's museum, geared toward kids ages 2 to 10, has three floors of lively hands-on experiences. Kids can participate in a television newscast, learn about dinosaurs by seeing what it's like to be a paleontologist, tell stories through pictures or radio, climb into a Life Flight helicopter, or revel in a kid-size town with grocery store, vehicles, a house, and a construction site. The family-friendly restaurants of the surrounding Gateway Center, including the HallPass food hall, are steps from the museum. ⊠ *444 W. 100 S, Downtown* ☎ *801/456–5437* ⊕ *www.discoverygateway.org* 🎟 *$14* ☉ *Closed Tues.*

Family History Library

This four-story library houses the world's largest collection of genealogical data, including books, maps, and census information. Mormons and non-Mormons alike come here to research their family history. ⊠ *35 N. West Temple, Temple Square* ☎ *801/240–6996* ⊕ *www.family-search.org/en/library/visit* ☉ *Closed Sun.*

The Gallivan Center

PLAZA/SQUARE | FAMILY | Sometimes dubbed Salt Lake City's "living room," the John W. Gallivan Center anchors downtown and offers an amphitheater, ice rink, and various art projects, and it hosts numerous events, including popular Food Truck Thursdays and several annual festivals. Down the stairs on the south side of this bustling plaza, you'll also find a strip of popular fast-casual restaurants, including Monkeywrench ice cream and Bangkok Terrace. ⊠ *239 S. Main St., Downtown* ☎ *801/535–6110* ⊕ *www.thegallivancenter.com.*

★ Granary District

NEIGHBORHOOD | If downtown Salt Lake City is growing fast, this historic manufacturing and railroad district on the southwest side of downtown is positively booming. Many of the neighborhood's handsome late-19th-century and early-20th-century warehouses and factory buildings have been converted into mixed-use developments, and in seemingly every direction, shiny new condos and apartments are going up. Many of the city's hottest drinking, dining, and shopping venues are in the Granary District, including Fisher Brewing, Laziz Kitchen, Water Witch, and The Pearl. West 900 South, between 300 West and South West Temple, is especially rife with buzzy places to eat and drink. ⊠ *Salt Lake City ✛ Bound by 600 South, S. West Temple St., and I–15* ⊕ *www.thegranary-district.com.*

The Leonardo

ART MUSEUM | FAMILY | Salt Lake's only museum devoted to the convergence of science, art, and technology hosts large-scale national touring exhibits as well as hands-on permanent exhibits dedicated to inspiring the imaginations of children. In this former library building, you'll be greeted by a main-floor lab space where revolving artists-in-residence offer a variety of free programs for kids to sculpt with clay, draw, design, or write. Head upstairs to the workshop, where volunteers help you build with repurposed household objects and deconstructed electronics. ⊠ *209 E. 500 S, Downtown* ☎ *801/531–9800* ⊕ *www.theleonardo.org* 🎟 *$13; additional fee for special exhibits.*

★ Liberty Park

CITY PARK | Salt Lake's oldest (and second-largest) park contains a wealth of intriguing amenities, including the Tracy Aviary, the Chase Home Museum, several playgrounds, a large pond, a swimming pool, and volleyball and tennis courts, on its eight square city blocks, which total about 80 acres. Weekly farmers' markets on Friday nights and the city's biggest Pioneer Day celebration (July 24) mark a busy summer schedule annually. Within walking distance of a number of inviting neighborhood restaurants, it's also a nice place for a stroll before or after brunch

Downtown and Central City

THE AVENUES

100 South
200 South
300 South
400 South
500 South
600 South
700 South
800 South
900 South

EAST CENTRAL

CENTRAL CITY

9TH & 9TH

EAST LIBERTY PARK

Liberty Park

Herman L Franks Park

1300 South
Browning Ave.
Roosevelt Ave.
Emerson Ave.
Kensington Ave.
Bryan Ave.
Logan Ave.
1700 South

E Street
F Street
500 East
600 East
700 East
800 East
900 East
1000 East
Lake Street
Windsor Street
Lincoln Street

Sights ▼
1 Church History Museum **D1**
2 Church of Jesus Christ of Latter-day Saints Conference Center **D1**
3 Clark Planetarium **B2**
4 Discovery Gateway Children's Museum **B2**
5 Family History Library **D1**
6 Gallivan Center **E3**
7 Granary District **C5**
8 The Leonardo **E4**
9 Liberty Park **G6**
10 Salt Lake City and County Building **E3**
11 Salt Lake City Public Library **E3**
12 The Tabernacle **D1**
13 Temple Square **D1**
14 Tracy Aviary & Botanical Garden **G7**

Restaurants ▼
1 Bambara **D2**
2 The Bayou **E4**
3 Café Trio Downtown **I5**
4 The Copper Onion **E3**
5 Current Fish & Oyster ... **F3**
6 Curry Fried Chicken **E5**
7 HallPass **B2**
8 HSL **F2**
9 Ivy & Varley **D2**
10 La-Cai Noodle House **E6**
11 Laziz Kitchen **D6**
12 Lucky 13 Bar and Grill .. **D7**
13 Manoli's **F6**
14 Oasis Cafe **G2**
15 Pago **I6**
16 Park Cafe **G7**
17 Pretty Bird Chicken **E2**
18 Red Iguana **A1**
19 Seasons Plant Based Bistro **E8**
20 Settebello Pizzeria Napoletana **C3**
21 Sweet Lake Biscuits & Limeade **D9**
22 Takashi **D3**
23 Tin Angel **D2**
24 Zest Kitchen & Bar **C3**

Quick Bites ▼
1 Eva's Bakery **D2**
2 Fillings & Emulsions **D8**
3 Goodly Cookies **I3**
4 Normal Ice Cream **E6**
5 Tulie Bakery **I5**

Hotels ▼
1 AC Hotel by Marriott Salt Lake City Downtown **C2**
2 Evo Hotel **B4**
3 The Grand America Hotel **D4**
4 Hyatt House Salt Lake City– Downtown **C2**
5 Hyatt Regency Salt Lake City **D2**
6 Kimpton Hotel Monaco Salt Lake City **D2**
7 Le Méridien Salt Lake Downtown **C2**
8 Little America Hotel **D4**
9 Peery Hotel, Tapestry Collection by Hilton **D3**
10 Salt Lake Marriott Downtown at City Creek **D2**

3

Salt Lake City DOWNTOWN AND CENTRAL CITY

or dinner. ⊠ *600 E. 900 S, East Side*
☎ *801/521–0962* ⊕ *www.slc.gov/parks*.

Salt Lake City and County Building
GOVERNMENT BUILDING | The castle-like
seat of city government was the city's
tallest building from its 1894 construction to 1973. On Washington Square,
at the spot where the original Mormon
settlers circled their wagons on their first
night in the Salt Lake Valley, this building
served as the state capitol for 19 years.
Hundreds of trees, including species
from around the world, and many
winding paths and seating areas make
the grounds a calm downtown oasis.
In summer the grounds host major Salt
Lake arts and music festivals. Free tours
are given on Monday at noon during the
summer and by request at other times
through Preservation Utah. ⊠ *451 S.
State St., Downtown* ☎ *801/535–7704*
⊕ *www.slc.gov* ☽ *Closed weekends*.

★ Salt Lake City Public Library
LIBRARY | **FAMILY** | Designed by Moshe
Safdie and built in 2003, this spectacular
contemporary structure has become
the city's cultural center and one of the
country's most architecturally noteworthy
libraries. Inspired by the Roman Colise-
um, it features a six-story walkable wall
that serves as both sculpture and func-
tion, allowing for great views and a path
up the building. From the rooftop garden
you get a 360-degree view of the valley
and mountains. Hemingway Café (the
on-site branch of the Salt Lake Roasting
Co. coffeehouse), the outstanding Art at
the Main gallery, a handful of shops, a
writing center, and a public radio station
provide ways to spend the entire day
here. Kids can fall in love with reading in
the Crystal Cave and Treehouse Room in
the huge children's section. Other noteworthy features include a Teen Lounge,
an extensive Alternative Press/Zine
Collection, and a collection of beehives
on the rooftop where visitors can learn
about beekeeping and honey harvesting.

There are several other libraries in the
system, including the Tudor-style Sprague
Library that opened in 1928 in the city's
popular Sugar House neighborhood.
⊠ *210 E. 400 S, Downtown* ☎ *801/524–
8200* ⊕ *about.slcpl.org/main-library*.

The Tabernacle
PERFORMANCE VENUE | The Salt Lake City
Tabernacle, also known simply as the
Tabernacle, is home to the famous
Tabernacle Choir at Temple Square and
an impressive organ with 11,623 pipes.
Visitors can hear organ recitals Monday
through Saturday at noon (and also at 2
pm across the street in the Conference
Center) and Sunday at 2 pm. You're also
welcome Thursday from 7:30 pm to
9:30 pm to listen to the choir rehearse
Sunday hymns, as well as from 9:30
am to 10 am as the choir performs for
the world's longest-running contin-
uous network broadcast, *Music and
the Spoken Word*. During the summer
months, choir rehearsals and *Music
and the Spoken Word* take place at
the Conference Center. ⊠ *50 N. West
Temple, Temple Square* ☎ *801/240–2534*
⊕ *www.churchofjesuschrist.org/learn/
salt-lake-tabernacle-temple-square*.

★ Temple Square
PLAZA/SQUARE | **FAMILY** | When Mormon
pioneer and leader Brigham Young first
entered the Salt Lake Valley, he chose
this spot at the mouth of City Creek Canyon for the headquarters of the Church
of Jesus Christ of Latter-day Saints, a
role it maintains to this day. The buildings
in Temple Square vary in age, from the
Tabernacle constructed in the 1860s to
the Conference Center constructed in
2000. The centerpiece of the square, the
striking Salt Lake Temple isn't open to the
general public but is a sacred pilgrimage
destination for members of the faith.
Built of blocks of granite hauled by oxen
and train from Little Cottonwood Canyon,
the Temple opened in 1893, 40 years to
the day after the start of its construction.

See emus, parrots, and bald eagles at Tracy Aviary & Botanical Garden.

Perhaps the most striking aspect of the Square is the attention to landscaping, which turns the heart of downtown Salt Lake City into a year-round oasis. The Church takes particular pride in its Christmas decorations, which make a nighttime downtown stroll, or horse-and-buggy ride, a must on December calendars. Some of the square's notable buildings include the **Beehive House,** Brigham Young's restored 1854 home; the **Family History Library,** which houses the world's largest collection of genealogical data, and where Mormons and non-Mormons alike can research their family histories; and the stately 1911 **Joseph Smith Memorial Building.** The Salt Lake Temple and parts of Temple Square are currently undergoing a four-year renovation and restoration, which is expected to be completed sometime in 2025. ⊠ *Main St. and N. Temple, Downtown* ☏ *801/240–8945* ⊕ *www.churchofjesus-christ.org/feature/templesquare.*

Tracy Aviary & Botanical Garden

ZOO | FAMILY | Easily walkable for even the smallest kids, this family-friendly facility in gracious Liberty Park features more than 100 species of birds found on the Western Hemispheric Flyway, a migratory pattern that includes Great Salt Lake. You will see emus, bald eagles, flamingos, parrots, several types of waterfowl, and maybe even a wandering peacock. There are bird shows and educational activities daily. ⊠ *589 E. 1300 S, East Side* ☏ *801/596–8500* ⊕ *www.tracyaviary.org* ⌺ *$13.*

🍴 Restaurants

Bambara

$$$$ | **MODERN AMERICAN** | In an ornate former bank lobby adjacent to swanky Hotel Monaco, the city's most esteemed hotel restaurant is as notable for its setting as for its exceptional food. The kitchen crafts big plates of seasonally sourced modern American fare, including seared elk loin with berry compote, sea scallops with corn and cannellini beans, and

fillet of beef with duck-fat potatoes and truffle aioli. **Known for:** stylish, see-and-be-seen dining room; lavishly prepared steaks and seafood; outstanding wine list. $ *Average main: $45* ⊠ *202 S. Main St., Downtown* ☎ *801/363–5454* ⊕ *www.bambara-slc.com* ⊘ *No dinner Sun. No lunch.*

The Bayou

$ | **CAJUN** | You'll find more than 200 microbrews, both bottled and on tap, at this lively, often crowded Louisiana-inflected bar and restaurant on the south side of downtown. The menu offers plenty of Cajun specialties, such as crawfish étouffée and blackened catfish sandwiches, along with more regionally American grub like fried chicken and pizza. **Known for:** savory alligator sausage cheesecake; gumbolaya (jambalaya smothered with crawfish gumbo); great live music many nights. $ *Average main: $15* ⊠ *645 S. State St., Downtown* ☎ *801/961–8400* ⊕ *www.utahbayou.com* ⊘ *Closed Mon. No lunch on weekends.*

Café Trio Downtown

$$ | **MODERN ITALIAN** | In this comfortable, modern dining room with clean lines and a great location near Trolley Square and 9th and 9th, you might whet your appetite with a selection of cheeses or flatbread, but save room for balsamic-drizzled stone-fired pizzas, hearty baked pastas, and roasted half chicken, all of which vie for attention at this chatter-filled Italian eatery. You'll want to linger for the crème brûlée, flavored martinis, and espresso. **Known for:** terrific weekend brunch; enchanting patio with a leafy pergola; knowledgeable, friendly service. $ *Average main: $19* ⊠ *680 S. 900 E, Downtown* ☎ *801/533–8746* ⊕ *www.triodiningslc.com.*

★ The Copper Onion

$$$ | **MODERN AMERICAN** | Celebrated chef-owner Ryan Lowder brings joy with the basics—artful salads, house-made pastas, and charcuterie—and then dazzles with mouthwatering locally sourced dishes, from Cast Iron Mary's Chicken to rainbow trout with charred lemon and Greek yogurt. Stop in at this chic modern downtown bistro before or after a film, gallery tour, or live theater on Salt Lake's Broadway. **Known for:** cocktails and after-dinner drinks next door at Copper Common bar; warmly lighted, romantic dining room; delicious charcuterie board. $ *Average main: $28* ⊠ *111 E. Broadway, Downtown* ☎ *801/355–3282* ⊕ *www.thecopperonion.com* ⊘ *No lunch weekdays.*

★ Current Fish & Oyster

$$ | **SEAFOOD** | Being in a city with a major international hub airport has its advantages, including access to daily shipments of incredibly fresh fish, which are the stars on the menu of this postindustrial former warehouse space with a soaring arched ceiling and exposed rafters and air ducts. Expect seafood sourced from East and West—consider Japanese Kumamoto oysters on the half shell, Gulf shrimp and grits, and Prince Edward Island mussels with house-smoked pork belly. **Known for:** ceviche and other raw bar specialties; affogato for dessert; stellar international wine list. $ *Average main: $20* ⊠ *279 E. 300 S, Salt Lake City* ☎ *801/326–3474* ⊕ *www.currentfishandoyster.com* ⊘ *No lunch weekends.*

Curry Fried Chicken

$ | **INDIAN** | Whether for a flavor-packed snack or a hearty meal, head to this bustling hole-in-the-wall café near the Salt Lake City and County Building for some of the best fried chicken in the city—this Indian-spiced treat is available with veggie curry and rice, hummus and pitas, or in a salad. You'll find plenty of other tasty Indian and Middle Eastern dishes here, too, including falafel wraps, chicken shawarma, vegetable samosas, and masala chai. **Known for:** hot curry fries; no alcohol; colorful, quirky decor. $ *Average main: $13* ⊠ *660 S. State St., Downtown* ☎ *801/924–9188* ⊕ *www.facebook.com/cfcslc* ⊘ *Closed Sun.*

★ HallPass

$ | INTERNATIONAL | Set in downtown's Gateway Center shopping village and offering several distinct dining stations and seating at gorgeous carved-wood tables, the city's first food hall opened in 2020 and has quickly become a trendy spot to eat and people-watch. The options are varied and consistently good and include Nashville hot chicken, Belgian-style waffles and crepes, slow-cooked ramen, prodigious lobster rolls, and Japanese-Mexican-fusion *izakaya* fare. **Known for:** large outdoor dining area; great mix of healthy and decadent international options; terrific craft beer bar. [$] *Average main: $13* ✉ *153 S. Rio Grande St., Salt Lake City* ☎ *801/415–9886* 🌐 *www.hallpassslc.com.*

★ HSL

$$$$ | MODERN AMERICAN | Within a short, pretty stroll of the Avenues and Capitol Hill, this outpost of the original, nationally acclaimed Handle restaurant in Park City turns heads with its stunningly plated, locavore-driven cuisine and a fetching interior with marble-top tables, a wood-beam ceiling, and a gleaming, tiled open kitchen. What's served on any given night varies according to what's in season, but you might encounter truffled agnolotti pasta filled with Swiss chard, corn, and goat's whey cream or slow-cooked pork shank with carrot-frisée salad, whipped ranch dressing, and apple butter. **Known for:** artful, Instagram-worthy food; exquisitely curated spirits, wine, and beer list; unusual, daily-changing dessert selection. [$] *Average main: $37* ✉ *418 E. 200 S, Downtown* ☎ *801/539–9999* 🌐 *www.hslrestaurant.com* ⏲ *Closed Sun. and Mon. No lunch.*

Ivy & Varley

$$ | MODERN AMERICAN | Downtown's largest restaurant patio—with its tranquil reflecting pool, canopy of ornamental trees, and eye-catching murals—is an idyllic setting for boozy weekend brunch with friends, dinner and drinks before a show at nearby Abravanel Hall, or a late-night snack between dance clubs. The reasonably priced contemporary American food is consistently good, too, from the braised Wagyu beef Benedict with truffle Mornay sauce at brunch to ahi tuna tartare and cashew-kimchi bowls for dinner. **Known for:** sophisticated cocktails; gorgeous outdoor space; lavender lemon bars with honey mousse. [$] *Average main: $19* ✉ *55 W. 100 S, Downtown* ☎ *801/895–2846* 🌐 *www.ivyandvarley.com.*

La-Cai Noodle House

$$ | VIETNAMESE | Named for a historic restaurant district in Ho Chi Minh City, this unassuming eatery south of downtown re-creates the cuisine of southern Vietnam. The menu ranges from traditional basics, like beef-brisket pho and stir-fried crispy egg noodles, to more creative fare, such as walnut shrimp in a creamy white sauce, salt-baked calamari, and a massive hot pot that's perfect for groups of two to four. **Known for:** pho and noodle soups; huge portions; hot and iced Vietnamese coffee. [$] *Average main: $19* ✉ *961 S. State St., Downtown* ☎ *801/322–3590* 🌐 *www.lacainoodlehouse.com* ⏲ *Closed Sun. No lunch.*

★ Laziz Kitchen

$$ | MIDDLE EASTERN | Run by a friendly husband-and-husband team who began with a hummus stand at the farmers' market, Laziz has grown into an outstanding full-service Lebanese restaurant in the burgeoning Granary District, with a cheerfully hip plant-filled dining room and street-side terrace. The most delicious strategy here is to make a feast of a selection of small plates: spiced *labneh*, eggplant baba ghanoush, grilled Halloumi cheese, kibbeh, fried cauliflower with garlic-cilantro pesto, red-wine-braised lamb shank, and maybe a *kafta* burger or two. **Known for:** shared dips and mezze appetizer platters; blueberry, lavender, and other kefir sodas; interesting list of Lebanese wines. [$] *Average main: $20* ✉ *912 Jefferson St. W,*

Salt Lake City ☎ *801/441–1228* ⊕ *www. lazizkitchen.com.*

Lucky 13 Bar and Grill

$ | **AMERICAN** | There may be no better place in the valley to order a monstrous burger (with intriguing toppings like hickory-smoked pastrami or peanut butter and bacon, plus house-baked buns) and wash it down with a local beer or a shot of whiskey. At this rollicking tavern near Smith's Ballpark baseball stadium, bacon lovers drool over the house-made slices on many signature burgers, but it's hard to resist Fungus Amongus, a burger with mushrooms sautéed in red wine and garlic, topped with Swiss cheese. **Known for:** attractive landscaped patio; mammoth burgers; locally produced whiskies. $ *Average main: $14* ⊠ *135 W. 1300 S, Downtown* ☎ *801/487–4418* ⊕ *www. lucky13slc.com.*

Manoli's

$$ | **GREEK** | Venture into this sleek, angular neighborhood bistro to savor some of the tastiest contemporary Greek food in Utah, best enjoyed with a selection from the nicely curated wine list (which lists some excellent Hellenic offerings). The menu is broken down into tapas-style vegetable, meat, and seafood plates, such as *piquillo* peppers with smoked feta and olive oil, charred octopus with bean salad and sherry vinaigrette, and pork-beef meatballs with a soul-warming cinnamon-tomato sauce. **Known for:** delicious apps and side dishes; ouzo and resin-y Skinos mastiha Greek liqueurs; Greek doughnuts with spiced-honey syrup. $ *Average main: $22* ⊠ *402 E. 900 S, Salt Lake City* ☎ *801/532–3760* ⊕ *www. manolison9th.com* ☽ *Closed Mon. No lunch weekdays.*

Oasis Cafe

$$ | **ECLECTIC** | From early morning to well into the evening, a selection of fine teas and espresso drinks, big breakfasts, and healthful entrées draw regulars to this café and its serene patio courtyard, and also to adjacent New Age bookstore and gift shop, the Golden Braid. The menu leans toward vegetarian and seafood selections, such as multigrain waffles and eggs Benedict Florentine in the morning and sesame-blackened ahi with sticky rice and peanut stir-fry with udon noodles later in the day. **Known for:** short stroll to the Avenues and City Creek Park; diverse, New Age vibe; seasonal house-made sorbets. $ *Average main: $22* ⊠ *151 S. 500 E, Downtown* ☎ *801/322–0404* ⊕ *www.oasiscafeslc.com.*

Oquirrh

$$$ | **MODERN AMERICAN** | An unprepossessing storefront eatery near the leafy Avenues district, Oquirrh (rhymes with "poker") is named for the snowcapped mountain range west of Downtown and focuses on seasonal fare with locally sourced ingredients. Boldly flavored dishes like house-made radiatori pasta with basil-cashew pesto and Niman ranch pork chops with feta and beet puree are presented artfully on handmade stoneware in an intimate, art-filled dining room. **Known for:** friendly, knowledgeable service; excellent French- and West Coast–centric wine selection; Sunday brunch. $ *Average main: $28* ⊠ *368 E. 100 S, Salt Lake City* ☎ *801/359–0426* ⊕ *www. oquirrhslc.com* ☽ *No lunch weekdays.*

★ Pago

$$$ | **MODERN AMERICAN** | More than living up to its promise of farm-to-table freshness, this welcoming, microscopic, chef-driven neighborhood bistro capitalizes on local artisan farmers, with big and small plates anchored around simple ingredients like radishes, beets, or mountain stream trout. There's plenty to satisfy big appetites, too, such as bavette steak with duck fat potatoes, and fettuccine with braised hen, *sofrito*, pistachio, chile, and lemon. **Known for:** cute, art-filled dining in 9th and 9th neighborhood; excellent service; scene-y weekend brunches. $ *Average main: $26* ⊠ *878 S. 900 E, East Side* ☎ *801/532–0777* ⊕ *www. pagoslc.com* ☽ *No lunch weekdays.*

The Park Cafe

$ | **AMERICAN** | Drop by this long-running café with a wall of windows facing the leafy trees of Liberty Park for a leisurely breakfast or lunch before strolling amid the greenery or visiting Tracy Aviary & Botanical Garden. Specialties include vegan hash with grilled potatoes and avocado, the bacon-and-egg-filled pancake sandwich, and a variety of burgers. **Known for:** cheeseburgers smothered in pork chile verde sauce; breakfast served all day; friendly neighborhood atmosphere. [$] *Average main: $9* ✉ *604 E. 1300 S, Downtown* ☎ *801/487–1670* 🌐 *www.theparkcafeslc.com* 🕒 *No dinner.*

Pretty Bird

$ | **AMERICAN** | As its name hints, this usually packed Downtown fast-casual eatery with counter service and a small seating area specializes in poultry, and the menu couldn't be simpler. Pick your spice level (from medium to the excruciatingly fiery "hot behind"), choose either a quarter bird or a boneless-chicken sandwich, and add some sides if you'd like (crinkle-cut fries, cider slaw, pickles). **Known for:** in midst of Downtown shopping and theater scene; astoundingly spicy fried chicken (as requested); interesting sides, like purple cider slaw. [$] *Average main: $14* ✉ *146 S. Regent St., Salt Lake City* 🌐 *www.prettybirdchicken.com* 🕒 *Closed Sun.*

★ **Red Iguana**

$$ | **MEXICAN** | Visitors are sometimes taken aback to find stunningly authentic, richly flavorful house-made moles, *chile verde*, carnitas, and other self-described "killer Mexican" dishes in Salt Lake City, and especially in a rambling old yellow-brick building on the other side of I–15 from Downtown. But the lines out the door attest to the longstanding adoration of the Red Iguana, which in addition to doling out great food also serves first-rate premium margaritas, good Mexican beers, and delicious and free salsa and chips. **Known for:** chilaquiles with a fried egg and pork chorizo; richly complex turkey and mole dishes; fried ice cream with shredded coconut and cinnamon-sugar. [$] *Average main: $19* ✉ *736 W. North Temple, Downtown* ☎ *801/322–1489* 🌐 *www.rediguana.com.*

Seasons Plant Based Bistro

$$ | **VEGETARIAN** | Along the Jefferson Street restaurant row in the Granary District, this sleek, contemporary space serves creative, beautifully presented vegan cuisine, much of it with Italian and French preparations. Dishes like mushroom Alfredo with wild mushrooms and house-made ravioli with butternut squash and brown-butter consommé are both hearty and robustly flavored. **Known for:** tasty veggie versions of Philly cheesesteaks, Cuban sandwiches, and burgers; fine selection of wine and craft beer; cheesecakes with daily-rotating flavors. [$] *Average main: $20* ✉ *916 S. Jefferson St., Downtown* ☎ *385/267–1922* 🌐 *www.seasonsslc.com* 🕒 *Closed Sun. and Mon.*

Settebello Pizzeria Napoletana

$$ | **PIZZA** | Two ambitious restaurateurs set out to re-create authentic, ultrathin-crust pizza from Naples using an oven, flour, cheese, and other ingredients shipped from the Old Country. The popular result of this undertaking is Settebello Pizzeria, which draws raves for its blistered-crust pies with simple, top-quality toppings, like crusted tomatoes, artichokes, and pancetta, and a few nontraditional options, like jalapeño marmalade and slow-cooked brisket. **Known for:** slow-cooked smoked-brisket pizza; festive high-ceilinged dining room; tasty frozen desserts in adjacent Capo Gelateria. [$] *Average main: $18* ✉ *260 S. 200 W, Downtown* ☎ *801/322–3556* 🌐 *www.settebello.net.*

★ **Sweet Lake Biscuits & Limeade**

$ | **SOUTHERN** | This supercasual café with a smattering of sidewalk tables serves up heavenly biscuits in an assortment of ways, from blueberry-biscuit pudding French toast to fried chicken biscuit sandwiches with spicy pickles and mustard.

Head to the refreshment stand at one end of the dining room to order a refreshing raspberry, habanero, or mint limeade. **Known for:** limeades with rotating seasonal flavors; biscuit eggs Benedict; strawberry "tall cake" with fresh cream. [$] *Average main: $12* ✉ *54 W. 1700 S, Downtown* ☎ *801/953–1978* 🌐 *www.sweetlakefresh.com* 🕑 *No dinner.*

★ Takashi

$$$ | JAPANESE | You'll often see chef-owner Takashi Gibo behind the sushi bar at this hip and lively Japanese restaurant across from the Gallivan Center. Takashi is known for sublime, melt-in-your mouth sushi as well as a slew of *izakaya*-style treats, like miso-grilled eggplant, baked marinated sablefish, and shiitake lamb shank in Japanese yellow curry. **Known for:** barbecue pork ribs; riceless sushi rolls wrapped in cucumber; superb wine and sake selection. [$] *Average main: $26* ✉ *18 W. Market St., Downtown* ☎ *801/519–9595* 🌐 *www.takashisushi.com* 🕑 *Closed Sun. No lunch Sat.*

Tin Angel

$$$ | SOUTHERN | This bustling, art-filled restaurant inside the airy, contemporary Eccles Theater draws plenty of folks for meals before or even during shows (there's a quick-bites intermission menu). Food here tends toward Southern American, with plenty of modern twists, such as barbecue bone-in ribs with sweet potato mash, and shrimp salad po'boys with root-vegetable chips. **Known for:** pretheater people-watching; fried pickles with ranch dressing; banana pudding. [$] *Average main: $26* ✉ *131 S. Main St., Downtown* ☎ *801/328–4155* 🌐 *www.thetinangel.com* 🕑 *No lunch.*

Zest Kitchen & Bar

$$ | VEGETARIAN | The charms of this festive bar and grill near downtown theaters and Pioneer Park include quirky decor (both a chandelier *and* a disco ball), a superfriendly staff, a focus on organic spirits and wines, and healthy farm-to-fork–inspired plant-based cuisine. Drop in for a thyme-infused grapefruit-vodka cocktail (with CBD on request) and cashew-quinoa–stuffed poblano pepper before a show or a smoothie, jackfruit pizza, or miso ramen bowl to break up an afternoon of exploring. **Known for:** luscious smoothies; creative vegetarian fare; extensive selection of teas and healthy elixirs. [$] *Average main: $19* ✉ *275 S. 200 W, Salt Lake City* ☎ *801/433–0589* 🌐 *www.zestslc.com* 🕑 *No lunch Mon.*

☕ Coffee and Quick Bites

Eva's Bakery

$ | BAKERY | Skip the overpriced breakfast at your downtown hotel and make a beeline for this enchanting Parisian-inspired boulangerie with tiled walls, marble café tables, and sidewalk seating out front. Start the day with beet-avocado toast, stuffed French toast oozing with lemon cream cheese and blueberry compote, or a fruit tart or almond croissant. **Known for:** exquisite French pastries; short walk to Gallivan Center and Temple Square; French toast stuffed with lemon cream cheese. [$] *Average main: $13* ✉ *155 S. Main St., Downtown* ☎ *801/355–3942* 🌐 *www.evasbakeryslc.com* 🕑 *No dinner.*

★ Fillings & Emulsions

$ | BAKERY | Employing a team of world-class pastry chefs, including acclaimed owner and Food Network competitor Adalberto Diaz, this sumptuous little cake shop produces artful and delicious sweet treats. Stop by and treat yourself to a guava tart or a slice of raspberry chocolate cheesecake. **Known for:** one-day classes on myriad topics; savory baked Cuban sandwich meat pies; colorful French macarons. [$] *Average main: $6* ✉ *1475 S. Main St., Salt Lake City* ☎ *385/229–4228* 🌐 *www.fillingsandemulsions.com* 🕑 *Closed Sun. No dinner.*

Goodly Cookies
$ | **BAKERY** | **FAMILY** | It's all about the cookie at this delightful little shop whose best sellers include the cobbler-inspired Peachy Keen and the ethereal White Chocolate Raspberry Delight. It's open till 11 pm most nights and midnight on weekends, making it ideal for satisfying your late-night sugar cravings. **Known for:** ice-cream sandwiches; gooey Brookie (a hybrid of chocolate chip and brownie); unusual flavors like pumpkin chai and strawberry banana. [$] *Average main: $4* ✉ *432 S. 900 E, Salt Lake City* ☎ *801/784–4848* 🌐 *www.goodlycookies.com* 🕒 *Closed Sun.*

★ **normal ice cream**
$ | **ICE CREAM** | Begun by a pastry chef from acclaimed HSL restaurant, this off-beat artisan icecream shop turns out exceptional all-natural soft-serve ice cream in a riot of interesting flavors (brown butter, spruce tip with salted caramel, apple cider sorbet, olive oil), along with "composed" cones with interesting toppings mixed in—like house-made cake bits, gingersnap cookies, and honeycomb. If you're looking for sweet picnic treats, pick up a pint or a slice of ice-cream cake. **Known for:** vegan sorbets in cool flavors (pomegranate, blood orange, etc.); choco tacos with horchata ice cream; creative ice-cream sandwiches. [$] *Average main: $6* ✉ *169 E. 900 S, Salt Lake City* ☎ *385/299–5418* 🌐 *www.normal.club.*

Tulie Bakery
$ | **BAKERY** | This cozy neighborhood bakeshop between Trolley Square and 9th and 9th turns out absolutely ethereal cookies (the salted caramel bars are legendary), tarts, and cakes, as well as sandwiches on soft and crusty savory breads. The soppressata and provolone and prosciutto-fig-gorgonzola sandwiches are among the favorites, and there's a full roster of espresso drinks and fine teas. **Known for:** fine Japanese green teas; breakfast toast with apricot honey and garlic chevre; olive oil–orange cake with brown-butter buttercream. [$] *Average main: $8* ✉ *863 E. 700 S, Downtown* ☎ *801/883–9741* 🌐 *www.tuliebakery.com* 🕒 *No dinner.*

Hotels

★ **AC Hotel by Marriott Salt Lake City Downtown**
$$ | **HOTEL** | Across from the convention center and Vivint Arena, this dapper midsize property—part of Marriott's hip AC boutique brand—stands out for its smartly designed rooms, each with plush duvets and linens, 55-inch flat-screen TVs, and bathrooms with rainfall showers, as well as a 24-hour gym and a spacious lobby with high ceilings and comfy chairs you can actually enjoy sitting in. **Pros:** many restaurants and bars within walking distance; airy, stylish rooms; nice restaurant and bar on site. **Cons:** busy downtown location; gym overlooks parking lot; fills up during conventions. [$] *Rooms from: $177* ✉ *225 W. 200 S, Downtown* ☎ *385/722–9600* 🌐 *www.marriott.com* 🛏 *164 rooms* 🍴 *No Meals.*

★ **Evo Hotel**
$$ | **HOTEL** | An innovative celebration of the area's fervor for outdoor recreation, this community-minded 50-room lodging opened in a converted warehouse in the Granary District in 2022 and features such novel amenities as a bouldering gym, a skatepark, a pair of sporting gear shops, bike-tuning and snowboard-waxing services, and winter- and summer-sports rentals. The crisp, contemporary rooms have private patios and well-designed gear storage, and local artwork fills the many stylish common spaces. **Pros:** in a trendy neighborhood; lots of interesting amenities for outdoorsy types; rooftop bar with great mountain views. **Cons:** activity-driven vibe may not suit those seeking quiet; a bit of a walk to downtown attractions; common spaces can be a little busy. [$] *Rooms from: $195* ✉ *660 S. 400 W, Downtown* ☎ *385/386–8585* 🌐 *www.evohotel.com* 🛏 *50 rooms* 🍴 *No Meals.*

★ The Grand America Hotel

$$$$ | **HOTEL** | Built to impress dignitaries and celebs attending the 2002 Winter Olympics, this 24-story luxury tower is Salt Lake City's most opulent hotel, a huge complex with similarly huge rooms (averaging 700 square feet), most of them with balconies and sweeping views. **Pros:** big, sumptuous rooms; excellent pool and plush full-service spa; closer to Granary District than many downtown hotels. **Cons:** expensive for SLC; immense hotel that can feel a little overwhelming; quality of restaurants is uneven. [$] *Rooms from: $332* ✉ *555 S. Main St., Downtown* ☎ *801/258–6000* 🌐 *www.grandamerica.com* 🛏 *775 rooms* 🍴 *No Meals.*

Hyatt House Salt Lake City–Downtown

$$$ | **HOTEL** | Depending on your needs, this mid-rise Hyatt across from Vivint Arena and the convention center works either as a moderately priced option with unfussy but contemporary standard rooms or as an ideal choice for longer stays if you book one of the suites with well-designed kitchens and ample sitting areas. **Pros:** superconvenient to attractions and dining; nice pool and hot tub; suites have stylish, fully outfitted kitchens. **Cons:** neighborhood can get very crowded during games and events; breakfast is pretty ordinary; lower floors receive a bit of road noise. [$] *Rooms from: $229* ✉ *140 S. 300 W, Downtown* ☎ *801/359–4020* 🌐 *www.hyatt.com* 🛏 *159 rooms* 🍴 *Free Breakfast.*

Hyatt Regency Salt Lake City

$$$ | **HOTEL** | The city's first true convention hotel, this sleek, glass tower opened in late 2022 and is connected to the Salt Palace Convention Center; however, it offers lots of appealing features for leisure travelers, too, including an expansive rooftop pool and terrace with cabanas, several restaurants and bars, and a well-equipped fitness center. **Pros:** great dining options, including a rooftop restaurant; fantastic mountain views from many rooms; central location. **Cons:** at a busy downtown intersection; often filled with conventioneers; a huge property that can feel a bit impersonal. [$] *Rooms from: $279* ✉ *170 S. West Temple, Downtown* ☎ *801/596–1234* 🌐 *www.hyatt.com* 🛏 *700 rooms* 🍴 *No Meals.*

★ Kimpton Hotel Monaco Salt Lake City

$$$ | **HOTEL** | This swank hotel resides in an ornate 14-story former bank tower (built in 1924), distinguished by a sophisticated, eclectic, and upbeat interior design and rooms offering extra touches like big-fringed ottomans, oversize framed mirrors, and lots of pillows. **Pros:** sparkling design, inside and out; exceptional restaurant; short walk to many fun bars and eateries. **Cons:** parking is $28 nightly; busy Downtown location; some rooms receive street noise. [$] *Rooms from: $259* ✉ *15 W. 200 S, Downtown* ☎ *801/595–0000, 800/805–1801* 🌐 *www.monaco-saltlakecity.com* 🛏 *223 rooms* 🍴 *No Meals.*

Le Méridien Salt Lake City Downtown

$$$ | **HOTEL** | This angular, glass-walled tower, part of Marriott's worldly and chic Le Méridien brand, opened in fall 2022 a short walk from Vivint Arena and Temple Square and stands out for its clean and contemporary design, cushy bedding, and well-designed bathrooms with Malin + Goetz bath products. **Pros:** chic rooms with floor-to-ceiling windows; steps from Gateway Center and Pioneer Park; rooftop pool and bar with great mountain views. **Cons:** $50 nightly charge for pets; parking is a bit pricey; a long walk to Granary District or Central City. [$] *Rooms from: $249* ✉ *131 S. 300 W, Downtown* ☎ *801/658–4600* 🌐 *www.marriott.com* 🛏 *144 rooms* 🍴 *No Meals.*

The Little America Hotel

$$ | **HOTEL** | **FAMILY** | This enormous but reliably comfortable hotel stands in the shadow of its world-renowned and much more expensive sister property, but Little America has even more rooms and its own loyal following. **Pros:** large indoor-outdoor pool; trees make the courtyard an oasis; closer to Granary District than many downtown hotels. **Cons:** restaurants and bar are rather ordinary; huge property that can feel a little impersonal; sometimes packed with conventioneers. [$] *Rooms from: $142* ✉ *500 S. Main St., Downtown* ☎ *801/596–5700* 🌐 *www.saltlake.littleamerica.com* 🛏 *850 rooms* 🍴 *No Meals.*

The Peery Salt Lake City Downtown, Tapestry Collection by Hilton
$$ | HOTEL | Since becoming part of Hilton's indie-spirited Tapestry collection, this elegant 1910 classic hotel with a distinctive gray exterior has undergone a complete top-to-bottom renovation, with a substantial increase in room rates to go with it. **Pros:** well-maintained and charmingly historic; two full-service restaurants on site; steps from several good bars and eateries. **Cons:** receives noise from traffic and nearby bars; tiny elevator; quirky heating and AC system. [$] *Rooms from: $191* ✉ *110 W. Broadway, Downtown* ☎ *801/521–4300, 800/331–0073* 🌐 *www.peeryhotel.com* 🛏 *73 rooms* 🍴 *No Meals.*

Salt Lake Marriott Downtown at City Creek
$$ | HOTEL | The more centrally located of Marriott's two large downtown convention hotels, this gleaming, 16-story hotel lies between the City Creek shopping mall and the Salt Lake Convention Center. **Pros:** steps from restaurants, shops, and Temple Square; upper floors have mountain views; on-site restaurant, lounge, and Starbucks. **Cons:** not a lot of character; breakfast is expensive; often booked up with conventions. [$] *Rooms from: $180* ✉ *75 S. West Temple, Downtown* ☎ *801/531–0800* 🌐 *www.marriott.com* 🛏 *510 rooms* 🍴 *No Meals.*

Nightlife

BARS AND LOUNGES

Bar X
COCKTAIL LOUNGES | Part-owned by *Modern Family* star and SLC native Ty Burrell, this trendy cocktail lounge with cozy banquette seating stands out for its extensive selection of spirits and Prohibition Era–inspired cocktails. Next door, sister establishment Beer Bar is a great place to sample local brews. ✉ *155 E. 200 S, Downtown* ☎ *801/355–2287* 🌐 *www.barxslc.com.*

★ **Beehive Distilling**
BARS | At the forefront of south Salt Lake's burgeoning spirits and craft brewing scene, this acclaimed small-batch gin and vodka producer has a stylish, post-industrial bar where you can sample expertly crafted cocktails and nibble on tasty apps and sandwiches. Serious enthusiasts might want to book one of Beehive's occasional behind-the-scenes tours. ✉ *2245 S. West Temple, Downtown* ☎ *385/259–0252* 🌐 *www.beehive-distilling.com.*

★ **Bodega + The Rest**
BARS | There's more than meets the eye to this modest-looking Downtown bar with pinball machines and cheap drinks. A locked door leads to "the Rest," a basement speakeasy decorated with quirky framed portraits, mounted animals, and odd bric-a-brac. Here you'll discover well-curated menus of creative cocktails and well-prepared modern American food. Reservations are advised for the speakeasy. ✉ *331 S. Main St., Downtown* ☎ *801/532–4042* 🌐 *www.bodegaslc.com.*

BTG Wine Bar
WINE BARS | Close to downtown hotels and attractions, this classy, expansive lounge (in the same historic building as the excellent Italian restaurant Caffè Molise) offers plenty of comfy seating and one of the most impressive lists of wines—by the glass and the bottle—in

town. Flights are a good way to try a few different sips, and there's a nice menu of tapas and rich desserts (consider the dark-chocolate cake), too. ⊠ *404 S. West Temple, Downtown* ☎ *801/359–2814* ⊕ *www.btgwinebar.com.*

★ The Pearl

COCKTAIL LOUNGES | This chic, contemporary cocktail bar opened in summer 2022 in the buzzy Granary District/Central 9th neighborhood and has quickly become a trendy go-to for artfully crafted drinks and Vietnamese street food—lemongrass pork skewers and crispy fish-sauce wings. On warm days, snag a seat on the patio to enjoy your ice-cold *ca phe,* a robust concoction of Averna amaro liqueur, Vietnamese coffee, chicory, and spices. Check the bar's Instagram page for details. ⊠ *917 S. 200 W, Downtown.*

Purgatory

BARS | A mix of LGBTQ+ folks, musicians, artists, and hipsters converge at this inclusive, mod-industrial tavern on the south side of downtown, which has a spacious enclosed patio strung with twinkly lights and a menu of decadent, internationally inflected bar bites, from pork belly *bao* to K-pop fries smothered in braised beef, kimchi, and *gyochu* mayo. The eclectic music's on point, and Purgatory frequently hosts parties, drag shows, and other festivities. ⊠ *62 E. 700 S, Downtown* ☎ *801/596–2294* ⊕ *www. purgatorybar.com.*

The Ruin

BARS | This stylish downtown lounge stands out for its well-crafted cocktails, like the Pearly Gates, with gin, citrus, bergamot, activated charcoal, and egg white. There's a nice selection of apps, salads, and sandwiches, too. ⊠ *159 S. Main St., Downtown* ☎ *801/869–3730* ⊕ *www.ruinslc.com.*

Scion Cider Bar

BARS | This friendly newcomer to the Granary District's hip Central 9th strip offers a vast selection of ciders from all over

the world, with about 20 available on tap and many others sold in bottles and cans. Scion also produces its own small-batch ciders, and the staff is incredibly knowledgeable—if you're new to cider sipping, they'll steer you in the right direction. Wine, beer, cider cocktails, and cheese and charcuterie plates are offered, too. ⊠ *916 Jefferson St. W, Downtown* ⊕ *www.scionciderbar.com.*

The Tavernacle Social Club

PIANO BARS | Dueling pianos (Wednesday through Saturday) and karaoke (Sunday to Tuesday) make for a festive atmosphere in this bar just east of downtown. The musicians only play requests, and if you don't like the current song, you can pay $1 to change it. The Quorum of the Queens drag brunch on Sunday is always a crowd-pleaser. ⊠ *201 E. 300 S, Downtown* ☎ *801/519–8900* ⊕ *www. tavernacle.com.*

★ Water Witch

BARS | This intimate, minimalist space on the west edge of downtown received a James Beard nomination for its exemplary farm-to-cocktail scene. Creative drinks using fresh herbs and extracts and artisan spirits are served with a flourish in colorful vessels. ⊠ *163 W. 900 S, Downtown* ☎ *801/462–0967* ⊕ *www. waterwitchbar.com.*

BREWPUBS AND MICROBREWERIES

Beerhive

Set in an atmospheric vintage brick downtown building with a lively patio out front, this hive of hops enthusiasts stocks perhaps the most exhaustive selection of craft beer in the city, with about two dozen IPAs alone. ⊠ *128 S. Main St., Downtown* ☎ *801/364–4268.*

★ Fisher Brewing Company

BREWPUBS | Opened in 2017 by a group of beer lovers that includes the great-great-grandson of the owner of the original Fisher Brewing, which flourished from the late 1800s to 1967, this lively taproom in the Granary District produces some of the finest beers in the city. Have a seat on the dog-friendly patio. Rotating food trucks dispense tasty fare. ⊠ *320 W. 800 S, Downtown* ☎ *801/487–2337* ⊕ *www. fisherbeer.com.*

Kiitos Brewing

BREWPUBS | This festive purveyor of first-rate craft beer is as known for its smooth Coconut Stout and tangy Blackberry Sour as for its impressive selection of vintage pinball and arcade games. ⊠ *608 W. 700 S, Downtown* ☎ *801/215–9165* ⊕ *www. kiitosbrewing.com.*

Squatters Pub Brewery

BREWPUBS | Arguably Utah's most famous microbrewery, Squatters' flagship downtown pub is lined with well-deserved awards from the Great American Beer Festival and World Beer Cup. The pub has friendly staff and an easygoing, casual vibe, although it can get crowded on weekends and when there are conventions in town. ⊠ *147 W. Broadway, Downtown* ☎ *801/363–2739* ⊕ *www. squatters.com.*

LGBTQ+

MILK+

BARS | Opened in 2022 in the lively Central 9th corridor, this big, beautifully designed LGBTQ+ club has a huge stage and dance floor, a game room with darts and pool tables, a patio, and a pretty substantial food menu, too—and yes, milk and cookies is one of the dessert options. Theme nights include karaoke Sunday and country-western Wednesday. ⊠ *49 E. 900 S, Downtown* ☎ *801/935–4424* ⊕ *www.milkslc.com.*

🎭 Performing Arts

MAJOR PERFORMANCE VENUES
★ Abravanel Hall

ARTS CENTERS | This immense, stately venue across from Temple Square is famed for its soaring glass lobby and Dale Chihuly sculpture and is home of the Utah Symphony and other distinguished

events like the Wasatch Speaker Series featuring names such as Dr. Sanjay Gupta, Rob Reiner, and Annie Leibovitz. ⊠ *123 W. South Temple, Downtown* ☎ *385/468–1010* ⊕ *www.saltlakecountyarts.org.*

★ Capitol Theatre

THEATER | This grand 1913 theater with a stunningly ornate exterior was built originally for vaudeville and has been masterfully restored. It presents works by Ballet West and the Utah Opera in addition to hosting the JazzSLC series and Broadway touring companies. ⊠ *50 W. 200 S, Downtown* ☎ *385/468–1010* ⊕ *www.saltlakecountyarts.org.*

★ Eccles Theater

THEATER | Notable for its five-story glass-wall lobby and starry-sky ceiling, this striking 2,500-seat venue with a smaller black box theater helped spur a revitalization of Regent Street, the narrow lane just east of it. The Eccles hosts major Broadway touring shows as well as big-name concerts. ⊠ *131 S. Main St., Salt Lake City* ☎ *385/468–1010* ⊕ *www. saltlakecountyarts.org.*

Rose Wagner Performing Arts Center

ARTS CENTERS | Comprising the Leona Wagner Black Box Theatre, the Jeanne Wagner Theatre, and the Studio Theatre, the Center is home to the Ririe-Woodbury Dance Company and the Repertory Dance Theatre and also provides performance space for many of the city's smaller theater companies, including Plan-B and Pygmalion Productions. ⊠ *138 Broadway, Downtown* ☎ *385/468–1010* ⊕ *www.saltlakecountyarts.org.*

DANCE
★ Ballet West

BALLET | This respected professional ballet company performs both classic and original works at the Capitol Theatre. Its inner-workings were featured in the multiseason reality show *Breaking Pointe.* ⊠ *Downtown* ☎ *801/869–6900* ⊕ *www. balletwest.org.*

Ririe-Woodbury Dance Company

MODERN DANCE | This is Salt Lake City's premier modern dance troupe, recognized for its innovation and commitment to community education. ✉ *Downtown* ☎ *801/297–4241* ⊕ *www.ririewoodbury. com.*

FILM

Brewvies Cinema Pub

FILM | Enjoy craft beer and tasty pub fare while you watch the new releases and indie films at this intimate cinema in the Granary District. ✉ *677 S. 200 W, Downtown* ☎ *801/322–3891* ⊕ *www. brewvies.com.*

Broadway Centre Cinemas

FILM | Salt Lake Film Society shows newly released, independent, and foreign films at this hugely popular downtown venue. ✉ *111 E. Broadway, Downtown* ☎ *801/321–0310* ⊕ *www.saltlakefilmsociety.org.*

MUSIC

★ **Utah Symphony**

MUSIC | The premier orchestra in the state, the Utah Symphony performs in the acoustically acclaimed Abravanel Hall and calls the Deer Valley Music Festival its summer home. ✉ *Downtown* ☎ *801/533–6683* ⊕ *www.usuo.org.*

OPERA

Utah Opera

OPERA | Since 1978, this company has performed new and classical works at the Capitol Theatre and throughout the state. ✉ *Downtown* ☎ *801/533–6683* ⊕ *www.usuo.org.*

THEATER

★ **Plan-B Theatre Company**

THEATER | The resident company of the Rose Wagner Performing Arts Center stages modest productions built on fine original scripts and timely social and cultural themes. ✉ *Downtown* ☎ *801/297–4200* ⊕ *www.planbtheatre.org.*

Shopping

ANTIQUES

Capital City Antique Mall

ANTIQUES & COLLECTIBLES | This expansive, multidealer emporium across from Publik Coffee Roasters specializes in antiques of all periods, plus jewelry and vintage clothing. You're sure to encounter some great finds. ✉ *959 S. West Temple, Downtown* ☎ *801/521–7207* ⊕ *www. capitalcityantiquemall.com.*

ART GALLERIES

★ **Phillips Gallery**

ART GALLERIES | The highly respected, longest-running gallery in Utah features three floors of local and regional artists' work, including mixed media, paintings, and sculptures. Check out the sculptures in the rooftop garden. ✉ *444 E. 200 S, Downtown* ☎ *801/364–8284* ⊕ *www. phillips-gallery.com.*

Urban Arts Gallery

ART GALLERIES | This expansive space at The Gateway is the retail arm of the nonprofit Utah Arts Alliance, which supports both emerging and established Utah artisans working in a wide range of disciplines, from painting and sculpture to T-shirts and jewelry. You'll find everything from $5 keepsakes to larger works costing several hundred dollars. It's a great place to find a memorable gift while supporting artists from a wide range of cultural and economic backgrounds. ✉ *The Gateway, 115 S. Rio Grande St., Downtown* ☎ *801/230–0820* ⊕ *www. urbanartsgallery.org.*

BOOKS

Ken Sanders Rare Books

BOOKS | More than 100,000 titles, including a number of rare first editions, await book lovers at this legendary store that has especially strong collections of literature about Utah, Mormons, and Western exploration. The store moved into a space at The Leonardo museum in fall 2022. ✉ *The Leonardo, 209 E. 500*

S, Downtown ☎ 801/521–3819 ⊕ www. kensandersbooks.com.

★ Weller Book Works

BOOKS | The name of this store has been synonymous with independent book sales in Salt Lake City since 1929. Catherine and Tony Weller are the third generation to operate this bookstore located at Trolley Square. Bibliophiles appreciate the airy space and helpful and knowledgeable staff. ⊠ 607 Trolley Sq., East Side ☎ 801/328–2586 ⊕ www. wellerbookworks.com.

CLOTHING

★ Hip & Humble

WOMEN'S CLOTHING | Look to this dapper little 9th and 9th lifestyle shop for casually stylish women's attire, from cheerful floral midi-dresses to handmade silver jewelry, platform sandals, and cotton totes. There's also a big selection of housewares and gifts, including hand-painted planters, charcuterie boards, and detox soaking-tub teas. ⊠ 1043 E. 900 S, Salt Lake City ☎ 801/467–3130 ⊕ www. hipandhumble.com.

★ IconoCLAD

SECOND-HAND | In this beloved consignment and vintage shop with two downtown locations, bargain-priced treasures abound, from previously worn to brand-new gear and clothing, plus fun gifts, LGBTQ Pride items, and much more. Keep an eye out for the friendly feline staffers working the aisles. ⊠ 414 E. 300 S, Salt Lake City ☎ 801/833–2272 ⊕ www.iconoclad.com.

The Stockist

WOMEN'S CLOTHING | This cosmopolitan fashion boutique carries women's and men's attire and lifestyle products from Aesop, Citizens of Humanity, Filson, Snow Peak, Richer Poorer, and dozens of other brands, both internationally renowned and emerging. ⊠ 875 E. 900 S, Salt Lake City ☎ 801/532–3458 ⊕ www. thestockistshop.com.

FOOD

★ Caputo's Market & Deli

FOOD | A must for stocking up on snacks and picnic goods before hiking, skiing, or just hanging out across the street in Pioneer Park, this culinary wonderland boasts a fantastic butcher shop, bean-to-bar chocolates, fine local and imported cheeses and charcuterie, Italian baked goods, and a deli that produces some of the tastiest to-go sandwiches in town. Caputo's has two other locations in the area. ⊠ 314 W. Broadway, Downtown ☎ 801/531–8669 ⊕ www.caputos.com.

Liberty Heights Fresh

FOOD | This gourmet grocery near Liberty Park and 9th and 9th is a go-to for high-quality (often organic) foods as well as delicious prepared items, such as rosemary ham–Brie–balsamic sandwiches and roasted-veggie lasagna with house-made pasta. ⊠ 1290 S. 1100 E, Salt Lake City ☎ 801/583–7374 ⊕ www. libertyheightsfresh.com.

GIFTS

Cahoots

SOUVENIRS | Arguably SLC's most irreverent little retailer, Cahoots is where you go when seeking the perfect smart-ass greeting card, campy T-shirt, LGBTQ Pride tchotchke, or NSFW gag gift. ⊠ 878 E. 900 S, Salt Lake City ☎ 801/538–0606 ⊕ www.facebook.com/cahoots.cards.

HOUSEHOLD GOODS

Atelier

HOUSEWARES | Located along a block of converted warehouse buildings just north of Pioneer Park, this stylish lifestyle boutique represents more than 30 local makers. You'll discover an extensive selection of ceramics, kitchen and bath accessories, planters, jewelry, and body-care products. ⊠ 337 Pierpont Ave., Downtown ☎ 801/410–0953 ⊕ www. atelierslc.com.

★ Salt & Honey Market

HOUSEWARES | A well-stocked, mod-industrial mercantile that very much captures the hipster spirit of the surrounding 9th and 9th neighborhood, Salt & Honey carries large and small items for every room of the house, from arty bowls and vases to fine jewelry, and some locally made apparel, too. There are two other locations in the area. ⊠ *926 E. 900 S, Salt Lake City* ☎ *385/368–6088* ⊕ *www.saltandhoneymarket.com.*

OUTDOOR AND GREEN MARKETS

★ Downtown Farmers' Market

MARKET | Farmers and artisan food producers proffer fresh fruit and veggies, flowers, and other goodies at this phenomenally popular—and quite extensive—downtown farmers' market at Pioneer Park each Saturday from June through late October. Local bakeries and restaurants also sell tasty treats ranging from fresh salsa to cinnamon rolls, and there's a central food truck plaza with live music, too. A smaller version of the market takes place on Thursday afternoon from 4 until dusk in Liberty Park from mid-June through September, and a winter market is held on Saturday morning at The Gateway from November through April. Additional farmers' markets take place around the city, generally in summer, in Sugar House, Murray, South Jordan, and several other locales. ⊠ *300 W. 300 S, Downtown* ☎ *801/328–5070* ⊕ *www.slcfarmersmarket.org.*

PLAZAS AND MALLS

City Creek Center

MALL | The centerpiece of a $1 billion downtown redevelopment across from Temple Square, this attractive indoor-outdoor mall with an enclosed footbridge spanning Main Street has brought upscale shopping to the city with stores like Apple, Anthropologie, Louis Vuitton, Lululemon, Nordstrom, Tiffany, and West Elm. And across the street from the east side of the mall, the upscale Harmons Grocery Store is one of the nicest markets in the city. Note that most stores are closed on Sunday. ⊠ *50 S. Main St., Downtown* ☎ *801/238–5329* ⊕ *www.shopcitycreekcenter.com.*

The Gateway

MALL | This mostly outdoor shopping center next to Vivint Arena amid the warehouses and scads of new condos and apartments on the west side of downtown is steadily undergoing a revitalization, with several new shops and galleries and the popular HallPass food hall having opened in recent years. The complex isn't old—it was built for the 2002 Olympics, but it had struggled for years to retain tenants and has only lately begun to rebound. Plans are still underway to create an ice rink as well as a luxury hotel inside the historic Union Pacific building, which anchors the complex. Popular businesses include Urban Arts Gallery, W.O.S.B. Collective, HEXEH skincare, Momi doughnuts, and a multiplex theater. ⊠ *S. Rio Grande St. and W. 100 S, Downtown* ☎ *801/456–0000* ⊕ *www.atthegateway.com.*

SPORTSWEAR AND OUTDOOR GEAR

Canyon Sports

SPORTING GOODS | This big and well-stocked downtown retailer geared toward skiing, snowboarding, and other winter-sports gear and apparel—both for sale and for rent—also stocks plenty of warm-weather items, including paddleboards, mountain bikes, tents, and more. You can also buy lift tickets. ⊠ *517 S. 200 W, Salt Lake City* ☎ *801/322–4220* ⊕ *www.canyonsports.com.*

★ Cotopaxi

SPORTING GOODS | The boldly colored backpacks, fleeces, running wear, and ski jackets hint at Cotopaxi's mission and aesthetic. Named for a massive Andean stratovolcano in Ecuador, the B Corporation shop sources its goods from Latin America and pays its makers a fair, sustainable wage while also giving back through charitable action. ⊠ *74 S.*

Main St., Salt Lake City ☏ *385/528–0855* ⊕ *www.cotopaxi.com.*

 # Activities

BASEBALL
Salt Lake Bees

BASEBALL & SOFTBALL | The AAA affiliate of the Los Angeles Angels plays at attractive Smith's Ballpark, its backdrop of the Wasatch Mountains making a fantastic place to enjoy a game. The season runs April through August. ⊠ *77 W. 1300 S, Downtown* ☏ *801/325–2337* ⊕ *www. slbees.com.*

BASKETBALL
Utah Jazz

BASKETBALL | Salt Lake's NBA team plays at the Vivint Arena. Basketball buffs should check out the statues of Hall of Famers John Stockton and Karl Malone outside. ⊠ *301 W. South Temple, Downtown* ☏ *801/325–2500* ⊕ *www.nba.com/jazz.*

BIKING
★ Contender Bicycles

BIKING | In trendy 9th and 9th, the store that vows to "make every bike a dream bike" is a must-visit for cyclists, offering a full slate of sales and services, including rentals. You might catch Tour de France veterans Levi Leipheimer or Dave Zabriskie stopping by to chat or ride with this shop's competitive team. ⊠ *989 E. 900 S, Downtown* ☏ *801/364–0344* ⊕ *www. contenderbicycles.com* ⊗ *Closed Sun.*

Capitol Hill and the Avenues

These picturesque, historic neighborhoods overlook the city from the foothills north of Downtown. Two days after entering the future Salt Lake City, Brigham Young brought his fellow religious leaders to the summit of the most prominent hill here, which he named Ensign Peak, to plan out their new home. New arrivals built sod homes into the hillside of what is now the Avenues. Two-room log cabins and adobe houses dotted the area. Meanwhile, on the western slope of the hill, fruit and nut trees were planted. Some still remain, as does a neighborhood known as Marmalade, with streets named Apricot, Quince, and Almond.

With the coming of the railroad came Victorian homes. The city's rich and prominent families built mansions along South Temple. As the city has grown over the years, wealthy citizens have continued to live close to the city but farther up the hill where the views of the valley are better. The lower Avenues has become a particularly appealing, if expensive, place to live, as most of its beautiful late-Victorian and early-20th-century homes have been gorgeously restored over the years.

The state capitol, for which Capitol Hill is named, was completed in 1915. State offices flank the capitol on three sides. City Creek Canyon forms its eastern boundary and is a wonderful spot for urban hiking. The Avenues denotes the larger neighborhood along the foothills, north of South Temple, extending from Capitol Hill east to the University of Utah.

Sights

The Cathedral of the Madeleine

CHURCH | Although the Salt Lake Temple just to the west is Salt Lake's most prominent religious landmark, this 1909 cathedral stands high above the city's north side and is a stunning house of worship in its own right. The exterior sports gargoyles, and its Gothic interior showcases bright frescoes, intricate wood carvings, and a 4,066-pipe organ. The highly regarded Madeleine children's choir gives concerts regularly (especially during the Christmas season). ⊠ *331 E. South Temple, The Avenues* ☏ *801/328–8941* ⊕ *www.utcotm.org.*

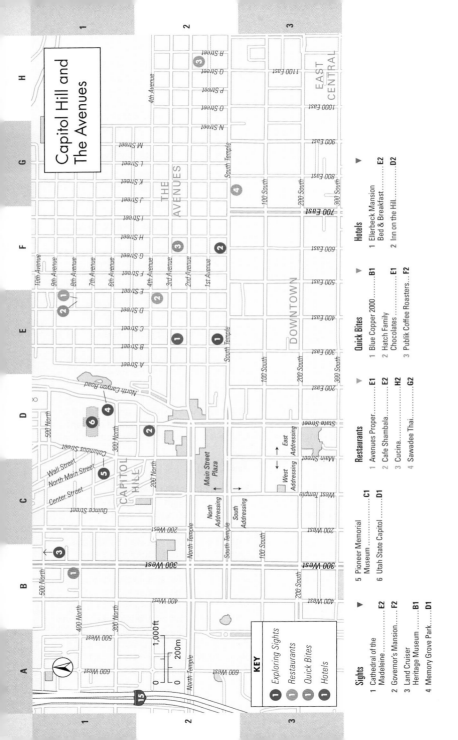

Capitol Hill and The Avenues

KEY

- ▶ 1 Exploring Sights
- ▶ 1 Restaurants
- ▶ 1 Quick Bites
- ▶ 1 Hotels

0 — 200m
0 — 1,000ft

▶ **Sights**

1 Cathedral of the
Madeleine................ **E2**
2 Governor's Mansion..... **F2**
3 Land Cruiser
Heritage Museum...... **B1**
4 Memory Grove Park..... **D1**
5 Pioneer Memorial
Museum.................. **C1**
6 Utah State Capitol...... **D1**

▶ **Restaurants**

1 Avenues Proper.......... **E1**
2 Cafe Shambala........... **E2**
3 Cucina.................... **H2**
4 Sawadee Thai............ **G2**

▶ **Quick Bites**

1 Blue Copper 2000........ **B1**
2 Hatch Family
Chocolates.............. **E1**
3 Publik Coffee Roasters... **F2**

▶ **Hotels**

1 Ellerbeck Mansion
Bed & Breakfast......... **E2**
2 Inn on the Hill.......... **D2**

Governor's Mansion

HISTORIC HOME | Built by silver-mining tycoon Thomas Kearns in 1902, this limestone structure—reminiscent of a French château with all its turrets and balconies—is now the official residence of Utah's governor. In its early days the mansion was visited by then-president Theodore Roosevelt and other dignitaries from around the world. The mansion was faithfully restored after Christmas lights caused a fire in 1993 that destroyed much of the interior. Free hour-long tours are given by Preservation Utah the first Wednesday of each month from April through November, by appointment only (call or book online at least 24 hours in advance). ⊠ *603 E. South Temple, The Avenues* ☎ *801/533–0858 Preservation Utah tours* ⊕ *governor.utah.gov/mansion.*

Land Cruiser Heritage Museum

OTHER MUSEUM | Nearly 100 models of Toyota Land Cruisers, some dating back to the early 1950s, fill this quirky museum that has something of a cult following among fans of old autos and four-wheel vehicle enthusiasts. In a rugged state like Utah, these rugged SUVs have quite a fan base, but folks come from all over the world, admiring the extensive collection of memorabilia, scale models, and artwork, plus a very cool 10-by-13-foot 3D map of the state of Utah. The museum is tucked away in a curious old industrial complex in the shadows of the 600 North overpass. ⊠ *470 W. 600 N, Capitol Hill* ☎ *505/615–5470* ⊕ *www.landcruiserhm. com* ⊠ *$15* ⊙ *Closed Sun.*

Memory Grove Park

CITY PARK | Severely damaged by a freak tornado in 1999, Memory Grove was carefully restored as a city park with veterans' monuments, beautiful landscaping, and the waters of City Creek. You can hike, jog, or bike on the paved road or dirt trails along **City Creek Canyon.** More trails commence here, including the 100-mile Bonneville Shoreline Trail. ⊠ *300 N.*

Canyon Rd., Capitol Hill ☎ *801/972–7800* ⊕ *www.slc.gov/parks.*

Pioneer Memorial Museum

HISTORY MUSEUM | Covering the pioneer era from the departure of the Mormons from Nauvoo, Illinois, to the hammering of the Golden Spike, this massive collection traces the history of pioneer settlers in 38 rooms—plus a carriage house—on four floors. Administered by the Daughters of Utah Pioneers, its displays include clothing, furniture, tools, wagons, and carriages. Be careful with kids—this museum is as cluttered as a westbound covered wagon loaded with all of a family's possessions. ⊠ *300 N. Main St., Capitol Hill* ☎ *801/532–6479* ⊕ *www.dupinternational.org* ⊠ *Free* ⊙ *Closed weekends.*

★ Utah State Capitol

GOVERNMENT BUILDING | The State Capitol, built in 1912, hosts Utah's legislature annually from January to March. The exterior steps offer marvelous views of the Salt Lake Valley. In the rotunda beneath the 165-foot-high dome, a series of murals, commissioned as part of a Works Progress Administration project during the Depression, depicts the state's history. Don't miss the gold-leafed State Reception Room, the original state supreme court, and the Senate gallery. Free guided tours are offered on weekdays from 9 to 3 (on the hour), except on holidays. ⊠ *350 N. State St., Capitol Hill* ☎ *801/538–1800* ⊕ *utahstatecapitol.utah. gov* ⊠ *Free* ⊙ *Closed weekends.*

🍴 Restaurants

★ Avenues Proper

$$$ | **MODERN AMERICAN** | One of two inviting restaurants run by the city's excellent Proper Brewing Company, this contemporary neighborhood bistro on a quiet street in the Avenues is a terrific option for a meal on the terrace on a sunny day or in the postindustrial dining room. Sample the flavorful house-brewed ales paired with eclectic comfort fare like steak , Korean pork belly bibimbap, and shrimp and grits. **Known for:** superb house-brewed beers; lovely sidewalk terrace; popular weekend brunches. $ *Average main: $23* ⊠ *376 8th Ave., The Avenues* ☎ *385/227–8628* ⊕ *www. avenuesproper.com.*

Cafe Shambala

$ | **TIBETAN** | Savory Tibetan food at bargain prices is the big attraction at this small, clean restaurant decorated with brightly colored Tibetan flags. You can indulge in hearty entrées such as spicy potatoes, chicken curry, and beef *phingsha*, a traditional Tibetan dish with vermicelli noodles, potatoes, dried mushrooms, and spices. **Known for:** bargain-priced lunch buffet; herbal teas; friendly service. $ *Average main: $12* ⊠ *382 4th Ave., The Avenues* ☎ *801/364– 8558* ⊕ *cafe-shambala.business.site* ⊗ *Closed Sun.*

★ Cucina

$$$ | **MODERN ITALIAN** | Foodies flock to this neighborhood café and food market for creative salads and colorful entrées like ahi tuna poke with guajillo chilies and mango, or lobster gnocchi in a saffron beurre blanc with dandelion pesto and candied oranges. Also on the menu are house-made soups and generous deli sandwiches. **Known for:** outstanding list of wines by the glass and bottle; hefty deli sandwiches to go; panna cotta with creative rotating preparations. $ *Average main: $27* ⊠ *1026 2nd Ave., The Avenues* ☎ *801/322–3055* ⊕ *www.cucinawinebar. com.*

Sawadee Thai

$$ | **THAI** | Head to this popular restaurant on the border between the Avenues and Central City—its brick walls and gorgeous artwork create a warm, inviting vibe—for authentic Thai fare. Starters like minced-fish cakes with red curry paste and Thai beef salad are perfect for sharing, and the main dishes—such as barbecue sweet-soy pork, pineapple fried rice, and duck in red curry sauce— arrive in generous portions. **Known for:** eggplant, garlic, and Thai basil stir fries; fragrant Thai iced tea; jackfruit with Thai sweet sticky rice. $ *Average main: $18* ⊠ *754 E. South Temple, The Avenues* ☎ *801/328–8424* ⊕ *www.sawadeethai-utah.com* ⊗ *Closed Sun.*

☕ Coffee and Quick Bites

Blue Copper 2000

$ | **CAFÉ** | This cozy branch of a well-established minichain is in an atmospheric old building a few blocks west of the capitol and is a perfect place to relax on the patio with an Earl Grey latte or flat white, maybe while enjoying a slice of raspberry shortbread. It's also a great stop for grabbing cold brew or kombucha to take with you on a hike in nearby City Creek Canyon. **Known for:** sidewalk seating; carefully sourced coffees; rich pastries and fluffy muffins. $ *Average main: $5* ⊠ *401 N. 300 W, Capitol Hill* ☎ *801/225– 2092* ⊕ *www.bluecopperslc.com.*

Hatch Family Chocolates

$ | **ICE CREAM** | **FAMILY** | For a sweet treat, stop by this friendly ice-cream parlor and candy shop. Jerry Hatch uses his mother's secret recipe for creamy caramel, and each piece of chocolate is hand-dipped and sold by weight. **Known for:** frozen chocolate-dipped bananas; espresso drinks, Italian sodas, and decadent hot chocolates; milk shakes and sundaes using house-made ice cream. $ *Average main: $5* ⊠ *376 8th Ave., The Avenues* ☎ *801/532–4912* ⊕ *www.hatchfamily-chocolates.com* ⊗ *Closed Sun. and Mon.*

★ Publik Coffee Roasters

$ | **CAFÉ** | This ubercool artisan-coffee purveyor has several locations around town, with this simple, streamlined shop in a converted service station in the Avenues arguably the most inviting, in part because of its handsome wooden tables and for its location along a block of lovely historic homes. Publik sources its fair-trade beans from high-quality farms throughout Latin America and Africa, and always offers an interesting array of seasonal espresso drinks, like the wintertime favorite Sweet Melissa, a honey syrup–infused latte with lemon balm, sage, and sweet mint. **Known for:** completely solar-powered; inviting, historic building; exceptional coffee and espresso drinks. [$] *Average main: $6* ✉ *502 3rd Ave., The Avenues* ☎ *385/229–4836* 🌐 *www.publikcoffee.com.*

Hotels

Ellerbeck Mansion Bed & Breakfast
$$ | B&B/INN | A stay in this gracious brick Victorian mansion with ornate trim, on a quiet tree-lined street, gives a real appreciation of what it might feel like to live in the charming and historic Avenues district. **Pros:** free parking; gorgeously appointed guest and common rooms; on-site café serves lunch, coffee, and pastries. **Cons:** sometimes books up for weddings; service can be a bit impersonal for a B&B; not a good fit for children. [$] *Rooms from: $167* ✉ *140 N. B St., Capitol Hill* ☎ *801/903–3916* 🌐 *www.ellerbeckbedandbreakfast.com* 🛏 *6 rooms* 🍴 *Free Breakfast.*

★ **Inn on the Hill**
$$ | B&B/INN | Owned and restored by former *Salt Lake Tribune* publisher Philip McCarthey, this spectacular turn-of-the-20th-century Renaissance Revival mansion makes a striking impression with its red-rock exterior and princely setting on the lower slopes of tony Capitol Hill. **Pros:** short walk from Temple Square and the state capitol; jetted tubs and radiant-heat bathroom floors in every room; exceptionally friendly and helpful staff. **Cons:** lots of steps and no elevator; no kids except in the carriage house; books up fast many weekends. [$] *Rooms from: $190* ✉ *225 N. State St., Capitol Hill* ☎ *801/328–1466* 🌐 *www.inn-on-the-hill.com* 🛏 *13 rooms* 🍴 *Free Breakfast.*

Nightlife

BARS AND LOUNGES

Garage on Beck
BARS | Once an auto garage in an industrial area north of Capitol Hill, this rollicking tavern draws a diverse crowd to its big patio for live rock, blues, and the like. The kitchen turns out tasty comfort food—think chicken or vegan wings with habanero-molasses "sludge" or burgers topped with candied jalapeños and crispy bacon. There's a popular Sunday brunch, too. ✉ *1199 Beck St., Capitol Hill* ☎ *801/521–3904* 🌐 *www.garageonbeck.com.*

★ **Mountain West Cider**
BARS | One of the state's first craft cider producers, Mountain West uses local ingredients—prickly pear puree and a wide variety of apples—to create its crisp and refreshing concoctions. In the cheerful tap room and sunny garden, where live bands often perform, you can sample the ciders along with local beers and spirits. It's on a quiet block in the Marmalade District, next door to the popular Red Rock Brewery. ✉ *425 N. 400 W, Capitol Hill* ☎ *801/935–4147* 🌐 *mountainwestcider.com.*

Performing Arts

Salt Lake Acting Company
THEATER | Recognized for its development of new regionally and locally written plays, this year-round company, which is based in a handsome old building, presents thought-provoking plays while promoting arts education for Utahns in kindergarten up through the university level. ✉ *168 W. 500 N, Capitol Hill* ☎ *801/363–7522* 🌐 *www.saltlakeactingcompany.org.*

Shopping

ART GALLERIES

★ Alice Gallery at Glendinning

ART GALLERIES | This gallery housed inside the gracious and historic Glendinning Home, which also houses the Utah Arts Council, features rotating exhibits that focus on contemporary Utah artists. It's beside the Governor's Mansion, on one of the prettiest streets in the city. ✉ *617 E. South Temple, The Avenues* ☎ *801/245–7272* ⊕ *artsandmuseums. utah.gov/alice-gallery.*

Activities

RECREATIONAL AREAS

★ City Creek Canyon

BIKING | A favorite of bikers as well as walkers and joggers, City Creek Canyon and its lush 6.5-mile trail—just east of the capitol—rewards visitors with dramatic views of the city and mountains. Part of the hike is along a pristine alpine stream. Cyclists can ride the trail on odd-number days from Memorial Day through Labor Day, and every day between Labor Day and Memorial Day, when the road is closed to vehicles. ✉ *N. Canyon Rd. at Bonneville Rd., Capitol Hill* ☎ *801/972– 7800* ⊕ *www.slc.gov/parks.*

Ensign Peak Nature Park

HIKING & WALKING | Close to City Creek Canyon and the Capitol building, this peaceful wildlife-rich habitat can be reached via a short, moderately steep trail of just under a mile, which leads to a 5,400-foot-elevation summit. Well-marked and-maintained, the trail ascends from a residential neighborhood, and there's usually plenty of free parking on the street. ✉ *1002 N. Ensign Vista Dr., Capitol Hill* ☎ *801/972–7800* ⊕ *www.slc. gov/parks.*

East Side and Sugar House

Home to the city's lofty University/Foot-hill District, the East Side is both a lively urban neighborhood and a scenic slice of nature, with its many trails twisting and turning into the Wasatch Range. Occupying what was once the eastern shoreline of ancient Lake Bonneville, the University of Utah is the state's largest higher-education institution and the oldest university west of the Missis-sippi. It's the cultural hub of University/Foothill, home to museums, the football stadium that was the site of the opening and closing ceremonies during the 2002 Winter Olympics, a 15,000-seat indoor arena, and numerous prominent medical and research facilities. Near campus, scenic Red Butte Garden and Arboretum is a great place to learn about plants that thrive in dry climates such as Utah's, and the gleaming copper-colored Natural History Museum of Utah is one of the city's must-see attractions.

A bit south, you'll find the charming Sugar House neighborhood. Utah pioneers tried to produce sugar out of beets at a mill here, and although sugar never made it to their tables, it is a sweet place to find eclectic shops and hip restaurants. The beautiful **Sprague Library** (✉ 2131 S. 1100 E), in a historic Tudor-style building, is worth a visit. Pick up picnic food and head for tiny Hidden Hollow Park, or cross 1300 East to the expansive Sugar House Park, which hosts the city's most spectacular fireworks and arts festival every July 4. Sugar House is a bit more commercial and built up than other parts of town, with plenty of chain franchises but also a good supply of independent eateries and retailers.

The Natural History Museum of Utah has a superb collection of fossils that have been discovered throughout the state.

Sights

Hogle Zoo

ZOO | FAMILY | This 42-acre zoo, nestled at the base of Emigration Canyon, has been a delightful destination for families since 1931. In the African Savanna you can spy zebras, giraffes, and ostriches; Asian Highlands showcases big cats in natural surroundings; Rocky Shores includes underwater viewing of polar bears, sea lions, seals, and otters; and Elephant Encounter has elephants and white rhinos in a simulated African plain. In between you'll find many exhibits with species native to the West, including wolves and bison. A children's zoo, interactive exhibits, and special presentations make visits informative for all ages. Just for fun is the Lighthouse Point Splash Zone, with a tube slide, the Zoo Train, and a carousel. ⊠ *2600 E. Sunnyside Ave., East Side* ☏ *801/584–1700* ⊕ *www. hoglezoo.org* 💲 *$22*.

★ Natural History Museum of Utah

SCIENCE MUSEUM | FAMILY | Stop and admire the sleek copper and granite form of this contemporary museum on the University of Utah campus before stepping inside to learn about the formation of the region's incredible landscape of parks, mountain ranges, lakes, and basins. Immerse yourself in prehistoric Utah, home to prolific research on dinosaurs and some of the most famous fossil recoveries in history. Superb rotating exhibits, which can touch on anything from environmental themes to the ancient cultures of Asia and Africa, typically take place once or twice a year. ⊠ *301 Wakara Way, University of Utah* ☏ *801/581–6927* ⊕ *www.nhmu.utah.edu* 💲 *$20*.

★ Red Butte Garden and Arboretum

GARDEN | FAMILY | With more than 21 acres of display gardens and another 80 undeveloped acres laced with 5 miles of hiking trails, this tranquil, mesmerizing nature space provides many enjoyable hours of strolling. Of special interest are the Perennial, Fragrance, and Water

East Side and Sugar House

0   1/2 mi

0   1/2 km

Salt Lake City EAST SIDE AND SUGAR HOUSE

3

Conservation gardens, the Daylily Collection, the Water Pavilion, and the Children's Garden. Lectures on everything from bugs to gardening in arid climates, workshops, and concerts are presented regularly. The popular Summer Concert Series attracts well-known musicians, from Bonnie Raitt to Pink Martini, as well as prominent performing arts companies like Ballet West. The pristine amphitheater seats approximately 3,000 people on its expansive lawn. The excellent Botanic Gift Shop offers books, soaps, sculptures, and fine gifts. ✉ *300 Wakara Way, University of Utah* ☎ *801/585–0556* 🌐 *www.redbuttegarden.org* 🎟 *$14.*

Sugar House Park

CITY PARK | FAMILY | Rolling grassy hills, athletic fields, multiple playgrounds, a creek, and a pond provide plenty of room to fly a kite or have a picnic at this big and popular neighborhood park. Take in stunning mountain views or head to the hill on the south end of the park—a go-to destination for sledding in winter. Odd fact: the park once housed a federal prison famous for incarcerating Utah's polygamists. ✉ *1330 E. 2100 S, East Side* 🌐 *www.sugarhousepark.org.*

This Is the Place Heritage Park

MUSEUM VILLAGE | FAMILY | Brigham Young and his band of Mormon followers descended into the Salt Lake Valley here. On July 24, 1847 (now a statewide holiday that is bigger than July 4 in many communities), he famously declared that this was the place for the Latter-day Saints to end their cross-country trek. A 60-foot-tall statue of Young, Heber Kimball, and Wilford Woodruff stands prominently in the park, which includes Heritage Village, a re-created 19th-century community and visitor center. In summer, volunteers dressed in period clothing demonstrate what Mormon pioneer life was like. You can watch artisans at work in historic buildings and take wagon or train rides around the compound. A 20-minute movie at the visitor center depicts the pioneers' trek across America. ✉ *2601 E. Sunnyside Ave., East Side* ☎ *801/582–1847* 🌐 *www.thisistheplace.org* 🎟 *Village: $16 summer, $8 winter. Monument: free* 🕒 *Closed Sun.*

Utah Museum of Fine Arts

ART MUSEUM | Spanning 74,000 square feet and offering more than 20 galleries, this well-regarded art museum on the University of Utah campus contains a vast permanent collection of Egyptian, Greek, and Roman relics, Italian Renaissance and other European paintings, and Chinese ceramics and scrolls. Special exhibits are mounted regularly, and a café and a sculpture court offer further diversions. ✉ *410 Campus Center Dr., University of Utah* ☎ *801/581–7332* 🌐 *www.umfa.utah.edu* 🎟 *$18* 🕒 *Closed Mon.*

🍴 Restaurants

★ Feldman's Deli

$ | SANDWICHES | A bustling space with high ceilings, brick walls, and live music some evenings, this contemporary take on a traditional Jewish deli is in a cheerful neighborhood on the south edge of Sugar House. It's a must for classic dishes—in enormous portions—of Reuben sandwiches, blintzes with fruit compote, matzo ball soup, and everything bagels with smoked sockeye salmon and a schmear. **Known for:** good local beers; authentic boiled bagels baked fresh daily; rugelach pastries. [$] *Average main: $15* ✉ *2005 E. 2700 S, East Side* ☎ *801/906–0369* 🌐 *www.feldmansdeli.com* 🕒 *Closed Sun. and Mon.*

Finca

$$$ | SPANISH | At this cozy neighborhood spot with a leafy covered patio and an intimate dining room with a fireplace, tuck into plates of Spanish *pintxos* and tapas—ham and cheese croquettes, grilled bread with roasted mushrooms, Moroccan-style lamb skewers—along with shareable larger platters of tagine and paella. The wine list of well-curated Spanish and Portuguese bottles is one of the best in the city. **Known for:** an exceptional wine list; hearty Valencia-style paella; Sunday brunch with breakfast paella. [$] *Average main: $27* ✉ *1513 S. 1500 E, East Side* ☎ *801/532–3372* 🌐 *www.fincaslc.com* 🕒 *No lunch Mon.–Sat.*

Mumbai House

$$ | INDIAN | You'll be enveloped in electrifying aromas the minute you step into this dark, intimate space that ranks among the best Indian restaurants in the state. You'll find all the standards, including soft garlic naan, chicken-coconut korma, piquant lamb vindaloo, fragrant tandoori dishes, and lots of vegetarian options. **Known for:** attentive service; several excellent shrimp dishes; rosewater lassi. [$] *Average main: $19* ✉ *2731 E. Parleys Way, East Side* ☎ *801/581–0222* 🌐 *www.mumbaihousecuisine.com* 🕒 *Closed Sun. No lunch.*

Ozora Izakaya

$$$ | JAPANESE | Sample small boldly flavored plates of yakisoba noodles, hamachi crudo, eggplant yakitori, and miso-glazed salmon at this airy, high-ceilinged Japanese restaurant in Sugar House. Ozora also offers a nice range of sushi rolls and sashimi. **Known for:** ample outdoor seating; extensive sushi menu; colorful and creative cocktails. [$] *Average main: $26* ✉ *1078 E. 2100 S, East Side* ☎ *801/845–0405* 🌐 *www.ozoraizakaya.com* 🕒 *No lunch Mon.–Thurs.*

★ **Ruth's Diner**

$ | AMERICAN | FAMILY | Families love the gussied-up old railcar that serves as Ruth's dining room and the best creek-side patio in the city—you just have to navigate your way up gorgeous Emigration Canyon to find it. Breakfast (served until 4 pm) has been the diner's trademark since 1930, and it starts with 3-inch-high biscuits followed by massive omelets like the King of Hearts (artichokes, garlic, mushrooms, and two cheeses). **Known for:** scenic canyon setting; live music on the patio in summer; long wait times on weekend mornings. [$] *Average main: $15* ✉ *4160 Emigration Canyon Rd., East Side* ☎ *801/582–5807* 🌐 *www.ruthsdiner.com.*

SOMI Vietnamese Bistro

$$$ | VIETNAMESE | The expertly prepared, contemporary Vietnamese food is but one reason for this buzzy, contemporary bistro's success—there's also a good wine list and a range of creative cocktails. The kitchen specializes in modern and traditional fare, along with some nods to countries that border Vietnam—try the piquant lemongrass beef noodle soup before graduating to steamed whole branzino fish with a ginger-scallion sauce and tender sliced Peking-style pork chops with sweet-and-sour sauce. **Known for:** slow-simmered beef-meatball pho; traditional Peking duck; fried bananas with toasted sesame and organic vanilla ice cream. [$] *Average main: $26* ✉ *1215 E. Wilmington Ave., East Side* ☎ *385/322–1158* 🌐 *www.somislc.com.*

★ **Table X**

$$$$ | MODERN AMERICAN | Serving artfully crafted modern American fare in a sceney cathedral-ceiling restaurant with tall black leather booths, a pair of esteemed chefs have created one of the most alluring dining destinations in the city. The five- and seven-course tasting menus change frequently and are based on what's in season, but recent offerings have included locally raised lamb shank accompanied by smoked and pickled alliums and saffron lamb jus and a vegetable "steak" topped with plum-zucchini caponata, leeks, and nasturtiums. **Known for:** fresh produce grown in the on-site garden; there's always a vegetarian menu option; daily-changing selection of house-made ice creams and sorbets. [$] *Average main: $75* ✉ *1457 E. 3350 S, Millcreek* ☎ *385/528–3712* 🌐 *www.tablexrestaurant.com* 🕒 *Closed Sun.–Tues. No lunch.*

Coffee and Quick Bites

Alchemy Coffee
$ | **CAFÉ** | In the Liberty Wells district a little west of Sugar House, this eclectically furnished café with cozy armchairs, rotating art exhibits, and high-ceiling rafters is an inviting place to while away a morning or afternoon. Veggie quiche with house-made aioli, thick-cut sourdough avocado toast, and well-crafted espresso drinks provide sustenance, and there's always good music playing. **Known for:** diverse crowd; sweet chocolate chai lattes; almond and chocolate croissants. [$] *Average main: $9* ✉ *390 E. 1700 S, Salt Lake City* ☎ *801/322–0735* 🌐 *www.alchemycoffee.com.*

★ Tea Zaanti
$ | **CAFÉ** | In a city known for healthy living and spiritualism, this Sugar House purveyor of exceptional loose-leaf teas, fine wines (by the bottle or in single-serving cans), and light but tasty snacks has a devoted following. Pick your tea from the lengthy menu—the blueberry matcha is a standout—and enjoy it hot, as a latte, or iced. **Known for:** dog-friendly patio; well-curated wine list; decadent drinking chocolates. [$] *Average main: $8* ✉ *1944 S. 1100 E, Salt Lake City* ☎ *801/906–8132* 🌐 *www.teazaanti.com* 🕒 *Closed Mon.*

Hotels

Salt Lake City Marriott University Park
$$ | **HOTEL** | Away from the downtown bustle and steps from hiking and biking trails as well as University of Utah attractions, this airy and inviting hotel is popular with business travelers but is actually a great choice if you'd rather be closer to nature and a little away from the bustle of downtown. **Pros:** near Natural History Museum and Red Butte Garden; sweeping Wasatch Mountain views; good on-site restaurant and bar, plus Starbucks. **Cons:** not many businesses within walking distance; expensive breakfast; 10- to 15-minute drive from Downtown. [$] *Rooms from: $179* ✉ *480 Wakara Way, University of Utah* ☎ *801/581–1000* 🌐 *www.marriott.com* 🛏 *247 rooms* 🍴 *No Meals.*

★ SpringHill Suites by Marriott Salt Lake City Sugar House
$$ | **HOTEL** | The first hotel in the city's colorful Sugar House neighborhood is a sleek all-suites lodging with large entertainment-work areas, a comfy lobby with a convenience market, and an East Side location near I–80 that's handy for hiking and skiing. **Pros:** free parking; across from a pretty park in a lively neighborhood; indoor pool with lots of natural light. **Cons:** pricey for the neighborhood; walls are a little thin; 10- to 15-minute drive from downtown. [$] *Rooms from: $195* ✉ *2206 S. 1330 E, Salt Lake City* ☎ *385/297–8300* 🌐 *www.marriott.com* 🛏 *125 rooms* 🍴 *Free Breakfast.*

University Guest House
$$ | **HOTEL** | Located on campus and operated by the University of Utah, this reasonably priced 30-suite hotel is favored by those doing business with the school or its hospital, but the general public is welcome, and those wanting to be near hikes in the East Side foothills as well as the Avenues appreciate this property's convenience and value. **Pros:** safe, quiet location on University of Utah campus; near Red Butte Garden and other East Side attractions; free parking and shuttle around campus and points nearby. **Cons:** 10- to 15-minute drive from downtown; some rooms are a little dark; books up well ahead during school events and conferences. [$] *Rooms from: $182* ✉ *110 Fort Douglas Blvd., University of Utah* ☎ *801/587–1000, 888/416–4075* 🌐 *www.universityguesthouse.com* 🛏 *30 suites* 🍴 *Free Breakfast.*

Nightlife

BARS AND LOUNGES
★ Osteria Amore

BARS | Although Ostia Amore is a full-service restaurant serving very good Italian fare, its bar is also one of the best spots near the University of Utah and the Avenues for a glass of wine—the selection is impressive, and the setting warm and inviting. On warm nights, sip and eat on the sidewalk patio. ⊠ *224 S. 1300 E, East Side* ☎ *385/270–5606* ⊕ *www. osteriaamore.com.*

BREWPUBS AND MICROBREWERIES
★ Hopkins Brewing

BREWPUBS | Grab a table in this handsome, brick-walled tap room and try some of the finest and most distinctive craft ales in the city, such as a crisp Sauvin Blanc Brut IPA produced with hops and Chardonnay grapes and a roasty Black Sesame Stout. The kitchen is known for its Thai-style and chipotle-honey wings. ⊠ *1048 E. 2100 S, East Side* ☎ *385/528–3275* ⊕ *www.hopkinsbrewingcompany.com.*

 Performing Arts

Pioneer Theatre Company

THEATER | This professional company, in residence at the University of Utah, stages classic and contemporary musicals and plays to consistently positive critical acclaim. ⊠ *300 S. 1400 E, University of Utah* ☎ *801/581–6961* ⊕ *www.pioneertheatre.org.*

 Shopping

BOOKS
The King's English Bookshop

BOOKS | FAMILY | With works by local authors, a wide selection of children's books, a dozen reading groups, and a community writing series, this converted cottage is a great place to browse and a terrific literary resource. ⊠ *1511 S. 1500 E, East Side* ☎ *801/484–9100* ⊕ *www. kingsenglish.com.*

 Activities

HIKING
★ Big Beacon Mount Wire Trail

HIKING & WALKING | One of the most popular treks on the East Side, this Big Beacon Trail leaves from Georges Hollow, near the Natural History Museum of Utah, and twists and turns for nearly 5 miles through wildflower meadows and sunny canyons to Mount Wire. Along the way, a popular (sometimes a bit too much so on weekends) side trail to Living Room cuts off to the side, providing some of the best views in the city. ⊠ *383 Colorow Rd., Salt Lake City.*

North and West Sides

The city's West Side is dominated by Salt Lake City International Airport, which is surrounded by mostly nondescript if perfectly pleasant chain hotels and restaurants. But the area is also home to Great Salt Lake State Park, which offers easier access than Antelope Island to the region's most famous body of water. The Interstate 15 corridor north of town passes through Bountiful and Layton, a couple of attractive bedroom communities at the foot of the Wasatch Range that have a smattering of noteworthy places to eat and some reasonably priced hotels.

 Sights

Great Salt Lake State Park

STATE/PROVINCIAL PARK | Parts of Great Salt Lake are as much as nine times saltier than the ocean and second only to the Dead Sea in salinity. What makes this massive body of water so briny? There's no outlet to the ocean, so salts and other minerals carried by rivers and streams become concentrated in this enormous evaporation pond. Easy access to this wonder is possible at

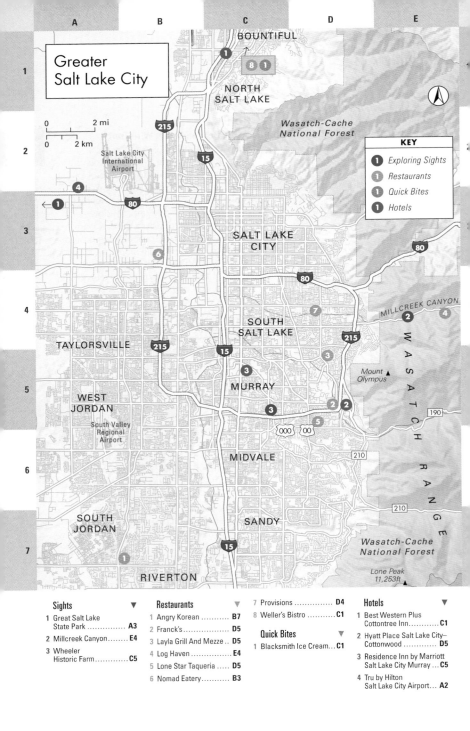

Greater Salt Lake City

BOUNTIFUL

NORTH SALT LAKE

Wasatch-Cache National Forest

SALT LAKE CITY

SOUTH SALT LAKE

TAYLORSVILLE

MURRAY

WEST JORDAN

South Valley Regional Airport

MIDVALE

SANDY

SOUTH JORDAN

RIVERTON

Salt Lake City International Airport

Mount Olympus

Wasatch-Cache National Forest

Lone Peak 11,253ft

MILLCREEK CANYON

W A S A T C H   R A N G E

0   2 mi
0   2 km

KEY

1 *Exploring Sights*

1 *Restaurants*

1 *Quick Bites*

1 *Hotels*

Sights ▼	Restaurants ▼	7 Provisions **D4**	Hotels ▼
1 Great Salt Lake State Park **A3**	1 Angry Korean **B7**	8 Weller's Bistro **C1**	1 Best Western Plus Cottontree Inn............. **C1**
2 Millcreek Canyon........ **E4**	2 Franck's.................. **D5**	**Quick Bites** ▼	2 Hyatt Place Salt Lake City–Cottonwood **D5**
3 Wheeler Historic Farm............. **C5**	3 Layla Grill And Mezze .. **D5**	1 Blacksmith Ice Cream... **C1**	3 Residence Inn by Marriott Salt Lake City Murray ... **C5**
	4 Log Haven **E4**		4 Tru by Hilton Salt Lake City Airport... **A2**
	5 Lone Star Taqueria **D5**		
	6 Nomad Eatery........... **B3**		

this state park on the lake's south shore, 16 miles west of Salt Lake City. A pavilion, souvenir shop, and dance floor honor the park's glory days when ballroom dancing and the lake brought thousands of visitors to its shores.

The state park used to manage the beaches north of the pavilion, but the lake is generally too shallow here for floating (Antelope Island State Park is better for that). What you can do here is walk down the boat ramp to Great Salt Lake State Marina and stick your legs in the water to experience the unique sensation of floating on water that won't let you sink. Your feet will bob to the surface, and you'll see tiny orange brine shrimp floating with you. Depending on water levels, you can also rent boats and stand-up paddleboards here and shower off at the marina. ✉ *13312 W. 1075 S, Magna* ☎ *801/828–0787* 🌐 *stateparks.utah.gov/parks/great-salt-lake* 🎟 *$5 per vehicle.*

🍴 Restaurants

Nomad Eatery

$ | **AMERICAN** | Located in something of a food desert amid the chain hotels southwest of Salt Lake City International Airport, this terrific adults-only gastropub—since it is inside Uinta Brewhouse Pub—serves elevated comfort fare. A nice option before or after a flight or on your way to or from Great Salt Lake State Park, Nomad doles out well-executed takes on comfort classics, from fish-and-chips to falafel salads.✉ **Known for:** friendly, easygoing staff; great beer from adjacent Uinta Brewhouse Pub; hefty burgers. [$] *Average main: $14* ✉ *Uninta Brewhouse Pub, 1722 S. Fremont Dr., West Side* ☎ *801/467–0909* 🌐 *www.nomad-eatery.com* ⏲ *Closed Sun.*

Weller's Bistro

$$ | **MODERN EUROPEAN** | A perfect option for a delicious feast of modern German-American fare before or after a visit to Antelope Island State Park, this dapper downtown Layton restaurant is also midway between Salt Lake City and Ogden. The made-from-scratch food is spot-on—try the Alsatian-style *flammküchen,* currywurst with fries, Parmesan-crusted pork schnitzel, or one of the tasty thin-crust pizzas. **Known for:** German apple pancakes at brunch; lots of tasty sides (spaetzle with mushroom sauce, sauerkraut with bacon); great selection of German and Austrian wines. [$] *Average main: $20* ✉ *197 N. Main St., Layton* ☎ *385/888–9531* 🌐 *www.wellersbistro.com* ⏲ *Closed Mon.*

☕ Coffee and Quick Bites

★ **Blacksmith Ice Cream**

$ | **ICE CREAM** | It's worth the 15-minute drive north of downtown Salt Lake to sample what may very well be the finest small-batch ice cream in the Rockies, or at least Utah. Innovative flavors at this bustling shop in cheerful downtown Bountiful include lavender studded with chunks of honeycomb and mango sticky rice. **Known for:** unusual ice-cream flavors; charming sidewalk seating in downtown Bountiful; house-baked waffle cones. [$] *Average main: $5* ✉ *180 S. Main St., Bountiful* ☎ *801/683–8951* 🌐 *www.instagram.com/blacksmithicecream* ⏲ *Closed Sun.*

🛏 Hotels

Best Western Plus Cottontree Inn

$$ | **HOTEL** | This clean and affordable two-story chain property is just off Interstate 15, less than 10 miles north of downtown and Capitol Hill, and on the way to Antelope Island and the northern suburbs. **Pros:** free parking; good base for exploring Salt Lake, Antelope Island, and Ogden; rooms well-insulated from street noise. **Cons:** dull freeway-adjacent setting; need a car to get around; prosaic decor. [$] *Rooms from: $145* ✉ *1030 N. 400 E* ☎ *801/292–7666* 🌐 *www.bestwestern.com* 🔑 *113 rooms* 🍴 *Free Breakfast.*

Wheeler Historic Farm is a family-friendly living history museum (and working farm) in suburban Murray.

Tru by Hilton Salt Lake City Airport

$$ | HOTEL | Among the dozen or so chain properties close to the airport, this boldly designed member of Hilton's budget-boutique Tru brand stands out for its smartly appointed rooms with 55-inch TVs, laminate-wood floors, and clean aesthetic. **Pros:** sleek design; free parking and airport shuttle; convenient to I-80 and Great Salt Lake State Park. **Cons:** bland office park setting; not too many frills; 15-minute drive from downtown. S *Rooms from: $135* ⊠ *206 N. Jimmy Doolittle Rd., Airport* ☏ *801/783–3170* ⊕ *www.hilton.com* ⤳ *90 rooms* ¶⊙ *Free Breakfast.*

Midvalley and South Valley

The swatch of suburban communities south of Salt Lake are divided into the Midvalley and South Valley regions, with more of the notable attractions, eateries, and businesses of interest to visitors in the former, chiefly in the towns of Murray, Millcreek, Cottonwood Heights, and Holladay, which has a particularly charming and lively downtown. In addition to being home to some interesting museums and parks, these areas also have some hotels and dining and nightlife options that are popular with winter skiers and summer hikers and bikers making their way to and from the Cottonwood Canyons.

Sights

★ Millcreek Canyon

CANYON | Running parallel to and just north of Big Cottonwood Canyon, this lush, steep-walled mountain canyon east of Millcreek and run by the Salt Lake County Parks office and the U.S. Forest Service is a wonderful destination for hiking, picnicking, camping, and mountain and road biking, and the meandering 9-mile drive up into the canyon is itself beautiful. There's also an inviting restaurant, Log Haven, located less than halfway up Mill Creek Canyon

Road. Certain trails are open to bikes only on odd- or even-numbered days, and dogs are welcome but can only be off-leash on odd-number days. There are about two-dozen well-maintained trails within the Millcreek Canyon system, ranging from shorter (3 to 5 miles) scrambles to challenging 13-mile round-trip adventures, but even the relatively quicker jaunts entail elevation gains of at least 1,000 feet. Good bets if you have only two or three hours include the 4.4-mile loop to Dog Lake and the 3-mile round-trip trek from Elbow Fork to Lambs Canyon Pass—wildflower viewing on these trails is especially dramatic from mid-June through mid-September. Although accessible on foot year-round, the upper section of the canyon closes to vehicles from November through around mid-June, depending on snowfall. Note that the upper half of Mill Creek Canyon Road is expected to be closed to road bikes due to road construction from 2024 through 2026. ⊠ *3800 Millcreek Canyon Rd., Millcreek* ☎ *385/468–7275* ⊕ *www. slco.org/parks* ⊑ *$5 per vehicle.*

Wheeler Historic Farm

FARM/RANCH | **FAMILY** | Now a 75-acre park and living history museum with numerous historic structures and a country store selling snacks, toys, and farm-related gifts, this verdant oasis and still-working farm on Little Cottonwood Creek in suburban Murray was settled in 1898 and is one of the only pioneer-era farmsteads left in the metro area. Activities here include cow-milking, observing the farm animals, tours of the impressive Victorian homestead (which is packed with farming implements and artifacts), and wagon rides and easy hikes on an extensive trail network. A very popular farmers' market is held here on summer Sundays. There's no charge to walk around the property, but tours and various activities have small fees. ⊠ *6351 S. 900 E, Murray* ☎ *385/468–1755* ⊕ *www.slco.org/ wheeler-farm.*

 Restaurants

The Angry Korean

$$ | **KOREAN** | With an irreverent name and somewhat remote suburban location in the District retail-dining center in South Jordan, this contemporary post-industrial space pulls in ardent fans of Korean food from points far and near. Once you've tucked into a plate of *kalbi* flame-grilled short ribs, beef bulgogi, fusion-style garlic-ginger tacos with Asian slaw, or a Korean fried shrimp po'boy slathered in house sweet-and-sour sauce, you'll understand what all the fuss is about. **Known for:** spicy house-made kimchi; crab and pork belly steamed buns; refreshing Italian sodas in a variety of flavors. Ⓢ *Average main: $17* ⊠ *11587 District Main Dr., South Jordan* ☎ *801/307–8300* ⊕ *www.theangrykorean.com* ⊗ *No dinner Sun.*

★ Franck's

$$$$ | **MODERN AMERICAN** | Celebrated for its art-filled dining room and lushly tree-shaded terrace, this romantic spot occupies a converted house in a historic neighborhood near the mouth of Big Cottonwood Canyon. The kitchen specializes in modern French and American fare, such as preserved-heirloom-tomato pie with cilantro aioli and toasted-Parmesan *sabayon*, and Franck's signature meat loaf with whipped potatoes and a champagne-lavender sauce. **Known for:** family-style platters that serve two to six people; well-chosen Old-World wine list; carrot cake with cream cheese frosting and a marbled chocolate shell. Ⓢ *Average main: $33* ⊠ *6263 S. Holladay Blvd., Cottonwood* ☎ *801/274–6264* ⊕ *www.francksfood.com* ⊗ *Closed Mon. No lunch.*

Layla Mediterranean Grill and Mezze

$$ | **MEDITERRANEAN** | Venture a few miles south from downtown to Holladay to enjoy savory Mediterranean dishes—with an emphasis on hearty Moroccan and Middle Eastern grills—in a crisp, contemporary dining space. Tangy spices enliven

Old-World favorites, such as shawarma and moussaka, and not-so-common dishes like *muhamarra* (think hummus but with walnuts) may tempt you away from your comfort zone. **Known for:** combination mezze platters; Lebanese-influenced cocktails; Turkish coffee ice cream. [$] *Average main: $22* ✉ *4751 S. Holladay Blvd., Holladay* ☎ *801/272–9111* 🌐 *www.laylagrill.com* 🕓 *Closed Sun. No lunch.*

★ Log Haven

$$$$ | MODERN AMERICAN | This elegant 1920s canyon retreat brings inventive takes on American wild game–focused cuisine by incorporating Asian ingredients with a Rocky Mountain style—consider grilled bison steak with charred Brussel sprouts and truffle aioli or roasted hen of the woods mushrooms with Calabrian chile–ricotta dumplings. With its romantic setting in a beautifully renovated log home amid the pine trees, waterfalls, and wildflowers of Millcreek Canyon, this is definitely a restaurant to remember. **Known for:** breathtaking views of the lush canyon; inventive cuisine; elaborate desserts. [$] *Average main: $39* ✉ *6451 E. Mill Creek Canyon Rd., Millcreek* ☎ *801/272–8255* 🌐 *www.log-haven.com* 🕓 *No lunch.*

Lone Star Taqueria

$ | MEXICAN | You can't miss this tiny lime green joint, marked by an old sticker-covered car off Fort Union Boulevard and often packed with skiers from the nearby Cottonwood canyons. The kitchen serves tasty, inexpensive Mexican food—including house special fish tacos, handmade tamales, burritos, and plenty of chilled Mexican beer. **Known for:** shrimp tacos with cilanto-jalapeño aioli; mammoth burritos; Mexican beers on tap. [$] *Average main: $9* ✉ *2265 E. Fort Union Blvd., Cottonwood* ☎ *801/944–2300* 🌐 *www.lstaq.com* 🕓 *Closed Sun. in summer.*

★ Provisions

$$ | MODERN AMERICAN | Renowned for its delicious weekend brunches and a bright and colorful dining room with a lively open kitchen, this modern American bistro with a focus on organic ingredients also turns out flavorful dinner fare. Brunch favorites include slow-roasted pork shoulder with poached eggs and wood-roasted blueberry pancakes, while homemade pappardelle with braised rabbit and smoked bacon stars among the dinner options. **Known for:** shareable, creative small plates; extensive list of artisan spirits; yuzu-mint coconut brûlée. [$] *Average main: $22* ✉ *3364 S. 2300 E, Millcreek* ☎ *801/410–4046* 🌐 *www.slcprovisions.com* 🕓 *No lunch weekdays.*

Hotels

★ Hyatt Place Salt Lake City–Cottonwood

$$ | HOTEL | This mid- to upscale pet-welcoming Hyatt mid-rise near the mouth of Big Cottonwood Canyon is a perfect roost for skiers and hikers but also a comfortable base for the metro area, with its access to I–215. **Pros:** outdoor pool and hot tub; nice views of Wasatch Range; convenient to I–215 and ski areas. **Cons:** pleasant but nondescript interior design; not many restaurants within walking distance; 20-minute drive from downtown SLC. [$] *Rooms from: $179* ✉ *3090 E. 6200 S, Cottonwood* ☎ *801/890–1280* 🌐 *www.hyatt.com* 🛏 *124 rooms* 🍴 *Free Breakfast.*

Residence Inn by Marriott Salt Lake City Murray

$$ | HOTEL | With a central suburbs location near I–15, this bright, light-filled all-suites property is handy for families and groups and within striking distance of downtown, the ski areas, and Utah County to the south. **Pros:** good soundproofing; full kitchens in every room; convenient base location for entire SLC region. **Cons:** breakfast area can be a zoo on ski-season weekends; humdrum suburban setting; 15- to 20-minute drive to downtown SLC. [$] *Rooms from: $156* ✉ *171 E. 5300 S, Murray* ☎ *801/262–4200* 🌐 *www.marriott.com* 🛏 *136 rooms* 🍴 *Free Breakfast.*

Nightlife

BARS AND LOUNGES

★ Porcupine Pub and Grille

BARS | Above a ski- and board-rental shop at the mouth of Big and Little Cottonwood Canyons, this lively pub offers a huge menu of hearty dishes, cocktails, and craft beers. Inside the large A-frame chalet-like building, you'll find bright polished wood floors and trim and a friendly vibe. ⊠ *3698 E. Fort Union Blvd., Cottonwood Heights* ☎ *801/942–5555* ⊕ *www.porcupinepub.com.*

BREWPUBS AND MICROBREWERIES

Bohemian Brewery

BREWPUBS | This rustic log cabin–inspired brewery near Cottonwood Canyon specializes in Eastern European beers, including crisp Czech pilsners and Bavarian weissbiers. Try to snag a seat by the towering stone fireplace ⊠ *94 E. 7200, Midvale* ☎ *801/566–5474* ⊕ *www. bohemianbrewery.com.*

Shopping

SPORTSWEAR AND OUTDOOR GEAR

Backcountry.com

SPORTING GOODS | One of the country's top outdoor-equipment retailers, Backcountry has a flagship store in West Valley City that comprises a small showroom and massive (200,000-square-foot) back room where you can shop or pick up products you've ordered online. Skiers, boarders, campers, and climbers all favor this place. ⊠ *2607 S. 3200 W, West Valley City* ☎ *801/736–6665* ⊕ *www.backcountry.com.*

Activities

GOLF

★ Stonebridge Golf Club

GOLF | One of the state's top public courses is just a five-minute drive from the airport and just 20 minutes from Downtown. The links-style course, designed by Gene Bates and Johnny Miller, offers 27 holes amid beautiful scenery. Water hazards come in the form of lakes and streams, and there are plenty of bunkers, but fairways are wide and generally quite forgiving. ⊠ *4415 Links Dr., West Valley City* ☎ *801/957–9000* ⊕ *www.golfstonebridgeutah.com* ⤣ *$50* 🏌. *Sunrise: 9 holes, 3291 yards, par 36; Creekside: 9 holes, 3270 yards, par 36; Sagebrush: 9 holes, 3368 yards, par 36.*

ICE SKATING

★ Utah Olympic Oval

ICE SKATING | The stunning venue was built for the 2002 Winter Olympics and is the home of the U.S. speed skating team. Watch the world's best skaters in major competitions every winter. It's open to the public October–March for myriad activities, including skating, curling, and running on the 442-meter indoor track. ⊠ *5662 S. Cougar La., Kearns* ☎ *801/968–6825* ⊕ *www.utaholympiclegacy.org/oval.*

SOCCER

Real Salt Lake

SOCCER | Since 2005, Real Salt Lake has competed in Major League Soccer. The gleaming Rio Tinto Stadium also hosts concerts and other events. ⊠ *9256 S. State St., Sandy* ☎ *801/727–2700* ⊕ *www.rsl.com.*

Side Trips from Salt Lake City

A 45-minute drive north of town, you can explore the shores of Great Salt Lake at Antelope Island State Park, which is famed for its massive herd of free-ranging bison along with scenic hiking trails and e-bike adventures.

For much of the year, and especially during the winter ski season, the gorgeous alpine resorts of Big Cottonwood and Little Cottonwood Canyons rank

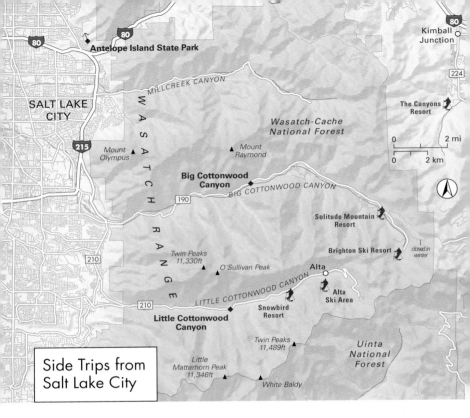

Side Trips from Salt Lake City

among the top reasons to visit Salt Lake City. The world-class ski areas of Alta, Brighton, Snowbird, and Solitude are nestled deep within these lush canyons and offer a variety of high-end lodgings and restaurants, although the majority of visitors to both places stay in Salt Lake or the nearby suburbs of Cottonwood Heights, Holladay, and Millcreek and visit for the day. From late spring through early autumn, these side-by-side canyons are famed for hiking, mountain biking, and other recreational pursuits.

Antelope Island State Park

25 miles north of Salt Lake City.

A visit to northern Utah isn't complete without a trip to the Great Salt Lake. The best way to experience this 1,700-square-mile body of water (it's a little smaller than the state of Delaware) is a half-day excursion to Antelope Island. There's no place in the country like this state park, home to millions of waterfowl and hundreds of bison and antelope, and surrounded by some of the saltiest water on earth. Drive the 7-mile narrow causeway that links the shoreline, then explore the historic ranch house and miles of hiking trails, and try a buffalo burger at the small café.

GETTING HERE AND AROUND

Take Exit 332 off Interstate 15, then drive west on Antelope Drive for 7 miles to the park entrance.

Sights

★ Antelope Island State Park

STATE/PROVINCIAL PARK | In the 19th century, settlers grazed sheep and horses on Antelope Island, ferrying them back and forth from the mainland across the waters of the Great Salt Lake. Today, the park is the most developed and scenic spot in which to experience the lake. Hiking and biking trails crisscross the island, and the lack of cover—cottonwood trees provide some of the only shade—gives the place a wide-open feeling and makes for some blistering hot days. You can go saltwater bathing at several beach areas, the most popular being Bridger Bay, which has a changing room with hot showers. Since the salinity level of the lake is always greater than that of the ocean, the water is extremely buoyant (and briny smelling). Faced with several years of drought, as of fall 2022 the lake was at its lowest water level since the 1840s, leading to even higher salinity and threatening the viability of the lake's ecosystem.

The island has historic sites, as well as desert wildlife and birds in their natural habitat. The most popular inhabitants are the members of a herd of between 500 and 700 bison descended from 12 brought here in 1893. Each October at the Buffalo Roundup more than 250 volunteers on horseback round up the free-roaming animals and herd them to the island's north end to be counted. The island's Fielding-Garr House, built in 1848 and now owned by the state, was the oldest continuously inhabited home in Utah until the last resident moved out in 1981. The house displays assorted ranching artifacts, and guided horseback riding is available from the stables next to the house. Be sure to check out the modern visitor center, and sample a bison burger at the stand that overlooks the lake to the north. If you're lucky, you'll hear coyotes howling in the distance. Access to the island is via a 7½-mile causeway, which is reached from I–15 about a 45-minute drive north of Salt Lake City. ✉ *4528 W. 1700 S, Syracuse* ☎ *801/773–2941* 🌐 *stateparks.utah.gov/parks/antelope-island* 🎟 *$15 per vehicle, $3 per pedestrian.*

🍴 Restaurants

You'll pass a smorgasbord of fast-food outlets in Davis County north of Salt Lake City, including most of the national chain restaurants and a few that are found mainly in Utah. Unless you go as far north as Ogden, there aren't too many choices.

Island Buffalo Grill

$ | BURGER | It may feel a little odd eating buffalo burgers at a bison sanctuary, but if you're a carnivore, you're in for a treat (the less expensive beef burgers are pretty tasty, too). There are no frills here, except for an unparalleled view. **Known for:** juicy buffalo burgers; expansive lake and beach views; snow cones. [$] *Average main: $9* ✉ *4528 W. 1700 S, Syracuse* ☎ *801/897–3452* 🌐 *www.islandbuffalogrill.com* 🕒 *No dinner. Closed Nov.–Feb.*

🏃 Activities

BIKING

Antelope E-Bikes

BIKING | Just across the causeway on Antelope Island, this popular outfitter rents e-bikes, which offer a perfect way to experience the surrounding state park. The company also leads e-bike (and bike-and-hike) tours and provides shuttle bus service from downtown Salt Lake City or the Clearfield FrontRunner rail station to the park. ✉ *Marina Parking Lot, 4528 W. 1700 S, Syracuse* ☎ *801/317–8549* 🌐 *www.antelopeebikes.com* 🎟 *Rentals from $30, guided tours from $99.*

HIKING

Antelope Island State Park offers plenty of space for both avid and casual hikers to explore, but keep a few things in mind. All trails are also shared by mountain bikers and horseback riders—not to mention the occasional bison. Trees are few and far between on the island, making for high exposure to the elements, so bring (and drink) plenty of water and dress appropriately. In the spring, biting insects make bug repellent a must-have. Pick up a trail map at the visitor center.

Once you're prepared, hiking Antelope Island can be a very enjoyable experience. Trails are fairly level except for a few places, where the hot summer sun makes the climb even more strenuous. Mountain ranges, including the Wasatch Front to the east and the Stansbury Mountains directly to the west, provide beautiful background in every direction, though haze sometimes obscures the view. Aromatic sage plants offer shelter for a variety of wildlife, so don't be startled if your next step flushes a chukar partridge, horned lark, or jackrabbit. A bobcat is a rarely seen island resident that will likely keep its distance.

Big Cottonwood Canyon

31 miles from Downtown Salt Lake City.

The histories of mining and skiing in Utah often go hand in hand, and that's certainly true of Big Cottonwood Canyon, with its adjacent ski resorts of **Brighton** and **Solitude.** In the mid-1800s, 2,500 miners lived at the top of this canyon in a rowdy tent city. The old mining roads make great hiking, mountain-biking, and backcountry ski trails. Rock climbers congregate in the lower canyon for excellent sport and traditional climbing. Opened in 1936, Brighton is the second-oldest ski resort in Utah and one of the oldest in North America. Just down the canyon, Solitude has undergone several incarnations since it opened in 1957 and has invested heavily in overnight accommodations and new base facilities in recent years. Among local ski areas, Big Cottonwood is quieter than Park City or neighboring Little Cottonwood Canyon, home of the Alta and Snowbird resorts. In summer, you can drive from Big Cottonwood Canyon to Park City via beautiful Guardsman Pass (it closes from fall through spring due to snow).

GETTING HERE AND AROUND

From downtown Salt Lake City it's a 40-minute drive to Big Cottonwood via I–80 and I–215, then Highway 190 E. Most downtown hotels offer free shuttles to the ski resorts, and Utah Transit Authority runs bus shuttles for $4.50 each way.

🍴 Restaurants

★ The Yurt at Solitude

$$$$ | **MODERN AMERICAN** | One of the most memorable and dramatic restaurant experiences in the state, dining in this secluded yurt begins with a guided ¼-mile snowshoe trek beneath a canopy of nighttime stars, and the dinner price—$175 per person—includes rentals, guides, corkage fee, and a grand four-course meal. The seasonally driven menu changes regularly, and The Yurt's chef describes the meal as he prepares it before your eyes in the cozy exhibition kitchen. **Known for:** unique snowshoeing tour to dinner; rich steaks and seafoods; festive yet intimate space. [$] *Average main: $175* ✉ *12000 Big Cottonwood Canyon Rd., Bldg. 15, Solitude* ☎ *385/282–7155* 🌐 *www.solitudemountain.com* 🕓 *Closed Mon., Tues., and in summer. No lunch.*

🛏 Hotels

★ The Inn at Solitude

$$$ | **RESORT** | Enjoy ski-in, ski-out convenience and VIP treatment at this well-appointed hotel with comfortable and spacious rooms and a slew of creature comforts, including an atmospheric bar, a lovely spa with a range of treatments, and an outdoor heated pool and hot tub. **Pros:** steps from lifts and ski village dining; outdoor heated pool and full-service spa; dazzling mountain views. **Cons:** social butterflies may find it a bit quiet; breakfast not included; no pets. [$] *Rooms from: $283* ✉ *12000 Big Cottonwood Canyon Rd., Solitude*

☎ *385/282–7155* 🌐 *www.solitudemountain.com* 🕓 *Closed May–mid-June and mid-Oct.–Nov.* 🛏 *46 rooms* 🍴 *No Meals.*

Silver Fork Lodge

$$ | **B&B/INN** | Log furniture and wood paneling give the rooms in the cozy and rustic 1940s ski lodge just down the road from Solitude and Brighton a warm and inviting feel; the views are unbeatable and the food in the excellent restaurant is a major attraction year-round (you can dine on the patio in summer). **Pros:** popular on-site restaurant; full breakfast included; free shuttle to ski lifts. **Cons:** not ski-in, ski-out; no in-room phones or TVs; three-night minimum during ski season. [$] *Rooms from: $185* ✉ *11332 E. Big Cottonwood Canyon Rd., Big Cottonwood Canyon* ☎ *801/533–9977* 🌐 *www.silverforklodge.com* 🛏 *6 rooms, 1 suite* 🍴 *Free Breakfast.*

Nightlife

Molly Green's

BARS | Ski bums and snowboarders come together to tip back a few at this retro-fun 1950s watering hole in the A-frame at the base of Brighton Ski Resort. ✉ *8302 S. Brighton Loop Rd., Brighton* ☎ *801/532–4731* 🌐 *www.brightonresort.com/molly-greens.*

Activities

BICYCLING

Solitude Mountain Resort

BIKING | Mountain bikers will love Solitude for its single-track trails that span 20 miles within Big Cottonwood Canyon as well as routes that connect neighboring canyons. Solitude Mountain Resort offers lift-served mountain biking with rentals available at Solitude Village on weekends from mid- to late June to early October. You can also rent disc-golf gear to play Solitude's popular 18-hole course. ✉ *12000 Big Cottonwood Canyon Rd.* ☎ *801/534–1400* 🌐 *www.solitudemountain.com.*

HIKING

Bloods Lake Trail

HIKING & WALKING | **FAMILY** | A favorite ramble in summer, this alpine trek accessed from scenic Guardsman Pass Road winds through aspen groves and around colorful wildflower meadows to a rippling lake with an elevation just under 10,000 feet. Pack a swimsuit—on hot days, a dip in the lake is the perfect reward for making this 2.7-mile trek. Beware that the trailhead parking fills up fast on weekend mornings—try to arrive early or late in the day. The trailhead is just 4 miles from Brighton resort in Big Cottonwood Canyon and extremely popular as a day trip from Salt Lake City as well. ✉ *S. Guardsman Pass Rd., Park City* ✥ *Just beyond Brighton Ski Resort.*

★ **Brighton Lakes Trail**

HIKING & WALKING | The upper section of Big Cottonwood Canyon is a glacier-carved valley with many side drainages that lead to picturesque alpine lakes. In the Brighton area, you can access beautiful mountain lakes (Dog, Mary, Martha, and Catherine), about a 4½-mile round-trip jaunt. The elevation at Brighton's parking lot is 8,700 feet and the lakes are at 9,400 to 10,000 feet, so take it easy, rest often, drink plenty of water, and keep an eye on the weather no matter the season. This beautiful hike along the Brighton Lakes Trail eventually ascends to Catherine Pass. From here you can choose to descend into Little Cottonwood's Albion Basin near Alta (but remember, you'll need a car for the 45-minute ride back to Brighton), or return back along the Brighton Lakes Trail. ✉ *Mary Lake La. at S. Brighton Loop Rd., Brighton.*

Lake Blanche Trail

HIKING & WALKING | This moderately challenging 7-mile round-trip trek leads to three stunning, glacially carved lakes, the largest of which is Lake Blanche—there's a beautiful waterfall, too. With an elevation gain of nearly 3,000 feet, this one will give you a pretty serious workout, but the scenery is amazing. The trailhead is just a 10-minute drive from Cottonwood Heights, less than midway before you get to Brighton. ⊠ *Lake Blanche Trailhead, Big Cottonwood Canyon Rd., Brighton* ⊕ *About 4½ miles from jct. with Hwy. 210.*

SKIING
Brighton Ski Resort
SKIING & SNOWBOARDING | The smallest of the Cottonwood resorts just outside Salt Lake City, Brighton is nonetheless a favorite among serious snowboarders, parents (who flock to the resort's ski school), and some extreme skiers and riders. There are no megaresort amenities here, just a nice mix of terrain for all abilities and a basic lodge, ski shop, and ski school. The snow is as powdery and deep as at nearby Alta and Snowbird, and advanced (and prepared) skiers can access extensive backcountry areas. There's something for everyone here at a fraction of the cost of the bigger resorts. ⊠ *8302 S. Brighton Loop Rd., Brighton* ☎ *801/532–4731* ⊕ *www. brightonresort.com* 🎟 *Lift tickets $125* ☞ *1,875-foot vertical drop; 1,050 skiable acres; 21% beginner, 40% intermediate, 39% advanced/expert; 4 high-speed quad chairs, 1 triple chair.*

★ Solitude Mountain Resort
SKIING & SNOWBOARDING | Since 1957, Solitude has offered Big Cottonwood Canyon's most intense ski experience. It's now anchored by a European-style village with lodges, condominiums, an upscale hotel, and some good restaurants. Downhill skiing and snowboarding are still the main attractions, with steep, pristine terrain in Honeycomb Canyon attracting the experts, and a mix of intermediate cruising runs and beginner slopes beckoning the less accomplished. You can enjoy relaxing after a hard day on the slopes at the comfortable Solitude Mountain Spa. ⊠ *12000 Big Cottonwood Canyon Rd., Solitude* ☎ *801/534–1400, 800/748–4754, 801/536–5777 snow report* ⊕ *www.solitudemountain.com* 🎟 *Lift tickets $110* ☞ *2,494-foot vertical*

drop; 1,200 skiable acres; 10% beginner, 40% intermediate, 50% advanced; 4 high-speed quad chairs, 2 quad chairs, 1 triple chair, 1 double chairs.

Solitude Nordic Center
SKIING & SNOWBOARDING | Accessible from Solitude and Brighton Villages, the Solitude Nordic Center has 12 miles of groomed cross-country trails, 6 miles of snowshoe trails, and a small shop offering rentals, lessons, food, and guided tours. For $20 you can use the trails all day; for $75 you can get a private lesson, rental, and all-day trail pass. ⊠ *12000 Big Cottonwood Canyon Rd.* ☎ *801/536–5774* ⊕ *www.solitudemountain.com.*

Little Cottonwood Canyon

25 miles from Brighton and Solitude, 20 miles from Salt Lake City.

Skiers have been singing the praises of Little Cottonwood Canyon since 1938, when the Alta Lifts Company pieced together a ski lift using parts from an old mine tram to become the **Alta Ski Resort,** the second such area in North America. With its 550 inches per year of dry, light snow and unparalleled terrain, this canyon is legendary among diehard snow enthusiasts. A mile down the canyon from Alta, **Snowbird Ski and Summer Resort,** which opened in 1971, shares the same mythical snow and terrain quality—the two areas are connected via the Mineral Basin area. You can purchase an Alta Snowbird One Pass that allows you on the lifts at both areas, making this a huge skiing complex.

But skiing isn't all there is to do here. Dazzling mountain-biking and hiking trails access the higher reaches of the Uinta-Wasatch-Cache National Forest, and the trails over Catherine Pass will put you at the head of Big Cottonwood Canyon at the Brighton Ski Area. Formed by the tireless path of an ancient glacier, Little Cottonwood Canyon cuts a swath through

Alta, Utah, is a dramatic place to enjoy the slopes or to take in the sights during the off-season.

these pristine woodlands. Canyon walls are composed mostly of striated granite, and traditional climbing routes of varied difficulty abound. At Snowbird's base area, modern structures house accommodations, restaurants, and bars. The largest of these buildings, the brutalist concrete (yet oddly alluring) Cliff Lodge, is an entire ski village under one roof. The resort presents a wide range of entertainment throughout the year, including pop and jazz concerts and Oktoberfest in fall.

GETTING HERE AND AROUND

To get here, take I–80 East to I–215 South, then hop off the highway at Exit 6 and venture into Little Cottonwood Canyon, following signs for Alta and Snowbird. The canyon's dramatic topography invites very occasional avalanches that block the road, the only entrance and egress. Note the $10 fee to enter the hiking areas in Albion Basin, past the main ski area in Alta.

VISITOR INFORMATION

CONTACTS Alta Chamber & Visitors Bureau. ☎ *435/633–1394* 🌐 *www.altacommunity.org.*

🍴 Restaurants

Steak Pit

$$$$ | **STEAKHOUSE** | Views and food take precedence over interior design at Snowbird's oldest restaurant, with a menu full of well-prepared steak and seafood entrees, including opulent Wagyu New York strip steaks and 16-ounce lobster tails. The dining room is warm and unpretentious, with some wood paneling and an expanse of glass. **Known for:** exceptional steaks with rich sauces; a number of high-ticket bottles on the extensive wine list; signature mud pie dessert. [$] *Average main: $44* ✉ *Snowbird Plaza Center, Level 1, Snowbird* ☎ *801/933–2222* 🌐 *www.snowbird.com* 🕒 *No lunch.*

Swen's

$$$$ | MODERN AMERICAN | With its sleek, contemporary vibe, warm lighting and wood accents, open kitchen, and floor-to-ceiling windows overlooking the fantastic ski terrain, this upscale restaurant in the ritzy Snowpine Lodge is Alta's hippest dining destination. The kitchen takes a farm-to-table approach to its hearty but creative mountain fare, with standout dishes like hamachi crudo and a succulent peppercorn-crusted rib-eye steak with mashed potatoes and Merlot-braised mushrooms. **Known for:** breathtaking mountain views; filling breakfasts; impressive wine list. $ *Average main: $47* ⊠ *10420 E. Hwy. 210, Alta* ☎ *801/742-6014* ⊕ *www.snowpine.com* ☉ *No dinner Mon. and Tues. No lunch.*

Hotels

Alta Lodge

$$$$ | B&B/INN | Many families have been booking the same week each year for several generations at this low-key but stylish 1939 lodge that's home to the famed Sitzmark Club bar as well as saunas and hot pools, which are set against a 30-foot wall of windows, to help you work out the kinks after a day on the slopes. **Pros:** steps from lift to Alta's steep slopes; magnificent Wasatch Mountain views; breakfast and dinner included during ski season. **Cons:** not many amenities for the price; no TVs in guest rooms; four-night minimum stay in high ski season. $ *Rooms from: $479* ⊠ *10230 E. Hwy. 210, Alta* ☎ *801/742-3500, 800/707-2582* ⊕ *www.altalodge.com* ☉ *Closed mid-Apr.–May and early Oct.–mid-Nov.* ⤴ *57 rooms* ⦿ *All-Inclusive.*

Alta's Rustler Lodge

$$$$ | HOTEL | Alta's sleekest lodge is a contemporary, full-service hotel with warmly decorated guestrooms and seating areas and exceptional views of the slopes. **Pros:** plush full-service spa; adjacent to Alta's ski lifts; superb, unpretentious service. **Cons:** avalanches are rare, but you could get snowed in; pricey, especially for a family; four-night minimum stay during ski season. $ *Rooms from: $700* ⊠ *10380 E. Hwy. 210, Alta* ☎ *801/742-4200* ⊕ *www.rustlerlodge. com* ☉ *Closed late Apr.–mid-Nov.* ⤴ *85 rooms* ⦿ *All-Inclusive.*

The Cliff Lodge

$$$$ | RESORT | The stark concrete walls of this 10-story structure, designed to complement the surrounding granite cliffs, enclose a self-contained ski-in, ski-out village with restaurants, bars, shops, and a high-end, two-story spa. **Pros:** central Snowbird ski village location; nice rooftop spa; several eateries and bars on site. **Cons:** stark, monolithic design isn't to every taste; furnishings are a bit dated; huge property that can feel impersonal. $ *Rooms from: $644* ⊠ *9320 Cliff Lodge Dr., Snowbird* ☎ *801/933-2222, 800/232-9542* ⊕ *www.snowbird.com* ⤴ *511 rooms* ⦿ *No Meals.*

★ Snowpine Lodge

$$$$ | RESORT | FAMILY | The level of luxury that's commonplace in Park City (along with the lofty prices to go with it), arrived in Alta in 2019 with the opening of this ultraposh slopeside retreat built using timber and stone from the original lodge on the site, and featuring a glamorous full-service spa with a heated outdoor pool, a swanky restaurant and hip gastropub, and stylishly kitted rooms and suites, many with mountain-view balconies. **Pros:** steps from ski lifts; excellent on-site restaurants; gorgeous full-service spa. **Cons:** multinight minimum stay during busy times; some might find it a bit glitzy for laid-back Alta; steep rates (with no meals included). $ *Rooms from: $637* ⊠ *10420 E. Hwy. 210, Alta* ☎ *801/742-2000* ⊕ *www.snowpine.com* ⤴ *63 rooms* ⦿ *No Meals.*

ⓨ Nightlife

★ The Gulch Pub

PUBS | The handsome gastropub in Alta's swanky Snowpine Lodge has big windows and an inviting terrace overlooking the slopes and plush leather seats and rustic stone columns. Upscale but easygoing, it's a terrific spot for a glass of wine or local IPA and light dining (from noon until evening) on tasty bar fare, such as kale Caesar salads, pickle-brined fried chicken, and New Haven–style white clam pizza. ⊠ *10420 E. Hwy. 210, Alta* ☎ *801/742–2000* ⊕ *www.snowpine.com.*

Activities

RECREATIONAL AREAS

★ Snowbird Resort

BIKING | **FAMILY** | The resort is transformed into a playground in summer with rides and games for children of all ages, plus concerts, outdoor sports, alfresco dining, and more. Thrill-seekers appreciate the mountain coaster, the alpine slide, the zipline, and the mountain flyer, which resembles a roller coaster. You'll also find a climbing wall, trampoline, ropes course, inflatables, and more. There are ample options to access stunning hiking terrain and views, including the tram to 11,000-foot Hidden Peak. Mountain biking is another favorite summer activity. Other than a mile-long beginner-to-intermediate single-track trail, the steep, rocky terrain here is not recommended for novices, but experienced riders love exploring this extensive network of rugged trails. Bike rentals are available. Summer tickets on the tram—which was completely overhauled in 2022 and now features cars with floor-to-ceiling windows and rooftop observation platforms—cost $40, and all-day passes are a good way to save on multiple activities, especially for families. ⊠ *Hwy. 210* ☎ *801/933–2200* ⊕ *www.snowbird.com.*

HIKING

Cecret Lake Trail

HIKING & WALKING | **FAMILY** | One of Little Cottonwood Canyon's most stunning trails, this moderately steep 1.8-mile round-trip climb from Albion Basin leads through colorful wildflower meadows to a peaceful high-country lake and can be completed in under 90 minutes. ⊠ *Alta* ⊹ *Trailhead: on Albion Basin Rd.*

★ Sunset Peak

HIKING & WALKING | The trailhead for the 4-mile out-and-back hike to Sunset Peak starts high in Little Cottonwood Canyon, above Alta Ski Resort, in Albion Basin. This is a popular area for finding wildflowers in July and August. After an initial steep incline, the trail wanders through flat meadows before it climbs again to Catherine Pass at 10,240 feet. From here intermediate hikes continue along the ridge in both directions. Continue up the trail to the summit of Sunset Peak for breathtaking views of the Heber Valley, Park City, Mount Timpanogos, Big and Little Cottonwood Canyons, and even a part of the Salt Lake Valley. You can alter your route by starting in Little Cottonwood Canyon and ending your hike in neighboring Big Cottonwood Canyon, by following the Catherine Pass as it descends along the Brighton Lakes Trail to Brighton Ski Resort (from which it's nearly an hour's drive back to Alta). ⊠ *Cecret Lake/Catherine Pass Trailhead, Albion Basin Rd., Alta.*

White Pine Trailhead

HIKING & WALKING | **FAMILY** | White Pine Trailhead, ¾ mile below Snowbird on the south side of the road, runs alongside gurgling Little Cottonwood Creek and accesses some excellent easy hikes to overlooks with great opportunities for spotting wildlife. If you want to keep going on more intermediate trails, continue up the trail to the lakes in White Pine Canyon, Red Pine Canyon, and Maybird Gulch. All of these hikes share a common path for the first mile. ⊠ *Hwy. 210, Snowbird.*

SKIING

★ Alta Ski Area

SKIING & SNOWBOARDING | Alta Ski Area has perhaps the best snow anywhere in the world—an average of nearly 550 inches a year, and terrain to match it. Alta is one of the few resorts left in the country that doesn't allow snowboarding. Sprawling across two large basins, Albion and Wildcat, Alta has a good mixture of expert and intermediate terrain, but relatively few beginner runs. Much of the best skiing (for advanced or expert skiers) requires either finding obscure traverses or doing some hiking. It takes some time to get to know this mountain, so if you can find a local to show you around you'll be ahead of the game. Albion Basin's lower slopes have a terrific expanse of novice and lower-intermediate terrain. Rolling meadows, wide trails, and light dry snow create one of the best places in the country for less-skilled skiers to learn to ski powder. Two-hour lessons start at $114. In addition to downhill skiing, Alta also has 3 km (2 miles) of groomed track for skating and classic skiing (on a separate ticket), plus a good selection of rental equipment. ⊠ *10230 Hwy. 210, Alta* ☎ *801/359–1078, 801/572–3939 snow report* ⊕ *www.alta.com* ⬛ *Lift tickets $139* ☞ *2,538-foot vertical drop; 2,614 skiable acres; 15% novice, 30% intermediate, 55% advanced; 3 high-speed quads, 1 triple chairs, 2 double chairs, 5 surface tows.*

★ Snowbird Resort

SKIING & SNOWBOARDING | For many skiers, this is as close to heaven as you can get. Soar aboard Snowbird's signature 125-passenger tram straight from the base to the resort's highest point, 11,000 feet above sea level, and then descend into a playground of powder-filled chutes, bowls, and meadows—a leg-burning top-to-bottom run of nearly 3,000 vertical feet if you choose. The terrain here is weighted more toward experts—35% of Snowbird is rated black diamond—and if there is a drawback to this resort, it's a lack of beginner terrain. The open bowls, such as Little Cloud and Regulator Johnson, are challenging; the Upper Cirque and the Gad Chutes are hair-raising. On deep-powder days—not uncommon at the Bird—these chutes are exhilarating for skiers who like that sense of a cushioned free fall with every turn. With a nod to intermediate skiers, Snowbird opened North America's first skier tunnel in 2006. Skiers and boarders ride a 600-foot magic carpet through the Peruvian Tunnel, reducing the trek to Mineral Basin. If you're looking for intermediate cruising runs, there's the long, meandering Chip's Run. After a day of powder turns, you can lounge on the 3,000-square-foot deck of Creekside Lodge at the base of Gad Valley. Beginner's lessons start at $155 and include lift ticket, tuition, and rentals. ⊠ *Hwy. 210, Snowbird* ☎ *801/933–2222, 801/933–2100 snow report* ⊕ *www. snowbird.com* ⬛ *Lift tickets $145* ☞ *2,900-foot vertical drop; 2,500 skiable acres; 27% novice, 38% intermediate, 35% advanced; 125-passenger tram, 4 quad lifts, 6 double chairs, 1 gondola, and a skier tunnel with surface lift.*

SKI TOURS

Ski Utah Interconnect Adventure Tour

SKIING & SNOWBOARDING | Strong intermediate and advanced skiers can hook up with the Ski Utah Interconnect Adventure Tour for a guided alpine ski tour that takes you to as many as six resorts (including Brighton, Solitude, Alta, and Snowbird) in a single day, all connected by backcountry ski routes with unparalleled views of the Wasatch Mountains. Guides test your ski ability before departure. The tour includes guide service, lift tickets, lunch, and transportation back to the point of origin. You'll even walk away with a finisher's pin. The Deer Valley Departure Tour operates Sunday, Monday, Tuesday, Wednesday, and Friday; the Snowbird Departure Tour operates Thursday and Saturday. Reservations are required. ☎ *801/534–1907* ⊕ *www. skiutah.com* ⬛ *From $475.*

Chapter 4

PARK CITY AND THE SOUTHERN WASATCH

4

Updated by
Tessa Woolf

 Sights
★★★★★

 Restaurants
★★★★★

 Hotels
★★★★★

 Shopping
★★★★★

 Nightlife
★★★★☆

WELCOME TO PARK CITY AND THE SOUTHERN WASATCH

TOP REASONS TO GO

★ **Outdoor fun:** Regardless of the season, Park City is the epicenter of mountain adventure.

★ **Two top-tier resorts:** No place in North America has two world-class and distinct resorts so close to one another, not to mention as expansive, dynamic, luxurious, and unique as Deer Valley and Park City Mountain Resort.

★ **Olympic spirit:** This town seems to contain more Olympians per capita than any town in the country, if not the world.

★ **Old Town Park City:** First laid out by silver miners in the late 1800s, Park City's historic Main Street is especially lively during big events like the Sundance Film Festival and Kimball Arts Festival.

★ **Sundance Resort:** At the base of Mount Timpanogos, Robert Redford's intimate resort pays homage to art and nature.

1 Park City. With a high desert climate, you'll smell both sagebrush and pine in this alpine outback. There are rivers, streams, and lakes to fish from and thousands of trails to hike and mountain bike.

2 Kimball Junction and Olympic Park. Just north of Park City, this burgeoning residential area is near the site of the Olympic Park, where ski events were conducted during the 2002 Salt Lake City Olympic Games.

3 Heber Valley. This valley is what the Salt Lake Valley probably looked like 50 years ago. It's still fairly pristine and with an agricultural and small town vibe. A winding river runs through the verdant valley on the west side, and horses still clop down the side streets. People come here for the golfing, fishing, and recreational opportunities near Kamas and in the Uinta Mountains. Close by is Midway, a Swiss-like village built on the west side where you can find pampered stays at European-like resorts and a dairy farm where you can get ice cream and learn to make cheese.

4 Sundance Resort. Robert Redford bought and preserved this swath of paradise under the snowy head of Mount Timpanogos and shares it with the public. The Provo River is also a famous blue-ribbon fly-fishing destination.

5 Provo. A youthful college town that's equally devoted to their raucous Freedom Festival in July and their fall football season at Brigham Young University (BYU). Be sure to wear blue on game days. The town is home to a gorgeous art museum on the campus of BYU as well as many orchard stands that run along the eastern edge near Provo Canyon. Provo Canyon is a great place to go tubing or have a picnic while you watch Bridal Veil Falls cascade down the cliffs.

6 American Fork. At the foot of the Wasatch Range, American Fork (named after the river) is a base from which you can access the Timpanogos Cave National Monument and the Alpine Loop Scenic Drive.

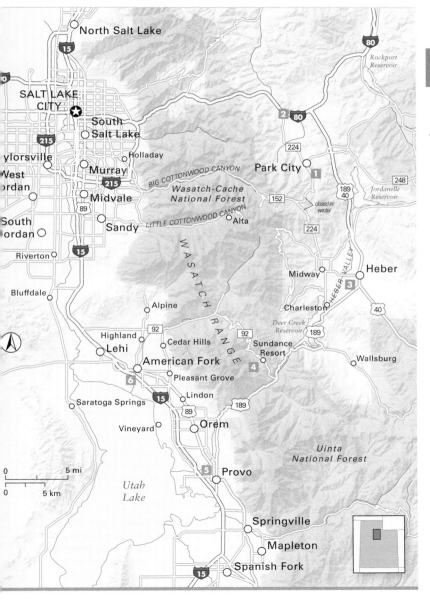

The Wasatch Range shares the same desert climate as the Great Basin, which it rims, but these craggy peaks rise to more than 11,000 feet and stall storms moving in from the Pacific, causing massive precipitations. The 160-mile stretch of verdure is home to 2 million people, or three-fourths of all Utahns.

Although its landscape is crisscrossed by freeways and dappled by towns large and small, the Wasatch still beckons adventurers with its alpine forests and wind-swept canyons. Where three geologically distinct regions—the Rocky Mountains, the Colorado Plateau, and the Basin and Range province—converge, the Wasatch Range combines characteristics of each. You'll find broad glacial canyons with towering granite walls, stream-cut gorges through purple, tan, and green shale, and red-rock bluffs and valleys.

Most people associate Park City with its legendary skiing in winter, but this is truly a year-round destination. Bright-blue lakes afford fantastic boating and water sports, and some of the West's best trout streams flow from the high country. Add miles of hiking and biking trails and you have a vacation that's hard to beat.

You can also find cultural activities and entertainment at every turn. The Sundance Film Festival, hosted by the Sundance Institute (which was founded by actor-director Robert Redford), attracts movie stars and independent filmmakers from all over. Major recording artists of all types play indoor and outdoor venues, and nightlife abounds in the city and

resorts, with an increasing number of nightclubs and music venues.

Planning

Getting Here and Around

AIR
Commercial air traffic flies in and out of Salt Lake City International Airport, which was renovated in 2020. The airport is less than an hour from all destinations in the Wasatch. Heber's airport is open to private planes only.

AIRPORT TRANSFERS
Shared shuttles are the best way to travel between the airport and Park City, with fares starting at $49 per person one-way. Once you arrive in Park City, a free, efficient Park City transit system operates a reliable network of bus routes, connecting Old Town, the local ski resorts, Kimball Junction, and most neighborhoods.

CONTACTS Canyon Transportation.
☎ 801/255–1841 ⊕ www.canyon-transport.com. **Park City Direct Shuttle.**
☎ 866/655–3010 toll-free, 435/655–3010
⊕ www.parkcitydirectshuttle.com.

CAR

Highway travel around the region is quick and easy. The major routes in the area include the transcontinental I–80, which connects Salt Lake City and Park City; and U.S. 40/189, which connects southwest Wyoming, Utah, and northwest Colorado via Park City, Heber City, and Provo. Along larger highways, roadside stops with restrooms, fast-food restaurants, and sundries stores are well spaced. Scenic routes and lookout points are clearly marked, enabling you to slow down and pull over to take in the views. Off the main highways, roads range from well-paved multilane blacktop routes to barely graveled backcountry trails. Watch out for wildlife on the roads just about anywhere in Utah.

Hotels

Chain hotels and motels dot I–15 all along the Wasatch Front and nearly always have availability. Every small town on the back side of the range has at least one good bed-and-breakfast, and most towns have both independent and chain motels. Park City lodging offers everything from cozy condominiums to high-end hotels, luxurious lodges, and well-run bed-and-breakfast inns. All this luxury means prices here tend to be higher than in other areas in the state during the winter. Prices drop significantly in the warmer months, when package deals or special rates are offered. Lodging in Provo tends to be most expensive during the week. Make reservations well in advance for winter holiday weekends and during January's Sundance Film Festival.

Hotel reviews have been shortened. For full information, visit Fodors.com.

What It Costs

	$	$$	$$$	$$$$
RESTAURANTS				
	under $16	$16–$22	$23–$30	over $30
HOTELS				
	under $125	$125–$200	$201–$300	over $300

CONDO RENTALS

The reservationists at **Deer Valley Resort Lodging** (☎ 435/645–6428 ⊕ www.deer-valley.com) are knowledgeable and the service is efficient at this high-end property-management company. Complimentary shuttle service to/from resorts and around town in Cadillac Escalades is a perk.

Natural Retreats Park City (☎ 435/275–4943 ⊕ www.naturalretreats.com) manages roughly 150 properties around town, ranging from two-bedroom condos to eight-bedroom ski homes. More than 90% of their properties are on the slopes or a short walk to the lifts. Your concierge will take care of everything from grocery delivery and private chefs to ski rental delivery, and each reservation includes daily housekeeping and shuttle service around town.

Restaurants

American cuisine dominates the Wasatch dining scene, with great steaks, barbecue, and traditional Western fare. There's also an abundance of good seafood, which the busier eateries fly in daily from the West Coast. Restaurants range from Swiss to Japanese, French, and Mexican. Hours vary seasonally, so it's a good idea to call ahead. Reservations are essential during winter holiday weekends and the Sundance Film Festival. Park City restaurants offer great deals, such as two-for-one entrées from spring to fall, so check the local newspaper for coupons or ask your concierge which eateries are offering discounts.

Visitor Information

CONTACTS Park City Convention and Visitors Bureau. ✉ *1850 Sidewinder Dr., #320, Park City* ☎ *800/453–1360* ⊕ *www.visitparkcity.com.* **Ski Utah.** ✉ *2749 E. Parleys Way, Suite 310, Salt Lake City* ☎ *801/534–1779, 800/754–8824* ⊕ *www.skiutah.com.* **Utah Valley Convention and Visitors Bureau.** ✉ *220 W. Center St., Suite 100, Provo* ☎ *801/851–2100, 800/222–8824* ⊕ *www.utahvalley.com.*

When to Go

Winter is long in the mountains (ski resorts buzz from November to mid-April) but much more manageable in the valleys. The snow stops falling in April or May, and a month later the temperatures are in the 80s. If you don't mind capricious weather, spring and fall are opportune seasons to visit, with lower rates and smaller crowds. Spring is also a good time for fishing, rafting on rivers swollen with snowmelt, birding, and wildlife viewing. In summer, water-sports enthusiasts flock to the region to fish, water-ski, windsurf, sail, stand-up paddleboard, kayak, and canoe. The Wasatch Mountains also draw people on foot, bike, and horseback seeking respite from the heat of the valley from June through Labor Day. Fall's colors rival those of New England. A fall tradition here is to drive along the Alpine Loop east of Provo or up Pine Canyon out of the Heber Valley.

Park City

The best-known areas of the Wasatch Mountains lie east of Salt Lake City. Up and over Parley's Canyon via I–80 you'll find the sophisticated mountain town of Park City, with its world-class ski resorts and myriad summer attractions.

After silver was discovered in Park City in 1868, it quickly became a rip-roaring mining town with more than two dozen saloons and a thriving red-light district. In the process, it earned the nickname "Sin City." A fire destroyed many of the town's buildings in 1898; this, combined with declining mining fortunes in the early 1900s, caused most of the residents to pack up and leave. It wasn't until 1946 that its current livelihood began to take shape in the form of the small Snow Park ski hill, which opened where Deer Valley Resort now sits.

Park City once again profited from the generosity of the mountains as skiing became popular. In 1963 Treasure Mountain Resort began operations with its skier's subway—an underground train and hoist system that ferried skiers to the mountain's summit via old mining tunnels. Facilities were upgraded over time, and Treasure Mountain became Park City Mountain Resort. Although it has a mind-numbing collection of condominiums, at Park City's heart is a historic downtown that rings with the authenticity of a real town with real roots.

GETTING HERE AND AROUND

The free Park City Shuttle operates from roughly 6 am to midnight in summer and winter. The schedule is more limited in fall and spring, so be sure to check schedules at the Transit Center on Swede Alley or on the buses.

Old Town is walkable, but the rest of greater Park City is best explored by bicycle in the spring, summer, and fall. More than 400 miles of bike trails help Park City earn accolades as one of the top cycling communities in the world, including the designation as a Gold Level Ride Center by the International Mountain Biking Association. Automobile traffic is relatively minimal and limited to slowdowns during morning and evening commutes and the post-ski exodus from the resorts. There are several local taxi businesses.

VISITOR INFORMATION

CONTACTS Park City Visitor Information Center. ✉ *1794 Olympic Pkwy., Kimball Junction* 🕿 *435/649–6100* ⊕ *www.visit-parkcity.com.*

FESTIVALS

Robert Redford's Sundance Film Festival comes to Park City every January, but the city hosts a number of other festivals and events that might sway your decision about when to visit.

★ Deer Valley Snow Park Amphitheater

CONCERTS | Everything from Utah Symphony performances to country music features on stage. Big name stars like Willie Nelson, Bonnie Raitt, Chris Isaak, and Judy Collins have graced the outdoor amphitheater, which sits on the resort's beginner ski area.

■ TIP→ **Go on Wednesday evening for free concerts with local and regional bands, and pack a picnic.** ✉ *2250 Deer Valley Dr. S, Park City* 🕿 *435/649–1000* ⊕ *www.deervalley.com.*

Park City Food & Wine Classic

FESTIVALS | Held in early July, this festival allows diners and wine-enthusiasts to sample from wineries, distilleries, and breweries from all over the world and to taste delicious fare from the region's best restaurants. Educational seminars are offered, and the festival culminates in a grand tasting at Montage Deer Valley.

■ TIP→ **It's increasingly popular, and many events now sell out in advance, so plan ahead.** ✉ *Park City* 🕿 *877/328–2783* ⊕ *www.visitparkcity.com.*

★ Park City Kimball Arts Festival

ARTS FESTIVALS | FAMILY | Celebrating visual and culinary art, this three-day festival, held the first weekend in August, is the biggest summer event in town. More than 200 artists from all over North America exhibit and offer their work to 40,000 festival attendees. Culinary vendors and beer and wine gardens offer plenty of refreshment to art lovers, and

live music is around every corner. ✉ *Main St., Park City* 🕿 *435/649–8882* ⊕ *www.parkcitykimballartsfestival.org.*

★ Sundance Film Festival

FESTIVALS | For 10 days each January, movie stars, film executives, and independent film lovers gather in a mountain setting for the Sundance Film Festival, hosted by Robert Redford's Sundance Institute. It's a chance to view the screenings of new, risk-taking documentaries, features, and other creative film projects from around the globe. Moviegoers can also participate in Q&A conversations with filmmakers, producers, and creatives after screenings. Participants can add their names to a waiting list even if shows are sold out. The festival is held at many venues in Park City, Sundance, Ogden, and downtown Salt Lake City, and there are music and culinary events as well.

■ TIP→ **Book your hotel months in advance. Skip the rental car and use the free shuttle. Park City's legendary ski slopes empty out while the filmgoers attend the screenings, so build in a day of crowd-free skiing.** ✉ *Park City* 🕿 *435/658–3456* ⊕ *www.sundance.org.*

◉ Sights

Kimball Art Center

ART MUSEUM | A thriving nonprofit community art center, this venue hosts national and regional exhibitions, sells art supplies, provides educational opportunities, including seminars and art classes for all ages, and hosts special events. ✉ *1251 Kearns Blvd., Park City* 🕿 *435/649–8882* ⊕ *www.kimballart-center.org* ⊡ *Free* ⊙ *Closed Mon.*

Park City Farmer's Market

MARKET | Held rain or shine each Wednesday from June through October, the Farmer's Market is always a good spot to pick up locally sourced bread, fruits and vegetables, flowers, and more. ✉ *Canyons Village, 4000 Canyons Resort*

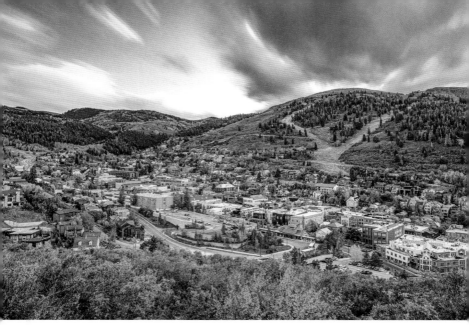

Park City has been known since its mining heyday as Utah's "Sin City."

Dr., Park City ☎ *435/671–1455* ⊕ *www.parkcityfarmersmarket.com.*

★ Park City Mountain Resort

AMUSEMENT PARK/CARNIVAL | FAMILY | In the warmer months, the resort transforms itself into a mountain amusement park, with attractions such as the Alpine Slide and the Alpine Coaster, ziplines, and a climbing wall. Visitors take a chairlift up the mountain to the Alpine Slide, then hop aboard special sleds that carry them down 3,000 feet of winding concrete and fiberglass track at speeds controlled by each rider. The gravity-propelled Alpine Coaster (which operates year-round) zooms through aspen-lined twists and turns at speeds up to 35 mph. Two ziplines offer a high-flying adrenaline rush as riders strap into a harness suspended from a cable. In addition to the climbing wall, there's a miniature golf course, trampolines, an adventure zone for younger children, and some of the West's best lift-served mountain biking and hiking. ⊠ *1345 Lowell Ave., Park City*

☎ *435/649–8111, 800/222–7275* ⊕ *www.parkcitymountain.com.*

Park City Museum

HISTORY MUSEUM | FAMILY | A must-see for history buffs, this museum is housed in the former library, city hall, and whistle tower on Main Street. With a two-story scale model of the 19th-century Ontario Mine, a 20th-century gondola hanging overhead, and the old jail below, this is an authentic tribute to Park City's mining and skiing past. Climb aboard a re-created Union Pacific train car, hold on to a quivering and noisy jack drill for a feel of the mining experience, and, if you dare, step inside a jail cell. Tours of historic Main Street also depart from here. ⊠ *528 Main St., Park City* ☎ *435/649–7457* ⊕ *www.parkcityhistory.org* ⊡ *$15.*

Park Silly Sunday Market

MARKET | A funky and constantly changing assortment of artisans, entertainers, and culinary vendors transform Old Town into a street festival complete with beer garden and Bloody Mary bar on Sunday, June through September. The Park Silly

Market strives to be a no-waste event with everything recycled or composted. Look for the free bike valet to park your ride while you walk through the crowds. ✉ *Lower Main St., Park City* ☎ *435/714–4036* ⊕ *www.parksillysundaymarket.com.*

 Restaurants

Apex

$$$$ | **STEAKHOUSE** | Suitably named as this restaurant is the highest year-round restaurant in Park City, Apex is also at the top of its class for dining and service. For dinner, it transforms into a mountainside steak house. **Known for:** vegan and children's menus; steak; superior service. Ⓢ *Average main: $50* ✉ *Montage Deer Valley, 9100 Marsac Ave., Park City* ☎ *435/604–1402* ⊕ *www.montagedeervalley.com.*

Café Terigo

$$$ | **ITALIAN** | This Main Street staple has delighted guests since the mid-1990s with a modern Italian menu in an airy café with the best patio in town. The restaurant serves well-prepared pasta and seafood dishes using only fresh ingredients for lunch and dinner. **Known for:** traditional Bolognese; hearty salads; alfresco dining. Ⓢ *Average main: $30* ✉ *424 Main St., Park City* ☎ *435/645–9555* ⊕ *www.cafeterigo.com* ⊙ *Call for seasonal hrs.*

★ Chimayo

$$$$ | **SOUTHWESTERN** | Chef Arturo Flores will delight you with tantalizing dishes such as duck breast enchiladas, tortilla soup (his grandmother's recipe), a giant ahi tuna taco, or melt-off-the-bone spareribs in this upscale Southwestern restaurant. Order a house-made margarita (try the serrano margarita for an extra kick), and enjoy the cozy and intimate feel of this popular eatery. **Known for:** upscale Southwestern fare; margaritas; friendly staff. Ⓢ *Average main: $40* ✉ *368 Main St., Park City* ☎ *435/649–6222* ⊕ *www.chimayorestaurant.com* ⊙ *No lunch.*

Deer Valley Café

$ | **AMERICAN** | **FAMILY** | An extension of the ski resort's famous culinary offerings, this gourmet grocery/café serves breakfast, lunch, and early dinner, and features menu items ranging from the famous Deer Valley turkey chili to shrimp tacos to a chicken tandoori wrap, and everything in between. The expansive outdoor deck provides waterfront alfresco dining and views of the ski resort. **Known for:** turkey chili; high-quality ingredients; casual dining year-round. Ⓢ *Average main: $10* ✉ *Deer Valley Plaza Bldg., Deer Valley Resort, 1375 Deer Valley Dr., Park City* ☎ *435/615–2400* ⊕ *www.deervalley.com* ⊙ *No dinner.*

El Chubasco

$ | **MEXICAN** | **FAMILY** | For quick and hearty traditional Mexican food, this popular place is perfect. Favorites are *camarones a la diabla* (spicy shrimp), chiles rellenos, and fish tacos. **Known for:** big burritos; extensive salsa bar; fast-casual dining. Ⓢ *Average main: $10* ✉ *1890 Bonanza Dr., Park City* ☎ *435/645–9114* ⊕ *www.elchubascoparkcity.com.*

The Farm

$$$ | **MODERN AMERICAN** | The team at The Farm relentlessly seeks new, fresh, and unique ingredients to infuse into memorable meals in the restaurant's open kitchen. Seasonal menus always spotlight items from the region's sustainable farms, including root vegetables, truffles, berries, and meat. **Known for:** charcuterie board; fresh ingredients; cozy atmosphere. Ⓢ *Average main: $30* ✉ *Canyons Village, 4000 Canyons Resort Dr., Park City* ☎ *435/615–8080* ⊕ *www.parkcitymountain.com* ⊙ *Call for seasonal hrs.*

★ Fireside Dining

$$$$ | **EUROPEAN** | **FAMILY** | After a day of playing in the snow, Empire Canyon Lodge's Fireside Dining is the perfect way to warm up as you eat in the timber-framed lodge surrounded by several stone fireplaces. You'll feel like a medieval lord as you go from fireplace to

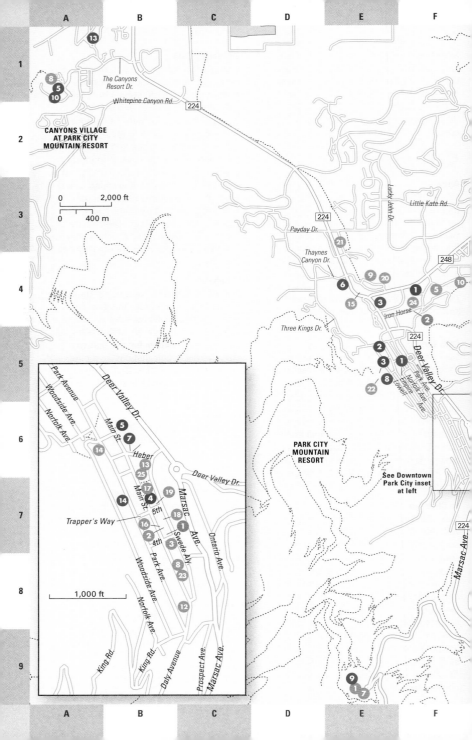

Sights ▼

1 Kimball Art Center **F4**
2 Park City
  Farmers Market.......... **E5**
3 Park City
  Mountain Resort......... **E5**
4 Park City Museum **B7**
5 Park Silly
  Sunday Market.......... **B6**

Restaurants ▼

1 Apex....................... **E9**
2 Café Terigo **B7**
3 Chimayo.................. **B7**
4 Deer Valley
  Grocery-Cafe........... **H6**
5 El Chubasco **F4**
6 The Farm................. **A1**
7 Fireside Dinning......... **E9**
8 Firewood................. **C8**
9 Five5eeds................ **E4**
10 Freshies Lobster Co...... **F4**
11 Glitretind Restaurant ... **G9**
12 Grappa **C8**
13 Handle **B6**
14 High West Saloon **A6**
15 Park City
  Roadhouse Grill **E4**
16 Purple Sage **B7**
17 Riverhorse on Main **B7**
18 Shabu **B7**
19 Tupelo **B7**
20 Twisted Fern.............. **E4**
21 Versante
  Hearth + Bar.............. **E3**
22 The Viking Yurt **E5**
23 Wasatch Brew Pub....... **C8**
24 Windy Ridge Café........ **F4**
25 Yuki Yama Sushi......... **B6**

Quick Bites ▼

1 Java Cow
  Cafe & Bakery........... **B7**
2 Ritual Chocolate Cafe ... **F4**

Hotels ▼

1 Chateau Après **F5**
2 The Chateaux
  Deer Valley **G8**
3 Doubletree by
  Hilton Park City–
  The Yarrow **E4**
4 Goldener Hirsch,
  Auberge Resorts
  Collection................ **G8**
5 Grand Summit
  Hotel..................... **A1**
6 Hotel Park City,
  Autograph Collection.... **E4**
7 Main & SKY.............. **B6**
8 Marriott's
  MountainSide **E5**
9 Montage Deer Valley.... **E9**
10 Pendry Park City **A1**
11 The St. Regis
  Deer Valley **H7**
12 Stein Eriksen Lodge
  Deer Valley **G9**
13 Waldorf Astoria
  Park City **A1**
14 Washington
  School House Hotel **B7**

4

Park City and the Southern Wasatch PARK CITY

Park City

Kearns Blvd.

189

KEY

1 *Exploring Sights*
1 *Restaurants*
1 *Quick Bites*
1 *Hotels*

fireplace to be served hearty fare like veal stew, elk, or a slice of perfectly roasted lamb cooked over a spit. **Known for:** dining around the fire; decadent dining options; lengthy meals. $ Average main: $110 ⊠ Empire Canyon Lodge, Deer Valley Resort, 9200 Marsac Ave., Park City ☎ 435/645–6632 ⊕ www.deervalley.com ⊗ No lunch; closed Mon. and Tues. in May–Nov.

Firewood

$$$$ | **AMERICAN** | At this lively establishment, dishes are cooked over an open flame, and antique leather chairs look out onto the open kitchen. Serving so-called heirloom American cuisine, the restaurant's seasonal, locally sourced menu changes frequently. **Known for:** open-fire cooking; locally sourced menu; downstairs nickel-topped bar. $ Average main: $36 ⊠ 306 Main St., Main Street ☎ 435/252–9900 ⊕ firewoodonmain.com ⊗ No lunch. Closed Sun. and Mon. in May–Nov.

★ Five5eeds

$ | **AUSTRALIAN** | This breakfast and lunch hot spot offers up nourishing dishes that look and taste like works of art. The restaurant manages to pull in flavors from all over the globe while using Utah-sourced ingredients with an Aussie twist, a nod to the owners' roots. **Known for:** iced coffee with ice cream; unique menu offerings; breakfast served all day. $ Average main: $14 ⊠ 1600 Snow Creek Dr., Suite #EF, Park City ☎ 435/901–8242 ⊕ www.five5eeds.com ⊗ No dinner.

★ Freshie's Lobster Co

$$ | **SEAFOOD** | It may seem a bit out of place in the land-locked mountains of Utah, but this casual restaurant started as a food truck run by East Coast natives, then became so popular that a brick-and-mortar location opened in 2016. Lobsters are flown in fresh daily, and the lobster roll is now nationally recognized as the "World's Best Lobster Roll" after taking home the win at a competition in Portland, Maine, in 2017. **Known for:** lobster

rolls; food truck traveling the region; casual atmosphere. $ Average main: $20 ⊠ 1915 Prospector Ave., Prospector ☎ 435/631–9861 ⊕ www.freshieslobster-co.com.

Glitretind Restaurant

$$$$ | **MODERN AMERICAN** | Beloved chef Zane Holmquist is the culinary king behind the restaurants within Stein Eriksen Lodge. Holmquist's inventive and soulful dishes are as much of a staple here as the wood trim, crisp white linens, crystal glasses, and fresh-cut flowers. **Known for:** top-notch service; excellent wine and beer pairings; Sunday brunch. $ Average main: $45 ⊠ Stein Erickson Lodge, Deer Valley Resort, 7700 Stein Way, Deer Valley ☎ 435/645–6455 ⊕ www.steinlodge.com/dining.

Grappa

$$$$ | **ITALIAN** | Heavy floor tiles, rustic bricks, and exposed timbers lend a warm, rustic farmhouse feel to this romantic spot. The menu offers appetizers, such as a grape-and-Gorgonzola salad with roasted walnuts, and hearty entrées, like Roman-style chicken, osso bucco, and horseradish-encrusted salmon. **Known for:** outdoor deck for summer dining; osso bucco; extensive wine list with several varieties of grappa. $ Average main: $40 ⊠ 151 Main St., Main Street ☎ 435/645–0636 ⊕ www.grapparestaurant.com ⊗ No lunch.

★ Handle

$$$ | **AMERICAN** | Handle was voted Best Restaurant in Park City in 2017 thanks to chef Briar Handly's inventive American dishes. Small plates make it easy to try everything, and you'll want to with dishes like buffalo cauliflower, smoked trout sausage, and the chef's famous fried chicken. **Known for:** chef's fried chicken; creative cocktails; inventive desserts. $ Average main: $30 ⊠ 136 Heber Ave., Old Town ☎ 435/602–1155 ⊕ www.handleparkcity.com ⊗ Closed Mon. and Tues. in May–Nov. No lunch.

★ High West Saloon

$$ | **AMERICAN** | Touted as the only ski-in, ski-out distillery in the world, High West Saloon sits at the base of Park City Mountain's Town Lift, serving hearty American fare with a locally focused menu that changes seasonally and delicious, handcrafted cocktails using the distillery's own whiskey and vodka. This lively restaurant and bar, housed in a historical home and livery, is a favorite among locals and visitors alike. **Known for:** whiskey; handcrafted cocktails; lively atmosphere. $ *Average main: $21* ⊠ *703 Park Ave., Old Town* ☎ *435/649–8300* ⊕ *www.highwest.com.*

Park City Roadhouse Grill

$ | **AMERICAN** | **FAMILY** | If you are looking for a place to grab a burger and delicious craft beer while your kids enjoy house-made mac-and-cheese, this roadhouse (formerly Squatters) is the spot. With a sleek and bustling brewpub vibe, it's a great place for either an evening out or a quick stop after a spin on your mountain bike to enjoy truffle fries and share a pint of pale ale. **Known for:** local favorite; one of the largest craft breweries in Utah with excellent beer; open all day. $ *Average main: $14* ⊠ *1900 Park Ave., Park City* ☎ *435/649–9868.*

Purple Sage

$$$ | **AMERICAN** | Plenty of purple-hue touches—velvet upholstered booths, hand-painted scrims, and Western murals—brighten the 1898 brick building that was once the local telegraph office. "Fancy cowboy" cuisine includes such dishes as grilled veal meat loaf with poblano peppers and pine nuts or the lime-grilled black tiger shrimp. In summer, eat on the back deck under the charming bistro lights. **Known for:** Western fare; meat loaf; intimate dining. $ *Average main: $30* ⊠ *434 Main St., Main Street* ☎ *435/655–9505* ⊕ *www.purplesageparkcity.com* ⊗ *No lunch.*

★ Riverhorse on Main

$$$$ | **AMERICAN** | With two warehouse loft rooms, exposed wood beams, sleek furnishings, and original art, this award-winning restaurant feels like a big-city supper club where chef-owner Seth Adams pairs imaginative fresh food with a world-class wine list in this elegant—but ski-town relaxed—atmosphere. The menu changes seasonally, but look out for the braised buffalo short rib, pan-roasted tomahawk pork chop, or signature macadamia-nut-crusted Alaskan halibut. **Known for:** Alaskan halibut; vegan and gluten-free friendly; Sunday brunch. $ *Average main: $42* ⊠ *540 Main St., Park City* ☎ *435/649–3536* ⊕ *www.riverhorseparkcity.com* ⊗ *No lunch.*

Shabu

$$$$ | **ASIAN** | The Wagyu hot rock, volcano sushi roll (tuna, wasabi, pineapple, jalapeño, and cilantro), and shabu-shabu (Japanese hot pot) are all favorites at this trendy eatery. If you are thirsty for something alcoholic, go for a Ginger Snap sake martini (saketini) in the red-hue dining room. **Known for:** excellent sushi; Wagyu hot rock; trendy spot. $ *Average main: $33* ⊠ *442 Main St., Main Street* ☎ *435/645–7253* ⊕ *www.shabuparkcity.com* ⊗ *No lunch.*

★ tupelo

$$$$ | **SOUTHERN** | Southern comfort dishes with a sophisticated twist are lovingly crafted at this warm and inviting restaurant started by veteran Park City chef Matt Harris, formerly at J&G Grill and the St. Regis Bar. Favorite dishes include out-of-this-world flaky buttermilk biscuits with honey butter and their take on beef & barley: Niman Ranch beef with barley risotto. **Known for:** Southern comfort food; craft cocktails; weekend brunch. $ *Average main: $50* ⊠ *1500 Kearns Blvd., Park City* ☎ *435/292–0880* ⊕ *tupeloparkcity.com* ⊗ *Closed Mon. and Tues.*

Twisted Fern
$$ | **MODERN AMERICAN** | **FAMILY** | The brainchild of chef/owner Adam Ross, this hot spot serves comfort food such as pork chops, cheesy short-rib sandwiches, and Utah trout hash. Dedicated to locally sourced and seasonal fare, Twisted Fern offers dinner daily in a welcoming atmosphere. **Known for:** patio dining; friendly staff; local food. [$] *Average main: $21* ✉ *1300 Snow Creek Dr., Suite RS, Park City* ☎ *435/731–8238* 🌐 *www.twisted-fern.com* 🕒 *No lunch.*

Versante Hearth + Bar
$$ | **AMERICAN** | **FAMILY** | Located in the newly remodeled Park City Peaks Hotel, Versante has become a favorite among locals. The welcoming, casual atmosphere paired with menu favorites such as flatbread pizzas, hearty pastas, and specialty cocktails is hard to beat. **Known for:** flatbread pizzas; local craft beers; welcoming atmosphere. [$] *Average main: $18* ✉ *Park City Peaks Hotel, 2346 Park Ave., Park City* ☎ *435/604–4012* 🌐 *www.parkcitypeaks.com* 🕒 *No lunch.*

The Viking Yurt
$$$$ | **EUROPEAN** | Don your Scandinavian sweater for a brisk sleigh ride (pulled by a snowcat rather than reindeer) through wintery pines up to this Nordic hut, built in a mountainous enclave in Park City Mountain Resort. After a hot cup of glogg, tuck into a European-style feast, featuring six hearty courses that might feature braised short ribs, lobster soup, and a traditional cheese course. **Known for:** reservations are essential; unique dining experience; traditional Nordic cuisine. [$] *Average main: $185* ✉ *Park City Mountain Resort, 1345 Lowell Ave., Old Town* ☎ *435/615–9878* 🌐 *www.thevikingyurt.com* 🕒 *Closed Apr.–Nov. No lunch.*

Wasatch Brew Pub
$$ | **AMERICAN** | **FAMILY** | It's hard to believe it's been more than 30 years since Wasatch became Park City's first brewery in the post-Prohibition era back in 1986. At the top of Main Street, this pub stays on top of its game with celebrated beers and down-to-earth yet elevated pub food. **Known for:** local craft beer; outdoor dining in summer; elevated pub food. [$] *Average main: $18* ✉ *250 Main St., Main Street* ☎ *435/649–0900* 🌐 *www.wasatchbeers.com.*

Windy Ridge Café
$$ | **AMERICAN** | **FAMILY** | Don't overlook Windy Ridge because of its industrial park neighborhood—the dining room is warm and inviting, and the baked goods are delicious. Lighter appetites might fancy the homemade chicken noodle soup and a Southwest salad, or if you've spent the day skiing or biking, tackle the meat loaf or a rack of smoked ribs. **Known for:** comfort food; warm atmosphere; to-go dinner packages. [$] *Average main: $20* ✉ *1250 Iron Horse Dr., Prospector* ☎ *435/647–0880* 🌐 *windyridgecafe.com.*

Yuki Yama Sushi
$$ | **SUSHI** | The name means "snow mountain" in Japanese, and the menu has a whirling blend of sushi, sashimi, and *maki*, as well as hot entrées, including noodle dishes. Observe sushi-making theatrics at the bar while they prepare the 84060 roll in homage to the local zip code, or retreat to the sunken seating of the tatami room. **Known for:** fresh sushi; sake; lively atmosphere. [$] *Average main: $18* ✉ *586 Main St., Main Street* ☎ *435/649–6293* 🌐 *www.yukiyamasushi.com* 🕒 *No lunch weekdays.*

☕ Coffee and Quick Bites

Java Cow Café & Bakery
$ | **ICE CREAM** | **FAMILY** | Java Cow has long been a staple on Main Street. Stop in for a panini, a caffeine pick-me-up, or delicious ice cream to satisfy your sweet tooth. **Known for:** excellent coffee; house-made ice cream; quick breakfast or lunch spot. [$] *Average main: $10* ✉ *402 Main St., Main Street* ☎ *435/647–7711* 🌐 *javacowparkcity.com.*

★ Ritual Chocolate Café

$ | **BAKERY** | **FAMILY** | Experience a rush of senses when you visit this fixture in Park City's culinary scene opened in 2015 by Robbie Stout and Anna Seear. Smell just-baked brownies with toasted Peruvian cocoa nibs and watch through an observation window as cocoa beans go into the factory's roll mill as a thick gritty paste, then come out smooth and flaky. **Known for:** sustainability; bean-to-bar craft chocolate; sipping chocolate. ⓢ *Average main: $15* ✉ *1105 Iron Horse, Park City* ☎ *435/200–8475* ⊕ *www.ritualchocolate. com.*

 Hotels

Chateau Après

$$ | **B&B/INN** | In one of the most expensive ski towns around, this reasonably priced classic skiers' lodge is a throwback to bygone ski days. **Pros:** comfortable rooms; close to the slopes; longtime local owners. **Cons:** limited parking; basic accommodations; no in-house restaurant. ⓢ *Rooms from: $165* ✉ *1299 Norfolk Ave., Park City* ☎ *435/649–9372, 800/357–3556* ⊕ *www.chateauapres. com* ⌂ *32 rooms* †◎† *Free Breakfast.*

The Chateaux Deer Valley

$$$$ | **HOTEL** | **FAMILY** | Just steps away from the Deer Valley lifts at Silver Lake Village, this modern interpretation of a luxury European château incorporates designer furnishings, heated towel racks, full kitchens in suites, gas fireplaces, and numerous windows with spectacular mountain views. **Pros:** luxury digs without stuffy atmosphere; great Italian dining at Cena; rooms can accommodate any family size. **Cons:** too far from Old Town to walk; the pool can get crowded during high season; evenings are quiet. ⓢ *Rooms from: $899* ✉ *7815 Royal St. E, Park City* ☎ *435/658–9500, 877/288–2978* ⊕ *www.the-chateaux.com* ⌂ *124 rooms* †◎† *Free Breakfast.*

Doubletree by Hilton Park City - The Yarrow

$$$ | **HOTEL** | Guests love its central location with easy access to Park City's ski resorts and to historic Main Street with its many upscale and casual restaurants, shopping options, and even a cinema close by. **Pros:** clean, basic rooms; heated outdoor pool is open all year; easy access to all Park City has to offer. **Cons:** location has no charm; traffic during peak season; confusing layout. ⓢ *Rooms from: $239* ✉ *1800 Park Ave.* ☎ *435/649–7000, 800/927–7694* ⊕ *www.doubletree3. hilton.com* ⌂ *181 rooms* †◎† *No Meals.*

Goldener Hirsch, Auberge Resorts Collection

$$$$ | **RESORT** | A beloved alpine escape for more than 30 years, this cozy and charming, Bavarian-style chalet got a modern upgrade in 2021 with the addition of two new buildings designed by Tom Kundig of Olson Kundig, named one of the AD100 design firms by *Architectural Digest*. The sleek buildings added contemporary accommodations to the property, as well as a new lobby and lounge area, ski lockers for guests, a fitness center and sauna, and the crown jewel: Deer Valley's only rooftop pool and hot tub with panoramic mountain views. **Pros:** rooftop pool and hot tub with mountain views; new, state-of-the-art accommodations; ski-in, ski-out access at Deer Valley Resort. **Cons:** expensive overnight parking; short drive to Main Street; limited nightlife options. ⓢ *Rooms from: $899* ✉ *7520 Royal St., Park City* ☎ *800/252–3373, 435/649–7770* ⊕ *aubergeresorts.com/goldenerhirsch* ⌂ *66 rooms* †◎† *No Meals.*

Grand Summit Hotel

$$$$ | **RESORT** | **FAMILY** | Located in the heart of Canyons Village, the hotel is just steps from a heated chairlift and golf course, making lodgings here ideal year-round. **Pros:** luxury accommodations; countless activities; on-site spa. **Cons:** very large, can sometimes feel cavernous; expensive daily resort fee;

no nightlife on property. $ Rooms from: $368 ⊠ 4000 Canyons Resort Dr., Park City ☎ 435/615–8040 front desk, 888/226–9667 reservations ⊕ www.parkcitymountain.com ⟿ 375 units ⃝ No Meals.

Hotel Park City, Autograph Collection

$$$$ | HOTEL | On the Park City golf course, this all-suites hotel is built in the tradition of the grand old stone-and-timber lodges of the West. **Pros:** close to town and the ski hills; grand lodge-style rooms with views; on 18-hole golf course. **Cons:** rooms are expensive; must drive to restaurants and resorts; long outdoor walk to some of the rooms. $ Rooms from: $569 ⊠ 2001 Park Ave., Park City ☎ 435/200–2000 ⊕ www.hotelparkcity.com ⟿ 100 suites ⃝ No Meals.

Main & SKY

$$$$ | HOTEL | Smack in the middle of Old Town, this contemporary hotel blends chic modern design with a mountain feel, and all 33 rooms are suites or residences, providing ample space to relax and take in the views of Park City and historic Old Town. **Pros:** prime location; large, luxurious rooms; great views. **Cons:** location on Main Street means no escaping the action; large suites mean expensive rates; pricey valet parking. $ Rooms from: $650 ⊠ 201 Heber Ave., Park City ☎ 435/658–2500 ⊕ www.skyparkcity.com ⟿ 33 suites ⃝ No Meals.

Marriott's MountainSide

$$$$ | HOTEL | Watch skiers go by from the heated outdoor pool at this timeshare hotel near the lifts in arguably the most ideal location at Park City Base Area, offering traditional rooms and one- and two-bedroom suites. **Pros:** ski-in, ski-out convenience; heated outdoor pool and hot tubs; helpful, pleasant staff. **Cons:** busy and somewhat congested area; rooms are plain; no great dining nearby. $ Rooms from: $400 ⊠ 1305 Lowell Ave., Park City ☎ 435/940–2000, 800/845–5279 ⊕ www.marriott.com ⟿ 365 rooms ⃝ No Meals.

★ Montage Deer Valley

$$$$ | RESORT | The breathtakingly luxurious resort hotel is nestled into Empire Pass at 9,000 feet above the sea like a jewel atop Park City's alpine crown, providing the ideal place to stay if you are looking to be completely pampered in a wilderness location. **Pros:** exquisite location with beautiful views; top-level dining; ample amenities and activities on site. **Cons:** remote location; car or shuttle required to get to Main Street; can feel cavernous at times. $ Rooms from: $805 ⊠ 9100 Marsac Ave., Park City ☎ 435/604–1300 ⊕ www.montagedeervalley.com ⟿ 154 rooms ⃝ No Meals.

Pendry Park City

$$$$ | RESORT | FAMILY | This swanky slope-side resort opened in Canyons Village in 2021, marrying the best of mountain living with modern design. **Pros:** multiple on-site dining options; rooftop pool and bar; great amenities for families. **Cons:** surrounding area is not very walkable; short drive to Main Street and other attractions; not much action in the off season. $ Rooms from: $495 ⊠ 2417 W. High Mountain Rd., Canyons Resort ☎ 435/800–1990 ⊕ www.pendry.com/park-city ⟿ 152 rooms ⃝ No Meals.

★ The St. Regis Deer Valley

$$$$ | RESORT | A 90-second ride up the funicular will take you to one of the most luxurious hotels at any alpine resort. **Pros:** glitz, glam, and butlers; ski-in, ski-out convenience; award-winning dining on property. **Cons:** additional restaurants are a drive away; layout is confusing, easy to get lost inside; après is popular with locals, get there early. $ Rooms from: $946 ⊠ 2300 Deer Valley Dr. E, Park City ☎ 435/940–5700, 866/932–7059 ⊕ www.marriot.com ⟿ 115 rooms, 66 suites ⃝ No Meals.

★ Stein Eriksen Lodge Deer Valley

$$$$ | RESORT | As enchanting as it gets for a slope-side retreat, this lodge is as perfectly groomed, timelessly gracious, and uniquely charming as its namesake

founder, the winner of an Olympic Gold Medal in 1952. **Pros:** award-winning dining on property; service is impeccable and exemplary; only five-star-rated spa in Park City. **Cons:** isolated location at 8,000-plus feet can be both inconvenient and difficult; rooms require a walk outside, which can be cold in the winter; free breakfast only in winter ski season. $ *Rooms from: $1397 ⊠ 7700 Stein Way, Park City* 🕾 *435/649–3700, 800/453–1302* ⊕ *www.steinlodge.com* ⤳ *171 rooms* ❑ *Free Breakfast.*

★ Waldorf Astoria Park City

$$$$ | **RESORT** | A sweeping staircase, Baccarat crystal chandelier, and 300-year-old marble fireplace lend grandeur to the first Waldorf Astoria hotel in an alpine location. **Pros:** celebrated restaurant; steps from the gondola; decadent spa. **Cons:** very little within walking distance; gondola nearby is very slow; only one dining option on site. $ *Rooms from: $740 ⊠ 2100 Frostwood Blvd., Park City* 🕾 *435/647–5500, 866/279–0843* ⊕ *www. waldorfastoriaparkcity.com* ⤳ *160 rooms* ❑ *No Meals.*

★ Washington School House Hotel

$$$$ | **B&B/INN** | Since 2011, this spectacular boutique hotel has been the hottest "must-stay" destination in Old Town Park City, providing beautifully designed and well-appointed rooms within a National Historic Registry landmark. **Pros:** central location; stellar service (they'll even pack and unpack for you); chefs provide delicious (included) breakfast and après-ski. **Cons:** not family-friendly; intimate common areas are shared with other guests; rooms fill up quickly, so book far in advance. $ *Rooms from: $875 ⊠ 543 Park Ave., Park City* 🕾 *435/649–3800, 800/824–1672* ⊕ *www.washingtonschoolhouse.com* ⤳ *12 rooms* ❑ *Free Breakfast.*

 Nightlife

In a state where nearly every town was founded by Mormons who eschewed alcohol and anything associated with it, Park City has always been an exception. Founded by miners with healthy appetites for whiskey and gambling, Park City has been known since its mining heyday as Utah's "Sin City." The miners are gone, but their legacy lives on in this town that has far more bars per capita than any other place in Utah.

Boneyard Saloon and Kitchen

BARS | This hot spot is in a somewhat unlikely place—in fact, you might think you're lost as you pull into the industrial-looking area in Prospector. But its off-Main location means it's popular with the locals, and ample parking is a huge plus. TVs lining the wall and a special weekend breakfast menu have made Boneyard the new go-to for Sunday football, and the rooftop deck has stunning views of the mountains. A sister restaurant of No Name on Main Street, Boneyard features beers on tap and an extensive bottle list. Head next door to Wine Dive (same ownership) to find 16 wines on tap and artisan pizza. ⊠ *1251 Kearns Blvd., Prospector* 🕾 *435/649–0911* ⊕ *www. boneyardsaloon.com.*

★ No Name Saloon

BARS | A Park City favorite anchoring Main Street's nightlife, this is a classic wood-backed bar with lots of memorabilia, a shuffleboard table, and a regular local clientele. The upstairs outdoor deck is great for enjoying cool summer nights, but heaters in the winter make this deck comfortable year-round. The eclectic decor looks like everything was purchased at a flea market, in the best way possible. If you are looking for some late-night grub, No Name has the best buffalo burgers in town. ⊠ *447 Main St., Park City* 🕾 *435/649–6667* ⊕ *www. nonamesaloon.net.*

Old Town Cellars

WINE BARS | The first of its kind in the area, this private label winery opened on Main Street in 2016. Stop in to learn about the urban wine-making process, buy a bottle of their house wine, or enjoy an après-ski tasting in their Bar & Lounge, where local beers and spirits are also available. Local meats and chocolate, available on their fare menu, pair perfectly with the experience. ✉ *408 Main St., Main Street* ☎ *435/649–3759* ⊕ *www.otcwines.com.*

The Spur Bar and Grill

BARS | If you are looking for live music, look no further than The Spur, which hosts bands seven nights a week. A renovation in 2016 more than doubled the size of The Spur, adding two additional bar areas and a Main Street entrance. The front room provides a lively bar atmosphere; head upstairs if you want to hear your conversation. The back room is where you'll find the live music and the dancing. A full kitchen means breakfast, lunch, and dinner are served until 10 pm. ✉ *352 Main St., Park City* ☎ *435/615–1618* ⊕ *www.thespurbarandgrill.com.*

Troll Hallen

COCKTAIL LOUNGES | If quiet conversation and a good single-malt scotch or Swiss raclette in front of a fire is your idea of nightlife, this is the place for you. ✉ *Stein Eriksen Lodge Deer Valley, 7700 Stein Way, Park City* ☎ *435/645–6455* ⊕ *www. steinlodge.com.*

Performing Arts

MUSIC

★ Mountain Town Music

MUSIC | **FAMILY** | This nonprofit organization books dozens of local, regional, and national musical acts in the Park City area, using many different venues around town, including the ski resorts and Main Street. No matter what show you go to, you're likely to see every age group represented and enjoying the music.

Most performances are free. ✉ *Park City* ☎ *435/901–7664* ⊕ *www.mountaintown-music.org.*

THEATER AND DANCE

Egyptian Theatre

THEATER | **FAMILY** | This historical building has been a Park City theater since its mining days in the 1880s. In 1922, the Egyptian Theatre was constructed on the site of the original Dewey Theatre that collapsed under record-breaking snow. Patrons enjoy an eclectic array of local and regional music, theater, and comedy in the 266-seat space. ✉ *328 Main St., Park City* ☎ *855/745–7469* ⊕ *www.egyptiantheatrecompany.org.*

🛍 Shopping

ART GALLERIES

Park City Gallery Stroll

ART GALLERIES | Main Street is packed with great art galleries, and the best way to see them all is the Park City Gallery Stroll, a free event hosted by the Park City Gallery Association on the last Friday of the month 6–9 pm, sun or snow. ✉ *Park City* ⊕ *www.parkcitygalleryassociation.com.*

BOOKS

Dolly's Bookstore

BOOKS | **FAMILY** | For many returning visitors, the first stop in town is Dolly's Bookstore to check on the two cats: Dolly and Pippi Longstocking. Oh, and to browse a great selection of regional books as well as national bestsellers. Dolly's also has a uniquely complete selection of children's books and toys. While you are at it, swing through neighboring Rocky Mountain Chocolate Factory to satisfy your sweet tooth. ✉ *510 Main St., Park City* ☎ *435/649–8062* ⊕ *www.dollysbookstore.com.*

CLOTHING

Mary Jane's

SHOES | This independently owned boutique has an eclectic selection of trendy clothing and designer jeans, lingerie, statement jewelry, shoes, and handbags. ⊠ *613 Main St., Park City* ☎ *435/645–7463* ⊕ *www.maryjanesshoes.com.*

Olive + Tweed

WOMEN'S CLOTHING | This artist-driven boutique sells local handmade jewelry, women's clothing accessories, home decor, baby items, and local art. ⊠ *608 Main St., Park City* ☎ *435/649–9392* ⊕ *www.oliveandtweed.com.*

FOOD AND CANDY

Rocky Mountain Chocolate Factory

CANDY | FAMILY | You'll find a quick fix for your sweet tooth here, and you can watch them make fudge, dozens of different caramel apples, and other scrumptious treats. There's another location at 1385 Lowell Avenue. ⊠ *510 Main St., Park City* ☎ *435/604–0652.*

HOUSEHOLD ITEMS

La Niche Gourmet & Gifts

HOUSEWARES | Classical music and the aroma of fresh-roasted coffee greet you at La Niche. While away an hour in this cozy collection of linens, home decorations, quilts, and cooking and decorating books, with an intimate espresso and gelato bar in the back. ⊠ *401 Main St., Park City* ☎ *435/649–2372.*

Activities

BIKING

In 2012, Park City was the first community ever designated a Gold Level Ride Center by the International Mountain Bicycling Association, thanks in large part to the relentless work of the Mountain Trails Foundation, which oversees and maintains more than 400 miles of area trails. The accolade is based upon bike shops, trail access, variety, and more. Pick up a map at any local bike shop or get details from the **Mountain Trails Foundation** (☎ 435/649–6839 ⊕ www.mountaintrails.org). You can join local road or mountain bikers most nights in the summer for free group rides sponsored by Park City bike shops.

Cole Sport

BIKING | Road bikers of all abilities can ride with a pack one evening a week from June to mid-September from this shop. You can rent mountain and road bikes here, too; be ready to ride at 6 pm. ⊠ *1615 Park Ave., Park City* ☎ *435/649–4806* ⊕ *www.colesport.com* ☞ *Call in advance for weekly schedule.*

Deer Valley Resort

BIKING | Mountain bikers from across the world flock to Deer Valley's single-track trails for mountain biking each summer, and it's easy to see why with the variety of terrain and bike offerings available. Nearly 70 miles of trails can be accessed from three chairlifts, spanning all levels of ability, including down-hill flow trails. Bike clinics and lessons, both group and private, are offered through the Deer Valley Mountain Bike School, and rentals are available at the base areas. Trails are open June through September. ⊠ *2250 Deer Valley Dr. S, Park City* ☎ *435/649–1000* ⊕ *www.deervalley.com.*

Park City Mountain Resort

BIKING | Utah's largest ski resort transforms into a summer adventure land for cyclists, with a lift-served bike park at Canyons Village and miles of cross-country and downhill trails across the whole resort. Park City Base Area provides a number of trails accessible directly from the base, or haul your bike up the lift for some downhill riding. Canyons Village is the home of Park City Bike Park, with a dozen downhill flow and jump trails, many of which are accessible to all skill levels. Lessons are available with certified instructors for those who are new to the sport, and cyclists can find bike rentals at both base areas. ⊠ *Park City Base Area, 1345 Lowell Ave., Park City* ☎ *435/649–8111* ⊕ *www.parkcitymountain.com.*

Silver Star Ski & Sport

BIKING | Look for Azalea, the English bulldog at Silver Star Ski & Sport. While the dog watches the shop, friendly staff help find the best bike or piece of outdoor equipment to suit your needs. In addition to the retail area of the store offering top-of-the-line gear and clothing, Silver Star offers cruiser, road, and mountain bike rentals. ⊠ *1825 Three Kings Dr. #85, Park City* ☎ *435/645–7827* ⊕ *www.silverstarskiandsport.com.*

White Pine Touring

BIKING | Every Thursday in summer, mountain bikers of all levels gather at 6 pm for a free guided mountain-bike ride. On the last Thursday of June, July, and August, the White Pine guides prepare a barbecue, too. There's also a women-only ride on Tuesday. For both rides, meet at the shop at 6 pm—earlier if you need to rent a bike. Guided road biking, mountain biking, climbing, and hiking tours are also available throughout the summer. In the winter, experience their Fat Bike Tours to ride snow-covered single-track on a bike. ⊠ *1790 Bonanza Dr., Park City* ☎ *435/649–8710* ⊕ *www.whitepinetouring.com.*

FLY-FISHING

The mountain-fed waters of the Provo and Weber Rivers and several smaller streams near Park City are prime trout habitat.

Park City Flyshop and Guide Service

FISHING | See Chris Kunkel, the owner of this shop, for good advice, guide service, and a modest selection of fly-fishing necessities. ⊠ *2065 Sidewinder Dr., Park City* ☎ *435/640–2864* ⊕ *www.pcflyshopguideservice.com.*

Trout Bum 2

FISHING | This full-service fly shop can outfit you with everything you need, then guide you to where the fish are. This shop has the largest selection of flies in town and is the only guide service in all of Park City to have access to the renowned Green River below Flaming Gorge Reservoir. Check the website for fishing reports of the area rivers and streams. ⊠ *4343 N. Hwy. 224, Suite 101, Park City* ☎ *435/658–1166, 877/878–2862* ⊕ *www.troutbum2.com.*

FRISBEE GOLF

Alpine Disc Golf

LOCAL SPORTS | Frisbee fans can try 18 holes of high-altitude disc golf at the Red Pine Lodge area at Canyons Village. You'll need a gondola pass, but there's no charge to play the course. Rent discs at Canyon Mountain Sports in the resort village. ⊠ *4000 Canyons Resort Dr., Park City* ☎ *435/649–8111* ⊕ *www.parkcitymountain.com* 🎟 *$24 for gondola ride.*

GOLF

Within 20 minutes of Park City are 12 golf courses. An equal amount of private and public courses provide a variety of terrain, views, and holes to play.

Canyons Golf

GOLF | This 97-acre course uses the mountainous terrain at the base of the ski resort for a challenging game. Six holes interact with ski runs, with more than 550 feet of elevation change throughout the course. With seven par-3s, the course is not for the faint of heart, but the views alone make it worth checking out no matter your level. ⊠ *4000 Canyons Resort Dr., Canyons Resort* ☎ *435/615–4728* ⊕ *www.parkcitymountain.com/golf* 🎟 *$95; rates drop to $70 during off-peak times* 🏌 *18 holes, 6256 yards, par 70.*

Park City Golf Club

GOLF | On this gorgeous and challenging 6,800-yard, par-72 public course, you'll love the views of ski runs, rising peaks, historic Main Street, and an occasional moose. Popular among locals, it's considered one of the best public courses in the area. Everything you need is in the pro shop in Hotel Park City, right along the course. ⊠ *1541 Thaynes Canyon Dr., Park City* ☎ *435/615–5800* ⊕ *www.parkcity.org/departments/park-city-golf-club* 🎟 *$26 for 9 holes, $33 with cart; $52 for 18 holes, $67 with cart* 🏌 *18 holes, 6800 yards, par 72.*

Few places in the world can show off such distinct geologic features in an area as small as the 50 to 70 miles along the Wasatch Front.

HIKING

The Wasatch Mountains surrounding Park City offer more than 400 miles of hiking trails, ranging from easy, meandering meadow strolls to strenuous climbs up wind-blown peaks. Getting away from civilization and into the aspens is easy, and lucky hikers might spy foxes, coyotes, moose, elk, deer, and red-tailed hawks. Many of the trails take off from the resort areas, but some of the trailheads are right near Main Street. For beginners, or for those acclimating to the elevation, the Rail Trail is a good place to start. Another alternative is to take the McLeod Creek Trail from behind The Market all the way to the Redstone Center. The Round Valley and Lost Prospector Trails are still mellow but slightly more challenging. To really get the blood pumping, head up Spiro or do a lengthy stretch of Mid-Mountain.

For interactive trail maps, up-to-date information about trail conditions and events, and answers to your trail questions, contact the nonprofit Mountain Trails Foundation (⊕ www.mountaintrails. org), whose mission is to promote, preserve, advocate for, and maintain Park City's local trail system. Maps detailing trail locations are available at most local gear shops.

HORSEBACK RIDING

Red Pine Adventures

HORSEBACK RIDING | This outfitter leads trail rides through thousands of acres of private land. ⊠ 2050 W. White Pine Canyon Rd., Park City ☎ 435/649–9445 ⊕ www. redpinetours.com ⌕ From $150.

Rocky Mountain Recreation

HORSEBACK RIDING | Saddle up for a taste and feel of the Old West with guided mountain trail rides, from one hour to all-day or overnight excursions, departing from several locations in the Park City area, complete with fantastic scenery and good cowboy grub. ⊠ Stillman Ranch, Oakley ☎ 435/645–7256 ⌕ From $66.

RAFTING

Utah Outdoor Adventures

WHITE-WATER RAFTING | This company specializes in half-day and full-day excursions, all of which are private groups. Tours take place on the Weber River on class II and class III rapids. Perfect for all age groups. ⊠ *3310 Mountain La., Park City* ☎ *801/703–3357* ⊕ *www.utahoutdooradventures.com* ✉ *$70.*

ROCK CLIMBING

White Pine Touring

ROCK CLIMBING | If you're looking for some hang time on the local rocks but don't know the area, White Pine Touring offers guided climbing tours, equipment rental, and private and group lessons. Reservations are required. ⊠ *1790 Bonanza Dr., Park City* ☎ *435/649–8710* ⊕ *www.whitepinetouring.com* ✉ *From $325.*

SKIING AND SNOWBOARDING

★ Deer Valley Resort

SKIING & SNOWBOARDING | FAMILY | Just to the south of downtown Park City, this resort set new standards in the ski industry by providing such amenities as ski valets and slope-side dining of the highest caliber. For such pampering, the resort has drawn rave reviews from virtually every ski and travel magazine, consistently rated #1 Ski Resort in America by *SKI* magazine. The careful layout of runs and the impeccable grooming makes this an intermediate skier's heaven. With the Empire Canyon and Lady Morgan areas, the resort also offers bona fide expert terrain. For many, part of the ski experience includes a two- to three-hour midday interlude of feasting at one of the many world-class dining locations on the mountain and catching major rays on the snow-covered meadow in front of Silver Lake Lodge. The ski experience fits right in with the resort's overall image. With lessons for kids from preschool through teens, Deer Valley's acclaimed children's ski school is sure to please both children and parents. Note: this is one of the only ski resorts in the United States that prohibits snowboards. ⊠ *2250 Deer Valley Dr., Park City* ☎ *435/649–1000, 800/424–3337 reservations* ⊕ *www.deervalley.com* ✉ *Lift ticket pricing varies; call for daily rates* ⌕ *3,000-foot vertical drop; 2,026 skiable acres; 27% beginner, 41% intermediate, 32% advanced; 101 total runs.*

★ Park City Mountain Resort

SKIING & SNOWBOARDING | FAMILY | Although this has been one of North America's most popular ski and snowboard destinations for quite some time, in 2015 Vail Resorts joined neighboring Canyons Resort to Park City Mountain, creating the largest ski resort in the United States. With more than 330 trails, 17 mountain peaks, 7,300 skiable acres, and 41 lifts, it is almost impossible to ski the entire resort in one day. The trails provide a great mix of beginner, intermediate, and advanced terrain, with Jupiter Peak providing the highest elevation and steepest terrain in town. Three distinct base areas provide a great starting point for the ski day—Park City Base Area has a variety of dining and retail options, along with a stellar après-ski scene. Park City is the only resort with lift access to Historic Main Street with Town Lift, allowing for guests staying near or on Main Street direct access to the slopes. Canyons Village, located on the other side of the mountain, gives ski-in/ski-out access to many of the base area's hotels and lodging properties. The resort is widely acclaimed for being a free-skiing and snowboarding mecca with official Olympic qualifying events each year; you're likely to see Olympic athletes training and playing on the slopes. ⊠ *1345 Lowell Ave., Park City* ☎ *435/649–8111* ⊕ *www.parkcitymountain.com* ✉ *Lift ticket prices change daily; check online for daily rate* ⌕ *3,200-foot vertical drop; 7,300 skiable acres; 8% beginner, 42% intermediate, 50% advanced; 41 lifts; 2 halfpipes (including 1 super pipe) and 8 terrain parks.*

Powderbird

SKIING & SNOWBOARDING | If you don't mind paying for it, the best way to find untracked Utah powder is with Wasatch Powderbird guides. A helicopter drops you on the top of the mountain, and a guide leads you back down. Itineraries are always weather dependent. Call to inquire about departures from Snowbird (Little Cottonwood Canyon) or Park City Mountain Resort (Canyons Village). ⌧ *3000 Canyons Resort Dr., Park City* ☎ *801/341–2455* ⊕ *www.powderbird. com* ⊠ *From $1260.*

White Pine Nordic Center

SKIING & SNOWBOARDING | Just outside Old Town, the White Pine Nordic Center offers around 20 km (12 miles) of set track, in 3-km (2-mile), 5-km (3-mile), and 10-km (6-mile) loops, plus cross-country ski instruction, equipment rentals, and a well-stocked cross-country ski shop. The fee to use the track is $24, or $16 after 3 pm. Reservations are required for their guided backcountry ski and snowshoe tours in the surrounding mountains. ⌧ *On Park City Golf Course, 1541 Thaynes Canyon Dr., Park City* ☎ *435/649–6249* ⊕ *www.whitepinetouring.com.*

SKI RENTALS AND EQUIPMENT

Many shops in Park City rent equipment for skiing and other sports. From old-fashioned rental shops that also offer discount lift tickets to luxurious ski-delivery services that will fit you in your room, you have dozens of choices. Prices tend to be slightly lower if you rent in Salt Lake City.

▣ TIP➔ **If you happen to be visiting during holidays, reserve skiing and snowboarding gear in advance.**

Breeze Winter Sports Rentals

SKIING & SNOWBOARDING | You can reserve your equipment online in advance with this company (often for less than day-of rentals), which has two locations in Park City. You'll find them near Canyons Village

and at Park City Base Area. They're owned by Vail Resorts, and you can expect good quality and service at a value price. ⌧ *4343 N. Hwy. 224, Park City* ☎ *435/655–7066, 888/427–3393* ⊕ *www. skirentals.com.*

Cole Sport

SKIING & SNOWBOARDING | With four locations from Main Street to Deer Valley, Cole Sport carries all your winter ski, snowboard, and snowshoe rental needs. Come back in summer for bikes, stand-up paddleboards, hiking gear, and more. No matter the season, Cole Sport offers expert fitting and advice, with a broad range of equipment. ⌧ *1615 Park Ave., Park City* ☎ *435/649–4806, 800/345–2938* ⊕ *www.colesport.com.*

Jans Mountain Outfitters

SKIING & SNOWBOARDING | For almost 40 years, this has been the locals' choice for gear rentals, with ski and snowboard equipment packages and clothing in winter, and bikes and fly-fishing gear in summer. With the most knowledgeable staff around, they'll assist you with any outdoor adventure. There are multiple locations, including the flagship Park Avenue store, Deer Valley, and Park City Mountain Resort. ⌧ *1600 Park Ave., Park City* ☎ *435/649–4949* ⊕ *www.jans.com.*

Park City Sport

SKIING & SNOWBOARDING | At the base of Park City Mountain Resort, this is a convenient place to rent ski and snowboard equipment, goggles, and clothing. You can drop off your personal gear at the end of a ski day, and they'll have it tuned and ready for you the next morning, with free overnight storage for customers. A second location on Main Street is across from the Town Lift. ⌧ *1335 Lowell Ave., #104, Park City* ☎ *435/940–1470* ⊕ *www. parkcitysport.com.*

Silver Star Ski & Sport

SKIING & SNOWBOARDING | This company rents, tunes, and repairs ski equipment, snowshoes, bike gear, and stand-up paddleboards. It doesn't get much more convenient for winter rentals/gear adjustments, as the shop is located at the base of the Silver Star lift at Park City Mountain Resort. ⊠ *1825 Three Kings Dr., #85, Park City* ☎ *435/645–7827* ⊕ *www. silverstarskiandsport.com.*

Ski Butlers
SKIING & SNOWBOARDING | The most prominent of a number of companies offering ski and snowboard delivery, Ski Butlers carries top-of-the-line Rossignol equipment. Their experts will fit you in your hotel room or condo and meet you at any of the resorts should something go wrong. You'll pay a little more, but you'll avoid the hassle of rentals when the snow is falling on your first morning in the mountains. ⊠ *Park City* ☎ *877/754–7754* ⊕ *www.skibutlers.com.*

Utah Ski & Golf
SKIING & SNOWBOARDING | Downhill equipment, snowshoes, clothing, and golf-club rental are available here, at Park City Base Area and the Town Lift, as well as in downtown Salt Lake City. ⊠ *698 Park Ave., Park City* ☎ *435/649–3020* ⊕ *www. utahskigolf.com.*

SKI TOURS
Ski Utah Interconnect Tour
SKIING & SNOWBOARDING | Strong intermediate and advanced skiers can hook up with the Ski Utah Interconnect Tour for a guided alpine ski tour that takes you to as many as six resorts, including Deer Valley and Park City, in a single day, all connected by backcountry ski routes with unparalleled views of the Wasatch Mountains. Guides test your ski ability before departure. The tour includes guide service, lift tickets, lunch, and transportation back to the point of origin. You'll even walk away with a finisher's pin. Reservations are required. ⊠ *Park City* ☎ *801/534–1907* ⊕ *www.skiutah.com* ⊠ *$395.*

★ White Pine Touring
SKIING & SNOWBOARDING | Specializing in telemark, cross-country, and alpine touring gear and guided tours, White Pine Touring also has top-of-the-line clothing, as well as mountain bikes, fat bikes, snowshoes, and climbing shoes. ⊠ *1790 Bonanza Dr., Park City* ☎ *435/649–8710* ⊕ *www.whitepinetouring.com.*

SNOWMOBILING
Park City Peaks Snowmobiling
SNOW SPORTS | Backcountry snowmobile tours are on one of Utah's largest private mountain ranches, just outside Park City. Clothing is available to rent. ⊠ *Office, 698 Park Ave.* ☎ *888/304–7669* ⊕ *www.powderutah.com* ⊠ *From $189 single rider.*

Red Pine Adventures
SNOW SPORTS | For a winter speed thrill of the machine-powered variety, hop on a snowmobile and follow your guide along private groomed trails adjacent to Park City Mountain Resort. Pick up is in Park City. ⊠ *2050 W. White Pine Canyon Rd., Park City* ☎ *435/649–9445* ⊕ *www. redpinetours.com* ⊠ *$250 single rider for 1½-hr tour; plus $50 double.*

Kimball Junction and Olympic Park

12 miles north of Park City.

Just north of Park City, the Utah Olympic Park was built for the 2002 Winter Olympics in Salt Lake City to host ski jumping, bobsled, and luge events. Nearby Kimball Junction was just a fork in the road then, but as the city has grown and become more expensive, it's become a popular residential location for city residents, who were drawn by both residential and commercial development as well as the open spaces of the Swaner Preserve.

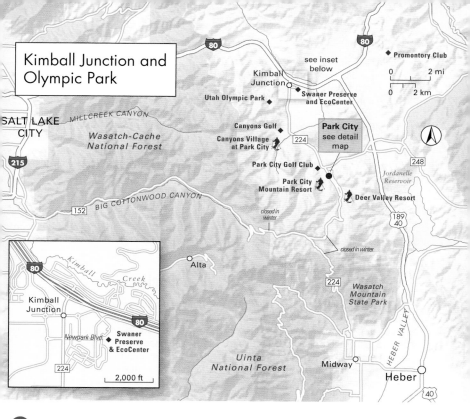

Kimball Junction and
Olympic Park

see inset
below

Promontory Club

80

Kimball
Junction

Swaner Preserve
and EcoCenter

Utah Olympic Park

0   2 mi
0   2 km

SALT LAKE
CITY

MILLCREEK CANYON

Wasatch-Cache
National Forest

Canyons Golf

224

Park City
see detail
map

215

Canyons Village
at Park City

Park City Golf Club

248

Jordanelle
Reservoir

Park City
Mountain Resort

152

BIG COTTONWOOD CANYON

Deer Valley Resort

189
40

closed in
winter

closed in winter

Kimball

Creek

Alta

224

Wasatch
Mountain
State Park

80

Kimball
Junction

80

Newpark Blvd.

Swaner
Preserve
& EcoCenter

224

2,000 ft

Uinta
National Forest

Midway

HEBER VALLEY

Heber

40

◉ Sights

Swaner Preserve and EcoCenter

NATURE PRESERVE | Home to more than
100 migratory and native birds (most
notably sandhill cranes) and small critters
(like the spotted frog), as well as foxes,
deer, elk, moose, and coyotes, this
1,200-acre preserve is both a bird-watch-
ers' paradise and an example of land
restoration in action. Naturalist-led walks,
snowshoe tours in winter, and other
events are hosted here throughout the
year. The EcoCenter is filled with interactive exhibits, such as a climbing wall
with microphones emitting the sounds
of the wetlands as climbers move
through habitats. The facility serves as
an exhibit in itself, given its eco-friendly
construction, incorporating everything
from recycled denim insulation to solar
panels. More than 10 miles of hiking and

biking trails and 15 wetland ponds give
visitors a great place to unwind and get
away from the urban life. ⊠ *1258 Center
Dr., Newpark* ☎ *435/649–1767* ⊕ *www.
swanerecocenter.org* ⊠ *Free (donation
appreciated)* ⊙ *Closed Mon. and Tues.*

★ Utah Olympic Park

SPORTS VENUE | FAMILY | An exciting legacy
of the 2002 Winter Olympics, this is a
mecca of bobsled, skeleton, luge, and ski
jumping. As it is one of the only places in
America where you can try these sports,
you might have to wait your turn behind
U.S. Olympians and aspirants who train
here year-round. In summer or winter,
screaming down the track in a bobsled at
nearly 80 mph with a professional driver
is a ride you will never forget. In summer,
check out the freestyle ski jumpers doing
flips and spins into a splash pool and
Nordic jumpers soaring to soft landings

on a synthetic outrun. Ride the ziplines or the Alpine Slide, or explore the adventure course. There's also an interactive ski museum and an exhibit on the Olympics; guided tours are offered year-round, or you can take a self-guided tour. ✉ *3419 Olympic Pkwy., Park City* ☎ *435/658–4200* 🌐 *www.utaholympiclegacy.com* 🎟 *Museum and self-guided tours free, guided tours $13.*

🍴 Restaurants

★ Hearth and Hill

$$$$ | AMERICAN | Started in 2017 by Brooks Kirchheimer, when he returned to his Park City hometown, this local favorite quickly became a hangout for those in search of comfort food and community. Built with floor-to-ceiling windows inside a modernized industrial space, the restaurant has plenty of elbow room, and the natural lighting and white-tiled open kitchen give the place a distinctive communal vibe. **Known for:** dog-friendly patio; chef-driven menu; spicy Korean fried chicken on a scallion potato waffle. [$] *Average main: $35* ✉ *1153 Center Dr., Newpark* ☎ *435/200–8840* 🌐 *hearth-hill.com.*

Maxwell's East Coast Eatery

$$ | ITALIAN | FAMILY | Located between the Swaner Preserve and a swath of shops, this casual Italian eatery is popular with locals and welcomes the late-night crowd. Nearly 2 feet in diameter, the "Fat Kid" pizzas will remind you of something you might see in Brooklyn or the Bronx—the "Goodfella" veggie pizza or the "Italian Stallion" meat-lovers version. **Known for:** East Coast–style pizza; sports bar; family-friendly. [$] *Average main: $21* ✉ *1456 Newpark Blvd., Newpark* ☎ *435/647–0304* 🌐 *www.facebook.com/MaxwellsParkCity.*

☕ Coffee and Quick Bites

Vessel Kitchen

$ | FAST FOOD | FAMILY | In a part of town where fast food reigns, Vessel Kitchen has a sustainable and healthy menu without sacrificing the fast-casual environment and reasonable prices. Here, you'll find hearty grain bowls, proteins such as braised beef and pork confit, and seasonal vegetables for sides. **Known for:** healthy dining; hearty grain bowls; fast-casual dining. [$] *Average main: $12* ✉ *1784 Uinta Way, #E1, Kimball Junction* ☎ *435/200–8864* 🌐 *www.vesselkitchen.com.*

🛏 Hotels

Holiday Inn Express & Suites Park City

$ | HOTEL | Just off the main Park City exit near I–80, this chain hotel has a mountain-lodge feel. **Pros:** affordable; walking distance to shops and restaurants; continental breakfast included. **Cons:** you'll need a car or to take free public bus to get to the resorts; close to interstate; rooms are small. [$] *Rooms from: $122* ✉ *1501 W. Ute Blvd., Park City* ☎ *435/658–1600, 877/662–6241* 🌐 *www.holidayinn.com* 🛏 *73 rooms* 🍴 *Free Breakfast.*

Newpark Resort

$$$ | HOTEL | At Newpark you'll find a busy shopping and dining scene on one side and a gorgeous nature preserve on the other. **Pros:** comfortable suites; affordable rates; within walking distance of shops and restaurants. **Cons:** a drive to ski resorts and Main Street; location is in congested area; not all rooms have views. [$] *Rooms from: $295* ✉ *1476 Newpark Blvd., Newpark* ☎ *435/649–3600, 877/649–3600* 🌐 *www.newparkresort.com* 🛏 *126 rooms, 24 townhomes* 🍴 *No Meals.*

Shopping

CLOTHING

Indigo Highway

WOMEN'S CLOTHING | This eclectic boutique, located in Newpark Town Center, is worth a visit. Here you'll find clothing, gifts, scented candles, Park City keepsakes, and more, all with a modern nomad twist. They sell handmade bags from all over the world (with notes about the women who made them) next to Park City embroidered caps. There's even a full section of small batch, artisanal apothecary items (think body oils, detoxifying bath salts, and more). ⊠ *1241 Center Dr. #L170, Newpark* ☎ *435/214–7244* ⊕ *www.indigohighway.com.*

OUTLET AND DISCOUNT STORES

Outlets Park City

OUTLET | **FAMILY** | Just west of Highway 224 when you exit I–80 toward the ski resorts, this is a bargain shopper's paradise, with dozens of outlets. Tourists spend lavishly here, and locals find deals year-round. Among the 70 stores are activewear brands like Columbia and Nike, plus fashion labels Banana Republic, Gap, Polo Ralph Lauren, Eddie Bauer, and J.Crew. ⊠ *6699 N. Landmark Dr., Park City* ☎ *435/645–7078* ⊕ *www. tangeroutlet.com.*

TOYS

J. W. Allen & Sons Toys & Candy

TOYS | **FAMILY** | Jam-packed with classic toys and modern fun, J. W. Allen & Sons rescues parents who forgot to pack toys for their kids on family vacation. Scary dinosaurs, giant stuffed bears, dolls, sleds, scooters, and kites are as irresistible as the candy. ⊠ *1675 W. Redstone Center, No. 105, Kimball Junction* ☎ *435/575–8697.*

🏃 Activities

GOLF

Promontory

GOLF | The only private club in the area to make selected tee times available to the general public, Promontory welcomes nonmembers on its challenging and sometimes windy Pete Dye–designed course. The club is renowned for extraordinary views and exemplary service. Six sets of tees on this course make for what some call the most level playing field on any course in Utah. ⊠ *8758 Promontory Ranch Rd., Park City* ☎ *435/333–4000* ⊕ *www.promontoryclub.com* 🖃 *$250 for nonmembers; check with hotel concierge for better price* 🖈 *. 18 holes, 7700 yards, par 72.*

HORSEBACK RIDING

Wind In Your Hair Riding

HORSEBACK RIDING | Only experienced riders who are looking for a get-up-and-go kind of mountain riding adventure are allowed on these trail rides, so there will be no inexperienced riders to slow you down, and the Paso Fino horses are noted for their smooth ride. Plan to tip the trail leader. Lessons are available for beginners. ⊠ *Cherry Canyon Ranch, 46 E. Cherry Canyon Dr., Wanship* ☎ *435/336–4795, 435/901–4644* ⊕ *www.windinyourhair.com* 🖃 *From $150.*

ICE-SKATING

Park City Ice Arena

ICE SKATING | The Olympic-size rink here provides plenty of space for testing out that triple-toe loop or slap shot. The hill outside the building is popular sledding terrain. ⊠ *600 Gillmor Way, Park City* ☎ *435/615–5700* ⊕ *www.parkcityice.org* 🖃 *$11.*

RAFTING

Park City Rafting

WHITE-WATER RAFTING | Two-hour, mostly class II rafting adventures are offered, as well as full-day trips that end with a class III splash. Given the Weber's mostly benign water, there are plenty of breaks between plunges to look for moose, deer, beavers, badgers, and feathered friends along the shore. ✉ *1245 Taggart La., Morgan* ☎ *435/655–3800, 866/467–2384* ⊕ *www.parkcityrafting. com* ⟴ *From $49.*

SNOW TUBING

Woodward Park City

SNOW SPORTS | FAMILY | Lift-served snow tubing (with seven lanes) and mini-snowmobile rentals bring families here. ✉ *3863 W. Kilby Rd., Park City* ☎ *435/658–2648* ⊕ *www.woodwardparkcity.com/tickets-passes/tubing* ⟴ *From $55.*

Heber Valley

20 miles south of Park City, 22 miles northeast of Sundance.

Bounded by the Wasatch Mountains on the west and the rolling foothills of the Uinta Mountains on the east, the Heber Valley, including the towns of Heber, Midway, and Charleston, is well-supplied with snow in winter for cross-country skiing, snowmobiling, and other snow sports. Summers are mostly cool and green. Events throughout the year entertain locals and visitors alike.

GETTING HERE AND AROUND

From Park City, head east on Highway 40 to enter the Heber Valley. The highway turns into Main Street, which leads straight through Heber City. Turn right on 100 South to reach the Swiss-influenced town of Midway. If you're coming from Sundance, take Highway 92 south, then Highway 189 east.

VISITOR INFORMATION

CONTACTS Heber Valley County Chamber of Commerce. ✉ *475 N. Main St., Heber Valley* ☎ *435/654–3666* ⊕ *www.gohebervalley.com.*

Sights

The Historic Heber Creeper: Heber Valley Railroad

TRAIN/TRAIN STATION | FAMILY | This steam train takes passengers on a nostalgic trip along a line that first ran in 1899, past the Deer Creek Reservoir and through beautiful Provo Canyon. It continues past Bridal Veil Falls, a veil-like waterfall near snow-capped Mount Timpanogos. Each car has been restored, and two of the engines are fully operational, steam-powered locomotives. The railroad offers special events, including cheese-tasting rides, the local favorite North Pole Express, Raft 'n Rails (pairing rafting with a train excursion), Reins 'n Trains (with horseback riding), and Wilderness. Lunch is available for an extra cost.

▰TIP→ **There's no climate control in the rail cars, so dress for the weather.** ✉ *450 S. 600 W, Heber* ☎ *435/654–5601* ⊕ *www. hebervalleyrr.org* ⟴ *Provo Canyon $30; Deer Creek $20; call for special event and activity trip prices.*

Mirror Lake Highway

SCENIC DRIVE | East of Park City, this scenic byway winds through aspens and ponderosa pines, skirts alpine lakes and waterfalls, and reaches 11,943-foot Bald Mountain. The ride is good, but getting out of the car is better. A spectacular hike is the 5-mile, five-lake Lofty Lake Loop, which starts at the Pass Lake Trailhead at mile 32. It's also a great place to snowshoe in the winter. Keep an eye out for moose, wildflowers, and changeable weather. Reward yourself with jerky from Samak Smoke House, a typical dry goods store near the Uinta-Wasatch-Cache National Forest's Kamas entrance. ✉ *Kamas* ☎ *435/783–4338* ⊕ *www.fs.usda. gov* ⟴ *$6 per car for 3-day pass* ☉ *Road closed in winter, depending on snowfall.*

Soldier Hollow Nordic Center

SPORTS VENUE | On the southern end of Wasatch Mountain State Park, this activity center was one site for the 2002

To the west of Heber Valley are the Wasatch Mountains; to the east are the Uinta Mountains.

Winter Olympics and still hosts the national championship Nordic ski events and other events, including powwows and sheepdog championships. It's open to the public year-round for hiking, horseback riding, cross-country skiing, tubing, and snowshoeing, as well as biathlon and other events. A beautiful lodge has food concessions, equipment rentals, and a souvenir shop. ✉ *Wasatch Mountain State Park, 2002 Soldier Hollow La., Midway* ☎ *435/654–2002* 🌐 *www.soldierhollow.com* 🎟 *Annual Trail Pass $150; biathlon range access plus $100.*

Wasatch Mountain State Park

STATE/PROVINCIAL PARK | FAMILY | This 22,000-acre preserve is 3 miles from Heber City and provides for a number of activities, ranging from serene hikes along winding mountain trails to golfing at one of the four 18-hole courses. Children have their own fishing pond near the visitor center. In winter, hiking turns to snowshoeing and cross-country or backcountry skiing along the Dutch Hollow, Snake Creek, or Pine Creek Trails winding up through stands of Gambel oak, aspen, and maple. ✉ *1281 Warm Springs Rd., Midway* ☎ *435/654–1791, 800/322–3770* 🌐 *stateparks.utah.gov* 🎟 *$10 per car.*

🍴 Restaurants

Café Galleria

$ | ITALIAN | FAMILY | This family-friendly restaurant claims to have the best pizza and bagels in the state, and they may not be far off. The wood-fired pizza oven cooks to perfection, and bagel sandwiches, available throughout the day, hit the spot. **Known for:** casual atmosphere; bagels; wood-fired pizza. [$] *Average main: $11* ✉ *101 W. Main St., Midway* ☎ *435/657–2002* 🌐 *www.thecafegalleria.com.*

☕ Coffee and Quick Bites

The Bagel Den

$ | CAFÉ | Locals love this bagel shop, where they can pick up a latte and a New York–style bagel made fresh daily. Try the pumpernickel, French toast, or pretzel bagels and add a schmear like bacon scallion or blueberry cream cheese. **Known for:** New York–style bagels; local favorite; delicious smoothies. [$] *Average main: $8* ✉ *570 N. Main St., Heber* ☎ *435/654–3193* 🌐 *www.thebagelden.com.*

Dairy Keen

$ | **FAST FOOD** | **FAMILY** | A welcome respite from chain fast food, this family-owned drive-in is loved by all the locals and serves the best shakes and burgers for miles around. Railroad artifacts line the walls, and an electric train entertains children as it passes over the booths. **Known for:** thick, creamy shakes; signature burgers; vintage vibe. [$] *Average main: $5* ✉ *199 S. Main St., Heber* ☎ *435/654–5336* 🌐 *www.dairykeen.com.*

Hotels

The Blue Boar Inn

$$$ | **B&B/INN** | Wrought-iron balconies, mountain views, and an antique alpenhorn give this château-style inn a warm, romantic feel. **Pros:** hospitable staff; romantic ambience; full breakfast. **Cons:** not the ideal place for boisterous little ones; 20-plus minutes to the ski resorts; dark decor. [$] *Rooms from: $260* ✉ *1235 Warm Springs Rd., Midway* ☎ *435/654–1400, 888/650–1400* 🌐 *www.theblueboarinn.com* 🛏 *12 rooms* 🍴 *Free Breakfast.*

Homestead Resort

$$$ | **HOTEL** | **FAMILY** | Park City silver miners once soaked in the hot springs of this resort, which has been in operation since 1886. **Pros:** a Bruce Summerhays–designed golf course; natural hot springs; family-friendly. **Cons:** far from ski resorts; rooms are basic; a bit sleepy. [$] *Rooms from: $249* ✉ *700 N. Homestead Dr., Midway* ☎ *435/654–1102, 800/327–7220* 🌐 *www.homesteadresort.com* 🛏 *147 rooms* 🍴 *No Meals.*

Zermatt Resort

$$$ | **RESORT** | **FAMILY** | This charming Swiss-style hotel is a restful retreat tucked into the idyllic countryside. **Pros:** immaculate rooms; stellar views; plenty to do. **Cons:** far from restaurants and ski resorts; expensive resort fee; very quiet. [$] *Rooms from: $269* ✉ *784 W. Resort Dr., Midway* ☎ *435/657–0180, 866/840–5087* 🌐 *www.zermattresort.com* 🛏 *427 rooms* 🍴 *No Meals.*

Activities

CAMPING

Wasatch Mountain State Park. The large campground at this busy state park has great facilities, including 36 holes of golf and a well-stocked fishing pond. Many of the sites are fairly open with scenic views; others are more shaded and private. It's a stunning setting, but it is closed in winter. There are 66 full hookups and 56 partial hookups from $20 per night. ✉ *1281 Warm Springs Rd., Midway* ☎ *435/654–1791; 800/322–3770 for reservations only* 🌐 *stateparks.utah.gov*

GOLF

Homestead Golf Club

GOLF | This incredible course, in the heart of the Heber Valley on the Homestead Resort, offers views of the Wasatch Mountains and plenty of fresh mountain air. GPS-enabled cart paths mean you won't get lost while looking at the scenery. ✉ *700 N. Homestead Dr., Midway* ☎ *435/654–5588, 800/327–7220* 🌐 *playhomesteadgc.com* 🎟 *$46 for 18 holes April and Oct.; $56 for 18 holes May–Sept.* 🏌 *18 holes, 7040 yards, par 72* 🕒 *Closed Nov.–Mar.*

Soldier Hollow Golf Course

GOLF | Reflecting the Olympic heritage, the names of the two 18-hole courses are Gold and Silver. While on these greens, golfers enjoy the beauty of both the Heber Valley to the east and stunning Mount Timpanogos to the west. The Gold course is considered a mountain course, with dramatic elevation changes within each hole. The Silver course is slightly shorter than Gold, but with longer and trickier greens. ⊠ *Wasatch Mountain State Park, 1370 W. Soldier Hollow La., Midway* ☎ *435/654–7442* ⊕ *stateparks. utah.gov/golf/soldier-hollow* ⊠ *$55 Mon.–Thurs.; $60 Fri.–Sun. and holidays (includes cart)* ⅄. *Gold: 18 holes, 7598 yards, par 72; Silver: 18 holes, 7335 yards, par 72.*

★ Wasatch Mountain Golf Course

GOLF | The setting within Wasatch Mountain State Park is spectacular, particularly at fall foliage time, and with the challenging Mountain Course as well as the gentler Lake Course, this is one of the most popular public courses in the state. The Mountain Course is designed around the natural contours of the surrounding Wasatch Mountains, and motorized carts are mandatory. Sometimes you can see deer and even moose while you golf. The easier Lake Course surrounds eight lakes and ponds and is a favorite with high, low, and no handicappers. The course's café serves breakfast, lunch, and dinner. ⊠ *Wasatch Mountain State Park, 975 Golf Course Dr., Midway* ☎ *435/654–0532* ⊕ *stateparks.utah.gov/ golf/wasatch/* ⊠ *$55 Mon.–Thurs.; $60 Fri.–Sun. and holidays (includes cart)* ⅄. *Mountain course: 18 holes, 6459 yards, par 71; Lake course: 18 holes, 6942 yards, par 72.*

HIKING

The path connecting the towns of Heber City and Midway is an easy walk with spectacular views of the Wasatch Range at a distance and, up close, the Provo River.

Jordanelle State Park

HIKING & WALKING | For a quiet experience, start your hike from the Rock Cliff Nature Center, under tall cottonwoods at the east end of Jordanelle State Park, which lies 10 miles east of Heber City. Hikers often report excellent wildlife viewing along this section of the upper Provo River. No dogs are allowed. ⊠ *515 Hwy. 319, Heber* ☎ *435/649–9540* ⊕ *stateparks. utah.gov.*

Soldier Hollow Nordic Center

HIKING & WALKING | FAMILY | Although the trail system here is more exposed than that in the northern end of Wasatch Mountain State Park, hikers will enjoy the stunning view of the east side of Mount Timpanogos as well as the vista of the Uinta Mountains to the east across the Heber Valley. Or, if you'd rather go faster than your feet can take you, rent an electric mountain bike at Soldier Hollow Lodge to zip down the trails. ⊠ *2002 Soldier Hollow La., Midway* ☎ *435/654–2002* ⊕ *www.soldierhollow.com* ☞ *To rent an electric bike costs $75 for ½ day and $110 for full day.*

Wasatch Mountain State Park

HIKING & WALKING | Hikers will find lots of foliage and wildlife here, on any number of trails in Dutch Hollow and Pine Canyon and along Snake Creek. ⊠ *1281 Warm Springs Rd., Midway* ☎ *435/654–1791* ⊕ *stateparks.utah.gov.*

HORSEBACK RIDING
Rocky Mountain Outfitters

HORSEBACK RIDING | Visitors can enjoy the spectacular back country of Wasatch Mountain State Park and surrounding areas on horseback year-round with Rocky Mountain Outfitters. Choose from a variety of ride durations and destinations with the nicest guides in the area. ☎ *435/654–1655* ⊕ *www.rockymtnoutfitters.com* ⊠ *$99 for 1½-hr ride.*

WATER SPORTS
Deer Creek State Park

FISHING | Consistently good fishing, mild canyon winds, and water warmer than you'd expect are responsible for Deer Creek State Park's popularity with windsurfers, sailors, swimmers, and those just kicking back in the mountain sunshine. The park is 5 miles south of Heber City. ⊠ *5566 Hwy. 314, Heber* ☎ *435/654–0171* ⊕ *stateparks.utah.gov* ⊠ *$15 day-use fee.*

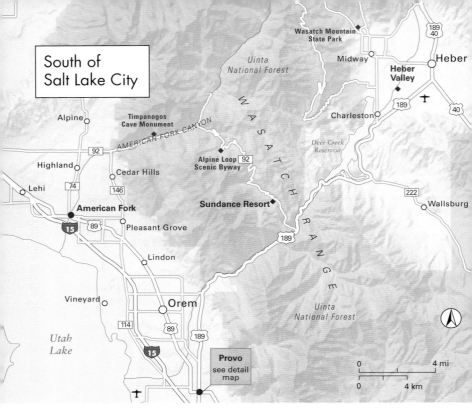

South of
Salt Lake City

Wasatch Mountain
State Park

Uinta
National Forest

Midway   Heber

Heber
Valley

189 40

189

40

Charleston

Deer Creek
Reservoir

Alpine

Timpanogos
Cave Monument

AMERICAN FORK CANYON

WASATCH RANGE

Highland

Cedar Hills

Alpine Loop 92
Scenic Byway

222

Wallsburg

Lehi

74

146

Sundance Resort

American Fork

89

Pleasant Grove

189

Lindon

Uinta
National Forest

Vineyard

Orem

114

89

189

Utah
Lake

15

Provo
see detail
map

0   4 mi
0   4 km

Jordanelle State Park

WATER SPORTS | This park has three recreation areas on a large mountain reservoir. The Hailstone area, 10 miles north of Heber City via U.S. 40, offers day-use areas, boat ramps, playgrounds, and a marina store where water toys (wave runners and the like) can be rented. To the east, across the reservoir on Highway 32, the Rock Cliff area and facilities are near the Provo River. To the north, Ross Creek is where some of the best fishing in the area can be found. ⊠ *515 Hwy. 319, Heber* ☎ *435/649–9540 Hailstone Main Park* ⊕ *stateparks.utah.gov* ✉ *Hailstone $20, Rock Cliff $10 and Ross Creek $10 per day use.*

Sundance Resort

35 miles south of Park City, 12 miles northeast of Provo.

As Thoreau had Walden Pond, so does Redford have Sundance. Lucky for the rest of us, the "Sundance Kid" shares his 5,000-acre bounty. Several miles up a winding mountain lane, Sundance Resort is a full-service ski resort with bustling slopes in winter, except during the Sundance Film Festival. In summer, it's a destination for filmmakers, writers, craftsmen, and artists of all sensibilities. It also caters to visitors looking to relax at spas, shop, or dine.

GETTING HERE AND AROUND
From Park City, take Highway 40 and 189 south. From Provo, head northeast on Highway 92.

The 11,750-foot Mount Timpanogos overlooks Sundance Resort.

◉ Sights

★ Sundance Mountain Resort

RESORT | Set on the eastern slopes of the breathtaking 11,750-foot Mount Timpanogos, the resort came into being when Robert Redford purchased the land in 1969. Though he sold the property in 2020, the 5,000-acre mountain resort continues to reflect Redford's legacy and commitment to the natural environment, outdoor exploration, and artistic expression. All resort facilities—constructed from materials such as indigenous cedar, fir, and pine and locally quarried stone—compliment the natural landscape. No matter the season, you'll find plenty of recreational opportunities, including hiking, biking, fly-fishing, horseback riding, alpine and cross-country skiing, snowboarding, snowshoeing, and ziplining. If you're looking for a more indulgent experience, relax with a body treatment in the Spa at Sundance or take one of many creative classes in the Art Studio. Dine in one of the on-site restaurants, like the cozy Tree Room or the hip western Owl Bar on a night when they play live music. The Sundance Film Festival, based in nearby Park City each January, is an internationally recognized showcase for independent films. Festival screenings and summer workshops are held at the resort. ⊠ *8841 N. Alpine Loop Rd., Sundance* ☎ *801/225–4107, 800/892–1600* ⊕ *www.sundanceresort.com* ✉ *Lift tickets $129* ☞ *2,150-foot vertical drop; 450 skiable acres; 35% novice, 45% intermediate, 20% advanced; 3 quad lifts, 1 triple chair, 1 surface lift.*

🍴 Restaurants

★ The Foundry Grill

$$$ | **AMERICAN** | Wood-oven pizzas, sizzling steaks, and spit-roasted chicken are among the hearty staples on the menu at this restaurant. Like the rest of Sundance, everything from the food presentation to the interior design is beautiful and fits right in with the eco-friendly, nature-first concept established by Redford. **Known for:** Sunday brunch; open kitchen; wood-burning pizza oven. [$] *Average main: $30* ✉ *Sundance Resort, 8841 N. Alpine Loop Rd., Sundance* ☎ *866/932–2295, 801/223–4220* 🌐 *www.sundanceresort.com.*

★ **The Tree Room**

$$$$ | **AMERICAN** | It's easy to imagine that you're a personal guest of Robert Redford at this intimate, rustic restaurant with Western memorabilia from the actor's private collection. With its warm wood interior and natural light, this cozy restaurant is a great place to tuck into for hours to eat delicious food, listen to the creek nearby, and forget about your worries. **Known for:** fine dining; candlelit atmosphere; interesting art. [$] *Average main: $37* ✉ *Sundance Resort, 8841 N. Alpine Loop Rd., Sundance* ☎ *866/627–8313* 🌐 *www.sundanceresort.com* ⏲ *No lunch.*

Hotels

★ **Sundance Mountain Resort**

$$$$ | **RESORT** | With 11,750-foot Mount Timpanogos serving as a backdrop, Robert Redford's resort is tucked into a 5,000-acre swath of lush wilderness and is a genuine tribute to arts and the natural world. **Pros:** retreat from urban hubbub; glorious scenery; culinary magic. **Cons:** cell reception is spotty; long drive to other restaurants and nightlife; limited ski terrain compared to other Utah resorts. [$] *Rooms from: $465* ✉ *8841 N. Alpine Loop Rd., Sundance* ☎ *801/225–4107, 800/892–1600* 🌐 *www.sundanceresort.com* 🛏 *95 rooms* 🍴 *No Meals.*

Nightlife

The Owl Bar

PUBS | Whether you feel like a quiet midday chess game or a more lively atmosphere at night, the Owl Bar is a good gathering space. Here you'll find live music on weekends and a wide selection of beers and spirits to accompany a limited but satisfying menu. Classic photographs of Paul Newman and Robert Redford as Butch Cassidy and the Sundance Kid hang on the walls, and with the worn plank floors, stone fireplace, and original 1890s rosewood bar (said to have been favored by Cassidy's Hole-in-the-Wall Gang) transported from Thermopolis, Wyoming, you might just feel like cutting loose. ✉ *Sundance Mountain Resort, 8841 N. Alpine Loop Rd., Sundance* ☎ *801/223–4222* 🌐 *www.sundanceresort.com.*

Performing Arts

Every January the Sundance Institute, a nonprofit organization supporting independent filmmaking, screenwriters, playwrights, composers, and other film and theater artists, presents the Sundance Film Festival. A world-renowned showcase for independent film, the 10-day festival is based in Park City, but has screenings and workshops at Sundance Mountain Resort.

Sundance Art Studio

ARTS CENTERS | The studio offers workshops in photography, jewelry making, wheel-thrown pottery, plein air acrylic and watercolor painting, and charcoal or pencil drawing. Mirroring the Sundance ethic, these classes blend the natural world with the artistic process. All workshops and classes are open to resort guests as well as day visitors, and you'll go away with a finished piece of art. ✉ *Sundance Mountain Resort, 8841 N. Alpine Loop Rd., Sundance* ☎ *801/225–4107* 🌐 *www.sundanceresort.com.*

Sundance Author Series

READINGS/LECTURES | For more than 15 years, the Sundance Author Series has brought literary and political icons like Sue Monk Kidd and Jimmy Carter to the Tree Room for an intimate brunch and lecture. As an added bonus, you'll walk away with a signed copy of the author's book. ✉ *Sundance Mountain Resort, 8841 N. Alpine Loop Rd., Sundance*

☎ 866/734–4428 ⊕ www.sundancere-sort.com.

Sundance Bluebird Café Concert Series
MUSIC | Each summer, Sundance brings a little Nashville to Utah with the Bluebird Café series. Singer-songwriters take the outdoor stage on select summer Fridays to share stories and music in the serene Utah mountains. ⊠ 8841 N. Alpine Loop, Sundance ☎ 801/223–4567 ⊕ www.sundanceresort.com.

 Shopping

General Store
JEWELRY & WATCHES | Step inside the Sundance catalog, which features distinctive home furnishings, clothing, and jewelry reflecting the rustically elegant Sundance style. Ask about many items that are organic or made of recycled materials. ⊠ Sundance Mountain Resort, 8841 N. Alpine Loop Rd., Sundance ☎ 801/223–4250 ⊕ www.sundanceresort.com.

Sundance Deli
FOOD | Selling foods from American cottage farmers and artisans as well as homemade oils, soaps, and bath salts, the Deli also has a juice bar and is a good place to get tea, coffee, shakes, pastries, deli meats, organic produce, and other tasty snacks. Stop here before your hike to pick up a fresh sandwich. ⊠ Sundance Mountain Resort, 8841 N. Alpine Loop Rd., Sundance ☎ 801/223–4211 ⊕ www.sundanceresort.com ⏾ Closed Sun.

 Activities

FLY-FISHING
The Provo River, minutes from Sundance Resort, is a fly-fishing catch-and-release waterway. Access to the rainbow, cut-throat, and German brown trout found in the river is year-round. Tours are provided by Wasatch Guide Service, and include all necessary gear and guides, and some may include drinks and snacks.

Wasatch Guide Service
FISHING | The preferred outfitter of Sundance Resort, Wasatch Guide Service provides access to some of the best fly-fishing in the state. Guides will take you to the world-class Provo River, right near Sundance Resort, or up to the Weber River to help you hook into fun runs of lively cutthroat or brown trout. They can even provide access to private waters and lesser-known streams. One guide to every two guests ensures personalized experiences, and they provide all necessary equipment. Half-day and full-day tours are available year-round, with lunch provided on the full-day tour. ⊠ Sundance ☎ 801/830–3316 ⊕ www.wasatchguideservice.com 💰 From $280 ½-day; from $400 full day.

HIKING
Hiking trails in the Sundance area vary from the easy 1.25-mile Nature Trail and the popular lift-accessed Stewart Falls Trail (3 miles) to the 7½-mile Big Baldy Trail, which leads past a series of waterfalls up steep, rugged terrain. You can access moderate- to expert-level trails from the resort base or chairlift. Select from three routes to summit 11,000-foot Mount Timpanogos. Guided naturalist hikes are available.

MOUNTAIN BIKING
You'll find more than 25 miles of ski lift–accessed mountain-biking trails at Sundance Resort, extending from the base of Mount Timpanogos to Ray's Summit at 7,250 feet. High-tech gear rentals are available for full or half days, as is individual or group instruction.

Sundance Mountain Outfitters
BIKING | Rent all the gear you need for mountain biking, skiing, or snowboarding. ⊠ 8841 N. Alpine Loop Rd., Sundance ☎ 801/223–4121 ⊕ www.sundanceresort.com.

SKIING
CROSS-COUNTRY

Enjoy terrain suitable for all skill levels on nearly 10 miles of groomed trails. Six miles of dedicated snowshoeing trails wind through mature aspen groves and pines. Lessons and equipment rentals, including telemark gear, are available for all techniques of cross-country skiing and snowshoeing at the Sundance Nordic Center.

DOWNHILL

Skiers and snowboarders at Sundance Resort will find 44 trails on 450 acres of varied terrain. Services include specialized ski workshops (including ladies' day clinics and personal coaching), a PSIA-certified ski school, and a ski school just for children, with programs that include all-day supervision, lunch, and ski instruction. Children as young as four are eligible for group lessons. Rentals are available for all skill levels. Night skiing is also available four nights a week.

Provo

45 miles southeast of Park City, 45 miles south of Salt Lake City.

With Mount Timpanogos to the east and Utah Lake to the west, Provo and the adjacent city of Orem make up one of the prettiest communities in the West. This two-city community is also one of the fastest growing.

Provo's historic downtown includes many small shops and family restaurants; in the newer sections you'll find malls, factory outlet stores, a variety of eateries, and the headquarters for several large corporations. The presence of Brigham Young University and the LDS Missionary Training Center imbue the community with a wholesome quality.

GETTING HERE AND AROUND

Highway 189 from Park City or Interstate 15 from Salt Lake City both deposit you into Provo's tidy grid of easy-to-navigate streets. The sprawling Brigham Young University campus and historic downtown are at its center, with shopping malls scattered in all directions. Giant Utah Lake is to the west.

FESTIVALS
America's Freedom Festival

FESTIVALS | FAMILY | Each June and July, the America's Freedom Festival combines a series of patriotic activities and contests. The event peaks with a hot-air balloon festival, the state's biggest Independence Day parade, and fireworks at BYU's 65,000-seat LaVell Edwards Stadium, dubbed the Stadium of Fire. ⊠ *Provo* ☎ *801/818–1776* ⊕ *www.freedomfestival. org.*

VISITOR INFORMATION

CONTACTS Utah County Convention and Visitors Bureau. ⊠ *220 W. Center St., Suite 100, Provo* ☎ *801/851–2100, 800/222– 8824* ⊕ *www.utahvalley.com.*

Sights

Brigham Young University

COLLEGE | Provo and the entire region are probably best known as the home of BYU. The university was established as the Brigham Young Academy in 1875, with a mandate to combine teaching about the sacred and the secular. It has grown into one of the world's largest church-affiliated universities, and still reflects the conservative nature of the Church of Jesus Christ of Latter-day Saints. Students must adhere to a strict dress and honor code, and refrain from alcohol, tobacco, coffee, and tea. BYU is known for its large variety of quality undergraduate and graduate programs, and is a considerable force in regional athletics. Heading up BYU attractions is a quartet of museums. A free guided university tour is offered weekdays on the hour, and reservations are recommended. ✉ *BYU visitor center, Campus Dr., Provo* 🕿 *801/422–4636* ⊕ *www.byu.edu.*

BYU Museum of Art

ART MUSEUM | The permanent collection of more than 17,000 works here includes primarily American artists, such as Maynard Dixon, Dorothea Lange, Albert Bierstadt, Minerva Teichert, and Robert Henri, and emphasizes the Hudson River School and the American impressionists. Rembrandt, Monet, and Rubens also turn up, along with some fine Far Eastern pieces. The museum's café overlooks the sculpture garden. ✉ *N. Campus Dr., southeast of LaVell Edwards Stadium, Provo* 🕿 *801/422–8287* ⊕ *moa.byu.edu* 🍽 *Free* 🕐 *Closed Sun.*

BYU Museum of Paleontology

SCIENCE MUSEUM | **FAMILY** | This museum, across from LaVell Edwards Stadium, features dinosaur bones, fossils, and tours for adults and children. Kids love the hands-on activities, which include several small tables of touchable artifacts. ✉ *1683 N. Canyon Rd., Provo* 🕿 *801/422–3680* ⊕ *geology.byu.edu/museum* 🍽 *Free* 🕐 *Closed weekends.*

BYU Museum of Peoples and Cultures

HISTORY MUSEUM | **FAMILY** | A student-curated collection of artifacts relating to cultures from all over the world is housed here. Clothing, pottery, rugs, weapons, and agricultural tools of Utah's Native American cultures are often on display. A permanent display includes artifacts from the first Provo Tabernacle that BYU students dug up in 2012. ✉ *2201 N. Canyon Rd., Provo* 🕿 *801/422–0020* ⊕ *mpc.byu.edu* 🍽 *Free* 🕐 *Closed weekends.*

Monte L. Bean Life Science Museum

SCIENCE MUSEUM | **FAMILY** | This museum at BYU, north of the bell tower, has extensive collections of birds, mammals, fish, reptiles, insects, plants, shells, and eggs from around the world, as well as revolving nature-art exhibits. You'll also see current NASA satellite images, wildlife art, and various interactive ecology exhibits. If you bring a toddler, head for the play area themed around animal habitats. ✉ *645 E. 1430 N, Provo* 🕿 *801/422–5050* ⊕ *mlbean.byu.edu* 🍽 *Free* 🕐 *Closed Sun.*

Provo Pioneer Village

MUSEUM VILLAGE | **FAMILY** | This museum re-creates what life was like for the first settlers in the mid-19th century. Original cabins and shops furnished with period antiques are staffed by volunteer history buffs. ✉ *500 W. 600 N, Provo* 🕿 *801/852–6609* ⊕ *www.provopioneervillage.org* 🍽 *Free* 🕐 *Closed Sept.–May.*

Splash Summit Waterpark

WATER PARK | **FAMILY** | There's plenty of family fun at this popular local water park, including more than 15 water play areas, slides, and pools. Float along the relaxing Rainforest River, catch a wave in the wave pool, or rent a cabana and cool off with a delicious Dole Whip. ✉ *1330 E. 300 N* 🕿 *385/309–2388* ⊕ *www.splashsummit.com* 🍽 *$25* 🕐 *Closed Sept.–May.*

Springville Museum of Art

ART MUSEUM | Springville, 10 miles south of Provo on I–15 or U.S. 89, is known for its support of the arts, and its museum is a must-stop for fine-arts fans. Built in 1937 to accommodate works by John Hafen and Cyrus Dallin, the museum now features mostly Utah artists, among them Gary Lee Price, Richard Van Wagoner, and James T. Harwood. It also has a collection of Soviet working-class impressionism and a sculpture garden with rotating exhibits. ✉ *126 E. 400 S, Springville* 🕿 *801/489–2727* ⊕ *www.smofa.org* 🍽 *Free* 🕐 *Closed Sun. and Mon.*

🍴 Restaurants

★ Communal

$$$$ | **AMERICAN** | This cozy restaurant will feel a lot like a Sunday dinner around a large communal table, and you'll feel like you're part of the family. Meals are sourced from local food purveyors, like

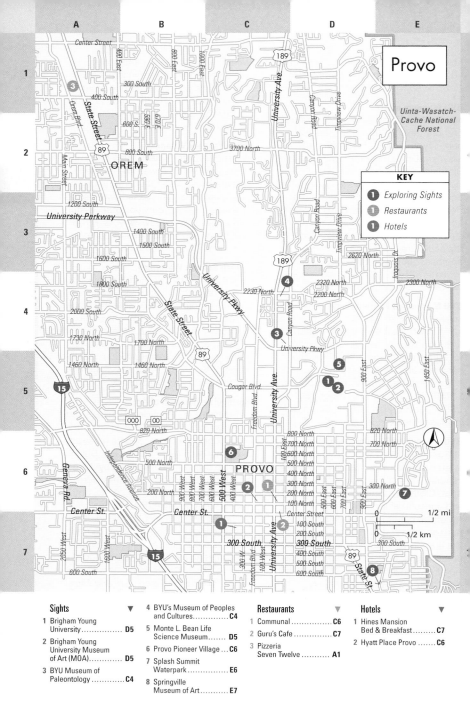

Provo

KEY

- ❶ Exploring Sights
- ❶ Restaurants
- ❶ Hotels

Uinta-Wasatch-Cache National Forest

Payson Spring Ranch, which supplies live trout to the restaurant just hours before you sit down to eat. **Known for:** locally sourced ingredients; communal dining; vibrant open kitchen. $ *Average main: $38 ⊠ 102 N. University Ave., Historic Downtown* ☎ *801/373–8000* ⊕ *www. communalrestaurant.com* ☯ *Closed Sun.*

Guru's Cafe

$ | **ECLECTIC** | The vegetarian-friendly fare includes cilantro-lime quesadillas and rice bowls; options for nonvegetarians include a Southwestern chipotle chicken wrap with a side of sweet-potato fries. An art deco portrait of Gandhi decorates one wall of this downtown hippie refuge; elsewhere you'll find metal sculptures and blue skyscapes. **Known for:** eclectic decor; menu variety; vegetarian-friendly. $ *Average main: $10 ⊠ 45 E. Center St., Provo* ☎ *801/375–4878* ⊕ *www.guruscafe.com.*

Pizzeria Seven Twelve

$ | **PIZZA** | With a name that comes from the ideal temperature for cooking pizza, the centerpiece of this bright, minimalist establishment is a wood-burning brick oven. Pizzas come topped with delectable items like *speck* (prosciutto) and *soppressata* (salami). **Known for:** local beer menu; varied pizza toppings; open kitchen. $ *Average main: $13 ⊠ 320 S. State St., #185, Orem* ☎ *801/623–6712* ⊕ *www.pizzeria712.com* ☯ *Closed Sun.*

Hotels

Hines Mansion Bed & Breakfast

$$ | **B&B/INN** | Quaint and charming, this bed-and-breakfast is located in an 1895 mansion, where much of the original woodwork, brick, and stained glass has been left intact. **Pros:** close to BYU; historic building with modern updates; unique and comfortable. **Cons:** bathtubs take up too much space; small rooms; inefficient layout in some rooms. $ *Rooms from: $165 ⊠ 383 W. 100 S, Provo* ☎ *801/374–8400, 800/428–5636* ⊕ *www.hinesmansion.com* ⇆ *9 rooms* ℠ *Free Breakfast.*

Hyatt Place Provo

$$ | **HOTEL** | Among the best lodging options in Provo, this dapper contemporary Hyatt boutique property is close to Brigham Young University and the city's many attractions while also providing convenience to Thanksgiving Point and mountains to the north and east. **Pros:** within walking distance of downtown Provo dining and sightseeing; mountain views from many rooms; convenient for exploring Mount Timpanogos. **Cons:** at a busy intersection; books up during conventions and university events; 45-minute drive to downtown SLC. $ *Rooms from: $199 ⊠ 180 W. 100 N, Provo* ☎ *801/609–2060* ⊕ *www.hyatt.com* ⇆ *133 rooms* ℠ *Free Breakfast.*

▼ Nightlife

Although Provo isn't completely "dry," the standards of BYU are evident in the city's dearth of nightlife options.

● Performing Arts

Because the university has a considerable interest in the arts, Provo is a great place to catch a play, dance performance, or musical production. BYU has a dozen performing groups in all. The BYU International Folk Dance Ensemble and BYU Ballroom Dance Company travel extensively but also perform at home.

BYU Franklin S. Harris Fine Arts Center

ARTS CENTERS | **FAMILY** | Most performances at BYU are held in this center, which houses a concert hall, recital hall, and three theaters. The ticket office is on the third floor, near the south entrance, and is open weekdays 9–5; there's another ticket office on the north side of the Marriott Center, ground level, with more convenient parking. ⊠ *800 E. Campus Dr., Provo* ☎ *801/422–4322, 801/422–2981 tickets* ⊕ *arts.byu.edu* ☯ *Closed Sun.*

4

Park City and the Southern Wasatch PROVO

Shopping

Shopping in the Provo–Orem area centers on four primary areas. In addition to the malls, visitors find shopping opportunities at boutiques and galleries in downtown Provo, especially along Center Street.

Provo Towne Centre

MALL | FAMILY | On the south end of Provo, this mall has mainstream retailers like JCPenney and Bath & Body Works, plus a food court and a Cinemark movie theater. It's open 10–6 Monday through Saturday and noon–6 on Sunday. ⊠ *1200 Towne Centre Blvd., Provo* ☎ *801/852–2400* ⊕ *www.provotownecentre.com.*

The Shops at Riverwoods

MALL | FAMILY | This mall is one of the newest in the area and home to upscale retailers like Jos. A. Banks and popular local boutiques, including Lonely Ghost and Called To Surf. Sitting near Provo Canyon, enjoy outdoor dining amid fresh canyon breezes. The mall is open Monday through Saturday 10–9. ⊠ *4801 N. University Ave., Provo* ☎ *801/802–8430* ⊕ *www.shopsatriverwoods.com* ⊗ *Closed Sun.*

University Place

MALL | FAMILY | Catering to the needs of BYU students, this mall also has everything from fashion retailers like Dillard's and H&M to footwear and furniture—more than 150 shops and restaurants in all. The mall is open Monday through Saturday 10–9. ⊠ *575 E. University Pkwy., Orem* ☎ *801/224–0694* ⊕ *www.universityplaceorem.com* ⊗ *Closed Sun.*

Activities

BIKING

In the Provo area, road cyclists may make a 100-mile circumnavigation of Utah Lake or tackle U.S. 189 through Provo Canyon or the Alpine Loop Scenic Byway. Mountain bikers can choose from a large selection of trails varying in degrees of difficulty.

Racer's Cycle Service

BIKING | For information about biking in the area, bicycle sales, and world-class service, call Racer's Cycle Service and talk to owner "Racer" Jared Gibson. Racer's Cycle Service is fully mobile with no brick-and-mortar store. ⊠ *Provo* ☎ *801/375–5873* ⊕ *www.racerscycleservice.com* ☞ *By appointment only.*

FISHING

Utah Lake State Park

BOATING | Fishing is popular at Utah Lake, which, at 96,600 acres, is the state's largest freshwater lake. In spring and fall it gets some of the best wind in Utah for windsurfing and sailing. Powerboating and canoeing are also popular. ⊠ *4400 W. Center St., Provo* ☎ *801/375–0731* ⊕ *stateparks.utah.gov* ⊡ *$10 Nov.–Mar., $15 Apr.–Oct.*

GOLF

You'll find 10 public courses within the Utah Valley, ranging from canyon or mountain settings to relatively flat and easy-to-walk terrain. Tee times are usually easy to get, and greens fees are reasonable.

Hobble Creek Golf Course

GOLF | The canyon setting at this affordable course east of Springville makes for a beautiful day, especially in fall when the hills explode with color. Golfers rave about the views and warn of tricky greens. This course is consistently rated a favorite among the public courses in Utah. The newly renovated Terrace Grill and full service pro shop are added conveniences. ⊠ *94 Hobble Creek Canyon Rd., Provo* ☎ *801/489–6297* ⊕ *www.springville.org/golf* ⊡ *$18 for 9 holes, $36 for 18 holes* ⅄ *18 holes, 6400 yards, par 71.*

Timpanogos Golf Club

GOLF | The 18-hole championship course wends around the beautiful shoreline of Utah Lake and wetlands, with excellent views of the Wasatch Mountains and

The Alpine Loop Scenic Byway is especially gorgeous in the fall.

the chance to spot birds along the way. The 7-hole Executive Course is great for beginners and juniors and is walk-on only. The individual and group lessons, as well as clinics, provide personalized instruction with PGA professionals. ✉ *380 E. Lakeview Pkwy., Provo* ☎ *801/852–7529* ⊕ *www. timpanogosgolf.com* ✉ *Greens fees from $32* 🏌 *18 holes, 6,900 yards, par 73.*

HIKING

Visitors to the southern part of the Wasatch find many trails from which to choose.

Bonneville Shoreline Trail

HIKING & WALKING | The 100-mile Bonneville Shoreline Trail from Brigham City to Nephi spans the foothills of the Wasatch Front following the eastern shoreline of ancient Lake Bonneville. The section near Provo begins at the Rock Creek trailhead and continues south along the foothills, past the Y trailhead, to the Hobble Creek Parkway trailhead. ✉ *Provo.*

Bridal Veil Falls

HIKING & WALKING | The trailhead to Bridal Veil Falls is 2½ miles up Provo Canyon; after the moderate climb, hikers are rewarded with a cold mountain waterfall shower. ✉ *Provo* ⊕ *www.utahvalley.com.*

Provo Parkway

HIKING & WALKING | The easy, paved Provo Parkway meanders along the Provo River from the mouth of Provo Canyon and provides a good mix of shade and sun. ✉ *Provo.*

ICE-SKATING

Peaks Ice Arena

ICE SKATING | **FAMILY** | A 2002 Olympic Hockey venue, this arena includes two ice sheets, and is open throughout the year for figure skating, hockey, and parties. ✉ *100 N. Seven Peaks Blvd., Provo* ☎ *801/852–7465* ⊕ *www.provo. org/community/peaks-ice-arena* ✉ *$6* ☾ *Closed Sun.*

ROCK CLIMBING

American Fork Canyon

ROCK CLIMBING | In the Uinta National Forest, 10 miles north of Provo, American Fork Canyon has northern Utah's best sport climbing, with dozens of fixed routes. The steep walls also offer face, slab, and crack climbs. It's also is home to Mount Timpanogos Cave, the mouth of which you can hike up to and explore with a headlamp and guide. ⊠ *Provo*.

American Fork

14 miles north of Provo.

American Fork serves as a good base for exploring Timpanogos Cave National Monument as well as other sights throughout the canyon.

 Sights

★ Alpine Loop Scenic Byway

SCENIC DRIVE | Beyond Timpanogos Cave, Highway 92 continues up American Fork Canyon before branching off to climb behind Mount Timpanogos itself. Designated the Alpine Loop Scenic Byway, this winding road offers stunning mountain views and fall foliage in the latter months before dropping into Provo Canyon to the south. The 14-mile round-trip Timpooneke Trail and the 14-mile round-trip Aspen Grove Trail, both off the byway, reach the summit of Mount Timpanogos. Also along this highway is the famed Sundance Resort. Closed, depending on snowfall, from late October to late May, the Alpine Loop is free to drive, but you need to purchase a National Forest pass ($6, good for three days) to park at any of the trailheads and recreation areas along the route. This is the roundabout way to get to scenic Provo Canyon and Deer Creek Reservoir from I–15 (if heading south from Salt Lake City); the more direct route is U.S. 189 east from near Orem and Provo (stop by Bridal Veil Falls on your way in). ⊠ *American Fork* ⊕ *www.utah.com/scenic-drive/alpine-loop.*

Timpanogos Cave National Monument

CAVE | **FAMILY** | Soaring to 11,750 feet, Mount Timpanogos is the centerpiece of a wilderness area of the same name and towers over Timpanogos Cave National Monument along Highway 92 within American Fork Canyon. After a somewhat strenuous hike up the paved 1½-mile trail to the entrance, you can explore three caves connected by two man-made tunnels. Stalactites, stalagmites, and other formations make the three-hour round-trip hike and tour worth the effort. No refreshments are available on the trail or at the cave, and the cave temperature is 45°F throughout the year, so bring water and warm clothes. Although there's some lighting inside the caves, a flashlight will make your explorations more interesting; it will also come in handy if you're heading back down the trail after dusk. These popular tours often sell out; it's a good idea to book online in advance, especially on weekends. ⊠ *2038 W. Alpine Loop Rd., American Fork* ☎ *801/756–5239 cave info, 877/444–6777 tickets* ⊕ *www.nps.gov/tica* ⊠ *Cave tours $12* ☉ *Cave closed Nov.–Apr.*

Chapter 5

NORTHERN UTAH

Updated by
Tessa Woolf

⊙ **Sights**
★★★★★

🍴 **Restaurants**
★★★★☆

🛏 **Hotels**
★★★☆☆

🛍 **Shopping**
★★★☆☆

🍸 **Nightlife**
★★★☆☆

WELCOME TO NORTHERN UTAH

TOP REASONS TO GO

★ **Ski Ogden:** Park City gets the accolades, but locals know that the snow is just as amazing, the slopes less crowded, and the prices much more reasonable at Snowbasin, Powder Mountain, and Nordic Valley.

★ **Hiking:** You'll find hiking adventures throughout the Ogden Valley.

★ **Logan Canyon Scenic Byway:** The magnificent, winding 39-mile stretch of U.S. 89 from Logan to Bear Lake is best enjoyed in the fall.

★ **Historic 25th Street, Ogden:** Once home to brothels and unsavory railside establishments, downtown Ogden's revitalized 25th Street and adjacent Nine Rails Creative District now abound with art galleries, museums, hip restaurants, and indie shops.

★ **Bear Lake:** A favorite retreat on the Utah–Idaho border during the hot summer months, this modestly developed lake has a reputation for azure-blue water and delicious raspberry milkshakes.

The region north of Salt Lake City stretches along the rugged Wasatch Range to the Idaho border and includes a couple of smaller cities with their own distinctive histories and personalities, Ogden and Logan, as well as the smaller community of Brigham City located between the two. Additionally, the Ogden Valley and Garden City (with surrounding Bear Lake) are hubs of outdoor recreation.

1 Ogden. Not counting the sprawling suburbs around Salt Lake City, Ogden is Utah's second-largest metropolis, a once rough-and-tumble railroad and fur-trading hub whose vibrant and historic downtown now teems with cool dining, galleries, and retail; its outskirts abound with gorgeous hiking and mountain biking trails.

2 Ogden Valley. Just a 15-minute drive over the mountains from Ogden, this sweeping mile-high valley is home to the villages of Eden and Huntsville, which flank the shores of massive Pineview Reservoir. The Ogden Valley is famed for its world-class ski resorts, Snowbasin and Powder Mountain.

3 Brigham City. The pleasant, all-American seat of Box Elder County makes a good stop en route between Ogden and Logan and a base for day trips to Golden Spike National Historical Park.

4 Logan. This picturesque collegiate community is home to Utah State University and offers a handsome downtown with some elegantly restored theaters where the Utah Festival Opera performs. There's also easy access to miles of breathtaking hiking trails, most of them off scenic U.S. 89, which winds through the sheer walls of nearby Logan Canyon.

5 Garden City. A tiny and mostly seasonal summer-vacation hub with a number of restaurants and hotels, Garden City hugs the western shore of enormous Bear Lake, which is half in Utah, half in Idaho.

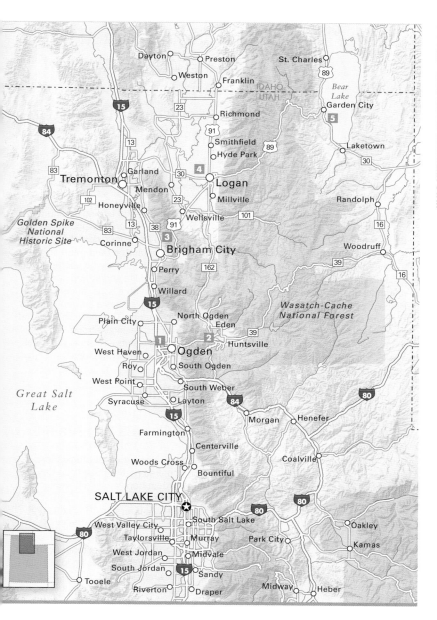

When you picture Utah, many envision the red-rock crags and canyons of the south, but the north, with its cattail marshes and pasture lands framed by the gray cliffs and towering conifers of the Wellsville Mountains and the Bear River Range, has its own kind of beauty—without the throngs of tourists you'll encounter in the south.

Here the Shoshones (Sacagawea's tribe) made their summer camps, living on roots, berries, and the plentiful game of the lowlands. In the 1820s and '30s mountain men came to trap beavers, foxes, and muskrats, taking time out for their annual rendezvous on the shores of Bear Lake. Some, like the famous Jim Bridger, married Native Americans and settled here; to this day, Cache, Rich, and Box Elder Counties are collectively known as "Bridgerland." In the 1850s Mormon pioneers were sent by Brigham Young to settle here, and their descendants still populate this rugged land. In 1869 an event occurred here that would change the face of the West, and indeed the nation, forever: the completion of the Transcontinental Railroad was celebrated officially at Promontory Summit.

The region is characterized by alternating mountain ranges and valleys, typical of the Basin and Range geologic province that extends westward into Nevada and California. Much of the landscape has remained unspoiled, thankfully preserved as part of the Uinta-Wasatch-Cache National Forest, and offers a range of outdoor activities for all seasons: hiking, mountain biking, kayaking, skiing,

snowmobiling, and birding among them. In more recent years, as Ogden has reimagined its historic downtown, the area has begun to attract more artists, foodies, and hipsters who appreciate the high quality of life and strong sense of community. With a large student population, Logan also has a burgeoning arts and maker scene. Overall, northern Utah enjoys an increasingly strong—if still slightly underrated—balance of natural and human-made attractions.

Planning

Getting Here and Around

There are three main strategies for visiting the area north of Salt Lake City. By far the most popular and convenient is by car—Ogden is 45 minutes north of Salt Lake City via Interstate 15, and Logan is four hours southeast of Boise via Interstate 84 to U.S. 89. Although central Ogden and to a lesser extent Logan can be explored on foot or using local buses, you really need a car to fully appreciate the region's best attractions. It is possible

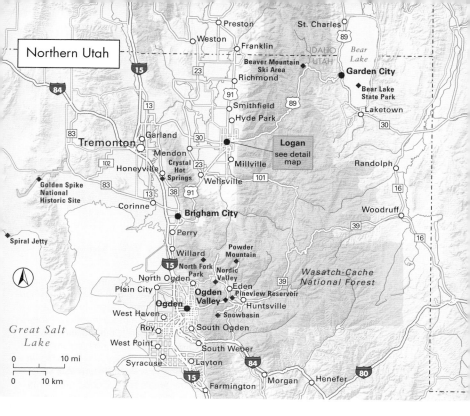

Northern Utah

to take a bus or commuter train to Ogden or Logan from Salt Lake City and rent a car once you arrive. Several major car rental agencies have offices in Ogden and there are a couple in Logan, too. The advantage with this strategy is that rental car rates are generally much lower at these local offices than at Salt Lake City International Airport.

The least expensive but also least practical option is using public transit to both reach and explore the towns in the area—this works best in Ogden and the Ogden Valley, which has a robust bus network. You could also use Lyft and Uber to get around in Ogden and Logan, but if you're making more than two or three trips a day, the cost may exceed that of renting a car.

BUS

The Utah Transit Authority (UTA) provides bus, FrontRunner commuter rail, and TRAX light-rail service throughout the Wasatch Front, and it can get you to a lot of places in Ogden and Brigham City as well as back and forth from Salt Lake City, but it's a slower and less flexible alternative to driving. Another option is using one of the region's shuttle bus companies. From the Salt Lake City airport, Express Shuttle can get you to Ogden and the Ogden Valley, and from the airport and downtown, Salt Lake Express stops in Ogden, Brigham City, and Logan on its way north to Idaho.

BUS CONTACTS Express Shuttle.
☏ 800/397–0773, 801/596–1600
⊕ www.expressshuttleutah.com. **Salt Lake Express.** ☏ 208/656–8824 ⊕ www.

saltlakeexpress.com. **Utah Transit Authority.** ☎ 801/743–3882 ⊕ *www.rideuta.com.*

CAR

The interstate cuts north from Salt Lake City through the region, joining U.S. 89, which winds up through Logan to Bear Lake, and also Interstate 84, which curves in a northwesterly direction to Idaho. U.S. 89 is also known as Logan Canyon Scenic Byway north of the city of Logan and is, as you might guess, stunning to drive. Off the main highways, roads range from well-paved multilane blacktop routes to barely graveled backcountry trails that may require high-clearance vehicles—if heading to trailheads or lakes in the national forest, it's a good idea to check websites or with local ranger offices for driving conditions, especially in winter or after rainy periods.

TRAIN

UTA's FrontRunner high-speed commuter train operates hourly Monday through Saturday, and every half-hour during weekday rush hour, between the downtowns of Ogden and Salt Lake City (and on south to Provo), with several stops in between. Fares are based on the distance traveled; it's $5.50 one way from Salt Lake City to Ogden.

TRAIN INFORMATION Utah Transit Authority. ☎ 801/743–3882 ⊕ *www.rideuta.com.*

Hotels

Chain hotels are the most likely options in this part of the state, although you will find a handful of B&Bs in Logan and some of the small villages in the Ogden Valley; the area also abounds with condo rentals that fill up—and can command steep rates—during ski season. Bear Lake, on the other hand, has very few hotels and virtually no chain properties but does have some family-friendly condos and vacation rentals (just remember that summer is high season in this area).

Restaurant and hotel reviews have been shortened. For full information, visit Fodors.com.

What It Costs			
$	$$	$$$	$$$$
RESTAURANTS			
under $16	$16–$22	$23–$30	over $30
HOTELS			
under $125	$125–$200	$201–$300	over $300

Planning Your Time

You can get a good sense of the region's key draws over a long weekend, divided between Ogden, Logan, and perhaps Bear Lake. For a more intensive exploration of northern Utah, **Ogden** serves as a great base, offering plenty of urban and outdoor activities. Plan on a day in Ogden to check out **Historic 25th Street** and the area's several good museums and outdoor attractions. More ardent fans of recreation will want to add at least a day in the **Ogden Valley,** with its abundance of hiking and boating opportunities and—in winter—world-class skiing and snowboarding at **Powder Mountain** and **Snowbasin.** The small city of **Brigham City** is worth a stop if you're planning to spend time at nearby **Golden Spike National Historical Park** and perhaps taking a soak at family-friendly **Crystal Hot Springs.** Heading north to the friendly college town of **Logan,** spend a day enjoying great opera in summer and some good museums and impressive hikes before venturing out on one of the state's most scenic drives through **Logan Canyon** on your way to **Bear Lake State Park,** where boating, swimming, or lounging await at Rendezvous Beach.

Restaurants

Ogden has become a real dining destination in recent years; its historic downtown is rife with cool little indie eateries, gastropubs, international restaurants, and coffeehouses, along with a handful of craft-beer bars and microbreweries. Logan has a smattering of notable eateries, too, but beyond these communities, you can mostly expect casual, Western-style grub (steaks, burgers, and the like). Note that many restaurants in this part of the state, especially beyond Ogden, don't serve alcohol and are closed on Sunday.

Visitor Information

Bear Lake Convention and Visitors Bureau
✉ *69 N. Paradise Pkwy., Garden City* ☎ *435/946–2197, 800/448–2327* ⊕ *www. bearlake.org.*

Cache Valley Visitors Bureau
✉ *199 N. Main St., Logan* ☎ *435/755–1890* ⊕ *www.explorelogan.com.*

When to Go

Northern Utah offers four seasons of outdoor fun. Be prepared for hot summer days and extremely cold winter nights, especially in the mountains. Spring brings vistas of verdant pastures under the still snowcapped mountains. Hot summer afternoons prepare you for a dip in Bear Lake followed by an evening at Logan's Festival Opera. On crisp fall days, breathtaking hues of red scrub oak, orange maple, and bright yellow aspen rub shoulders with blue-green firs. Winter is the domain of skiers, snowshoers, and snowmobilers. This region drops dozens of inches of snow annually in the valleys and hundreds of inches in the mountains. You'll never battle hordes of tourists in this less-discovered part of the state, but you might have to wait in a line of locals for a raspberry shake at Bear Lake on a summer weekend.

Ogden

35 miles north of Salt Lake City.

Even though it was settled several years prior to Salt Lake City's 1847 Mormon influx, Ogden has nonetheless been trumped by the capital city for most of its history.

More recently, however, a thriving outdoor recreation industry, the Hill Air Force Base, Weber State University (and its 26,000 students), three ski areas just over the mountains in Ogden Valley, and the renovation of Historic 25th Street have brought jobs, recreation, and redevelopment to a community that was once a seedy railroad junction abundant with rowdy bars and bordellos. With a population of 88,000, the city is a small, affordable alternative to Salt Lake City with similarly great access to hiking and skiing as well as an emerging cluster of hip places to eat, shop, drink, and view art. The oldest town in Utah, Ogden was founded by mountain man Miles Goodyear, who settled here with his family in the early 1840s. The Mormons arrived in the area in 1847, and in 1869 Ogden became a hub for the Transcontinental Railroad. The city quickly became a major Western crossroads.

On the first Friday of each month, 20 or so downtown galleries, shops, and restaurants showcase the work of local artists during a neighborhood stroll that stretches from the gallery inside Union Station to the Eccles Community Art Center in the emerging Nine Rails Creative District. One of the most interesting stops is The Monarch, a multi-use business incubator and arts space housed in a restored 1920s parking garage that contains galleries as well as captivating murals.

GETTING HERE AND AROUND

Ogden lies about 40 minutes north of Salt Lake City on Interstate 15, with a few suburbs and Hill Air Force Base in between. Slower but parallel U.S. 89 hugs the foothills of the Wasatch Mountains and offers an alternative route and a shortcut for drivers headed to the Ogden Valley. Most visitors get here by car, but FrontRunner trains and UTA buses are public-transit options that make sense if you're planning to spend most of your time downtown, which is quite pedestrian-friendly.

VISITOR INFORMATION

VISITOR INFORMATION Visit Ogden.
✉ *2411 Kiesel Ave., Suite 401, Ogden* ☎ *800/255–8824, 801/778–6250* ⊕ *www. visitogden.com.*

 Sights

Eccles Community Art Center

ARTS CENTER | FAMILY | Housed in an imposing 1893 Queen Anne mansion with soaring turrets, this vibrant community arts center with a focus on diversity and inclusion presents a permanent collection of works by regional and national artists. There are also rotating shows exhibited throughout the building's public spaces and a sculpture garden with flowers and a stunning fountain. The center also offers a wide range of performing and visual arts classes and special events. ✉ *2580 Jefferson Ave., Ogden* ☎ *801/392–6935* ⊕ *www.ogden4arts.org* ✉ *Free* ⊗ *Closed Sun.*

★ George S. Eccles Dinosaur Park

CITY PARK | FAMILY | This 5-acre park near the mouth of Ogden Canyon is the stomping ground for about 100 life-size dinosaur models and the delighted children who come to see them. A playground with dinosaurs to crawl on appeals to younger kids, and adults can brush up on their geology and paleontology inside two natural history museums. You can watch technicians working with

excavated dinosaur bones in the paleontology lab. A particularly good gift shop brims with dinosaur toys and souvenirs. ✉ *1544 E. Park Blvd., Ogden* ☎ *801/393–3466* ⊕ *www.dinosaurpark.org* ✉ *$7* ⊗ *Closed Sun. and Mon. in winter.*

Hill Aerospace Museum

MILITARY SIGHT | FAMILY | You can view the exteriors of nearly 100 military aircraft dating from the early years of flight to the present at this impressive 30-acre indoor-outdoor museum at the north end of Hill Air Force Base, about 7 miles south of downtown Ogden. There are also missiles, military vehicles, munitions, uniforms, and thousands of other artifacts. ✉ *Hill Air Force Base, 7961 Wardleigh Rd., Roy* ☎ *801/825–5817* ⊕ *www.aerospaceutah.org* ✉ *Free* ⊗ *Closed Sun. and Mon.*

★ Historic 25th Street

STREET | The centerpiece of downtown Ogden's highly successful renaissance, this broad, lively street with restaurants, bars, and shops set inside handsomely restored 19th-century buildings is a great spot for a stroll any time of day. Historical markers tell the story of the pubs, brothels, and gambling houses that thrived here a century ago, an anomaly in heavily Mormon Utah. The three-block stretch from Union Station to Washington Boulevard is especially vibrant, but the action continues a couple of blocks north to 23rd Street, where you'll find the Salomon Center (an indoor complex of gyms and fitness enterprises that includes a bowling alley, surfing and wakeboarding park, climbing wall, and indoor wind tunnel) and a big multiscreen movie theater at the corner of Kiesel Avenue. As you venture east, beyond Grant Avenue and between 24th and 26th Streets, you'll encounter the rapidly emerging Nine Rails Creative District, a hub of galleries, start-up businesses, and creative endeavors that's anchored around the multiuse Monarch Building (✉ 455 25th St.), with its art studios and

Ogden's George S. Eccles Dinosaur Park has life-size models of dinosaurs for the kids to play on as well as two natural history museums for the adults.

murals. ✉ *25th St. at Washington Blvd.* ⊕ *www.historic25.com.*

Ogden Botanical Gardens

GARDEN | This tranquil 11-acre urban oasis set along the Ogden River Parkway is operated by the University of Utah and contains a series of theme gardens— rose, Oriental, water conservation, edible, cottage—connected by a network of meandering paths, some of which flank the river. One garden has been designed for people with mobility challenges, and an arboretum features trees that are ideal for planting beneath powerlines, as they never exceed 25 feet in height. On warm days, the conifer garden is a fragrant spot offering plenty of shade. There are also attractive picnic areas and lawns that invite relaxing. ✉ *1750 Monroe Blvd., Ogden* ☎ *801/399–8080* ⊕ *www.ogden-botanicalgardens.org.*

★ Ogden Nature Center

NATURE PRESERVE | **FAMILY** | Although close to Interstate 15 on the north side of the city, this quiet 152-acre center abounds with opportunities to view and interact with nature. It's home to thousands of trees, plus vibrant marshlands and ponds, with nature trails that are popular year-round (cross-country skiers take to them in winter). It's possible to view Canada geese, great blue herons, red foxes, mule deer, and porcupines roaming the grounds (you can get especially good views from a small observatory tower), as well as rescued bald eagles, owls, and other spectacular species. The eco-consciously designed visitor center has interesting exhibits as well as activities for kids, while the education building shows rotating art exhibits and the excellent Nest gift shop sells nature-oriented goods. ✉ *966 W. 12th St., Ogden* ☎ *801/621–7595* ⊕ *www.ogdennature-center.org* ⬧ *$5* ⊙ *Closed Sun.*

Treehouse Museum

CHILDREN'S MUSEUM | **FAMILY** | Offering a hands-on learning experience where children literally can step into a story, this downtown museum is filled with imaginative interactive exhibits geared generally to those under 12. Visit Jack's

Fairy Tale Diner, a Japanese House, the Jupiter Train Locomotive, or the German House Puppet Theater. Other fun activities include songs, theater, and art workshops. Admission is actually slightly higher ($8) for kids than adults. ✉ *347 22nd St., Ogden* ☎ *801/394–9663* 🌐 *www.treehousemuseum.org* 🎫 *$5* 🕒 *Closed Sun.*

Union Station

OTHER MUSEUM | **FAMILY** | Incorporating elements from Ogden's original 1870s train depot that was destroyed by a fire in 1923, the impressive Spanish Revival replacement has been developed into a landmark cultural center with two art galleries and four diverse museums. The Browning Firearms Museum celebrates the many achievements of the museum's namesake and showcases the sporting and military firearms that were popular in the Old West before Browning formed his own company. The Browning–Kimball Classic Car Museum pays tribute to the golden age of automobiles with a small but dazzling collection of restored cars from the first half of the 20th century. The Utah State Railroad Museum thrills train enthusiasts with its meandering exhibits detailing all phases of Utah's railroad history; a highlight is the outdoor Eccles Rail Center, which includes half a dozen restored train cars. The smallest museum of the bunch, the Utah Cowboy & Western Heritage Museum, features the Utah Cowboy Hall of Fame and honors artists, rodeo champions, entertainers, musicians, ranchers, and writers who have promoted the Western lifestyle. The Myra Powell Gallery mounts monthly photography exhibits, while the Gallery at the Station showcases local art in an enclosed passenger platform. ✉ *2501 Wall Ave., Ogden* ☎ *801/629–8680* 🌐 *ogdencity.com/2230/Union-Station* 🎫 *$7 (combined admission for all museums)* 🕒 *Closed Sun. and Mon.*

🍴 Restaurants

Harp & Hound

$ | **AMERICAN** | A hot spot among artists, hikers, musicians, LGBTQ+ folks, and college students, this festive gastropub serves up elevated comfort fare, like blackened salmon tacos, barbecue chicken pizzas, meatless "wings" with buffalo sauce, and garlic-mushroom-Swiss burgers. There's an excellent tap and cocktail list, and in the basement, you'll find the hip and diverse Funk and Dive speakeasy, an inviting spot for cocktails and live music. **Known for:** lots of vegan options; eclectic crowd and great people-watching; popular weekend brunch. [$] *Average main: $13* ✉ *2550 Washington Blvd., Ogden* ☎ *801/621–3483* 🌐 *www.harphound.com.*

Hearth on 25th

$$$ | **MODERN AMERICAN** | With an emphasis on wood-fired cooking and farm-to-table seasonality, the menu at this dapper but casual gem includes salmon and octopus with creative preparations and house-made pastas, breads, and dressings. On warm days, dine on the patio overlooking the historic district and the Wasatch Mountains while enjoying the wine on tap, a huge selection of whiskeys, and a seasonally changing array of fresh desserts. **Known for:** yak, rabbit, elk, and other wild game dishes; addictive truffle fries; market with pastas, olive oils, and gourmet groceries to go. [$] *Average main: $24* ✉ *195 25th St., Suite 6, Ogden* ☎ *801/399–0088* 🌐 *www.hearth25.com* 🕒 *Closed Sun. and Mon. No lunch.*

Pig & a Jelly Jar

$ | **SOUTHERN** | **FAMILY** | This funky, down-home diner with graffiti-covered brick walls serves hearty Southern food throughout the day, starting with fried chicken and biscuits and ham hash in the morning and moving on to catfish and chips and brown sugar–and–maple barbecue pork sandwiches later in the day. Save room for the beignets or cinnamon biscuits for dessert, and snag a jar of pineapple-lemon-rosemary or blueberry-lavender jam on your way out. **Known for:** shareable family-style platters; Nashville-style hot chicken; champagne cocktails mixed with house-made jams. [$] *Average main: $12* ✉ *227 25th St., Ogden* ☎ *801/605–8400* 🌐 *www.pigandajellyjar.com.*

Slackwater Pizzeria & Pub

$ | **PIZZA** | This casual eatery boasts hundreds of craft beers, mountain views, and a festive, friendly vibe. Try the boldly unorthodox pizza toppings, which are internationally inspired, verdant, and piled high; the gyro trip pie with a peppered-lemon base, shaved lamb, and tzatski drizzle is especially good. **Known for:** après-ski fun on the heated patio; live music and Ping-Pong; innovative brick-oven pizzas. [$] *Average main: $15* ✉ *209 24th St., Ogden* ☎ *801/399–0637* 🌐 *www.slackwaterpizzeria.com.*

★ **Tona Sushi Bar and Grill**

$$ | **JAPANESE** | This chic little Japanese spot has a modern focus, offering much more than just sushi rolls (although the phenomenal rolls alone, such as the smokin' hot *machi* with rosemary-smoked *hamachi*, fennel, Thai chili, orange slices, and citrus soy, would keep the doors open). Tona goes light on the sauce and heavy on the freshest ingredients, with an expansive menu that features artfully plated grilled mackerel with a raspberry-soy glaze, udon with chicken and tempura prawns, and flash-seared ahi with freshly cut pineapples. **Known for:** ocean-trout crudo and other creatively presented sashimi; extensive sake selection; house-made cheesecake with raspberry puree. [$] *Average main: $18* ✉ *210 25th St., Ogden* ☎ *801/622–8662* 🌐 *www.tonarestaurant.com* 🕒 *Closed Sun. and Mon.*

WB's Eatery

$ | **MODERN AMERICAN** | Plush armchairs, exposed air ducts, rotating contemporary art, and brick walls create a salon ambience in this high-ceiling space inside the Monarch Building in the trendy Nine Rails Creative District. Specializing in fine coffees and wines, WB's also turns out well-crafted café fare throughout the day, including brûléed grapefruit and ham-and-egg toasties at breakfast and grilled-shrimp bowls, Brussel sprouts tostadas, and fig-and-prosciutto bruschetta during the afternoon and evening hours. **Known for:** stunning, art-filled interior; delectable cheese and meat boards; craft beverages and snacks to go in the specialty market. [$] *Average main: $12* ✉ *455 25th St., Ogden* ☎ *385/244–1471* 🌐 *www.wbseatery.com.*

☕ Coffee and Quick Bites

Wasatch Roasting Company

$ | **CAFÉ** | Tucked inside a narrow historic downtown building festooned with colorful murals and graffiti, this funky café has well-trained baristas and sources its coffee beans from small, high-quality growers. Choose from well-crafted espresso drinks, single-origin coffees by whatever brewing method you choose (Chemex, French press, and so on), or one of the many nitro options, from on-tap cascara to kombucha. **Known for:** potent nitro cold brew (available by the can); affogato with premium ice cream; colorful "Aerosol Art Gallery" on the patio. [$] *Average main: $6* ✉ *2436 Grant Ave., Ogden* ☎ *801/689–2626* 🌐 *www.wasatchroasting.com.*

🛏 Hotels

Courtyard by Marriott Ogden

$$ | **HOTEL** | This eight-story chain property looks and feels a bit like any other Courtyard Marriott but stands out for its excellent downtown location a block from Historic 25th Street, its spacious rooms with sitting areas, and a wealth of fitness and leisure amenities, including an indoor pool, hot tub, and 24-hour gym. **Pros:** mountain views from even-number rooms; free parking; steps from 25th Street dining and retail. **Cons:** breakfast

Union Station houses four museums and two art galleries.

costs extra; cookie-cutter decor and design; in a busy part of downtown. [$] *Rooms from: $144* ✉ *247 24th St., Ogden* ☎ *801/627–1190* 🌐 *www.marriott.com* 🛏 *193 rooms* 🍴 *No Meals.*

★ Hampton Inn and Suites Ogden

$$ | **HOTEL** | Gray marble, bright bay windows, and soaring ceilings with ornate crown molding greet you in the lobby of this art deco beauty with airy guest rooms and gorgeous mountain and city views. **Pros:** elegant, historic architecture; suites are among the largest rooms downtown; steps from Historic 25th Street. **Cons:** frequently fills up with business travelers; no pool; on a very busy street. [$] *Rooms from: $129* ✉ *2401 Washington Blvd., Ogden* ☎ *801/394–9400* 🌐 *www.hilton.com/en/hampton* 🛏 *145 rooms* 🍴 *Free Breakfast.*

Hilton Garden Inn Ogden UT

$$ | **HOTEL** | A modern low-rise that's right in the heart of downtown and steps from attractions, restaurants, and shopping, this well-outfitted outpost of the reliable Hilton Garden brand has a slew of handy perks, including a full-service restaurant, an indoor pool and hot tub, a gym, and a striking glass-pavilion lobby with a bar and fireplace. **Pros:** some suites have jetted tubs or gas fireplaces; decent restaurant and lounge with room service; across from multiplex theater and Salomon Center fitness studios. **Cons:** a bit pricier than other downtown hotels; breakfast costs extra; rooms get some traffic noise. [$] *Rooms from: $179* ✉ *2271 S. Washington Blvd., Ogden* ☎ *801/399–2000* 🌐 *www.hilton.com* 🛏 *134 rooms* 🍴 *No Meals.*

🍸 Nightlife

The Angry Goat

PUBS | With one of the best craft beer lists in Utah and a terrific selection of artisan spirts, this inviting gastropub with exposed-brick walls and a handful of sidewalk tables also turns out delicious comfort food, from lamb burgers to steamed mussels. It opens early on weekends for a very popular and boozy brunch. ✉ *2570 Washington*

Blvd., Ogden ☎ 801/675–5757 ⊕ www. angrygoatpk.com.

Lighthouse Lounge

LIVE MUSIC | A longtime favorite for drinks and live music (sometimes without a cover) amid the bustle of Historic 25th Street, the Lighthouse has comfy seating as well as a long old-fashioned bar and local art on the walls. ⊠ *130 25th St., Ogden ☎ 801/392–3901 ⊕ lighthouse-ogden.com.*

Roosters Brewing

BREWPUBS | On Historic 25th Street, this long-time favorite brewpub (housed in a building from 1892) serves up an eclectic roster of house brews, including the popular O-Town Nut Brown ale, plus steak, sandwiches, and pizzas with locally made cheeses. Hang on the patio on warm days or watch the weather from the glass-enclosed sunroom year-round. ⊠ *253 25th St., Ogden ☎ 801/627–6171 ⊕ www.roostersbrewingco.com.*

★ UTOG Brewing Company

BREWPUBS | With an industrial-chic vibe, retractable garage-door-style windows, and an impressively extensive selection of house brews, UTOG gives Salt Lake City's many acclaimed breweries a run for their money. The Mandarina Kolsch is a refreshing choice on a warm night, while the heady Red Eye Imperial Red Ale will warm your soul on a winter night. Brats, cheesesteaks, and other pub fare is served, too. ⊠ *2331 Grant Ave., Ogden ☎ 801/689–3476 ⊕ www.utogbrewing.com.*

The Yes Hell

COCKTAIL LOUNGES | A dimly lit tavern and live-music lounge with an irreverent spirit—from its name to the beer taps with creepy doll heads—the Yes Hell brings in some great rock, blues, and soul performers. Order a few street food–style tacos (smoked carnitas and vegan soy chorizo) to go with your local IPA or craft cocktail. ⊠ *2430 Grant Ave., Ogden ☎ 801/903–3671 ⊕ www.theyeshell.com ⊗ Closed Sun. and Mon.*

 Performing Arts

Ogden Amphitheater

CONCERTS | FAMILY | Throughout the summer, you can attend free concerts and movie screenings at this open-air venue off Historic 25th Street, with gorgeous mountain views. ⊠ *Municipal Gardens, 343 25th St. ☎ 801/629–8307 ⊕ www.ogdencity.com/709/Amphitheater.*

★ Peery's Egyptian Theater

THEATER | Built in the 1920s but then abandoned for many years, this restored art deco jewel with a working Wurlitzer pipe organ received a splendid restoration in 1997 and now hosts concerts ranging from world music to blues, jazz, and country acts, as well as an ongoing film series and touring musicals. ⊠ *2415 Washington Blvd., Ogden ☎ 801/689–8700 ⊕ www.egyptiantheaterogden.com.*

Val A. Browning Center for the Performing Arts

ARTS CENTERS | FAMILY | Theater, music, and dance performances by students and visiting artists are offered frequently at Weber State University's excellent performing arts center, home stage for the Ogden Symphony Ballet Association. ⊠ *3950 W. Campus Dr. ☎ 801/626–7015 ⊕ www.weber.edu/browningcenter.*

Shopping

ARTWORK

Gallery 25

ART GALLERIES | More than 50 local and regional contemporary artists sell their art at this terrific co-op gallery that's been going strong along Historic 25th Street since 2000. ⊠ *268 25th St., Ogden ☎ 801/334–9881 ⊕ www.gallery25utah.com ⊗ Closed Sun.*

The Local Artisan Collective

ART GALLERIES | You can buy art and take classes at this vibrant community art space in the Junction District downtown. More than 60 artists working in pottery, glass, fiber, jewelry, toy-making, and several other disciplines create and sell here. ⊠ *2371 Kiesel Ave., Ogden* ☎ *801/399–2787* ⊕ *www.localartiscollective.com* ⏱ *Closed Sun.*

FOOD

★ Beehive Cheese

FOOD | Just a 10-minute drive southeast of Ogden, this artisan creamery has become famous in recent years for its creamy yet nutty cheddars, including the signature lavender-coffee-rubbed Barely Buzzed variety, which appears on cheese platters at some of the country's top restaurants. Other flavored varieties of note include apple-walnut-smoked and Hatch chili. You can sample and buy them, along with other tasty products, at this friendly shop. ⊠ *2440 E. 6600 S, Suite 8, Uintah* ☎ *801/476–0900* ⊕ *www.beehivecheese. com.*

★ Farmers Market Ogden

MARKET | **FAMILY** | Find an eye-opening selection of fresh local produce, gourmet goods, live music, and local art at one of Utah's largest and most popular farmers' markets. The main summer market runs late June through mid-September from 9 am to 2 pm along Historic 25th Street. There's also a shorter fall market from late September through late October, and a winter version of the market from mid-January to late February. ⊠ *25th St. from Wall St. to Washington Blvd., Ogden* ☎ *385/389–1411* ⊕ *www.farmersmarketogden.com.*

SPORTING GOODS

Alpine Sports

SPORTING GOODS | If you're in Utah for a ski vacation, you can't beat Alpine Sports for high-performance winter gear, stylish outdoor apparel, and design-conscious gadgets and accessories. The selection here is painstakingly curated by buyers who know their stuff, and you can't walk through the door without falling in love with something a little outside your budget. Rentals, tuning, and repair are also available. ⊠ *1165 Patterson St.,*

Ogden ☎ *801/393–0066* ⊕ *www.alpinesportsutah.com.*

TEXTILES AND SEWING

Needlepoint Joint

CRAFTS | **FAMILY** | Needlepointers, knitters, quilters, and crochet enthusiasts from miles around flock to this fantastic little shop to find patterns, yarn, thread, and instruction. ⊠ *241 25th St., Ogden* ☎ *801/394–4355* ⊕ *www.needlepointjoint.com* ⏱ *Closed Sun. and Mon.*

Activities

More than 250 miles of trails for hiking, mountain biking, and horseback riding surround the Ogden area, and the scenic roads are perfect for biking enthusiasts. The Weber and Ogden Rivers provide high-adventure rafting and kayaking while Olympic-caliber skiing is just up the canyon in the Ogden Valley.

BASEBALL

★ Lindquist Field

BASEBALL & SOFTBALL | One of the best minor-league ballparks in America, this "rookie ball" farm club of the Los Angeles Dodgers—known officially as the Ogden Raptors—plays from June to August. The mountain views are dazzling. ⊠ *2330 Lincoln Ave., Ogden* ☎ *801/393–2400* ⊕ *www.ogden-raptors.com.*

BIKING

The Bike Shoppe

BIKING | Founded in 1976, this shop favored by serious bike enthusiasts sells and repairs top-of-the-line brands and offers bike rentals by the day. You can also rent snowshoes and wetsuits. ⊠ *4390 Washington Blvd., Ogden* ☎ *801/476–1600* ⊕ *www.thebikeshoppe. com* ⏱ *Closed Sun.*

HIKING

With its numerous green spaces and proximity to rugged mountains and canyons east of downtown, Ogden is a terrific hiking destination. You can be out on an easy stroll along the river or a challenging trek to a lofty peak in no time. Most of the top hikes are mapped and described on the Ogden Trails Network and Trails Foundation of Northern Utah websites. For less strenuous, family-friendly treks, consider venturing out along the 4½-mile Ogden River Parkway, which runs west to east on the north side of town. If you're up for a demanding but stunning adventure that will reward you with grand views from soaring outlooks, you might follow the Beus Canyon Trail to the 9,570-foot summit of Mount Ogden—this all-day hike is about 11 miles round trip. The North and South Skyline Trails are also favorite higher-elevation treks.

★ Ogden Trails Network
HIKING & WALKING | The city's official and definitive hiking resource—with maps, details, and hiking etiquette and tips—details more than 25 adventures around the area, including local favorites like the Ogden River Parkway, Waterfall Canyon, Beus Canyon, and Bonneville Shoreline Trails. Some of these destinations are also open to mountain biking. ⊠ *Ogden* ☎ *801/629–8214* ⊕ *www.ogdencity. com/545/Ogden-Trails-Network.*

Trails Foundation of Northern Utah
HIKING & WALKING | FAMILY | This local nonprofit organization is dedicated to preserving and maintaining trails throughout Weber County. The online trail map includes detailed elevation information and covers adventures in Ogden but also well beyond into the Ogden Valley as well as north and south along the Wasatch Range ⊠ *Ogden* ☎ *801/393–2304* ⊕ *www.tfnu.org.*

RECREATION CENTERS
WSU Outdoor Adventure & Welcome Center
LOCAL SPORTS | Located on the campus of Weber State University, this outstanding outdoor recreation center offers community programs, guided tours, and many other resources that are available to both locals and visitors. The new 17,000-square-foot state-of-the-art center

opened in 2021 and features a 55-foot climbing wall, a rooftop rappelling and rigging area, and an expanded equipment rental center, where you can pick up kayaking, rafting, winter sports, camping, and biking equipment and lots of other gear. ⊠ *Weber State University, 4022 Taylor Ave., Ogden* ☎ *801/626–6373* ⊕ *www. weber.edu/outdoor* ⊙ *Closed Sun.*

Ogden Valley

8 miles east of Ogden City.

Locals call it "the valley," as if it were the only valley in the world. It's sleepy and slow around these parts, but once you see the valley, anchored by Pineview Reservoir and surrounded by the spectacular Wasatch Mountains, you'll see why residents feel this way. Home to the quaint pioneer towns of Huntsville, Eden, and Liberty and filled with world-class skiing, accessible water sports, and great fishing, golf, climbing, hiking, biking, and camping, the Ogden Valley is a recreation mecca still largely waiting to be discovered.

GETTING HERE AND AROUND
Most visitors approach the valley from Ogden via 12th Street, which becomes Highway 39. Pineview Reservoir lies at the center of the valley and resembles an airplane with the nose pointing west and wings (arms of the lake) extending north and south. You can drive around the reservoir in about 30 minutes without stops, and a car is definitely the best way to get around this area and visit the famed ski areas. From Salt Lake City, Trapper's Loop (Highway 167) is the scenic shortcut from I–84 to the south end of the reservoir. It's beautiful in spring and fall and well maintained for access to the Snowbasin ski resort in the winter.

Pineview Reservoir resembles the shape of an airplane from above.

Sights

New World Distillery

DISTILLERY | In a handsome barnlike building on the outskirts of the small ski town of Eden, this acclaimed small-batch distillery offers tastings as well as (paid) tours, which include tastings. Known for bourbon, vodka, and barrel-conditioned gin, New World also makes a crisp tequila-like agave spirit and an agave liqueur flavored with Utah tart cherries. Tours are typically offered only on weekends, including some Sundays. ⊠ *4795 E. 2600 N, Eden* ☏ *385/244–0144* ⊕ *www.newworlddistillery.com* ✉ *Tours $20* ◷ *Closed Sun. and Mon. No tours May–Oct.*

Pineview Reservoir

BODY OF WATER | FAMILY | In summer, this 2,800-acre lake dotted with several marinas and sandy beaches is festooned with colorful umbrellas and the graceful arcs of water-skiers and wakeboarders. In winter it's a popular spot for ice-fishing. Middle Inlet, Cemetery Point, and Anderson Cove are the three developed beaches, and Anderson Cove also allows overnight camping. The Cove has a boat launch. The beaches at Pineview Trailhead, North Arm, and Spring Creek are free and have restrooms but no other amenities. ⊠ *End of Cemetery Point Rd., Huntsville* ☏ *801/625–5112* ⊕ *www. visitogden.com* ✉ *From $15 day use; access to some beaches is free* ◷ *Beach amenities closed Oct.–Apr.*

🍽 Restaurants

Carlos & Harley's

$$ | MEXICAN | Inside the colorful 1890s-era Eden General Store, a few blocks from the north shore of Pineview Reservoir, this fun Tex-Mex restaurant specializes in the kind of food that effectively sustains the area's many skiers, hikers, boaters, and other outdoorsy sorts. Think big plates of chile con queso, bacon-wrapped jalapeño poppers, shrimp fajitas, pork tamales, and slow-roasted-pork carnitas tacos. **Known for:** buzzy, chatter-filled dining room; four types of fresh-made salsa; margaritas on the outdoor patio. $ *Average main: $18* ✉ *5510 E. 2200 N, Eden* ☎ *801/745–8226* ⊕ *www.carlosandharleys.com.*

Gray Cliff Lodge Restaurant

$$$ | AMERICAN | Set in scenic Ogden Canyon, this romantic restaurant with lace tablecloths, linen napkins, and mountain and forest views is a time-honored destination for classic Continental fare, such as slow-roasted prime rib, grilled mountain trout, and sage-stuffed lamb chops with mint jelly. The fireplace makes this a fun gathering spot for pre- or after-dinner drinks in winter. **Known for:** surf-and-turf combos; unabashed old-school vibe; leisurely Sunday brunches. $ *Average main: $28* ✉ *508 Ogden Canyon* ☎ *801/392–6775* ⊕ *www.graycliflodge. com* ⊗ *Closed Mon.–Wed. No lunch.*

Mad Moose Café

$ | CAFÉ | FAMILY | This super-chill, family-friendly eatery is a perfect stop for delicious flavored coffee drinks and traditional breakfast fare early in the day or burgers, panini sandwiches, and ice-cream desserts after your outdoor adventures. **Known for:** Ivory Moose (white chocolate–hazelnut) lattes; burgers with lots of different topping combos; milk shakes, smoothies, and ice-cream floats. $ *Average main: $9* ✉ *2429 N. Hwy. 158, Suite 6, Eden* ☎ *801/452–7425* ⊕ *www. madmoosecafe.com.*

Shooting Star Saloon

$ | AMERICAN | The oldest remaining saloon in the state—in operation since the 1880s—is a beloved favorite hangout for skiers in winter and bikers in summer. The menu doesn't stray far from beer and burgers, but after a long day of outdoor play, the burgers hit the spot. **Known for:** the Star Burger (double cheeseburger topped with a Polish hot dog); Saint Bernard head mounted on the wall; decent selection of local craft brews. $ *Average main: $9* ✉ *7350 E. 200 S, Huntsville* ☎ *801/745–2002* ⊕ *www.visitogden.com.*

Hotels

There are no real hotels or motels in the Ogden Valley, but you will find a few tucked-away B&Bs and condos that accommodate groups of all sizes.

Alaskan Inn and Spa

$$$ | HOTEL | On a scenic stretch of Highway 39 in Ogden Canyon, between Ogden and Pineview Reservoirs, this rustic but upscale riverside lodge with cabins is perfect for a quiet getaway that's not too far from civilization, yet offers easy access to hiking, boating, and Ogden Valley skiing. **Pros:** lush setting beneath craggy mountains peaks; next to Gray Cliff Lodge restaurant and a kayak and Jet Ski rental agency; massage and spa services available. **Cons:** rooms facing road can get some traffic noise; 15-minute drive from downtown Ogden; log cabin vibe doesn't suit every taste. $ *Rooms from: $279* ✉ *435 Ogden Canyon, Ogden* ☎ *801/621–8600* ⊕ *www. alaskaninn.com* ⟿ *23 rooms* ⊗⊙ *Free Breakfast.*

Atomic Chalet B&B

$$ | B&B/INN | With comfortable beds, cathedral ceilings, and three windows offering sweeping Ogden Valley views, each of the three rooms in this contemporary B&B near Pineview Reservoir is perfect for a good night's sleep during a weekend of skiing or hiking. **Pros:** 15- to 20-minute drive from Ogden Valley ski areas; friendly, helpful hosts; picturesque, tranquil grounds. **Cons:** in a small, quiet town; not suitable for kids under 16; two-night minimum on ski-season weekends. $ *Rooms from: $149* ✉ *6917 E. 100 S, Huntsville* ☎ *801/425–2813* ⊕ *www.atomicchalet.com* ⟿ *3 rooms* ⊗⊙ *Free Breakfast.*

★ Compass Rose Lodge

$$$ | B&B/INN | The gorgeous contemporary design, charming small-town location, hip coffeehouse, welcoming hosts, and light-filled sitting areas are—amazingly—not even the coolest things

about this stylish boutique inn: that honor belongs to the silo-shape Huntsville Astronomic and Lunar Observatory, which adjoins the inn and offers unforgettable viewing experiences of the cosmos. **Pros:** stunning steampunk–meets–ski lodge design; steps from Utah's oldest bar, the Shooting Star Saloon; half-price "star walk" observatory tours for guests. **Cons:** fills up on weekends, especially in ski season; not too many dining options in town; slightly spendy for the area. [$] *Rooms from: $299 ✉ 198 S. 7400 E, Huntsville ☎ 385/279–4460 🌐 www.compassroselodge.com 🛏 15 rooms 🍴 Free Breakfast.*

Moose Hollow at Wolf Creek Resort

$$ | **TIMESHARE** | **FAMILY** | The individually decorated condos at Wolf Creek's Moose Hollow property—all with full kitchens, stone fireplaces, decks or patios, vaulted ceilings, and massive log beams—are just a few miles from Powder Mountain and within walking distance of Wolf Creek's scenic 18-hole golf course. **Pros:** spacious units with kitchens; outdoor pool; gorgeous views of the lake and mountains. **Cons:** two-night minimum stay during busy times; no pets; no housekeeping during stay. [$] *Rooms from: $150 ✉ N. Huntsman Path at Moose Hollow Dr. ☎ 801/745–3737 🌐 www.wolfcreekrentals.com 🛏 30 units 🍴 No Meals.*

Activities

BOATING

Club Rec

BOATING | **FAMILY** | This outdoor recreation shop rents Jet Skis, speedboats, double-decker pontoon boats, and other watercraft so you can enjoy Pineview Reservoir to the fullest. In the winter time, a guided tour of Monte Cristo is one of the best snow adventures in the West. In addition to the main store, there are a few satellite locations in the area. *✉ 3718 N. Wolf Creek Dr., Eden ☎ 801/745–3038 🌐 www.clubrecutah.com.*

HIKING

★ Snowbasin

HIKING & WALKING | Beginning at an elevation of 6,500 feet, Snowbasin offers 26 miles of hiking and mountain-biking trails of varying degrees of difficulty, many of them ascending through bowls filled with summer wildflowers to the dramatic 9,350-foot summit of Mount Ogden. On weekends, you can ride the gondola ($16) to Needles Lodge, eat lunch, and then hike along the ridge to the peak. June through September, the resort hosts the popular Blues, Brews & BBQ every Sunday, bringing free musical acts to the base of the mountain. *✉ 3925 Snowbasin Rd., Huntsville ☎ 801/620–1000, 888/437–5488 🌐 www.snowbasin.com.*

SKIING

If you're staying in Ogden and want to head for the mountains for a day of skiing or snowboarding, you can catch the Ski Bus (🌐 www.rideuta.com), which runs between several downtown Ogden hotels and the ski resorts in the Ogden Valley. Black Diamond Shuttle (🌐 www.blackdiamondshuttle.com) also offers taxi service from hotels and Salt Lake City International Airport.

Nordic Valley

SKIING & SNOWBOARDING | **FAMILY** | Utah's smallest ski resort was used for downhill training for the 2002 Olympics. A great place to learn, this charming family-oriented resort is one of the most affordable in the state, and the whole mountain is lighted for night skiing and boarding. *✉ 3567 E. Nordic Valley Way, Eden ☎ 801/745–3511 🌐 www.nordicvalley.com 🎫 Lift tickets from $59 ☞ 965-foot vertical drop; 140 skiable acres; 36% beginner, 45% intermediate, 18% advanced; 2 double chairs, 1 triple chair, 1 surface lift.*

North Fork Park

SKIING & SNOWBOARDING | The 14 well-maintained miles of cross-country trails here, plus 6 miles of snowshoe trails, are perfect for all experience levels and also popular in summer for hiking and biking. Cross-country ski and snowshoe rentals are available. ☒ *4150 E. 5950 N, Liberty* ☏ *801/648–9020* ⊕ *www. ogdennordic.com* ✉ *Day passes: $10 (hiking), $8 (biking), $5 (snowshoeing).*

★ Powder Mountain

SKIING & SNOWBOARDING | This classic ski resort offers huge terrain—more skiable acres than any other resort in North America—even though it doesn't have as many lifts (nine all together) as some of Utah's destination resorts. Two terrain parks and a half-pipe are popular with snowboarders. Snowcat skiing (for an additional $25) and night skiing are also popular. Although plenty challenging, the intermediate options (40% of the 154 runs) are heavenly in contrast to nearby Snowbasin, which is generally steeper and more exposed. You won't find fancy lodges or haute cuisine here, but with caps on passes (3,000 per season and 1,500 per day), crowds are nonexistent, and the laid-back slope-side eateries serve everything from scones and hot soup to flame-broiled burgers at the Powder Keg. ☒ *6965 E. Hwy. 158, Eden* ☏ *801/745–3772* ⊕ *www.powdermountain.com* ✉ *Lift tickets $115* ⌖ *2,205-foot vertical drop; 8,464 skiable acres; 25% beginner, 40% intermediate, 35% advanced; 4 quad chairs, 1 triple chair, 3 surface lifts.*

★ Snowbasin

SKIING & SNOWBOARDING | A vertical drop of 2,959 feet and a dramatic start at the pinnacle of Mount Ogden made this resort just 17 miles from Ogden the perfect site for the downhill ski races during the 2002 Olympic Winter Games. With nine lifts accessing more than 3,000 acres with 104 runs of steep, skiable terrain, this is one of Utah's largest resorts.

It also offers miles of Nordic trails for cross-country skiing. Served in spectacular lodges, the on-mountain food consistently ranks among the best in the state, and the resort also scores high marks for service, lifts, and grooming. ☒ *3925 E. Snowbasin Rd. (Hwy. 226), Huntsville* ☏ *801/620–1000, 888/437–5488* ⊕ *www. snowbasin.com* ✉ *Lift tickets $155* ⌖ *2,959-foot vertical drop; 3,000 skiable acres; 20% beginner, 50% intermediate, 30% advanced; 2 high-speed gondolas, 1 tram, 1 high-speed six-pack chair, 2 high-speed quad chairs, 3 triple chairs, 2 surface lifts.*

Brigham City

21 miles north of Ogden.

People passing through Brigham City are charmed by its sycamore-lined Main Street and old-fashioned downtown, but they may not realize they are in one of Utah's most progressive towns.

Northrop Grumman, which manufactures rocket motors about 30 minutes west of here (originally Orbital ATK), has brought in a lot of highly paid, well-educated professionals who have settled here and molded the city to their liking. The local art and history museum outclasses those in many of the state's larger cities, and the annual Peach Days Celebration brings sizable crowds over Labor Day weekend to honor the town's most famous local crop. The region's star attraction, though, is Golden Spike National Historic Park, which honors one day in history that changed North America: May 10, 1869. That's the date the Union Pacific and Central Pacific railroad officials met to drive their symbolic golden spike in celebration of the completion of the First Transcontinental Rail route. It happened at Promontory Summit, an ironically desolate spot about 30 miles west of Brigham City.

At Golden Spike National Historical Park, visitors can see replicas of famed locomotives.

GETTING HERE AND AROUND

Brigham City lies just to the east of I–15 on Highway 89/91. Like many cities settled by LDS pioneers, it's laid out on a grid system, with Main Street running north–south and each street numbered by 100s as you head in all four directions. Head north on Main to get to the quaint center of town. Highway 89/91 to Logan bypasses the town.

VISITOR INFORMATION

CONTACTS Box Elder Chamber of Commerce. ✉ *6 N. Main St., Brigham City* ☎ *435/723–3931* ⊕ *www.boxelderchamber.com.*

FESTIVALS

Peach Days Celebration

FESTIVALS | FAMILY | In honor of the famous local crop, this popular event has been held the Wednesday to Saturday after Labor Day since 1904—the longest continually celebrated harvest festival in Utah. There's a Peach Queen pageant, two parades, a carnival, theater and concerts, classic car and motorcycle shows, art and crafts booths, and, of course, freshly baked peach cobbler. ✉ *Brigham City* ☎ *435/723–3931* ⊕ *www. boxelderchamber.com/peach-days* ⬚ *Free admission.*

Sights

★ Bear River Migratory Bird Refuge

NATURE PRESERVE | Established in 1928 to conserve the Bear River habitat for migratory waterfowl and wildlife, this 80,000-acre U.S. Fish and Wildlife Service refuge is just west of Brigham City. You can observe wildlife along a 12-mile driving route and 1½ miles of walking trails, with ducks, geese, pelicans, herons, swans, shore birds, and more than 200 other kinds of birds arriving in various seasons. The Wildlife Education Center contains interactive displays and observation decks. ✉ *2155 W. Forest St., Brigham City* ☎ *435/723–5887* ⊕ *www.fws.gov/refuge/bear-river-migratory-bird* ⊗ *Wildlife Education Center closed Sun. and Mon.*

Brigham City Museum of Art & History
ART MUSEUM | More than 10,000 objects from Box Elder County's 170-year history tell the story of the area's early settlement and Mormon cooperative periods. This well-designed, modern museum also includes a permanent collection of more than 300 works of art, with several rotating exhibitions throughout the year. ✉ *24 N. 300 W, Brigham City* ☎ *435/723–6769* 🌐 *www.brighamcitymuseum.org* 🕒 *Closed Sun. and Mon.*

Crystal Hot Springs
HOT SPRING | **FAMILY** | Originally used as a winter camp by the Shoshones, this popular recreation area has one of the world's largest natural hot and cold springs. Mixing water from the two springs allows for a variety of pools with temperatures ranging from 80°F to 105°F. The complex in Honeyville, about 11 miles north of Brigham City, has its own campground, hot tubs, a large soaker pool, a cold freshwater swimming pool, two water slides, and a lap pool. ✉ *8215 N. Hwy. 38, Honeyville* ☎ *435/339–0038* 🌐 *www.crystalhotsprings.net* 🎟 *$18 pool; $20 pool and slide.*

★ **Golden Spike National Historical Park**
HISTORIC SIGHT | The Union Pacific and Central Pacific Railroads met here at Promontory Summit on May 10, 1869, to celebrate the completion of the first transcontinental rail route. Today, the National Park Service runs the site, which includes a visitor center and two beautifully maintained locomotives that are replicas of the originals that met here for the "wedding of the rails." Every May 10 (and on Saturday and holidays in summer), a reenactment of the driving of the golden spike is held, and throughout summer you can watch the trains in action on demonstration runs a few times a day. You can also walk a 1½-mile trail around the site and drive two scenic auto tour routes that reveal the terrain and engineering feats involved in creating this remote stretch of the rail line. In August, boiler stoking, rail walking, and buffalo-chip throwing test participants' skills at the Railroader's Festival. The Winter Steam Festival around Christmas gives steam buffs opportunities to photograph the locomotives in the cold, when the steam from the smokestacks forms billowing clouds. To get here, it's about a 40-minute drive west from Brigham City and a 90-minute drive north of Salt Lake City. ✉ *6200 N. 22300 West, Promontory* ☎ *435/471–2209* 🌐 *www.nps.gov/gosp* 🎟 *$20 per vehicle.*

★ **Spiral Jetty**
PUBLIC ART | This 1,500-foot-long, 15-foot-wide earthen creation that juts in a spiral out into Great Salt Lake was created by artist Robert Smithson in 1970 and is often photographed by passengers in planes flying overhead. The jetty, 16 miles from the Golden Spike site via a dirt road, was submerged for much of the subsequent 30 years, before the lake level fell precipitously in 2002 revealing the structure again. The snail shell–shape land art structure is considered one of the most remote sculptures in modern American art history, and it is Utah's state work of art. ✉ *N. Rozel Flats Rd. W, Rozel Point* ☎ *212/989–5566* 🎟 *Free.*

🍴 Restaurants

★ **Idle Isle Café**
$ | **AMERICAN** | **FAMILY** | It feels like you've wandered onto the set of *The Andy Griffith Show* at this quaint 1921 café—the oldest continually operating restaurant in Utah—with a menu specializing in old-fashioned comfort foods like pot roast and au gratin potatoes, chicken-fried steak, and hot turkey sandwiches with gravy. Save room for ice cream or a shake—or perhaps some sweet treats from the Idle Isle candy factory across the street. **Known for:** hefty sandwiches; authentic 1920s soda fountain; idleberry pie (with blueberries, blackberries, and boysenberries). [$] *Average main: $12* ✉ *24 S. Main St., Brigham City*

☎ 435/734–2468 🌐 www.idleislecafe.com 🕒 Closed Sun.

Maddox Ranch House

$$ | **AMERICAN** | **FAMILY** | Just a little south of Brigham City, this down-home log-cabin-style eatery is one of the most celebrated family-owned restaurants in Utah, a favorite since the late 1940s. The Maddox family serves stick-to-your-ribs Western fare—the fried chicken, Porterhouse steaks and bison rib eyes are big enough to satisfy a ranch hand, especially if you factor in generous sides of vegetables, potatoes, and homemade soups, plus fresh-baked dinner rolls served with raspberry honey-butter. **Known for:** attached retro burger drive-in with carhop service; fresh peach pie; no alcohol. *[$] Average main: $21 ✉ 1900 S. U.S. 89, Perry ☎ 435/723–8545, 800/544–5474 🌐 www.maddoxfinefood.com 🕒 Closed Sun. and Mon.*

Hotels

Best Western Brigham City

$ | **HOTEL** | Less than 2 miles off Interstate 15 on the edge of downtown Brigham City, this two-story Best Western with views of the mountains is a convenient, affordable base for exploring the area, from Bear Lake to Promontory. **Pros:** good prices; pet-friendly; less than 30 minutes from Logan and Ogden. **Cons:** ho-hum design; no elevator; nothing much within walking distance. *[$] Rooms from: $115 ✉ 480 Westland Dr., Brigham City ☎ 435/723–0440 🌐 www.bestwestern.com 🛏 53 rooms 🍴 Free Breakfast.*

Logan

25 miles northeast of Brigham City.

Mormon pioneers created the permanent settlement of Logan in 1859, but the town didn't become prominent until 1888, when it was chosen as the site for Utah's land-grant agricultural college, now called Utah State University (USU). Logan is now the hub of the dramatic Cache Valley, which is walled in on the west by the imposing Wellsville Mountains (often touted as having the steepest incline of any range in the country) and on the east by the Bear River Range (a subrange of the Wasatch).

Historic Main Street is best explored on foot and contains a number of noteworthy buildings. In addition to the USU campus and its handful of museums, Logan draws visitors in summer for its nationally acclaimed Utah Festival Opera and is a great little city for outdoor recreation. The Logan Canyon Scenic Byway (U.S. 89) leads east from town and offers terrific hiking, and there are some fun family-friendly ski areas nearby as well. It's also within day-tripping distance of Bear Lake's western shore beaches.

GETTING HERE AND AROUND

Head up U.S. 89 from Brigham City through Sardine Canyon and you'll arrive at the beautiful Cache Valley and the city of Logan. Although downtown is quite walkable, you'll find a car the most convenient way to get here and explore the scenic attractions in the vicinity.

VISITOR INFORMATION

Cache Valley Visitors Bureau

✉ 199 N. Main St., Logan ☎ 435/755–1890 🌐 www.explorelogan.com.

Sights

American West Heritage Center

MUSEUM VILLAGE | **FAMILY** | On U.S. 89/91 en route to Logan from points south, this 160-acre living history museum interprets the Cache Valley's development from 1820 to 1920. At the farm, antique implements are on display, draft horses still pull their weight, pony and train rides entertain the kids, and docents dressed in period clothing demonstrate sheepshearing and carding and offer bison tours. Baby Animal Days is popular in the spring, and the fall corn maze is actually quite challenging. Late July's Pioneer Festival features additional displays and reenactments, along with food booths, cowboy poetry readings, ice-cream making, and concerts. ✉ *4025 S. U.S. 89/91, Wellsville* ☎ *435/245–6050* ⊕ *www. awhc.org* ✆ *$7* ☉ *Closed Sun. and Mon.*

Hardware Wildlife Management Area

FARM/RANCH | FAMILY | In winter, it's worth taking the picturesque mountain drive about 25 miles east of Logan to Blacksmith Fork Canyon, where the Utah Division of Wildlife Resources feeds 500 to 600 elk during the snowy months. A 20-minute sleigh ride takes you up close to the majestic creatures. Dress warmly in layers. The visitor center is only open December through early February, when tours are offered, but from spring through fall, the area is also popular for hiking and wildlife viewing. ✉ *Off Hwy. 101, Hyrum* ☎ *435/753–6206, 435/753–6168* ⊕ *wildlife.utah.gov/hardware-visit. html* ✆ *Free* ☉ *Visitor center closed mid-Feb.–early Dec.*

★ **Logan Canyon Scenic Byway**

SCENIC DRIVE | Connecting the Cache Valley and Logan to Bear Lake, the Logan Canyon Scenic Byway (U.S. 89) is perhaps best known for its vibrant fall colors. A photographer's dream in autumn, the canyon also thrills snowmobilers in the winter and wildflower watchers in spring. Towering limestone walls follow the path of the Logan River through the Bear River Mountains and provide ample opportunity for rock climbing. Hiking, fishing, biking, and horseback riding are also popular all along this route. High in the canyon's mountains, Tony Grove Lake and its campground provide a serene escape, and a trail from the lake leads to Naomi Peak, the highest point in the Bear River Mountains. ✉ *U.S. 89, Logan.*

Logan Tabernacle

HISTORIC SIGHT | It took Mormon settlers 27 years to build the tabernacle, which they completed in 1891. Today's tabernacle is a venue for concerts and lectures.

You can also tour the building or search for information about your family history at the genealogical research facility. ✉ *50 Main St., Logan* ☎ *435/227–0013.*

★ **Tony Grove Lake and Naomi Peak**

SCENIC DRIVE | From Logan, U.S. 89 continues for 30 miles up Logan Canyon before topping out at the crest of the Bear River Range (from which it continues another 10 miles to Bear Lake). For a particularly satisfying excursion that leads to awesome hiking and mountain biking, drive the well-signed 7-mile side road to Tony Grove Lake. At more than 8,000 feet, this subalpine jewel is surrounded by cliffs and meadows filled in summer with a stunning profusion of wildflowers. A short trail circles the lake. Mountain bikers and hikers alike can access a prime wilderness area via the 3.3-mile one-way route from the lake to the 9,984-foot summit of Naomi Peak, which offers 80-mile views on clear days. With a gain almost 2,000 feet in elevation, the hike passes through conifer forests and open meadows and along subalpine basins and rocky ledges. A shorter hike to White Pine Lake, which begins on the same trail and splits after a quarter of a mile, is also lovely. ✉ *Tony Grove Rd., Logan* ⊕ *www.fs.usda.gov/uwcnf* ✆ *$7 per vehicle.*

★ **Utah State University**

COLLEGE | Established in 1888 as a small agricultural school, USU now enrolls around 27,000 students and is an intellectual and technological leader in land, water, space, and life enhancement. The scenic, 400-acre campus is best toured by starting at the historic Old Main administration building east of downtown Logan—look for the bell tower. Inside the building you'll find the Museum of Anthropology, which contains an impressive collection of prehistoric and contemporary Native American artifacts and cultural works. The first Saturday of each month features family-friendly exploration of a specific country through its food,

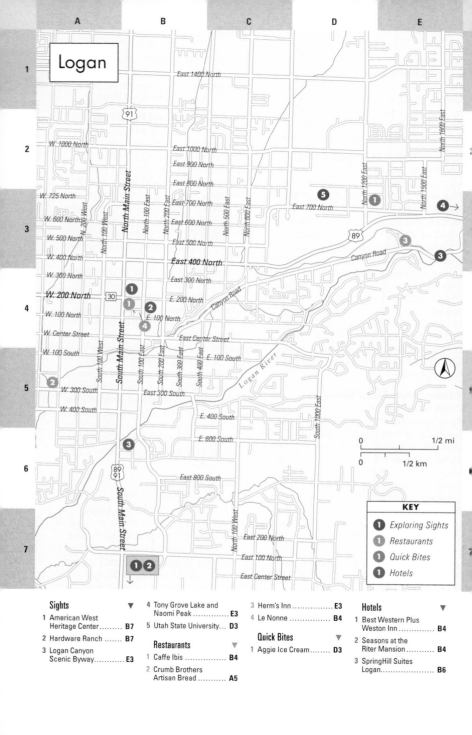

Logan

Sights ▼

1 American West Heritage Center......... **B7**
2 Hardware Ranch **B7**
3 Logan Canyon Scenic Byway............. **E3**
4 Tony Grove Lake and Naomi Peak **E3**
5 Utah State University... **D3**

Restaurants ▼

1 Caffe Ibis **B4**
2 Crumb Brothers Artisan Bread **A5**
3 Herm's Inn **E3**
4 Le Nonne **B4**

Quick Bites ▼

1 Aggie Ice Cream........ **D3**

Hotels ▼

1 Best Western Plus Weston Inn **B4**
2 Seasons at the Riter Mansion **B4**
3 SpringHill Suites Logan..................... **B6**

art, crafts, and music. Also worth a stop is the Nora Eccles Harrison Museum of Art, which is in a striking contemporary building a few blocks northeast of the campus Quad and contains a permanent collection as well as mounting rotating shows. You can also pick up a map here of sculptures and public art visible throughout the campus. ✉ *Old Main Hill at Champ Dr., Logan* ☎ *435/797–1000* 🌐 *www.usu.edu.*

🍴 Restaurants

Caffe Ibis

$ | **CAFÉ** | Inside this handsome café with ample seating and live music on weekend evenings, you'll see shiny brass canisters brimming with shade-grown, organic, fair-trade coffee beans ground daily at the local off-site roastery. In addition to tasty drinks, Ibis serves a nice array of breakfast and lunch entrées, such as avocado toast with farm eggs and roasted-veggie sandwiches. **Known for:** superbly crafted coffee drinks; hip and down-to-earth crowd; weekend brunch. [$] *Average main: $11* ✉ *52 Federal Ave., Logan* ☎ *435/753–4777* 🌐 *www.caffeibis.com* 🕒 *No dinner.*

★ Crumb Brothers Artisan Bread

$ | **BAKERY** | The thick-crusted artisan breads served in this airy, verdant, and much beloved bakery are fantastic on their own or in an impressive roster of freshly prepared sandwiches, like the bacon, avocado, egg, and provolone on ciabatta or the banh mi on a crisp baguette, available vegan or with pork belly. Some of the most creative fare incorporates house-made organic bread as an ingredient, from bread pudding to panzanella, and there's an ever-changing array of ethereal pastries. **Known for:** daily-rotating pizzettas with inventive toppings; pretty garden patio; beer, wine, and champagne cocktails. [$] *Average main: $9* ✉ *291 S. 300 W, Logan* ☎ *435/753–0875* 🌐 *www.crumbbrothers.com* 🕒 *No dinner.*

★ Herm's Inn

$ | **AMERICAN** | Famous for its pizza-size cinnamon swirl pancakes, this popular breakfast and lunch spot is often jam-packed with students from Utah State University or hikers headed to Logan Canyon, but it's worth the wait. The meat-lover's breakfast skillet with eggs, toast, ham, bacon, sausage, and cheddar will fuel you up before a big hike, while the burger on marble rye topped with caramelized garlic and onions, Swiss cheese, and garlic mayo is a lunchtime specialty. **Known for:** patio with fireplace overlooking Logan Canyon; killer breakfasts; open Sunday (which is rare for the area). [$] *Average main: $10* ✉ *1435 Canyon Rd., Logan* ☎ *435/792–4321* 🌐 *www.hermsinn.com* 🕒 *No dinner; closed Mon.*

Le Nonne

$$ | **ITALIAN** | Housed in a courtly converted Victorian home, this sophisticated restaurant features northern Italian cuisine—such as rigatoni *amatriciana*, sweet-potato ravioli, and thinly sliced, oven-baked steak *tagliata* with sun-dried tomatoes—crafted by a chef born and raised in Tuscany. Live jazz some evenings wafts through the cozy dining room and the outdoor patio nestled in a garden. **Known for:** romantic dining room with attentive service; pre-theater dining; nicely curated wine list. [$] *Average main: $22* ✉ *129 N. 100 E, Logan* ☎ *435/752–9577* 🌐 *www.lenonne.com* 🕒 *No lunch; closed Sun.*

☕ Coffee and Quick Bites

★ Aggie Ice Cream

$ | **CAFÉ** | **FAMILY** | The pride and joy of Utah State University dairy students, this historic ice-cream shop on campus has been making ice cream "from cow to cone" for 100 years. The luscious creations use milk from cows that live on USU's farm and a recipe and production process that's been perfected over the last century. **Known for:** lines out the door on hot days; Aggie Blue Mint–flavored ice

Utah State University in Logan has an impressive Museum of Anthropology as well as a nice art museum.

cream; thick shakes and malts. $ *Average main: $5* ⊠ *Nutrition & Food Science Bldg., USU, 750 N. 1200 E, Logan* ☎ *435/797–2109, 888/586–2735* ⊕ *www.aggieicecream.usu.edu* ▬ *No credit cards* ⊘ *Closed Sun.*

Hotels

Best Western Plus Weston Inn

$$ | **HOTEL** | This reasonably priced, centrally located Best Western is ideal for being close to downtown dining and attractions, and with free parking and a hot breakfast, it's a good value. **Pros:** walking distance of theaters and restaurants; good-size indoor pool; free parking in front of or near your room. **Cons:** standard chain furnishings; small bathrooms; some street noise. $ *Rooms from: $149* ⊠ *250 N. Main St., Logan* ☎ *435/752–5700* ⊕ *www.bestwestern.com* ⤴ *89 rooms* ❍ *Free Breakfast.*

★ The Riter Mansion

$$ | **B&B/INN** | In a quiet residential area just a short walk from Main Street, this beautifully restored Greek Revival–Georgian mansion is perfect for a romantic getaway or as a cozy retreat, its suites warmly decorated and outfitted with whirlpool baths and, in many cases, fireplaces. **Pros:** surrounded by fragrant gardens and mature shade trees; within walking distance of downtown; fantastic breakfasts. **Cons:** sometimes booked for weddings and events; not a good option for kids; antique-y aesthetic may not please modernists. $ *Rooms from: $149* ⊠ *168 N. 100 E, Logan* ☎ *435/752–7727* ⊕ *www.theritermansion.com* ⤴ *6 rooms* ❍ *Free Breakfast.*

SpringHill Suites by Marriott Logan

$$ | **HOTEL** | Logan's most upscale hotel offers bright and modern all-suite accommodations that are nicely outfitted for families and for longer stays, each with separate sitting areas, refrigerators and microwaves, high-end pull-out sleeper sofas, and flat-screen TVs. **Pros:** very nice indoor pool and fitness center; substantial complimentary breakfast buffet; quiet but fairly central location. **Cons:**

sometimes books up with convention-eers; 15-minute walk to city center; no pets. $ *Rooms from: $159* ⊠ *635 S. Riverwoods Pkwy., Logan* ☏ *435/750–5180* ⊕ *www.marriott.com* ⮆ *115 suites* ⦿ *Free Breakfast.*

Performing Arts

★ Ellen Eccles Theatre

MUSIC | This European-style theater, with ornate balconies, murals, and frescoes, was built in 1923 and restored to its original grandeur in 1993. Cache Valley Center for the Arts brings about a dozen national touring productions here each year, including musicals, dance, comedy, and concerts. ⊠ *43 S. Main St., Logan* ☏ *435/752–0026* ⊕ *www.cachearts.org.*

★ Utah Festival Opera & Musical Theatre

OPERA | Each summer this highly respected company presents a five-week season at Logan's Utah Theatre, Ellen Eccles Theatre, and the Dasante Building. Featuring nationally renowned performers from across the country, the productions dazzle. ⊠ *59 S. 100 W, Logan* ☏ *435/750–0300, 800/262–0074* ⊕ *www.utahfestival.org.*

🛍 Shopping

COSMETICS

The Spirit Goat

COSMETICS | Just steps from Main Street, this family-owned shop specializes in skin care products made from goat's milk. Filled with aromatic fragrances like cranberry orange, citrus, and lavender, the quaint shop has an in-store workshop and brims with more than 80 varieties of soaps, plus body lotions and other gifts. ⊠ *28 Federal Ave., Logan* ☏ *435/512–9040* ⊕ *www.spiritgoat.com.*

FOOD

Cox Honeyland and Gifts

OTHER SPECIALTY STORE | Specializing in honey products, this Logan landmark, operated by the Cox family for four

generations, offers pure raw honey, fresh fudge and candy, gift baskets, and skin and body items. ⊠ *1780 S. Hwy. 89, Logan* ☏ *435/752–3234* ⊕ *www.coxhoney.com* ⊗ *Closed Sun.*

MARKETS

Cache Valley Gardeners' Market

MARKET | From early May through mid-October, Utah's oldest local farmers' market is held every Saturday from 9 to 1, outside the Cache Historic Court-house. The market features regional produce vendors, locally made goods, and live music. ⊠ *199 N. Main St., Logan* ☏ *435/754–7402* ⊕ *gardenersmarket.org.*

Activities

The beautiful Cache Valley is a stunning destination for outdoor adventures. Dom-inated by mountains east and west and by the lazy Bear River snaking through the bottomlands, it's ideal for fly-fishing on the Logan River and Blacksmith Fork as well as birding and paddling in marsh-es. Road cyclists pedal out to the long, flat country roads of the scenic Cache Valley or venture up Logan and Black-smith Fork Canyons. Mountain bikers can spend an afternoon on the 9-mile round-trip from Wood Camp, in Logan Canyon, to the 1,500-year-old Jardine juniper tree that grows on a high ridge offering views of Wyoming and Idaho. Hiking trails for all abilities are just minutes away from downtown Logan, while more arduous treks await you in Uinta-Wasatch-Cache National Forest, especially out around Tony Grove and White Pine Lakes.

BIKING AND HIKING

★ Logan Canyon

HIKING & WALKING | You'll find some gor-geous hikes just a few miles up Logan Canyon from town, starting with the popular and easy Logan River Trail, which meanders along the river for nearly 4 miles and is suitable for all skill levels. The wide passageway accommodates dogs and even strollers, and it passes both the family-friendly Stokes Nature Center and picturesque Second Dam, which has a lovely picnic area. A few miles' drive farther east of the Logan River Trailhead, you'll reach the parking lot for the Crimson Trail, a more rugged but also rewarding 5-mile loop along the dramatic China Wall crag that offers eye-popping views throughout the canyon. Note that it entails an elevation gain of about 1,345 feet, and it is a bit steep in places. Just a mile farther up U.S. 89, park near Guinavah-Malibu Campground to access the famed Wind Caves Trail, which is a 3½-mile hike that's only moderately challenging and ascends about 1,000 feet through wildflower-strewn meadows and conifer forests to a fanciful triple-arch rock formation sometimes nicknamed the "Witch's Castle." ⊠ *Logan River Trailhead, 2696 U.S. 89, Logan* ⊕ *www.fs.usda.gov/uwcnf.*

SKIING

Beaver Mountain Ski Area

SKIING & SNOWBOARDING | FAMILY | Family-owned and operated since 1939, this locals' favorite is a 21-mile drive from Logan and offers skiing like it was before it became an expensive sport. See aerial tricks or try night skiing (until 9 pm) at the two terrain parks. There aren't any trendy nightspots at the foot of this mountain, just an old-fashioned A-frame lodge with burgers and chili. ⊠ *12400 E. 12900 N, Logan* ☏ *435/946–3610* ⊕ *www.skithebeav.com* 🎟 *Lift tickets $60* ⌖ *1,700-foot vertical drop; 828 skiable acres; 48 runs; 35% beginner, 40% intermediate, 25% advanced; 3 triple chairs, 1 double chair.*

Cherry Peak Resort

SKIING & SNOWBOARDING | FAMILY | Twenty minutes from Logan, Utah's newest ski area, is also the state's most affordable place to board or ski. Night skiing and tubing make this a fun place for families, as do summertime concerts, mountain biking, and a water slide. ⊠ *3200 E. 11000 N, Richmond* ☏ *435/200–5050* ⊕ *www.skicpr.com* 🎟 *Lift ticket $39*

⊘ *Closed Sun.* ⌖ *1,265-foot vertical drop; 400-plus skiable acres; 30% beginner, 35% intermediate, 35% advanced; 3 triple chair lifts, 1 surface lift.*

Garden City

41 miles northeast of Logan.

Nearly 6,000 feet above sea level and quite remote, Bear Lake straddles the Utah–Idaho border. Known for its vibrant blue water rivaling Lake Tahoe, it's one of the most beautiful alpine lakes in America. Garden City (population 615), on the lake's western shore and reached via scenic U.S. 89 from Logan, offers most of the lake area's few dining and lodging options, which tend to book up quickly during the warmer months (some are closed in winter). From here, it can take 90 minutes to circle the 109-square-mile lake by car, especially if it's a busy summer weekend (and in winter, the road around the lake is sometimes closed due to snow).

The area's abundance of raspberries is celebrated each year in early August at Raspberry Days. A parade, a rodeo, fireworks, and entertainment are almost eclipsed by the main event: sampling myriad raspberry concoctions. Garden City is a perfect base for swimming, boating, fishing, Jet Skiing, and a chance to sample the region's famous raspberry shakes. In winter, those in the know come to enjoy the miles of snowy terrain, which offer cross-country skiing and snowmobiling.

GETTING HERE AND AROUND

Garden City is where you'll find most of the services and businesses in the Bear Lake region. It has a walkable downtown, but you need a car to get around the area.

VISITOR INFORMATION

CONTACTS Bear Lake Convention and Visitors Bureau. ⊠ *69 N. Paradise Pkwy., Garden City* ☏ *435/946–2197, 800/448–2327* ⊕ *www.bearlake.org.*

Sights

★ Bear Lake State Park

BODY OF WATER | FAMILY | Eight miles wide and 20 miles long, Bear Lake is an unusually radiant shade of blue, thanks to limestone particles suspended in the water. The Utah half of the lake is a state park. Along the south shore of Bear Lake, Highway 30 traces an old route used by Native Americans, mountain men, and settlers following the Oregon Trail. Harsh winters persuaded most settlers to move on before the first snows, but hardy Mormon pioneers settled in the area and founded Garden City. From town you can stroll along a ¼-mile boardwalk through a small wetlands preserve to the lakeshore, and there's a large marina just to the north. The park operates a few other recreation areas along other parts of the shore, including **Rendezvous Beach** to the south, which has a marina and burger stand, and **Cisco Beach** on the lake's quieter eastern shore, where the lake bottom drops off quickly, making it a favorite spot among anglers and scuba divers. The lake is home to four species of fish found nowhere else, including the Bonneville cisco, which draws anglers during the January spawning season. ✉ *U.S. 89 at Hwy. 30, Garden City* ☎ *435/946–3343* 🌐 *stateparks.utah.gov/parks/bear-lake* 🎫 *From $15 per vehicle.*

Restaurants

★ Campfire Grill

$$$ | MODERN AMERICAN | FAMILY | Located within Garden City's distinctive Conestoga Ranch glamping resort, this rambling and scenic seasonal restaurant (housed in a tent with a firepit overlooking the property's covered wagons) is the most distinctive dining destination in town, and one of the most upscale too. Serving creative American fare throughout the day—including a popular brunch on Sundays—this open-air eatery offers delicious pancakes with maple-macerated berries, shrimp with smoked-cheddar grits, an array of wood-fired pizzas, and other enticing dishes. **Known for:** Wagyu burgers and meat loaf; open-air dining with glorious lake views; s'mores and ice cream. [$] *Average main: $25* ✉ *427 N. Paradise Pkwy., Garden City* ☎ *385/626–7395* 🌐 *www.campfiregrillrestaurant.com* ⏲ *Closed Oct.–mid-May.*

LaBeau's Drive-in

$ | FAST FOOD | The Bear Lake region is well known for its locally grown raspberries, and this is the most popular spot in town to enjoy a thick and creamy raspberry shake. Choose from 45 other shake flavors along with a menu of old-fashioned hamburgers, hot dogs, and chicken sandwiches, and if you haven't tried Utah's signature condiment, "fry sauce" (i.e., ketchup and mayo), LaBeau's is a good place for that too. **Known for:** pastrami burgers; people-watching at outdoor picnic tables; thick milkshakes in dozens of flavors. [$] *Average main: $9* ✉ *69 N. Bear Lake Blvd.* 🌐 *www.labeaus.com* ⏲ *Closed Sun. and late Sept.–late May.*

Coffee and Quick Bites

Ruca's

$ | CAFÉ | Specializing in *aebleskivers* (fluffy, round Danish pancakes) topped with Nutella and strawberries and any number of other sweet toppings along with overstuffed sandwiches, this cute counter-service eatery is a fun spot for breakfast or lunch all summer long. This is also Bear Lake's go-to for espresso and coffee drinks, and there's an extensive menu of gourmet milk shakes, too. **Known for:** Danish aebleskivers; raspberry milkshakes; outdoor seating overlooking the lake. [$] *Average main: $10* ✉ *284 S. Bear Lake Blvd., Garden City* ☎ *435/946–3691* 🌐 *www.facebook.com/Rucasbearlake* ⏲ *Closed Mon.–Thurs. and mid-Oct.–mid-May.*

Hotels

The Bluebird Inn Family Vacation Retreat
$$$$ | **HOUSE** | This charming lodging option on the western shore of Bear Lake happens to be just over the border in Idaho, set on a grassy bluff near Bear Lake West Golf Course and offering two vacation homes decorated with country furnishings and colorful quilts. **Pros:** cozy lodging option for large families; grand lake and mountain views; 10-minute drive to downtown Garden City. **Cons:** only one restaurant within walking distance; no TVs; some may find the decor too frilly. [$] *Rooms from: $349* ✉ *423 U.S. 89* ☎ *435/881–7246* 🌐 *www.thebluebirdinn.com* 🛏 *1 2-bedroom house, 1 5-bedroom house* 🍴 *No Meals.*

Ideal Beach Resort
$$$ | **RESORT** | **FAMILY** | A private beach awaits at this traditional family-friendly condo resort offering two- to four-bedroom accommodations that vary in size and amenities, but all with fully equipped kitchens and easy access to pools, hot tubs, saunas, tennis, miniature golf, a children's playground, and a kids' activity center. **Pros:** tons of activities for families; five-minute drive from Garden City dining; direct beach access. **Cons:** with so many kids around, it can get a little loud; some units could use updating; expensive in summer high season. [$] *Rooms from: $244* ✉ *2176 S. Bear Lake Blvd., Garden City* ☎ *435/946–3364* 🌐 *www.idealbeachresort.com* 🛏 *60 units* 🍴 *No Meals.*

Activities

BIKING
Cyclists of all abilities can enjoy all or any portion of the level 48-mile ride on the road circling Bear Lake. The paved Lakeside Bicycle Path curves from Bear Lake Marina south and east along the shore, with several rest stops. Interpretive signs relate stories about Bear Lake's history and local lore.

BOATING
Personal watercraft, kayaks, pontoons, and motorboats are available at the Bear Lake Marina and in the surrounding towns. Prices vary from about $70 per hour for a PWC to $150 an hour and up for large motorboats capable of towing water-skiers and wakeboarders. Be advised that the winds at this mountain lake can change 180 degrees within minutes (or go from 30 knots to completely calm), so be cautious. Life jackets are required for everyone on board vessels up to 40 feet.

FISHING
The Logan River and Blacksmith Fork are blue-ribbon trout streams. You can pull Bear Lake cutthroat out of Bear Lake from mid-April through June, or join the locals in dip-netting Bear Lake cisco when they come to shore to spawn in January. Warm-water species are found in abundance in Mantua Reservoir, 4 miles east of Brigham City on Highway 89. In the Bear River you'll find mostly carp. For a novelty fishing experience, boat out to the middle of Tony Grove Lake and use a long line with plenty of sinkers to land one of the rare albino rainbow trout that frequent the depths of the lake.

HIKING
At 9,980 feet, Naomi Peak is the highest point of the Bear River Range in Uinta-Wasatch-Cache National Forest. The 3.2-mile Naomi Peak Trail starts in the parking lot of the Tony Grove Campground and gains almost 2,000 feet in elevation. You hike through conifer forests and open meadows and along subalpine basins and rocky ledges. A shorter hike to White Pine Lake, which begins on the same trail and splits after a quarter of a mile, is also lovely. To reach the trailhead, take Highway 89 southwest from Garden City for approximately 15 miles to the Tony Grove turnoff, then follow the signs. Closer to Garden City is the Limber Pine Nature Trail, a popular and easy hike (1 mile round-trip) at the summit between Logan Canyon and Bear Lake that features interpretive information especially designed for children.

Chapter 6

DINOSAURLAND AND EASTERN UTAH

6

Updated by
Stina Sieg

 Sights
★★★★☆

 Restaurants
★★☆☆☆

 Hotels
★★☆☆☆

 Shopping
★☆☆☆☆

🍸 Nightlife
☆☆☆☆☆

WELCOME TO DINOSAURLAND AND EASTERN UTAH

TOP REASONS TO GO

★ **Flaming Gorge:** With its red canyon walls and blue-green water, the Flaming Gorge National Recreation Area is the most jaw-dropping spot in northeastern Utah.

★ **Dinosaurs:** Come to Dinosaur National Monument to see the famed dinosaur fossils or just to explore some truly remote country.

★ **Ancient art:** Explore the towering cliffs near Vernal and Price to find numerous displays of ancient petroglyphs and pictographs, drawn once upon a time by members of the Fremont tribe.

★ **Biking Vernal:** Explore the countless mountain biking trails, many of them former cow trails, in the high desert surrounding the area's largest community.

★ **Solitude:** The San Rafael Swell is one of the least crowded desert recreation areas in a region that's already known for its sparse population.

This section of Utah is large, but it's easy to get around, with little traffic between its sparsely spaced towns. The main highways to explore this area are U.S. 191 and U.S. 40.

1 Vernal. The largest city in the region (though still pretty small) and a major hub for Dinosaurland.

2 Dinosaur National Monument. Home to ancient dinosaur fossils and stunning landscapes.

3 Flaming Gorge National Recreation Area. An astounding reservoir and 91-mile-wide canyon with excellent fishing and boating.

4 Roosevelt. A small town close to the Uintah and Ouray Reservation.

5 Duchesne. A good stopping point for visits to Fred Hayes State Park at Starvation.

6 Price. Home to several major dinosaur sites and the San Rafael Swell.

7 Helper. A former mining town with a dramatic red-rock backdrop being transformed by artists.

8 Mirror Lake Scenic Byway. A gorgeous road that takes you through the Uinta Mountains.

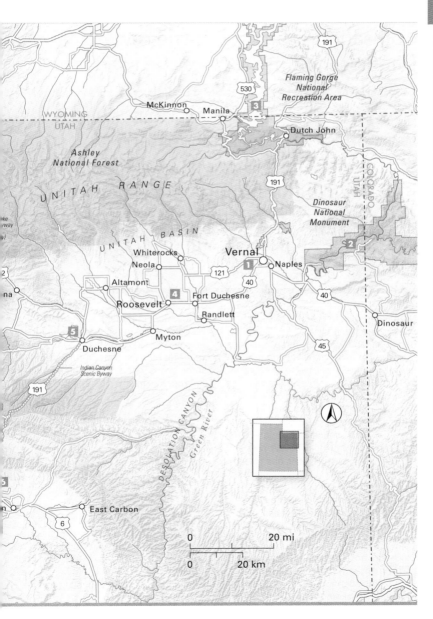

WYOMING
UTAH

Flaming Gorge
National
Recreation Area

191

530

McKinnon   Manila

3

Dutch John

Ashley
National Forest

191

U N I T A H   R A N G E

COLORADO
UTAH

Dinosaur
National
Monument

U N I T A H   B A S I N

ke
way

Whiterocks

Vernal

Neola

1   Naples

2

121

40

Altamont

na

4   Fort Duchesne

Roosevelt

40

Randlett

5

Myton

Dinosaur

Duchesne

45

Indian Canyon
Scenic Byway

191

DECORATION CANYON

Green River

East Carbon

6

20 mi

0

0   20 km

The rugged beauty of Utah's northeastern corner, wedged neatly between Wyoming to the north and Colorado to the east, is the reward for those willing to take the road less traveled. Neither I–80 nor I–70 enters this part of the state, so most visitors who pass through the western United States never even see it—that is part of its appeal. Small towns, rural attitudes, and a more casual and friendly approach to life are all part of the eastern Utah experience.

Northeastern Utah is home to superb boating and fishing at Flaming Gorge, Red Fleet, and Steinaker Reservoirs. Hundreds of miles of hiking and mountain-biking trails (available to cross-country skiers, snowmobilers, or snowshoers in winter) crisscross the region. The Green and Yampa Rivers entice white-water rafters as well as less ambitious float-trippers. The pine- and aspen-covered Uinta Mountains offer campers and hikers hidden, pristine lakes and streams surrounded by amazing mountain views. Even if you don't get out of the car, exploring this region on the road takes you through vast red-rock basins, over high mountain passes, and between geologic folds in the earth.

Dinosaurs once dominated this region, and in many ways, they still do. Excavation sites such as Dinosaur National Monument make northeastern Utah one of the most important paleontological research areas in the world. Paleontology labs and fossil displays can be found at roadside stops and on off-road adventures, along with kitschy dino statues and impressive life-size skeleton casts.

Ancient Native American cultures also left their marks throughout the region. Cliff walls and boulders are dotted with thousands of examples of rock art of the Fremont people (AD 600 to 1300), so called because they inhabited the region near the Fremont River. Today, the Uintah and Ouray Reservation is the second largest in the United States. It covers a significant portion of eastern Utah, though much of the reservation's original land grant was reclaimed by the U.S. government for its mineral and timber resources. The Ute Tribe, whose 3,000-some members inhabit the land, hold powwows and host other cultural ceremonies available to the public.

Museums throughout the region are full of fascinating pioneer relics, and there are a number of restored homesteads in and around Vernal. The rich mining and railroad history of the Price–Helper area fuels the tall tales you're certain to hear of outlaws, robberies, mine disasters, and heroes of the past.

Planning

Getting Here and Around

AIR

The closest major airport is Salt Lake City International Airport—two hours from Price and three hours from Vernal; it's served by most major airlines.

CAR

Both U.S. 40 and U.S. 191 are well maintained but have some curvy, mountainous stretches. Away from major towns, be prepared for much smaller dirt roads. Keep your vehicle fueled up because gas stations can be far apart, and some are closed on Sunday. Watch for wildlife on the road, especially at night. Price is the largest city on U.S. 6, the major route between the Wasatch Front and the southeastern part of the state. Dinosaur National Monument (which spans the Utah–Colorado border) is about 3½ hours east of Salt Lake City on U.S. 40, or 2½ hours northeast of Price via U.S. 191 and U.S. 40. Flaming Gorge is 40 miles north of Vernal via U.S. 191. The Uinta Mountains and the High Uintas Wilderness area are about 1½ hours east of Salt Lake City, first via I–80, U.S. 40, and Highway 248 to Kamas, and then via Highway 150.

Hotels

Many hotels and motels in eastern Utah are chains, and you can expect clean, comfortable rooms and standard amenities. The area's lodges make for a nice change of pace when desired, surrounding you with natural beauty and more individualized rooms and services. Though it goes against logic, many hotels here offer cheaper rates on weekends than weekdays, due to the high number of workers who stay during the week. On weekends, hotels and motels do their best to attract tourists.

Restaurant and hotel reviews have been shortened. For full information, visit Fodors.com.

What It Costs			
$	$$	$$$	$$$$
RESTAURANTS			
under $16	$16–$22	$23–$30	over $30
HOTELS			
under $125	$125–$200	$201–$300	over $300

Planning Your Time

The two biggest draws in this area are the **Flaming Gorge National Recreation Area** and **Dinosaur National Monument.** While it's reasonable to see the fossils on display at Dinosaur in just a day, you'll get a better sense of the park's untouched natural beauty if you stay overnight. Nearby **Vernal** has plenty of hotels and motels to choose from. Likewise, you can spend a day or several hiking the trails and playing in the water at **Flaming Gorge.** A good base for your adventures is **Price,** a pleasant town about 90 miles from the stunning **San Rafael Swell,** a huge, oval-shape, geologic dome that's far from everything but worth the trek. You could easily spend a few days exploring these unique areas. If you can make the time, a one or multiday excursion on the **Green, White,** or **Yampa River** would be an unforgettable—and occasionally heart-pounding—addition to your stay.

Restaurants

Because the towns in eastern Utah are small, dining options are generally more casual and less innovative than you may find in big cities. The best dining in this part of the state can be found in upscale lodges—including Red Canyon Lodge and Flaming Gorge Resort, both near the Flaming Gorge National Recreation Area—which pride themselves on gourmet menus. Vernal, historically a farming and ranching town, has good steak houses and tasty diner eats. Price has a mix of diverse restaurants representing its immigrant railroad and mining history. Bear in mind that most locally owned restaurants are closed on Sunday.

The area also has a handful of brewpubs, the best of which is the trendy Vernal Brewing Company, which serves its own beers on tap, along with an assortment of burgers, pizzas, and other pub favorites.

Visitor Information

VISITOR INFORMATION Bureau of Land Management. ⊠ *125 S. 600 W, Price* ☎ *435/636–3600* ⊕ *www.blm.gov/ut.* **Visit Dinosaurland.** ⊠ *152 E. 100 N, Vernal* ☎ *800/477–5558* ⊕ *www.dinoland.com.*

When to Go

In northeastern Utah most museums, parks, and other sights extend their hours from Memorial Day to Labor Day or through the end of September. (Some museums and parks are open only in summer.) Summer (when temperatures can reach 100°F) also brings art festivals,

pioneer reenactments, rodeos, and other celebrations. Spring and autumn are cooler and less crowded. Some campgrounds are open year-round, but the drinking water is usually turned off after Labor Day. In winter you can cross-country ski or snowshoe on many of the hiking trails.

Vernal

173 miles east of Salt Lake City, 22 miles east of Fort Duchesne.

Vernal, the county seat of Uinta County, is the hub of Dinosaurland, mixing the region's ancient heritage with a certain kitschy charm—think down-home diners and giant dino statues. Dinosaurs aren't the only things they're proud of in Vernal, though. The town claims a connection to the ancient Fremont people, a rowdy ranching past, and more than a passing acquaintance with outlaws like Butch Cassidy, who frequented the area whenever he felt it was safe to be seen around town.

Legend has it that the saloonkeepers of Vernal gave Butch's gang the name "Wild Bunch," muttering "There goes that wild bunch" whenever the outlaws rolled in. Now the largest town (population 10,000) in the northeast corner of the state, this cattle-ranching and oil-and-gas community is one of the few Utah towns founded by non-Mormons. However, it was its remote location, far from government authorities, that led to its early reputation as a wild and lawless place. These days it's more of a tame, friendly spot to cool your heels between trips to outlying areas; it's also full of opportunities for biking and river adventures.

GETTING HERE AND AROUND
Though secluded, it's easy to get to Vernal. From Salt Lake City, head 25 miles via I–80, then 145 miles east via U.S. 40/U.S. 191; from Price go east on U.S. 40. Most of Vernal's attractions are right on Main Street. From Vernal, take

Butch Cassidy, the Robin Hood of Utah

One of the West's most notorious outlaws was born and raised in southern Utah by Mormon parents, and his footprints and legends are scattered over southern and eastern Utah like buckshot. Butch Cassidy (born Robert LeRoy Parker in 1866) started out as a migrant cowboy dabbling in rustling. A brief career as a butcher in Wyoming earned him the nickname "Butch," and "Cassidy" was likely the name of his old rustling mentor.

By 1896 he'd formed a gang of accomplices and had turned from rustling to the more lucrative pursuits of bank and train robberies. His Wild Bunch of loosely knit companions fancied themselves the "Robin Hoods" of the West. Outraged by the way wealthy cattle barons were squeezing out the smaller ranchers, the outlaws justified their lifestyle choice by sharing their bounty with the local people, who often struggled in the harsh environment of the Utah desert. Of course, the fact that this generosity helped buy allies and protectors in the area didn't hurt. Butch Cassidy was well known for being shrewd, quick-witted, and charming.

The only major heist he pulled in Utah was in Price Canyon, near Helper, with his friend Elza Lay. Butch and Elza stole $8,800 in gold coins from the Pleasant Valley Coal Mine office by shoving a gun in the paymaster's belly while 200 men stood nearby waiting for their pay. The steps from the Castle Gate store, where the robbery occurred, are still on display at Helper's Mining & Railroad Museum. The Wild Bunch often wintered near Vernal in Browns Park—a major hideout along the so-called Outlaw Trail, which stretched from Mexico to Montana. Many of the buildings are still visible and on display to visitors today.

After masterminding one of the longest strings of successful bank and train robberies in America, Cassidy eventually escaped to Argentina with Harry Longabaugh (the Sundance Kid) and Longabaugh's girlfriend, Etta Place. What happened then is a source of continuing mystery. Some believe Cassidy and Longabaugh were killed there; others swear the two returned to the American West, living out their days in peaceful anonymity.

U.S. 40 east to reach Dinosaur National Monument, or head north on U.S. 191 to explore the Flaming Gorge National Recreation Area.

VISITOR INFORMATION
CONTACTS Vernal Area Chamber of Commerce. ⊠ 134 W. Main St., Vernal ☎ 435/789–1352 ⊕ www.vernalchamber.com. **Visit Dinosaurland.** ⊠ 152 E. 100 N, Vernal ☎ 800/477–5558 ⊕ www.dinoland.com.

Sights

Browns Park Recreation Area
MUSEUM VILLAGE | FAMILY | If you're looking for a glimpse of the Wild West, head to Browns Park. Lying along a quieter stretch of the Green River and extending into Colorado, this area features plenty of high-desert scenery, a national waterfowl refuge, and a history complete with notorious outlaws of the late 1800s. You can explore several buildings on the John Jarvie Historic Ranch site and visit the museum, where a video details the ranch's history. Buildings date from

1880 to the early 1900s, and there's also a cemetery containing the graves of a few men who met violent ends nearby. In addition to his ranch, Jarvie ran a post office, store, and river ferry, and his spread was a major hideout on the so-called Outlaw Trail. The area also includes several campgrounds, OHV (off-highway vehicle) trails, and river-rafting opportunities. Reach Browns Park by driving 65 miles north of Vernal on U.S. 191, then 22 miles east on a gravel road, following signs to the ranch. ⊠ *Browns Park Rd., Browns Park* ☎ *435/885–3307 John Jarvie Ranch* ⊕ *www.blm.gov/utah* ⊠ *Free.*

Daughters of Utah Pioneers Museum

HISTORY MUSEUM | **FAMILY** | This museum provides a window into the daily lives of the pioneers. The large collection of artifacts (most donated by descendants of the area's early settlers) range from a working loom to guns to a mortician's tools. Most everything is displayed in period rooms, including a shop, a house, and a doctor's office. ⊠ *186 S. 500 W, Vernal* ☎ *435/789–0352* ⊠ *Free* ⊙ *Closed Sept.–May and Sun.–Tues.*

★ Dry Fork Canyon

INDIGENOUS SIGHT | **FAMILY** | An impressive array of Native American petroglyphs and pictographs adorn the 200-foot-high cliffs in Dry Fork Canyon, making the 22-mile round-trip drive from Vernal well worth your time. Two trails leading to the rock art are on McConkie Ranch, a privately owned property that asks only for a $5 per vehicle donation and respect for the site. Make sure to bring sturdy shoes because both short paths have steep and rough spots. If you call the ranch's number, Jean McConkie McKenzie, who was born and still lives here, will show you her collection of arrowheads and antiques. Her mother, Sadie, first opened the rock art to the public in 1930. ⊠ *3500 Dry Fork Canyon Rd., Vernal* ☎ *435/789–6733* ⊠ *$5 per vehicle donation requested.*

Flaming Gorge–Uintas National Scenic Byway

SCENIC DRIVE | Past Red Fleet Reservoir north of Vernal, U.S. 191 begins to ascend the eastern flank of the Uinta uplift as you head toward Flaming Gorge. The section of U.S. 191 and Highway 44 between Vernal and Manila, Utah, is known as the Flaming Gorge–Uintas National Scenic Byway. Within a distance of 30 miles the road passes through 18 uptilted geologic formations, including the billion-year-old exposed core of the Uinta Mountains, with explanatory signs. The route also provides plenty of opportunity for wildlife-watching and fossil hunting, with several nature trails. Before setting out, pick up a guide at the Utah Field House of Natural History. ⊠ *U.S. 191, Vernal.*

Uintah County Heritage Museum

HISTORY MUSEUM | **FAMILY** | Inside the Uintah County Heritage Museum are collections of Fremont and Ute Indian artifacts, including baskets, water jugs, and beadwork, as well as pioneer items like carriages, guns, saddles, and old-fashioned toys. Be sure to check out the wooden cataract boats built by local river-running legend A. K. Reynolds. They're still in great shape considering they date back to the late 1940s. The most off-beat installation is a collection of kitschy handmade porcelain dolls modeled after the nation's First Ladies, from Martha Washington to Nancy Reagan. ⊠ *155 E. Main St., Vernal* ☎ *435/789–7399* ⊕ *www.uintahmuseum.org* ⊠ *Free (donation requested)* ⊙ *Closed Sun.*

★ Utah Field House of Natural History State Park Museum

SCIENCE MUSEUM | **FAMILY** | Around 150 million years ago, this was the stomping ground of dinosaurs, and you can see rock samples, fossils, Fremont and Ute nation artifacts, and a viewing lab where you can watch paleontologists restore actual fossils. The biggest attraction for kids is undoubtedly the outdoor Dinosaur

Garden with its 18 life-size models of prehistoric creatures, including a T. rex and a woolly mammoth. The Field House also doubles as a visitor center for all of Dinosaurland, so stop here for maps and guides for the entire area. ⌧ 496 E. Main St., Vernal ☎ 435/789–3799 ⊕ stateparks. utah.gov ⌦ $8.

 ## Restaurants

Antica Forma

$$ | **ITALIAN** | **FAMILY** | With a branch in Moab, as well, this popular pizza spot offers Neapolitan-style pies with scrumptious crusts and high-end touches, including house-made fresh mozzarella. There's also a long list of pastas and appetizers, and it's all served from a spacious downtown location that can get absolutely mobbed on Friday and Saturday. **Known for:** personal-size pizzas, enough for one hungry person or two less-ravenous people; beer and wine available (not a given in rural Utah); house-made pizza dough, including a gluten-free option. $ Average main: $19 ⌧ 251 E. Main St., Vernal ☎ 435/374–4138 ⊕ www.anticaforma. com ⊙ Closed Sun.

Betty's Cafe

$ | **AMERICAN** | **FAMILY** | This friendly, no-frills diner has the look of a fast-food joint but brings in tons of locals and tourists alike for meals that will leave you full all day. While lunch is tasty here, too, this is the best spot in Vernal for breakfast. **Known for:** giant portions; huge cinnamon rolls and other baked goods; famed fried potatoes. $ Average main: $12 ⌧ 416 W. Main St., Vernal ☎ 435/781–2728 ⊙ No dinner.

Dinosaur Brew Haus

$ | **AMERICAN** | This friendly joint serves higher quality food than your average sports pub, with an emphasis on burgers and sandwiches. Snack on peanuts and watch a game on one of the TVs while you wait for your food, or drop a coin in the jukebox and shoot some pool. **Known**

for: specialty burgers, including the "Brew Haus" with sliced corn beef; good selection of local microbrews on tap; excellent sweet potato fries. $ Average main: $13 ⌧ 550 E. Main St., Vernal ☎ 435/781–0717 ⊕ www.facebook.com/ dinosaurbrewhaus.

Plaza Mexicana

$$ | **MEXICAN** | Festive, colorful interiors and authentic Mexican specialties make Plaza Mexicana a sure bet if you need a break from Vernal's ubiquitous diners and steak houses. There are about 20 varieties of burritos to choose from, as well as a large selection of seafood options. **Known for:** huge portions; fantastic homemade salsas; extensive menu. $ Average main: $20 ⌧ 55 E. Main St., Vernal ☎ 435/781–2931.

Swain Brothers Restaurant

$$$ | **STEAKHOUSE** | This spacious steak house right downtown has a gigantic menu, venturing far from your favorite cuts to pastas, seafood, and Mexican dishes. The atmosphere is hip, with friendly service, and there's a full bar with signature cocktails. **Known for:** large portions; fantastic prime rib and other steaks; weekend brunch. $ Average main: $23 ⌧ 29 S. Vernal Ave., Vernal ☎ 435/781–8700 ⊕ www.facebook.com/ swainbrothers.

Vernal Brewing Company

$$ | **MODERN AMERICAN** | One of the rare breweries in this corner of the state, this gastropub also stands out for its creative takes on pub favorites, including burgers, pizza, and sandwiches. Located downtown, the interior has a big-city warehouse feel, with large windows, tall ceilings, and exposed pipes. **Known for:** innovative burger menu (try the "VBC," with candied bacon and onion marmalade); chicken skillet pie; hip atmosphere. $ Average main: $16 ⌧ 55 S. 500 E, Vernal ☎ 435/781–2337 ⊕ www.vernal-brewing.com ⊙ Closed Sun.

Hotels

Dinosaur Inn & Suites
$$ | **HOTEL** | **FAMILY** | Located blocks from all downtown attractions, this independent hotel is the best known lodging in Vernal and is perfect for families, with a pool to cool the kids down on hot days. **Pros:** pool makes it a good choice for families; rooms have a microwave, refrigerator, and coffeemaker; complimentary hot breakfast buffet. **Cons:** traffic noise in some rooms; higher priced than many other Vernal motels; can book up quickly in the summer. [$] *Rooms from: $131* ✉ *251 E. Main St., Vernal* ☎ *435/789–2660* 🌐 *www.dinoinn.com* 🛏 *60 rooms* 🍴 *Free Breakfast.*

Ledgestone Hotel Vernal
$ | **HOTEL** | This central, newer hotel is one of the most comfortable and affordable places in Vernal to spend a night, with a fully furnished kitchen (small dining table included) in each room. **Pros:** full kitchens make this perfect for long stays; large rooms; right downtown. **Cons:** no pool; no breakfast; more geared toward work trips than family stays. [$] *Rooms from: $99* ✉ *679 W. Main St., Vernal* ☎ *435/789–4200* 🌐 *ledgestonehotel.com* 🛏 *78 rooms* 🍴 *No Meals.*

SpringHill Suites by Marriott Vernal
$$$ | **HOTEL** | One of the most stylish places to stay in Vernal, this all-suites hotel features large rooms decorated in neutral colors, all with a sofa bed in an attached lounging area. **Pros:** hot complimentary breakfast; microwaves and mini-refrigerators in all rooms; indoor pool and hot tub. **Cons:** not in walking distance of town; more expensive than most nearby properties; no pets. [$] *Rooms from: $249* ☎ *435/781–9000* 🌐 *www.marriott.com* 🛏 *97 suites* 🍴 *Free Breakfast.*

Performing Arts

THEATER

Outlaw Trail Theater
PERFORMANCE VENUE | **FAMILY** | In late June and early July, enjoy musicals, melodramas, or comedies under the stars. Shows typically run Monday through Saturday. ✉ *Western Park Outdoor Amphitheater, 302 E. 200 S, Vernal* 🌐 *www.outlawtrailtheater.org.*

Shopping

Ashley Trading Post
OTHER SPECIALTY STORE | This extensive shop specializes in Native American beadwork and other jewelry, as well as Navajo weavings, Pendleton blankets, and even antique firearms. If you can't make it in, check out its large online store. ✉ *236 E. Main St., Vernal* ☎ *435/789–8447* 🌐 *www.cowboysandindiansonline.com.*

Fullbright Studios
ART GALLERIES | Stop here to enjoy artist Randy Fullbright's collection of gorgeous Dinosaur National Monument photographs. His paper castings of petroglyphs make nice mementos, too. ✉ *216 E. Main St., Vernal* ☎ *435/789–2451* 🌐 *www.randyfullbright.com.*

Activities

BIKING

Because Dinosaurland is lesser known than other parts of the state, bikers can often escape the crowds and enjoy some scenic solitude. The Uinta Basin has some 140 miles of trails. Bring plenty of water, snacks, and sunblock.

Altitude Cycle
BIKING | To talk to knowledgeable cyclists about local trails off-the-beaten path, stop in here; they can set you up with trail guides, repairs, and accessories. Ask for a map of biking hot spot McCoy Flats, just 6½ miles out of town, off Highway

Get close to Dinosaur National Monument by rafting down the Green or Yampa River.

40. There you'll find 35 miles of trails to explore. There's also a branch in Price. ⊠ *580 E. Main St.* ☎ *435/781–2595.*

BOATING

Red Fleet State Park

BOATING | FAMILY | Like the other reservoirs in the region, this one, just 10 miles north of Vernal, is great for boating and fishing. Visitors come to see the colorful sandstone formations surrounding the lake and the section of 200-million-year-old dinosaur tracks reachable by a short hike or by boat. Enjoy the scenery, trails, and more at your leisure when you camp in the park. RV hookups and dry camping are available, and you can also rent a tepee in the warmer months. ⊠ *Off Hwy. 191, Vernal* ☎ *435/789–4432* ⊕ *stateparks.utah.gov; utahstateparks. reserveamerica.com for camping reservations* ⚑ *$10 day use.*

Steinaker State Park

BOATING | Boating and waterskiing enthusiasts love this park, 7 miles north of Vernal. With 825 surface acres, Steinaker Reservoir relinquishes a fair number

of largemouth bass and rainbow trout. There's a sandy swimming beach, hiking trails, and nearby wildlife-viewing areas. A campground with full RV hookups and covered group pavilions also makes this a popular spot. ⊠ *U.S. 191, Vernal* ☎ *435/789–4432* ⊕ *stateparks.utah.gov; utahstateparks.reserveamerica.com for camping reservations* ⚑ *$10 day use.*

HIKING

Dinosaur National Monument Quarry Visitor Center

HIKING & WALKING | Check with the rangers at this visitor center, 20 miles east of Vernal, for information about the numerous hiking trails in the area. ⊠ *11625 E. 1500 S, Dinosaur National Monument* ☎ *435/781–7700* ⊕ *www.nps.gov/dino.*

Jones Hole Creek

HIKING & WALKING | One of the most beautiful hikes in the area begins at the Jones Hole National Fish Hatchery, 40 miles northeast of Vernal on the Utah–Colorado border, and follows Jones Hole Creek through riparian woods and canyons, past petroglyphs and wildlife. The full trail is a moderate 8½-mile round trip to the Green River and back, but you can stop halfway at Ely Creek and return for an easier, but still lovely, 4¼-mile hike. There are numerous trails in this area that are unmarked and not maintained, but easy to follow if you use reasonable caution. ⊠ *24495 E. Jones Hole Hatchery Rd., Vernal* ☎ *435/789–4481.*

Dinosaur National Monument

20 miles east of Vernal.

Dinomania rules at this 330-square-mile park that straddles the Utah–Colorado border. Although the main draw is obviously the ancient dinosaur fossils, the park's setting is something to savor as well, from craggy rock formations to waving grasslands to the Green and Yampa Rivers. The best part is that complete solitude is easy to find, as desolate wilderness surrounds even the busiest spots within the park.

GETTING HERE AND AROUND

Coming from Vernal, go east about 10 miles to the town of Jensen, via U.S. 40. Once there, be on the lookout for Utah Highway 149 on your left, and then follow the signs to the park. Note that the dinosaur fossils and the Quarry Exhibit Hall are both on the Utah side of the monument.

 Sights

Cub Creek Road

SCENIC DRIVE | This scenic 20-mile round-trip drive goes from the Quarry Visitor Center east to the Josie Morris Cabin. Josie's sister, Ann Bassett, was reputedly the "Etta Place" of Butch Cassidy legends. Morris lived alone for 50 years at her isolated home. Along the drive, watch for ancient rock art, geological formations, views of Split Mountain, the Green River, and hiking trails. The route is dubbed the "Tour of the Tilted Rocks" in the $1 guidebook sold at the visitor center. ⊠ *Dinosaur National Monument.*

Island Park Road

SCENIC DRIVE | A scenic drive on the unpaved Island Park Road, along the northern edge of the park, passes not only some impressive Fremont petroglyph panels but also the Rainbow Park Campground, a beautiful place to spend a night or two on the banks of the Green River. Be sure to check with the visitor center about road conditions as it can be impassable when wet and there is no winter maintenance. ⊠ *Dinosaur National Monument.*

★ Quarry Exhibit Hall

The Monument's astoundingly large collection of fossils was discovered by Earl Douglass in 1909, when he stumbled upon eight enormous dinosaur vertebrae exposed on a sandstone ridge. Although most of the park's acreage is in Colorado, the Utah side features its prime attraction: the Quarry Exhibit Hall. Here you can view more than 1,500 genuine fossils, displayed in their original burial positions in an excavated river bed, several stories high, 150-feet long, and now enclosed by a large, airy museum. A "touch wall" allows you to run your hands over some of the ancient bones, and various displays and dinosaur replicas help you put the jumble of bones in their prehistorical context. Before going to the Exhibit Hall, stop by the Quarry Visitor Center near the Monument's west entrance. There you can view a short video and see displays that give an overview of the site and its paleontological significance. Then hop a shuttle (in summer) or drive (in winter) up to the Exhibit Hall.

■ TIP→ **Use one of the interactive kiosks to identify the massive bones embedded in the wall, or, better yet, flag down a ranger, who can add interesting tidbits about the bones and their excavation.** ⊠ *Hwy. 149, 20 miles east of Vernal, Dinosaur National Monument* ☎ *435/781–7700* ⊕ *www.nps.gov/dino* 🚗 *$25 per vehicle to enter monument.*

⚡ Activities

CAMPING

You can camp at six spots inside the national monument, but only two are developed sites. Both campgrounds are along the Green River, have a bit of shade, and are surrounded by canyon scenery. The **Green River Campground** is only open when the water is turned on, from approximately April to October, and it has a boat ramp for rafters with permits; camping is $18 per night. The **Split Mountain Campground** is open year-round, but only larger groups can camp there from approximately April to October. After the water is turned off in the fall, it's open to all, and vault toilets are available. Reservations are not accepted at either campground, except for groups at Split Mountain in the summer. There are 80 sites at Green River and 22 more at Split Mountain (only 7 of which accommodate RVs). Make reservations at ⊕ recreation.gov ☎ 435/781–7759.

HIKING

When embarking on any hike in Dinosaur, bring plenty of water and sun protection as most trails have little to no shade. Dehydration is a real concern (especially in summer) with the dry air and elevation changes. Pets are not allowed on most trails.

Desert Voices Nature Trail

HIKING & WALKING | Four miles past the Quarry Visitor Center, the moderate 1½-mile trail has interpretive signs that describe the arid environment you're hiking through. You can make a longer hike by using the **Connector Trail** to link up with the Sound of Silence Trail. ⊠ *Dinosaur National Monument.*

Sound of Silence Trail

HIKING & WALKING | More challenging than the Desert Voices Trail, this 3-mile trail begins 2 miles past the Dinosaur Quarry and delivers excellent views of Split Mountain. To hike both trails without returning to your car, use the easy ¼-mile **Connector Trail,** which links the two, making a trek of about 5 miles total. ⊠ *Dinosaur National Monument.*

RAFTING

The best way to experience the geologic depths of Dinosaur National Monument is to take a white-water rafting trip on the Green or Yampa River. Joining forces near Echo Park in Colorado, the two waterways have each carved spectacular canyons through several eons' worth of rock, and contain thrilling white-water rapids. River-running season is typically May through September.

▣ **TIP → Permits are required for all boaters.**

Adrift Dinosaur

WHITE-WATER RAFTING | FAMILY | The closest guide service to Dinosaur National Monument, this outfitter offers one-day or multiday rafting trips on the Green and Yampa Rivers. Note that a pass to Dinosaur National Monument must be purchased separately beforehand. ⊠ *9500 E. 6000 S, Jensen* ☎ *435/789–3600, 800/824–0150* ⊕ *www.adrift.com* ⛵ *From $109 (day trip, including lunch).*

Dinosaur River Expeditions

WHITE-WATER RAFTING | FAMILY | The only locally owned outfitter in Dinosaur National Monument, this company offers daily and multiday whitewater trips on the Green and Yampa Rivers. ⊠ *2279 N. Vernal Ave., Vernal* ☎ *800/345–7238* ⊕ *www.dinosaurriverexpeditions.com* ⛵ *From $105.*

OARS Dinosaur

WHITE-WATER RAFTING | FAMILY | In operation since 1969, OARS offers one-day and multiday rafting trips on both calm and white waters on the Green and Yampa Rivers. ⊠ *221 N. 400 E, Vernal* ☎ *800/342–8243* ⊕ *www.greenriverrafting.com* ⛵ *From $119.*

Flaming Gorge was named by explorer John Wesley Powell for its "flaming, brilliant red" color.

Flaming Gorge National Recreation Area

40 miles north of Vernal (to Flaming Gorge Dam).

If you are standing in front of the Flaming Gorge or its reservoir with a crowd of people, you'll likely hear gasps and exclamations of amazement. The sheer size of these bodies of water is astounding, as are the red, narrow walls on either side of the gorge. Though not far from the suburban town of Vernal, the Flaming Gorge area offers a lesson in stillness and serenity. The lake and 91-mile gorge also have some of the best boating and fishing in the state. The Flaming Gorge Reservoir stretches north into Wyoming, but most facilities lie south of the state line in Utah.

GETTING HERE AND AROUND

From Vernal, getting to the gorge is a straight shot north via U.S. 191. Follow the highway for about 38 miles, which will take you into some magnificent country at high elevations. Then, simply follow the signs to the gorge. The road will veer downward for a few miles before you reach it. From Salt Lake City, go 30 miles east via I–80 past Evanston, Wyoming. Take the Fort Bridge exit, and drive to Manila via Highway 414, which becomes Highway 43. Once in Manila, turn right on Highway 44 for 38 miles until you reach U.S. 191 and follow signs.

VISITOR INFORMATION

CONTACTS Flaming Gorge Dam Visitor Center. ⊠ *U.S. 191, Flaming Gorge National Recreation Area* ☎ *435/885–3135* ⊕ *www.flaminggorgecountry.com.* **Red Canyon Visitor Center.** ⊠ *Hwy. 44, Flaming Gorge National Recreation Area* ☎ *435/889–3713* ⊕ *www.flaminggorge-country.com.*

Sights

Sheep Creek Canyon Geological Area

SCENIC DRIVE | A scenic 13-mile drive on paved and gravel roads crosses the Sheep Creek Canyon Geological Area, which is full of upturned layers of rock, craggy pinnacles, and hoodoos. Watch for a herd of bighorn sheep, as well as a popular cave alongside the road. In the fall, salmon return to Sheep Creek to spawn; a kiosk and several bridges provide unobtrusive viewing. The area, 28 miles west of Greendale Junction off U.S. 191 and Highway 44, is open from May to October. ✉ *Forest Service Rd. 218, Flaming Gorge National Recreation Area* ☎ *435/784–3445* ⏲ *Closed Nov.–Apr.*

Spirit Lake Scenic Backway

SCENIC DRIVE | This 17-mile round-trip add-on to the Sheep Creek Canyon Loop road leads past the **Ute Lookout Fire Tower,** which was in use from the 1930s through the 1960s. ✉ *Flaming Gorge National Recreation Area.*

Swett Ranch

MUSEUM VILLAGE | This isolated homestead belonged to Oscar and Emma Swett and their nine children through most of the 1900s. The U.S. Forest Service has turned the ranch into a working historical site, complete with restored and decorated houses and buildings. ✉ *Off U.S. 191, Flaming Gorge National Recreation Area* ✣ *At Greendale Junction of U.S. 191 and Hwy. 44, stay on U.S. 191; about ½ mile north of junction there's a sign for 1½-mile dirt road to ranch* ☎ *435/784–3445* 🌐 *www.flaminggorgecountry.com* 🎟 *Free* ⏲ *Closed early Sept.–Memorial Day.*

Hotels

Flaming Gorge Resort

$$ | **HOTEL** | With motel rooms and condo-style suites, a good American-cuisine restaurant, and a store just a short drive from the water, this is a practical home base for enjoying Flaming Gorge. **Pros:** almost all rooms come with private porches or decks; many lodging options for groups, including suites and trailers; good on-site restaurant (important for a remote area). **Cons:** rooms are simple; most room rates increase $10 a night for each additional adult beyond 1; can be very busy in summer. [$] *Rooms from: $179* ✉ *1100 E. Flaming Gorge Resort Rd., off U.S. 191, Dutch John* ☎ *435/889–3773* 🌐 *www.flaminggorgeresort.com* 🛏 *46 rooms* 🍴 *No Meals.*

★ **Red Canyon Lodge**

$$ | **RESORT** | **FAMILY** | A pleasant surprise in the woods, this lodge is surrounded by well-built, handcrafted log cabins with kitchenettes (some with wood-burning stoves) that face a private trout-stocked lake. **Pros:** beautiful setting; cabins are comfortable for families or groups (up to six people per cabin); excellent restaurant. **Cons:** must book a year in advance for summer months; Wi-Fi only in restaurant; no air-conditioning. [$] *Rooms from: $169* ✉ *2450 W. Red Canyon Lodge, Dutch John* ☎ *435/889–3759* 🌐 *www.redcanyonlodge.com* 🛏 *18 cabins* 🍴 *No Meals.*

Activities

BIKING

Because it mixes high-desert vegetation—blooming sage, rabbit brush, cactus, and wildflowers—and red-rock terrain with a cool climate, Flaming Gorge is ideal for road and trail biking. The easy 3-mile round-trip **Bear Canyon–Bootleg** ride begins south of the dam off U.S. 191 at the Firefighters' Memorial Campground and runs west to an overview of the reservoir. For the intermediate rider, **Dowd Mountain Hideout** is an 11-mile ride with spectacular views through forested single-track trail, leaving from Dowd Springs Picnic Area off Highway 44. Flyers describing cycling routes are at area visitor centers or online at 🌐 *www.flaminggorgecountry.com.* Several local lodges rent bikes.

BOATING AND FISHING

Flaming Gorge Reservoir provides ample opportunities for boating and water sports of all kinds. Most boating facilities close from October through mid-March.

Old-timers maintain that Flaming Gorge provides the best lake fishing in the state, yielding rainbow and lake trout, smallmouth bass, and kokanee salmon. The Green River below Flaming Gorge Dam has been identified as one of the best trout fisheries in the world, with plentiful rainbow and brown trout. Note that the Green doesn't allow any live bait, while the lake allows the use of crawdads or worms, but no other live bait.

Fed by cold water from the bottom of the lake, this is a calm, scenic stretch of the Green River, ideal for risk-averse folk or for families who want to take smaller children on rafting trips but don't want to worry about them falling into white water.

Cedar Springs Marina

BOATING | Only 1 mile from Flaming Gorge Dam, this full-service marina is a great resource for any boating trip. Here you can rent a boat, take a lake tour, or hire a fishing guide. It's also the spot to launch, fuel up, or rent a slip. Most important to many visitors: it's home to the casual hangout **The Snag,** a floating grill with a full bar (a big deal in rural Utah) and a good selection of pub eats. Both visitors and locals fill up the place Friday through Sunday, Memorial Day through Labor Day. ⊠ *2675 N. Cedar Springs Rd., Dutch John* ☎ *435/889–3795* ⊕ *www.cedarspringsmarina.com.*

Dutch John Resort at Flaming Gorge

BOATING | Boat rentals, guided fishing trips, and daily float trips on the Green River are available here. The **Green River Grill and Steakhouse** offers three meals a day, plus boxed lunches, of casual American fare. ⊠ *1050 South Blvd., Dutch John* ☎ *435/885–3191* ⊕ *dutchjohnresort.com.*

Lucerne Valley Marina

BOATING | Seven miles east of Manila you'll find this full-service marina, with just about any amenity you may need for your water adventure. There's a launch, slips, boat and stand-up paddleboard rentals, fishing licenses, mechanical services, and gas. You can even rent a houseboat or floating cabin. The casual **Lucerne**

Lakeside Grill has a small menu, including burgers, tacos, and fish-and-chips. ⊠ *5570 E. Lucerne Valley Rd.* ☎ *435/784–3483, 888/820–9225* ⊕ *www.flaminggorge.com.*

HIKING

There's plenty of hiking in the Flaming Gorge area and any of the local visitor centers or lodges can recommend trails best suited to your ability level. From the Red Canyon Visitor Center, three different hikes traverse the **Canyon Rim Trail** through the pine forest: an easy ½-mile round-trip trek leads to the Red Canyon Rim Overlook (above 1,300-foot cliffs), a moderate 3½-mile round-trip hike finds you at the Swett Ranch Overlook, and a 7-mile round-trip hike winds through brilliant layered colors to the Green River at the canyon's bottom below the dam. In the Sheep Creek Canyon Geological Area, the 4-mile **Ute Mountain Trail** leads from the Ute Lookout Fire Tower down through pine forest to Brownie Lake, and back the same way. The **Tamarack Lake Trail** begins at the west end of Spirit Lake (on Highway 44, go past the Ute Lookout Fire Tower turnoff and take F.S. Road 221 to Spirit Lake) and goes to Tamarack Lake and back for a moderate 3-mile trek, round-trip.

Roosevelt

50 miles southwest of Flaming Gorge.

Roosevelt, a small town named for Theodore Roosevelt, lies between blocks of the sovereign land of the Uintah and Ouray Reservation. Despite being right on U.S. 191, its main drag is quite walkable and quaint, with shops and restaurants behind vintage storefronts—and even a one-screen theater that dates back to the 1930s.

It's also the center of the Uintah and Ouray Reservation (⊕ www.utetribe. com). The over 4.5 million acres of the reservation is spread out in a patchwork-like fashion across the Uinta Basin and northeastern Utah, all the way to the

The Northern Ute Powwow is held every July 4 in Roosevelt, the center of the Uintah and Ouray Reservation.

eastern edge of the state. Fort Duchesne is the tribal headquarters for the Uintah and Ouray branch of the Ute Tribe. Because it's sometimes difficult to tell whether you're on reservation land, public land, or private land, you should stay on main roads unless you have permission to be on the reservation lands.

GETTING HERE AND AROUND

Roosevelt's location between Price and Vernal on U.S. 40 makes it an ideal place to get out and stretch your legs while driving through the region's beautiful countryside. If you're headed here from Price, go north on U.S. 191 for 83 miles.

WHEN TO GO

Each July 4 weekend, the **Northern Ute Powwow** has drumming, dancing, and singing competitions featuring top performers from throughout North America. The powwow is one of the largest in the West and is free to the public. All are welcome to attend and camp on the grounds. Other attractions include a rodeo, golf and softball tournaments, and an art-and-crafts fair. The tribe also celebrates Ute

Bear Dances in spring, Sundances in July and August, and a smaller powwow held over Thanksgiving weekend at the tribal gymnasium in Fort Duchesne.

Sights

Ouray National Wildlife Refuge

OTHER ATTRACTION | FAMILY | Established in 1960, this refuge consists of 11,987 acres of land along the Green River. Here you can see more than 200 species of migratory birds in spring and fall, mule deer and golden eagles year-round, and bald eagles in early winter. An information kiosk at the refuge has a bird checklist and other leaflets. The best times to visit are in the early morning and early evening. The park is open from sunrise to sunset. ⊠ 19001 E. Wildlife Refuge Rd., off Hwy. 88, Randlett ⊕ 15 miles east of Roosevelt on U.S. 40, then 13 miles south on Hwy. 88 ☎ 435/545–2522 ⊕ www.fws.gov/refuge/ouray ☞ Free ⊘ Visitor center is closed weekends, though the park is open daily.

🍴 Restaurants

Marion's Variety

$ | **DINER** | **FAMILY** | Open since the 1930s, this family-run soda fountain is delightfully old-timey, with a black-and-white checkerboard floor and sparkly red stools. Many people come for the ice-cream treats, and there's also a pretty long list of burgers, sandwiches, and other diner staples. **Known for:** ice-cream sodas and thick shakes; family business for four generations; barbecue burgers marinated in a sweet, tangy sauce. [$] *Average main: $6* ✉ *29 N. Main St., Roosevelt* ☎ *435/722–2143.*

🛏 Hotels

Best Western Plus Landmark Hotel

$$ | **HOTEL** | **FAMILY** | Ample amenities, including one of the few indoor pools in the region, make this chain hotel a reliable choice. **Pros:** hot breakfast; large rooms (with kitchenettes available for a small upcharge); indoor pool open year-round. **Cons:** rates are high for the area; rooms nearest the highway can be noisy; few nearby attractions. [$] *Rooms from: $170* ✉ *2477 E. U.S. 40, Ballard* ✥ *1.8 miles east of Roosevelt U.S. 40* ☎ *435/725–1800, 800/780–7234* 🌐 *www.bestwestern.com* 🛏 *96 rooms* 🍴 *Free Breakfast.*

Frontier Grill & Motel

$ | **HOTEL** | This mom-and-pop motel is right in the heart of town and offers simple but updated rooms at a reasonable price. **Pros:** convenient downtown location; great adjacent restaurant; most rooms have been updated. **Cons:** aging facilities and interior design; breakfast is not included; small bathrooms. [$] *Rooms from: $89* ✉ *75 S. 200 E* ☎ *435/722–2201* 🌐 *www.frontiermotelandgrill.com* 🛏 *54 rooms* 🍴 *No Meals.*

★ **The Lodge at Falcon's Ledge**

$$$ | **B&B/INN** | With an emphasis on escaping the workaday world, this small and comfortable lodge is found on a 600-acre private ranch, catering to fly-fishers and hunters. **Pros:** gorgeous setting with dark skies; exquisite food; great fishing. **Cons:** no children under 12 allowed; no TVs in rooms; breakfast is continental. [$] *Rooms from: $229* ✉ *Hwy. 87, Altamont* ✥ *15 miles north of Duchesne or 25 miles west of Roosevelt* ☎ *435/253–7336* 🌐 *www.falconsledge.com* 🛏 *9 rooms* 🍴 *Free Breakfast.*

🎟 Performing Arts

FILM

Roosevelt Theatres

THEATER | **FAMILY** | For a nostalgic dose of Americana, catch a show at the **Echo Drive-In** on summer weekends. For a year-round movie fix, the **Roosevelt Twin Theatre** and historic one-screen **Uinta Theatre** are both located right downtown. ✉ *250 W. Hwy. 40, Roosevelt* ☎ *435/722–2095* 🌐 *www.rooseveltmovies.com.*

🏃 Activities

FISHING

Ute Tribe Fish & Wildlife Department

FISHING | Information about camping, sporting, and photo safaris on the Uintah and Ouray Reservation is available from the Ute Tribe Fish & Wildlife Department. You can purchase fishing permits from Fort Duchesne's Ute Plaza Supermarket, as well as Ute Petroleum, a gas station in Myton. ✉ *Fort Duchesne* ☎ *435/722–5511* 🌐 *www.utetribe.com.*

Duchesne

28 miles southwest of Roosevelt, 54 miles northeast of Price.

A small town in a small county of the same name, Duchesne is probably best known for its proximity to Fred Hayes State Park at Starvation and the park's fishing-friendly reservoir.

GETTING HERE AND AROUND

From Price, take U.S. 191 north for 54 miles.

VISITOR INFORMATION

CONTACTS Duchesne County Chamber of Commerce. ✉ *50 E. 200 S, Roosevelt* ☎ *435/722–4598* ⊕ *www.uintabasin.org.*

 ## Sights

Fred Hayes State Park at Starvation

This state park's original name, Starvation State Park, was most likely in recognition of the early homesteaders and cattlemen who battled bitter winters, short growing seasons, and other hardships in the area. In 2019, it was renamed in memory of a beloved director of the Utah Division of Parks and Recreation. Boaters and anglers come to cast for walleye, yellow perch, and smallmouth bass in the park's 3,500-acre reservoir. There are six campgrounds within the park, two of which are developed. Bring sunscreen, as there is little natural shade on site. Note that dogs must be on a leash at all times. ✉ *Hwy. 311* ☎ *800/322–3770 camping reservations, 435/738–2326* ⊕ *stateparks.utah.gov; www.reserveamerica.com (camping reservations)* 🖘 *$10 per vehicle* ⛺ *Camping reservations are available up to four months in advance.*

Price

120 miles southeast of Salt Lake City, 54 miles southwest of Price.

Thousands of visitors travel to Price every year to experience Utah's past through fossils, exhibits, and preservation sites at the Prehistoric Museum, USU Eastern. For being a quite small, mostly blue-collar town, one may not expect to find much excitement here, but they'd be wrong. This comfortable town is easy to stroll through and spend time in, with plenty of affordable hotels and a few beloved restaurants. Two large festivals draw throngs of people each summer, as well. While Price began as a Mormon farming settlement in the late 1800s, in 1883 the railroad arrived, bringing with it immigrants from around the world to mine coal reserves. As the town expanded, coal became the cash crop of the area, and mining remains an important part of the town's identity to this day.

GETTING HERE AND AROUND

To get to Price from Salt Lake City, travel on I–15 South for 50 miles, and then take U.S. 6 for 70 miles toward the southeastern corner of the state. This drive contains many of the area's breathtaking views and rock formations. Be aware that mountain and canyon roads can seem unpredictable if you're not used to them. If you're heading to Price from Green River or the surrounding area, take U.S. 191 north for 65 miles. From Vernal, it's a straight shot down U.S. 191 southwest; the section from Duchesne to Helper (called the Indian Canyon Scenic Byway) is a particularly scenic drive.

The town is easy to navigate, with most of the main attractions on or close to Main Street.

WHEN TO GO

Greek Festival Days

FESTIVALS | FAMILY | A sizable number of Greek immigrants arrived in the area of Price to work in the mines throughout the early 1900s. This annual festival in mid-July celebrates that heritage with two days of traditional Greek food, dance, and music. You can even tour the Assumption Greek Orthodox Church, which hosts the event. ✉ *Assumption Greek Orthodox Church, 61 S. 200 E, Price* ☎ *435/637–0704.*

Price City International Days

FESTIVALS | FAMILY | Typically held at the end of July, this three-day festival uses music, dance, and food (plus a parade) to celebrate the many nationalities and cultures that make up the Price community. It's right on the heels of the statewide

The San Rafael Swell looks otherworldly at sunset.

Pioneer Days festivities, which is always on July 24. ✉ *Pioneer Park, 100 E. 550 N, Price* ☎ *435/636–3701* ⊕ *www.castle-country.com* ✉ *Free.*

VISITOR INFORMATION

CONTACTS Carbon County Office of Tourism and Visitors Center. ✉ *751 E. 100 N #2600, Price* ☎ *435/636–3701* ⊕ *www.castle-country.com.*

 Sights

Cleveland-Lloyd Dinosaur Quarry at Jurassic National Monument

OTHER ATTRACTION | FAMILY | Paleontologists and geologists have excavated more than 12,000 dinosaur bones from the Cleveland-Lloyd Dinosaur Quarry, making this the densest concentration of Jurassic fossils ever found. Since the quarry's discovery by herders in the 1920s, scores of dinosaur remains have been uncovered here, and much of what the world knows about the Allosaurus was discovered on these grounds. Although many of the bones found in the quarry now reside in museums around the world, a trip to the remote landscape surrounding the quarry pit is worth the journey. Paleontologists still come here for digs every year. The visitor center, which generates its own electricity from rooftop solar panels, has a reconstructed dinosaur skeleton and exhibits about the quarry, and the area has some short hiking trails. The center is 15 miles on a gravel road from the nearest services, so bring food and water and dress for desert conditions. It's 33 miles south of Price: take Highway 10 south to the Cleveland/Elmo turnoff and follow the signs.

■ **TIP→ There's free admission for ages 15 and younger.** ✉ *Off Hwy. 10, Price* ☎ *435/636–3600* ⊕ *www.blm.gov/ut* ✉ *$5* ⊗ *Closed Mon.–Wed. and Nov.–Mar.*

Indian Canyon Scenic Byway

SCENIC DRIVE | This section of U.S. 191 climbs north from the Price and Helper vicinity, cresting at Indian Creek Pass at an elevation of 9,100 feet. It then begins a long descent into the Uinta Basin area, ending at Duchesne. The winning, 43-mile route takes you through canyons, over plateaus, and into the heart of the geology and natural beauty that define this part of Utah. Take it slow and watch for fallen rocks and rockslides, which often litter the road. There are plenty of scenic viewpoints along the way. Expect at least one hour of driving. ✉ *U.S. 191, Helper.*

★ Nine Mile Canyon

INDIGENOUS SIGHT | The hundreds of petroglyphs etched into the boulders and cliffs of Nine Mile Canyon may be one of the world's largest outdoor art galleries. They're attributed to the Fremont and Ute peoples, who lived in much of what is now Utah more than a thousand years ago. The canyon also shelters the remnants of many early homesteads, stage stops, and ranches. It's important not to touch the fragile rock art because oils from your fingers can damage them. The scenic drive through Nine Mile Canyon spans about 100 miles round-trip. ✉ *Nine Mile Canyon Rd., Price ⊹ To reach canyon, go 7½ miles southeast of Price on U.S. 6 and then turn north on Soldier Creek Rd., which eventually connects with Nine Mile Canyon Rd.* ☎ *435/637–3701* ⊕ *www.castlecountry. com/nine-mile-canyon.*

The Prehistoric Museum, USU Eastern

SCIENCE MUSEUM | **FAMILY** | Ever since the 1910s, archaeologists have been coming to this rural area to excavate rare natural treasures, including dinosaur bones, eggs, skeletons, and fossilized tracks. These are all on exhibit at Utah State University Eastern's Prehistoric Museum. For families, this museum offers a small but excellent kids' discovery area where children can experiment with excavating dino bones all on their own. A second hall is devoted to indigenous peoples, with displays of beadwork, clay figurines, a walk-in teepee, and other area artifacts. You can't miss the museum's gigantic mammoth and saber-toothed tiger replicas. ✉ *155 E. Main St., Price* ☎ *435/613–5060, 800/817–9949* ⊕ *www. usueastern.edu/museum* ✉ *$6.*

Price Mural

PUBLIC ART | The 200-foot-long mural inside the Price Municipal Building is a visual narration of the history of the town and of Carbon County, beginning with the first trappers and white settlers. The painting took artist Lynn Fausett almost four years to complete back in the late 1930s. ✉ *200 E. Main St., Price* ☎ *435/637–5010* ✉ *Free.*

★ San Rafael Swell Recreation Area

NATURE SIGHT | **FAMILY** | Tremendous geological upheavals pushed through the Earth's surface eons ago, forming a giant oval-shape dome of rock about 80 miles long and 30 miles wide, giving rise to the name "swell." Over the years, the harsh climate beat down the dome, eroding it into a wild array of multicolor sandstone and creating buttes, pinnacles, mesas, and canyons that spread across nearly 1 million acres—an area larger than the state of Rhode Island.

Managed by the Bureau of Land Management, the Swell offers visitors spectacular sights similar to those in Utah's national parks but without the crowds. In the northern Swell, the Wedge Overlook peers into the Little Grand Canyon with the San Rafael River below, for one of the most scenic vistas in the state. The strata at the edges of the southern Swell are angled nearly vertical, creating the San Rafael Reef. Both are known for fantastic hiking, canyoneering, and mountain biking. As recently as 2018, proposals have been made to designate the Swell a national monument; until then, the San Rafael Swell remains one of the little-known natural wonders of the American West.

Interstate 70 bisects the San Rafael Swell and is the only paved road in the region. Although there are many off-road opportunities, the main gravel road and many of the graded dirt roads through the Swell are accessible to two-wheel-drive vehicles. The Swell is about 25 miles south of Price (typically considered the main gateway to the Swell), and the setting is so remote that it's essential you bring whatever supplies you might need, including plenty of water, food, and a spare tire. For directions on how to access the San Rafael Swell viewing area from Green River, turn to the Green River section of the Moab and Southeastern Utah chapter. **TIP→ Always keep your wits about you, as flash flooding can be deadly, especially in the Swell's narrow slot canyons.** ✉ *BLM Field Office, 125 S. 600 W, Price* ☎ *435/636–3600* 🌐 *www.blm.gov.*

🍴 Restaurants

Farlaino's Café
$ | **AMERICAN** | **FAMILY** | Found in a historic building along Main Street, this casual diner has the feel of an old-time soda fountain and serves up home-style American fare for breakfast, lunch, and early dinner (it closes at 7 pm). Full of local color, this has been the spot for big portions and low prices for decades. **Known for:** hand-cut curly fries; giant pancakes; low prices (great for families). [$] *Average main: $10* ✉ *87 W. Main St., Price* ☎ *435/637–9217* ⏲ *Closed Sun.*

Greek Streak
$ | **GREEK** | **FAMILY** | In what used to be a Greek coffeehouse in the early 1900s, this low-key café is a reminder of Price's strong Greek heritage. The menu features traditional recipes from Crete, including gyros and dolmades. **Known for:** long-time local favorite; baklava and other Greek pastries; delicious lemon-rice soup. [$] *Average main: $11* ✉ *84 S. Carbon Ave., Price* ☎ *435/637–1930* ⏲ *Closed Sun.*

★ **Sherald's Frosty Freeze**
$ | **FAST FOOD** | **FAMILY** | If you hanker for the nostalgia, and the prices, of an old-fashioned hamburger stand, you're in luck. Order at the window and eat outside at picnic tables, or have friendly carhops deliver your meal right to your vehicle. **Known for:** delectably thick milkshakes in a multitude of flavors; delicious burgers and fries; long lines. [$] *Average main: $6* ✉ *434 E. Main St., Price* ☎ *435/637–1447* 🌐 *www.sheralds-frostyfreeze.com* ⏲ *Closed Sun.*

🛏 Hotels

The Greenwell Inn & Convention Center
$ | **HOTEL** | **FAMILY** | With more amenities than most of the area's hotels but still reasonably priced, the Greenwell is a great choice for most travelers, especially families. **Pros:** convenient downtown location; beautiful indoor pool and hot tub; great value. **Cons:** older property with simple rooms; on a busy road; motel-style room entrances are a downside in inclement weather. [$] *Rooms from: $65* ✉ *655 E. Main St., Price* ☎ *435/637–3520, 800/666–3520* 🌐 *www.greenwellinn.com* 🛏 *136 rooms* 🍴 *No Meals.*

Legacy Inn
$ | **HOTEL** | **FAMILY** | If you want to save a bit of cash, but not scrimp on amenities, this simple but updated motel is one of the best bets in town. **Pros:** great value; easy access to freeway; free continental breakfast. **Cons:** simple roadside motel; rooms are a little small and dark; not in walking distance to downtown Price. [$] *Rooms from: $80* ✉ *145 N. Carbonville Rd., Price* ☎ *435/637–2424* 🌐 *www.legacyinnutah.com* 🛏 *33 rooms* 🍴 *Free Breakfast.*

Nine Mile Ranch
$$ | **B&B/INN** | Ben Mead grew up in beautiful Nine Mile Canyon and started this "bunk and breakfast" establishment years ago on his working cattle ranch, where guests can stay in the comfy house or rent one of the rustic cabins. **Pros:** a true cowboy experience; beautiful setting with dark-as-can-be nighttime skies; perfect for large gatherings, with Dutch oven dinners available for groups of 14 or more. **Cons:** breakfast is only for B&B guests and not included with a cabin rental; cabins are rustic, with solar

lights and bathrooms located behind the buildings; bedding not included with cabin rental. $ *Rooms from: $130 ⊠ Nine Mile Canyon Rd., Mile Post 24 ⊹ To reach ranch, travel 7 miles southeast of Price to Wellington via Hwy. 6, then make left onto Soldier Creek Canyon Rd., which will become Nine Mile Canyon Rd., and drive north for 25 miles ☎ 435/637–2572 ⊕ 9mileranch.com ⤴ 4 rooms ⦿ Free Breakfast.*

Ramada by Wyndham Price

$ | **HOTEL** | **FAMILY** | A bright, lovely atrium is the stunning centerpiece of this reliable chain option, featuring comfy rooms with a long list of standard amenities (mini-refrigerator, microwave, desk, and more). **Pros:** many amenities, including a restaurant and separate bar; pleasant and well-lit interiors; large pool. **Cons:** not in walking distance of downtown Price; more expensive than many nearby properties; books up quickly (especially when conventions are in town). $ *Rooms from: $114 ⊠ 838 Westwood Blvd., Price ☎ 435/637–8880, 877/492–4803 ⊕ www.ramada.com ⤴ 151 rooms ⦿ Free Breakfast.*

Nightlife

Sports Page Bar

BARS | Inside the Ramada hotel, this bar offers pool and big-screen TVs to watch the night's game. Karaoke nights, live music, open mikes, and theme parties also make this a fun peek into Price's nightlife. *⊠ Ramada by Wyndham Price, 838 Westwood Blvd., Price ☎ 435/637–8880 ⊕ www.ramada.com.*

Activities

Carbon County covers a wide range of geography, from mountains to gorges to plateaus. Hundreds of miles of hiking and biking trails crisscross the region.

GOLF

Carbon Country Club

GOLF | The 18-hole championship course at the Carbon Country Club is open to the public. The course has a pleasant, relaxing atmosphere that will make even the most novice of players feel welcome. And if you happen to be a little over par, the sandstone cliffs and waterfall will be enough to distract you from an off-game day. *⊠ 3055 N. U.S. 6, Price ☎ 435/637–2388 ⊕ www.carboncountryclub.com ⛳ $30 ⚑ 18 holes, 6,159 yards, par 70.*

HIKING AND MOUNTAIN BIKING

The canyons and surrounding desert-scapes of Price include trails reminiscent of the slickrock of Moab, minus the crowds. Head to the visitor center in Price for a mountain biking guide that shows several trails you can challenge yourself on, including Nine Mile Canyon. Adventurous hikers can use many of these trails as well. Altitude Cycle is a great source of information for those looking to explore.

Altitude Cycle

BIKING | This is Price's go-to bike shop for trail details, repairs, and area information. *⊠ 82 N. 1st W ☎ 435/637–2453.*

Helper

10 miles north of Price.

Sitting under sheer red-rock cliffs, Helper is a tiny town that's coming into its own more and more. Just a few years ago, it seemed the place might dry up and blow away, but it's since become a haven for artists, who have opened up galleries in buildings that used to be boarded up. The main drag is now also dotted with a few coffee shops, a good restaurant, and little stores that cater to visitors looking to bring home something fun from this quirky little spot.

Helper has never fit the small-town Utah mold. Unlike most places in the state, it wasn't settled by Mormons but instead grew out of necessity in the late 1880s due to its proximity to the rail line. Designed to be the division point between the eastern and western terminals of the Denver & Rio Grande Western Railroad, it was named after the "helper" locomotives used to get the trains up the steep nearby mountain and into the Salt Lake Valley. It quickly became a hub for the various settlers. Miners converged here to drink and visit houses of ill repute, and immigrants arrived to set up shops, bars, and restaurants. From the beginning, it had a diversity that's still uncommon in the state.

Sandwiched between several mining camps, Helper remained a supply and service town for decades and continued strong until the 1960s. By the 1970s, however, mining started to decline, and the town began to lose its usefulness. The 1980s and 1990s were especially rough, a period to which a few remaining shuttered stores and abandoned houses are still a testament. There is still some sleepiness in the air here, but that's diluting each year as Helper gets hipper. The biggest annual shot of vitality comes in the summer, during the popular Helper Arts, Music, and Film Festival.

While Helper is one of the most fun towns in the region to visit, it doesn't have many lodging options besides short-term rentals. If you're looking for a traditional hotel, it's best to stay in Price, only 10 minutes away.

GETTING HERE AND AROUND
From Salt Lake City, travel south on I–15 for 50 miles, then southeast on Highway 6 for about another 60 miles. Helper is also a stop for Amtrak's *California Zephyr*, and the station's downtown location makes exploring this little place without a car very easy.

WHEN TO GO
The annual Helper Arts, Music, and Film Festival (⊕ www.helperartsfest.com), spread over three days in mid-August, is the biggest event in town. Come celebrate Helper's local artists with outdoor concerts, art and crafts booths, open galleries, and a children's art yard. The festival shuts down Helper's main drag, making it easy to stroll through downtown and peek in the growing number of galleries starting to pop up.

◉ Sights

Helper's Mining & Railroad Museum
HISTORY MUSEUM | FAMILY | Located within the old Hotel Helper in the town's National Historic District, this excellent museum doubles as a visitor center. A labyrinth of rooms spread over four floors depict everyday activities of Helper's past and include uncountable trinkets, toys, clothing, and tools from the various businesses and homes here. Some visitors come just for the incredible historic photographs, including several by Dorothea Lange of a nearby coal camp in the 1930s. The museum also features one of the best collections in the state of WPA paintings from Utah artists, including Price's own Lynn Fausett. An exhibit on railroad and mining equipment is located outdoors. ⊠ *294 S. Main St., Helper* 🕾 *435/472–3009* ⊕ *www.helpercity.net/museum* 🎫 *$8 suggested donation* ⊗ *Closed Sun.*

Spring Canyon
GHOST TOWN | FAMILY | The Helper area—in particular the area around Spring Canyon, 4 miles to the west—probably holds the state's best concentration of ghost towns. Spring Canyon Road winds past the remnants of several, including the towns of Spring Canyon, Standardville, Latuda, and Mutual. If you're lucky, you might catch a glimpse of "the White Lady"—a ghost rumored to haunt the Latuda mine office. You can get a map of all the ghost towns in the Helper area at the Helper Museum information desk. ⊠ *Spring Canyon Rd., Helper* 🕾 *435/637–3009.*

🍴 Restaurants

Balance Rock Eatery & Pub
$ | **AMERICAN** | **FAMILY** | With tall ceilings and a second-floor mezzanine, this downtown pub looks like a reformed Wild West saloon and serves up American fare and Utah-made microbrews all day long. It's best known for its generous breakfasts and juicy burgers, and while you're here, make sure to browse the eclectic assortment of gift items for sale on the upper level. **Known for:** homemade potato chips; all-day breakfast; live music by local bands. [$] *Average main: $14* ✉ *148 S. Main St., Helper* ☎ *435/472–0403* 🕒 *No dinner Sun.*

Groggs Pinnacle Brewing Company
$$ | **AMERICAN** | This small, casual pub between Helper and Price is out of the way but worth the drive for its huge selection of burgers, pizzas, salads, and steak-house favorites. Start your meal with one of the many appetizers, and make sure to try one of the craft beers on tap. **Known for:** tasty burgers in more than a dozen varieties (including its Rodeo Burger, with pulled pork added); microbrews on tap; friendly, welcoming vibe. [$] *Average main: $17* ✉ *1653 N. Carbonville Rd., Helper* ☎ *435/637–2924* 🌐 *www.groggspinnaclebrewing.com.*

☕ Coffee and Quick Bites

Marsha's Sammich Shop-N-Bakery
$ | **CAFÉ** | This casual downtown gathering spot is a great place to get a sense of what's going on in Helper, plus a cup of coffee and a homebaked treat (the cinnamon rolls, in particular, sell out early). Marsha, one of the town's many colorful characters, also serves made-to-order breakfasts, burgers, soups, and sandwiches until 6 pm. **Known for:** delicious cinnamon rolls (especially when heated up); homemade soups; sandwiches with homemade bread (all the turkey selections are especially popular). [$] *Average main: $10* ✉ *69 S. Main St., Helper* ☎ *435/472–2253* 🕒 *Closed Sun. and Mon.*

🛍 Shopping

ART GALLERIES

★ **Steven Lee Adams Fine Arts**
ART GALLERIES | Painter Steve Adams has transformed Helper's historic JCPenney building into a glorious showcase for his impressionist takes on nature scenes from all over the world. He shares the space with painter Tim Morse, whose depictions of the Southwest are graphic and vibrant. Most days you can see at least one of them working in this huge studio and gallery. Lofty ceilings with a stuffed elk and motorcycles on display make this a memorable spot to peruse. ✉ *125 S. Main St., Helper* ☎ *801/318–3300* 🌐 *www.stevenleeadams.com.*

GIFTS

Bug + Bird Mercantile
ANTIQUES & COLLECTIBLES | This fun downtown shop is full of vintage clothing and accessories, local art, furniture, and many treasures that defy a category. Chat with the store's friendly owner, Jana, about the happenings around town including any events you shouldn't miss. ✉ *52 S. Main St.* ☎ *480/216–0889* 🌐 *www.facebook.com/bugandbirdmercantile.*

Mirror Lake Scenic Byway

Kamas is 16 miles east of Park City, 42 miles east of Salt Lake City.

Although the Wasatch may be Utah's best-known mountain range, the Uinta Mountains, the only major east–west mountain range in the United States, are its tallest, topped by 13,528-foot Kings Peak. This area, particularly in the High Uintas Wilderness where no vehicles are allowed, is great for pack trips, horseback day rides, hiking, and overnight backpacking in summer. The Uintas are ribboned with streams and dotted with small lakes set in rolling meadows.

From Salt Lake City, take I–80 and Highway 32 south to Kamas. You can access the Uinta Mountains either from Kamas or Evanston, Wyoming. From Kamas, go 65 miles east via Highway 150. From Evanston, travel 30 miles south on the same highway.

 ## Sights

Mirror Lake
BODY OF WATER | **FAMILY** | A mile north of the crest of Bald Mountain Pass on Highway 150, this is arguably the best known lake in the High Uintas Wilderness. At an altitude of 10,000 feet, it offers a cool respite from summer heat. It's easy to reach by car, and families enjoy fishing, hiking, and camping along its rocky shores. Its campgrounds provide a base for hikes into the surrounding mountains, and the Uinta Highline Trail accesses the 460,000-acre High Uintas Wilderness Area to the east. ✉ *UT 150, mile marker 32* ⊕ *www.fs.usda.gov.*

★ Mirror Lake Scenic Byway
SCENIC DRIVE | This scenic road begins in Kamas and winds its way up to the High Uinta country. The 65-mile drive follows Highway 150 through heavily wooded canyons past mountain lakes and peaks, cresting at 10,687-foot Bald Mountain Pass. Because of heavy winter snows, much of the road is closed from October to June. A three-day pass is required to use facilities in the area. You can purchase a pass at self-serve sites along the way, or at the Chevron, Kamas Food Town, or Samak Smoke House in Kamas. You can buy a guide to the byway from the Uinta-Wasatch-Cache National Forest's Kamas Ranger District office in Kamas. ✉ *Kamas Ranger District, 50 E. Center St., Kamas* ☎ *435/783–4338 Wasatch-Cache National Forest, Kamas Ranger District* ⊠ *$6 for 3-day pass.*

Upper Provo Falls
WATERFALL | If you are driving the Mirror Lake Scenic Byway, this is a good place to stop en route to Mirror Lake, near mile marker 24, where you can stroll the boardwalk to the terraced falls cascading with clear mountain water. ✉ *Hwy. 150, mile marker 24.*

 ## Hotels

The Cabins at Bear River Lodge
$$$ | **MOTEL** | **FAMILY** | Log cabins in the forest let you reconnect with nature via a range of on-site activities without giving up creature comforts. **Pros:** peaceful getaway in beautiful setting; plenty of activities; comfortable cabins. **Cons:** prices seem high for the level of amenities; no other restaurants within 30 miles; lower-level floors can be noisy. Ⓢ *Rooms from: $299* ✉ *Mirror Lake Hwy., mile marker 49* ☎ *435/642–6289* ⊕ *www.bearriverlodge.com* ↪ *14 cabins* ⦿*No Meals.*

 ## Activities

If you are staying at The Cabins at Bear River Lodge, you'll find it to be an ideal jumping-off spot to explore the Uinta Mountains. Well-informed employees can steer you to the right hiking trails for you, and the lodge rents sporting equipment you may not wish to carry with you, including fishing gear, ATVs, snowmobiles, cross-country skis, sleds, and snowshoes.

Chapter 7

CAPITOL REEF NATIONAL PARK

7

Updated by
Andrew Collins

🏕 Camping	🛏 Hotels	🏃 Activities	👁 Scenery	🎡 Crowds
★★☆☆☆	★☆☆☆☆	★★★★☆	★★★★★	★★★☆☆

WELCOME TO CAPITOL REEF NATIONAL PARK

TOP REASONS TO GO

★ **The Waterpocket Fold:** See a remarkable example of a monocline—a fold in the Earth's crust with one very steep side in an area that is otherwise horizontal. This one's almost 100 miles long.

★ **Fewer crowds:** Although visitation has more than doubled (to more than 1.4 million per year) since 2011, Capitol Reef is less crowded than nearby parks, such as Zion and Bryce Canyon.

★ **Fresh fruit:** Pick apples, pears, apricots, and peaches in season at the pioneer-planted orchards at historic Fruita. These trees still produce plenty of fruit.

★ **Rock art:** View pictographs and petroglyphs left by Native Americans who lived in this area from AD 600 to 1300.

★ **Rugged adventures:** Give yourself an extra day to explore the less-traveled but mesmerizing landscapes of remote Cathedral Valley (high-clearance vehicle required) and the South District (where a passenger car is suitable).

Forming the spine of this 378-square-mile park is the massive natural feature known as the Waterpocket Fold, which runs roughly 100 miles northwest to southeast. Capitol Reef itself is named for a formation along the fold near the Fremont River. A historic pioneer settlement, the green oasis of Fruita is easily explored on foot, and the 8-mile Scenic Drive provides a photogenic overview of the canyons and rock formations that populate the park. Colors here range from deep, rich reds to sage greens to crumbling gray sediments. The absence of large towns nearby ensures ideal conditions for stargazing in the dark night skies.

1 Fruita. This historic pioneer village is at the accessible heart of Capitol Reef. Here you'll find the lone park visitor center as well as verdant fruit orchards, some historic buildings, the main campground, and trailheads to several wonderful hikes. This is also where the free section of the Scenic Drive begins.

2 Scenic Drive. Winding 8 miles through the park, this aptly named road is the best way to get an overview of Capitol Reef's highlights, and it's easily accessible for all vehicles (although also the part of the park where a fee is charged). It takes about 90 minutes to drive to the end and back, but allow double that time to explore the interesting sights along the way.

3 North (Cathedral Valley) District. The views are stunning and the silence deafening in the park's remote northern section. High-clearance vehicles are required, as is crossing the Fremont River. Driving in this valley is next to impossible after it's rained, so check at the visitor center about current weather and road conditions.

4 South (Waterpocket) District. More and more visitors are taking the time to discover the eye-popping scenery of the park's southern reaches, which are accessed via Notom-Bullfrog Road from the north and Burr Trail Road from the west and southeast. High-clearance vehicles are required to drive into Upper Muley Twist Canyon, and rain can cause road closures, so check conditions in advance.

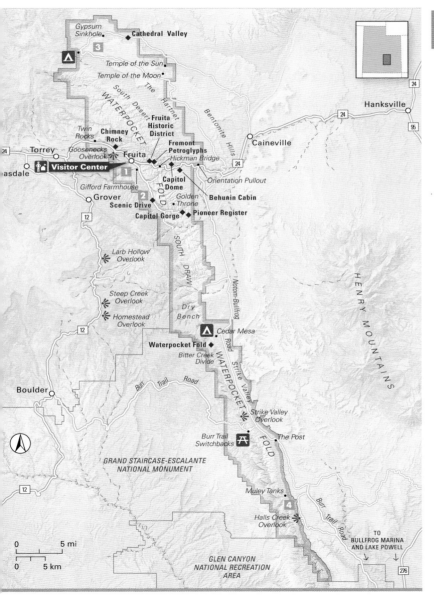

Gypsum
Sinkhole
3
Cathedral Valley

Temple of the Sun
Temple of the Moon

The Hartnet

WATERPOCKET

South Desert

Bentonite Hills

Hanksville

24

24

95

Twin
Rocks
**Chimney
Rock**
**Fruita
Historic
District**

Caineville

Torrey
Goosenecks
Overlook
Fruita
**Fremont
Petroglyphs**
Hickman Bridge

24

asdale
Visitor Center

FOLD

**Capitol
Dome**
Orientation Pullout

24

Gifford Farmhouse
Grover
2
Scenic Drive
Golden
Throne
Behunin Cabin

Capitol Gorge
Pioneer Register

12

Larb Hollow
Overlook

SOUTH
DRAW

Notom-Bullfrog

Steep Creek
Overlook

Homestead
Overlook

Dry
Bench

12

Cedar Mesa

Waterpocket Fold

Bitter Creek
Divide

WATERPOCKET

Strike Valley Road

H
E
N
R
Y

M
O
U
N
T
A
I
N
S

Burr
Trail
Road

Boulder

12

Strike Valley
Overlook

FOLD

Burr Trail
Switchbacks
The Post

GRAND STAIRCASE-ESCALANTE
NATIONAL MONUMENT

Muley Tanks

Burr
Trail
Road

4

12

Halls Creek
Overlook

0   5 mi

0   5 km

GLEN CANYON
NATIONAL RECREATION
AREA

TO
BULLFROG MARINA
AND LAKE POWELL

276

Ask regulars visitors to southern Utah's five national parks to name a favorite, and a surprising number will name Capitol Reef—at the very least, the consensus is that it's the most underrated of the group. With some of the most dramatic colors and geological shapes in the West, this kaleidoscopic landscape is a feast for the eyes. The Moenkopi Formation is a rich, red-chocolate hue; deep blue-green juniper and pinyon trees stand out against it. Sunrise and sunset bring out the colors in explosions of copper, platinum, and orange, then dusk turns the cliffs purple and blue.

The park, established in 1971, preserves the Waterpocket Fold, a giant wrinkle in the earth that extends 100 miles between Thousand Lake Mountain and Lake Powell. When you climb high onto the rocks or into the mountains, you can see this remarkable geologic wonder and the jumble of colorful cliffs, massive domes, soaring spires, and twisting canyons that surround it. It's no wonder early pioneers called this part of the country the "land of the sleeping rainbow."

Beyond incredible sights, the fragrance of pine and sage rises from the earth, and canyon wrens serenade you as you sit along the banks of the Fremont River, a narrow little creek that can turn into a swollen, raging torrent during desert flash floods. The river sustains cottonwoods, varied wildlife, and verdant valleys rich with fruit trees. During the harvest, your sensory experience is complete when you bite into a perfect ripe peach or apple from the park's orchards. Your soul, too, will be gratified here. You can walk the trails and drive the picturesque roads with relatively few crowds, except during busier periods. All around you are signs of those who came before: ancient Native Americans of the Fremont culture, Mormon pioneers who settled the land, and other courageous explorers who traveled the canyons.

Planning

Getting Here and Around

The nearest major airports are in Salt Lake City and Las Vegas, about 3½ and 5½ hours away by car, respectively. St. George Regional Airport (3½ hours away) is a handy, smaller airport with direct flights from several major cities in the West, Cedar City Municipal Airport (3 hours) has direct daily service on Delta from Salt Lake City, and Canyonlands Regional Airport in Moab (2 hours away) has direct daily service on United Airlines from Denver and Delta Airlines from Salt Lake City.

Capitol Reef has no shuttle service as in nearby Zion and Bryce Canyon National Parks, so you'll need your own transportation.

You can approach Capitol Reef country from several routes, including Highways 24 and 72 from Interstate 70 (and Moab), Highway 12 from Bryce Canyon National Park, and Highway 20 to U.S. 89 to Highway 62 from Interstate 15. All are well-maintained, safe roads that bisect rich agricultural communities steeped in Mormon history (especially in the nearby towns of Bicknell and Loa). Highway 24 runs across the middle of Capitol Reef National Park, offering scenic views the entire way. If spending time in the park's South District, the best approach is via Highway 12 to Burr Trail Road in Boulder.

Inspiration

Capitol Reef National Park: The Complete Hiking and Touring Guide, by Rich Stinchfield, is an outstanding companion for hiking and exploring.

The Capitol Reef Reader, edited by Stephen Trimble, shares writings about the park by almost 50 authors, with nearly 100 photos, many taken by the editor during decades of hiking Capitol Reef's trails.

Capitol Reef: Canyon Country Eden, by Rose Houk, is an award-winning collection of photographs and lyrical essays on the park.

Park Essentials

ACCESSIBILITY
Capitol Reef has few trails that are accessible to people in wheelchairs. The visitor center, museum, film, and restrooms are all accessible, as is the campground amphitheater where evening programs are held. The Fruita Campground has five campsites and a restroom that are fully accessible; so is the boardwalk to the petroglyph panel on Highway 24, 1.2 miles east of the visitor center.

CELL PHONE RECEPTION
Cell phone reception is nearly nonexistent in the park, although you may pick up a weak signal in a few spots. There's a pay phone at the Fruita Campground.

PARK FEES AND PERMITS
There is no fee to enter the park, but it's $20 per vehicle (or $10 per bicycle and $15 per motorcycle) to travel on the Scenic Drive beyond the Fruita Campground. You can pick up a free backcountry camping permit at the visitor center.

PARK HOURS
The park is open 24/7 year-round. It's in the Mountain time zone.

Hotels

There are no lodging options within Capitol Reef, but you'll find plenty of appealing places to stay in the nearby town of Torrey. See the Southwest Utah chapter for recommendations.

HOTEL AND RESTAURANT PRICES
Hotel and restaurant reviews have been shortened. For full information visit Fodors.com. Hotel prices are the lowest cost of a standard double room in high season. Restaurant prices are the

average cost of a main course at dinner, or if dinner is not served, at lunch.

What It Costs			
$	$$	$$$	$$$$
RESTAURANTS			
under $16	$16–$22	$23–$30	over $30
HOTELS			
under $125	$125–$200	$201–$300	over $300

Restaurants

Inside Capitol Reef you won't find any restaurants, though in summer the small Gifford House store sells baked goods and ice cream. Nearby Torrey has a number of excellent restaurants, though.

Visitor Information

PARK CONTACT INFORMATION Capitol Reef National Park. ⊠ *Hwy. 24* ☎ *435/425–3791* ⊕ *www.nps.gov/care.*

When to Go

Spring through early summer and fall are the most bustling seasons in the park. It's slightly less busy in midsummer, when days can be hot and thunderstorms can sometimes cause flooding, but the park is still fairly busy at this time. Winter is the quiet period. Although Capitol Reef is less crowded than Zion, Bryce Canyon, and Arches, visitation has increased dramatically in recent years, and the campground fills quickly (and is by reservation only). Annual rainfall is scant, but when it does rain (typically from late spring through summer), flash floods can wipe out park roads. Snowfall is usually light.

FESTIVALS AND EVENTS

Harvest Time Scarecrow Festival. Events for this month-long celebration marking the end of the busy season are held throughout Wayne County in October. In addition to a scarecrow contest, there are plenty of family-friendly events, including live music, arts and crafts, pumpkin carving, and a Halloween party. ⊕ www.entradainstitute.org

Wayne County Fair. The great American county fair tradition is at its finest in Loa, 30 miles west of the park, in mid-August. A demolition derby, a rodeo, horse shows, and a parade are all part of the fun. You'll also find crafts such as handmade quilts, agricultural exhibits, children's games, and plenty of good food. ⊕ waynecountyutah.org

Fruita

In the 1880s, Nels Johnson became the first homesteader in the Fremont River valley, building his home near the confluence of Sulphur Creek and the Fremont River. Other Mormon settlers followed and established small farms and orchards, creating the village of Junction. The orchards thrived, and by 1900 the name was changed to Fruita. The orchards, less than a mile from the visitor center, are preserved and protected as a Rural Historic District.

 Sights

GEOLOGICAL LANDMARKS

Capitol Dome

NATURE SIGHT | The rock formation that gave the park its name, this giant sandstone dome is visible in the vicinity of the Hickman Bridge trailhead on Highway 24, 1.9 miles east of the visitor center. ⊠ *Hwy. 24, Capitol Reef National Park.*

Chimney Rock

NATURE SIGHT | Even in a landscape of spires, cliffs, and knobs, this deep-red landform, 3.9 miles west of the visitor

Did You Know?

The 3.5-mile round-trip trek up to Chimney Rock has some steep switch-backs, but the journey yields panoramic views. The trailhead is 3 miles from the park visitor center, near the entrance. It is forbidden to rock climb on it.

center, is unmistakable. ⊠ *Hwy. 24, Capitol Reef National Park.*

HISTORIC SIGHTS

Behunin Cabin

NOTABLE BUILDING | FAMILY | In 1883, Elijah Cutler Behunin used blocks of sandstone to build this rudimentary cabin in which he and his family of 15(!) resided. Floods in the lowlands made life too difficult, and he moved just a year later. The house, 5.9 miles east of the visitor center, is empty, but you can peek through the window to see the interior. ⊠ *Hwy. 24, Capitol Reef National Park.*

Fremont Petroglyphs

INDIGENOUS SIGHT | Between AD 600 and 1300, the Capitol Reef area was occupied by Native Americans who were eventually referred to by archaeologists as the Fremont, after the park's Fremont River. A nice stroll along a boardwalk bridge, 1.1 miles east of the visitor center, allows close-up views of ancient rock art depicting bighorn sheep as well as trapezoidal figures, often shown wearing headdresses and ear baubles. ⊠ *Hwy. 24, Capitol Reef National Park.*

★ Gifford House Store and Museum

HISTORIC HOME | FAMILY | A mile south of the visitor center in a grassy meadow with the Fremont River flowing by, this is an idyllic shady spot in the Fruita Historic District to enjoy a sack lunch (if you have packed one), complete with tables, drinking water, grills, and a convenient restroom. The store sells reproductions of pioneer tools and items made by local craftspeople; there's also locally made fruit pies and ice cream to enjoy with your picnic. ⊠ *Scenic Dr., by the Fruita Campground, Capitol Reef National Park.*

TRAILS

★ Chimney Rock Trail

TRAIL | You're almost sure to see ravens drifting on thermal winds around the deep-red Mummy Cliff that rings the base of this loop trail that begins with a steep climb to a rim above dramatic

Chimney Rock—from here you're treated to impressive vistas of the western ridge of the Waterpocket Fold. This 3.6-mile loop has a 590-foot elevation change and can be a bit strenuous in hot weather, as there's no shade. Allow three to four hours. *Moderate–Difficult.* ⊠ *Capitol Reef National Park* ✛ *Trailhead: Hwy. 24, about 3 miles west of visitor center.*

★ Cohab Canyon Trail

TRAIL | You can access this 3.4-mile round-trip hike from near the campground in Fruita or from the Hickman Bridge parking lot on Highway 24; the Fruita approach is the more dramatic. From the campground, it's a steep climb to the mouth of the canyon and then a level hike through a wash with amazing color and texture. You'll find miniature arches, skinny side canyons, and honeycombed patterns on canyon walls where wrens make nests. When you get to Frying Pan, continue a little longer to where you can see Highway 24. Here you can hear the river and easily turn around, maybe taking the short (though steep) side treks to the South (0.6 miles round-trip) and North (0.2 miles round-trip) Fruita Overlooks on your way back. Allow two hours, including the side trails to the overlooks. *Moderate.* ⊠ *Capitol Reef National Park* ✛ *Trailheads: Scenic Dr. by campground, or Hwy. 24, about 2 miles east of visitor center.*

Fremont River Trail

TRAIL | What starts as a quiet little stroll beside the river turns into an adventure. The first 0.3 miles of the trail wanders past orchards next to the Fremont River. After you pass through a narrow gate, the trail changes personality and you're in for a steep climb on an exposed ledge with drop-offs. The views at the top of the 480-foot ascent are worth it. It's 2.1 miles round-trip; allow 90 minutes. *Moderate.* ⊠ *Capitol Reef National Park* ✛ *Trailhead: The parking lot for the picnic area just north of the Fremont River.*

Goosenecks Trail

TRAIL | FAMILY | This quick little stroll provides a great introduction to Capitol Reef and the surrounding landscape. You'll enjoy the dizzying views from the overlook. It's only 0.2 miles round-trip to the overlook. *Easy.* ⊠ *Capitol Reef National Park* ⊹ *Trailhead: Hwy. 24, about 3 miles west of visitor center.*

Hickman Bridge Trail

TRAIL | This extremely popular trail leads to a natural bridge of Kayenta sandstone, with a 133-foot opening carved by intermittent flash floods. Early on, the route climbs a set of steps along the Fremont River. The trail splits, leading along the right-hand branch to a strenuous uphill climb to the Rim Overlook and Navajo Knobs. Stay to your left to see the bridge, and you'll encounter a moderate up-and-down trail with an elevation gain. Up the wash on your way to the bridge is a Fremont granary on the right side of the small canyon. Allow about two hours for the 1.8-mile round-trip, which has an elevation gain of about 400 feet. *Moderate.* ⊠ *Capitol Reef National Park* ⊹ *Trailhead: Hwy. 24, 2 miles east of visitor center.*

★ Sunset Point Trail

TRAIL | FAMILY | The trail starts from the same parking lot as the Goosenecks Trail, on your way into the park about 3 miles west of the visitor center. Benches along this easy, 0.8-mile round-trip invite you to sit and meditate surrounded by the vast, colorful canyons and soaring mesas and mountain peaks. At the trail's end, you'll be rewarded with incredible vistas into the park. As the name suggests, it's a wonderful spot to watch the sunset. *Easy.* ⊠ *Hwy. 24, Capitol Reef National Park.*

SCENIC DRIVES
★ Utah Scenic Byway 24

SCENIC DRIVE | A roughly 15-mile section of this 65-mile designated byway between Loa and Hanksville passes right through the heart of Capitol Reef National Park. Colorful rock formations in all their hues of red, cream, pink, gold, and deep purple extend from one end of the route to the other. The landscape is most colorful within the park, but the views are pretty impressive the entire route, even as you continue through the lush green mountains west of Loa. ⊠ *Hwy. 24.*

VISITOR CENTERS
Capitol Reef Visitor Center

VISITOR CENTER | FAMILY | Watch a park movie, talk with rangers, or peruse the many books, maps, and materials for sale in the bookstore. Towering over the center, which is just off Highway 24 about 11 miles east of Torrey, you'll view The Castle, one of the park's most prominent rock formations. ⊠ *Scenic Dr., just south of Hwy. 24, Capitol Reef National Park* ☎ *435/425–3791* ⊕ *www. nps.gov/care.*

Scenic Drive

This paved 8-mile road, simply called "Scenic Drive," starts at the visitor center and winds south through the Fruita Historic District and colorful sandstone cliffs into Capitol Gorge. This section covers the sites you'll encounter south of Fruita, after you reach the pay station (1½ miles south of the visitor center). Off Scenic Drive, unpaved Grand Wash Road jogs east into an imposing canyon. Where the pavement ends at Capitol Gorge, the canyon walls become steep and impressive. This additional 2-mile section makes for a fun adventure but is also susceptible to severe and dangerous flash floods, especially from June through early September. In summer 2022, a sudden thunderstorm turned the road into a river, destroying several cars and temporarily stranding about 60 visitors (no one was hurt). ■TIP➜ **Check weather forecasts and with the visitor center before setting out.**

Temple of the Sun, a monolith in Capitol Reef's Cathedral Valley, is a favorite with photographers.

Sights

GEOLOGICAL LANDMARKS

The Waterpocket Fold

NATURE SIGHT | This giant wrinkle, technically what's called a monocline, in the earth's crust extends almost 100 miles between Thousand Lake Mountain and Lake Powell. You can glimpse the fold by driving south on Scenic Drive after it branches off Highway 24, past the Fruita Historic District. For a more complete immersion, enter the park via the Burr Trail, 36 miles from Boulder. Roads through the park's South District are unpaved and sometimes very rough—they can be impassable after rain, so check with the visitor center for current road conditions. ⊠ *Capitol Reef National Park.*

HISTORIC SIGHTS

Pioneer Register

HISTORIC SIGHT | Travelers passing through Capitol Gorge in the 19th and early 20th centuries etched the canyon wall with their names and the date. Directly across the canyon from the Pioneer Register and about 50 feet up are signatures etched into the canyon wall by an early United States Geologic Survey crew. Though it's illegal to write or scratch on the canyon walls today, plenty of damage has been done by vandals over the years. You can reach the register via an easy hike from the sheltered trailhead at the end of Capitol Gorge Road; the register is about 10 minutes along the hike toward the sandstone Tanks. ⊠ *Off Scenic Dr., Capitol Reef National Park.*

SCENIC DRIVES

★ Capitol Gorge

SCENIC DRIVE | The narrow, unpaved road that begins at the end of Scenic Drive twists along the floor of the gorge and was a route for pioneer wagons traversing this part of Utah starting in the 1860s. After every flash flood, pioneers would laboriously clear the route so wagons could continue to go through. The gorge was the main automobile route into the area until 1962, when Highway 24 was built. This 2-mile drive with striking views of the surrounding cliffs leads to one of the park's most popular hikes, to several "tanks" eroded into the sandstone that fill naturally with rainwater and snow-melt. ⊠ *Scenic Dr., Capitol Reef National Park* ⊹ *The unpaved road begins at end of Scenic Drive.*

TRAILS

★ Capitol Gorge Trail and the Tanks

TRAIL | FAMILY | Starting at the Pioneer Register, about a ½ mile from the Capitol Gorge parking lot, this ½-mile trail continues to a short uphill climb to the Tanks—holes in the sandstone, formed by erosion, that fill with rainwater and snowmelt. After a scramble up about ¼ mile of steep trail with cliff drop-offs, you can look down into the Tanks and see a natural bridge below the lower tank. Including the walk to the Pioneer Register, allow an hour to 90 minutes for this interesting hike, one of the park's most popular. *Easy .* ⊠ *Capitol Reef National Park* ⊹ *Trailhead: End of Scenic Dr.*

The Golden Throne Trail

TRAIL | As you hike to the base of The Golden Throne, you may be lucky enough to see one of the park's elusive desert bighorn sheep, but you're more likely to spot their split-hoof tracks. The challenging but rewarding hike sees a steady elevation gain of nearly 800 feet and sheer drop-offs. The Golden Throne is hidden until you near the end of the trail, when suddenly this huge sandstone monolith appears before you. If you hike near sundown, the throne burns gold. The round-trip hike is 4 miles and takes two to three hours. *Difficult.* ⊠ *Capitol Reef National Park* ⊹ *Trailhead: End of Capitol Gorge Rd.*

Grand Wash Trail

TRAIL | FAMILY | At the end of unpaved Grand Wash Road you can continue on foot through Bear Canyon all the way to Highway 24; if you'd rather avoid paying the $20 fee for Scenic Drive, you can also park at the Grand Wash Trailhead on Highway 24 and hike in from there. This mostly level hike takes you through a wide wash between canyon walls and is an excellent place to study the geology up close. Its round-trip hike is 4.4 miles; allow two to three hours. Check the weather conditions before you start, as this wash is prone to flooding after thunderstorms. Another (more strenuous) hiking option from the same starting point is the rugged 3.4-mile round-trip trail (it's fairly steep) to Cassidy Arch. *Easy.* ⊠ *Capitol Reef National Park* ⊹ *Trailhead: End of Grand Wash Rd., off Scenic Dr., or on Hwy. 24, 2.7 miles east of Hickman Bridge parking lot.*

North (Cathedral Valley) District

This primitive, rugged area was named for its sandstone geological features, which are reminiscent of Gothic cathedrals. Visiting is quite the backroad adventure, so not many people make the effort to drive on roads that can exact a brutal toll on your nerves and your vehicle. But if you have a high-clearance, four-wheel-drive vehicle and an adventurous spirit, the rewards of seeing ancient natural wonders are worth the effort. The selenite crystals of Glass Mountain attract rockhounds for a closer look, but no collecting is allowed. Sunset and sunrise at the Temple of the Sun and Temple of the Moon monoliths are especially colorful and photogenic.

Sights

SCENIC DRIVES

Cathedral Valley Loop

SCENIC DRIVE | The north end of Capitol Reef, along this backcountry road, is filled with towering monoliths, panoramic vistas, water crossings, and a stark desert landscape. The area is remote and the road through it unpaved and extremely rough, so don't even think about entering without a suitable mountain bike or high-clearance vehicle, some planning, and a cell phone (although reception is virtually nonexistent, you'll want to download maps to it before you get here). The trail through the valley is a 58-mile loop that you can begin at River Ford Road, 11¾ miles east of the visitor center off Highway 24; allow half a day. If your time is limited, consider touring just Caineville Wash Road, which takes about two hours by ATV or four-wheel-drive vehicle. If you are planning a multiday trip, there's a primitive campground about halfway through the loop. Pick up a self-guided tour brochure at the visitor center. ⊠ *Hartnet Rd., off Hwy. 24, Capitol Reef National Park.*

South (Waterpocket) District

Of the two sections of Capitol Reef National Park that require more effort and time to explore, the narrow South District (sometimes called the Waterpocket District) is far more accessible than Cathedral Valley—and the breathtaking scenery and relative absence of crowds makes it well worth seeking out. As long as you're visiting in dry weather, it's possible to explore this narrow, roughly 40-mile-long section of the striking Waterpocket Fold geological fault with a passenger car, although high-clearance vehicles allow access onto some of the rougher side roads. Late spring through summer is when rain is more likely; always check with the visitor center before setting out. Even brief recent storms (along with snow in winter) can render the unpaved roads in this part of the park virtually impassable, regardless of how high your vehicle's clearance is.

Most visitors explore this part of the park via the Loop-the-Fold route, a 125-mile circular route that takes four to six hours to drive—although you should allow a

full day if you're planning any side hikes. From the Capitol Reef Visitor Center, drive east 9 miles on Highway 24, then turn right onto Notom-Bullfrog Road and follow it south 33 miles (it becomes unpaved after about 17 miles). Then turn right (east) onto Burr Trail Road, driving up over the Waterpocket Fold via the famous Burr Trail Switchbacks; after about 5 miles, Burr Trail leaves Capitol Reef and enters Grand Staircase–Escalante National Monument. From here for the next 30 miles to Highway 12 in Boulder, the road is paved. When you reach Highway 12, it's an easy, paved 36-mile drive back to Torrey, and 10 more miles east on Highway 24 to return to the visitor center. An easier option for exploring the South District is spending the night in Boulder or Escalante and making a day trip from there (the Burr Trail Switchbacks and Upper Muley Twist Canyon hiking are less than 90 minutes from Boulder).

Sights

SCENIC DRIVES

★ Burr Trail Switchbacks

SCENIC DRIVE | Offering some of the most eye-popping scenery of any drive in southern Utah, the 67-mile Burr Trail twists and turns from the town of Boulder all the way to tiny Bullfrog, which lies at the tip of one of the many fingers of Lake Powell, within Glen Canyon National Recreation Area. Only an 8½-mile stretch of Burr Trail passes through Capitol Reef National Park, but it's arguably the most spectacular section. It's especially dramatic if approaching from the west from Boulder through Grand Staircase–Escalante National Monument. When you reach the Capitol Reef National Park border, the road becomes unpaved but is still generally (unless there's been heavy rain or snow) passable with a passenger car. It curves through juniper-dotted, red-rock countryside, offering sweeping views of the Strike Valley, the Studhorse Peaks, and—in the distance—the

Henry Mountains. After about 3 miles, you'll crest the upper, western ridge of the Waterpocket Fold, a 100-mile-long monocline in the earth's crust, and then zigzag some 800 feet down a series of dramatic switchbacks to the lower end of the fold. From here, Burr Trail Road continues southeast past the junction with Notom-Bullfrog Road (where a left turn leads back up to Torrey) toward the small village of Bullfrog. ⊠ *Burr Trail Rd., Capitol Reef National Park* ⊕ *www.nps.gov/glca/planyourvisit/driving-the-burr-trail.htm.*

TRAILS

Headquarters Canyon Trail

TRAIL | **FAMILY** | Among the hikes in Capitol Reef's South District, this typically quiet (you may have it all to yourself) trek offers a great reward—it leads into a narrow slot canyon with soaring cliff walls—but requires relatively little effort. It takes only about an hour to complete this 2.2-mile round-trip trail with an elevation gain of about 400 feet. *Easy.* ⊠ *Capitol Reef National Park* ⊕ *Trailhead: Burr Trail Rd., 2.3 miles south of junction with Notom-Bullfrog Rd.*

★ Upper Muley Twist Canyon Trail

TRAIL | The entire Muley Twist canyon runs about 12 miles north to south, crossing Burr Trail Road. It was used as a pass by pioneers traveling by wagon through the Waterpocket Fold and got its name because it was so narrow that it could "twist a mule." The Upper section has the most impressive scenery. There are two ways to tackle this trek. If using a high-clearance vehicle, you can drive 3.2 miles from Burr Trail along a rough but pretty road to the Strike Valley Overlook parking lot. If you're using a passenger vehicle, you'll need to park at the Upper Muley Twist Canyon trailhead, which is just 0.3 miles off Burr Trail, and then hike the remaining 2.9 miles to the Strike Valley Overlook parking lot. Just remember, the latter approach adds an extra (although very flat) 5.8 miles round-trip of hiking to this 10.3-mile trail, so

plan accordingly. From the Strike Valley Overlook lot, it's a pretty easy and level 3.4-mile round-trip hike to Saddle Arch, a dramatic sandstone formation. But for the most magical scenery, from here you'll want to continue on the 5.6-mile Rim Route loop, following it counter-clockwise as it passes over slickrock (you'll need to scramble up steep ridges in places) and through juniper and pinyon forests, providing dazzling views of fantastic rock formations, the Waterpocket Fold, and the Strike Valley down below. The trails in this part of the park aren't maintained (rock cairns and occasional signs mark the way), so bring a map, along with plenty of water—it can get very hot here in summer. *Difficult.* ⊠ *Capitol Reef National Park* ⊕ *Trailhead: Off Burr Trail, west of the Switchbacks.*

🚶 Activities

BIKING

Bicycles are allowed only on established roads in the park. Highway 24 receives a substantial amount of through traffic, so it's not the best place to pedal. The Scenic Drive is better, but the road is narrow, and you have to contend with drivers dazed by the beautiful surroundings. It's best to traverse it in the morning or evening when traffic is reduced, or in the off-season. Four-wheel-drive roads are certainly less traveled, but they are often sandy, rocky, and steep. The Cathedral Valley (North District) Loop is popular with mountain bikers (but also with four-wheelers). You cannot ride your bicycle in washes or on hiking trails, with the exception of the short trail that connects the visitor center to the Fruita Campground.

South Draw Road

BIKING | This is a very strenuous but picturesque ride that traverses dirt, sand, and rocky surfaces, crossing several creeks that may be muddy. It's not recommended in winter or spring because of deep snow at higher elevations. The route starts at an elevation of 8,500 feet on Boulder Mountain, 13 miles south of Torrey, and ends 15¾ miles later at 5,500 feet in the Pleasant Creek parking area at the end of Scenic Drive. ⊠ *Bowns Reservoir Rd., 7½ miles east of Hwy. 12, Capitol Reef National Park.*

CAMPING

Campgrounds—both the highly convenient Fruita Campground and the two backcountry sites—in Capitol Reef fill up fast between March and October.

Cathedral Valley Campground. This small (just six sites), basic (no water, pit toilet), no-fee campground in the park's remote northern district touts sprawling views, but the bumpy road there is hard to navigate and requires a high-clearance vehicle. ⊠ *Hartnet Junction, on Caineville Wash Rd.* ☎ *435/425–3791.*

Cedar Mesa Campground. Wonderful views of the Waterpocket Fold and Henry Mountains surround this primitive (pit toilet, no water), no-fee campground with five sites in the park's southern district. ⊠ *Notom-Bullfrog Rd., 23 miles south of Hwy. 24* ☎ *435/425–3791.*

Fruita Campground. Near the orchards and the Fremont River, the park's developed (flush toilets, running water), shady campground has 71 sites and is a great place to call home for a few days. The nightly fee is $25, and those nearest the Fremont River or the orchards are the most coveted. ⊠ *Scenic Dr., about 1 mile south of visitor center* ☎ *435/425–3791* ⊕ *www.recreation.gov.*

EDUCATIONAL PROGRAMS
RANGER PROGRAMS

Evening Program. Learn about Capitol Reef's geology, Native American cultures, wildlife, and more at the Fruita Campground amphitheater about a mile from the visitor center. Programs typically begin around sunset. ⊕ www.nps.gov/care/planyourvisit/ranger-programs.htm

Junior Ranger Program. Each child who participates in this self-guided, year-round program completes a combination of activities in the Junior Ranger booklet and attends a ranger program or watches the park movie.

Ranger Talks. Typically, the park offers a daily morning geology talk at the visitor center and a daily afternoon petroglyph-panel talk. Occasional geology hikes, history tours, and moon and stargazing tours are also offered.

FOUR-WHEELING

You can explore Capitol Reef in a four-wheel-drive vehicle on a number of exciting backcountry routes, with the Cathedral Valley/North District Loop especially thrilling. Keep in mind that all vehicles must remain on designated roadways. Road conditions can vary greatly depending on recent weather—if there's been heavy rain or snow, even the best four-wheel-drive vehicle may not be enough to tackle some of these roads.

HIKING

Many trails in Capitol Reef involve some significant elevation gains, but there are a handful of easy-to-moderate hikes. A short drive from the visitor center takes you to a dozen trails near the Fruita Historic District, but you'll discover some memorable hikes in the other areas, including the South District.

Chapter 8

ZION NATIONAL PARK

8

Updated by
Andrew Collins

 Camping
★★★★☆

 Hotels
★★★★☆

 Activities
★★★★☆

 Scenery
★★★★★

Crowds
★★★★★

WELCOME TO ZION NATIONAL PARK

TOP REASONS TO GO

★ **Eye candy:** Pick just about any trail in the park and it's all but guaranteed to culminate in an astounding viewpoint full of pink, orange, and crimson rock formations.

★ **Car-free exploring:** From February through November, Zion Canyon Scenic Drive can only be explored by free shuttle bus, making it a relatively peaceful road even when the park is crowded.

★ **Botanical wonderland:** Zion Canyon is home to more than 1,000 species of plants, more than anywhere else in Utah.

★ **Animal tracks:** Zion has expansive hinterlands where furry, scaly, and feathered residents are common. Hike long enough and you'll encounter deer, elk, rare lizards, birds of prey, and other fantastic fauna.

★ **Unforgettable canyoneering:** Zion's array of rugged slot canyons is one of the richest places on Earth for scrambling, rappelling, climbing, and descending.

The heart of Zion National Park is Zion Canyon, which follows the North Fork of the Virgin River for 6½ miles beneath cliffs that rise 2,000 feet from the river bottom. The Kolob Canyons area is considered by some to be more beautiful, and because it's isolated from the rest of the park, it's less crowded.

1 Zion Canyon. This area defines Zion National Park for most people. Free shuttle buses are the only vehicles allowed in the heart of the canyon February through November. Cars are permitted in the lower part of the canyon (which borders the town of Springdale) as well as Upper East Canyon, which are traversed via Highway 9. The backcountry is accessible via the West Rim Trail and The Narrows.

2 Kolob Canyons. The northwestern half of Zion is a secluded wonderland that can be reached only via a separate entrance off Interstate 15 or via Kolob Terrace Road, north of Virgin. It encompasses Kolob Arch and Lava Point, one of the highest points in the park.

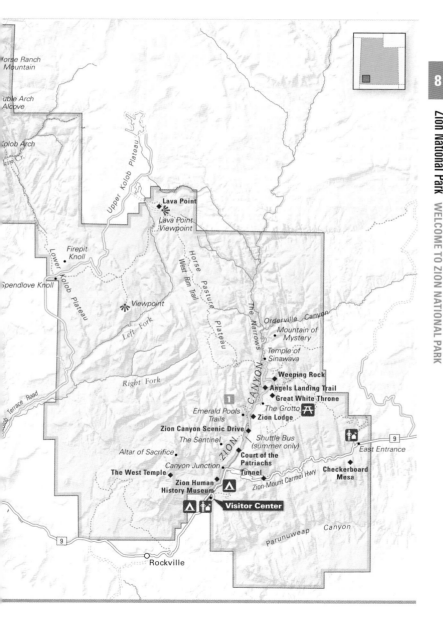

Horse Ranch
Mountain

uble Arch
Alcove

olob Arch

kin' Cr.

Upper Kolob Plateau

Lava Point
Lava Point
Viewpoint

Firepit
Knoll

Lower Kolob Plateau

Spendlove Knoll

Horse Pasture Plateau

West Rim Trail

Viewpoint

Left Fork

The Narrows

Orderville Canyon

Mountain of
Mystery

Temple of
Sinawava

Right Fork

Weeping Rock

Angels Landing Trail

Great White Throne

ZION CANYON

The Grotto

Emerald Pools
Trails

Zion Lodge

Zion Canyon Scenic Drive

The Sentinel

Altar of Sacrifice

Shuttle Bus
(summer only)

East Entrance

9

Z.I.O.N.

Court of the
Patriachs

The West Temple

Canyon Junction

Tunnel

Checkerboard
Mesa

Zion Human
History Museum

Zion-Mount Carmel Hwy

Visitor Center

mab Terrace Road

Parunuweap Canyon

9

Rockville

The walls of Zion Canyon soar more than 2,000 feet above the valley. Bands of limestone, sandstone, and lava in the strata point to the distant past. Greenery high in the cliff walls indicates the presence of water seepage or a spring. Erosion has left behind a collection of domes, fins, and blocky massifs bearing the names of cathedrals and temples, prophets and angels.

Trails lead deep into side canyons and up narrow ledges to waterfalls, serene spring-fed pools, and shaded spots of solitude. So diverse is this place that 85% of Utah's flora and fauna species are found here. Some, like the tiny Zion snail, appear nowhere else in the world.

The Colorado River helped create the Grand Canyon, while the Virgin River—a muddy tributary—carved Zion's features. Because of the park's unique topography, distant storms and spring runoff can transform a tranquil slot canyon into a sluice, and flood damage does sometimes result in extended trail closures, as happened in 2019 to three trails near the Grotto and Zion Lodge sections of Zion Canyon.

Planning

Getting Here and Around

AIR

Harry Reid International Airport in Las Vegas is approximately 3 hours by car from Zion; Salt Lake City's airport is 4½ hours by car.

The nearest airport to Zion's main (southern) entrance in Springdale is in St. George, which lies 40 miles west via Highway 9 and Interstate 15. From here, the park's less-visited Kolob Canyons entrance is 30 miles northeast.

CAR

You can access the main section of the park via Highway 9 (aka the Zion–Mt. Carmel Highway) and famously scenic Zion Canyon Scenic Drive; however, on the latter road, private cars are prohibited from February through November (with the exception of overnight guests at Zion Lodge). During these times, you can explore Zion Canyon Scenic Drive via free and frequent shuttle buses that depart from the Zion Canyon Visitor Center. Shuttles also bring visitors from neighboring Springdale to the visitor center.

Park Essentials

PARK FEES AND PERMITS

Entry, good for seven days, to Zion National Park costs $35 per vehicle, $20 per person entering on foot or by bicycle, and $30 by motorcycle.

Wilderness permits ($15) are required for backcountry camping and overnight hikes. Climbing and canyoneering parties need to buy one of these permits before using technical equipment to explore the park.

ACCESSIBILITY

Both visitor centers, all shuttle buses, and Zion Lodge are fully accessible to people in wheelchairs. Several campsites (sites A24 and A25 at the Watchman Campground, and sites 103, 114, and 115 at the South Campground) are reserved for people with disabilities, and two trails—Riverside Walk and Pa'rus Trail—are accessible with some assistance.

CELL PHONE RECEPTION

Cell phone reception is good in Springdale but spotty in the park. There are public phones at the Zion Canyon Visitor Center and Zion Lodge.

PARK HOURS

The park, open daily year-round, 24 hours a day, is in the Mountain time zone.

Hotels

There's one accommodation inside the park, the rustic and handsome Zion Lodge and its surrounding historic cabins. But you'll find plenty of (generally pricey) lodgings in the park-adjacent town of Springdale and a smaller number of mostly less expensive options to the east of the park in Orderville and Kanab. West of Springdale, both Hurricane and the city of St. George also offer good value and plenty of choices.

Restaurants

Only one full-service restaurant operates within the park, Red Rock Grill at the famed Zion Lodge (along with the adjacent snack bar, the Castle Dome Café), but in Springdale, just outside the park's south entrance, you'll find a sizable selection of both casual and sophisticated eateries. To the east, options are more limited, but nearby Kanab has an increasingly noteworthy dining scene.

HOTEL AND RESTAURANT PRICES

Hotel and restaurant reviews have been shortened. For full information visit Fodors.com. Hotel prices are the lowest cost of a standard double room in high season. Restaurant prices are the average cost of a main course at dinner, or if dinner is not served, at lunch.

What It Costs			
$	$$	$$$	$$$$
RESTAURANTS			
under $16	$16–$22	$23–$30	over $30
HOTELS			
under $125	$125–$200	$201–$300	over $300

8

Zion National Park PLANNING

Visitor Information

CONTACTS Zion National Park. ✉ *Hwy. 9, Springdale* ☎ *435/772–3256* ⊕ *www.nps. gov/zion.*

When to Go

Zion is the most heavily visited national park in Utah, receiving more than 5 million visitors each year. Locals used to call the spring and fall the shoulder seasons because traffic would drop off from the highly visited summer months; not anymore. These days the park is busy from March through November. Summer in the park is hot and mostly dry, punctuated by sudden cloudbursts that can create flash flooding and spectacular waterfalls. Expect afternoon thunderstorms between July and September. Whether the day starts out sunny or not, wear sunscreen and drink lots of water, even if you aren't exerting yourself or spending much time outside. The sun is very powerful at this elevation. Winters are mild at lower desert elevations but chilly in the higher Kolob Canyons section of the park. It's possible to encounter snow from November to mid-March, and although most park programs are suspended in winter, it is a wonderful and solitary time to see the canyons.

■ **TIP**→ **The temperature in Zion often exceeds 100°F in July and August.**

Zion Canyon

Although this area comprising the soaring 6-mile main canyon cut by the Virgin River as well as Upper East Canyon along Highway 9 makes up only the southeastern third of Zion National Park, this is where the vast majority of the 5 million annual visitors spend their visits. There's no denying the beauty and scale of the solid rock cliffs that dwarf the stream-fed valley below—indeed, this part of the park is so popular because it contains some of its most iconic attractions and hikes, from Angels Landing and The Court of the Patriarchs to Zion Lodge and Canyon Overlook.

Zion Canyon is also easy to access and contains the park's main visitor center, which sits right at the border with the cute town of Springdale, an excellent base with plenty of lodging and dining options. Highway 9 (aka Zion–Mount Caramel Highway) traverses this portion of the park from the south entrance in Springdale through the dramatic Zion–Mt. Caramel Tunnel to the east entrance. You can drive this road year-round, and you'll find plenty of pullouts for hopping out, stretching your legs, and snapping photos; several popular trailheads are located along here, too.

The most spectacular section of the main canyon is accessed via spectacular Zion Canyon Scenic Drive, but from about February through November (check the visitor center or park website for exact hours), you can only visit this road by free shuttle bus—unless you're overnight at Zion Lodge, in which case you can drive your own car to that point. You'll find trailheads to several legendary hikes along this drive.

It's a good idea to bring insect repellent, as the trails along the Virgin River can get buggy from spring through early fall. Note, also, that the hikes to Weeping Rock, Hidden Canyon, and Observation Point were closed due to a major rock slide in 2019, and as of this writing, no reopening date has been announced. Check with the visitor center for further updates.

 Sights

GEOLOGICAL LANDMARKS
★ **The Narrows**

NATURE SIGHT | This sinuous, 16-mile crack in the earth where the Virgin River flows over gravel and boulders is one of the world's most stunning gorges. If you hike through it, you'll find yourself surrounded—sometimes nearly boxed in—by smooth walls stretching high into the heavens. Plan to get wet, and be aware that deadly flash floods can occur here, especially in spring and summer. Always check on the weather before you enter. ⊠ *Zion National Park* ⊕ *Begins at Riverside Walk, at end of Zion Canyon Scenic Drive.*

HISTORIC SIGHTS
Zion Human History Museum
HISTORY MUSEUM | This informative museum tells the park's story from the perspective of its human inhabitants, among them Ancestral Puebloans and early Mormon settlers. Permanent exhibits illustrate how humans have dealt with wildlife, plants, and natural forces. Temporary exhibits have touched on everything from vintage park-employee photography to the history of Union Pacific Railroad hotels. Don't miss the incredible view of Towers of the Virgin from the back patio. ⊠ *Zion Canyon Scenic Dr., ½ mile north of south entrance, Zion National Park* ☎ *435/772–3256* ⊕ *www. nps.gov/zion* ⊠ *Free.*

SCENIC DRIVES
★ Zion Canyon Scenic Drive
SCENIC DRIVE | **FAMILY** | Vividly colored cliffs tower 2,000 feet above the road that meanders north from Highway 9 at Canyon Junction along the floor of Zion Canyon. As you roll through the narrow, steep canyon, you'll pass The Court of the Patriarchs, The Sentinel, and The Great White Throne, among other imposing rock formations. From roughly February through November, unless you're staying at the lodge, you can access Zion Canyon Scenic Drive only by riding the park shuttle. The rest of the year, you can drive it yourself. ⊠ *Off Hwy. 9 at Canyon Junction, Zion National Park.*

Zion–Mount Carmel Highway and Tunnels
SCENIC DRIVE | Two narrow tunnels as old as the park itself lie between the east entrance and Zion Canyon on this breathtaking 12-mile stretch of Highway 9. One was once the longest man-made tunnel in the world. As you travel the (1.1-mile)

passage through solid rock, five arched portals along one side provide fleeting glimpses of cliffs and canyons. When you emerge you'll find that the landscape has changed dramatically. Large vehicles require traffic control and a $15 permit, available at the park entrance, and have restricted hours of travel. This includes nearly all RVs, trailers, dual-wheel trucks, and campers. The Canyon Overlook Trail starts from a parking area between the tunnels. ⊠ *Hwy. 9, 5 miles east of Canyon Junction, Zion National Park* ⊕ *www.nps.gov/zion/planyourvisit/the-zion-mount-carmel-tunnel.htm.*

SCENIC STOPS
Checkerboard Mesa
NATURE SIGHT | It's well worth stopping at the pull-out 1 mile west of Zion's east entrance to observe the distinctive waffle patterns on this huge white mound of sandstone. The stunning crosshatch effect visible today is the result of eons of freeze-and-thaw cycles that caused vertical fractures, combined with erosion that produced horizontal bedding planes. ⊠ *Hwy. 9, Zion National Park.*

The Court of the Patriarchs
NATURE SIGHT | This trio of peaks bears the names of, from left to right, Abraham, Isaac, and Jacob. Mount Moroni is the reddish peak on the far right that partially blocks the view of Jacob. Hike the trail that leaves from The Court of the Patriarchs viewpoint, 1½ miles north of Canyon Junction, to get a much better view of the sandstone prophets. ⊠ *Zion Canyon Scenic Dr., Zion National Park.*

TRAILS
★ Angels Landing Trail
TRAIL | As much a trial as a trail, this serpentine path beneath The Great White Throne, which you access from the Lower West Rim Trail, is one of the park's most challenging and genuinely thrilling hikes. It had also been on the verge of becoming a victim of its own popularity, suffering badly from overcrowding, until the park service instituted

a permit system in 2022, which has greatly reduced the number of hikers at any given time and vastly improved the experience. You now must apply online at ⊕ *recreation.gov* (both seasonal and day-before lotteries are held, and the cost is $6) for the chance to hike the famed final section beyond Scout Lookout. Once you've ascended from the Lower West Rim Trail, you'll encounter Walter's Wiggles, an arduous (but not at all scary) series of 21 switchbacks built out of sandstone blocks that leads up to Scout Lookout. From here, assuming you've secured a permit, you'll continue along a narrow, steadily rising ridge with sheer cliffs that drop some 1,400 feet on either side. Chains bolted into the rock face serve as handrails in the steepest places. In spite of its hair-raising nature, and taking into consideration that 14 people have fallen to their deaths on this hike since 2000, the climb doesn't require technical skills and is quite safe as long as you step deliberately and use the handrail chains. Still, children and those uneasy about heights should not attempt this hike. Allow 2½ hours round-trip to hike to Scout Lookout (2 miles), which is itself an impressive viewpoint, and four to five hours if you continue to where the angels (and birds of prey) play. The total hike is about 4.5 miles round-trip from the Grotto shuttle stop. *Difficult.* ⊠ *Zion National Park* ⊹ *Trailhead: Off Zion Canyon Scenic Dr. at the Grotto* ⊕ *www.nps.gov/zion/planyourvisit/angels-landing-hiking-permits.htm.*

★ Canyon Overlook Trail

TRAIL | FAMILY | The parking area just east of Zion–Mount Carmel Tunnel leads to this highly popular trail, which is about 1 mile round-trip and takes about an hour to finish. From the breathtaking overlook at the trail's end, you can see The West and East Temples, The Towers of the Virgin, The Streaked Wall, and other Zion Canyon cliffs and peaks. The elevation change is 160 feet. There's no shuttle to this trail, and the parking area often fills up—try to

come very early or late in the day to avoid crowds. *Easy–Moderate.* ⊠ *Zion National Park* ⊹ *Trailhead: Off Hwy. 9 just east of Zion–Mt. Carmel Tunnel.*

Emerald Pools Trail

TRAIL | FAMILY | Multiple waterfalls cascade (or drip, in dry weather) into algae-filled pools along this trail that begins along the Virgin River on Zion Canyon Scenic Drive. The path leading to the lower pool is paved but is too steep and narrow to be appropriate for wheelchairs, at least not without assistance. If you've got any energy left, keep going past the lower pool. The ½ mile from there to the middle and then upper pools becomes rocky and somewhat steep but offers increasingly scenic views. A less crowded and exceptionally enjoyable return route follows the Kayenta Trail, connecting to the Grotto Trail. Allow 50 minutes for the 1¼-mile round-trip hike to the lower pool, and an hour more each round-trip to the middle (2 miles) and upper pools (3 miles). *Lower, easy. Upper and Middle, moderate.* ⊠ *Zion National Park* ⊹ *Trailhead: Off Zion Canyon Scenic Dr., at Zion Lodge or the Grotto.*

Grotto Trail

TRAIL | FAMILY | This level, 1-mile round-trip trail takes you from Zion Lodge to the lovely, tree-shaded Grotto picnic area, traveling much of the way parallel to the park road. Allow 20 minutes or less for this easy stroll through meadows and beneath a light tree canopy. From here, you can cross the footbridge over the Virgin River to connect with the Kayenta Trail, which leads south to the Emerald Pools trails or north to the West Rim Trail and eventually up to Angels Landing (for which a permit is required). *Easy.* ⊠ *Zion National Park* ⊹ *Trailhead: Off Zion Canyon Scenic Dr. at the Grotto.*

★ The Narrows Trail

TRAIL | After leaving the paved ease of Riverside Walk (aka the Gateway to The Narrows Trail) behind, this famous and challenging trek entails walking on the riverbed itself. You'll find a pebbly shingle or dry sandbar path, but when the walls of the canyon close in, you'll be forced into the chilly waters of the Virgin River. A walking stick and proper water shoes are a must. Be prepared to swim, as chest-deep holes may occur even when water levels are low. More than half of the entire hike takes place at least partially wading or even possibly swimming in the water, but the views of the sheer canyon walls are something else. Always check the weather forecast and with park rangers about the likelihood of flash floods—a hiker was swept to her death following a sudden thunderstorm in summer 2022. A day trip up the lower section of The Narrows is about 4.7 miles one-way to the turnaround point at Big Spring. Allow at least five to seven hours round-trip. *Difficult.* ⊠ *Zion National Park* ⚐ *Trailhead: Off Zion Canyon Scenic Dr., at end of Riverside Walk.*

Pa'rus Trail

TRAIL | FAMILY | This relatively flat, paved walking and biking path parallels and occasionally crosses the Virgin River and offers a great way to take in some of Zion Canyon's most impressive vistas while using a wheelchair or stroller, spending time with your pooch (leashed dogs are welcome), or simply enjoying a relaxing ramble or bike ride. Starting at the South Campground, ½ mile north of the South Entrance, the walk proceeds north along the river to the beginning of Zion Canyon Scenic Drive and is 3.5 miles round-trip. Along the way you'll take in great views of The Watchman, The Sentinel, The East and West Temples, and The Towers of the Virgin. Keep an eye out for bicycles zipping by. *Easy.* ⊠ *Zion National Park* ⚐ *Trailhead: At South Campground.*

Riverside Walk

TRAIL | FAMILY | This 2.2-mile round-trip hike that's also sometimes referred to as the Gateway to The Narrows Trail shadows the Virgin River. In spring, wildflowers bloom on the opposite canyon wall in lovely hanging gardens. The trail, which begins at the end of Zion Canyon Scenic Drive, is one of the park's most visited, so be prepared for crowds. Riverside Walk is paved and suitable for strollers and wheelchairs, though some wheelchair users may need assistance. Round-trip it takes about 90 minutes. At the end, the much more challenging The Narrows Trail begins. *Easy.* ⊠ *Zion National Park* ⚐ *Trailhead: Off Zion Canyon Scenic Dr. at the Temple of Sinawava.*

Watchman Trail

TRAIL | FAMILY | For a dramatic view of Springdale and a great introduction to the park's landscape, including lower Zion Creek Canyon and The Towers of the Virgin, this moderately taxing adventure begins on a service road east of the Watchman Campground. Some springs seep out of the sandstone, nourishing the hanging gardens and attracting wildlife. There are a few sheer cliff edges, so supervise children carefully. Plan on two hours to complete this 3.3-mile round-trip hike with a 368-foot elevation change. *Moderate.* ⊠ *Zion National Park* ⚐ *Trailhead: At Zion Canyon Visitor Center.*

VISITOR CENTERS

Zion Canyon Visitor Center

VISITOR CENTER | FAMILY | Learn about the area's geology, flora, and fauna at the outdoor interpretive exhibits next to a gurgling stream. Inside, a large shop sells everything from field guides to souvenirs. Zion Canyon shuttle buses leave regularly from the center and connect with Springdale as well as making several stops along the canyon's beautiful Scenic Drive; ranger-guided shuttle tours depart once a day from Memorial Day to late September. Within a short walk you can also access the small Zion Nature Center, the park's two main campgrounds, and both the Watchman and Pa'rus hiking trails. During busy periods, the visitor center and surrounding plaza can feel like a bit of a zoo (and spaces can be tough to come by in the parking lot); try

Take a shuttle or scenic horseback ride within the walls of Zion Canyon.

to arrive very early or late in the day if you can. ✉ *Zion Park Blvd. at south entrance, Springdale* ☎ *435/772–3256* 🌐 *www.nps.gov/zion.*

🍴 Restaurants

Castle Dome Café
$ | **CAFÉ** | Next to the shuttle stop at Zion Lodge, this small, convenient, fast-food restaurant has a lovely shaded patio. You can grab a banana, burger, smoothie, or salad to go, order local brews from the Beer Garden cart, or enjoy a dish of ice cream while soaking up the views of the surrounding geological formations. **Known for:** quick option for pre- or posthiking; gorgeous views; nice beer selection. [$] *Average main: $8* ✉ *Zion Lodge, Zion Canyon Scenic Dr., Zion National Park* ☎ *435/772–7700* 🌐 *www.zionlodge.com* ⏲ *Closed Dec.–Feb.*

Red Rock Grill
$$ | **AMERICAN** | The dinner fare at this restaurant in Zion Lodge includes steaks, seafood, and Western specialties, such as pecan-encrusted trout and cheddar-jalapeño-topped bison cheeseburgers; salads, sandwiches, and hearty Navajo tacos are lunch highlights; and, for breakfast, you can partake of the plentiful buffet or order off the menu. Photos showcasing the surrounding landscape adorn the walls of the spacious dining room; enormous windows and a large patio (which can be buggy) take in the actual landscape. **Known for:** there can be a wait for a table at busy times; astounding canyon views from dining room and patio; only full-service restaurant in the park. [$] *Average main: $21* ✉ *Zion Lodge, Zion Canyon Scenic Dr., Zion National Park* ☎ *435/772–7760* 🌐 *www.zionlodge.com.*

🛏 Hotels

★ Zion Lodge
$$$ | **HOTEL** | For a dramatic setting inside the park, you'd be hard-pressed to improve on a stay at the historic Zion Lodge: the canyon's jaw-dropping beauty surrounds you, access to trailheads is easy, and guests can drive their cars on

the lower half of Zion Park Scenic Drive year-round. **Pros:** ideal location if planning a long day hike in the canyon; incredible views; bike rentals on-site. **Cons:** pathways are dimly lit; spotty Wi-Fi, poor cell service; books up months ahead. [$] *Rooms from: $237* ✉ *Zion Canyon Scenic Dr., Zion National Park* ☎ *888/297–2757, 435/772–7700* 🌐 *www.zionlodge.com* 🛏 *122 rooms* 🍴 *No Meals.*

Kolob Canyons

Overlooked by many park visitors, Kolob Canyons and Kolob Terrace offer windows into an entirely different habitat than that of Zion Canyon. About 45 minutes from Springdale, the Kolob Canyons section showcases the red rocks of the park's northwest corner. It's accessible from I–15 at Exit 40, and nothing in the appearance of the unassuming visitor center here hints at the lush red canyons that cut into the mountains behind it. The entire 5-mile road is within park boundaries, with two trailheads offering day hikes and one trailhead leading into the vast backcountry.

Kolob Terrace Road runs to lava fields, a reservoir, and a beautiful campground, Lava Point, in the heart of the park's backcountry. Unlike Kolob Canyons Road, much of this road is outside park boundaries, hopscotching through Bureau of Land Management and private land. Look for evidence of prehistoric volcanic activity, with black rock prevailing here rather than the red clay and white sandstone that characterizes much of the rest of the park. There are several noteworthy peaks to see, several trailheads through which to access the backcountry, and, finally, Kolob Reservoir, which has somewhat low water levels, due to drought in recent years.

Sights

SCENIC DRIVES

★ Kolob Canyons Road

SCENIC DRIVE | Receiving relatively little traffic, Kolob Canyons Road climbs 5 miles into red rock canyons that extend east-to-west along three forks of Taylor Creek and La Verkin Creek. The beauty starts modestly at the junction with Interstate 15, but as the road twists and turns higher, the red walls of the Kolob finger canyons rise suddenly and spectacularly. From Kolob Canyons Viewpoint at the end of the drive, take in views of Nagunt Mesa, Shuntavi Butte, and Gregory Butte, each rising to nearly 8,000 feet in elevation. The entire round-trip drive can be completed in about an hour, without hikes. Kolob Canyons Road does sometimes close as a result of heavy snowfall. ✉ *Zion National Park* ✣ *Off I–15, Exit 40.*

Kolob Terrace Road

SCENIC DRIVE | Starting around 4,000 feet above the floor of Zion Canyon, and without the benefit of the canyon's breezes and shade, the landscape at the beginning of this less-traveled park road is arid—browns and grays and ambers—but not without rugged beauty. The 21-mile stretch begins 19 miles west of Springdale via the village of Virgin and winds north. As you travel along, peaks and knolls emerge from the high plateau, birds circle overhead, and you might not see more than a half-dozen cars. The drive meanders out of the park boundary and then back in again, accessing a few prominent backcountry trailheads, all the while overlooking the cliffs of North Creek. It eventually climbs into the cooler alpine wilderness, to elevations of nearly 8,000 feet.

A popular day-use trail (a $15 wilderness permit is required) leads past fossilized dinosaur tracks to The Subway, a stretch of the stream where the walls of the slot canyon close in so tightly as to form a near tunnel. Farther along the road is the Wildcat Canyon trailhead, which connects to the path overlooking North Guardian Angel. The road then leaves the park and terminates at Kolob Reservoir, beneath 8,933-foot Kolob Peak. Although paved, this narrow, twisting road is not recommended for RVs. Because of limited winter plowing, the road is closed from November or December through April or May. Although there's no fee station on this road, you are required to have paid the park entrance fee, which you can do in Springdale or at the Kolob Canyons Visitor Center. ⊠ *Zion National Park* ✛ *Enter the park about 6½ miles north of Hwy. 9 in Virgin.*

SCENIC STOPS

★ Kolob Canyons Viewpoint

VIEWPOINT | **FAMILY** | The big payoff for entering the northwestern Kolob Canyons section of the park off Interstate 15, this spectacular viewpoint lies at the end of 5-mile Kolob Canyons Road. You'll be treated to a beautiful view of Kolob's "finger" canyons from the several picnic tables spread out beneath the trees. The parking lot has plenty of spaces, a pit toilet, and an overlook with a display pointing out the area's most prominent geological features. Restrooms and drinking water are available at the start of the drive, at Kolob Canyons Visitor Center. ⊠ *Zion National Park* ✛ *End of Kolob Canyons Rd.*

Lava Point Overlook

VIEWPOINT | Infrequently visited, this area has a primitive campground and, just beyond the park boundary, two nearby reservoirs that offer the only significant fishing opportunities near the park. Lava Point Overlook, one of the park's highest viewpoints, provides vistas of Zion Canyon from the north. The higher elevation here makes it much cooler than the Zion Canyon area. Park visitors looking for a respite from crowds and heat find the campground a nice change of pace—the six sites are available by reservation only, May through September. ⊠ *Zion National Park* ✛ *Lava Point Rd., off Kolob Terrace Rd.*

Lee Pass

VIEWPOINT | This hairpin turn on Kolob Canyons Road has a roadside pullout that provides the opportunity to glimpse deep into the canyon carved by the South Fork of Taylor Creek. This is the trailhead for the 14-mile round-trip Kolob Arch hike, which also connects you to the main section of Zion National Park via the backcountry (if overnighting in the backcountry, a wilderness permit is required). ⊠ *Kolob Canyons Rd., Zion National Park* ✛ *4 miles east of Kolob Canyons Visitor Center.*

TRAILS

La Verkin Creek Trail to Kolob Arch

TRAIL | In the park's northwest corner, this 14-mile round-trip hike with an elevation gain of a little over 1,000 feet leads to one of the largest freestanding arches ever discovered. Kolob Arch spans nearly the length of a football field (287 feet) and is reached via this pleasant trail alongside La Verkin Creek and beneath the vivid red cliffs of Shuntavi Butte and Timber Top Mountain. Multiple campsites are available to make this an overnight itinerary (a wilderness permit is required for overnight stays). You can connect with the Hop Valley Trail to head into the main section of Zion National Park. *Difficult.* ⊠ *Zion National Park* ✛ *Trailhead: At Lee Pass, on Kolob Canyons Rd.*

★ Taylor Creek Trail

TRAIL | This trail in the Kolob Canyons area descends parallel to Taylor Creek, sometimes crossing it, sometimes shortcutting benches beside it. The historic Larson Cabin precedes the entrance to the canyon of the Middle Fork, where the trail becomes rougher. After the old Fife Cabin, the canyon bends to the right into Double Arch Alcove, a large, colorful grotto with a high blind arch (or arch "embryo") towering above. To Double Arch it's 5 miles round-trip, and takes about four hours. The elevation change is 450 feet. *Moderate.* ⊠ *Zion National Park* ✛ *Trailhead: At Kolob Canyons Rd., about 1½ miles east of Kolob Canyons Visitor Center.*

Timber Creek Overlook Trail

TRAIL | **FAMILY** | Don't miss this short hike at the end of Kolob Canyons Road. Covered with desert wildflowers in spring and early summer, it's barely a mile round-trip on a sandy, relatively exposed plateau above the surrounding valleys. Get a good look at the Kolob Canyons "skyline," including Shuntavi Butte in the shadow of 8,055-foot Timber Top Mountain. The last few hundred yards are a little rockier with a 100-foot ascent, but even kids and novice hikers shouldn't have any trouble with it. At the picnic area at the trailhead, you might spy lizards, chipmunks, squirrels, and the occasional long-eared, black-tailed jackrabbit. *Easy. ⊠ Zion National Park ⊹ Trailhead: At end of Kolob Canyons Rd.*

VISITOR CENTERS

Kolob Canyons Visitor Center

VISITOR CENTER | Stop here at this small visitor center just off Interstate 15 to pay your entrance fee and pick up books, maps, and information on exploring the Kolob Canyons section of the park. ⊠ *3752 E. Kolob Canyons Rd., Exit 40 off I–15, Zion National Park* ☎ *435/772–3256* ⊕ *www.nps.gov/zion.*

Activities

ADVENTURE TOURS

★ Zion Adventures

HIKING & WALKING | **FAMILY** | Since 1996, this well-respected company has guided, equipped, and offered advice on a wide range of desert adventures, including some of the top hikes in the park. Countless trekkers heading upstream on The Narrows carry Zion Adventures walking sticks and neoprene Aqua Sox footwear. The company offers special family adventures, including rock climbing and canyoneering, as well as bike tours and rentals, multiday canyoneering experiences, rock-climbing courses, photography tours, and workshops. ⊠ *36 Lion Blvd., Springdale* ☎ *435/772–1001* ⊕ *www.zionadventures.com* ⊠ *From $89.*

Zion Guru

HIKING & WALKING | **FAMILY** | With a holistic approach to adventure, this guide service teaches canyoneering skills to beginners as young as age five and guides advanced tours as well. They offer half- and full-day rock-climbing and guided hikes, including into The Narrows, as well as yoga and wellness experiences. They also rent e-bikes and gear for The Narrows and run a shuttle service to park trailheads. ⊠ *792 Zion Park Blvd., Springdale* ☎ *435/632–0462* ⊕ *www.zionguru.com* ⊠ *From $188.*

AIR TOURS

Zion Helicopters

AIR EXCURSIONS | This flightseeing operation 10 miles west of the park's Springdale entrance offers exhilarating helicopter rides over the park, starting with relatively affordable 12-minute quick zips over the canyon, up to 90-minute excursions that include landing on a private red-rock butte. The company also offers Bryce Canyon and Lake Powell flights. ⊠ *3050 Hwy. 9, Virgin* ☎ *435/668–4185* ⊕ *www.zionhelicopters.com* ⊠ *From $99.*

BIKING

Zion Cycles

BIKING | This shop just outside the park rents bikes by the hour or longer, sells parts, and has a full-time mechanic on duty. You can pick up trail tips and other advice from the staff here. They also offer guided road-biking treks in the park and mountain-biking excursions elsewhere in southern Utah. ⊠ *868 Zion Park Blvd., Springdale* ☎ *435/772–0400* ⊕ *www.zioncycles.com* ⊠ *Guided tours from $189.*

CAMPING

Lava Point Campground. This high-alpine (elevation 7,890 feet) section of the park off Kolob Terrace Road has six primitive tent sites and is typically open May through September. In 2022, Lava Point began requiring reservations (rates are $20 nightly). ⊠ *Kolob Terrace Rd., 15 miles northeast of Kolob Terrace entrance* ☎ *877/444–6777* ⊕ *www.recreation.gov.*

South Campground. All the sites here are under big cottonwood trees that provide some relief from the summer sun. The campground operates on a reservation system ($20 nightly). ⊠ *Hwy. 9, ½ mile north of south entrance* ☎ *877/444– 6777* ⊕ *www.recreation.gov.*

Watchman Campground. This large camp- ground with both tent and RV sites on the Virgin River operates on a reservation system ($20 nightly for tent sites, $30 for RV sites). ⊠ Access road off Zion Canyon Visitor Center parking lot ☎ *877/444– 6777* ⊕ *www.recreation.gov.*

HORSEBACK RIDING

Canyon Trail Rides

HORSEBACK RIDING | FAMILY | Easygoing one-hour and half-day guided rides are available (minimum age 7 and 10 years, respectively). These friendly folks have been around for years and are the only outfitter for trail rides inside the park. Reservations are recommended and can be made online. The maximum weight is 220 pounds, and the season runs from March through October. ⊠ *Across from Zion Lodge, Zion National Park* ☎ *435/679–8665* ⊕ *www.canyonrides. com* ⊠ *From $50.*

BRYCE CANYON NATIONAL PARK

Updated by
Andrew Collins

⛰ Camping	🛏 Hotels	🏃 Activities	👁 Scenery	👥 Crowds
★★★★☆	★★★★☆	★★★☆☆	★★★★★	★★★★☆

WELCOME TO BRYCE CANYON NATIONAL PARK

TOP REASONS TO GO

★ **Hoodoo heaven:** The boldly colored, gravity-defying limestone tentacles reaching skyward—called hoodoos—are Bryce Canyon's most recognizable attraction.

★ **Famous fresh air:** With some of the clearest skies in the nation, this park offers views that, on a clear day, can extend more than 100 miles and into three states.

★ **Spectacular sunrises and sunsets:** The deep orange and crimson hues of the park's hoodoos are intensified by the light of the sun at either end of the day.

★ **Dramatically different zones:** From the highest point of the rim to the canyon base, the park spans 2,000 feet, so you can explore three unique climatic zones: spruce-fir forest, ponderosa-pine forest, and pinyon pine–juniper forest.

★ **Snowy fun:** Bryce averages around 80 inches of snowfall annually and is a popular destination for cross-county skiers and snowshoe enthusiasts.

Bryce Canyon National Park isn't a single canyon, but rather a series of natural amphitheaters on the eastern edge of the Paunsaugunt Plateau. The park's scenic drive runs along a formation known as The Pink Cliffs and offers more than a dozen amazing overlooks. A smart strategy is to drive without stops to the end of the 18-mile road and turn around, stopping at the scenic overlooks—which will then all be conveniently on the right side of the road on the return drive. From the main park road you can also access the most popular hiking trails down into the canyons. A handful of roads veer east of the scenic drive to access other points of interest. For relief from the frequent heavy traffic and scarce parking in the northern half of the park during the spring–fall high season, leave your car outside the park and ride the free (once you've paid the park entrance fee) shuttle buses.

1 Bryce Canyon North. The Bryce Amphitheater is the heart of the park. It's home to the historic Lodge at Bryce Canyon as well as Sunrise, Sunset, and Inspiration Points. Walk to Bryce Point at sunrise to view the mesmerizing collection of massive hoodoos known as The Silent City. This is also the northern terminus of the 23-mile Under-the-Rim Trail, which ventures into the Bryce Canyon backcountry. It can be a challenging three-day adventure or a half-day of fun via one of the four access points from the main road. Several primitive campgrounds line the route.

2 Bryce Canyon South. Rainbow and Yovimpa Points are at the end of the scenic road and offer breathtaking scenery. Here you can hike a short trail to see some ancient bristlecone pines and look south into Grand Staircase–Escalante National Monument.

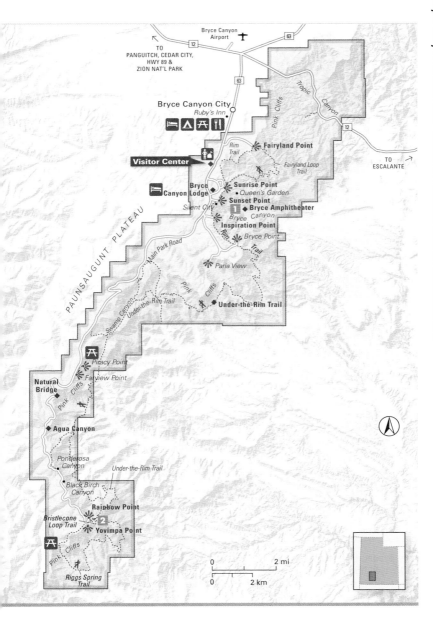

Bryce Canyon Airport

63

TO
PANGUITCH, CEDAR CITY,
HWY 89 &
ZION NAT'L PARK

12

63

Bryce Canyon City
Ruby's Inn

Pink Cliffs

Tropic Canyon

12

Rim Trail

Fairyland Point

TO
ESCALANTE

Fairyland Loop Trail

Visitor Center

Bryce
Canyon Lodge

Sunrise Point
Queen's Garden
Sunset Point
1 Bryce Amphitheater

Silent City

Bryce Canyon

Inspiration Point

Bryce Point

Main Park Road

Rim Trail

Paria View

P A U N S A U G U N T   P L A T E A U

Pink Cliffs

Under-the-Rim Trail

Swamp Canyon

Under-the-Rim Trail

Piracy Point

Fairview Point

Natural Bridge

Pink Cliffs

Agua Canyon

Ponderosa Canyon

Under-the-Rim Trail

Black Birch Canyon

Rainbow Point

Bristlecone Loop Trail

2 Yovimpa Point

Pink Cliffs

Riggs Spring Trail

0   2 mi

0   2 km

A land that captures the imagination and the heart, Bryce is a favorite among the Southwest's national parks. Among Utah's five national parks, it and Arches are also the most easily explored as most of the major attractions are along picturesque and well-maintained park roads.

Designated a national park in 1928 and settled by Mormon pioneers in the late 19th century, this vast landscape of spectacular rock formations had been occupied by the indigenous Paiute people since at least AD 1200. Bryce Canyon is famous for its fanciful hoodoos, best viewed at sunrise or sunset, when the light plays off the red rock.

In geological terms, Bryce is actually an amphitheater, not a canyon. The hoodoos in the amphitheater took on their unusual shapes because the top layer of rock—caprock—is harder than the layers below it. When erosion undercuts the soft rock beneath the cap too much, the hoodoo tumbles. Bryce continues to evolve today, but the hoodoos are a permanent feature; old ones may die, but new ones are constantly forming as the amphi-theater rim recedes.

Planning

Getting Here and Around

The closest airport is in Cedar City, a little under two hours west of Bryce—it has daily flights on Delta to Salt Lake City. An hour farther south, St. George Regional Airport has flights to several western cities. The nearest major airports are in Salt Lake City and Las Vegas, about four hours away.

You reach the park via Highway 63, just off of Highway 12, which connects U.S. 89 just south of Panguitch with Torrey, near Capitol Reef. Among Utah's national parks, it's a pretty easy one to explore, with nearly all of its key attractions along the park's well-maintained 18-mile park road. Although Bryce's main road has no driving restrictions, you may encounter heavy traffic and full parking lots from spring through fall. During these busy months, it's a good idea to take the free shuttle bus to explore the most popular attractions and trails in the Bryce Amphitheater.

Shuttles operate from April through late October. Buses start at 8 am and run every 10 to 15 minutes until 8 pm in summer and 6 pm in early spring and October. The route begins at the Shuttle Station north of the park, where parking is available (visitors can also park at Ruby's Inn or Ruby's Campground outside the park entrance and catch the shuttle there).

Park Essentials

PARK FEES

The entrance fee is $35 per vehicle for a seven-day pass and $20 for pedestrians or bicyclists. If you leave your private vehicle outside the park at the shuttle staging area or Ruby's Inn or Campground, the one-time entrance fee is $35 per party and includes transportation on the shuttle.

A backcountry permit, available from the visitor center, is required for camping in the park's interior, allowed only on the Under-the-Rim and Rigg's Spring Loop Trails, both south of Bryce Point. The cost is $10 for a permit, plus $5 for each person in your party. Campfires are not permitted. Camping in either of the park's designated campgrounds costs $20 nightly for tent sites and $30 for RV sites.

ACCESSIBILITY

Some of the park's facilities, which were generally constructed between 1930 and 1960, have been upgraded for wheelchair accessibility, although in some cases assistance is still required. The Sunset Campground offers two sites with wheelchair access, and the Sunrise building at the Lodge at Bryce Canyon has accessible rooms and parking. Few trails, however, can be managed in a standard wheelchair due to the sandy, rocky, or uneven terrain. The ½-mile section of the Rim Trail between Sunrise and Inspiration Points is wheelchair accessible. And the 1-mile Bristlecone Loop Trail at Rainbow Point has a hard surface and could be used with assistance, but several grades do not meet accessibility standards. Most of the overlooks on the scenic park road have accessible parking and either paved or level but unpaved paths that are accessible to wheelchairs.

CELL PHONE RECEPTION

Cell phone reception is hit-or-miss in the park, with some of the higher points along the main road your best bet. The lodge and visitor center have limited (it can be slow during busy periods) Wi-Fi.

PARK HOURS

The park is open 24/7, year-round. It's in the Mountain time zone.

Hotels

Although there are a handful of functional but pricey lodgings just outside the park in Bryce Canyon City, there's only one accommodation inside the park: the Lodge at Bryce Canyon. This is an appealing option, though, with a few rooms in the main historic building, a number of charmingly rustic cabins, and two pleasant midcentury motel-style units—they all have a fantastic setting, nestled in the evergreens and a short walk from Sunrise and Sunset Points. Keep in mind that lodgings in and around Bryce Canyon fill up fast in summer. The nearby towns of Tropic and Panguitch are also good bases, and they tend to have more last-minute availability.

Restaurants

Dining options within the park are limited to a pair of options at the Lodge at Bryce Canyon. Just outside the park, Bryce Canyon City has mediocre options, but you'll find better places to eat if you venture a bit farther to Tropic or Panguitch.

HOTEL AND RESTAURANT PRICES

Hotel and restaurant reviews have been shortened. For full information visit Fodors.com. Hotel prices are the lowest cost of a standard double room in high season. Restaurant prices are the average cost of a main course at dinner, or if dinner is not served, at lunch.

What It Costs

	$	$$	$$$	$$$$
RESTAURANTS				
	under $16	$16–$22	$23–$30	over $30
HOTELS				
	under $125	$125–$200	$201–$300	over $300

Visitor Information

PARK CONTACT INFORMATION Bryce Canyon National Park. ☏ *435/834–5322* ⊕ *www.nps.gov/brca.*

When to Go

Around Bryce Canyon National Park, elevations approach and surpass 9,000 feet, making for temperamental weather, intermittent and seasonal road closures due to snow, and downright cold nights well into June. The air is cooler on the rim of the canyon than it is at the lower altitudes within the Bryce Amphitheater.

▇TIP→ **Bryce Canyon receives the greatest crowds from April through October. During this period, traffic on the main road can be heavy and parking limited, so consider taking one of the park shuttle buses. RV access is also limited to a handful of lots and camping areas, most of them near the park entrance, during these months.**

If it's solitude you're looking for, come to Bryce from November through March. The park is open all year long, and during these cooler months you might just have a trail all to yourself. And when Bryce is blanketed beneath a layer of snow, the contrast of the red hoodoos is incredibly dramatic.

FESTIVALS AND EVENTS

Bryce Canyon Winter Festival. This mid-February event in nearby Bryce Canyon City features cross-country ski races, snow-sculpting contests, ski archery, ice-skating, and kids' snow boot races. Clinics to hone skills such as snowshoeing and photography also take place, and there's plenty of entertainment, too. ⊕ visitbrycecanyoncity.com/bryce-canyon-winter-festival

Quilt Walk Festival. During the bitter winter of 1864, Panguitch residents set out over the mountains to fetch provisions from the town of Parowan, 40 miles away. Legend says the men, frustrated and ready to turn back, laid a quilt on the snow and knelt to pray. Soon they realized the quilt had kept them from sinking into the snow. Spreading quilts before them as they walked, leapfrog style, the men traveled to Parowan and back. This four-day gathering in June commemorates the occasion with a quilt show and classes, a tour of pioneer homes, dinner-theater, and other events. ⊕ www.quiltwalk.org

Bryce Canyon North

Bryce Amphitheater is the park's scenic and social—it can get crowded—hub. Here you'll find the visitor center, the lodge, both campgrounds, and the park's most iconic trails and viewpoints. A convenient free shuttle runs a loop through this area, stopping at eight main spots where you can get out and explore. It also connects with the nearby town of Bryce Canyon City, so you don't need to bring your vehicle if you're staying at one of that town's hotels.

The 23-mile Under-the-Rim Trail, Bryce Canyon's longest, leads under the rim of the park's plateau and edges this natural amphitheater. Hiking the entire trail requires an overnight stay, but you can connect with it via some shorter trails in the park. On clear nights, the stargazing can be amazing.

Sights

HISTORICAL SIGHTS

★ The Lodge at Bryce Canyon

NOTABLE BUILDING | Architect Gilbert Stanley Underwood was already a national park specialist, having designed lodges at Zion and the Grand Canyon, before turning his T square to Bryce in 1924. With its distinctive, wavy, hunter-green shingle roof and artful interior, this National Historic Landmark has been faithfully restored, right down to the lobby's huge limestone fireplace and log and wrought-iron chandelier. Inside the historic building, the only remaining hotel built by the Grand Circle Utah Parks Company, are a restaurant and gift shop, comfy sitting areas, and information on park activities. Just a short walk from the rim trail, the lodge's landscaped brick terrace is an enchanting place to relax after a hike. The lodge also offers accommodations in several historic log cabins and two lodge-inspired but motel-style buildings nearby on the wooded grounds. ⊠ *Off Main Park Rd., Bryce Canyon National Park* ☏ *435/834–8700* ⊕ *www.brycecanyonforever.com* ⊗ *Closed late Nov.–Mar.*

SCENIC DRIVES

★ Main Park Road

SCENIC DRIVE | Snaking for miles along the canyon's rim, the park's only true thoroughfare accesses more than a dozen scenic overlooks between the entrance and Rainbow Point. Major overlooks are rarely more than a few minutes walk from the parking areas, and from many of these spots, you can see more than 100 miles on clear days. Remember that all overlooks lie east of the road, meaning that you may be looking into the sun early in the day but can enjoy spectacular color and light closer to dusk. Allow two to three hours to travel the entire 36-mile round-trip—more if you set out on any hikes along the way. The road is open year-round but sometimes closes temporarily after heavy snowfalls. Be on the lookout for wildlife crossing the road.

Trailers are not allowed at Bryce Point and Paria View, and vehicles longer than 20 feet are prohibited from parking at most of the major stops in and around the Bryce Amphitheater from mid-May through late October; during these months, you can travel throughout the park via the free shuttle and park your larger vehicle at the shuttle station parking lot in Bryce Canyon City. ⊠ *(Hwy. 63), Bryce Canyon National Park.*

SCENIC STOPS

Bryce Point

VIEWPOINT | Reached via a narrow 2-mile spur road off the main park road, Bryce Point is where the park's fairly easy Rim Trail (which you can hike from here to Inspiration Point or even all the way to Sunrise Point) meets with the more challenging and remote Under-the-Rim Trail, and it's also the southernmost vista point into the Bryce Amphitheater—and a favorite place to watch the sunrise. After absorbing views of the Black Mountains and Navajo Mountain, you can follow the Under-the-Rim Trail to explore beyond the Bryce Amphitheater to the cluster of top-heavy hoodoos known collectively as The Hat Shop. Or, take a left off the Under-the-Rim Trail and hike the challenging Peek-A-Boo Loop Trail down into the amphitheater. ⊠ *Bryce Point Rd., 5 miles south of park entrance, Bryce Canyon National Park.*

Fairyland Point

VIEWPOINT | The viewpoint nearest to the park entrance, this scenic overlook adjacent to Boat Mesa, ½ mile north of the visitor center and a mile off the main park road, has splendid views of Fairyland Canyon and its delicate, fanciful forms. The Sinking Ship and other formations stand before the grand backdrop of the Aquarius Plateau and distant Navajo Mountain. Nearby is the Fairyland Loop trailhead—it's a stunning five-hour hike, and in winter it's a favorite trail for snowshoeing. ⊠ *Off Main Park Rd., Bryce Canyon National Park.*

★ Inspiration Point

VIEWPOINT | One of the best—though often most crowded—places in the park to watch the sunset, this lofty prom-ontory with sweeping vistas into the Bryce Amphitheater is easily accessed by car—the parking lot is down a short and well-signed spur road near the start of Bryce Point Road. But for a more exciting approach and a bit of fresh air and exercise, consider hiking to this dramatic spot via the relatively easy and flat Rim Trail; from Sunset Point, it's a ¾-mile trek south, and from Bryce Point, it's a 1½-mile hike northwest. From either direction, the views are spectacular for virtually the entire hike. ⊠ *Inspiration Point Rd., Bryce Canyon National Park.*

North Campground Viewpoint

VIEWPOINT | **FAMILY** | Across the road and slightly east of the Bryce Canyon Visitor Center, this popular campground has a couple of scenic picnic areas plus a general store and easy access to the Rim Trail and Sunrise Point. ⊠ *N. Campground Rd., Bryce Canyon National Park.*

★ Sunrise Point

VIEWPOINT | Named for its stunning views at dawn, this overlook a short walk from the Lodge at Bryce Canyon is one of the park's most beloved stops. It's also the trailhead for the Queens Garden Trail and the southern end of the Fairyland Loop Trail. You can also walk to Sunrise Point along the easy Rim Trail from Sunset Point (to the south) or the North Camp-ground (to the north). ⊠ *Sunrise Point Rd., Bryce Canyon National Park.*

Sunset Point

VIEWPOINT | Watch the late-day sun paint the hoodoos from this famous overlook a short walk from the Lodge at Bryce Can-yon (or you can drive here via the short spur road off the main park road). You'll be treated to a striking view of Thor's Hammer, a delicate formation similar to a balanced rock. Sunset Point is also the access point for the tremendously popular hike 550 feet down into the amphitheater on the Navajo Loop Trail. ⊠ *Sunset Point Rd., Bryce Canyon National Park.*

TRAILS

Fairyland Loop Trail

TRAIL | Hike into whimsical Fairyland Can-yon on this trail that gets more strenuous and less crowded as you progress along its 8 miles. It winds around hoodoos, across trickles of water, and finally arrives at a natural window in the rock at Tower Bridge, 1½ miles from Sunrise Point and 4 miles from Fairyland Point. The pink-and-white badlands and hoodoos surround you the whole way. Don't feel like you have to go the whole distance to make it worthwhile. But if you do, allow at least five hours round-trip with 1,900 feet of elevation change. *Difficult.* ⊠ *Bryce Canyon National Park* ⊹ *Trailheads: At Fair-yland Point and Sunrise Point.*

The Hat Shop Trail

TRAIL | The sedimentary haberdashery sits 2 miles from the trailhead. Hard gray caps balance precariously atop narrow pedes-tals of softer, rust-color rock. Allow three to four hours to travel this somewhat strenuous but rewarding 4-mile round-trip trail, the first part of the longer Under-the-Rim Trail. *Moderate.* ⊠ *Bryce Canyon National Park* ⊹ *Trailhead: At Bryce Point, 5½ miles south of park entrance.*

Navajo Loop Trail

TRAIL | **FAMILY** | One of Bryce's most pop-ular and dramatic attractions is this steep descent via a series of switchbacks lead-ing to Wall Street, a slightly claustropho-bic hallway of rock only 20 feet wide in places, with walls 100 feet high. After a walk through The Silent City, the northern end of the trail brings Thor's Hammer into view. A well-marked intersection offers a shorter way back via the Two Bridges Trail or continuing on the Queens Garden Trail to Sunrise Point. For the short version allow at least an hour on this 1½-mile trail with 515 feet of elevation change. *Moderate.* ⊠ *Bryce Canyon National Park* ⊹ *Trailhead: At Sunset Point.*

Peek-A-Boo Loop Trail

TRAIL | The reward of this steep trail is The Wall of Windows and The Three Wise Men formations. Start at Bryce, Sunrise, or Sunset Point and allow four to five hours to hike the 5½-mile trail or 7-mile double-loop. Horses use this trail spring–fall and have the right-of-way. *Difficult.* ✉ *Bryce Canyon National Park* ✣ *Trailheads: Bryce, Sunset, or Sunrise Points.*

★ **Queens Garden Trail**

TRAIL | **FAMILY** | This hike is the easiest way down into the amphitheater, with 450 feet of elevation change leading to a short tunnel, quirky hoodoos, and lots of like-minded hikers. It's the essential Bryce "sampler." Allow two hours total to hike the 1½-mile trail plus the ½-mile rim-side path and back. *Easy.* ✉ *Bryce Canyon National Park* ✣ *Trailhead: At Sunrise Point.*

Under-the-Rim Trail

TRAIL | Starting at Bryce Point, the trail travels 23 miles to Rainbow Point, passing through The Pink Cliffs, traversing Agua Canyon and Ponderosa Canyon, and taking you by several springs. Most of the hike is on the amphitheater floor, characterized by up-and-down terrain among stands of ponderosa pine; the elevation change totals about 1,500 feet. It's the park's longest trail, but four trailheads along the main park road allow you to connect to the Under-the-Rim Trail and cover its length as a series of day hikes. Allow at least two days to hike the route in its entirety, and although it's not a hoodoo-heavy hike, there's plenty to see to make it a more leisurely three-day affair. *Difficult.* ✉ *Bryce Canyon National Park* ✣ *Trailheads: At Bryce Point, Swamp Canyon, Ponderosa Canyon, and Rainbow Point.*

VISITOR CENTERS

★ **Bryce Canyon Visitor Center**

VISITOR CENTER | **FAMILY** | Even if you're eager to hit the hoodoos, the visitor center—just to your right after the park entrance station—is the best place to start if you want to know what you're looking at and how it got there. Rangers staff a counter where you can ask questions or let them map out an itinerary of "must-sees" based on your time and physical abilities. There are also multimedia exhibits, Wi-Fi, books, maps, backcountry camping permits for sale, and the Bryce Canyon Natural History Association gift shop, whose proceeds help to support park programs and conservation. ✉ *Hwy. 63, Bryce Canyon National Park* ☎ *435/834–5322* 🌐 *www.nps.gov/brca.*

🍴 Restaurants

★ **The Lodge at Bryce Canyon Restaurant**

$$$ | **AMERICAN** | With a high-beam ceiling, tall windows, and a massive stone fireplace, the dining room at this historic lodge set among towering pines abounds with rustic western charm. The kitchen serves three meals a day (reservations aren't accepted, so be prepared for a wait), and the dishes—highlights of which include buffalo sirloin steak, burgundy-braised bison stew, and almond-and-panko-crusted trout—feature organic or sustainable ingredients whenever possible. **Known for:** good selection of local craft beers; delicious desserts, including a fudge-brownie sundae and six-layer carrot cake; hearty breakfasts. [$] *Average main: $28* ✉ *Off Main Park Rd., Bryce Canyon National Park* ☎ *435/834–8700* 🌐 *www.brycecanyonforever.com* ⏲ *Closed late Nov.–late Mar.*

Valhalla Pizzeria & Coffee Shop

$ | **PIZZA** | **FAMILY** | A quick and casual 40-seat eatery across the parking lot from the Lodge at Bryce Canyon, this pizzeria and coffee shop is a good bet for an inexpensive meal, especially when the lodge dining room is too crowded. Coffee shop choices include an espresso bar, house-made pastries, and fresh fruit, or kick back on the tranquil patio in the evening and enjoy fresh pizza or salad. **Known for:** convenient and casual; decent beer and wine selection; filling pizzas. [$] *Average main:*

$14 ✉ *Off Main Park Rd., Bryce Canyon National Park* ☎ *435/834–8709* 🌐 *www.brycecanyonforever.com/pizza* 🕒 *Closed mid-Sept.–mid-May.*

Hotels

★ The Lodge at Bryce Canyon

$$$ | **HOTEL** | This historic, rugged stone-and-wood lodge close to the amphitheater's rim offers western-inspired rooms with semiprivate balconies or porches in two motel-style buildings; suites in the historic inn; and cozy, beautifully designed lodgepole pine-and-stone cabins, some with cathedral ceilings and gas fireplaces. **Pros:** steps from canyon rim and trails; lodge is steeped in history and has loads of personality; cabins have fireplaces and exude rustic charm. **Cons:** closed in winter; books up fast; no TVs or air-conditioning. [$] *Rooms from: $232* ✉ *Off Main Park Rd., Bryce Canyon National Park* ☎ *435/834–8700, 877/386–4383* 🌐 *www.brycecanyonforever.com* 🕒 *Closed late Nov.–Mar.* 🛏 *113 rooms* 🍴 *No Meals.*

Bryce Canyon South

The biggest draw in the generally less-crowded southern end of the park is Rainbow Point and the short trails near here, including Riggs Loop. There are also several scenic overlooks along the way, and while these all show different perspectives on Bryce Canyon's amazing rock formations, they can also start to feel a bit repetitive. Most of them face East and are therefore most photogenic later in the day, when the sun is behind you (or very early, to catch the sunrise). Natural Bridge is one of the most dramatic, as the viewing area offers an up-close view of the massive arch for which it's named. Agua Canyon and Piracy Point are also worth a stop if time allows. A good strategy is to drive to Rainbow Point without stopping, and then work your way back north, making stops at the various overlooks along the way.

Sights

SCENIC DRIVES AND OVERLOOKS

Agua Canyon

VIEWPOINT | This overlook in the southern section of the park has a nice view of several standout hoodoos. Look for the top-heavy formation called The Hunter, which actually has a few small hardy trees growing on its cap. As the rock erodes, the park evolves; snap a picture because The Hunter may look different the next time you visit. ✉ *Main park road, Bryce Canyon National Park.*

★ Natural Bridge

VIEWPOINT | Formed over millions of years by wind, water, and chemical erosion, this 85-foot-tall, rusty-orange arch formation—one of several rock arches in the park—is an essential photo op. Beyond the parking lot lies a rare stand of aspen trees, their leaves twinkling in the wind. Watch out for distracted drivers at this stunning viewpoint. ✉ *Main park road, Bryce Canyon National Park.*

★ Rainbow and Yovimpa Points

VIEWPOINT | Just a half-mile apart, Rainbow and Yovimpa Points offer two spectacular panoramas facing opposite directions. Rainbow Point's best view is to the north overlooking the southern rim of the amphitheater and giving a glimpse of Grand Staircase–Escalante National Monument; Yovimpa Point's vista spreads out to the south. On an especially clear day you can see all the way to Arizona's highest point, Humphreys Peak, 150 miles away. Yovimpa Point also has a shady and quiet picnic area with tables and restrooms. You can hike between them on the easy Bristlecone Loop Trail or tackle the more strenuous 9-mile Riggs Spring Loop Trail, which passes the tallest point in the park. This is the outermost auto stop on the main road, so visitors often drive here first and make

Yovimpa Point looks to the south of Bryce Canyon, offering a spectacular view.

it their starting point, then work their way back to the park entrance. ✉ *End of main park road, 18 miles south of park entrance, Bryce Canyon National Park.*

TRAILS
Bristlecone Loop Trail
TRAIL | This 1-mile trail with a modest 200 feet of elevation gain lets you see the park from its highest points of more than 9,000 feet, alternating between spruce and fir forest and wide-open vistas out over Grand Staircase–Escalante National Monument and beyond. You might see yellow-bellied marmots and dusky grouse, critters not typically found at lower elevations in the park. Allow about an hour. *Easy.* ✉ *Bryce Canyon National Park* ⊹ *Trailhead: At Rainbow Point parking lot.*

Activities

Many visitors explore Bryce Canyon by car and by just venturing along the Rim Trail or to some of the scenic overlooks, but it really pays off to make at least one hike down into the canyon. If you're

not used to these lofty elevations, you may have to stop to catch your breath at times. It gets warm in summer but rarely uncomfortably hot, so hiking farther into the depths of the park isn't necessarily difficult, but if it's your first time here or you're not an experienced hiker, consider starting out with one of the shorter treks, such as the Navajo Loop.

AIR EXCURSIONS
Bryce Canyon Airlines & Helicopters
AIR EXCURSIONS | For a bird's-eye view of Bryce Canyon National Park, take a dramatic helicopter ride or airplane tour over the fantastic sandstone formations. Longer full-canyon tours and added excursions to sites such as the Grand Canyon, Monument Valley, Lake Powell, and Zion are also offered. Flights last from 35 minutes to four hours. ☎ *435/834–8060* ⊕ *www.rubysinn.com/scenic-flights* ✈ *From $125.*

CAMPING
The two campgrounds in Bryce Canyon National Park fill up fast, especially in summer, and are family-friendly. All are

drive-in, except for the handful of back-country sites that only backpackers and gung-ho day hikers ever see.

North Campground. A cool, shady retreat in a forest of ponderosa pines, this is a great home base for exploring Bryce Canyon. You're near the general store, the Lodge, trailheads, and the visitor center. It's reservation only late May–September and first-come, first-served the rest of the year. Be aware that some sites feel crowded and not private. ⊠ *Main park road, ½ mile south of visitor center* ☎ *435/834–5322.*

Sunset Campground. This serene alpine campground is across (on the west side of) the main park road but still within walking distance of the Lodge at Bryce Canyon and many trailheads. The 100 or so sites are first-come, first-served tend to fill up by early afternoon July though September, so try to arrive early. The Sunset Campground is open only mid-April through October. ⊠ *Main park road, 2 miles south of visitor center* ☎ *435/834–5322.*

HIKING

To get up close and personal with the park's hoodoos, set aside a half-day to hike into the amphitheater. Remember, after you descend below the rim, it generally takes twice as much time and effort to get back up. The air is warmer the lower you go, and the altitude can have you huffing and puffing if you're unused to it. The uneven terrain calls for lace-up shoes on even the well-trodden, high-traffic trails and sturdy hiking boots for the more challenging ones. No below-rim trails are paved. Bathrooms are at most trailheads but not down in the amphitheater.

HORSEBACK RIDING

Many of the park's hiking trails were first formed beneath the hooves of cattle wranglers. Today, hikers and riders share many trails. A few outfitters can set you up with a gentle mount and lead you to the park's best sights. Not only can you cover more ground than you would walking, but equine traffic has the right-of-way at all times. Treks usually last from about 1½ to 3 hours. People under the age of 7 or who weigh more than 220 pounds are prohibited from riding.

Canyon Trail Rides

HORSEBACK RIDING | FAMILY | Descend to the floor of the Bryce Canyon Amphitheater via horse or mule—most visitors have no riding experience, so don't hesitate to join in. A two-hour ride (children as young as seven can participate) ambles along the amphitheater floor through Queens Garden before returning to Sunrise Point. The three-hour expedition (children must be at least 10 years old) follows Peek-A-Boo Loop Trail, winds past Fairyland, and passes The Wall of Windows before returning to Sunrise Point. Two rides a day of each type leave in the morning and early afternoon. Rides are offered April–September. ⊠ *Lodge at Bryce Canyon, Off Hwy. 63, Bryce Canyon National Park* ☎ *435/679–8665, 435/834–5500 Bryce Canyon reservations* ⊕ *www.canyonrides.com* ⊠ *From $75.*

Chapter 10

SOUTHWESTERN UTAH

10

Updated by
Andrew Collins

 Sights
★★★★★

 Restaurants
★★★★☆

 Hotels
★★★★☆

 Shopping
★★★☆☆

 Nightlife
★★☆☆☆

WELCOME TO SOUTHWESTERN UTAH

TOP REASONS TO GO

★ **Amazing national parks:** This part of the state contains Zion, Bryce Canyon, and Capitol Reef National Parks and Grand Staircase–Escalante National Monument.

★ **Traveling through history:** Imagine life during the pioneer days as you explore the historic sites and museums of St. George and the ghost towns outside Springdale and Kanab.

★ **Scenic highways:** With its hair-raising twists and turns, spectacular Highway 12 dips through rugged canyons and climbs over dramatic mountain passes from Panguitch to Torrey. Highway 9 and U.S. 89 also offer spectacular scenery.

★ **Sleeping under the stars:** Watch the stars as you stay overnight at a historic ranch or a B&B or in a canvas tent at one of the region's growing crop of luxury glamping resorts.

★ **Blissing out:** Treat yourself at a luxuriant spa, shoot a round of golf, and partake of sophisticated resort dining with views of red rock canyons in and around St. George.

Southwestern Utah contains three of Utah's most popular national parks, as well as the massive (and increasingly popular) Grand Staircase–Escalante National Monument. The area also has Utah's fastest-growing city, St. George, which has become a retirement destination for many seniors due to its rugged beauty and climate. Even the smaller communities in the region are growing along with the popularity of the nearby parks.

1 Cedar City. Home to Southern Utah University, this bustling community has some of the region's top cultural draws.

2 Brian Head. This alpine hamlet is most famous as the state's southernmost ski town, but in summer it's popular for hiking and mountain biking.

3 St. George. This fast-growing desert metropolis boasts a slew of diversions, from upscale golf and spa resorts to a historic downtown filled with excellent museums and lively eateries.

4 Springdale. Within walking distance of the most popular entrance to Zion National Park.

5 Kanab. Once a hub of Old Hollywood filmmaking, this funky high-desert hamlet is convenient to several parks and has a small but sophisticated dining scene and boutique lodging.

6 Orderville. The largest town in the lush and sparsely populated Sevier River valley between Kanab and Panguitch.

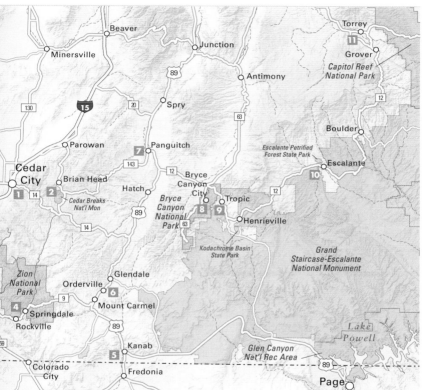

7 Panguitch. You can count on this low-key town in the Sevier River valley for inexpensive, casual lodgings and eateries within striking distance of Bryce Canyon and Cedar Breaks.

8 Bryce Canyon City. This touristy hub of motels and gift shops has a great location if not much in the way of curb appeal.

9 Tropic. Tiny Tropic has a cute downtown and several appealing eateries and hotels.

10 Escalante. Since the designation of surrounding Grand Staircase–Escalante National Monument, this picturesque village on Highway 12 has become one of the region's top recreation hubs.

11 Torrey. Visitors to Capitol Reef National Park typically eat, stay, and relax in this pretty settlement on the Fremont River.

Just two hours north of the glittering lights of Las Vegas, by way of Interstate 15, lies one of the most beautiful and distinctive regions of the United States. Home to Zion, Bryce, and Capitol Reef National Parks as well as the vast and stunning wilderness of Grand Staircase–Escalante National Monument, this outdoor mecca is anchored by the fast-growing city of St. George, which is itself surrounded by shimmering white and red sandstone and blackened lava formations.

Elsewhere in the region, you'll find small recreational base communities—such as Cedar City, Springdale, Kanab, Escalante, and Torrey—all of which offer plenty of charms, from hip coffeehouses and fine art galleries to breathtaking scenic drives and rugged hikes.

Southwestern Utah is a landscape of both adrenaline thrills and peaceful relaxation—head for one of the swanky spa resorts in St. George for a rejuvenating getaway. Seasonal entertainment, like the renowned Utah Shakespeare Festival, and a growing number of noteworthy dining options and one-of-a-kind lodgings make this a region worth spending several days in, even beyond the national parks. You'll find southern Utah's best alpine skiing in Brian Head and opportunities for mountain biking, horseback trail rides, jeep tours, and wildlife viewing throughout the region, and St. George

has a clutch of renowned golf courses. As you venture to some of the more remote sections of the area, visiting canyons and mesas rich with Native American history and where Butch Cassidy and the Sundance Kid once roamed, it's easy to feel as though you've traveled back in time. And at night, when the dark alpine sky pulses with stars, you can almost imagine you're on another planet.

MAJOR REGIONS

South–Central Washington County. Many of southwestern Utah's Mormon settlers arrived from the American South and brought the name "Dixie" with them, a nickname for the area that's quickly falling out of favor but still appears on many signs. Sunny and dry-hot St. George, the region's main population center, offers a growing mix of eclectic eateries, swanky resort hotels, affordable chain motels, and plenty to see and do in the way of historic attractions and recreational pursuits. Many residents from northern climes migrate here during cold months. To the north, Cedar City is smaller but also has plenty of attractions and services, and tiny Brian Head is renowned for winter skiing and daytime hiking and biking.

Along U.S. 89. From the Arizona border, U.S. 89, which is known as the Heritage Highway for its role in shaping Utah history, winds west through Paria Canyon and then turns north in Kanab and meanders through the Sevier River valley past Panguitch on its way into the center of the state. The small towns along this route are excellent bases for visiting nearby Zion and Bryce Canyon National Parks.

Along Highway 12. Branching off from U.S. 89, this designated Scenic Byway passes near Bryce Canyon National Park before twisting and turning through 1.9 million-acre Grand Staircase–Escalante National Monument and then cutting north of dramatic mountains toward Capitol Reef National Park. Here as well, you'll find several towns to stay in and explore.

Planning

Getting Here and Around

Most visitors to the region drive or (in rare cases) take the bus here from Las Vegas (two hours away) or Salt Lake City (a little over four hours), but the airport in St. George is served by most major airlines and is a good option if you're spending most of your trip in southwestern Utah. Just keep in mind that among these cities, Las Vegas has the greatest number of direct flights and often cheaper airfare and better deals on rental cars. However you get here, you absolutely need a car to get around. Most major car

rental agencies have offices in downtown St. George as well as out at the airport. Enterprise and Budget also have offices at the small airport in Cedar City, which has regularly scheduled flights from Salt Lake City.

AIR

Small, modern, and convenient St. George Regional Airport (SGU) has daily flights to Salt Lake City (Delta), Denver (United), Los Angeles (American), and Phoenix (also American). Even smaller Cedar City Regional Airport (CDC) also has daily service to Salt Lake City (Delta). Las Vegas's Harry Reid International Airport (LAS) is 120 miles south of St. George, and Salt Lake International Airport is 300 miles north. Salt Lake Express buses make numerous trips per day between Harry Reid Airport and St. George and a handful of trips north from St. George to Salt Lake City, with a stop in Cedar City.

AIRPORT CONTACTS Harry Reid International Airport. ✉ 5757 Wayne Newton Blvd., Las Vegas ☎ 702/261–5211 ⊕ www.harryreidairport.com. **St. George Regional Airport.** ✉ 4550 S. Airport Pkwy., St. George ☎ 435/627–4080 ⊕ www. flysgu.com. **Cedar City Regional Airport.** ✉ 2560 Aviation Way St., Cedar City ☎ 435/867–9408 ⊕ www.cedarcity. org/76/Airport.

AIRPORT SHUTTLE Salt Lake Express. ✉ 805 S. Bluff St., St. George ☎ 208/656–8824 ⊕ www.saltlakeexpress.com.

CAR

Interstate 15, the main corridor through southwestern Utah, connects St. George and Cedar City with Las Vegas and Salt Lake City and also intersects with Interstate 70 about 75 miles north of Cedar City. It's actually quite pretty for a major highway, but the scenery becomes even more dramatic as you venture onto the region's main two-lane highways, especially Highway 9 through Springdale and

Zion National Park; Highways 14 and 143 through Brian Head and Cedar Breaks National Monument; U.S. 89 through Paria Canyon, Kanab, and Panguitch; and Highway 12 through Red Canyon, Tropic, Escalante, and Torrey.

■ TIP→ **If you travel between I–15 and U.S. 89 via Highway 9, you must pay the $35 admission fee to Zion National Park even if you don't plan to stop and visit. If you're planning to visit Zion and at least two other parks, however, it makes sense to buy an Interagency Annual Pass for $80.**

In winter, Highway 143—the primary access road to Brian Head and Cedar Breaks National Monument—occasionally closes when there's heavy snowfall, and Highway 148 shuts down all winter, typically from mid-November through February. The Utah Department of Transportation provides free, up-to-the-minute interactive road conditions. You can also download the app or check conditions online (⊕ *udottraffic.utah.gov*).

Keep in mind that services are few and far between on back roads in this part of the state, especially as you head east from the Interstate 15 corridor. Cell service can be spotty in these areas, too. It's best to download maps and top off your gas tank before you set out to explore these areas.

Hotels

As southern Utah's national parks have skyrocketed in popularity in recent years, hotel rates in towns nearest the parks have also soared, especially during the spring–fall high season, when demand can dramatically exceed supply. Springdale, which borders Zion National Park, is now one of Utah's priciest towns to spend the night in, and at busy times, rates in Bryce Canyon City and Torrey can also get steep. If you don't mind staying a half-hour to an hour from the parks, towns like Escalante, Panguitch, Kanab,

and Hurricane typically offer better prices. You'll find the largest and most diverse inventory of hotels, from budget motels to posh resorts, in the largest city, St. George, which is especially affordable during the sweltering summer months. Cedar City has a number of economical and midpriced lodging options, too, although summer tends to be more expensive, especially during the Utah Shakespeare Festival season. You'll find a growing number of vacation rentals throughout the area—these can be a good alternative to conventional lodgings during busy periods. And the latest trend in the small towns in and around the national parks (and Grand Staircase–Escalante National Monument) are trendy, sometimes downright posh, glamping resorts. Several of these have opened since 2020, and others are planned.

Wherever you plan to stay, it's prudent to book well in advance (at least a month, if possible) if visiting in summer, and also during spring and fall weekends. In the area's remote regions (along the U.S. 89 and Highway 12 corridors), never show up without a reservation. If it's a busy time, you may find out that you're miles from the nearest available hotel room. Also keep in mind that from around mid-November to mid-April, many hotels in and around the national parks close for the season. In St. George and Hurricane (and the ski town of Brian Head), hotels do typically stay open year-round; in fact, the winter is becoming quite popular in St. George, since it has the warmest climate in the state.

HOTEL AND RESTAURANT PRICES

Hotel and restaurant reviews have been shortened. For full information visit Fodors.com. Hotel prices are the lowest cost of a standard double room in high season. Restaurant prices are the average cost of a main course at dinner, or if dinner is not served, at lunch.

What It Costs

	$	$$	$$$	$$$$
RESTAURANTS				
	under $16	$16–$22	$23–$30	over $30
HOTELS				
	under $125	$125–$200	$201–$300	over $300

Planning Your Time

No matter which area you visit or what adventure you're pursuing, you'll spend a lot of time driving in this expansive region connected by a fairly limited network of paved roads. There's a silver lining, though: there's awe-inspiring scenery along virtually all of the region's roads—even Interstate 15.

Speaking of which, the Interstate 15 corridor—including St. George and Cedar City—offers a range of cultural and out-doorsy diversions, from attending theater and music concerts to touring historic homesteads to increasingly urbane dining and shopping. There's also amazing hiking, wildlife viewing, biking, and other recreational pursuits even in these relatively more developed areas.

As you head east from here and explore the national parks (Bryce Canyon, Capitol Reef, Zion) and national monuments (Grand Staircase–Escalante, Cedar Breaks), pretty much every activity available to visitors involves some kind of outdoor pursuit. But exciting, memorable experiences abound for every age and experience level. The national parks as well as the towns outside of them all have scenic drives with accessible overlooks and easy hikes. And throughout the entire region, fans of extreme adventure will find challenging, breathtaking hikes that can last from several hours to several days, plus ample opportunities for off-road driving, mountain and road biking, canyoneering, and more.

Restaurants

Over the past 20 years or so, southwestern Utah's dining scene has improved by leaps and bounds. This is especially true of the region's biggest city, St. George, which offers a good mix of regional American and international options. Cedar City, Hurricane, Springdale, and even tiny towns like Kanab, Escalante, Boulder, and Torrey all have at least two or three noteworthy options as well.

Utah has unique wine and liquor laws, but these days, most of the nicer restaurants in bigger communities serve local craft beer along with wine and sometimes cocktails. Still, especially in smaller towns, it's a good idea to call ahead and confirm if alcohol is served and also how late dinner is served, as many establishments close by 8 or 9 in these more remote communities.

Restaurant reviews have been shortened. For full information, visit Fodors.com.

When to Go

Year-round, far southwestern Utah is the warmest region in the state. St. George is usually the first city in Utah to break 100°F every summer (or even spring), and winters are mild at these lower desert elevations. Despite the summer's heat, many people visit from June to September—prime season for national park touring—making the off-season winter months preferable if you wish to avoid crowds and sweltering (but arid) heat. With milder weather, spring and fall have become increasingly popular, especially on weekends. If you do decide to brave the heat, wear sunscreen and drink lots of water, regardless of your activity level, but also pack some warmer clothes if you're venturing into the national parks, Brian Head, or the U.S. 89 and Highway 12 corridors, as even in July and August, nights cool down significantly in these high-elevation climates.

Cedar City

250 miles southwest of Salt Lake City.

The region's rich iron-ore deposits captured the attention of Mormon leader Brigham Young. He ordered a Church of Jesus Christ of Latter-day Saints mission be established here in what is now southwestern Utah's second-largest community, with a population of about 36,500 (up from just 13,000 in 1990).

The first ironworks and foundry opened in 1851 and operated for only eight years; problems with the furnace, flooding, and hostility between settlers and regional Native Americans eventually put out the flame. Residents then turned to ranching and agriculture for their livelihoods, and Cedar City has thrived ever since as an agricultural and, since the founding of Southern Utah University in 1897, educational point of the state.

Since 1962, the university campus has been home to the city's most beloved event, the Utah Shakespeare Festival, with a season that continues to expand as its reputation grows. It's just a couple of blocks from the beautiful architecture of the festival theaters to Cedar City's endearing downtown of old-school shops and inviting restaurants.

Much of the city's newer development has happened on the south side, near Exit 57 of I–15, which is also where you'll find the newest chain hotels, including Courtyard by Marriott, Hampton Inn, and Holiday Inn Express along with a number of fast-casual restaurants. This suburban-feeling area lacks downtown's charm but is handy as a base for exploring the area and nearby attractions, such as Brian Head Ski Resort, Cedar Breaks National Monument, and even Bryce Canyon National Park, which is 90 minutes away.

GETTING HERE AND AROUND
Interstate 15 cuts through Cedar City. Though downtown is walkable, you'll want a car to explore farther afield.

VISITOR INFORMATION
CONTACTS Visit Cedar City and Brian Head. ✉ *581 N. Main St., Cedar City* ☎ *435/586–5124* ⊕ *www.visitcedarcity. com.*

 Sights

Frontier Homestead State Park Museum
HISTORY MUSEUM | FAMILY | This interactive living-history museum devoted to the county's early iron industry is home to a number of interesting attractions, including a bullet-scarred stagecoach that ran in the days of Butch Cassidy and the oldest standing home in all of southern Utah, built in 1851. Local artisans demonstrate pioneer crafts, and numerous mining artifacts and tools are on display. ✉ *585 N. Main St., Cedar City* ☎ *435/586–9290* ⊕ *www.frontierhomestead.org* ⊠ *$4* ⊗ *Closed Sun. in Sept.–Apr.*

IG Winery
WINERY | In a state with few wineries, this popular operation in downtown Cedar City sources grapes from respected vineyards in California's Napa and Sonoma valleys, Washington's Columbia Valley, and Oregon's Rogue Valley. The Bordeaux-style reds are well-crafted, though spendy, while more moderately priced Tempranillo and Sangiovese also have plenty of fans. With exposed brick walls and hardwood floors, the handsome tasting room is hung with local art and warmed by a fireplace in winter. There's also a sunny patio, and live bands perform regularly. ✉ *59 W. Center St., Cedar City* ☎ *435/867–9463* ⊕ *www.igwinery. com* ⊗ *Closed Mon.*

Southern Utah Museum of Art
ART MUSEUM | Set in a striking modern building that opened in 2016 and was designed to resemble the region's canyons and rock formations, this excellent

regional art museum with a peaceful sculpture garden is part of Southern Utah University's cultural compound, along with the Utah Shakespeare Festival theaters. The galleries feature selections from the museum's permanent collection of some 2,000 works—including pieces by Renoir, Dalí, Picasso, and Thomas Hart Benton—along with rotating shows that shine a light on emerging regional artists as well as students and faculty. ⊠ *13 S. 300 W, Cedar City* ☎ *435/586–5432* ⊕ *www.suu.edu/suma* ⊙ *Closed Sun.*

 ## Restaurants

★ Centro Woodfired Pizzeria

$ | **PIZZA** | You can watch your handmade artisanal pizza being pulled from the fires of the brick oven, then sit back and enjoy a seasonal pie layered with ingredients like house-made fennel sausage and wood-roasted cremini mushrooms. The creamy vanilla gelato layered with a balsamic reduction and sea salt is highly addictive. **Known for:** house-made sausage; good wine and beer list; creative desserts. Ⓢ *Average main: $15* ⊠ *50 W. Center St., Cedar City* ☎ *844/385–3285* ⊕ *www.centropizzeria.com.*

Milt's Stage Stop

$$$ | **STEAKHOUSE** | Cabin decor, friendly service, and canyon views are the hallmarks of this dinner spot 10 minutes southeast of downtown Cedar City by car. Expect traditional, hearty steak house cuisine: teriyaki beef kebabs, prime rib, and shrimp scampi, accompanied by loaded baked potatoes, deep-fried zucchini, and similar sides. **Known for:** scenic alpine setting; hefty steaks and seafood; apple crisp à la mode. Ⓢ *Average main: $29* ⊠ *3560 E. Hwy. 14, Cedar City* ☎ *435/586–9344* ⊕ *www. miltsstagestop.com* ⊙ *No lunch.*

Porkbelly's Eatery

$$ | **AMERICAN** | As the name suggests, this airy contemporary restaurant is a meat-lover's paradise. Starting with tri-tip

eggs Benedict and chicken and waffles at breakfast, pulled-pork sandwiches, carne asada nachos, and bacon-mushroom-cheddar burgers follow. **Known for:** mammoth portions of meat-centric fare; smoked baby back ribs on weekends; the chicken bomb (a jalapeño stuffed with cream cheese and sausage and wrapped in chicken and bacon). Ⓢ *Average main: $18* ⊠ *565 S. Main St., Cedar City* ☎ *435/586–5285* ⊕ *www.porkbellyseatery.com* ⊙ *Closed Sun. and Mon.*

Rusty's Ranch House

$$$ | **STEAKHOUSE** | Locals have long considered the meals at this fun, if a bit touristy, Old West–style roadhouse some of the best in the region. They serve steaks, barbecue brisket and baby back ribs, towering burgers, sweet coconut shrimp, and other classics. **Known for:** extensive cocktail selection; quirky Western vibe; Granny's hot-caramel apple cobbler. Ⓢ *Average main: $28* ⊠ *2275 E. Hwy. 14, Cedar City* ☎ *435/586–3839* ⊕ *www.rustysranchhouse.com* ⊙ *Closed Sun. No lunch.*

 ## Coffee and Quick Bites

Bristlecone

$ | **CAFÉ** | Drop by this airy, contemporary, downtown coffeehouse—which adjoins a yoga studio that offers a wide range of classes—for the best espresso drinks in town, including bourbon barrel–aged cold brew and crème brûlée cappuccinos. There's also an extensive menu of flavored lemonades and fresh-squeezed juices, plus tasty breakfast items like blackberry parfait and chai oatmeal. **Known for:** outstanding, locally roasted coffee beans; yoga and pilates classes; healthy breakfast fare and salads. Ⓢ *Average main: $8* ⊠ *67 W. Center St., Cedar City* ☎ *435/708–0000* ⊕ *www. bristleconeco.com.*

★ The French Spot

$$ | **FRENCH** | This tiny takeout patisserie in the center of downtown is a favorite stop for lattes and cold brew; crepes and salads; heartier dinner specials (salmon,

filet mignon, ratatouille); and ethereal pastries and sweets, including a rotating selection of chocolate, berry, lemon, and seasonal tarts. Although primarily a to-go option that's perfect for stocking up before a hiking or biking adventure, in warm weather, you can also dine on the cute patio out front. **Known for:** picnic supplies to enjoy before a show at the nearby Utah Shakespeare Festival; scrambled-egg breakfast croissants with ham, bacon, Gruyère, or smoked salmon; colorful macarons. $ *Average main: $17* ✉ *5 N. Main St., Cedar City* ☎ *347/886–8587* ⊕ *www.thefrenchspotcafe.com.*

Hotels

Abbey Inn & Suites

$ | **MOTEL** | A few blocks from the interstate and near Southern Utah University, this two-story economical motel has spacious rooms with exterior entrances, refrigerators, microwaves, and—in the case of suites—kitchens and jetted tubs. **Pros:** centrally located; reasonable rates; nice indoor pool and fitness center. **Cons:** road noise for some rooms; bland setting amid fast-food restaurants and chains; cookie-cutter room decor. $ *Rooms from: $118* ✉ *940 W. 200 N, Cedar City* ☎ *435/586–9966, 800/325–5411* ⊕ *www.abbeyinncedar.com* ⤶ *83 rooms* ⦿l *Free Breakfast.*

★ Big Yellow Inn

$$ | **B&B/INN** | Many of the rooms in this stately Georgian Revival inn are more reminiscent of Colonial Williamsburg than the Utah high desert, but they contain the kinds of plush amenities you'll appreciate if celebrating a special occasion or a grand theater weekend—think stone fireplaces, large balconies, and claw-foot tubs or Jacuzzis. **Pros:** a few minutes' walk to Shakespeare Festival and downtown dining; in a pleasant, leafy residential neighborhood; elegant, rambling old home. **Cons:** books up in advance during summer festival season; frilly, old-fashioned room decor; on a slightly busy street. $ *Rooms from: $139* ✉ *234 S. 300 W, Cedar City*

☎ *435/586–0960* ⊕ *www.bigyellowinn. com* ⤶ *12 rooms* ⦿l *Free Breakfast.*

 Performing Arts

★ Utah Shakespeare Festival

THEATER | Since 1962, Cedar City has been Bard-crazy, staging productions of Shakespeare's plays from mid-June through mid-October in three Southern Utah University campus theaters, the largest of which is an open-air replica of Shakespeare's Globe Theatre. The Tony award–winning festival that has featured Jeremy Irons, Ty Burrell, and Bradley Whitford over the years also presents literary seminars, backstage tours, cabarets showcasing festival actors, and an outdoor pre-show with Elizabethan performers. Try to book well in advance, as many performances sell out. ✉ *195 W. Center St., Cedar City* ☎ *435/586–7878, 800/752–9849* ⊕ *www.bard.org.*

Shopping

Bulloch's Drug Store

CANDY | **FAMILY** | Built in 1917 and remodeled to retain its historic character, this landmark building in downtown Cedar City contains an old-fashioned drug store, complete with a soda fountain from the 1950s. Enjoy ice cream, shakes, sundaes, and malts, or try one of the uniquely flavored sodas. And then pick up a few treats at the candy counter, or browse the adjacent gift shops where you'll find a tempting selection of toys and souvenirs. ✉ *91 N. Main St., Cedar City* ☎ *435/586–9651* ⊕ *www.bullochdrug.com.*

★ Red Acre Farm

OTHER FOOD & DRINK | **FAMILY** | Run by the engaging mother-daughter team of Symbria and Sara Patterson, this organic and biodynamic farm in a fertile valley 6 miles north of Cedar City is a wonderful side trip for visitors of all ages. The farmstand fashioned out of recycled materials stocks seasonal fruits and veggies, plus eggs, cheese, baked goods, and jams.

You can also learn about sustainable agriculture on a free farm tour (given twice monthly) and visit with the friendly goats, pig, dairy cow, and llama, and a two-bedroom suite in the farmhouse is available for overnight stays. ✉ *2322 W. 4375 N, Cedar City* ☎ *435/865–6792* ⊕ *www. redacrefarmcsa.org.*

Activities

HIKING
Coal Creek Trail
HIKING & WALKING | FAMILY | It's easy, even if you're pushing a stroller, to get out into nature in sunny, mile-high Cedar City. Perfect for strolling, jogging, biking, or running, this 3.4-mile paved multipurpose trail starts in Bicentennial Park and cuts in a southeasterly direction right through the center of town, paralleling the scenic creek for which it's named and eventually joining with the similarly paved Cedar Canyon Trail. Other non-paved hiking trails spur off from the Cedar Creek Trail and into the surrounding foothills. ✉ *Bicentennial Park, 660 W. 1045 N, Cedar City* ⊕ *www.cedarcity.org.*

Brian Head

29 miles east of Cedar City.

This tiny town's Brian Head Resort is Utah's southernmost and highest ski area at well over 9,000 feet, but the area's summer recreation, especially mountain biking, has also boomed in recent years, thanks in part to the town's refreshing alpine air and close proximity to Cedar Breaks National Monument. You can explore more than 200 miles of hiking and biking trails, many of which are served by chairlifts or shuttles.

Winter is still the high season here, so book early on weekends and expect higher room rates. During the fall (October and November) and spring (April and May) shoulder seasons, some businesses shut down in this village with fewer than 200 year-round residents.

GETTING HERE AND AROUND
From Cedar City, the easiest route here is via picturesque Highway 14 east to Highways 143 and 148 north, but taking I–15 north to tiny Parowan and then following Highway 143 through the dramatic mountains is nearly as fast (either route takes about 45 to 60 minutes) and even more scenic. This latter route is also your only option in winter, when the southern route closes due to snow.

Sights

Brian Head Peak Observation
SCENIC DRIVE | This 11,312-foot stone lookout hut was built by the Civilian Conservation Corps (CCC) in 1935 atop the highest summit in Iron County. You can see for miles in every direction, as far as Nevada and Arizona, enjoying especially dramatic views of nearby Cedar Breaks National Monument. The windy and dramatic nearly 3-mile drive along bumpy and unpaved Forest Road 047 from Highway 143 (take it slowly) is part of the fun; when there's snow, the last section of road is closed to vehicles, but you can still hike or snowshoe up to the top. You can also hike to the summit from the junction of Rocky Road and Highway 143—the rugged and picturesque trek is about 3½ miles each way. ✉ *End of Forest Rd. 047, Brian Head* ⊕ *www.fs.usda. gov/dixie* 🎫 *Free.*

★ Cedar Breaks National Monument
NATIONAL PARK | Cedar Breaks is a 3-mile-long natural amphitheater that plunges a half-mile into the Markagunt Plateau, offering spectacular scenery and fewer crowds than at the area's better known national parks. Mostly short alpine hiking trails trace the rim, meandering past wildflowers in summer. You can get a nice view of these distinctive red-rock formations that bear a strong resemblance to those of Bryce Canyon at the

handful of overlooks along Highway 148—which means hikers, skiers, and snowshoers can usually find solitude along the trails.

Winter is one of the best times to visit, when snow drapes the red-orange formations. As of this writing, the park service was constructing an attractive and much-needed new visitor center by the Sunset Trailhead parking area—it's slated to open in late summer 2023. From here, you can hike the 1-mile round-trip Sunset Trail, which is paved and wheelchair accessible, or embark on the most memorable of the park's hikes, the 5-mile round-trip South Rim Trail. This latter trek is moderately challenging, but if time is short, just hike the first mile to the Spectra Point viewpoint for an eye-popping panorama. Across Highway 148, the easy 0.6-mile round-trip Nature Trail connects with the Point Supreme Campground, which has 25 tent and RV sites. In winter, call ahead for conditions (the road is sometimes closed due to heavy snowfall), and keep in mind that visitor facilities are closed from October through late May. ✉ *Hwy. 148, Brian Head* ✣ *3½ miles north of Hwy. 14* ☎ *435/586–9451* 🌐 *www.nps.gov/cebr* 🎫 *$10 per person (free under the age of 16)* 🕓 *Visitor center closed mid-Oct.–late May.*

🛏 Hotels

The Brian Head Lodge & Spa

$$ | RESORT | FAMILY | With its stunning scenery and prime location, this modern mission-style lodge is a welcoming base for outdoor adventures and offers a number of amenities, including a bar and grill, outdoor deck, indoor pool, and hot tubs, plus a spa where you can enjoy a range of body and beauty treatments. **Pros:** comfortable base for outdoor recreation; game room is popular with families; mountain views. **Cons:** not as close to slopes as Cedar Breaks Lodge; rooms lack kitchenettes; on-site restaurant gets mixed reviews. [$] *Rooms from: $139* ✉ *314 Hunter Ridge Rd., Brian Head* ☎ *435/677–9000* 🌐 *www.bwpbrianheadhotel.com* 🛏 *112 rooms* 🍴 *Free Breakfast.*

🏃 Activities

SKIING AND SNOWBOARDING

Brian Head Ski Resort

SKIING & SNOWBOARDING | Eight lifts (including two high-speed quads) transport skiers to the 71 runs (evenly divided among expert, intermediate, and beginner terrain) at Utah's highest ski area, which covers more than 650 acres and encompasses a vertical drop of about 1,400 feet, with peak elevation nearing 11,000 feet. A half-pipe, trails, and a terrain park attract snowboarders. From the upper slopes, you can see the red-rock cliffs of Cedar Breaks National Monument to the southwest. During summer and fall, the resort is a favorite with mountain bikers and hikers. ✉ *329 S. Hwy. 143, Brian Head* ☎ *435/677–2035* 🌐 *www.brianhead.com* 🎫 *Lift tickets from $42.*

St. George

50 miles southwest of Cedar City.

Believing the mild year-round climate ideal for growing cotton, Brigham Young dispatched 309 LDS families in 1861 to found St. George. They were to raise cotton and silkworms and to establish a textile industry, to make up for textile shortages resulting from the Civil War.

Flash forward to the early 2020s, and St. George is the fastest-growing metropolitan area in the country—the city population has soared from about 11,500 to nearly 100,000 over the past four decades. It's the cultural and recreational hub of southern Utah, a favorite place to relocate for both retirees (who appreciate the warm winters) and younger families and entrepreneurs (lured by the high

Cedar Breaks National Monument offers both spectacular scenery and fewer crowds than nearby Bryce Canyon National Park.

quality of life, stunning scenery, and growing number of restaurants, shops, and other services). It's a popular destination (and base for nearby Zion National Park) year-round, but fall through spring is especially appealing and free of summer's sometimes oppressive heat. One very popular draw is the **Dixie Roundup** (⊕ www.stgeorgelions.com), a three-day rodeo held every mid-September since the 1930s.

Although the metro area sprawls in all directions, except where soaring red-rock hills (mostly to the north) prevent expansion, St. George has an attractive, pedestrian-friendly downtown anchored by a stately white stucco–clad Mormon temple that dates to 1877. Other appealing areas include historic Santa Clara, a small village several miles west of downtown with a cluster of well-preserved pioneer homes, and the town of Ivins, which is home to the Sedona-esque Kayenta Art Village and is also the gateway for exploring gorgeous Snow Canyon State Park.

GETTING HERE AND AROUND
This increasingly sprawling city is bisected by Interstate 15, and although the very heart of downtown is pedestrian-friendly, you need a car to visit outlying attractions.

Sights

Brigham Young Winter Home and Office
HISTORIC HOME | Mormon leader Brigham Young spent the last seven winters of his life in the warm, sunny climate of St. George. Built of adobe on a sandstone-and-basalt foundation and now a museum, this two-story home, with pretty green and red trim and well-tended gardens, contains a portrait of Young over one fireplace and furnishings from the late 19th century. Visits are by guided tour. ⊠ *67 W. 200 N, St. George* ☎ *435/673–2517* ⊕ *history. churchofjesuschrist.org/landing/historic-sites* ☒ *Free.*

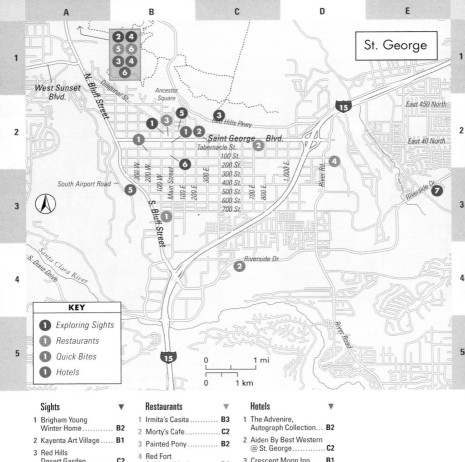

St. George

KEY
- ● Exploring Sights
- ● Restaurants
- ● Quick Bites
- ● Hotels

★ Kayenta Art Village

ARTS CENTER | In the heart of an upscale, contemporary planned community in Ivins, not far from Tuacahn Center for the Arts and Snow Canyon State Park, this beautifully situated arts colony contains several of southern Utah's top galleries, including Gallery 873, known for jewelry and ceramics; Kayenta Desert Arboretum & Desert Rose Labyrinth, which visitors can freely stroll through; Zia Pottery Studio, a co-op operated by talented local potters; and several others. Set against a red-rock landscape, it's an enchanting neighborhood to stroll through, especially during the Art in Kayenta outdoor festival in mid-October. Also check to see what's on at the Center for the Arts at Kayenta—which presents lectures, movies, theater, and concerts—or grab a bite at the excellent Xetava Gardens Cafe. ⊠ *875 Coyote Gulch Ct., Ivins* ☎ *435/688–8535* ⊕ *www.kayentautah.com.*

★ Red Hills Desert Garden

GARDEN | Opened in 2015 as the state's first botanic garden devoted to desert conservation, this beautiful space in the red hills on downtown's northern edge is ideal for a peaceful stroll and learning about water-efficient plants. More than 5,000 of them—including fragrant mesquite trees, prickly pear cactus, blue agave, Joshua trees, weeping yucca, and desert willows—thrive here, along with a meandering stream that's stocked with desert suckers, Virgin River chub, and other native species. Paths also lead past a number of boulders that preserve the tracks of dinosaurs that roamed here some 200 million years ago. The garden adjoins rugged Pioneer Park, a 52-acre expanse of rock-climbing and hiking terrain, with barbecue pits, picnic pavilions and tables, and both short and long trails. ⊠ *375 E. Red Hills Pkwy., St. George* ☎ *435/673–3617* ⊕ *www.redhillsdesert-garden.com.*

★ Snow Canyon State Park

STATE/PROVINCIAL PARK | FAMILY | Named not for winter weather but after a pair of pioneering Utahans named Snow, this breathtaking 7,400-acre red rock wonderland—about 10 miles northwest of St. George and located entirely within Red Cliffs Desert Reserve—abounds with natural wonders, many of which are easily explored from the well-marked parking areas. The best strategy is to enter from the south from Ivins and drive north along the 4½-mile park road to Highway 18, which leads south back to St. George.

Nearly 40 miles of hiking trails lead to lava cones, petrified dunes, cactus gardens, and high-contrast vistas. Great options if you have only a couple of hours include the short trek to the soaring slot canyon known as Jenny's Canyon and the slightly longer (it takes an hour) Lava Tube Trail. Upper Galoot is a pretty picnic area with grills as well as a short trail lined with interesting interpretative signs about the desert tortoise. From the campground you can scramble up huge sandstone mounds and look across the entire valley. Park staff lead occasional guided hikes. ⊠ *1002 Snow Canyon Dr., Ivins* ☎ *435/628–2255* ⊕ *stateparks.utah.gov/parks/snow-canyon* 🎫 *$15 per vehicle.*

St. George Art Museum

ART MUSEUM | FAMILY | The downtown centerpiece of St. George's growing art scene occupies an attractively reimagined former sugar-beet warehouse. The permanent collection celebrates the works of mostly regionally based potters, photographers, and painters, many of them depicting the region's spectacular landscapes. Rotating exhibits highlight local history and lore and showcase emerging contemporary talents. There's also a Family Discovery Center, with materials for kids to create their own works. ⊠ *47 E. 200 N, St. George* ☎ *435/627–4525* ⊕ *www.sgcity.org/*

artmuseum 🎫 *$15 suggested donation* ⏲ *Closed Sun. and Mon.*

St. George Children's Museum

CHILDREN'S MUSEUM | FAMILY | Next to Town Square Park and the downtown library and set inside a former school building with a striking red-stone exterior, this well-designed museum contains two floors of touch-friendly exhibits, including an earthquake-simulation table, a science discovery lab, a transportation center with planes and an auto shop, and a miniature version of St. George's red-rock–framed Tuacahn Amphitheatre. ✉ *86 S. Main St., St. George* ☎ *435/986–4000* 🌐 *www.sgchildrensmuseum.org* 🎫 *$7* ⏲ *Closed Sun.*

St. George Dinosaur Discovery Site

SCIENCE MUSEUM | FAMILY | Unearthed in 2000 by property developers, this site preserves and exhibits ancient footprints left by dinosaurs from the Jurassic Period millions of years ago. A modern museum displays dinosaur fossils and replicas and presents several short informative videos about the Jurassic era. There's an interactive area for children and a Dino Park outside the museum with shaded picnic tables and a Walk Through Time exhibit. ✉ *2180 E. Riverside Dr., St. George* ☎ *435/574–3466* 🌐 *www.utahdinosaurs.org* 🎫 *$8* ⏲ *Closed Tues.*

🍴 Restaurants

Irmita's Casita

$ | MEXICAN | FAMILY | A reliable standby for tasty Mexican-American fare since 1993, this humble spot serves affordable, no-nonsense food that can be quite spicy if requested. Specialties include pork tortas, massive burritos smothered in red or green sauce, and shrimp enchiladas. **Known for:** steak chilaquiles at breakfast; chicken mole poblano; Mexican soft drinks and juices. [$] *Average main: $12* ✉ *95 W. 700 S, St. George* ☎ *435/703–9162* 💳 *No credit cards* ⏲ *Closed Sun. and Mon.*

Morty's Cafe

$ | MODERN AMERICAN | FAMILY | At this funky, updated downtown take on a burger joint, the brick walls are hung with local art for sale. Creatively topped beef and veggie burgers are offered, plus breakfast burritos, several varieties of quinoa salad, and thick milkshakes. **Known for:** breakfast sandwiches and burritos served all day; three-bean veggie burgers with chipotle mayo; cheesecake milkshakes. [$] *Average main: $9* ✉ *702 E. St. George Blvd., St. George* ☎ *435/359–4439* 🌐 *www.mortyscafe.com* ⏲ *Closed Sun.*

★ **The Painted Pony**

$$$$ | MODERN AMERICAN | A charming patio overlooking Ancestor Square with contemporary Southwestern art on the walls provides a romantic setting for enjoying contemporary American fare with an emphasis on seasonal ingredients, many from the owners' private organic garden. Consider sage-smoked quail with a tamarind glaze, followed by a juniper-brined bone-in pork chop with stuffed pears and smoked-tomato relish, and don't pass up the standout sides that include sweet cornbread pudding, truffle potato chips, and Stilton fritters. **Known for:** knowledgeable servers; one of the best wine lists in town; seasonally changing bread pudding. [$] *Average main: $34* ✉ *2 W. St. George Blvd., St. George* ☎ *435/634–1700* 🌐 *www.painted-pony.com* ⏲ *No lunch Sun.*

Red Fort Cuisine of India

$$ | INDIAN | On the east side of town, enjoy authentic Indian cuisine in this attractive high-ceilinged space with trompe l'oeil murals, palm leaf–ceiling fans, and comfy booths. Well-seasoned lamb coconut korma, Assam pineapple shrimp, and *baygan bharta* (roasted eggplant) are standouts, and there's an extensive selection of chutneys and breads. **Known for:** very good wine list; efficient, outgoing staff; rose and mango lassis. [$] *Average main: $18* ✉ *148 S. 1470 E, St. George* ☎ *435/574–4050* 🌐 *www.redfortcuisine.com* ⏲ *Closed Tues. No lunch.*

★ **Rylu's Bistro**

$$$ | **CONTEMPORARY** | In a handsomely restored little house in the tree-lined, historic village of Santa Clara—about 15 minutes west of downtown St. George—this sweet, cozy neighborhood restaurant with seating in a colorful front garden serves extraordinarily tasty, locally sourced contemporary American–Mediterranean fare. It's worth the trip to this slightly off-the-beaten-path locale to savor coconut *labneh* with spicy harissa, charred heirloom tomatoes, and hazelnut dukkah and seared skirt steak with jalapeño-parsley *chermoula*. **Known for:** exceptional farm-to-table cuisine; charming, historic setting; thoughtful wine list (and inexpensive corkage fee if you bring your own bottle). [$] *Average main: $28* ✉ *2862 Santa Clara Dr., St. George* ☎ *435/412–5120* 🌐 *www.rylusbistro.com* 🕓 *Closed Sun. and Mon. No lunch.*

★ **Xetava Gardens Cafe**

$$ | **MODERN AMERICAN** | This beautifully designed adobe oasis in the Kayenta Art Village in Ivins, about 10 miles northwest of St. George, offers gracious indoor and outdoor seating, the latter overlooking fragrant high-desert gardens and the surrounding red-rock ramparts. Pronounced zay-tah-vah, the space began as a coffee bar and is still a source of lattes and mochas, but you'll also find an eclectic selection of globally inspired all-day fare, including blue-corn waffles, ham ciabattas, peach-glazed organic chicken, and wild mushroom burgers. **Known for:** steps from several art galleries; well-curated beer, wine, and cocktail list; croissant bread pudding with caramel sauce. [$] *Average main: $20* ✉ *815 Coyote Gulch Ct., Ivins* ☎ *435/656–0165* 🌐 *www.xetava.com* 🕓 *Closed Tues. and Wed. No dinner Mon.*

Coffee and Quick Bites

★ **Farmstead**

$ | **BAKERY** | This hip sidewalk café and bakery on the ground floor of a downtown St. George apartment building is a pleasing option for both decadent sweets—think passionfruit-coconut–glazed doughnuts and blood-orange tarts—and filling sandwiches on crusty house-baked breads. Notable drink options include brown sugar–cinnamon lattes and high-octane cold brews. **Known for:** sensational doughnuts and pastries; shaded sidewalk seating; hearty sandwiches and pizzas. [$] *Average main: $9* ✉ *18 S. 200 W, St. George* ☎ *435/986–7777* 🌐 *www.farmsteadbakery.com* 🕓 *Closed Mon. and Tues. No dinner.*

FeelLove Coffee

$ | **CAFÉ** | Head to this local chainlet's light-filled, high-ceilinged east side location—near the Virgin River bike and jogging trail—for well-crafted coffees, teas, and lemonades as well as an assortment of tasty, generally healthy, dishes. Start the day with some BLT avocado toast or a turmeric-tofu scramble, and for lunch, try the harvest berry salad. **Known for:** lots of vegan options; Thai, matcha, and other sweet tea lattes; fresh-baked desserts. [$] *Average main: $10* ✉ *558 E. Riverside Dr., St. George* ☎ *435/922–1717* 🌐 *www.feellovecoffee.com* 🕓 *No dinner.*

Hotels

★ **The Advenire, Autograph Collection**

$$$ | **HOTEL** | A strikingly contemporary, upscale hotel that's directly across the street from the buzzy shopping and dining of Ancestor Square, this stylish member of Marriott Bonvoy's indie-spirited Autograph Collection exudes hipness with its hardwood floors, bold-print pillows and chairs, high-tech entertainment centers, and cushy bedding. **Pros:** stylish, cosmopolitan decor; superb on-site restaurant; steps from downtown dining and retail. **Cons:** neighborhood can be crowded and noisy; steep pet fee; parking is valet only ($18) unless you find a spot on the street. [$] *Rooms from: $255* ✉ *25 W. St. George Blvd., St. George* ☎ *435/522–5022* 🌐 *www.theadvenirehotel.com* 🛏 *60 rooms* 🍴 *No Meals.*

Aiden by Best Western @ St. George

$$ | MOTEL | FAMILY | Within walking distance of downtown, this retro-inspired member of Best Western's stylish Aiden boutique hotel brand is a great value with an attractive pool, hot tub, and sun deck, and rates include a full breakfast buffet and free bike rentals. **Pros:** central location; soda–ice cream float bar that's a hit with kids; cool mid-century modern design. **Cons:** no gym; on a busy road; rooms set around a parking lot. [$] *Rooms from: $189* ✉ *316 E. St. George Blvd., St. George* ☎ *435/673–3541* 🌐 *www.aidenstg.com* 🛏 *30 rooms* 🍴 *Free Breakfast.*

Crescent Moon Inn

$$ | B&B/INN | The eight apartment-style units in this adobe Pueblo Revival–style property overlooking a reservoir in scenic and relaxing Kayenta Art Village have kitchens, balconies or patios, and homey contemporary furnishings. You can rent cruiser bikes for $20 a day, take a dip in the large community pool, and hike to your heart's content at nearby Snow Canyon State Park. Rates drop significantly the more nights you stay. **Pros:** full kitchens; close to galleries and a great café; peaceful setting with red rock views. **Cons:** condo vibe and self check-in isn't for everyone; 20-minute drive to downtown St. George; no staff on site. [$] *Rooms from: $195* ✉ *1504 Crescent Moon Trail, Ivins* ☎ *435/879–9076* 🌐 *www.thecrescentmooninn.com* 🛏 *8 rooms* 🍴 *No Meals.*

The Inn at Entrada

$$$ | RESORT | Hikers, spagoers, and—above all—golfers flock to this plush boutique resort set amid the red-rock canyons northwest of downtown, surrounded by a world-class Johnny Miller–designed golf course that was completely rebuilt in 2022 and offering a top-notch spa, pool, and fitness facility. **Pros:** adjoins one of the top golf courses in the state; attractive Southwest-inspired contemporary decor; terrific spa. **Cons:** 10- to 15-minute drive from downtown dining; thin walls; can get very expensive depending on time of year. [$] *Rooms from: $280* ✉ *2588 W. Sinagua Trail, St. George* ☎ *435/634–7100* 🌐 *www.innatentrada.com* 🛏 *57 rooms* 🍴 *No Meals.*

★ Inn on the Cliff

$$ | HOTEL | It's all about the panoramic views at this exceptionally well-maintained mid-century modern boutique hotel set high on a ridge overlooking downtown St. George and the red rocks beyond. **Pros:** reasonable rates for such a nice property; stunning views; continental breakfast delivered to your room. **Cons:** breakfast is a bit meager; too far to walk from downtown; restaurant closed on Sunday. [$] *Rooms from: $189* ✉ *511 S. Tech Ridge Dr., St. George* ☎ *435/216–5864* 🌐 *www.innonthecliff.com* 🛏 *27 rooms* 🍴 *Free Breakfast.*

★ Red Mountain Resort

$$$ | RESORT | This luxurious red-rock hideaway, with its stunning surroundings near the mouth of Snow Canyon, offers a range of outdoor adventures and fitness and wellness options, from fitness classes, hikes, and yoga sessions to red clay–lavender body wraps and warm Himalayan salt stone massages. **Pros:** world-class spa and fitness facilities; handsome contemporary design fits in with natural surroundings; a range of meal, spa, and activity packages available. **Cons:** caters more to activity-seekers than those looking to relax; 15-minute drive northwest of St. George; all those potential treatment, activity, and meal add-ons can get pricey. [$] *Rooms from: $260* ✉ *1275 E. Red Mountain Circle, Ivins* ☎ *435/673–4905, 877/246–4453* 🌐 *www.redmountainresort.com* 🛏 *106 units* 🍴 *No Meals.*

🍸 Nightlife

★ George's Corner

BARS | A lively hub of bustling Ancestor Square, this welcoming tavern is open all day for casual dining but is also one of the city's relatively few late-night options for drinks and live music. The spacious bar decorated with historic black-and-white photos of the area offers a nice selection of cocktails and regional craft brews. ⊠ *2 W. St. George Blvd., St. George* ☎ *435/216–7311* ⊕ *www.georgescornerrestaurant.com.*

Performing Arts

★ Tuacahn Center for the Arts
CONCERTS | At this magnificent outdoor amphitheater nestled in a natural red-sandstone cove, you can watch touring Broadway musicals and concerts by noted pop artists. ⊠ *1100 Tuacahn Dr., Ivins* ☎ *800/746–9882 box office* ⊕ *www.tuacahn.org.*

Activities

BIKING
Cyclists from all over the world are drawn to St. George's 60-plus miles of paved bike trails, which meander past the black lava flows and red rocks of Snow Canyon State Park and connect with a half-dozen other parks around the city. Mountain bikers should check out the interconnected 6-mile Prospector–Church Rocks Trail in nearby Washington—it also boasts mesmerizing red rock views.

Visit ⊕ trails.greaterzion.com for an interactive map.

Bicycles Unlimited
BIKING | A trusted southern Utah biking resource, this shop rents mountain and road bikes and also offers maps and advice about great rides in the area. ⊠ *90 S. 100 E, St. George* ☎ *435/673–4492* ⊕ *www.bicyclesunlimited.com.*

GOLF

★ Entrada at Snow Canyon Country Club
GOLF | Opened in 1996 and completely redesigned to the tune of $7 million in 2022 by David McLay Kidd, this challenging course is surrounded by a spectacular lava rock–desert landscape and consistently ranks among the top courses in the Southwest for its perfectly manicured greens and stylish clubhouse. This is a private course, but it is accessible to guests staying at The Inn at Entrada, which offers stay-and-play packages and lessons. ⊠ *2511 W. Entrada Trail, St. George* ☎ *435/986–2200* ⊕ *www.golfentrada.com* 🏷 *From $130* 🏌 *18 holes, 7,065 yards, par 71.*

The Ledges Golf Course
GOLF | Seven miles north of St. George, this state-of-the-art course designed by Matt Dye features meticulously maintained greens and an impressive backdrop of red rock combined with panoramic views of Snow Canyon State Park. The difficult back nine can be a bit intimidating for less experienced golfers. ⊠ *1585 Ledges Pkwy., St. George* ☎ *435/634–4640* ⊕ *www.ledges.com* 🏷 *From $85* 🏌 *18 holes, 7,200 yards, par 72.*

HIKING
St. George is a hiking mecca, not only because it's a good base for exploring Zion National Park, but because it has miles of gorgeous trails through the surrounding red rock mountains on the north edge of town. These include the Owen's Loop, City Creek, and Paradise Rim Trails in the southwest corner of Red Cliffs Desert Reserve and the entirety of Snow Canyon State Park.

Springdale

40 miles east of St. George.

Although tiny, this gorgeously situated town of around 630 residents has more than doubled in population since 1990, thanks in large part to its being directly adjacent to Zion National Park. Nearly all of the town's growing number of upscale hotels, restaurants, and shops are along Highway 9, or Zion Park Boulevard, within walking or easy shuttle-bus distance of the park's main visitor center.

GETTING HERE AND AROUND

You'll need a car to get to Springdale, via Highway 9, but getting around once you're here can be easily managed without one. The complimentary Zion Canyon shuttle bus—available from March through November (as well as in late December and on weekends in February and March)—makes getting from one end of Springdale to the other stress-free, with bus stops throughout town and connecting service to the free shuttle into Zion National Park. It's also a pleasant town to stroll through. In winter, when there are fewer crowds, a car is handy for getting around town or visiting the park.

Sights

Grafton

GHOST TOWN | FAMILY | A stone school, dusty cemetery, and a few wooden structures are all that remain of the nearby town of Grafton, which is between Springdale and Hurricane, a few miles west of the turnoff onto Bridge Road in Rockville. This ghost town, which has a dramatic setting with striking views of Zion's peaks, has been featured in several films, including *Butch Cassidy and the Sundance Kid.* ⊠ *End of W. Grafton Rd., Springdale.*

Restaurants

The Bit & Spur

$$ | SOUTHWESTERN | This laid-back Springdale institution has been delighting locals and tourists since the late 1980s, offering a well-rounded menu that includes fresh fish and pasta dishes, but the emphasis is on creative Southwestern fare, such as roasted-sweet-potato-and-pork tamales and chili-rubbed rib-eye steak. Craft beers and the popular house-made sangria complement the zesty cuisine. **Known for:** creative margaritas; live music; outdoor dining by a fountain beneath shade trees. Ⓢ *Average main: $22* ⊠ *1212 Zion Park Blvd., Springdale* ☎ *435/772–3498*

⊕ *www.bitandspur.com* ⊗ *No lunch. Closed Mon.–Thurs. in Dec. and Jan.*

★ King's Landing Bistro

$$$ | MODERN AMERICAN | Ask to be seated on the patio—with dramatic views of the area's red rock monoliths—when dining at this casually stylish bistro at the popular Driftwood Lodge. The artfully presented cuisine tends toward creative American with Mediterranean influences—think king salmon with saffron couscous, roast chicken with artichoke-olive tapenade, and charred Spanish octopus with chorizo and baba ghanoush. **Known for:** interesting artisanal cocktail list; emphasis on local and seasonal produce and vegetables; rich desserts, including a classic tiramisu. Ⓢ *Average main: $28* ⊠ *1515 Zion Park Blvd., Springdale* ☎ *435/772–7422* ⊕ *www.klbzion.com* ⊗ *Closed Sun. and Mon. No lunch.*

Oscar's Cafe

$$ | SOUTHWESTERN | FAMILY | Prepare for an active day with a filling breakfast, or reward yourself after a long hike with lunch or dinner at this welcoming Southwestern café with a big, inviting patio offering stunning mountain views. The pork *verde* breakfast burrito and huevos rancheros are hearty and delicious, and excellent lunch and dinner options include flame-broiled garlic burgers topped with provolone cheese and shrimp tacos with a creamy lime sauce. **Known for:** blue-corn nachos with cheese and guacamole; creative burgers; large heated patio. Ⓢ *Average main: $18* ⊠ *948 Zion Park Blvd., Springdale* ☎ *435/772–3232* ⊕ *www.oscarscafe.com.*

Park House Cafe

$ | AMERICAN | Notable for its big patio with fantastic views into the park and for one of the better selections of vegan and vegetarian dishes in town, this funky little café decorated with colorful artwork serves plenty of tasty meat and egg dishes, too. The grilled ham Benedict has plenty of fans, as do buffalo burgers with Havarti cheese and apple-pear-berry salads with organic greens, feta, and walnuts. **Known for:** breakfast served all day; full slate of espresso drinks and smoothies; ice cream sundaes and banana splits. $ *Average main: $14* ⊠ *1880 Zion Park Blvd., Springdale* ☎ *435/772–0100* ⊕ *www.parkhousecafezion.com* ⊗ *No dinner.*

Spotted Dog Café

$$ | **MODERN AMERICAN** | At this upscale, light-filled restaurant with an eclectic menu that's rich on fresh pastas and creative meat and seafood dishes, the staff makes you feel right at home even if you saunter in wearing hiking shoes. The exposed wood beams and large windows that frame the surrounding trees and rock cliffs set a Western mood, with tablecloths and original artwork supplying a dash of refinement. **Known for:** interesting but accessible wine list; lovely patio for alfresco dining; much of the produce is grown on site. $ *Average main: $22* ⊠ *Flanigan's Inn, 428 Zion Park Blvd., Springdale* ☎ *435/772–0700* ⊕ *flanigans.com/dine/* ⊗ *No lunch.*

★ Zion Canyon Brew Pub

$$ | **AMERICAN** | Relax after a rugged day of hiking with a flight of ales or a juicy elk burger in the beer garden of southern Utah's oldest craft beer maker, Zion Brewery, which is just steps from the park's southern entrance. The kitchen turns out excellent pub grub, such as stout-glazed buffalo meat loaf and beer-battered fish-and-chips, and there's live music most weekend evenings. **Known for:** serves food later than most places in town; excellent craft beers; lovely setting overlooking the Virgin River. $ *Average main: $20* ⊠ *95 Zion Park Blvd., Springdale* ☎ *435/772–0336* ⊕ *www.zionbrewery.com.*

Zion Pizza & Noodle Co.

$$ | **ITALIAN** | **FAMILY** | Creative pizzas and a kickback atmosphere in a former church make this a great place to replenish after a trek through the canyon. Meat lovers appreciate the Cholesterol Hiker pizza,

topped with pepperoni, Canadian bacon, and Italian sausage, but the Thai chicken and rosemary-garlic pies are also delicious. **Known for:** stone-slate pizzas with creative toppings; lovely garden seating; good craft beer list. $ *Average main: $18* ⊠ *868 Zion Park Blvd., Springdale* ☎ *435/772–3815* ⊕ *www.zionpizzanoodle.com* ⊗ *No lunch. Closed Dec.–Feb.*

Coffee and Quick Bites

★ Deep Creek Coffee Company

$ | **CAFÉ** | Stop by this cheerful coffeehouse with hanging plants and several tables on a spacious side patio to fuel up before your big park adventure or to grab some healthy sustenance for later. Hearty acai and miso-quinoa bowls, toast with goat cheese and fresh strawberries, bagels with the requisite schmears, breakfast burritos, and house-made granola are among the tasty offerings. **Known for:** opens at 6 am daily; potent house-made cold brew; delicious smoothies. $ *Average main: $10* ⊠ *932 Zion Park Blvd., Springdale* ☎ *435/669–8849* ⊕ *www.deepcreekcoffee.com* ⊗ *No dinner.*

Hotels

★ Cable Mountain Lodge

$$$ | **HOTEL** | This contemporary lodge with a large swimming pool and a serene full-service spa is the closest hotel in Springdale to Zion—it's a scenic five-minute walk over a footbridge across the Virgin River. **Pros:** steps from Zion National Park's south entrance; many suites have full kitchens; beautiful picnic area along river with gas grills and tables. **Cons:** no breakfast (but a coffeehouse and market steps away); not all rooms have park views; sometimes books up weeks in advance. $ *Rooms from: $269* ⊠ *147 Zion Park Blvd., Springdale* ☎ *435/772–3366, 877/712–3366* ⊕ *www.cablemountainlodge.com* ⇆ *52 rooms* ⊠| *No Meals.*

Cliffrose Springdale, Curio Collection by Hilton

$$$$ | **HOTEL** | The canyon views, acres of lush lawns and flowers, and pool and two-tier waterfall hot tubs at this stylish riverside hotel make it more than a place to rest your head, and you could throw a rock across the river and hit Zion National Park. **Pros:** close to Zion's south entrance; enchanting grounds and views; excellent restaurant and full-service spa. **Cons:** steep rates; lots of foot and car traffic nearby; no elevator. [$] *Rooms from: $356* ✉ *281 Zion Park Blvd., Springdale* ☎ *435/772–3234* 🌐 *www.cliffroselodge.com* 🛏 *50 rooms* 🍴 *No Meals.*

★ **Desert Pearl Inn**

$$$$ | **HOTEL** | Offering rooms of 650 square feet or larger with vaulted ceilings, oversize windows, sitting areas, small kitchens with wet bars and dishwashers, and pleasing contemporary decor, this riverside lodge is special. **Pros:** spacious, smartly designed rooms; excellent Camp Outpost Co. restaurant next door; rooms facing river have balconies or terraces. **Cons:** often books up well in advance; breakfast not included; pets not permitted. [$] *Rooms from: $379* ✉ *707 Zion Park Blvd., Springdale* ☎ *435/772–8888, 888/828–0898* 🌐 *www.desertpearl.com* 🛏 *72 rooms* 🍴 *No Meals.*

The Driftwood Lodge

$$$ | **HOTEL** | The bright and contemporary rooms at this friendly, upscale roadside lodge have balconies or patios and great views of the Virgin River and surrounding canyons, along with refrigerators and large flat-screen TVs. **Pros:** many rooms overlook the river and park; superb restaurant; attractive pool and picnic area. **Cons:** least expensive rooms have limited view or balcony; breakfast not included; limited pet reservations must be booked by phone. [$] *Rooms from: $269* ✉ *1515 Zion Park Blvd., Springdale* ☎ *435/772–3262* 🌐 *www.driftwoodlodge.net* 🛏 *63 rooms* 🍴 *No Meals.*

Flanigan's Resort

$$$$ | **HOTEL** | A tranquil, nicely landscaped inn with canyon views and a small pool, Flanigan's offers spacious, elegantly appointed accommodations, including two private villas and suites that sleep six; some units have a patio or a deck. **Pros:** easy shuttle ride or pleasant walk to Zion Canyon Visitor Center; a meditation maze on the hilltop; one of the better restaurants in town. **Cons:** not all rooms have views; smaller property that tends to book up quickly; breakfast isn't complimentary (and isn't available in winter). [$] *Rooms from: $399* ✉ *450 Zion Park Blvd., Springdale* ☎ *435/772–3244* 🌐 *flanigans.com* 🛏 *34 rooms* 🍴 *No Meals.*

Under Canvas Zion

$$$$ | **RESORT** | This high-end, Insta-worthy glamping compound enjoys an eye-popping setting just west of the minimally trafficked Kolob Terrace entrance to Zion National Park. The swanky, eco-friendly canvas tents are spacious and have private bathrooms, and amenities include a restaurant with firepits serving tasty breakfast and dinner fare (and free s'mores kits), live music some evenings, yoga classes, and games for kids. And although there's no electricity, USB battery packs are provided for you to charge your phones. **Pros:** far from the crowds of Springdale and the main park entrance; incredible Zion-adjacent setting; downright plush bedding and furnishings. **Cons:** can be uncomfortably hot in summer; a bit of a drive from area restaurants; spendy for tent accommodations (however gorgeously appointed) with no Wi-Fi or electricity. [$] *Rooms from: $399* ✉ *3955 Kolob Terrace Rd., Hurricane* ☎ *888/496–1148* 🌐 *www.undercanvas.com* 🛏 *48 units* 🍴 *No Meals.*

🛍 Shopping

David J. West Gallery
ART GALLERIES | The radiant photography of artist David West captures Zion's natural setting in its full grandeur, along with Bryce, Cedar Breaks, Arches, and other stunning spots throughout Utah and the Southwest. The gallery also stocks contemporary landscape paintings by Michelle Condrat and geologically inspired pottery by Bill Campbell. ✉ *801 Zion Park Blvd., Springdale* ☎ *435/772–3510* ⊕ *www.davidjwest.com.*

★ Worthington Gallery
ART GALLERIES | The emphasis at this superb gallery in a circa-1880s pioneer home is on regional art, including pottery, works in glass, jewelry, beguiling copper wind sculptures by Lyman Whitaker, and paintings by more than a dozen artists that capture the dramatic beauty of southern Utah. ✉ *789 Zion Park Blvd., Springdale* ☎ *435/772–3446* ⊕ *www.worthingtongallery.com.*

Kanab

43 miles southeast of Springdale.

In the 1920s, Kanab became a Hollywood vision of the American West. Soaring vermilion sandstone cliffs and sagebrush flats with endless vistas lured filmmakers to the area, which has appeared in more than 170 movies and TV shows, including *Stagecoach, My Friend Flicka, Fort Apache, The Outlaw Josey Wales, Maverick,* and many others. And although Kanab is no longer a major filming location, old movie posters and photos now cover the walls of many local businesses.

This town of about 4,800 now prospers as a convenient, scenic, and relatively affordable base for visiting three of the nation's top national parks: Zion, Bryce Canyon, and the Grand Canyon (North Rim). It's also an excellent base for visiting Grand Staircase–Escalante and Pipe Spring National Monuments as well as the mesmerizing landscapes of the Paria Canyon–Vermilion Cliffs Wilderness. It's also become a mecca among animal lovers, who come here to visit Best Friends Animal Sanctuary. As the town's popularity continues to soar, Kanab has developed an impressive crop of hip boutique hotels and one of southern Utah's better restaurant scenes.

GETTING HERE AND AROUND
U.S. 89 cuts right through town, with U.S. 89A breaking off to the south into northern Arizona. You can walk to many hotels and restaurants within town, but a car is a must for exploring the area.

VISITOR INFORMATION
CONTACTS Big Water BLM Visitor Center. ✉ *20 Revolution Way, off U.S. 89, 57 miles east of Kanab, Big Water* ☎ *435/675–3200* ⊕ *www.blm.gov/visit/big-water-visitor-center.* **Kanab BLM Visitor Center.** ✉ *745 E. U.S. 89, Kanab* ☎ *435/644–1300* ⊕ *www.blm.gov/visit/kanab-visitor-center.*

👁 Sights

★ Best Friends Animal Sanctuary
WILDLIFE REFUGE | FAMILY | On a typical day, this 3,700-acre compound 7 miles north of town houses some 1,600 rescued animals, mostly dogs and cats but also horses, rabbits, farm animals, and even wildlife in need of shelter. They receive dozens of visitors who come to take one of the free 90-minute tours (offered four times daily); a special tour of Dogtown, Cat World Headquarters, Bunny House, Parrot Garden, or one of the other animal-specific areas of the sanctuary; a walk through the animal cemetery; or even a hike in adjacent Angel Canyon. Founded in 1984 and with several other adoption centers and offices around the country, Best Friends is the largest animal sanctuary in the United States and one of the world's most successful and influential no-kill animal rescue advocacy

organizations. It's a rewarding visit if you love animals, and if you have the time and interest, you and your family can volunteer for a day at this amazing place. The organization also operates the Best Friends Roadhouse and Mercantile, a unique pet-centric hotel and gift shop. All tours should be booked online or by phone, even if same day. ⊠ *5001 Angel Canyon Rd., Kanab* ☎ *435/644–2001* ⊕ *www.bestfriends.org.*

Coral Pink Sand Dunes State Park

STATE/PROVINCIAL PARK | This sweeping, 3,730-acre expanse of pink sand about 20 miles west of Kanab is the result of eroding sandstone. Funneled through a notch in the rock, wind picks up speed and carries grains of sand into the area— the undulating formations can reach heights of 100 feet and move as much as 50 feet per year. It's a giant playground for dune buggies, ATVs, and dirt bikes. If you just want a quick scamper through the dunes, park in one of the small roadside lots; there's no fee collected at these areas, and they're farther away from where vehicles zoom through the sand and so tend to be quieter. Children love to play in the sand, but check the surface temperature; it can get very hot. ⊠ *Coral Sand Dunes Rd. (Hwy. 43), Kanab* ⊕ *11 miles southwest of U.S. 89* ☎ *435/648–2800* ⊕ *stateparks.utah.gov/ parks/coral-pink/* ☜ *$10 per vehicle.*

Kanab Heritage House Museum

HISTORIC HOME | One of the most stately residences in southern Utah, this 1890s redbrick gingerbread Victorian home in the center of town is surrounded by herb and flower gardens and contains many of the original owners' furnishings. Guided tours are offered throughout the day, and historical demonstrations are present- ed from time to time. Visits provide an interesting look at pioneer life in the Southwest. ⊠ *115 S. Main St., Kanab* ☎ *435/644–3506* ⊕ *www.kanabheritage- house.com* ⊙ *Closed Sun., and Mon.– Thurs. in Oct.–mid-May.*

★ Paria Canyon–Vermilion Cliffs Wilderness

NATURE PRESERVE | In this extremely remote 112,500-acre expanse of otherworldly canyons, cliffs, and mesas that straddles the Utah–Arizona border south of Grand Staircase–Escalante National Monument and along the Arizona border, you'll find the subjects of some of the most famous and photographed rock formations in the Southwest, including "The Wave," an undu- lating landscape of waves frozen in striated red, orange, and yellow sandstone that can be accessed by permit only—it's reached via a somewhat strenuous 6.4-mile round- trip hike. The area has a number of other spectacular features, several of them a bit easier to access, such as the moderately easy 3.7-mile Wire Pass Trail, which leads to the longest slot canyon in the world, 13-mile Buckskin Gulch.

For any visits to this wilderness, part of which falls within Vermilion Cliffs National Monument, it's essential that you check with the area's BLM ranger offices in Kanab or Big Water (near Lake Powell) for guidance and conditions (deadly flash floods can occur with little warning in some of these slot canyons); staff can also provide permit information about visiting The Wave (aka Coyote Buttes North) and Coyote Buttes South. Or consider visiting the area on tour through one of the reputable outfitters in Kanab or Escalante, such as Dreamland Safari Tours, Forever Adventure Tours, and Paria Outpost & Outfitters. The parking lot for the Wire Pass Trailhead, a good place to start your explorations of the area, is 45 miles east of Kanab via U.S. 89 (turn right onto House Rock Valley Road shortly after milemarker 26 and continue 8.5 miles down the unpaved road).

Only 64 people are granted permits to visit The Wave each day, and all are awarded by online lottery (48 of them by advanced lottery up to four months in advance, and 16 of them by daily lottery issued two days in advance).

Visit 🌐 www.blm.gov/node/7605 for details. ✉ *Wire Pass Trailhead parking lot, House Rock Valley Rd., Paria* ☎ *435/644–1300* 🌐 *www.blm.gov/visit/paria-canyon-vermilion-cliffs-wilderness-area* 🎟 *$6 per person day use; reservations and permits required for some hikes.*

Paria Movie Set Day Use Site

GHOST TOWN | Surrounded by stunning striated bluffs and rock formations, here in this remote valley you can visit two ghost towns at once at the Paria (sometimes called Pahreah) townsite and movie set, one settled by hardy pioneers and one built by Hollywood but lost in 1998, briefly rebuilt, and then lost to a fire in 2006. In fact, floods also caused the demise of the original settlements along the Paria River, with the original town fully abandoned by around 1930. Films shot here include the 1962 Rat Pack comedy *Sergeants 3*, the Gregory Peck film *Mackenna's Gold*, and the famous Clint Eastwood Civil War western, *The Outlaw Josey Wales*, which was released in 1976, making it the last of the site's movie productions. To get here, drive 33 miles east of Kanab on U.S. 89, turning left—shortly after mile marker 31—at the Old Town Paria rock marker, and following the unpaved road about 4½ miles north to the parking area and wooden restroom. ✉ *Paria Valley Rd., Paria* ☎ *435/644–1300* 🌐 *www.blm.gov/visit/paria-movie-set-day-use-site.*

Pipe Spring National Monument

NATIONAL PARK | A 20-minute drive southwest of Kanab, this 40-acre plot of stone buildings and sagebrush- and red rock–dotted hillsides with a pond and gardens preserves a site where indigenous Kaibab Paiute people thrived for a thousand years, followed by Spanish missionaries and Mormon pioneers in the mid-19th century. A modern visitor center contains artifacts and interactive exhibits and presents a short video detailing the history of this community and its reliance on the natural springs that run beneath it. Rangers give guided tours and crafts demonstrations during the summer months, but any time of year you can explore the grounds, buildings, orchards, and horse and cattle corrals on your own and hike the ½-mile Ridge Trail for an astounding view of the Arizona Strip, as this region is known. ✉ *406 N. Pipe Springs Rd., off Hwy. 389, Fredonia* ☎ *928/643–7105* 🌐 *www.nps.gov/pisp* 🎟 *$10.*

🍴 Restaurants

Peekaboo Canyon Wood Fired Kitchen

$$ | **VEGETARIAN** | This inviting, art-filled restaurant at The Flagstone inn has one of the only all-vegetarian menus in southern Utah, but even avowed carnivores have been known to rave about the green chile–and–Swiss cheese Impossible burgers and the inventive pizzas—including the "hot mess," with vegan Italian sausage, chèvre, shishito and serrano peppers, and a bourbon sauce. There's an impressive selection of craft beers and ciders. **Known for:** large patio with sandstone tables; Impossible burgers and meatballs; salted-caramel crunch cake for dessert. [$] *Average main: $17* ✉ *The Flagstone Boutique Inn & Suites, 233 W. Center St., Kanab* ☎ *435/689–1959* 🌐 *www.peekabookitchen.com* 🕒 *Closed Sun. and Mon.*

Rocking V Cafe

$$$ | **SOUTHWESTERN** | This upbeat, art-filled eatery inside the town's former post office focuses on slow-cooked meals made from scratch, such as the Kanab-A-Dabba-A-Doo burger, a half-pound patty topped with Hatch chilies, bacon, cheddar, and avocado, and a chargrilled bison tenderloin with a fig demi-glace. Several excellent vegan options are available, too, such as yellow coconut curry with miso-marinated tofu. **Known for:** excellent margaritas; attractive patio; bread pudding with rotating preparations. [$] *Average main: $25* ✉ *97 W. Center St., Kanab* ☎ *435/644–8001* 🌐 *www.rockingvcafe.com* 🕒 *Closed Tues. and Wed.*

A permit to hike The Wave, a spectacular formation in Coyote Buttes North (in Paria Canyon-Vermillion Cliffs Wilderness), is one of the toughest permits to secure in Utah.

★ Sego

$$ | **MODERN AMERICAN** | Folks have been known to drive for an hour or more to partake of the outstanding modern American and Asian fare served in this charmingly intimate dining room just off the lobby of the romantic Canyons Boutique Hotel in Kanab. The small-plates–focused menu here changes often according to what's fresh, but recent standouts have included a pork belly and watermelon salad, foraged mushrooms with artichokes and goat cheese, and seared duck-breast lo mein with sambal and jalapeño cream. **Known for:** creative, globally inspired cooking; stellar wine and cocktail list; romantic yet unfussy vibe. $ *Average main: $22* ✉ *Canyons Boutique Hotel, 190 N. 300 W, Kanab* ☎ *435/644–5680* ⊕ *www.segokanab.com* ⊗ *Closed Sun. and Thurs. No lunch.*

★ Vermillion 45

$$$ | **MEDITERRANEAN** | The sophisticated contemporary Mediterranean fare served in this snazzy bistro with a cathedral ceiling and an open kitchen would hold its own in any big city. Start off your evening with escargot with herbed garlic butter or French onion soup, before graduating to gnocchi with sautéed lobster tail or pan-seared duck breast with a cherry reduction and truffle-dusted potatoes. **Known for:** charcuterie and cheese boards; outstanding wine and cocktail selection; house-made gelato. $ *Average main: $23* ✉ *210 S. 100 E, Kanab* ☎ *435/644–3300* ⊕ *www.vermillion45.com* ⊗ *Closed Mon. and Tues.*

Wild Thyme Cafe

$$$ | **MODERN AMERICAN** | Using herbs and produce from the on-site organic garden and sourcing meat and seafood from top-quality purveyors, the kitchen at this contemporary neighborhood bistro serves up delicious Southwestern fare. Fire-grilled Idaho trout and slow-braised, chargrilled cowboy pork ribs with barbecue sauce and an agave-mustard vinaigrette are a couple of house specialties, and there's also a nice selection of bowls featuring sesame tofu, falafel cakes, Jamaican-spiced pork, and other tasty proteins. **Known for:** pretty deck with red-rock views; outstanding list of creative cocktails; flourless dark chocolate cake. $ *Average main: $25* ⊠ *198 S. 100 E, Kanab* ☎ *435/644–2848* ⊕ *www.wildthymekanab.com.*

Coffee and Quick Bites

★ Kanab Creek Bakery
$ | **CAFÉ** | Drop by this intimate and urbane bakery-café with an expansive patio for some of the tastiest breakfast and lunch fare for miles around, as well as fine espresso drinks, teas, raw juice blends, and a small but well-chosen selection of beer and wine. The Belgian–French-inspired menu features sweet (crepes with jam and delectable pastries) and savory dishes, with croque monsieur, salade Nicoise, and avocado-hummus-tomato panini standing out among the latter. **Known for:** cheerful patio (but limited indoor) seating; heavenly croissants, Belgian chocolate chip cookies, and other sweet treats; fantastic breakfasts. $ *Average main: $10* ⊠ *238 W. Center St., Kanab* ☎ *435/644–5689* ⊕ *www.kanabcreekbakery.com* ⊘ *Closed Mon. and Tues. No dinner.*

Hotels

★ Best Friends Roadhouse & Mercantile
$$ | **MOTEL** | The nationally renowned, Kanab-based Best Friends Animal Society runs this smartly designed, pet-centric motel that offers a slew of amenities for travelers with four-legged friends, including a fenced dog park and water feature, pet treats and beds, built-in cubbies for snuggling and napping, and dog-walking and pet-visit services. **Pros:** hip, modern design; pets stay free (up to four, of any size); staying here supports a great cause. **Cons:** not a great fit if you're not a fan of pets; on a busy road; a bit pricey. $ *Rooms from: $200* ⊠ *30 N. 300 W, Kanab* ☎ *435/644–3400* ⊕ *www.*

bestfriendsroadhouse.org ⊃ *40 rooms* ⦿ *Free Breakfast.*

★ The Canyons Lodge
$ | **HOTEL** | With cattle-print throw pillows, papier-mâché mounted deer heads, log walls, and custom beds with rattan or carved-wood headboards, the playful vibe at this quirky 16-room boutique inn sets it apart from the usual budget-friendly lodgings in the Zion and Bryce area. **Pros:** fun and quirky ambience; good base for Zion, Bryce, and the North Rim of the Grand Canyon; there's a small pool. **Cons:** the least expensive rooms are tiny; complimentary breakfast is at nearby sister property; some road noise. $ *Rooms from: $112* ⊠ *236 N. 300 W, Kanab* ☎ *435/644–3069* ⊕ *www.canyonslodge.com* ⊃ *16 rooms* ⦿ *Free Breakfast.*

Parry Lodge
$ | **HOTEL** | Constructed in 1929, this landmark lodge hosted dozens of movie stars during Kanab's movie location heyday and is now a fun and simple, well-located base for budget-minded parks visitors. **Pros:** fascinating "old Hollywood" ambience; large pool; reasonably priced. **Cons:** some rooms are quite small; no elevator; breakfast costs extra. $ *Rooms from: $104* ⊠ *89 E. Center St., Kanab* ☎ *435/644–2601* ⊕ *www.parrylodge.com* ⊃ *89 rooms* ⦿ *No Meals.*

Activities

HIKING
Sand Caves
HIKING & WALKING | **FAMILY** | A little north of town and not to be confused with the touristy Moqui Cave, which is less than a mile up the road, these man-made sandstone caves were created in the early 1970s as part of a sand-mining operation and are reached via a slightly steep half-mile scramble. It's fun exploring these caverns and gazing out at the pinon-dotted hills below. ⊠ *U.S. 89 at Angel Canyon Rd., Kanab.*

★ Squaw Trail

HIKING & WALKING | FAMILY | With a trail-head right on the north side of downtown, this rugged 3-mile round-trip hike offers tremendous views of Kanab Valley and the surrounding high-desert landscape. Although a bit steep in places, the total elevation gain of about 800 feet is manageable for most and the trail is very well-maintained—and the eye-popping scenery is worth the effort, especially considering how much less crowded this hike is than those at nearby national parks. ⊠ *N. 100 E at W. 600 N, Kanab.*

ADVENTURE TOURS

★ Dreamland Safari Tours

ADVENTURE TOURS | This long-respected Kanab-based outfitter with around 20 super-knowledgeable guides offers myriad half- and full-day excursions throughout the surrounding countryside, from slot canyon and sunset photography trips near town to adventures a bit farther afield. Tours take place in the Paria Canyon Wilderness and Vermilion Cliffs National Monument, in Grand Staircase–Escalante National Monument, and around the North Rim of the Grand Canyon and nearby Marble Canyon. Multiday "desert safari" and photography tours are offered as well. ⊠ *Kanab* ☎ *435/291–1083* ⊕ *www.dreamland-tours.net* ☞ *From $99.*

★ Paria Outpost & Outfitters

ADVENTURE TOURS | Husband-and-wife owners Steve and Susan Dodson and their small team of guides are among the best experts on the Paria Canyon–Vermilion Cliffs Wilderness area and Grand Staircase–Escalante National Monument (especially the southern sections). The company offers photo workshops and guided tours of all the key destinations in these wilderness areas, including The Wave, as well as shuttle services if you're doing a one-way hike through Buckskin Gulch or Paria Canyon. Tours leave from the office on U.S. 89, about 42 miles east of Kanab, which also has a single-room overnight accommodation and a barbecue restaurant that's open only for groups by advance reservation. Note that all services are cash only. ⊠ *U.S. 89, between mile makers 21 and 22, Paria* ☎ *928/691–1047* ⊕ *www.paria. com* ☞ *From $125.*

Orderville

22 miles north of Kanab.

This easygoing farming town of about 600, along with the neighboring unincorporated communities of Mount Carmel and Mount Carmel Junction, lies at the southern end of the picturesque U.S. 89 corridor, about a 20-minute drive from both Zion National Park's east entrance and the many restaurants and shops of Kanab. Services here are a bit limited, but a handful of lodgings and eateries serve the growing number of visitors who appreciate the convenience to Zion and Bryce Canyon, minus the crowds. Don't miss the studio of Maynard Dixon, who was rightly considered one of the finest painters of the American West. And if you're here in early August, you can attend the festive and family-friendly Kane County Fair.

GETTING HERE AND AROUND

Tiny Orderville and even smaller Mount Carmel Junction are along U.S. 89, between Kanab (about 20 miles south) and Panguitch (about 45 miles north). A car is a must in these parts.

Sights

Maynard Dixon Living History Museum and Gallery

ART MUSEUM | Midway between Orderville and Mount Carmel Junction, you can tour the final summer residence of the famous painter of Western life and landscapes. Dixon lived from 1875 to 1946 and was married to the renowned WPA photographer Dorothea Lange, and, following their divorce, to San Francisco muralist Edith Hamlin. He and Hamlin summered on this property from 1939 until his death; shortly after, she scattered his ashes on a ridge behind the property, which consists of the original log cabin structure and an exceptional Western Art gallery, both of which are maintained by the nonprofit Thunderbird Foundation for the Arts. From mid-April through mid-November, self-guided and docent-led tours (by appointment only) are offered. The gallery and gift shop are open daily year-round. ✉ *2200 S. State St., (U.S. 89), Mount Carmel* ☎ *435/648–2653* 🌐 *www.thunderbirdfoundation.com* 🎟 *Gallery free, self-guided tours $20, guided tours $40.*

🍴 Restaurants

Cordwood

$$$ | **MODERN AMERICAN** | Edison bulbs, timber walls, local landscape photos, and actual stacked cords of wood impart a rustic-elegant ambience at this casually upscale restaurant just 4 miles beyond Zion National Park's eastern entrance, at Zion Mountain Ranch. Bison, beef, and lamb raised on Utah and Colorado ranches form the backbone of a contemporary American menu that also always features at least one vegetarian option and usually trout or salmon as well. **Known for:** great wine list; beef and bison steaks and burgers; close to Zion. [$] *Average main: $29* ✉ *Zion Mountain Ranch, 9065 W. Hwy. 9, Mount Carmel Junction* ☎ *435/648–2555* 🌐 *www.zmr.com/dining.*

🛏 Hotels

Arrowhead Country Inn & Cabins

$$ | **B&B/INN** | **FAMILY** | In a lush valley framed by towering white cliffs, across the road from the Maynard Dixon Living History Museum, this bucolic compound consists of well-appointed cabins, a verdant horse pasture, apple orchards, a pool and hot tub, and a farm market and bakery. The spacious accommodations have plenty of country charm (some have fireplaces) as well as modern conveniences like Roku TVs and fast Wi-Fi. **Pros:** delicious breakfasts and organic coffee included; kids love the farm animals and horses; some cabins have full kitchens. **Cons:** no refunds if cancelling within 21 days of arrival; few restaurants and services nearby; no pets. [$] *Rooms from: $169* ✉ *2155 S. State St., (U.S. 89), Orderville* ☎ *435/648–2569* 🌐 *www.arrowheadbb.com* 🔑 *11 units* 🍽 *Free Breakfast.*

Best Western East Zion Thunderbird Lodge

$$ | **MOTEL** | About 13 miles beyond the east entrance of Zion National Park, this low-slung motel with clean, spacious rooms decorated with rustic lodge-style furniture is a good option if you also want to be within an hour's drive of Bryce Canyon National Park. **Pros:** restaurant serves delicious pies; outdoor heated pool, hot tub; well-manicured grounds and nine-hole golf course. **Cons:** no elevator; limited dining options nearby; breakfast not included. [$] *Rooms from: $163* ✉ *U.S. 89 and Hwy. 9, Mount Carmel* ☎ *435/648–2203 hotel direct* 🌐 *www.bestwestern.com* 🔑 *61 rooms* 🍽 *No Meals.*

★ **East Zion Resort**

$$$ | **RESORT** | **FAMILY** |–Operated by one of the area's leading adventure tour companies, this eco-chic resort spread across three properties in the heart of Orderville offers a variety of distinctive, contemporary, and beautifully appointed accommodations, including tiny houses, treehouse-inspired lofts, and fully climate-controlled yurts and canvas glamping tents. **Pros:** Jeep rentals available on site; good base for visiting both Zion and Bryce Canyon; excellent food-truck-style restaurant. **Cons:** the resort's three sections are a short drive from one another; not many dining options nearby; slightly pricey for the area. [$] *Rooms from: $231* ✉ *490 E. State St., Orderville* ☎ *833/378–9466* 🌐 *www.eastzionresort.com* 🔑 *29 units* 🍽 *No Meals.*

Zion Mountain Ranch

$$$ | **RESORT** | **FAMILY** | This peaceful ranch-style resort with more than 50 handsomely furnished cabins and lodge-style vacation homes that sleep from 2 to 15 guests lies a mere 4 miles from the east entrance of Zion National Park and offers a variety of activities, including horseback riding, jeep tours, and guided hikes. **Pros:** rustic-chic aesthetic; spectacularly scenic surroundings; excellent restaurant. **Cons:** some decor is a bit dated; spotty Wi-Fi; half-hour drive to Kanab's restaurants. [$] *Rooms from: $239* ✉ *9065 W. Hwy. 9, Mount Carmel Junction* ☎ *435/648–2555, 866/648–2555* 🌐 *www.zmr.com* 🛏 *53 cabins* 🍴 *No Meals.*

Zion Ponderosa Ranch Resort

$$$ | **RESORT** | **FAMILY** | Just a few miles beyond Zion National Park's east entrance and about 16 miles northwest of Mount Carmel Junction, this scenic, 4,000-acre ranch offers a varied lineup of lodgings and a dizzying array of activities. **Pros:** lots of family-friendly activities; tranquil setting near Zion's east entrance; off-season packages include breakfast and Jeep tours. **Cons:** pool gets crowded in summer; least expensive cabins lack a private bath; few dining options nearby. [$] *Rooms from: $234* ✉ *Twin Knolls Rd., Orderville* ☎ *435/648–2700* 🌐 *www.zionponderosa.com* 🛏 *31 cabins* 🍴 *No Meals.*

Activities

ADVENTURE TOURS

East Zion Experiences

ADVENTURE TOURS | Although this outfitter that also runs Orderville's beautiful East Zion Resort offers some family-friendly, low-impact Jeep and UTV (utility terrain vehicle) tours of slot canyons in the area, it excels with more extreme adventures—canyoneering, rappelling, and via ferrata (using iron steps to scale steep rock faces). Tours last from two to nine hours, and no experience is required for most. The company also rents electric surfboards, stand-up paddleboards, and kayaks to use on Jackson Flat Reservoir in Kanab as well as e-bikes to cruise around the reservoir. ✉ *500 E. State St., Orderville* ☎ *855/635–9100* 🌐 *www.eastzionexperiences.com* 🎟 *From $45.*

HIKING

Red Hollow Canyon

HIKING & WALKING | **FAMILY** | For a highly rewarding and relatively easy hiking adventure close to town, take this 2-mile round-trip trek that ends in a dramatic, sheer-walled, red-rock slot canyon. ✉ *Red Hollow Dr., off 100 E, Orderville.*

Panguitch

45 miles north of Orderville.

At 6,500 feet, this low-key town with 1,750 full-time residents has a handful of moderately priced motels and casual restaurants, making it a pleasant, cool-aired base for visiting Bryce Canyon (24 miles southeast) and Cedar Breaks (30 miles west). Main Street is lined with late-19th-century buildings, and the early homes and outbuildings are noted for their distinctive brick architecture.

GETTING HERE AND AROUND

Panguitch is along U.S. 89 at its junction with Highway 143, a winding and scenic route past rippling Panguitch Lake that leads west to Cedar Breaks National Monument toward Cedar City. One of the state's most beautiful roads, U.S. 89 is known as the Heritage Highway for its role in shaping Utah history. Panguitch is also near the start of gorgeous Highway 12, which leads east to Bryce Canyon and Grand Staircase–Escalante.

VISITOR INFORMATION

CONTACTS Garfield County Office of Tourism. ✉ *Panguitch* ☎ *800/444–6689, 435/676–1160* 🌐 *www.brycecanyoncountry.com.*

Sights

★ Red Canyon

CANYON | This arresting 7,400-foot-elevation landscape of dark green Ponderosa pines and Douglas fir trees is part of Dixie National Forest. You'll see fiery-red sandstone pinnacles and hoodoos, as well as clear blue sky, as you make your way via Highway 12 from Panguitch to Bryce Canyon—at one point the road even passes beneath a dramatic red-rock arch. Have a picnic and a short stroll on one of the several trails that lead from the Red Canyon Visitor Center (open daily, late May to early September). Longer treks—the Hoodoo Loop, Ledges, and Losee Canyon Trails all showcase the rewarding scenery—are worth checking out if you have a bit more time. Some trails are well-suited to mountain biking, horseback riding, and cross-country skiing, and the paved 5-mile Red Canyon Trail is ideal for road biking. There's also a campground. ✉ *5375 Hwy. 12, Panguitch* ☎ *435/676–2676* 🌐 *www.fs.usda.gov/recarea/dixie/recarea/?recid=24942.*

Restaurants

Burger Barn

$ | **BURGER** | **FAMILY** | Order at the window and snag an outdoor table at this laid-back burger joint in a little red barn near Panguitch Lake, a great option en route to Cedar Breaks National Monument or Cedar City. The one-third-pound Black Angus steak burgers here come with a variety of toppings (bacon, onion rings), and the menu also has barbecue choices such as pulled pork or beef brisket sandwiches, fish-and-chips, sweet-potato fries, and shakes and ice cream. **Known for:** giant burgers and smoked meats; pretty setting near an alpine lake; ice-cream sundaes. [$] *Average main: $9* ✉ *75 S. Hwy. 143, Panguitch* ☎ *435/676–2445* 🕘 *Closed mid-Sept.–mid-May.*

Cowboy's Smokehouse Café

$$$ | **BARBECUE** | From the Western-style interior and creaky floors to the smoker out back, this rustic café has an aura of Texan authenticity—there are cowboy collectibles and game trophies lining the walls. No surprise that barbecue is the specialty here, with ample portions of favorites such as ribs, mesquite-flavored beef, and pulled pork and the restaurant's own house-made sauce, along with lighter sandwiches and salads. **Known for:** German sausage platter; prodigious steaks; delicious desserts, including fruit cobbler and pies. [$] *Average main: $23* ✉ *95 N. Main St., Panguitch* ☎ *435/676–8030* 🌐 *www.thecowboysmokehouse.com* 💳 *No credit cards* 🕘 *Closed Sun. and late-Nov.–mid-Mar.*

Hotels

Church's Blue Pine Motel

$ | **MOTEL** | This single-story 1930s-era motel in Panguitch's cute historic district doesn't look like much from the outside, but the rooms are clean, have refrigerators and microwaves, and are among the most affordable within striking distance of Bryce, Zion, and Cedar Breaks. **Pros:** you can pull your car right up to your room; in the center of town; rock-bottom rates. **Cons:** walls are a bit thin; very basic furnishings; not a lot to do right in Panguitch. [$] *Rooms from: $79* ✉ *130 N. Main St., Panguitch* ☎ *435/676–8197, 800/299–6115* 🌐 *www.bluepinemotel.com* 🛏 *20 rooms* 🍴 *No Meals.*

★ Cottonwood Meadow Lodge

$$ | **B&B/INN** | Set in a sweeping valley along the main road between Panguitch and Hatch, this sweet and secluded 50-acre ranch comprises four roomy cottages decorated with stylish Western-style furnishings—leather sofas, indigenous artwork, bearskin rugs, hand-carved beds and tables—and outfitted with well-equipped kitchens. **Pros:** peaceful, scenic setting; convenient to Bryce and Zion; self-catering and large sitting

Grand Staircase–Escalante National Monument is the area's main draw.

areas make rooms nice for families. **Cons:** few dining options nearby; no AC and no pets allowed; fills up well ahead on summer weekends. [$] *Rooms from: $185* ✉ *Mile marker 123, U.S. 89, Panguitch* ☎ *435/676–8950* 🌐 *www.brycecanyoncabins.com* 🛏 *4 cabins* 🍴 *No Meals.*

Mountain Ridge Cabins and Lodging
$ | **HOTEL** | In the tiny village of Hatch, 15 miles south of Panguitch, you'll find this nicely maintained and reasonably priced campus of cozy cabins and standard hotel rooms, all of them spotlessly clean and attractively decorated with modern furnishings, large flat-screen TVs, refrigerators, microwaves, and high-quality bedding. **Pros:** you can park right in front of your room; within walking distance of a couple of restaurants; convenient for exploring Bryce and Zion. **Cons:** least expensive rooms are quite small; in a tiny town; on a slightly busy road. [$] *Rooms from: $129* ✉ *106 S. Main St., Hatch* ☎ *435/735–4300, 877/877–9939* 🌐 *www.mountainridgelodging.com* 🕓 *Closed Jan.–Apr.* 🛏 *24 rooms* 🍴 *No Meals.*

Shopping

Bryce Canyon Trading Post
CRAFTS | Near Red Canyon a little east of U.S. 89, this rambling emporium carries high-quality Native American turquoise jewelry, beadwork, textiles, and other fine crafts, plus a number of souvenirs related to the nearby national parks. ✉ *2938 Hwy. 12, Panguitch* ☎ *435/676–2688.*

Bryce Canyon City

25 miles southeast of Panguitch.

Consisting primarily of shops, restaurants, gas stations, and services to serve the increasing number of visitors to Bryce Canyon National Park, Bryce Canyon City was incorporated as a town in 2007, though it isn't much of one. Although most of the businesses are mediocre and overpriced, they offer the only additional services on the doorstep of the park.

GETTING HERE AND AROUND

Highway 63 passes right through town on the way to Bryce Canyon National Park's main entrance, which is less than a mile south. The park's shuttle bus stops at several points in town.

Sights

Bryce Wildlife Adventure

SCIENCE MUSEUM | FAMILY | Imagine a zoo frozen in time: this 14,000-square-foot private museum contains more than 1,600 butterflies and 1,100 taxidermy animals in tableaux mimicking actual terrain and animal behavior. The animals and birds come from all parts of the world. An African room has baboons, bush pigs, Cape buffalo, and a lion. There's also a collection of about 40 living fallow deer that kids delight in feeding and ATV and bike rentals for touring scenic Highway 12 and the Paunsaugunt Plateau. ✉ *1945 W. Hwy. 12, Bryce Canyon City* ☎ *435/834–5555* 🌐 *www.brycewildlifeadventure.com* 🎟 *$8* 🕒 *Closed Nov.–Mar.*

Restaurants

Bryce Canyon Pines Restaurant

$$ | AMERICAN | FAMILY | Inside the Bryce Canyon Pines Motel, about 5 miles northwest of Bryce Canyon City, this down-home, family-friendly roadhouse decorated with Old West photos and memorabilia serves reliably good stick-to-your-ribs breakfasts, hefty elk burgers, rib-eye steaks, and Utah rainbow trout. But the top draw here is homemade pie, which comes in a vast assortment of flavors, from banana-blueberry cream to boysenberry. **Known for:** delectable pies; convenient Highway 12 location; plenty of kids' options. [$] *Average main: $17* ✉ *Hwy. 12, mile marker 10, Bryce Canyon City* ☎ *435/834–5441* 🌐 *www.brycecanyonrestaurant.com.*

Hotels

Best Western Plus Bryce Canyon Grand Hotel

$$$$ | HOTEL | If you appreciate creature comforts but can do without much in the way of local personality, this four-story hotel just outside the park fits the bill—rooms are quite comfortable, with plush bedding, spacious bathrooms, and modern appliances, and there's an outdoor pool and pleasant patio. **Pros:** clean, spacious rooms; attractive pool; short drive or free shuttle ride from Bryce Canyon. **Cons:** the closest restaurants aren't very good; very pricey during busy times; standard chain ambience. [$] *Rooms from: $359* ✉ *30 N. 100 E, Bryce Canyon City* ☎ *866/866–6634, 435/834–5700* 🌐 *www.brycecanyongrand.com* 🛏 *164 rooms* 🍴 *Free Breakfast.*

Bryce Canyon Pines Motel

$$ | MOTEL | Most rooms in this motel in the sweeping high desert 6 miles southwest of the park entrance and close to Red Canyon have pleasant views of the surrounding pine trees and the mountains in the distance. **Pros:** guided horseback rides through Red Canyon; outdoor pool and hot tub; lively restaurant famed for homemade pies. **Cons:** thin walls; no shuttle bus to the park; furnishings are a bit dated. [$] *Rooms from: $145* ✉ *Hwy. 12, mile marker 10, Bryce Canyon City* ☎ *435/834–5441* 🌐 *www.brycecanyonmotel.com* 🛏 *46 rooms* 🍴 *No Meals.*

Under Canvas Bryce Canyon

$$$$ | RESORT | FAMILY | The latest outpost of this popular luxury glamping brand opened in a juniper forest outside Widtsoe, a hiccup of a village about 15 miles north of the national park entrance, in summer 2022 and offers safari-chic canvas tents decked out with tasteful West Elm furnishings, private baths with eco-friendly products, and USB battery packs to keep your toys charged, plus a restaurant serving locally sourced breakfast and dinner fare. **Pros:** secluded

and stunning setting on 750 high-desert acres; nightly campfires with complimentary s'mores; lots of activities—yoga, live music. **Cons:** relatively short season; a 20-minute drive from the park and area restaurants; expensive. [$] *Rooms from: $385* ✉ *1325 S. Johns Valley Rd., Bryce Canyon City* ☎ *888/496–1148* 🌐 *www.undercanvas.com* 🕒 *Closed late Sept.–mid-May* 🛏 *50 tents* 🍴 *No Meals.*

Shopping

Ruby's Inn General Store

SOUVENIRS | On a busy evening, this giant mercantile bustles with tourists plucking through souvenirs that range from sweatshirts to wind chimes. There are also selections of Western wear, children's toys, holiday gifts, and groceries (albeit with pretty high prices). You'll also find camping equipment. Need a folding stove, sleeping bag, or fishing gear? You will find it at Ruby's. You can also cross Main Street to where this ever-expanding complex has added a line of shops trimmed like an Old West town, complete with candy store and rock shop. ✉ *26 S. Main St., Bryce Canyon City* ☎ *435/834–5484* 🌐 *www.rubysinn.com/rubys-inn-store.*

Tropic

12 miles southeast of Bryce Canyon City.

Just a few miles farther from the national park than Bryce Canyon City but considerably cuter and more charming, tiny Tropic (population 480) is a convenient base for exploring the region's majestic rock formations—many of which you can see from town. You'll find a handful of eateries and lodgings here, some of them excellent. Keep in mind that many businesses shut down or greatly slow down in winter.

GETTING HERE AND AROUND

Just down the hill from Bryce Canyon, tiny Tropic is along Highway 12.

Restaurants

★ **i.d.k. Barbecue**

$ | BARBECUE | FAMILY | This casually hip, counter-service restaurant with picnic tables outfitted with big rolls of paper towels serves tender pulled pork, smoked chicken, and beef brisket barbecue, along with classic sides like mac-and-cheese, baked beans, potato salad, and cornbread. You can enjoy your barbecue as a platter or sandwich, or take things to another level and try it smothered over nachos or in a loaded baked potato. **Known for:** nice variety of both sweet and spicy sauces; chalkboard menu with creative staff recommendations; peach cobbler. [$] *Average main: $12* ✉ *161 N. Main St., Tropic* ☎ *435/679–8353* 🌐 *www.idkbarbecue.com* 🕒 *Closed Sun.*

★ **The Stone Hearth Grille**

$$$$ | MODERN AMERICAN | With sweeping panoramas toward Bryce Canyon from the back deck, an art-filled dining room with a stone fireplace, and some of the most accomplished modern American fare within an hour's drive of the park, this refined yet unpretentious restaurant on the outskirts of tiny Tropic is well worth a splurge. Favorites here include the salad of citrus-roasted-carrots with avocado and coconut cream, the bone-in grilled pork chops with cheddar-potato fondue, and several preparations of local grass-fed steaks. **Known for:** breathtaking views; great children's menu; well-curated wine list. [$] *Average main: $34* ✉ *1380 W. Stone Canyon La., Tropic* ☎ *435/679–8923* 🌐 *www.stonehearthgrille.com* 🕒 *Closed Nov.–Feb. No lunch.*

Hotels

Bryce Trails Bed & Breakfast

$$$ | **B&B/INN** | This contemporary B&B set in a sagebrush canyon just outside Tropic's small downtown offers a number of noteworthy perks, including a delicious made-from-scratch breakfast, close access to a trail that leads right into the park, and individually decorated rooms hung with the dazzling landscape photography of owner Edgars Erglis—one-on-one photography classes are offered, too. **Pros:** friendly hosts who know a lot about the area; superb, hearty breakfast included; within hiking distance of Bryce Canyon. **Cons:** not a good fit for children; two-night minimum during some busy periods; about a mile from downtown restaurants. $ *Rooms from: $229* ✉ *1001 Bryce Way, Tropic* ☎ *435/231–4436* ⊕ *www.brycetrail.com* ⇥ *7 rooms* ⏐⊙⏐ *Free Breakfast.*

Bybee's Steppingstone Motel

$ | **MOTEL** | This cheerfully decorated, economical, and intimate seven-unit boutique property in tiny downtown Tropic is just 15 minutes east of the park and on the way toward Escalante. **Pros:** individually decorated rooms; short walk from several restaurants; Keurig coffee-makers and tea kettles in rooms. **Cons:** check-in office has limited hours; pets not allowed; no breakfast (but oatmeal and granola bars are provided). $ *Rooms from: $119* ✉ *21 S. Main St., Tropic* ☎ *435/574–9432* ⊕ *www.bybeesteppingstone.com* ⊙ *Closed Dec.–Mar.* ⇥ *7 rooms* ⏐⊙⏐ *No Meals.*

★ Stone Canyon Inn

$$$ | **B&B/INN** | Although technically not in the park, this stunningly situated luxury inn lies just east of Bryce Canyon, and rooms and the excellent on-site restaurant, The Stone Hearth Grille, have astounding views of the park's hoodoos—there's even a trailhead nearby that accesses some of Bryce's best trails. **Pros:** the most luxurious rooms in the area; fantastic restaurant on site; soaking tubs and fireplaces in some rooms. **Cons:** on the pricey side; not within walking distance of downtown shops and restaurants; no breakfast. $ *Rooms from: $205* ✉ *1380 W. Stone Canyon La., Tropic* ☎ *435/679–8611, 866/489–4680* ⊕ *www.stonecanyoninn.com* ⇥ *15 rooms* ⏐⊙⏐ *No Meals.*

Escalante

38 miles northeast of Tropic.

Though the Domínguez and Escalante expedition of 1776 came nowhere near this area, the town's name does honor the Spanish explorer. It was bestowed nearly a century later by a member of a survey party led by John Wesley Powell, charged with mapping this remote region. Today, this friendly little town of about 800 serves as the northern gateway to Grand Staircase–Escalante National Monument.

Politicians and activists continue to battle over the size of this immense monument (it's larger than Utah's five national parks combined) that was established by the Clinton administration in 1996; it was reduced by about 50% in 2017 by President Trump and then restored to its original size in 2021 by President Biden. As of this writing, Utah state officials were suing the Biden administration with the intention of once again reducing the monument's size. Whatever its eventual boundaries, the region grows ever more famous and popular with each passing year, and the influx of visitors has resulted in a steady boom of new lodgings, eateries, and tour operators. It's popular here year-round, but especially during the more temperate spring and fall seasons. Held over two weeks in mid-September, the Escalante Canyons Art Festival is an especially fun time to visit.

The best place to learn about the monument's remote and dazzling landscape is downtown's striking LEED-certified Escalante Interagency Visitor Center, which contains engaging exhibits and screens an informative film. The center's knowledgeable BLM, forest service, and national park employees readily dispense brochures and advice (including the latest road and weather conditions) on hiking, camping, and exploring within in the monument. The BLM visitor center in Cannonville, between Escalante and Tropic, is also handy.

GETTING HERE AND AROUND

Scenic Highway 12, which is one of the prettiest drives in the state (especially the section north to Boulder), passes right through the heart of Escalante. You can explore the vast Grand Staircase–Escalante National Monument via mostly unpaved and sometimes pretty rough roads, ideally with a four-wheel-drive vehicle, although in dry weather, a passenger car can handle some areas. To really venture off the beaten path into some of the most interesting and remote parts of the park, consider renting a custom-designed high-clearance vehicle from Epic Jeep Rentals. Most of the park's access points are off Highway 12. It costs nothing to enter the park, but fees apply for camping and backcountry permits.

CONTACTS Epic Jeep Rentals. ✉ *1605 Pine Creek Rd., Escalante* ☎ *435/293–4639* ⊕ *www.jlurentals.com.*

VISITOR INFORMATION

CONTACTS Cannonville BLM Visitor Center. ✉ *10 Center St., Cannonville* ☎ *435/826–5640* ⊕ *www.blm.gov/visit/cannonville-visitor-center.* **Escalante Interagency Visitor Center.** ✉ *755 W. Main St., Escalante* ☎ *435/826–5499* ⊕ *www.blm.gov/visit/escalante-interagency-visitor-center.*

Sights

★ Calf Creek Recreation Area

NATURE SIGHT | FAMILY | One of the more easily accessible and rewarding adventures in the national monument, this picturesque canyon rife with oak trees, cacti, and sandstone pictographs is reached via the 6-mile round-trip Lower Calf Creek Falls Trail, which starts at the Calf Creek Campground, 15 miles east of Escalante and 12 miles south of Boulder along scenic Highway 12. The big payoff, and it's especially pleasing on warm days, is a 126-foot spring-fed waterfall. The pool at the base is a beautiful spot for a swim or picnic. ✉ *Hwy. 12, Escalante* ☎ *435/826–5499* ⊕ *www.blm.gov/visit/calf-creek-recreation-area-day-use-site* 💲 *$5 per vehicle.*

Escalante Petrified Forest State Park

STATE/PROVINCIAL PARK | FAMILY | This park just 2 miles northwest of downtown protects a huge repository of petrified wood, easily spotted along two short but moderately taxing hiking trails (the shorter and steeper of the two, the Sleeping Rainbows Trail, requires some scrambling over boulders). Of equal interest is the park's Wide Hollow Reservoir, which has a swimming beach and is popular for kayaking, stand-up paddleboarding, trout fishing, and birding. Keep an eye out for Escalante Rock Shop, just before you reach the park border, which sells petrified wood and other geological wonders. ✉ *710 N. Reservoir Rd., Escalante* ☎ *435/826–4466* ⊕ *stateparks.utah.gov/parks/escalante-petrified-forest/* 💲 *$10 per vehicle.*

★ Grand Staircase–Escalante National Monument

NATIONAL PARK | This breathtaking, immense, and often difficult-to-access wilderness became a national monument in 1996. And although its federal status continues to generate controversy that has led to reductions and subsequent

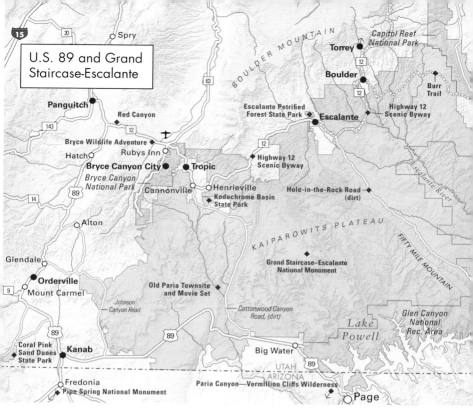

U.S. 89 and Grand
Staircase-Escalante

Spry

20

Capitol Reef
National Park

BOULDER MOUNTAIN

Torrey

12

Boulder

12

63

Burr
Trail

Panguitch

143

Red Canyon

12

Escalante Petrified
Forest State Park

Escalante

Highway 12
Scenic Byway

Escalante River

Bryce Wildlife Adventure

Hatch

Rubys Inn

Highway 12
Scenic Byway

Bryce Canyon City

Tropic

12

Bryce Canyon
National Park

89

14

Cannonville

Henrieville

Kodachrome Basin
State Park

Hole-in-the-Rock Road
(dirt)

Alton

KAIPAROWITS PLATEAU

FIFTY MILE MOUNTAIN

Glendale

Orderville

9

Mount Carmel

Old Paria Townsite
and Movie Set

Johnson
Canyon Road

Grand Staircase–Escalante
National Monument

Cottonwood Canyon
Road, (dirt)

Lake
Powell

Glen Canyon
National
Rec. Area

89

89

Coral Pink
Sand Dunes
State Park

Kanab

Big Water

89

UTAH
ARIZONA

Fredonia

Pipe Spring National Monument

Paria Canyon—Vermilion Cliffs Wilderness

Page

restorations of its boundaries, this nearly 1.9-million-acre tract of red-rock canyons, stepped escarpments (the Grand Staircase), sheer rock ridges, and sweeping mesas continues to beguile hikers, canyoneers, and other outdoors enthusiasts. Unlike parks and monuments operated by the National Park Service, Grand Staircase–Escalante is administered by the Bureau of Land Management (BLM), and visiting its key attractions requires a bit more research and effort than, for example, Bryce or Capitol Reef, which are relatively more compact and accessible.

The best way to plan your adventures within the park is by stopping by one of the four visitor centers in the area, the best of these being the stunning Escalante Interagency Visitor Center in downtown Escalante. The smaller BLM Visitor Center in Cannonville is also helpful, or if

you're entering the monument from the south, check out the BLM Visitor Centers in Kanab and Big Water. Given that many of the monument's top attractions are in remote areas with limited signage and access via unpaved (and sometimes very rough) roads, many visitors hire one of the area's many experienced outfitters and guides—this is an especially smart strategy if it's your first time in the area. Some of the monument's top attractions are big draws—including Calf Creek Recreation Area and the several hikes and vistas along Hole-in-the-Rock Road (see Escalante), the Burr Trail (see Boulder), and the Paria Movie Set and Paria Canyon–Vermilion Cliffs Wilderness (see Kanab). ⊠ *Escalante Interagency Visitor Center, 755 W. Main St., Escalante* ☎ *435/826–5499* ⊕ *www.blm.gov/ programs/national-conservation-lands/*

utah/grand-staircase-escalante-national-monument.

Hell's Backbone Road

SCENIC DRIVE | For a scenic, topsy-turvy backcountry drive or a challenging mountain-bike ride, follow 35-mile Hell's Backbone Road (aka Forest Road 153) from Escalante, where it begins as Posey Lake Road, to Boulder. Built by the Civilian Conservation Corps in the early 1930s, it's a gravel-surface alternate route to scenic Highway 12. You can make the drive with an ordinary passenger car in summer (it's impassable in winter), assuming dry conditions, but a four-wheel-drive vehicle is more comfortable. Allow about two hours to drive it. At roughly the midway point, the dramatic 109-foot-long Hell's Backbone Bridge, which crosses over a breathtaking 1,500-foot chasm, makes for a memorable photo op. ⊠ *Hell's Backbone Rd., Escalante.*

★ Highway 12 Scenic Byway

SCENIC DRIVE | Keep your camera handy and steering wheel steady along this entrancing 123-mile route that begins at U.S. 89 south of Panguitch and meanders in a generally northeasterly direction through Red Canyon, the south end of Bryce Canyon National Park, and the towns of Escalante and Boulder, before climbing Boulder Mountain and winding through Dixie National Forest to Torrey, just west of Capitol Reef National Park. The roughly 25-mile stretch from Escalante to Boulder is the most spectacular. Allow time to pull off and stop at the many scenic overlooks; almost every one will give you an eye-popping view, and interpretive signs let you know what you're looking at. Pay attention while driving, though. The road is sometimes twisting and steep—the section over Hogback Ridge, with its sheer drop-offs on both sides, will really get your heart pumping. ⊠ *Hwy. 12.*

Hole-in-the-Rock Road

SCENIC DRIVE | On the way to southeastern Utah in 1879, Mormon pioneers chipped and blasted a narrow passageway in solid rock, through which they lowered their wagons. The Hole-in-the-Rock Trail, now an extremely rugged 60-mile unpaved washboard road that's officially known as BLM 200, leads south from Highway 12, 5 miles southeast of Escalante, to the actual hole-in-the-rock site in Glen Canyon Recreation Area. The original passageway ends where the canyon has been flooded by the waters of Lake Powell—you can hike the half-mile from the end of the road to a dramatic viewpoint overlooking the lake.

Just keep in mind that it can take up to three hours to drive to the end of the road, and high-clearance vehicles are best (and a requirement when muddy—check with the Escalante Interagency Visitor Center before setting out). However, there are some amazing hiking spots located along the route, including Zebra Slot Canyon (at mile 8.5) and Devil's Garden (at mile 12), which are less daunting to reach. Other worthwhile hikes and stops along the route include Peek-A-Boo Gulch (off Dry Fork Road, at mile 26) and Dance Hall Rock (at mile 36). ⊠ *Hole-in-the-Rock Rd., Escalante* ⊕ *www.nps.gov/glca/learn/historyculture/holeintherock.htm.*

★ Kodachrome Basin State Park

STATE/PROVINCIAL PARK | **FAMILY** | Yes, this remarkable landscape in Cannonville, about 40 miles southwest of Escalante, is named after the old-fashioned color photo film, and once you see it you'll understand why the National Geographic Society gave it the name. The stone spires known as "sand pipes" are found nowhere else in the world. Hike any of the trails to spot some of the 67 pipes in and around the park. The short Angel's Palace Trail takes you quickly into the park's interior, up, over, and around some of the badlands. Note that the oft-photographed Shakespeare Arch collapsed in 2019; although the trail leading to what is now a pile of rubble is still open, it's not as interesting as the Angel's Palace or Panorama Trails. ✉ *Off Cottonwood Canyon Rd., Cannonville* ✥ *9 miles southeast of Cannonville* ☎ *435/679–8562* 🌐 *stateparks.utah.gov/parks/kodachrome-basin* 🎟 *$10 per vehicle.*

🍴 Restaurants

★ Escalante Outfitters Restaurant

$ | **AMERICAN** | This warm and inviting log cabin–style restaurant—operated by a popular tour operator that also runs a camp store and cabin and camping compound—is a great place to sit back and relax after a day of hiking, fly-fishing, or road-tripping. Try one of the creatively topped pizzas, a veggie sandwich, or an apple-pecan-arugula salad, or drop in for a well-crafted (Fair Trade) coffee and a light breakfast to kick off the day. **Known for:** excellent craft beer selection; friendly crowd; fine coffees, quiches, and pastries in the morning. [$] *Average main: $14* ✉ *310 W. Main St., Escalante* ☎ *435/215–7953* 🌐 *www.escalanteoutfitters.com* 🕑 *Closed Wed. and Dec.–Feb.*

Georgie's Outdoor Mexican Cafe

$ | **MEXICAN** | **FAMILY** | This quirky food truck–style café beside Canyons of Escalante RV Park doles out filling and flavorful Mexican and Southwestern standbys, including prodigious chicken or beef burritos with Oaxacan and Jack cheese and house-made green salsa, and seasoned-cod tacos with aioli. There's ample seating on the cheerful patio. **Known for:** flan with weekly rotating flavors; lavender lemonade and other nonalcoholic drinks; colorfully painted outdoor seating area. [$] *Average main: $13* ✉ *495 W. Main St., Escalante* ☎ *435/826–4782* 🌐 *www.facebook.com/georgiesoutdoormexicancafe* 🕑 *Closed Sun. and Mon.*

Nemo's Drive-Thru

$ | **BURGER** | **FAMILY** | Dive into one of the hefty burgers at this local fast-food spot set in a low-slung mid-century building on Main Street—there's no indoor seating, just order at the counter and enjoy your meal at one of the green picnic tables. Bison, beef, and veggie patties are available, along with beer-battered-cod baskets, corn dogs, pulled pork sandwiches, and homemade ice cream and shakes. **Known for:** pralines-and-cream milkshakes; mushroom-and-Swiss burgers; old-fashioned, family-friendly ambience. [$] *Average main: $11* ✉ *40 E. Main St., Escalante* ☎ *435/826–4500* 🌐 *www.burgeralien.com* 🕑 *Closed Sun.*

☕ Coffee and Quick Bites

★ Kiva Koffeehouse

$ | **CAFÉ** | This fun stop along scenic Highway 12, 13 miles east of Escalante, was constructed by the late artist and inventor Bradshaw Bowman, who began building it when he was in his eighties and spent two years finding and transporting the 13 Douglas-fir logs surrounding the structure. The distinctive eatery with amazing views serves a daily-changing array of made-from-scratch soups, bagel sandwiches, tamales, oatmeal pancakes, salads, and decadent desserts, plus exceptional coffee and espresso drinks. **Known for:** breathtaking canyon views; creative, farm-to-table breakfast and lunch fare; sticky date pudding, apple crumb pie, and other treats. [$] *Average main: $10* ✉ *Hwy. 12, Escalante* ✥ *Between mileposts 73 and 74* ☎ *435/826–4550* 🌐 *www.kivakoffeehouse.com* 💳 *No credit cards* 🕑 *Closed Mon. and Tues. and Nov.–Feb. No dinner.*

Hotels

★ Entrada Escalante Lodge

$$ | **B&B/INN** | Each of the eight rooms in this smart, contemporary lodge in downtown Escalante has a patio with grand views of the surrounding mountains, plus plenty of cushy perks like French presses and fresh-ground coffee, plush bedding, and 50-inch smart TVs. **Pros:** convenient downtown location; spacious rooms with Grand Staircase views; pets are welcome in some rooms. **Cons:** books up well ahead many weekends; in a very secluded, small town; great coffee but no breakfast. [$] *Rooms from: $179* ✉ *480 W. Main St., Escalante* ☎ *435/826–4000* 🌐 *www.entradaescalante.com* 🕒 *Closed Jan. and Feb.* 🛏 *8 rooms* 🍴 *No Meals.*

Escalante Outfitters Cabins

$ | **B&B/INN** | If you don't care about frills but do plan on adventuring in the area, consider one of this property's seven simple but cute log cabins, which share a bathhouse, or the large family cabin that sleeps four and has its own bathroom; tent sites are also available. **Pros:** firepit, grills, and picnic tables; pet-friendly; guided tours available on site. **Cons:** cabins are tiny; you may have to wait in line for a shower; some cabins have only bunk beds. [$] *Rooms from: $55* ✉ *310 W. Main St., Escalante* ☎ *435/215–7953* 🌐 *www.escalanteoutfitters.com* 🕒 *Closed Dec.–Feb.* 🛏 *8 cabins* 🍴 *No Meals.*

Escalante Yurts

$$$ | **B&B/INN** | **FAMILY** | Sitting on a peaceful pinon- and sagebrush-shaded mesa a couple of miles north of town, this mini glamping compound comprises seven warmly outfitted yurts, each with year-round climate control, top-of-the-line linens, a patio with gas grill, a well-stocked kitchen or kitchenette, and an ample sitting area with a TV. **Pros:** plenty of space between each yurt allows lots of privacy; peaceful setting that's ideal for stargazing; four-wheel-drive Jeep rentals available on-site. **Cons:** Wi-Fi can be a little slow; pets not allowed; not within walking distance of town. [$] *Rooms from: $289* ✉ *1605 N. Pine Creek Rd., Escalante* ☎ *435/826–4222, 844/200–9878* 🌐 *www.escalanteyurts.com* 🛏 *7 yurts* 🍴 *Free Breakfast.*

★ Slot Canyons Inn

$$ | **B&B/INN** | In a dramatic, New Mexico adobe-style building, this upscale inn with spacious rooms and lots of big windows is 5 miles west of town—at the mouth of a canyon on the edge of the national monument—and has hikes right outside its door, as well as hosts who are happy to provide guidance on regional treks. **Pros:** utterly peaceful, enchanting setting; within a short hike of petroglyphs and dramatic cliffs; many rooms have jetted soaking tubs. **Cons:** remote location; the cheapest room is a little small; not within walking distance of town. [$] *Rooms from: $149* ✉ *3680 Hwy. 12, Escalante* ☎ *435/826–4901* 🌐 *www.slotcanyonsinn.com* 🛏 *11 rooms* 🍴 *Free Breakfast.*

★ Yonder Escalante

$$$ | **RESORT** | **FAMILY** | Of the several hip glamping resorts that have opened in southern Utah in recent years, this sprawling compound on the west side of Escalante might just offer the best balance of a gorgeous contemporary design—accommodations are in sleekly restored Airstream trailers and cozy glass-walled cabins—and an inviting communal spirit, thanks to an inviting patio served by a food truck, a huge pool, and a drive-in movie theater with seating in vintage autos. **Pros:** fun common spaces that are perfect for making new friends; lots of thoughtful amenities; expansive view of the high desert and mountains. **Cons:** social atmosphere isn't for everyone; no private bathrooms (but the common bathhouses are gorgeously appointed); not within walking distance of town. [$] *Rooms from: $209* ✉ *2020 W. Hwy. 12, Escalante* ☎ *435/274–7222* 🌐 *www.stayyonder.com* 🛏 *32 units* 🍴 *No Meals.*

Nightlife

★ 4th West Pub
BARS | In a part of the world where nightlife typically consists of listening to coyotes howl beneath a starlit sky, it's nice to have one good late-night ("late" meaning 10 or 11 pm, depending on the season) option. The stylishly converted, circa-1940s service station is a great place to socialize, shoot pool, and sip craft beer and cocktails. There's live music, art classes, trivia matches, and other fun events on some evenings, and the kitchen turns out tasty bar snacks, from nachos to panini. ⊠ *425 W. Main St., Escalante* ☎ *435/826–4525* ⊕ *www.4wpub.com.*

Shopping

★ Escalante Mercantile & Natural Grocery
FOOD | Although ostensibly a grocery store—and one with an excellent selection of organic produce, fine cheeses and baked goods, prepared foods to go, and other gourmet items—this friendly market in a historic brick house also features a coffeehouse and smoothie café with patio seating and a small gallery with well-curated art, crafts, and gifts. ⊠ *210 W. Main St., Escalante* ☎ *435/826–4114* ⊕ *www.facebook.com/escalantemerc.*

Serenidad Gallery
ART GALLERIES | This gallery and shop features watercolors of local scenes by owner Harriet Priska, along with antiques, Native American jewelry and pottery, petrified wood, rocks, and other colorful crafts and gifts. ⊠ *170 S. 100 W, Escalante* ☎ *435/826–4720* ⊕ *www.facebook.com/serenidadgalleryescalanteutah.*

Activities

ADVENTURE TOURS
Excursions of Escalante
LOCAL SPORTS | Hiking, backpacking, photography, and canyoneering tours in the Escalante region are custom-fit to your needs and abilities by experienced guides. Canyoneers have the chance to explore slot canyons, moving through slot chutes and rappelling down walls and other obstacles. All gear and provisions are provided whether it's a day hike or multiday adventure. ⊠ *125 E. Main St., Escalante* ☎ *800/839–7567, 435/826–4714* ⊕ *www.excursionsofescalante.com* ☜ *From $165.*

FISHING
Escalante Outfitters
FISHING | FAMILY | Guided fly-fishing excursions as well as engaging natural history tours of Grand Staircase–Escalante National Monument and Boulder Mountain are offered by this outfitter that also runs a downtown shop with camping gear, a café, and an affordable lodging with small sleeping cabins and campsites. ⊠ *310 W. Main St., Escalante* ☎ *435/215–7953* ⊕ *www.escalanteoutfitters.com* ☜ *From $45.*

HIKING
Escape Goats
HIKING & WALKING | FAMILY | This noted family-owned outfit offers a variety of day and evening hikes, multiday backpacking trips, and photo and artist tours, which can be customized to any ability or age. Half- and full-day "herbal" tours acquaint participants with the medicinal and healing qualities of flora that grows naturally in Grand Staircase–Escalante. The company provides shuttle services, too. ⊠ *Escalante* ☎ *435/826–4652* ⊕ *www.escalantecanyonguides.com* ☜ *From $100.*

★ Utah Canyon Outdoors
HIKING & WALKING | Run by a young husband and wife team with extensive experience in Utah as naturalists and guides, this stellar outfitter operates an outdoor gear shop and coffeehouse in a charming little converted house in downtown Escalante. In addition to full-day hikes through slot canyons and the area's other dramatic features, the company also offers Escalante yoga experiences.

✉ *325 W. Main St., Escalante* ☎ *435/826–4967* ⊕ *www.utahcanyonoutdoors.com* 💲 *From $150.*

Torrey

67 miles north of Escalante.

Established in the 1880s by Mormon settlers who took advantage of the town's location on the Fremont River to build a canal to irrigate fields and ranches, Torrey is best known today as a base for visitors to Capitol Reef National Park, whose western border is just a few miles east. Giant cottonwood trees line the canal, which flows through the center of this pretty community that enjoys a cool elevation of nearly 7,000 feet. Although it's still a tiny town, Torrey's population has grown from 180 in 2010 to around 270, as new businesses catering to Capitol Reef visitors continue to open.

GETTING HERE AND AROUND

Extending west from Capitol Reef National Park, Highway 24 passes through the center of Torrey, where it joins scenic Highway 12, which leads south to Boulder and Escalante.

VISITOR INFORMATION

Capitol Reef Country Tourism. ✉ *Torrey* ☎ *435/425–3365* ⊕ *www.capitolreef.org.*

Sights

★ Etta Place Cider

DISTILLERY | This modern cidery on the west side of town honors the prolific orchards that have thrived in and around Torrey and Capitol Reef since pioneers began settling here in the late 19th century. And the name honors Etta Place, the storied companion of the Sundance Kid, who holed up with the notorious, though charming, outlaw at his hideout with Butch Cassidy near Torrey. Since planting its first 50 trees in 2012, this boutique cider operation has developed a critical following for its clean and crisp

dry, off-dry, and gingered hard ciders. One-hour tours provide an interesting look at the cider-making process and include a tasting; it's recommended that you book online, at least a couple of hours before you arrive. The on-site bottle shop also sells cheeses, meats, and other foods to snack on while you sip. ✉ *700 W. Main St., Torrey* ☎ *435/425–2727* ⊕ *www.ettaplacecider.com* 💲 *$10 for a tour and tasting* ⊗ *Closed Mon.–Wed.*

Larb Hollow Overlook

VIEWPOINT | The arresting 35-mile drive along Highway 12 from Boulder to Torrey climbs high up through the evergreen-dotted mountains of Dixie National Forest and passes a handful of dramatic pullouts where you can stop to stretch your legs, dine alfresco at a picnic table, and soak up the eye-popping easterly views of Capitol Reef and Escalante. Interpretive signs discuss the area's history and show the names of mountain peaks and geological features in the distance. At around 9,000 feet in elevation and offering restrooms and plenty of parking, Larb Hollow is one of the most inviting of these overlooks. Homestead and Wildcat Rest Area are other scenic options. ✉ *Hwy. 12, 15 miles southeast of Torrey, Teasdale* ⊕ *www.fs.usda.gov/recarea/fishlake/recarea/?recid=12190* ⊗ *Closed Nov.–Apr.*

🍴 Restaurants

★ Chak Balam

$$ | **MEXICAN** | But for a smattering of colorful *papel picado* (cut paper) flags strung along the ceiling and some neon Mexican beer signs, this unassuming eatery on the east side of Torrey lacks much in the way of ambience. The plates brimming with vibrant sauces, fresh vegetables, and tender steak, chicken, and seafood, however, hint at why this relatively new Mexican restaurant has such a passionate following. **Known for:** Mexican Jarritos-brand soft drinks and both local and Mexican beers; filling

Scenic Highway 12 from Boulder to Torrey is one of Utah's best drives. One of the most arresting lookout points is at Larb Hollow, 15 miles southeast of Torrey.

breakfast fare; sautéed octopus and shrimp tacos. [$] *Average main: $21 ✉ 12 Sand Creek Rd., Torrey ☎ 435/425–2877 ⊕ www.facebook.com/ChakBalam.2021.*

Hunt & Gather

$$$$ | **MODERN AMERICAN** | Try to snag a table on the tree-shaded semicovered patio at this contemporary upscale bistro on the west edge of downtown—it's especially romantic for enjoying a margarita or a glass of cider from neighboring Etta Place Cider. Run by a husband-and-wife team with extensive experience at some of Salt Lake City's top restaurants, this locavore-minded eatery specializes in creatively prepared dishes focused on both "hunted" (elk filet, duck breast) and "gathered" (wild mushrooms, mountain trout) ingredients. **Known for:** nightly-changing array of house-made desserts; superb charcuterie-and-cheese boards; red-rock views from the patio. [$] *Average main: $35 ✉ 599 W. Main St., Torrey ☎ 435/425–3070 ⊕ www.huntandgatherrestaurant.com ⊘ Closed Mon. and Tues. No lunch.*

The Rim Rock Patio

$ | **PIZZA | FAMILY** | One of the closest dining options to Capitol Reef National Park, this casual and lively pizza and barbecue place is located at The Rim Rock Inn, which has its own respectable but more expensive restaurant, but The Patio is perfect for tasty, reasonably priced food and beer after a long hike. Save room for the chunky homemade brownie with ice cream. **Known for:** pizzas and beer; eye-popping Capitol Reef views from the patio; serves food later than most places in town. [$] *Average main: $12 ✉ Rim Rock Inn, 2523 E. Hwy. 24, Torrey ☎ 435/425–3389 ⊕ www.therimrock.net ⊘ Closed Nov.–Apr. No lunch.*

★ Torrey Grill & BBQ

$$ | **BARBECUE | FAMILY** | Located a little west of town in the middle of Thousand Lakes RV Park, this festive barbecue joint offers chuckwagon-style outdoor seating around firepits. Think elevated comfort food, with dishes like dry-rub smoked pork spare ribs, spiced-rubbed grilled salmon, and chargrilled rib-eye steaks

packed with flavor, and delicious side dishes and desserts, too. **Known for:** corn muffins with pecan-honey butter; slow-smoked half chicken; make-your-own s'mores. [$] *Average main: $22* ✉ *1110 W. Hwy. 24, Torrey* ☎ *917/363-4124* 🌐 *www.torreygrillandbbq.com* 🕒 *Closed Sun. and Nov.–Mar. No lunch.*

Coffee and Quick Bites

★ Capitol Burger

$ | **BURGER** | **FAMILY** | This cheerful food truck, which doles out superb burgers with imaginative toppings, along with fries and soft drinks, parks in different parts of Torrey (often beside The Chuckwagon hotel)—check their Facebook page for the latest hours and address. Favorites among these over-the-top creations include the burger topped with gooey mac-and-cheese, smoked bacon, coal-roasted green chilies, and whole grain mustard; and another slathered with pulled pork, cream cheese, pickled jalapeños, and barbecue sauce. **Known for:** vegan Impossible burgers can be substituted for any order; creative burger toppings; typically parks in areas with pleasant, shaded seating. [$] *Average main: $10* ✉ *Torrey* ✣ *Location varies; check Facebook page* ☎ *801/362-0226* 🌐 *www.facebook.com/capitolburgertruck.*

★ Color Ridge Farm & Creamery

$ | **ICE CREAM** | **FAMILY** | Husband and husband Joseph Shumway and A. C. **Known for:** three- and five-flavor ice cream flights; farm-to-cone ice cream; plenty of outdoor seating. [$] *Average main: $5* ✉ *135 E. Main St., Torrey* ☎ *435/425-2155* 🌐 *www.colorridge.com* 🕒 *Closed Tues. and Wed.*

Hotels

Capitol Reef Resort

$$ | **HOTEL** | **FAMILY** | A relaxing and well-kept home base with excellent amenities and a wide range of accommodations—from traditional hotel rooms to luxurious cabins to authentically designed tents and Conestoga wagons—this hilltop lodging lies just a few miles west of Capitol Reef's western border, and many rooms have patios and balconies that overlook the not-so-distant sandstone cliffs. **Pros:** good restaurant and gift shop; astounding Capitol Reef views; nice gym and outdoor pool. **Cons:** breakfast not included in rates; sometimes books up with weddings; pets not allowed. [$] *Rooms from: $194* ✉ *2600 E. Hwy. 24, Torrey* ☎ *435/425-3761* 🌐 *www.capitolreefresort.com* 🛏 *149 rooms* 🍴 *No Meals.*

The Chuckwagon

$$ | **HOTEL** | **FAMILY** | This pleasant, shaded, and centrally located complex, which stands out for its friendly service and immaculate rooms, offers cozy and economical motel-style rooms, larger and more contemporary suites, and more charming stand-alone cabins that sleep up to six. **Pros:** very reasonable rates; several restaurants and shops within walking distance; large outdoor pool. **Cons:** family atmosphere may not please those seeking quiet; the handful of smaller, original rooms are a bit rustic; breakfast not included. [$] *Rooms from: $159* ✉ *12 W. Main St., Torrey* ☎ *435/425-3335, 800/863-3288* 🌐 *www.chuckwagonlodge.com* 🕒 *Closed Nov.–Mar.* 🛏 *28 rooms* 🍴 *No Meals.*

Cowboy Homestead Cabins

$$ | **B&B/INN** | Perfect if you want to be near the restaurants and services of Torrey but on a quiet, picturesque property a bit outside town, this relaxing hideaway comprises six custom-built contemporary

cabins with minimally stocked kitchenettes, soft bedding, front porches, and charcoal grills. **Pros:** peaceful location; dramatic views of red-rock cliffs; friendly dogs to play with. **Cons:** not within walking distance of town; cabins are right next to one another; no common spaces or amenities. [$] *Rooms from: $159* ✉ *2345 Cowboy Rd., Torrey* ✣ *Off Hwy. 12* ☎ *435/691–4384, 888/854–5871* 🌐 *www.cowboyhomesteadcabins.com* 🛏 *6 cabins* 🍴 *No Meals.*

★ The Lodge at Red River Ranch
$$$ | **B&B/INN** | Each of the 15 individually appointed rooms at this elegant but unpretentious 2,200-acre ranch hideaway has a wood-burning fireplace, efficient climate control and Wi-Fi, and either a patio or a balcony with grand views of orchards, the Fremont River, and the surrounding red-rock cliffs. **Pros:** Western and Native American artwork and antiques; outstanding farm-to-table restaurant; most luxurious accommodations in Capitol Reef region. **Cons:** breakfast, though delicious, is not included in the rates; a 25-minute drive to the national park; several miles west of Torrey's restaurants and shops. [$] *Rooms from: $249* ✉ *2900 Hwy. 24, Teasdale* ☎ *435/425–3322* 🌐 *www.redriverranch.com* 🛏 *15 rooms* 🍴 *No Meals.*

The Rim Rock Inn
$$ | **MOTEL** | On a bluff with outstanding views of red-rock palisades, this motel with clean, basic, and reasonably priced rooms (a basic breakfast is included) is one of the closest to the western entrance of Capitol Reef National Park. **Pros:** two distinctive dining options on site; affordable; set on 10 rugged acres. **Cons:** not within walking distance of town; rooms lack personality; pretty basic breakfast. [$] *Rooms from: $129* ✉ *2523 E. Hwy. 24, Torrey* ☎ *435/425–3398* 🌐 *www.therimrock.net* ⏲ *Closed late Oct.–Mar.* 🛏 *19 rooms* 🍴 *Free Breakfast.*

Torrey Schoolhouse B&B Inn
$$ | **B&B/INN** | One of the more interesting and historic lodging options in the Capitol Reef region, this stately three-story building with thick sandstone walls served as the local schoolhouse from 1917 to 1954 and has been transformed into a romantic inn with rooms individually decorated with a mix of antiques and newer pieces. **Pros:** delicious breakfast included; several restaurants within walking distance; most rooms have great mountain and red-rock views. **Cons:** pets not permitted; not appropriate for kids; family-style, single-seating breakfast isn't ideal if you don't enjoy socializing at 8:30 in the morning. [$] *Rooms from: $150* ✉ *150 N. Center St., Torrey* ☎ *435/491–0230* 🌐 *www.torreyschoolhouse.com* ⏲ *Closed Nov.–Mar.* 🛏 *10 rooms* 🍴 *Free Breakfast.*

Shopping

ART GALLERIES

Gallery 24
ART GALLERIES | This attractive gallery on the east side of town sells contemporary fine art from Southern Utah–based artists that includes paintings, photography, ceramics, and sculpture. ✉ *875 E. Hwy. 24, Torrey* ☎ *435/425–2124* 🌐 *www.gallery24.biz.*

★ The Torrey Gallery
ART GALLERIES | In a neatly restored pioneer home off Main Street, this handsome gallery specializes in regional art. Its offerings include paintings, sculpture, and photographs, as well as antique and contemporary Navajo rugs discovered by the longtime collectors who own the gallery. ✉ *160 W. Main St., Torrey* ☎ *435/425–3909* 🌐 *www.torreygallery.com.*

CRAFTS

Torrey Trading Post

CRAFTS | Come here for Native American jewelry and pottery, T-shirts, wood carvings, stone figures, gifts for children, and more. The trading post also rents out a handful of deluxe and camping cabins. ⊠ *25 W. Main St., Torrey* ☎ *435/425–3716* ⊕ *www.torreytradingpost.com.*

Activities

ADVENTURE TOURS

★ Sleeping Rainbow Adventures

ADVENTURE TOURS | **FAMILY** | Founded by a pair of former Capitol Reef National Park employees with a deep knowledge of and passion for the region, this versatile outfitter offers a wide range of tours geared to a wide range of interests: stargazing, photography, yoga, backpacking, Jeep exploring, and hiking. They're an especially great option if you're wanting to explore some of the harder-to-reach areas of the national park, including Cathedral Valley and the Waterpocket Fold and Upper Muley Twist Canyon. They also offer hikes and jeep tours through the slot canyons of Grand Staircase–Escalante National Monument. ⊠ *Torrey* ☎ *435/893–3039* ⊕ *www.sradventures. com* ⊠ *From $100.*

Chapter 11

ARCHES
NATIONAL PARK

Updated by
Stina Sieg

🔺 Camping	🛏 Hotels	🤸 Activities	👁 Scenery	👥 Crowds
★★☆☆☆	★★★★☆	★★★☆☆	★★★★★	★★★★★

WELCOME TO ARCHES NATIONAL PARK

TOP REASONS TO GO

★ **Arch appeal:** Nowhere in the world has as large an array or quantity of natural arches.

★ **Legendary landscape:** A photographer's dream—no wonder it's been the chosen backdrop for many Hollywood films.

★ **Treasures hanging in the balance:** Landscape Arch and Balanced Rock, in particular, look like they might topple any day. And they could—the features in this park erode and evolve constantly.

★ **Fins and needles:** Fins are thin, parallel walls of eroding rock that slowly disintegrate into towerlike "needles." The spaces around and between them will carve their way into your memories like the wind and water that formed them.

★ **Moab:** Known as Utah's "adventure capital," this small, busy town is a great base from which to explore by foot, bicycle, balloon, watercraft, boat, and four-wheeler.

Southeastern Utah's Arches National Park boasts some of the most unimaginable rock formations in the world. Off U.S. 191, Arches (along with Canyonlands National Park) is in Moab, 230 miles southeast of Salt Lake City and 27 miles south of Interstate 70.

1 Devils Garden. Eighteen miles from the visitor center, this is the end of the paved road in Arches. It has the park's only campground, a picnic area, and access to drinking water. Trails in Devils Garden lead to Landscape Arch and several other noteworthy formations.

2 The Fiery Furnace. About 14 miles from the visitor center this area is so labeled because its orange spires of rock look much like tongues of flame. Reservations are required, and can be made up to six months in advance, to join the twice-daily ranger-guided treks. Or you can obtain a permit to visit the Fiery Furnace on your own, but only experienced, well-prepared hikers should attempt this option.

3 Delicate Arch/Wolfe Ranch. A spur road about 11.7 miles from the visitor center leads to the moderately strenuous 3-mile round-trip trail and viewpoints for the park's most famous feature—Delicate Arch. To see it from below, follow the road to the viewpoint, then walk to either easily accessible viewing area.

4 The Windows. Reached on a spur 9.2 miles from the visitor center, here you can see many of the park's natural arches from your car or on an easy rolling trail.

5 Balanced Rock. This giant rock teeters atop a pedestal, creating a 128-foot formation of red rock grandeur right along the roadside, about 9 miles from the visitor center.

6 Petrified Dunes. Just a tiny pull-out about 5 miles from the visitor center, stop here for pictures of acres and acres of petrified sand dunes.

7 The Courthouse Towers. The Three Gossips, Sheep Rock, and The Tower of Babel are all here. Enter this section of the park 3 miles past the visitor center. The Park Avenue Trail winds through the area.

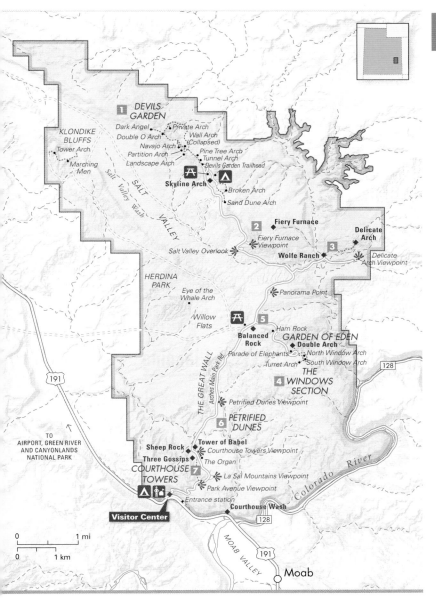

1 DEVILS GARDEN

KLONDIKE BLUFFS
Tower Arch

Marching Men

Dark Angel
Double O Arch
Navajo Arch
Partition Arch
Landscape Arch

Private Arch
Wall Arch (Collapsed)
Pine Tree Arch
Tunnel Arch
Devils Garden Trailhead

Skyline Arch

SALT VALLEY

Salt Valley Wash

Broken Arch

Sand Dune Arch

2 Fiery Furnace

Fiery Furnace Viewpoint

Salt Valley Overlook

Wolfe Ranch 3

Delicate Arch

Delicate Arch Viewpoint

HERDINA PARK

Eye of the Whale Arch

Panorama Point

Willow Flats

5

Ham Rock

GARDEN OF EDEN

Balanced Rock

Double Arch

Parade of Elephants

North Window Arch

Turret Arch

South Window Arch

THE GREAT WALL

Arches Main Park Rd

THE WINDOWS SECTION 4

Petrified Dunes Viewpoint

6 PETRIFIED DUNES

Sheep Rock

Tower of Babel

Courthouse Towers Viewpoint

Three Gossips

The Organ

COURTHOUSE TOWERS 7

La Sal Mountains Viewpoint

Park Avenue Viewpoint

Entrance station

Courthouse Wash

Visitor Center

191

TO AIRPORT, GREEN RIVER AND CANYONLANDS NATIONAL PARK

128

128

Colorado River

0   1 mi
0   1 km

MOAB VALLEY

191

Moab

More than 1.5 million visitors come to Arches annually, drawn by the red rock landscape and its red-rock formations carved by wind and water. The park is named for the 2,000-plus sandstone arches that frame horizons, cast precious shade, and are in a perpetual state of gradual transformation, the result of constant erosion.

Fancifully named attractions like The Three Penguins, Queen Nefertiti, and The Tower of Babel stir curiosity, beckoning visitors to stop and marvel. Immerse yourself in this spectacular landscape, but don't lose yourself entirely—summer temperatures frequently exceed 100°F, and water is hard to come by inside the park boundaries. Bringing hydration and snacks with you is a must.

It's easy to spot some of the arches from your car, but take the time to step outside and walk beneath the spans and giant walls of orange rock. This gives you a much better idea of their proportion. You may feel as writer Edward Abbey did when he awoke on his first day as a park ranger in Arches: that you're walking in the most beautiful place on Earth.

It's especially worthwhile to visit as the sun goes down. At sunset, the rock formations glow, and you'll often find photographers behind their tripods waiting for magnificent rays to descend on Delicate Arch or other popular sites. The Fiery Furnace earns its name as its narrow fins glow red just before the sun dips below the horizon. Full-moon nights are particularly dramatic in Arches as the creamy white Navajo sandstone reflects light and eerie silhouettes are created by towering fins and formations.

■TIP→ **Do not arrive at the park without checking first to see if a timed-entry reservation is needed. A pilot program was introduced in 2022 requiring visitors to purchase a reservation for trips between early April and early October. This may or may not be in place in coming years.**

Planning

Getting Here and Around

The park entrance is just off U.S. 191 on the north side of downtown Moab, 28 miles south of Interstate 70 and 130 miles north of the Arizona border. Arches is also about 30 miles from the Island in the Sky section and 80 miles from the Needles District of Canyonlands National Park. If you're driving to Arches from points east on Interstate 70, consider taking Exit 214 in Utah (about 50 miles west of Grand Junction) and continuing south on picturesque Highway 128, the Colorado River Scenic Byway, about 50 miles to Moab. Bear in mind that services can be sparse on even major roads in these parts.

Branching off the main 18-mile park road are two spurs, one 2½ miles to the Windows section and one 1.6 miles to Delicate Arch trailhead and viewpoint. Including these spurs, the entire out-and-back drive is about 45 miles long. There are several four-wheel-drive roads in the park; always check at the visitor center for conditions before attempting to traverse them. The entrance road into the park often has long backups midmorning to early afternoon during busy periods. You'll encounter less traffic early in the morning or at sunset (though sunset is still a very busy time at Delicate Arch).

Park Essentials

PARK FEES AND PERMITS

Admission to the park is $30 per vehicle, $25 per motorcycle, and $15 per person entering on foot or bicycle, valid for seven days. To encourage visitation to the park during less busy times, a $55 Southeast Utah Parks Pass grants you admission to both Arches and Canyonlands National Parks as well as Natural Bridges and Hovenweep National Monuments for one year. If you plan to visit even more national parks in a year, the best deal is an America the Beautiful Pass, giving you entry to all national parks, U.S. Fish and Wildlife sites, Bureau of Land Management areas, and more.

▤ TIP → **Do not arrive at the park without checking first if a timed-entry reservation is needed. A pilot program was introduced in 2022 requiring visitors to purchase a reservation for trips between early April and early October. This may or may not be in place in coming years.**

ACCESSIBILITY

Not all park facilities meet federally mandated accessibility standards, but as visitation to Arches increases, the park continues efforts to increase accessibility. Visitors with mobility impairments can access the visitor center, all park restrooms, and two campsites at the Devils Garden Campground (4H is first-come, first served, while site 7 can be reserved up to six months in advance March–October). The Park Avenue Viewpoint is a paved path with a slight decline near the end, and both Delicate Arch and Balanced Rock Viewpoints are partially hard-surfaced. For those with visual disabilities, visitor center exhibits include audio recordings and some tactile elements. You can also request an audio version of the park brochure (or listen to it on the park website ⊕ *www.nps.gov/ arch*). Large-print and braille versions of park information are also available at the visitor center.

PARK HOURS

Arches National Park is open year-round, seven days a week, around the clock. It's in the Mountain time zone.

CELL PHONE RECEPTION

Cell phone reception is spotty in the park and in general is strongest whenever the La Sal Mountains are visible. There are pay phones outside the visitor center.

Visitor Information

CONTACTS Arches National Park.
✉ *N. U.S. 191, Arches National Park*
☏ *435/719–2299* ⊕ *www.nps.gov/arch.*

When to Go

The busiest times of year are spring and fall. In the spring blooming wildflowers herald the end of winter, and temperatures in the 70s and 80s bring the year's largest crowds. The crowds remain steady in summer as the thermostat often exceeds 100°F and above in July and August. Sudden dramatic cloudbursts create rainfalls over red rock walls in late-summer "monsoon" season.

Fall means clear, warm days and crisp, cool nights. The park is much quieter in winter, and from December through February you can hike many of the trails in relative solitude. Snow occasionally falls in the valley beneath the La Sal Mountains, and when it does, Arches is a photographer's paradise, with a serene white dusting over slickrock mounds and natural rock windows.

Hotels

Though there are no hotels or cabins in the park itself, in the surrounding area every type of lodging is available, from economy chain motels to B&Bs and high-end, high-adventure resorts. It's important to know when popular events are held, however, as accommodations can, and do, fill up weeks ahead of time.

HOTEL AND RESTAURANT PRICES
Hotel and restaurant reviews have been shortened. For full information visit Fodors.com. Hotel prices are the lowest cost of a standard double room in high season. Restaurant prices are the average cost of a main course at dinner, or if dinner is not served, at lunch.

What It Costs

	$	$$	$$$	$$$$
RESTAURANTS				
	under $16	$16–$22	$23–$30	over $30
HOTELS				
	under $125	$125–$200	$201–$300	over $300

Restaurants

In the park itself, there are no dining facilities and no snack bars. Supermarkets, bakeries, and delis in downtown Moab will be happy to make you food to go. If you bring a packed lunch, there are several picnic areas from which to choose.

Devils Garden

18 miles north of the visitor center.

At the end of the paved road in Arches, Devils Garden is the most developed area of the park and includes the park's only campground. It's also the site of the busiest trailheads, and you can fill up your bottle here before heading out.

Sights

GEOLOGICAL FORMATIONS
Skyline Arch
NATURE SIGHT | FAMILY | A quick walk from the parking lot at Skyline Arch, 16½ miles from the park entrance, gives you closer views and better photos. The short trail is less than a ½ mile round-trip and takes only a few minutes to travel. Mostly flat, this is an especially great hike for little kids or people whose mobility issues keep them from longer treks, though you should still be cautious of uneven ground. ⌧ *Devils Garden Rd., Arches National Park.*

SCENIC DRIVES
★ Arches Main Park Road
SCENIC DRIVE | FAMILY | The main park road and its two short spurs are extremely scenic and allow you to enjoy many park sights from your car. The main road leads through The Courthouse Towers, where you can see Sheep Rock and The Three Gossips, then alongside The Great Wall, The Petrified Dunes, and Balanced Rock. A drive to the Windows section takes you to attractions like Turret Arch, The North Window, and Double Arch, and you can see Skyline Arch along the roadside as you approach the Devils Garden Campground. The road to Delicate Arch allows hiking access to one of the park's main features. Allow about two hours to drive the 45-mile round-trip, more if you explore the spurs and their features and stop at viewpoints along the way. ⌧ *Arches National Park.*

A hike to "the Windows" is a 1-mile round-trip.

TRAILS

Broken Arch Trail

TRAIL | An easy walk across open grassland, this loop trail passes Broken Arch, which is also visible from the road. The arch gets its name because it appears to be cracked in the middle, but it's not really broken. The trail is 1¼ miles round-trip, but you can extend your adventure to about 2 miles round-trip by continuing north past Tapestry Arch and through the Devils Garden Campground. *Easy.* ⊠ *Arches National Park* ⊹ *Trailhead: Off Devils Garden Rd., 16½ miles from park entrance.*

★ Devils Garden Trail

TRAIL | Landscape Arch is a highlight of this trail but is just one of several arches within reach, depending on your ambitions. It's an easy 0.9-mile one-way (mostly gravel, relatively flat) trip to Landscape Arch, one of the longest stone spans in the world. Beyond Landscape Arch the scenery changes dramatically and the hike becomes more strenuous as you must climb and straddle slickrock fins and negotiate some short, steep inclines.

Finally, around a sharp bend, the stacked spans that compose Double O Arch come suddenly into view. Allow up to three hours for this round-trip hike of just over 4 miles.

For a still longer (about a 7-mile round-trip) and more rigorous trek, venture on to see a formation called Dark Angel and then return to the trailhead on the primitive loop, making the short side hike to Private Arch. The hike to Dark Angel is a difficult route through fins. Other possible (and worthwhile) detours lead to Navajo Arch, Partition Arch, Tunnel Arch, and Pine Tree Arch. Allow about five hours for this adventure, take plenty of water, and watch your route carefully. Pick up the park's useful guide to Devils Garden, or download it from the website before you go. *Moderate–Difficult.* ⊠ *Arches National Park* ⊹ *Trailhead: On Devils Garden Rd., end of main road, 18 miles from park entrance.*

Landscape Arch Trail

TRAIL | This natural rock opening, which measures 306 feet from base to base and looks like a delicate ribbon of rock bending over the horizon, is the longest geologic span in North America. In 1991, a slab of rock about 60 feet long, 11 feet wide, and 4 feet thick fell from the underside, leaving it even thinner. You reach it via a rolling, gravel, 1.8-mile-long trail. *Easy–Moderate.* ⊠ *Arches National Park* ⚑ *Trailhead: At Devils Garden Rd., at end of main road, 18 miles north of park entrance.*

Tower Arch Trail

TRAIL | Check with park rangers before attempting the dirt road through Salt Valley to the Klondike Bluffs parking area. If rains haven't washed out the road, a trip to this seldom-visited area provides a solitude-filled hike culminating in a giant rock opening. Allow from two to three hours for this 2.6-mile round-trip hike, not including the drive. *Moderate.* ⊠ *Arches National Park* ⚑ *Trailhead: At Klondike Bluffs parking area, 24½ miles from park entrance, 7¾ miles off main road.*

Fiery Furnace

14 miles north of the park entrance.

Fewer than 10% of the park's visitors ever descend into the chasms and washes of the Fiery Furnace (a permit or a ranger-led hike is the only way to go), but you can gain an appreciation for this twisted, unyielding landscape from the Fiery Furnace Overlook. At sunset, the rocks glow a vibrant flamelike red, which gives the formation its daunting moniker.

Sights

TRAILS

Fiery Furnace Trail

TRAIL | This area of the park has taken on a near-mythical lure for park visitors, who are drawn to challenging yet breathtaking terrain. Rangers strongly discourage inexperienced hikers from entering here—in fact, you can't enter without watching a video about how to help protect this very special section of the park and obtaining a

permit ($10). Reservations can be made up to six months in advance to get a spot on the 2-mile round-trip ranger-led hikes ($16), offered mid-April–September, through this unique formation. A hike through these rugged rocks and sandy washes is tiring but fascinating. Hikers will need to use their hands at times to scramble up and through narrow cracks and along vertigo-inducing ledges above drop-offs, and there are no trail markings. If you're not familiar with The Furnace, you can easily get lost or cause damage, so watch your step and use great caution. The less intrepid can view The Fiery Furnace from the overlook off the main road. *Difficult.* ⊠ *Arches National Park* ⚑ *Trailhead: Off main road, about 14 miles from park entrance.*

Sand Dune Arch Trail

TRAIL | **FAMILY** | You may return to the car with shoes full of bright-red sand from this giant sandbox in the desert—it's fun exploring in and around the rock. Set aside five minutes for this shady, 530-yard walk and plenty of time if you have kids, who will love playing amid this dramatic landscape. Never climb on this or any other arch in the park, no matter how tempting—it's illegal, and it could lead to damage to the fragile geology or even someone getting hurt. The trail intersects with the Broken Arch Trail—you can visit both arches with an easy 1.2-mile round-trip walk. *Easy.* ⊠ *Arches National Park* ⚑ *Trailhead: Off Arches Scenic Dr., about 16½ miles from park entrance.*

Delicate Arch/ Wolfe Ranch

13 miles north of the park entrance.

The iconic symbol of the park and the state (it appears on many of Utah's license plates), Delicate Arch is tall and prominent compared with many of the spans in the park—it's big enough that it could shelter a four-story building. The arch is a remnant of an Entrada Sandstone fin; the rest of the rock has eroded and now frames the La Sal Mountains in the background. Drive 2.2 miles off the main road to the viewpoint to see the arch from a distance, or hike right up to it from the trailhead that starts near Wolfe Ranch. The trail, 1.2 miles off the main road, is a moderately strenuous 3-mile round-trip hike with no shade or access to water and several steep stretches. It's especially picturesque shortly after sunrise or before sunset. Be forewarned that the parking lot can get very busy and finding a spot is not guaranteed.

Sights

HISTORIC SIGHTS
Wolfe Ranch

HISTORIC HOME | Civil War veteran John Wesley Wolfe and his son started a small ranch here in 1888. He added a cabin in 1906 when his daughter Esther and her family came west to live. Built out of Fremont cottonwoods, the rustic one-room cabin still stands on the site. Look for remains of a root cellar and a corral as well. Even older than these structures is the nearby Ute rock-art panel by the Delicate Arch trailhead. About 150 feet past the footbridge and before the trail starts to climb, you can see images of bighorn sheep and figures on horseback, as well as some smaller images believed to be dogs. ☒ *Off Delicate Arch Rd., Arches National Park.*

TRAILS
★ **Delicate Arch Trail**

TRAIL | To see the park's most famous freestanding arch up close takes effort and won't offer you much solitude—but it's worth every step. The 3-mile round-trip trail ascends via steep slickrock, sandy paths, and along one narrow ledge (at the very end) that might give pause to anyone afraid of heights. Plus, there's almost no shade. First-timers should start early to avoid the midday heat in summer. Still, at sunrise, sunset, and

every hour in between, it's the park's busiest trail. Bring plenty of water, especially in the warmer months, as heatstroke and dehydration are very real possibilities. Allow two to three hours, depending on your fitness level and how long you care to linger at the arch. If you go at sunset or sunrise, bring a headlamp or flashlight. Don't miss Wolfe Ranch and some ancient rock art near the trailhead. *Moderate–Difficult.* ☒ *Arches National Park ⚛ Trailhead: On Delicate Arch Rd., 13 miles from park entrance.*

The Windows

11¾ miles north of the park entrance.

As you head north from the park entrance, turn right at Balanced Rock to find this concentration of natural windows, caves, and needles. Stretch your legs on the easy paths that wind between the arches and soak in a variety of geological formations.

Sights

GEOLOGICAL FORMATIONS
Double Arch

NATURE SIGHT | **FAMILY** | In the Windows section of the park, 11¾ miles from the park entrance, Double Arch has appeared in several Hollywood movies, including *Indiana Jones and the Last Crusade.* From the parking lot you can also take the short and easy Windows Trail to view The North Window, The South Window, and Turret Arch. ☒ *The Windows Rd., Arches National Park.*

TRAILS
Double Arch Trail

TRAIL | **FAMILY** | If it's not too hot, it's a simple walk to here from the Windows Trail. This relatively flat trek leads to two massive arches that make for great photo opportunities. The ½-mile round-trip gives you a good taste of desert flora and fauna. *Easy.* ☒ *Arches National Park*

⊕ *Trailhead: 2½ miles from main road, on Windows Section spur road.*

The Windows Trail

TRAIL | FAMILY | An early stop for many visitors to the park, a trek through The Windows gives you an opportunity to get out and enjoy the desert air. Here you'll see three giant openings in the rock and walk on a trail that leads right through the holes. Allow about an hour on this gently inclined, 1-mile round-trip hike. As most visitors don't follow the "primitive" trail around the backside of the two windows, take advantage if you want some desert solitude. The primitive trail adds an extra half-hour to the hike. *Easy.* ⊠ *Arches National Park* ⊕ *Trailhead: On the Windows Rd., 12 miles from park entrance.*

Balanced Rock

9¼ miles north of the park entrance.

One of the park's favorite sights, this rock is visible for several minutes as you approach—and just gets more impressive and mysterious as you get closer. The formation's total height is 128 feet, with the huge balanced rock rising 55 feet above the pedestal. Be sure to hop out of the car and walk the short (⅓-mile) loop around the base.

 ## Sights

TRAILS

Balanced Rock Trail

TRAIL | FAMILY | You'll want to stop at Balanced Rock for photo ops, so you may as well walk the easy, partially paved trail around the famous landmark. This is one of the most accessible trails in the park and is suitable even for small children. The 15-minute stroll is only about ⅓ mile round-trip. *Easy.* ⊠ *Arches National Park* ⊕ *Trailhead: Approximately 9¼ miles from park entrance.*

VISITOR CENTERS

Arches Visitor Center

VISITOR CENTER | FAMILY | With well-designed hands-on exhibits about the park's geology, wildlife, and history, helpful rangers, a water station, and a bookstore, the center is a great way to start your park visit. It also has picnic tables and something that's rare in the park: cell service for many carriers. ⊠ *N. U.S. 191, Arches National Park* ☎ *435/719–2299* ⊕ *nps.gov/arch.*

Petrified Dunes

5 miles north of the visitor center.

 ## Sights

SCENIC STOPS

Petrified Dunes

NATURE SIGHT | FAMILY | Just a tiny pull-out, this memorable stop features acres upon acres of reddish-gold, petrified sand dunes. There's no trail here, so roam as you like while keeping track of where you are. If you do lose your way, heading west will take you back to the main road. ⊠ *Arches National Park* ⊕ *6 miles from park entrance.*

Courthouse Towers

3 miles north of the visitor center.

This collection of towering rock formations looks unreal from a distance and even more breathtaking up close. The Three Gossips does indeed resemble a gaggle of wildly tall people sharing some kind of secret. Sheep Rock is right below, with the massive Tower of Babel just a bit north. Enter this section of the park 3 miles past the visitor center. The extremely popular Park Avenue Trail winds through the area.

Sights

SCENIC STOPS

Courthouse Wash Panel

INDIGENOUS SIGHT | FAMILY | Although this rock-art panel fell victim to an unusual case of vandalism in 1980, when someone scoured the petroglyphs and pictographs that had been left by four cultures, you can still see ancient images if you take a short walk from the parking area on the left-hand side of the road, heading south. At less than a mile out and back, this makes for a good hike for families. ✉ *U.S. 191, about 2 miles south of Arches entrance, Arches National Park.*

TRAILS

Park Avenue Trail

TRAIL | The first named trail that park visitors encounter, this is a relatively easy, 1.8-mile round-trip walk (with only one small hill but a somewhat steep descent into the canyon) amid walls and towers that vaguely resemble a New York City skyline. You'll walk under the gaze of Queen Nefertiti, a giant rock formation that some observers think has Egyptian-looking features. If you are traveling with companions, make it a one-way, 1-mile downhill trek by having them pick you up at the Courthouse Towers Viewpoint. Allow about 45 minutes for the one-way journey. *Easy–Moderate.* ✉ *Arches National Park* ⊹ *Trailhead: 2 miles from park entrance on main park road.*

Activities

Arches lies in the middle of one of the adventure capitals of the United States. Thousand-foot sandstone walls draw rock climbers from across the globe. Hikers can choose from shady canyons or red-rock ridges that give you vast views of the desert below The Colorado River forms the southeast boundary of the park and can give you every grade of white-water adventure. Moab-based outfitters can set you up for just about any sport you may have a desire to try: mountain biking, ATVs, dirt bikes, four-wheel-drive vehicles, kayaking, climbing, stand-up paddleboarding, and even skydiving. Within the park, it's best to stick with basics such as hiking, sightseeing, and photography. Climbers and other adventure seekers should always inquire at the visitor center about restrictions, which can also be seen on the park's website.

BIRD WATCHING

Within the park you'll definitely see plenty of the big, black, beautiful ravens. Look for them perched on top of a picturesque juniper branch or balancing on the bald knob of a rock. Noisy black-billed magpies populate the park, as do the more melodic canyon and rock wrens. Lucky visitors may spot a red-tailed hawk and hear its distinctive call. Serious birders will have more fun visiting the Nature Conservancy's Scott and Norma Matheson Wetlands Preserve, 5 miles south of the park. The wetlands are home to more than 200 species of birds including the wood duck, western screech owl, indigo bunting, and plumbeous vireo.

CAMPING

Campgrounds in and around Arches range from sprawling RV parks with myriad amenities to quaint, shady retreats near a babbling brook. The Devils Garden Campground in the park is a wonderful spot to call home for a few days, though it is often full and lacks an RV dump station. More than 350 campsites are operated in the vicinity by the Bureau of Land Management—their sites on the Colorado River and near the Slickrock Trail are some of the nicest (and most affordable, at just $20/night) in the area. The most centrally located campgrounds in Moab generally accommodate RVs.

Devils Garden Campground. This campground is one of the most unusual—and gorgeous—in the West, and in the national park system, for that matter. ✉ *End of main road, 18 miles from park entrance* ☎ *435/719–2299, 877/444–6777 for reservations* ⊕ *www.recreation.gov.*

HIKING

Getting out on any one of the park trails will surely cause you to fall in love with this Mars-like landscape. But remember, you are hiking in a parched desert environment and approximately 1 mile above sea level. Many people succumb to heat and dehydration because they do not drink enough water. Park rangers recommend a gallon of water per day per person, plus electrolytes.

★ Fiery Furnace Walk

HIKING & WALKING | Join a park ranger on a 2½-hour scramble through a labyrinth of rock fins and narrow sandstone canyons. You'll see arches and other eye-popping formations that can't be viewed from the road. You should be very fit and not afraid of heights or confined spaces for this moderately strenuous experience. Wear sturdy hiking shoes, sunscreen, and a hat, and bring at least a liter of water. Guided walks into The Fiery Furnace are offered mid-April through September, usually a few times a day (hours vary), and leave from the Fiery Furnace Viewpoint, about 15 miles from the park visitor center. Tickets must be reserved ahead (⊕ www.recreation.gov) and are available beginning six months in advance and up to four days before the day of the tour. Children under five are not allowed. Book early as the program usually fills months prior to each walk. ⊠ Arches National Park ⊹ Trailhead: On Arches Scenic Dr. ☏ $16 ⊗ Guided hikes not offered Oct.–mid-Apr.

ROCK CLIMBING AND CANYONEERING

Rock climbers travel from across the country to scale the sheer red-rock walls of Arches National Park and surrounding areas. Most climbing routes in the park require advanced techniques. Permits are not required, but climbers are strongly encouraged to register for a free permit, either online or at a kiosk outside the visitor center. Climbers are responsible for knowing park regulations, temporary route closures, and restricted routes. Two popular routes ascend Owl Rock in The Garden of Eden (about 10 miles from the visitor center); the well-worn route has a difficulty of 5.8, while a more challenging option is 5.11 on a scale that goes up to 5.13-plus. Many climbing routes are available in the Park Avenue area, about 2.2 miles from the visitor center. These routes are also extremely difficult climbs. No commercial outfitters are allowed to lead rock-climbing excursions in the park, but guided canyoneering (which involves ropes, rappelling, and some basic climbing) is allowed, and permits are required for canyoneering. Before climbing, it's imperative that you stop at the visitor center and check with a ranger about climbing regulations.

Desert Highlights

ROCK CLIMBING | This guide company takes adventurous types on descents and ascents through canyons on customizable half- and full-day trips around Moab. Expect scrambling, hiking, and rappelling, mostly on BLM land. Packrafting trips are also available, as are guided hikes in Arches and Canyonlands. Most trips have a two-person minimum, and all trips are private, meaning the only ones on the adventure will be your group and your guide. ⊠ 16 S. 100 E, Moab ☏ 435/259–4433 ⊕ www.deserthighlights.com ☏ From $124.

CANYONLANDS NATIONAL PARK

12

Updated by
Stina Sieg

 Camping
★★★☆☆

 Hotels
★★★☆☆

 Activities
★★★★☆

 Scenery
★★★★☆

 Crowds
★★★★☆

WELCOME TO CANYONLANDS NATIONAL PARK

TOP REASONS TO GO

★ **Endless vistas:** The view from Island in the Sky stretches for miles as you look out over millennia of sculpting by wind and rain.

★ **Seeking solitude:** Needles, an astoundingly beautiful part of the park to explore on foot, sees very few visitors—it can sometimes feel like you have it all to yourself.

★ **Radical rides:** The Cataract Canyon rapids and the White Rim Trail are world-class adventures by boat or bike.

★ **Native American artifacts:** View rock art and Ancestral Puebloan dwellings in the park.

★ **Wonderful wilderness:** Some of the country's most untouched landscapes are within the park's boundaries, and they're worth the extra effort needed to get there.

★ **The night skies:** Far away from city lights, Canyonlands is ideal for stargazing.

Canyonlands National Park, in southeastern Utah, is divided into three distinct land districts, as well as the separate Horseshoe Canyon, so it can be a little daunting to visit. It's exhausting, but not impossible, to explore Island in the Sky and Needles on the same day. For many, rafting through the waterways is the best way to see the park. The Green and Colorado Rivers, while very different today as a result of man-made dams from when John Wesley Powell explored them in the mid-1800s, are spectacular.

1 Island in the Sky. From any of the overlooks here you can see for miles and look down thousands of feet to canyon floors. Chocolate-brown canyons are capped by white rock, and deep-red monuments rise nearby.

2 Needles. Pink, orange, and red rock is layered with white rock and stands in spires and pinnacles around grassy meadows. Extravagantly red mesas and buttes interrupt the horizon as in a picture postcard of the Old West.

3 The Maze. Only the most intrepid adventurers explore this incredibly remote mosaic of rock formations. There's a reason Butch Cassidy hid out here.

4 Horseshoe Canyon. Plan on several hours of dirt-road driving to get here, but the famous rock-art panel "Great Gallery" is a grand reward at the end of a long hike.

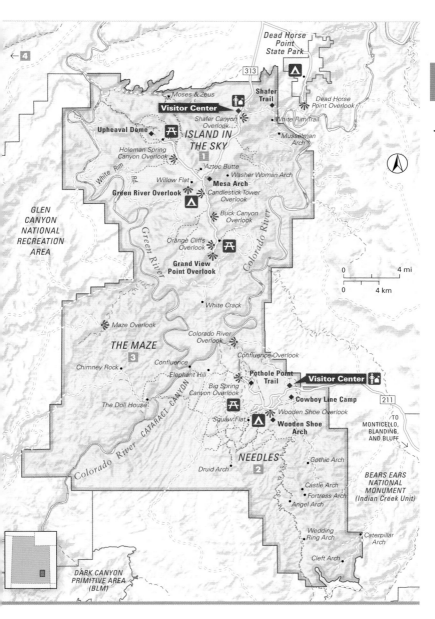

← 4

Dead Horse Point State Park

313

Shafer Trail

Moses & Zeus

Visitor Center

Dead Horse Point Overlook

Shafer Canyon Overlook

White Rim Trail

Upheaval Dome

ISLAND IN THE SKY

Musselman Arch

Holeman Spring Canyon Overlook

1

Aztec Butte

White Rim Rd.

Willow Flat

Mesa Arch

Washer Woman Arch

Green River Overlook

Candlestick Tower Overlook

GLEN CANYON NATIONAL RECREATION AREA

Buck Canyon Overlook

Green River

Colorado River

Orange Cliffs Overlook

Grand View Point Overlook

0   4 mi

0   4 km

White Crack

Maze Overlook

Colorado River Overlook

THE MAZE

3

Confluence Overlook

Chimney Rock

Confluence

Pothole Point Trail

Visitor Center

Elephant Hill

Big Spring Canyon Overlook

211

The Doll House

Cowboy Line Camp

TO MONTICELLO, BLANDING, AND BLUFF

Colorado River *CATARACT CANYON*

Wooden Shoe Overlook

Squaw Flat

Wooden Shoe Arch

NEEDLES

2

Gothic Arch

Druid Arch

BEARS EARS NATIONAL MONUMENT (Indian Creek Unit)

Castle Arch

Fortress Arch

Angel Arch

Wedding Ring Arch

Caterpillar Arch

Cleft Arch

DARK CANYON PRIMITIVE AREA (BLM)

The endless views here of red-rock buttes, mesas, and signature canyons can feel like something out of a dream. While many national parks in the West are filled with snack bars and gift shops, Canyonlands offers a real taste of remote wilderness that can be explored to whatever extent you'd like, from a scenic drive to a multiday backpacking trip.

The park likely owes its existence to Bates Wilson, a former superintendent of nearby Arches National Park. While there had been calls to create a new park here for years, he fiercely advocated for Canyonlands' creation in the late 1950s and led many government officials on scenic Jeep tours and cookouts here. The secretary of the interior at the time, Stuart Udall, was so impressed that he lobbied for the park's creation upon his return to Washington. Then-president Lyndon B. Johnson officially established the park in 1964.

Canyonlands is truly four parks in one, but the majority of visitors explore the panoramic vistas of Island in the Sky and barely venture anywhere else. For a more in-depth exploration of the park, plan a day to explore the Needles District and see Canyonlands from the bottom up. Float down the Green and Colorado Rivers on a family-friendly rafting trip, or take on the white water in legendary Cataract Canyon.

Planning

Getting Here and Around

The closest airport to Moab is Canyonlands Field Airport; Grand Junction, Colorado (110 miles from Moab), is the closest midsize airport with regularly scheduled service from multiple destinations.

Off U.S. 191, Canyonlands' Island in the Sky Visitor Center is 29 miles from Arches National Park and 32 miles from Moab on Highway 313 west of U.S. 191; the Needles District is 80 miles from Moab and reached via Highway 211, 34 miles west of U.S. 191. ■ TIP→ **Highway 211 was closed in the summer of 2022 due to flash flooding damage. At this writing its reopening date is unclear. Check with the Bureau of Land Management before planning to take this route.**

Before starting a journey to any of Canyonlands' three districts, make sure your gas tank is topped off, as there are no services inside the large park. The Maze is especially remote, 135 miles from Moab, but actually a bit closer (100 miles) from Capitol Reef National Park. In the Island in the Sky District, it's about 12 miles from the entrance station to Grand View Point, with a 5-mile spur to Upheaval Dome. The Needles scenic drive is 10 miles from the entrance station, with two spurs, about 3 miles each. Roads in the Maze—suitable only for high-clearance, four-wheel-drive vehicles—wind for hundreds of miles through the rugged canyons. Within the park, it's critical that you park only in designated pull-outs or parking areas.

Park Essentials

PARK FEES AND PERMITS

Admission is $30 per vehicle, $15 per person on foot or bicycle, and $25 per motorcycle, good for seven days. Your Canyonlands pass is good for all the park's districts. There's no entrance fee to the Maze District of Canyonlands. A $55 local park pass grants you admission to both Arches and Canyonlands as well as Natural Bridges and Hovenweep National Monuments for one year.

You need a permit for overnight backpacking, four-wheel-drive camping, river trips, and mountain-bike camping. Online reservations can be made four months in advance on the park website (www.nps. gov/cany). Four-wheel-drive day use in Salt, Horse, and Lavender Canyons and all motorized vehicles and bicycles on the Elephant Hill and White Rim Trails also require a permit, which you can obtain online up to 24 hours before your trip or in person at visitor centers.

ACCESSIBILITY

There are currently no trails in Canyonlands accessible to people in wheelchairs, but Grand View Point, Buck Canyon Overlook, and Green River Overlook at Island in the Sky are all wheelchair-accessible. In Needles, the visitor center, restrooms, Squaw Flat Campground, and Wooden Shoe Overlook are wheelchair-accessible. The visitor centers for Island in the Sky and the Needles District are also accessible, and the park's pit toilets are accessible with some assistance.

PARK HOURS

Canyonlands National Park is open 24 hours a day, seven days a week, year-round. It is in the Mountain time zone.

CELL PHONE RECEPTION

Cell phone reception may be available in some parts of the park, but not reliably so. Public telephones are at the park's visitor centers.

Hotels

There is no lodging in the park. Most visitors—especially those focused on Island in the Sky—stay in Moab or perhaps Green River, but the small towns of Blanding and Bluff—which have a smattering of motels and inns—are also convenient for exploring the Needles District.

Restaurants

There are no dining facilities in the park, although the Needles Outpost Campground, a mile from the Needles Visitor Center, has a small solar-powered store with snacks and drinks. Moab has a multitude of dining options, and there are a few very casual restaurants in Blanding (in Blanding, restaurants don't serve alcohol and are typically closed Sunday), plus a couple of excellent eateries a bit farther south in Bluff.

HOTEL AND RESTAURANT PRICES

Hotel and restaurant reviews have been shortened. For full information visit Fodors.com. Hotel prices are the lowest cost of a standard double room in high season. Restaurant prices are the average cost of a main course at dinner, or if dinner is not served, at lunch.

What It Costs			
$	$$	$$$	$$$$
RESTAURANTS			
under $16	$16–$22	$23–$30	over $30
HOTELS			
under $125	$125–$200	$201–$300	over $300

Visitor Information

CONTACTS Canyonlands National Park.
✉ Moab ☎ 435/719–2313 ⊕ www.nps.gov/cany.

When to Go

Gorgeous weather means that spring and fall are most popular. Canyonlands is seldom crowded, but in spring backpackers and four-wheelers populate the trails and roads. During Easter week, some of the four-wheel-drive trails in the park are used for Jeep Safari, an annual event drawing thousands of visitors to Moab.

The crowds thin out by July as the thermostat reaches 100°F and higher for about four weeks. It's a great time to get out on the Colorado or Green River winding through the park. October can be a little rainy, but the region receives only 8 inches of rain annually.

The well-kept secret is that winter, except during occasional snow storms, can be a great time to tour the park. Crowds are gone, snowcapped mountains stand in the background, and key roads in Island in the Sky and Needles are well-maintained (although it's wise to check the park website for conditions). Winter here is one of nature's most memorable shows, with red rock dusted white and low-floating clouds partially obscuring canyons and towers.

Island in the Sky

Standing at one of the overlooks at Island in the Sky, it's hard to fully take in what looks like an oil painting a thousand feet below. Rivers and rain have eroded the desert floor for millennia, creating mesas, towers, and the park's famously deep canyons, all with an earthy red hue. While the view alone is worth the trip, getting onto one of the district's hiking trails or four-wheel-drive roads will get you up close with its rough beauty. Though a shade over 30 miles from Moab, this is the most accessible—and far most visited—section of the park.

Sights

SCENIC DRIVES
Island in the Sky Park Road
SCENIC DRIVE | This 12-mile-long main road inside the park is bisected by a 5-mile side road to the Upheaval Dome area. To enjoy dramatic views, including the Green and Colorado River basins, stop at the overlooks and take the short walks. Once you get to the park, allow at least two hours—and ideally four—to explore. ✉ Island in the Sky.

SCENIC STOPS
Green River Overlook
VIEWPOINT | From the road it's just 100 yards to this stunning view of the Green River to the south and west. It's not far from the Island in the Sky (Willow Flat) Campground. ✉ About 1 mile off Upheaval Dome Rd., Island in the Sky ✛ 7 miles from visitor center.

White Rim Overlook Trail
VIEWPOINT | The cliffs fall away on three sides at the end of this level, 1.8-mile out-and-back hike until you get a dramatic view of the White Rim and Monument Basin. There are restrooms at the trailhead. ✉ Grand View Point, Island in the Sky.

TRAILS

Aztec Butte Trail

TRAIL | The highlight of the 2-mile round-trip hike is the chance to see Ancestral Puebloan granaries. The view into Taylor Canyon is also nice. *Moderate.* ⊠ *Island in the Sky* ✛ *Trailhead: Upheaval Dome Rd., about 7 miles from visitor center.*

★ Grand View Point Trail

TRAIL | This 360-degree view is the main event for many visitors to Island in the Sky. Look down into the deep canyons of the Colorado and Green Rivers, which have been carved by water and erosion over the millennia. Many people just stop at the paved overlook and drive on, but you'll gain a breathtaking perspective by strolling along this 2-mile round-trip, flat cliffside trail. On a clear day you can see up to 100 miles to the Maze and Needles Districts of the park and each of Utah's major laccolithic mountain ranges: the Henrys, Abajos, and La Sals. *Easy.* ⊠ *End of main park road, Island in the Sky* ✛ *12 miles from visitor center.*

★ Mesa Arch Trail

TRAIL | If you don't have time for the 2,000 arches in nearby Arches National Park, you should take the easy, ½-mile round-trip walk to Mesa Arch. After the overlooks, this is the most popular trail in the park. The arch is above a cliff that drops 800 feet to the canyon bottom. Through the arch, views of Washerwoman Arch and surrounding buttes, spires, and canyons make this a favorite photo opportunity. *Easy.* ⊠ *Off main park road, Island in the Sky* ✛ *6 miles from visitor center.*

Shafer Trail

TRAIL | This rough trek that leads to the 100-mile White Rim Road was probably first established by ancient Native Americans. In the early 1900s the local Shafer family started using it to drive cattle into the canyon. John "Sog" Shafer is credited with improving the narrow and rugged trail, and it was further upgraded during the uranium boom, in order for miners to haul ore by truck from the canyon floor. But make no mistake: it's still a harrowing descent. Check out the road's winding, 5.2-mile route down canyon walls from the Shafer Canyon Overlook before you drive it to see why it's mostly used by daring four-wheelers and energetic mountain bikers. Off the main road, less than 1 mile from the park entrance, it descends 1,500 feet to the White Rim. Check with the visitor center about road conditions before driving the Shafer Trail. It's often impassable after rain or snow. ⊠ *Island in the Sky.*

★ Upheaval Dome Trail

TRAIL | This mysterious crater is one of the wonders of Island in the Sky. Some geologists believe it's an eroded salt dome, but others think it was made by a meteorite. Either way, it's worth the steep hike to see it and decide for yourself. The moderate hike to the first overlook is about a ½-mile each way; energetic visitors can continue another ½-mile to the second overlook for an even better perspective. The trail is steeper and rougher after the first overlook. The round-trip to the second overlook is 2 miles. The trailhead has restrooms and a picnic area. *Moderate.* ⊠ *End of Upheaval Dome Rd., Island in the Sky* ✛ *11 miles from visitor center.*

Whale Rock Trail

TRAIL | If you've been hankering to walk across some of that famed, pavement-smooth stuff they call slickrock, the hike to Whale Rock will make your feet happy. This 1-mile round-trip adventure, which culminates final 100-foot climb and features some potentially dangerous drop-offs, takes you to the very top of the whale's back. Once you get there, you are rewarded with great views of Upheaval Dome and Trail Canyon. *Moderate.* ⊠ *Island in the Sky* ✛ *Trailhead: Upheaval Dome Rd., 10 miles from visitor center.*

VISITOR CENTERS
Island in the Sky Visitor Center

VISITOR CENTER | The gateway to the world-famous White Rim Trail, this visitor center 21 miles from U.S. 191 draws a mix of mountain bikers, hikers, and tourists happy to see the area by car. This is a great stop to use the restroom, stock up on water, and buy maps and books for the journey ahead. Check the website or with the center for a daily schedule of ranger-led programs. ✉ *Off Hwy. 313, Island in the Sky* ☎ *435/259–4712* ⊘ *Closed Tues. and Wed. in Jan.–mid-Feb.*

Needles

Lower in elevation than Island in the Sky, Needles is more about on-the-ground exploration than far-off vistas, but it's an especially good area for long-distance hiking, mountain biking, and four-wheel driving. The district is named for its massive sandstone spires, with hundreds of the formations poking up toward the sky. There are also several striking examples of Native American rock art here, well worth the hikes to reach them. With relatively few visitors, Needles makes for a quiet place to set up camp and recharge for a few days before returning to busy nearby Moab.

◉ Sights

HISTORIC SIGHTS
Cowboy Camp

This fascinating stop on the 0.6-mile round-trip **Cave Spring Trail** is an authentic example of cowboy life more than a century ago. You do not need to complete the entire trail (which includes two short ladders and some rocky hiking) to see the 19th-century artifacts at Cowboy Camp. ✉ *End of Cave Springs Rd., Needles* ✛ *2.3 miles from visitor center.*

SCENIC DRIVES
Needles District Park Road

SCENIC DRIVE | You'll feel like you've driven into a Hollywood Western as you roll along the park road in the Needles District. Red mesas and buttes rise against the horizon, blue mountain ranges interrupt the rangelands, and the colorful red-and-white needles stand like soldiers on the far side of grassy meadows. Definitely hop out of the car at a few of the marked roadside stops, including both overlooks at Pothole Point. Allow at least two hours in this less-traveled section of the park. ✉ *Needles.*

SCENIC STOPS
Wooden Shoe Arch Overlook

VIEWPOINT | FAMILY | Kids will enjoy looking for the tiny window in the rock that looks like a wooden shoe with a turned-up toe. If you can't find it on your own, there's a marker to help you. ✉ *Off main park road, Needles* ✛ *2 miles from visitor center.*

TRAILS
★ Cave Spring Trail

TRAIL | FAMILY | One of the best and most interesting trails in the park takes you past a historic cowboy camp, precontact rock art, and great views. Two wooden ladders and one short, steep stretch may make this a little daunting for the extremely young or old or those with mobility issues, but it's also a short hike (0.6 miles round-trip) with some shady spots. *Moderate.* ✉ *Needles* ✛ *Trailhead: End of Cave Springs Rd., 2.3 miles from visitor center.*

★ Joint Trail

TRAIL | Part of the Chesler Park Loop, this trail follows a series of deep, narrow fractures in the rock. A shady spot in summer, it will give you good views of the Needles formations for which the district is named. The loop travels briefly along a four-wheel-drive road and is 10.7 miles round-trip; allow at least five hours to complete it. *Difficult.* ✉ *Needles*

⚐ Trailhead: Elephant Hill parking lot, 6 miles from visitor center.

Pothole Point Trail

TRAIL | FAMILY | Microscopic creatures lie dormant in pools that fill only after rare rainstorms. When the rains do come, some eggs hatch within hours and life becomes visible. If you're lucky, you'll hit Pothole Point after a storm. The dramatic views of the Needles and Six Shooter Peak make this easy, 0.6-mile out-and-back hike worthwhile. Plan for about 45 minutes. There's no shade, so wear a hat and take plenty of water. *Easy.* ✉ *Off main road, Needles* ⚐ *5 miles from visitor center.*

Slickrock Trail

TRAIL | Wear a hat and carry plenty of water if you're on this trail—you won't find any shade along the 2.4-mile round-trip loop. This is the rare frontcountry site where you might spot one of the few remaining native herds of bighorn sheep in the national park system. Nice panoramic views. *Easy.* ✉ *Needles* ⚐ *Trailhead: Main park road, 6 miles from visitor center.*

VISITOR CENTERS

Needles District Visitor Center

VISITOR CENTER | FAMILY | This gorgeous building is 34 miles from U.S. 191 via Highway 211, near the park entrance. Needles is remote, so it's worth stopping to inquire about road, weather, and park conditions. You can also use the restroom, refill water bottles, and get books, trail maps, and other information. Note that during part of the winter, it's only open Friday and Saturday. ✉ *Off Hwy. 211, Needles* ☎ *435/259–4711* ⊘ *Closed Sun.–Thurs. in Dec.–mid-Feb.*

Maze

The most remote district of the park, The Maze is hours away from any town and is accessible only via high-clearance, four-wheel-drive vehicles. A trip here should not be taken lightly. Many of the hikes

are considered some of the most dangerous in the world, and self-sufficiency is critical. But the few who do choose to visit this wild tangle of rock and desert are richly rewarded with unforgettable views and a silent solitude that's hard to find anywhere else. Plan to spend at least several days here, and bring all the water, food, and gas you'll need.

◉ Sights

VISITOR CENTER

Hans Flat Ranger Station

VISITOR CENTER | Only experienced and intrepid visitors will likely ever visit this remote outpost—on a dirt road 46 miles east of Highway 24 in Hanksville. The office is a trove of books, maps, and other documents about the unforgiving Maze District of Canyonlands, but rangers will strongly dissuade any inexperienced off-road drivers and backpackers from proceeding into this truly rugged wilderness. There's a vault toilet, but no water, food, or services of any kind. If you're headed for the backcountry, permits cost $36 per group plus $5 per person for up to 14 days. Rangers offer guided hikes in Horseshoe Canyon on most weekends in spring and fall.

▤ **TIP→ Call the ranger station for road conditions leading to Horseshoe Canyon/ Hans Flat as rain can make travel difficult.** ✉ *Jct. of Recreation Rds. 777 and 633, Maze* ☎ *435/259–2652.*

Horseshoe Canyon

Remote Horseshoe Canyon is not contiguous with the rest of Canyonlands National Park. Added to the park in 1971, it has what may be America's most significant surviving examples of rock art. While the canyon can usually be accessed by two-wheel-drive vehicles via a graded dirt road, it's still 2½ hours from Moab. And the road conditions can change abruptly, so visitors without a

Serious mountain bikers traverse all 100 miles of White Rim Road.

four-wheel-drive vehicle should always consult the park's road conditions hotline before departing. Rangers lead hikes here in the spring and fall.

Sights

Horseshoe Canyon Trail

TRAIL | This remote region of the park is accessible by dirt road, and only in good weather. Park at the lip of the canyon and hike 7 miles round-trip to the Great Gallery, considered by some to be the most significant rock-art panel in North America. Ghostly life-size figures in the Barrier Canyon style populate the amazing panel. The hike is moderately strenuous, with a 700-foot descent. Allow at least six hours for the trip and take a gallon of water per person. There's no camping allowed in the canyon, although you can camp on top near the parking lot. *Difficult.*

■ TIP→ Call Hans Flat Ranger Station before heading out because rain can make the access road a muddy mess. Also, make sure to use a map as GPS can be unreliable

here. ⊠ *Horseshoe Canyon ⇪ Trailhead: 32 miles east of Hwy. 24.*

Activities

BIKING

Mountain bikers from all over the world like to brag that they've conquered the 100 miles of White Rim Road. The trail's fame is well deserved: it traverses steep roads, broken rock, and dramatic ledges, as well as long stretches that wind through the canyons and look down onto others. If you're biking White Rim without an outfitter, you'll need careful planning, vehicle support, and much-sought-after backcountry reservations. Permits are available no more than four months, and no less than two days, prior to the permit start date. There is a 15-bike, three-vehicle limit for groups. Day-use permits are also required and can be obtained at the Island in the Sky visitor center or reserved 24 hours in advance at ⊕ www. recreation.gov.

In addition to the company listed below, Rim Tours, Western Spirit Cycling Adventures, and Escape Adventures (all in Moab) offer tours in Canyonlands.

Magpie Cycling

BIKING | Professional guides and mountain biking instructors lead groups (or lone riders) on half-day, daylong, and multiday bike trips exploring the Moab region's most memorable terrain, including the White Rim, Needles, and The Maze. If you need to rent a bike, Magpie can meet you at its preferred shop, Poison Spider Bicycles (☒ 497 N. Main St., Moab☏ 435/259–7882). ☒ Moab ☏ 435/259–4464 ⊕ www.magpiecycling. com ☙ Day tours from $190; 3-day White Rim Trail tours from $945.

CAMPING

Canyonlands campgrounds are some of the most beautiful in the national park system. At the Needles District, campers will enjoy fairly private campsites tucked against red-rock walls and dotted with pinyon and juniper trees. At Island in the Sky, starry nights and spectacular vistas make the small campground an intimate treasure. Hookups are not available at either of the park's campgrounds; however, some sites are long enough to accommodate units up to 28 feet long.

Needles Campground. The defining features of the campsites at Squaw Flat are house-size red-rock formations, which provide some shade, offer privacy from adjacent campers, and make this one of the more memorable campgrounds in the national park system. Sites can be reserved online from spring through fall and cost $20 per night.☒ Off main road, about 3 miles from park entrance, Needles ☏ 435/259–4711 ⊕ www.recreation.gov.

Willow Flat Campground. From this little campground on a mesa top, you can walk to spectacular views of the Green River. Most sites have a bit of shade from juniper trees. The 12 sites are first-come, first-served and cost $15

per night. ■**TIP→ The campground has no water.** ☒ Off main park road, about 7 miles from park entrance, Island in the Sky ☏ 435/259–4712.

FOUR-WHEELING

Nearly 200 miles of challenging backcountry roads lead to campsites, trailheads, and natural and cultural features in Canyonlands. All the roads require high-clearance, four-wheel-drive vehicles, and many are inappropriate for inexperienced drivers. The 100-mile White Rim Trail, for example, can be extremely challenging, so make sure that your four-wheel-drive skills are well honed and that you are capable of making basic vehicle repairs. Carry at least one full-size spare tire, extra gas, extra water, a shovel, a high-lift jack, and—October through April—chains for all four tires. Double-check to see that your vehicle is in top-notch condition, as you definitely don't want to break down in the interior of the park: towing expenses can exceed $1,000.

Day-use permits, available at the park visitor centers or 24 hours in advance through the park website, are required for motorized and bicycle trips on the Elephant Hill and White Rim Trails. For overnight four-wheeling trips, you must purchase a permit for $30 plus $5 per person, which you can reserve no more than four months and no fewer than two days in advance by visiting ⊕ www.recreation.gov or contacting the Backcountry Reservations Office (☏435/259–4351). Cyclists share all roads, so be aware and cautious of their presence. Vehicular traffic traveling uphill has the right-of-way. Check at the visitor center for current road conditions before taking off into the backcountry. You must carry a washable, reusable toilet with you in the Maze District and carry out all waste.

Winding around and below the Island in the Sky mesa top, the dramatic, 100-mile **White Rim Road** is not just for bikers. It offers a once-in-a-lifetime driving experience for four-wheeling as well. As you tackle Murphy's Hogback, Hardscrabble

Hill, and more formidable obstacles, you will get some fantastic views of the park. Attempting to travel the loop in one day is not recommended—plan instead to camp overnight with advance reservations, which can be made up to four months prior (book ASAP for busy spring and fall weekends). Day-use permits, which are available at the park visitor center or 24 hours in advance through the park website, are required for motorized and bicycle trips on White Rim Road. Bring plenty of water, a spare tire, and a jack, as no services are available on the road. White Rim Road starts at the end of the Shafer Trail.

The remote, rugged **Flint Trail** is the most popular in the Maze District, but it's not an easy ride. It has 2 miles of switchbacks that drop down the side of a cliff face. You reach the Flint Trail from the Hans Flat Ranger Station, 46 miles from the closest paved road. From Hans Flat to the end of the road at the Doll House it's a 41-mile drive that takes at least six hours one-way. The Maze is not recommended as a day trip, so you'll have to purchase an overnight backcountry permit for $36 plus $5 per person. Despite its remoteness, the Maze District can fill to capacity during spring and fall, so plan ahead.

The first 3 miles of the **Elephant Hill Trail** in the Needles District are passable by all vehicles, but don't venture out without asking about road conditions. For the rest of the trail, only 4X4 vehicles are allowed. The route is so difficult that many people get out and walk—it's faster than you can drive it in some cases. The trek from the Elephant Hill Trailhead to Devil's Kitchen is 3½ miles; from the trailhead to the Confluence Overlook, it's a 14½-mile out-and-back and requires at least eight hours. Don't attempt this without a well-maintained 4X4 vehicle and spare gas, tires, and off-road knowledge. A

day-use permit, which is available at the park visitor center or 24 hours in advance through the park website, is required for motorized and bicycle trips on the Elephant Hill Trail.

HIKING

At Canyonlands National Park you can immerse yourself in the intoxicating colors, smells, and textures of the desert.

TIP→ Make sure to bring water and electrolytes as dehydration is the number-one cause of search-and-rescue calls here.

Island in the Sky has several easy and moderate hikes that are popular with day-trippers, including the Aztec Butte Trail, Grand View Point Trail, Upheaval Dome Trail, and Whale Rock Trail. If you're up for a strenuous day of hiking, try the 8-mile Syncline Loop Trail, which follows the canyons around Upheaval Dome.

Both the Cave Spring Trail and Slickrock Trail are popular with day-trippers to the **Needles** section of Canyonlands and are suitable for most hikers young or old, though the former requires one to climb two wooden ladders. Others are considerably more difficult and require experience.

Chesler Park is a grassy meadow dotted with spires and enclosed by a circular wall of colorful "needles." One of Canyonlands' more popular trails, the Chesler Viewpoint Trail, leads through the area to the famous Joint Trail, one of the park's star attractions, though a moderately difficult hike.

Chapter 13

MOAB AND SOUTHEASTERN UTAH

Updated by
Stina Sieg

 Sights
★★★★★

 Restaurants
★★★☆☆

 Hotels
★★★☆☆

 Shopping
★★☆☆☆

 Nightlife
★☆☆☆☆

WELCOME TO
MOAB AND SOUTHEASTERN UTAH

TOP REASONS TO GO

★ **Otherworldly beauty:**
The terra-cotta expanse of open desert here is unparalleled.

★ **Get out and play:**
Mountain and road biking, rafting, rock climbing, hiking, four-wheeling, and cross-country skiing are all wildly popular.

★ **Creature comforts:**
Though remote, southeastern Utah—and Moab, in particular—has a vast array of lodging and dining options, including elegant bistros, fancy hotels, and quaint bed-and-breakfasts.

★ **Catch a festival:**
Especially in the spring and summer months, this area is chock-full of gatherings focused on art, music, and recreation.

★ **Another state of being:**
There's something about being in such intense beauty so far from everything that creates a friendly, informal culture in which time and money aren't the main focus. Once that red dirt gets in your blood, you might never leave.

1 Moab. This increasingly busy heart of the area is full of shops, restaurants, and hotels.

2 Green River. Stock up on supplies and gas before heading off on farther-flung adventures.

3 Hanksville. Close to nothing but the Fremont River, popular with summer boaters.

4 Monticello. Near Bears Ears National Monument.

5 Blanding. Close to several natural wonders and two Native American reservations.

6 Natural Bridges National Monument. The remote park has one of the largest natural bridges in the world.

7 Bluff. A tiny, arty town with a big personality.

8 Mexican Hat. A little dot on the San Juan River close to Monument Valley, the Valley of the Gods, and Goosenecks State Park.

9 Lake Powell. One of the biggest recreation draws in the Southwest, despite its falling water levels.

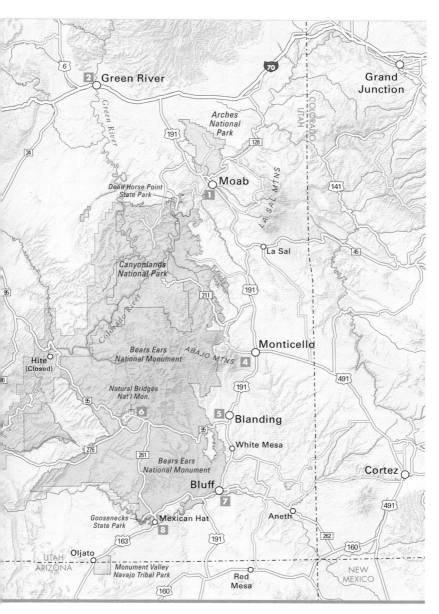

The West is full of remote, beautiful communities buoyed by outdoor recreation, but there's something special about southeastern Utah.

Even as the area gets busier (Moab, especially), the offbeat soul here can still be felt. This is an area full of converts—and not so much in a religious sense. These are people formerly from suburbs or cities who came here long ago for vacation and never truly left. They may have spent just a few days surrounded by the vast desert and the clean, welcoming rivers, but in that short time, the land became a part of them.

Although the towns tend to be visually simple in this part of the state, the scenery that surrounds them is awe-inspiring. You can see pictures of these canyons, arches, and natural bridges, but no words come close to their enormous presence.

Visitors arrive for all sorts of activities, from running the gorgeous stretch of the Colorado River near Moab to exploring the unique landscape of the area's national parks and monuments. Some are history buffs, excited to explore the ancient ruins and rock art left behind by Native American tribes. Whatever brings you to this unique, disarming landscape, you'll quickly understand how hard it can be to leave.

Small but unbelievably busy in spring, summer, and fall, Moab is on the Colorado River, south of I–70 on U.S. 191. More than 100 miles from any large town, it's close to nothing, and its residents are just fine with that.

From Green River to Mexican Hat, this large swath of desert has a very small population. The most easily reached destinations are the small towns right on U.S. 191 or I–70, but some of the most beautiful stops require substantial but worthwhile detours off these main roads. Lake Powell, about three hours southwest of Moab, remains a favorite among visitors and locals alike.

Utah scenery is dramatic, from the wide span of water at Lake Powell to the huge, sandstone formations (called "mittens") in Monument Valley. Around Green River you'll encounter a world of agriculture and boating, with melon stands popping up in the late summer and fall. Farther south you'll see the influence of Native American culture, including ancient rock art and dwellings. Along the way to Mexican Hat, you'll enjoy Navajo tacos and handmade jewelry.

Planning

Getting Here and Around

AIR

The nearest decent-size airport to southeastern Utah is Walker Field Airport in Grand Junction, Colorado, 110 miles from Moab, but you can catch a regional flight directly to Canyonlands Regional Airport Moab. You can rent a car at the Moab Airport, but advanced reservations are essential.

CONTACTS Grand Junction Regional Airport. ⊠ 2828 Walker Field Dr., Grand Junction ☎ 970/244–9100 ⊕ www.gjairport. com. Canyonlands Regional Airport. ⊠ 94

W. Aviation Way, Moab ☎ *435/259–4849* ⊕ *www.moabairport.com.*

CAR

To reach southeastern Utah from Salt Lake City, take I–15 to U.S. 6 and then U.S. 191 south. From Colorado or more eastern locations, use I–70 or U.S. 491. Take U.S. 191 from either Wyoming or Arizona. Most roads are well-maintained two-lane highways, though snow can be a factor during winter travel. Be sure your car is in good working order and keep the gas tank topped off, as there are long stretches of empty road between towns.

Hotels

Every type of lodging is available in southeastern Utah, from economy chain motels to B&Bs and high-end, high-adventure resorts. Some of the best values in Moab are condominiums available for rent.

CONTACTS Moab Property Management. ✉ *11850 Hwy. 191, Suite A6* ☎ *435/259–5125, 800/505–5343, 435/514–7281* ⊕ *www.moabutahlodging.com.*

HOTEL AND RESTAURANT PRICES
Hotel and restaurant reviews have been shortened. For full information visit Fodors.com. Hotel prices are the lowest cost of a standard double room in high season. Restaurant prices are the average cost of a main course at dinner, or if dinner is not served, at lunch.

What It Costs			
$	$$	$$$	$$$$
RESTAURANTS			
under $16	$16–$22	$23–$30	over $30
HOTELS			
under $125	$125–$200	$201–$300	over $300

Restaurants

Including a few surprising twists, Moab-area restaurants have anything you might crave. The other smaller towns in southeastern Utah don't have quite the culinary kaleidoscope and focus mainly on all-American cuisine.

When to Go

The most enjoyable times to be in this part of Utah are the beginning and end of high season, March and October, respectively. April and May have the best weather—and the biggest crowds. May to September is the best time to hit the river, but that is also when the towns and national parks are filled with people, and the temperatures can be downright fiery. From the beginning of November through the end of February some restaurants and stores shut down, and things can get eerily quiet. To compensate, almost all hotels offer steep discounts, which can make visiting in the off-season a steal.

Moab

When you first drive down crowded Main Street (Moab's commercial, downtown strip), you might not get the town's appeal right away. T-shirt shops and touristy restaurants line the wide thoroughfare, and crowds of people are often everywhere. But don't let Moab's impersonal exterior fool you; take a few walks, visit some of the town's locally owned stores and eateries, and talk to some of the residents, and you'll realize this is a town centered on community. Local theater, local radio, and local art rule. At its core, this is a frontier outpost, where people have had to create their own livelihoods for more than 100 years.

In the late 1880s, it was settled as a farming and ranching community. By the 1950s it became a center for uranium mining after Charlie Steen found a huge deposit of the stuff outside town. After about a decade of unbelievable monetary success, there was a massive downturn in the mining industry, and Moab plunged into an economic free fall. Then came tourism. Moab was able to rebuild itself with the dollars of sightseers, four-wheelers, bikers, and boaters. Today the town is dealing with environmental and development issues while becoming more and more popular with tourists and second-homeowners from around the world. No matter how much it changes, though, one thing never will: this town has a different flavor than any other in the state.

GETTING HERE AND AROUND
Although Moab is friendly to bikes and pedestrians, the only practical way to reach it is by car or plane. If you're coming from the south, U.S. 191 runs straight into Moab. If you're arriving from Salt Lake City, travel 50 miles via I–15, then go 150 miles southeast via U.S. 6, and finally 30 miles south via U.S. 191. Signs for Moab will be obvious past Green River.

▤ TIP→ **If you are approaching from the east on I–70, a fun way to reach Moab is by taking Exit 214, which leads you into the town of Cisco, and then driving down the Upper Colorado River Scenic Byway—Route 128—into Moab. The views of the river, rocks, and mesas are second to none.**

SHUTTLES
If you need a ride to or from your trailhead or river trip put-in point, a couple of Moab companies provide the service (and also provide airport shuttle service by reservation), with vehicles large enough to handle most groups. Coyote's website is worth checking out for trail and river conditions and other information. Inquiries for Roadrunner are handled by Dual Sport, under the same ownership.

SHUTTLES Coyote Shuttle. ✉ *55 W. 300 S, Moab* ☎ *435/260–2097* ⊕ *www.coyoteshuttle.com.* **Roadrunner Shuttle.** ✉ *Moab* ☎ *435/259–9402* ⊕ *www.roadrunnershuttle.com.*

VISITOR INFORMATION
CONTACTS Discover Moab Information Center. ✉ *25 E. Center St., Moab* ☎ *435/259–8825* ⊕ *www.discovermoab.com.*

Sights

★ Dead Horse Point State Park
STATE/PROVINCIAL PARK | FAMILY | One of the gems of Utah's state park system, right at the edge of the Island in the Sky section of Canyonlands, this park overlooks a sweeping oxbow of the Colorado River some 2,000 feet below. Dead Horse Point itself is a small peninsula connected to the main mesa by a narrow neck of land. As the story goes, cowboys used to drive wild mustangs onto the point and pen them there with a brush fence. There's a nice visitor center with a coffee shop and museum. The park's Intrepid trail system is popular with mountain bikers and hikers alike. If it's a nice day, be sure to walk the 4-mile rim trail loop and drive to the park's eponymous point. ✉ *Hwy. 313, Canyonlands National Park* ☎ *435/259–2614, 800/322–3770 camping reservations* ⊕ *stateparks.utah.gov* ⊠ *$20 per vehicle (up to 8 people).*

Lower Colorado River Scenic Byway— Highway 279
SCENIC DRIVE | If you're interested in Native American rock art, Highway 279 northwest of Moab is a perfect place to spend a couple of hours immersed in the past. To get there, go north from Moab on U.S. 191 for about 3½ miles before turning left onto Highway 279. If you start late in the afternoon, the cliffs will be glowing orange as the sun sets. Along the first part of the route you'll see signs reading **"Indian Writings."** Park only

in designated areas to view the petro-glyphs on the cliff side of the road. At the 18-mile marker you'll see **Jug Handle Arch.** A few miles beyond this point the road turns to four-wheel-drive only and takes you into the Island in the Sky District of Canyonlands. Do not continue onto Island in the Sky unless you are in a high-clearance four-wheel-drive vehicle with a full gas tank and plenty of water. Allow about two hours round-trip for the scenic byway drive.

▬TIP→ **If you happen to be in Moab during a heavy rainstorm, Highway 279 is also a good option for viewing the amazing water-falls caused by rain pouring off the cliffs on both sides of the Colorado River.** ✉ *Hwy. 279, Moab.*

Moab Museum

HISTORY MUSEUM | FAMILY | This small, centrally located museum focuses on the people, places, and events that have shaped the canyon country around Moab and Grand County. Exhibits feature everyone from indigenous peoples to Euro-American prospectors, ranchers, and farmers. There's also a big emphasis on mining history as this area was once the "Uranium Capital of America" before the local outdoor recreation boom. ✉ *118 E. Center St., Moab* ☎ *435/259–7985* ⊕ *www.moabmuseum.org* ✆ *$10* ☾ *Closed Sun. and Mon.*

Scott and Norma Matheson Wetlands Preserve

NATURE SIGHT | FAMILY | Jointly owned and operated by The Nature Conservancy and the Utah Division of Wildlife Resources, this preserve offers a chance to slow down from the hubbub of town and experience world-class bird-watching. The 900-acre oasis makes for great strolling while on the lookout for more than 200 species, including great blue herons, sandhill cranes, and a large number of neotropical migratory songbirds, from chats to western tanagers to black-head-ed grosbeaks. Sightings of deer and wild turkey are fairly common, but there

are also rare glimpses of more elusive mammals like beaver and river otters, not to mention mountain lions and bobcats. Always remember to respect the wildlife and keep an appropriate distance.

An information kiosk greets visitors just inside the preserve, and a boardwalk winds through the property to several viewpoints, including the Colorado River, a native fish project area, and a water control structure. If you have a little more time, take the new trail east to the Central Pond for spectacular views of the mountains and opportunities to spot waterfowl and other native species. ✉ *934 W. Kane Creek Blvd., Moab* ⊹ *Turn northwest off U.S. 191/Main St., at Kane Creek Blvd. and continue past a 3-way stop, continue on Kane Creek for approx-imately another ½ mile. Parking is on the right* ☎ *801/531–0999* ⊕ *www.nature.org* ✆ *Free.*

★ Upper Colorado River Scenic Byway—Highway 128

SCENIC DRIVE | One of the most sce-nic drives in the Four Corners region, Highway 128 intersects U.S. 191, 3 miles south of Arches. The 44-mile highway runs along the upper Colorado River, with 2,000-foot red rock cliffs rising on both sides. This gorgeous river corridor is home to a winery, orchards, and a couple of luxury lodging options. It also offers a spectacular view of world-class climbing destination Fisher Towers before winding north to Interstate 70. Give yourself an hour to 90 minutes to drive it, though be aware that traffic can get congested in the summer. For the full experience, go through the ghost town of Cisco by taking Exit 214 if you're heading east on I–70 and stop by the delightful **Buzzard's Belly General Store.** Full of snacks, soda, art, and fun knickknacks, it's an off-beat take on a general store, and you'll likely want to take some pictures to show your friends. ✉ *Hwy. 128, Moab.*

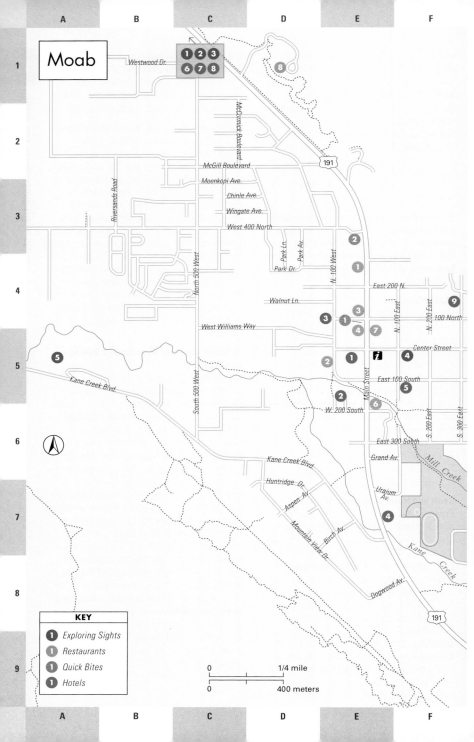

Moab

KEY

- **1** Exploring Sights
- **1** Restaurants
- **1** Quick Bites
- **1** Hotels

0 ——— 1/4 mile

0 ——— 400 meters

Sights ▼

1 Colorado River Scenic Byway— Highway 128..............**C1**
2 Colorado River Scenic Byway— Highway 279.............**C1**
3 Dead Horse Point State Park **C1**
4 Moab Museum..........**F5**
5 Scott and Norma Matheson Wetlands Preserve.....**A5**

Restaurants ▼

1 Antica Forma.............**E4**
2 Desert Bistro **E5**
3 Jailhouse Cafe **E4**
4 Miguel's Baja Grill **E5**
5 Milt's Stop and Eat......**G6**
6 Moab Diner...............**E6**
7 Moab Garage Co.........**E5**
8 Sunset Grill **D1**

Quick Bites ▼

1 Quesadilla Mobilla.......**E4**
2 Sweet Cravings Bakery + Bistro **E3**

Hotels ▼

1 Best Western Plus Canyonlands Inn.........**E5**
2 Gonzo Inn **E5**
3 Hoodoo Moab, Curio Collection by Hilton **E4**
4 Moab Red Stone Inn **E7**
5 Moab Rustic Inn **F5**
6 Moab Springs Ranch....**C1**
7 Red Cliffs Lodge **C1**
8 Sorrel River Ranch Resort & Spa **C1**
9 Sunflower Hill Inn........**F4**

Rosetree Ln.
Nichols Ln.
E. 200 South
Sundial St.
Bowen Dr.
Locust Ln.
Mill Creek Dr.
Oak St.
Sand Flats Rd.
Mill Creek Dr.
Tusher St.
Walker St.
Hillside Dr.
S. 400 East

🍴 Restaurants

Antica Forma

$$ | **ITALIAN** | **FAMILY** | Come hungry to Moab's best pizza joint, which offers an extensive list of thin-crust wood-fired pies, each more-or-less individually sized (you might leave stuffed). The ambience is pretty simple, but the interior is low-key and welcoming. **Known for:** gourmet pizzas, from the simple margherita on; extensive craft beer selection; linguine with meatballs and other pasta favorites. [$] *Average main: $19* ✉ *267 N. Main St., Moab* ☎ *435/355–0167* 🌐 *www.antica-forma.com* 🕑 *Closed Sun. in winter.*

★ **Desert Bistro**

$$$$ | **SOUTHWESTERN** | One of the jewels of the local culinary scene, this elegant restaurant serves adventurous cuisine with a Southwestern flair, all in a historic brick building in downtown Moab. The menu shifts with the seasons but always includes a good selection of game and fish, including elk and Chilean seabass. **Known for:** house-made desserts; bacon-wrapped bison tenderloin; full bar. [$] *Average main: $38* ✉ *36 S. 100 W, Moab* ☎ *435/259–0756* 🌐 *www.desertbistro.com* 🕑 *Closed Tues. and early Dec.–early Mar.* ☞ *No lunch.*

Jailhouse Café

$ | **AMERICAN** | A local institution for decades, this downtown spot *only* does breakfast from 7 to noon—and does it famously well. Expect all your morning favorites, plus a few surprises, served out of a pink 1880s-era home that also once served as the county courthouse (the kitchen was a jail cell). **Known for:** ginger and Swedish pancakes; "soul bacon" (thick-cut slices that are sourced and cut especially for Jailhouse); inventive varieties of eggs Benedict. [$] *Average main: $12* ✉ *101 N. Main St., Moab* ☎ *435/259–3900* 🌐 *facebook.com/MoabsBreakfastsPlace* 🕑 *Usually closed Nov.–Feb* ☞ *No lunch or dinner.*

Miguel's Baja Grill

$$ | **MEXICAN** | Right on the main drag, this friendly spot serves up south-of-the-border fare with the culinary spirit of Baja, California. That means in addition to expected Mexican favorites (burritos, enchiladas, quesadillas, etc.), Miguel's is also known for its excellent fresh seafood dishes (yes, even in the desert). **Known for:** big portions; Baja fish tacos; ceviche, a tangy blend of raw fish, onions, tomatoes, and more. [$] *Average main: $21* ✉ *51 N. Main St., Moab* ☎ *435/259–6546* 🌐 *www.miguelsbajagrill.net* 🕑 *Closed Dec.–Feb. No lunch.*

Milt's Stop & Eat

$ | **FAST FOOD** | **FAMILY** | Since 1954, this unassuming little drive-in stand has been the place to stop for burgers and shakes, especially when you're ravenous from being on the river. There's a wide variety of hamburger options (even including elk and veggie), and hand-cut fries, tater tots, and onion rings are among the classic sides. **Known for:** thick shakes with an impressive list of flavors; classic and specialty burgers made with grass-fed beef; friendly, vintage feel. [$] *Average main: $7* ✉ *356 Millcreek Dr., Moab* ☎ *435/259–7424* 🌐 *www.miltsstopandeat.com* 🕑 *Usually closed late Dec. and Jan.*

Moab Diner

$ | **DINER** | **FAMILY** | Quick and reliable, this no-frills diner opens early and closes late, dishing up large portions of all-American fare at a decent price. People come for the all-day breakfast, the grass-fed beef burgers, and a great selection of soda-fountain favorites, including shakes and sundaes. **Known for:** signature green chili; centrally located; Sweetwater Potatoes (fried with their skins on and seasoned with bacon, green onions, and spices). [$] *Average main: $13* ✉ *189 S. Main St., Moab* ☎ *435/259–4006* 🌐 *www.moabdiner.com* 🕑 *Closed Sun.*

Moab Garage Co.

$ | **ECLECTIC** | Set in a vintage redbrick storefront on downtown Moab's busiest block, this urbane café and ice-cream shop also offers enough hearty savory dishes throughout the day—plus a well-curated selection of beer and wine— to serve as a legit breakfast or lunch option. Consider the Liège-style waffles with fresh berries or avocado toast early in the day, or a veggie "meatball" or fancy grilled cheese sandwich (the preparation of the latter changes daily), Cobb salad, or street tacos in the afternoon. **Known for:** nitro-infused ice cream in surprising flavors; superb coffee; transforms into a speakeasy in the evening. $ *Average main: $9 ⊠ 78 N. Main St., Moab ☎ 435/554–8467 ⊕ moabgarageco.com ⊘ Closed Tues. No dinner.*

Sunset Grill

$$$ | **AMERICAN** | Looming high over Moab, this cliffside home of former uranium kingpin Charlie Steen offers gorgeous views of the Colorado River and surrounding red rocks, especially at sunset. The traditional American fare—including filet mignon, prime rib, pasta dishes and house-made desserts—is classic and upscale, making for the kind of place people take their parents for a fancy night out. **Known for:** linguine Olivia (a lemony, creamy pasta dish bursting with crabmeat, shrimp, and garlic); stunning views; slow-roasted prime rib. $ *Average main: $25 ⊠ 900 N. Main St., Moab ☎ 435/259–7146 ⊕ www.moabsunsetgrill.com ⊘ Closed Sun. No lunch.*

☕ Coffee and Quick Bites

Quesadilla Mobilla

$ | **FUSION** | Moab's bright-yellow gourmet food truck is permanently parked in the heart of town, where it offers a shaded spot under water-misters to dig into its extremely thick and tasty meat and veggie quesadillas. Not strictly Mexican or Southwestern, the food here is more of an inventive fusion with nontraditional ingredients, and the menu even includes a vegan option or two. **Known for:** the Enchanted Chicken, packed with green chili, corn, refried beans, and cheese; the best food truck in town; delicious cookies and cold drinks. $ *Average main: $11 ⊠ 95 N. Main St., Moab ☎ 435/260–0289 ⊕ www.quesadillamobilla.com ⊘ Usually closed Veterans Day–early Mar.*

★ Sweet Cravings Bakery + Bistro

$ | **BAKERY** | In addition to doling out some of the largest and most delicious cookies and cinnamon rolls you've ever tried, this cheerful bakery-café presents a terrific roster of breakfast and lunch panini, wraps, sandwiches, and soups. Here, the baked goods are all from scratch (with many gluten-free options), the produce is local, the meats are preservative-free, and the coffee is 100% Rainforest Alliance and organic. **Known for:** hefty cinnamon rolls; strawberry chicken salad wrap; local produce and ingredients. $ *Average main: $14 ⊠ 397 N. Main St., Moab ☎ 435/259–8983 ⊕ www.cravemoab.com ⊘ No dinner.*

Hotels

Best Western Plus Canyonlands Inn

$$$ | **HOTEL** | **FAMILY** | The confluence of Main and Center Streets is the epicenter of Moab, and this comfortable, contemporary, impeccably clean hotel anchors the intersection, providing a perfect base for families. **Pros:** close to many restaurants; sparkling, contemporary rooms; complimentary breakfast. **Cons:** central location can feel a bit crowded at busy times; books up far in advance (September and October usually require a year advance notice); pool is closed in winter (but hot tub stays open year-round). $ *Rooms from: $300 ⊠ 16 S. Main St., Moab ☎ 435/259–2300 ⊕ www.bestwestern.com ⤳ 80 rooms ⦿ Free Breakfast.*

The Gonzo Inn
$$$ | **HOTEL** | This eclectic inn stands out for its fun design, brightly colored walls, desert-inspired art, and varnished adobe construction. **Pros:** unique, spotless, and hip; steps to Main Street; pool and hot tub. **Cons:** interior hallways can be dark; no elevator; not all rooms have a good view. [$] *Rooms from: $300* ✉ *100 W. 200 S, Moab* ☎ *435/259–2515* 🌐 *www.gonzo-inn.com* 🛏 *43 rooms* 🍴 *Free Breakfast.*

★ **Hoodoo Moab, Curio Collection by Hilton**
$$$$ | **HOTEL** | Moab's only four-star hotel is right downtown, though also standing next to the area's famed red rocks, giving you the best of both worlds, surrounded by the kind of luxury that's hard to find in rural Utah. **Pros:** in-house restaurant and spa; boutique hotel with upscale services; interiors have lots of locally inspired character. **Cons:** it can take a sec to learn to navigate the winding hallways; high luxury comes with a high price tag; not yet pet-friendly, but may allow pets on a one-on-one basis. [$] *Rooms from: $400* ✉ *111 N. 100 W, Moab* ☎ *435/355–0595* 🌐 *www.hilton.com* 🛏 *117 rooms* 🍴 *No Meals.*

Moab Red Stone Inn
$$ | **HOTEL** | One of the best bargains in town, this timber-frame motel offers small, clean rooms at the south end of the Moab strip near restaurants and shops. **Pros:** walking distance of many restaurants and shops; the price is right; all rooms have small kitchenettes. **Cons:** pool is at sister property across busy Main Street; no frills; rooms close to the road are noisy. [$] *Rooms from: $134* ✉ *535 S. Main St., Moab* ☎ *435/259–3500, 800/772–1972* 🌐 *www.moabred-stone.com* 🛏 *52 rooms* 🍴 *No Meals.*

Moab Rustic Inn
$$ | **HOTEL** | One of the best values amid Moab's increasingly pricey lodging landscape, this homey downtown property is, as the name suggests, rustic—but the 35 rooms are clean and comfortable and provide space for families or friends traveling together. **Pros:** terrific value; pets allowed at no extra cost (but guests with pets must book directly with the hotel); nice pool and barbecue area. **Cons:** simple (but comfortable) furnishings; downtown location is busy at times; can book up months in advance, especially the apartments. [$] *Rooms from: $140* ✉ *120 E. 100 S, Moab* ☎ *435/259–6177* 🌐 *www.moabrusticinn.com* 🛏 *35 rooms* 🍴 *Free Breakfast.*

Moab Springs Ranch
$$$$ | **APARTMENT** | In addition to bungalows and town homes, this 18-acre historic property offers an expansive, private, shaded meadow, where guests can rest on lounge chairs and hammocks, wade in a cold-water spring, and even barbecue their dinner on an outdoor grill. **Pros:** scenic setting is a respite; boutique accommodations; sits on a bike path into town. **Cons:** about a mile walk to downtown; some U.S. 191 traffic noise; only a few of the units allow dogs. [$] *Rooms from: $344* ✉ *1266 N. Hwy. 191, Moab* ☎ *435/259–7891* 🌐 *www.moabsprings-ranch.com* 🛏 *41 units* 🍴 *No Meals.*

Red Cliffs Lodge
$$$$ | **RESORT** | Director John Ford discovered this working cattle ranch in the late 1940s and used it as the setting for several of his westerns, and you can feel transported into one as you gaze onto the Colorado River and high canyon walls from your simple but elegant room. **Pros:** beautiful spot, with peaceful canyon and river views; many luxury amenities and great restaurant; private cabins are woodsy but modern. **Cons:** drive to town can be long during busy season; spotty cell service; not all rooms have river or creek views. [$] *Rooms from: $340* ✉ *Hwy. 128, mile marker 14, Moab* ☎ *435/259–2002, 866/812–2002* 🌐 *www.redcliffslodge.com* 🛏 *110 rooms* 🍴 *No Meals.*

★ **Sorrel River Ranch Resort & Spa**

$$$$ | **RESORT** | One of the premier luxury resorts in the Southwest, this swanky wellness retreat on the banks of the Colorado River is the place to be when you need to escape the modern world—so long as money is no object. **Pros:** swanky spa and restaurant; luxurious rooms and countless amenities; red-rock setting along the Colorado River. **Cons:** drive to town is long during the busy season; steep rates; not all-inclusive, so most activities cost extra. [$] *Rooms from: $1062* ✉ *Hwy. 128, Moab* ✣ *Mile marker 17.5* ☎ *435/259–4642* 🌐 *www.sorrelriver.com* 🛏 *56 cabins* 🍴 *No Meals.*

★ **Sunflower Hill Inn**

$$$ | **B&B/INN** | Near the heart of downtown Moab, this historic inn is one of the most charming B&Bs in the region, with elegant rooms surrounded by lawns, gardens, and wondrous shade (a real treat in sunny Moab). **Pros:** just blocks from restaurants and shops; beautifully appointed rooms; most rooms have jetted tubs. **Cons:** children younger than 10 are discouraged; with only six rooms, it can fill up quickly; driveway to the parking area is narrow and a little difficult to maneuver. [$] *Rooms from: $270* ✉ *185 N. 300 E, Moab* ☎ *435/259–2974* 🌐 *www.sunflowerhill.com* 🕒 *Closed Thanksgiving wk and mid-Dec.–Jan. 1* 🛏 *6 rooms* 🍴 *Free Breakfast.*

Shopping

ART GALLERIES

Moab's many art galleries and shops celebrate the perfect weather of spring and fall with a series of exhibits. Art Walks are held the second Saturday of the month from April through June and September through November. Stroll the streets (5–8 pm) to see and purchase original works by Moab and regional artists.

Lema's Kokopelli Gallery

ART GALLERIES | The Lema family has built a reputation for fair prices on a large selection of Native American and Southwest-theme jewelry, art, pottery, rugs, and more. Everything sold here is authentic. ✉ *70 N. Main St., Moab* ☎ *435/259–5055* 🌐 *www.kokopellioutlet.com.*

Moab Made

ART GALLERIES | Featuring all local artists and artisans, the fun shop is a great place to find a personal gift for someone or that perfect piece of art to help you remember your Utah trip. The offerings here are diverse, including prints, jewelry, ceramics, and calendars. The more you look around this creative, colorful space, the more pieces you'll find you want. ✉ *82 N. Main St., Moab* ☎ *435/210–0650* 🌐 *www.moabmade.com.*

Tom Till Gallery

ART GALLERIES | Moab photographer Tom Till is internationally known for his stunning original photographs of the Arches and Canyonlands areas, as well as other regions of the world. His gallery features mostly images of southeastern Utah but also includes other gorgeous, remote places to fuel your wanderlust. Till and fellow photographer Bryan Haile offer personally guided, instructional photography tours of the surrounding area. You'll see many iconic spots and some lesser-known gems and learn how to capture them in photos. While the gallery is open daily through the height of the tourist season, opening times are variable from November through February, with the gallery also open by appointment. ✉ *61 N. Main St., Moab* ☎ *435/259–9808* 🌐 *tomtill.com.*

BOOKS

Back of Beyond Books

BOOKS | A Main Street treasure, this comprehensive shop features books on the American West, environmental studies, Native American cultures, water issues, and western history, as well as rare antiquarian books on the Southwest. There's also a nice nook for kids. ⊠ *83 N. Main St., Moab* ☎ *435/259–5154* ⊕ *www. backofbeyondbooks.com.*

CRAFTING

Desert Thread

KNITTING | Small-town yarn shops are as scarce as hen's teeth, and this one is especially sweet. Run by sisters Cathy and Rosie, it offers a wide selection of beautiful yarn, from fancy to simple, as well as needles, finished pieces, jewelry, and books. If you're sticking around the area for a while, you can sign up for a class or attend the weekly group knit night. ⊠ *29 E. Center St., Moab* ☎ *435/259–8404* ⊕ *www.desertthread. com.*

SUPPLIES

Dave's Corner Market

FOOD | You can get most anything you may need here for your travels, including some of the best cappuccino and Colombian coffee in town. The store is also the heartbeat of the local community, where everyone gossips, discusses local politics, and swaps info on the best hiking and adventure spots. ⊠ *401 Mill Creek Dr., Moab* ☎ *435/259–6999.*

GearHeads Outdoor Store

OTHER SPECIALTY STORE | If you forget anything for your camping, climbing, hiking, or other outdoor adventure, you can get a replacement here. GearHeads is packed with essentials and fun extras like booties and packs for your dog, water filtration straws, and cool souvenirs. The store's owners invented a high-end LED flashlight that has become very popular with the U.S. military, available at the store. ⊠ *471 S. Main St.* ☎ *435/259–4327* ⊕ *www.moabgear.com.*

Moonflower Community Cooperative

FOOD | A peek into the crunchy side of Moab, Moonflower is owned by 1,800 members, though anyone can shop here. The centrally located market is a great place to pick up produce, grab-and-go deli items, house-made baked goods (including vegan options), and hot breakfast and lunch choices. There's also a wide selection of essential oils, soaps, other personal-care products. When you first walk in, check out the vibrant bulletin board full of community events. ⊠ *39 E. 100 N, Moab* ☎ *435/259–5712* ⊕ *moonflower.coop.*

Walker Drug and General Store

DEPARTMENT STORE | A Moab landmark since the 1950s, this is as close as you'll get to a department store for more than 100 miles. Besides pharmacy and drugstore items, you can buy forgotten camping supplies, swimsuits, hats, sunglasses, souvenirs, and almost anything else. The pharmacy section is closed on weekends. ⊠ *290 S. Main St., Moab* ☎ *435/259–5959* ⊕ *www.facebook.com/ walkerdrugmoabut/.*

 # Nightlife

Woody's Tavern

BARS | A staple with Moab locals and visitors alike, Woody's is a unpretentious spot to grab a cold beer in the center of town. The bar's exterior has a Wild West saloon flavor (complete with a fake front), and its interior is more modern but down-home, with pool tables, foosball, and a long wooden bar where you can order a domestic or craft Utah brew. It often hosts karaoke and live music, too. Expect big crowds during Moab's busiest times, especially the Easter Jeep Safari. ⊠ *221 S. Main St., Moab* ☎ *435/259–3550.*

⚡ Activities

AIR EXCURSIONS

Redtail Air Adventures

AIR EXCURSIONS | This company's daily, regional tours give you an eagle's-eye view of the park, and you'll walk away with a new respect for and understanding of the word "wilderness." The Canyonlands Tour, one of several flightseeing options, lasts for one hour. There are also options to see Arches, as well. A two-person minimum applies. ⊠ *Canyonlands Field Airport, 94 W. Aviation Way, Moab ⊹ Off U.S. 191 ☎ 435/259–7421 ⊕ flyredtail.com ✈ From $219 per person.*

CAMPING

Campgrounds in and around Moab range from sprawling RV parks with myriad amenities to quaint, shady retreats near a babbling brook. More than 350 campsites are operated in the vicinity of Moab and Arches National Park by the Bureau of Land Management. The BLM campgrounds along the Colorado River on Highway 128 are some of the most scenic (and affordable) in the area, but most sites cannot be reserved, so it pays to scout your site as early as you can.

Big Bend. Directly across from the eastern cliffs of Arches National Park, this spot on the Colorado River has 23 sites at $20 per night and can accommodate both tents and RVs. There's a sandy beach and shade but no drinking water or hook-ups. Only the three group sites can be reserved. All others are available on a first-come, first-served basis. ⊠ *7.5 miles from U.S. 191 Moab ☎ 435/259–2100 ⊕ www.blm.gov; www.recreation. gov* (group camping reservations).

Dead Horse Point State Park. The park features miles of mountain-biking trails and electrical hookups at every RV site. It's a beautiful setting with 52 sites, but there are no water hookups (though water is available). RV sites are $50 per night, with tent-only sites at $40

(which require up to a 300-foot walk from your car). Yurts, which accommodate up to six people, are available for $150 per night, with a two-night minimum. ⊠ Dead Horse Point State Park, Rte. 313 ● 18 miles off U.S. 191, near the entrance to Canyonlands National Park ☎ *435/259–2614 ⊕ stateparks.utah. gov; www.reserveamerica.com* (camping reservations).

Goose Island Campground. The first campground north of Moab on stunningly beautiful Hwy. 128, this campground is suitable for RVs and tents, offering red rock views and a riverside location. There's no drinking water, but it's close to town. Like all the BLM campgrounds, its 18 sites go for $20 per night. ⊠ *1.4 miles from U.S. 191 on Rte. 128, Moab ⊕ www.blm.gov.*

FOUR-WHEELING

There are thousands of miles of four-wheel-drive roads in and around Moab suitable for all levels of drivers. Seasoned 4x4 drivers might tackle the daunting Moab Rim, Elephant Hill, or Poison Spider Mesa. Novices will be happier touring Long Canyon or Hurrah Pass. If you're not afraid of precipitous cliff edges, the famous Shafer Trail may be a good option for you. Almost all of Moab's river-running companies also offer four-wheeling excursions.

Coyote Land Tours

FOUR-WHEELING | **FAMILY** | Imposing Mercedes-Benz Unimog trucks (which dwarf Hummers) take you to parts of the backcountry where you could never wander on your own. Also available are technical driving tours that challenge drivers with imposing rock formations, washes, and assorted obstacles, and there are tamer sunset excursions and camp-style ride-and-dine trips. They stand by their money-back "great time" guarantee. ⊠ *Moab ☎ 435/260–6056 ⊕ www. coyotelandtours.com ✈ From $59.*

High Point Hummer & ATV

FOUR-WHEELING | **FAMILY** | You can rent UTVs (utility terrain vehicles) or the very distinctive three-wheel Vanderhall cars here, or get a guided tour of the back-country in open-air Hummers or UTVs that seat up to six people. The enthusiastic owners love families and small, intimate groups. Despite the name, ATVs are no longer offered. ⊠ *301 S. Main St., Moab* ☎ *435/259–2972, 877/486–6833* ⊕ *www.highpointhummer.com* ⊲ *From $89 for Hummer tours.*

HIKING

For a great view of the Moab Valley and surrounding red-rock country, hike up the steep **Moab Rim Trail.** For something a little less taxing, try the shady, cool path of **Grandstaff Canyon,** which is off Route Highway 129. At the end of the trail you'll find giant Morning Glory Arch towering over a serene pool created by a natural spring. If you want to take a stroll through the heart of Moab, hop on the **Mill Creek Parkway,** which winds along the creek from one side of town to the other. It's paved and perfect for bicycles, strollers, or joggers. For a taste of slickrock hiking that feels like the backcountry but is easy to access, try the **Corona Arch Trail** off Highway 279. You'll be rewarded with two large arches hidden from view of the highway. The Moab Information Center has a free hiking trail guide.

MOUNTAIN BIKING

Moab is where mountain biking first got Americans' attention in a big way, and the region has earned the well-deserved reputation as the mountain-biking capital of the world. Riders of all ages and skill levels are drawn to the many rugged roads and trails found here. One of the area's best known and most challenging routes, the **Whole Enchilada** is nearly 27 miles of mostly single-track, plus some double-track and fire roads. Descending more than 7,000 feet from the Manti–La Sal National Forest to the Colorado River, it should only be attempted by experienced riders. Expect a rugged trail, perilous drop-offs, and sweeping views of the desert floor far below.

Another popular route is the **Slickrock Trail,** a stunning area of steep Navajo Sandstone dunes a few miles east of Moab. Beginners should master the 2⅓-mile practice loop before attempting the longer, and very challenging, 10-mile loop.

More moderate rides can be found on the **Gemini Bridges** or **Monitor and Merrimac Trails,** both found off U.S. 191 north of Moab. **Klondike Bluffs,** north of Moab, is an excellent novice ride, as are sections of the newer trails in the **Klonzo Trails** system.

The Moab Information Center carries a free biking trail guide. Mountain-bike rentals range from $40 for a good bike to $85 for a top-of-the-line workhorse. If you want to go on a guided ride, expect to pay between $125 and $170 per person for a half-day, and $155 to $250 for a full day, including the cost of the bike rental. You can save money by joining a larger group to keep the per-person rates down; even a party of two will save drastically over a single rider. Several companies offer shuttles to and from the trailheads.

Chile Pepper Bike Shop

BIKING | For mountain bike rentals, sales, service, and gear, plus espresso, stop here before you set out. ⊠ *702 S. Main St., Moab* ☎ *435/259–4688* ⊕ *www. chilebikes.com.*

Dual Sport Utah

BIKING | If you're into dirt biking, this is the only outfitter in Moab specializing in street-legal, off-road dirt-bike tours and rentals. You can also rent pedal-assist, electric bikes. Follow the Klondike Bluffs Trail to Arches, or negotiate the White Rim Trail in Canyonlands in a fraction of the time you would spend on a mountain bike. ⊠ *197 W. Center St., Moab* ☎ *435/260–2724* ⊕ *www.dualsportutah. com* ⊲ *$300 for rentals.*

Escape Adventures

BIKING | FAMILY | With offices in Moab and Las Vegas, this tour company and outfitter focuses on biking excursions, many of which incorporate hiking and rafting. While it offers some road bike trips (including a few that allow electric bikes) the company is best known for mountain biking across the West. Popular Moab-based tours include a four-day trip on the White Rim Trail and a five-day adventure in The Maze, both rugged and remote sections of Canyonlands National Park. Trips run the gamut from challenging to family-friendly. ⊠ *391 S. Main St., Moab* ☎ *800/559–1978, 435/259–7423 Moab Cyclery* ⊕ *www.escapeadventures.com* ⊠ *From $999 for a tour-day mountain bike tour in Canyonlands.*

★ Poison Spider Bicycles

BIKING | In a town of great bike shops, this fully loaded store is one of the best. Poison Spider serves the thriving road-cycling community as well as mountain bikers. Rent, buy, or service your bike here. You can also arrange for shuttle and guide services and purchase merchandise. Want to ship your bike to Moab for your adventure? Poison Spider will store it until you arrive, and the staff will reassemble it for you and make sure everything is in perfect working order. ⊠ *497 N. Main St., Moab* ☎ *435/259–7882, 800/635–1792* ⊕ *www.poisonspiderbicycles.com.*

Rim Tours

BIKING | Reliable, friendly, and professional, Rim Tours has been taking guests on guided one-day or multiday mountain-bike tours, including Dead Horse Point single-track (half- or full day) and the White Rim Trail (multiday, inside Canyonlands National Park) since 1985. E-bike tours are also available. Bike skills a little rusty? Rim Tours also offers mountain bike instructional tours. Group rates are available. ⊠ *1233 S. U.S. 191, Moab* ☎ *435/259–5223* ⊕ *www.rimtours.com* ⊠ *Starts at $175.*

Western Spirit Cycling Adventures

BIKING | Head here for fully supported, go-at-your-own-pace, multiday mountain-bike, gravel-bike, and road-bike tours throughout the western states, including trips to Canyonlands, Bears Ears, and the 140-mile Kokopelli Trail, which runs from Grand Junction, Colorado, to Moab. Guides versed in the geologic wonders of the area cook up meals worthy of the scenery each night. Ask about family rides and road-bike trips, too. Electric bicycles are available. ⊠ *478 S. Mill Creek Dr., Moab* ☎ *435/259–8732, 800/845–2453* ⊕ *www.westernspirit.com* ⊠ *From $1195.*

MULTISPORT OUTFITTERS

Outdoor lovers wear many hats in Moab: boaters, bikers, and even Jeep-drivers. Here are a few companies that cater to a range of adventure seekers.

★ Adrift Adventures

BOATING | FAMILY | This outfitter takes pride in well-trained guides who can take you via foot, raft, kayak, 4X4, jet boat, stand-up paddleboard, and more, all over the Moab area, including the Colorado and Green Rivers, and on Arches Jeep and hiking adventures. It's also one of only two companies to have a special-use permit to go into the backcountry of Arches and Canyonlands National Parks. They also offer history, movie, and rock-art tours. They've been in business since 1977 and have a great reputation around town. ⊠ *378 N. Main St., Moab* ☎ *435/259–8594, 800/874–4483* ⊕ *www.adrift.net* ⊠ *From $70.*

Moab Adventure Center

ADVENTURE TOURS | FAMILY | At the prominent storefront on Main Street you can schedule most any type of local adventure experience you want, including rafting, Hummer tours, scenic flights, hikes, balloon rides, and a couple of excellent bus overview tours of Arches highlights. You can also purchase clothing and outdoor gear for your visit. ⊠ *225 S. Main St., Moab* ☎ *435/259–7019,*

866/904–1163 ⊕ www.moabadventure-center.com ⊠ From $89.

NAVTEC Expeditions

ADVENTURE TOURS | FAMILY | Doc Williams was the first doctor in Moab in 1896, and some of his descendants never left, sharing his love for the area through this rafting, canyoneering, and 4X4 company. Whether you want to explore the region by boat, boots, or wheels, you'll find a multitude of one-day and multiday options here. NAVTEC is one of only two companies with a special-use permit to go into the backcountry of Arches and Canyonlands National Parks. ⊠ 321 N. Main St., Moab ☎ 435/259–7983 ⊕ www.navtec.com ⊠ From $95.

RIVER EXPEDITIONS

On the Colorado River northeast of Arches and very near Moab, you can take one of America's most scenic—but not intimidating—river-raft rides. The river rolls by the red Fisher Towers as they rise into the sky in front of the La Sal Mountains. A day trip on this stretch of the river will take you about 15 miles. Outfitters offer full-, half-, or multiday adventures here. Upriver, in narrow, winding Westwater Canyon near the Utah–Colorado border, the Colorado River cuts through the oldest exposed geologic layer on Earth. Most outfitters offer this trip as a one-day getaway, but you may also take as long as three days to complete the journey. A permit is required from the Bureau of Land Management (BLM) in Moab to run Westwater Canyon.

Canyonlands by Night & Day

BOAT TOURS | FAMILY | Since 1963 this outfitter has been known for its Sound and Light Show Jet Boat Tour, a two-hour, after-dark boat ride on the Colorado River (March–October). While illuminating the canyon walls with 40,000 watts, the trip includes music and narration highlighting Moab's history, Native American legends, and geologic formations along the river. A dutch oven dinner is included, though you can exclude it and save $10. Daytime jet boat tours are offered, too, as well as tours by Hummer, airplane, and helicopter (land and air tours are offered year-round). ⊠ 1861 U.S. 191, Moab ☎ 435/259–2628, 800/394–9978 ⊕ www.canyonlandsbynight.com ⊠ Boat tour with dinner from $79.

OARS Canyonlands Rafting

WHITE-WATER RAFTING | FAMILY | This well-regarded outfitter can take you for several days of rafting the Colorado, Green, and San Juan Rivers. OARS is an authorized concessionaire in Canyonlands National Park and Dinosaur National Monument and also offers trips outside the parks. Note that trips in the Moab area do not meet at the office but instead originate wherever your tour guide indicates. ⊠ 2540 U.S. 191, Moab ☎ 435/259–5865, 800/346–6277 ⊕ www.oars.com/utah ⊠ From $119.

Sheri Griffith River Expeditions

WHITE-WATER RAFTING | FAMILY | In addition to trips through the white water of Cataract, Westwater, and Desolation Canyons, on the Colorado and Green Rivers, this company also offers specialty expeditions for women, writers, photographers, and families. One of their more luxurious expeditions features dinners cooked by a professional chef and served on linen-covered tables. Cots and other sleeping amenities also make roughing it a little more comfortable. ⊠ 2231 S. U.S. 191, Moab ☎ 435/259–8229, 800/332–2439 ⊕ www.griffithexp.com ⊠ From $195.

ROCK CLIMBING

Rock climbing is an integral part of Moab culture. The area's rock walls and towers bring climbers from around the world, and a surprising number end up sticking around and building a life in this desert community. Moab offers some of the best climbing challenges in the country, and any enthusiast will find bliss here.

Desert Highlights

ROCK CLIMBING | This guide company takes adventurous types on descents and ascents through canyons on customizable half- and full-day trips around Moab. Expect scrambling, hiking, and rappelling, mostly on BLM land. Packrafting trips are also available, as are guided hikes in Arches and Canyonlands. Most trips have a two-person minimum, and all trips are private, meaning the only ones on the adventure will be your group and your guide. ⊠ *16 S. 100 E, Moab* ☎ *435/259–4433* ⊕ *www.deserthighlights.com* 🖼 *From $124.*

★ Moab Cliffs & Canyons

ROCK CLIMBING | In a town where everyone seems to offer rafting and 4X4 expeditions, Moab Cliffs & Canyons focuses on canyoneering, climbing, and rappelling—for novice and veteran adventurers. Prices vary according to how many people sign up. This is the outfitter that provided technical assistance to the crew on the movie *127 Hours*. ⊠ *253 N. Main St., Moab* ☎ *435/259–3317, 877/641–5271* ⊕ *www.cliffsandcanyons. com* 🖼 *From $125.*

Pagan Mountaineering

ROCK CLIMBING | Climbers in need of gear and advice on local terrain should speak with the knowledgeable staff here, who can help plot your adventure. ⊠ *59 S. Main St., No. 2* ☎ *435/259–1117.*

Green River

70 miles west of the Colorado state line and about 50 miles northwest of Moab.

The town of Green River and the namesake waterway that runs through it are historically important. Early Native Americans used the river for centuries; the Old Spanish Trail crossed it, and the Denver & Rio Grande Railroad bridged it in 1883. Some say the "green" refers to the color of the water; others claim it's named for the plants along the riverbank.

And yet another story gives the credit to a mysterious trapper named Green. Whatever the etymology, Green River remains a sleepy little town—a low-key break from some of the more hip tourist communities in southern Utah.

Green River has a few affordable dining and lodging options and the excellent John Wesley Powell River History Museum. Each September the fragrance of fresh melons—cantaloupe, watermelon, honeydew, and canary—fills the air, especially during Melon Days, a family-fun harvest celebration held annually on the third weekend of the month.

GETTING HERE AND AROUND

Reaching Green River is as easy as finding I–70. The town is 180 miles southeast of Salt Lake City, 100 miles west of Grand Junction, Colorado, and 50 miles northwest of Moab. Though most people arrive here by car, the town is served by both Amtrak and Greyhound.

 Sights

Green River State Park

STATE/PROVINCIAL PARK | **FAMILY** | A shady respite on the banks of the Green River, this park is best known for its golf course. It's also the starting point for boaters drifting along the river through Labyrinth and Stillwater Canyons. Fishing and bird-watching are other favorite pastimes here. ⊠ *450 S. Green River Rd., Green River* ☎ *435/564–3633, 435/564–8882 golf course, 800/322–3770 for campground reservations* ⊕ *stateparks. utah.gov* 🖼 *$7 per vehicle.*

★ John Wesley Powell River History Museum

HISTORY MUSEUM | **FAMILY** | Learn what it was like to travel down the Green and Colorado Rivers in the 1800s in wooden boats. A series of displays tracks the Powell Party's arduous, dangerous 1869 journey, and visitors can watch the award-winning film *Journey Into the Unknown* for a cinematic taste of the

The ghostly figures etched in the walls of Sego Canyon date back some 4,000 years.

white-water adventure. The center also houses the River Runner's Hall of Fame, a tribute to those who have followed in Powell's wake. River-theme art occupies a gallery, and there's a dinosaur exhibit on the lower level. ✉ *1765 E. Main St., Green River* ☎ *435/564–3427* 🌐 *www.johnwesleypowell.com* 🎟 *$7* 🕒 *Closed Sun.*

Sego Canyon Rock Art Interpretive Site
INDIGENOUS SIGHT | **FAMILY** | Sego is one of the most dramatic and mystifying rock-art sites in the entire state. Large, ghost-like rock-art figures painted and etched by Native Americans approximately 4,000 years ago cover these canyon walls. There's also art left by the Ute from the 19th century. Distinctive for their large anthropomorphic figures, and for horses, buffalo, and shields painted with red-and-white pigment, these rare drawings are a must-see. A well-preserved ghost town is also nearby. ✉ *I–70, Exit 187, Thompson Springs* ✣ *25 miles east of Green River on I–70, at Exit 187 go north onto Hwy. 94 through Thompson Springs* ☎ *435/259–2100 Bureau of Land Management Office in Moab* 🌐 *www.blm.gov.*

🍴 Restaurants

Ray's Tavern
$ | **AMERICAN** | In little downtown Green River, Ray's is something of a western legend and a favorite hangout for river runners. The bar that runs the length of this 1940s restaurant reminds you this is still a tavern and a serious watering hole—but all the photos and rafting memorabilia make it also comfortable for families. **Known for:** legendary burgers; great people-watching; homemade apple pie. [$] *Average main: $12* ✉ *25 S. Broadway, Green River* ☎ *435/564–3511.*

Tamarisk Restaurant
$ | **AMERICAN** | **FAMILY** | Views of the Green River make this a restorative stop after a long drive. Though the interior has gotten hipper in recent years, the breakfast, lunch, and dinner menus are filled with the same classic diner favorites the

spot has been serving up for decades. **Known for:** famous views of the Green River; Navajo tacos; green chili burgers. $ *Average main: $14* ✉ *1710 E. Main St., Green River* ☎ *435/564–8109* ⊕ *www.tamariskrestaurant.com.*

Hotels

★ River Rock Inn Bed & Breakfast

$$ | **B&B/INN** | This reimagined roadside motel has morphed into Green River's only boutique lodging, with an upscale western motif and individually decorated rooms right in the heart of downtown. **Pros:** pool is perfect for cooling down on hot days; the best lodging in Green River; oversize showers. **Cons:** about 50 miles from Arches National Park; not pet-friendly; closes in the winter months. $ *Rooms from: $170* ✉ *20 W. Main St., Green River* ☎ *435/564–7625* ⊕ *www.riverrockinnutah.com* ⊗ *Closed early Jan. and Feb.* ⇥ *12 rooms* ⦿ *Free Breakfast.*

River Terrace

$$ | **HOTEL** | The peaceful setting, on the bank of the Green River, is conducive to a good night's rest, and this nicely maintained hotel is conveniently less than 2 miles off Interstate 70, although nearly an hour's drive from Arches. **Pros:** shady riverside location (be sure to request a river-view room); pool for cooling off on hot days; on-site restaurant. **Cons:** in a sleepy town with few attractions; not within walking distance of downtown Green River; about 50 miles north of Moab. $ *Rooms from: $141* ✉ *1740 E. Main St., Green River* ☎ *435/564–3401, 877/564–3401* ⊕ *www.river-terrace.com* ⇥ *50 rooms* ⦿ *Free Breakfast.*

🏃 Activities

RIVER FLOAT TRIPS

Bearing little resemblance to its name, Desolation Canyon acquaints those who venture down the Green River with some of the last true American wilderness: a lush, verdant canyon, where the rapids promise more laughter than fear. It's a favorite destination of canoe paddlers, kayakers, and novice rafters. May through September, raft trips can be arranged by outfitters in Green River or Moab. South of town the river drifts at a lazier pace through Labyrinth and Stillwater Canyons, and the stretch south to Mineral Bottom in Canyonlands is best suited to canoes and motor boats.

For additional river-trip outfitters, see the Moab Activities section.

Colorado River and Trail Expeditions

RAFTING | **FAMILY** | This well-known outfitter has been offering trips on the Green and Colorado Rivers since the 1970s. On the Green River, you can choose from a relaxing one-day float through Gray Canyon up to a six-day adventure through the high cliffs and moderate rapids of Cataract Canyon. There are many trips to choose from, and knowledgeable staff can walk you through the best one for your needs. ✉ *255 1000 N, Green River* ☎ *800/253–7328* ⊕ *www.crateinc.com* ⌨ *One-day rafting trips from $99.*

Holiday River Expeditions

WHITE-WATER RAFTING | **FAMILY** | Since 1966, this outfitter has offered one-day and multiday trips on the San Juan, Green, and Colorado Rivers, including inside Canyonlands National Park. They also offer multisport trips, women's, LGBTQ+, and BIPOC retreats, and bike adventures, including to the San Rafael Swell and the Canyonlands' White Rim Trail as well as the remote Maze

District. ✉ *2075 E. Main St., Green River* ☎ *435/564–3273, 800/624–6323* 🌐 *www.bikeraft.com* 🎫 *From $270.*

Hanksville

57 miles southwest of Green River via Hwy. 24, 95 miles northwest of Natural Bridges National Monument via Hwy. 95.

In its early years, Hanksville was the closest settlement to Robbers Roost country, a hangout for Butch Cassidy and his crew of outlaws, the Wild Bunch. Today, it's mostly popular with rafters, as it's at the confluence of the Fremont and Muddy Rivers, which combine to make the isolated, scenic Dirty Devil River. Named by the famed John Wesley Powell expedition for its less-than-clear water, it offers seasonal floats for adventurous river runners. During its busiest times, Hanksville will have traffic jams so long they'll make your head spin (often with travelers returning from or heading to Lake Powell). The high season here runs from March through June and September through November, though some services are available year-round. With gas, food, and a few shops—and one strange little roadside "art garden"—this is a surprisingly pleasant stop in the middle of nowhere.

GETTING HERE AND AROUND

To get to tiny Hanksville from Green River, head west on I–70 for about 10 miles, then take Exit 149 onto Highway 24. You'll head southwest about 45 miles to Hanksville.

VISITOR INFORMATION

CONTACTS Bureau of Land Management. ✉ *380 S. 100 W, Hanksville* ☎ *435/542–3461* 🌐 *www.blm.gov.*

Sights

Carl's Critter Garden

OTHER ATTRACTION | FAMILY | It's impossible to miss this delightfully weird roadside collection of massive scrap-metal sculptures, from huge dinosaurs to tiny, buglike creatures. The longer you stay, the more details you see, and somehow the small sign reading "Welcome to the Center of the Universe" feels right on. The "garden" promotes love and is free, though it does take donations in a little box. ✉ *Hwy. 24, Hanksville* ✥ *From Whispering Pines Motel, head west about 0.6 mile on Hwy. 24. It's directly across from post office* 🎫 *Free.*

Goblin Valley State Park

STATE/PROVINCIAL PARK | FAMILY | Hundreds of orange, mushroom-like rocks known as "hoodoos" rise up from the desert floor about 30 miles northwest of Hanksville. Short, easy trails wind through the bizarre goblins making it a fun walk for kids and adults. Be forewarned that during busy times of the year, there may be a wait time to enter the park. ✉ *Hwy. 24, Green River* ☎ *435/275–4584* 🌐 *stateparks.utah.gov* 🎫 *$20 per vehicle.*

Restaurants

Duke's Slickrock Grill

$$ | SOUTHWESTERN | Learning into the area's Wild West past, this casual spot has cowboy hats and cow skulls on the walls, a cardboard cutout of John Wayne—and some of the best smoked meats around. It offers Southwestern takes on breakfast, lunch, and dinner, all in generous portions, and even has a bar to hang out in after a long day of driving or river rafting. **Known for:** tasty, heaping nachos; house-smoked ribs and brisket; full bar. [$] *Average main: $16* ✉ *245 E. Hwy. 24, Hanksville* ☎ *435/542–3235* 🌐 *www.dukesslickrock.com* ⏲ *Closed early Nov.–Feb.*

Stan's Burger Shak

$ | **BURGER** | **FAMILY** | This casual burger joint connected to a gas station is probably the best-known stop between Lake Powell and Capitol Reef. Even if you're not hungry, it's worth a visit for the incredibly thick shakes that rise out of their cups, but just be ready for some long lines on busy days. **Known for:** shakes in an array of flavors, from peach cobbler to cookie dough; juicy double cheeseburgers; delicious homemade onion rings. [$] *Average main: $12* ✉ *150 S. Hwy. 95, Hanksville* ☎ *435/542–3330* 🌐 *www.stansburgershak.com.*

Hotels

Whispering Sands Motel

$$ | **MOTEL** | The real gems of this roadside motel are the updated cabins with warm, wooden walls and big windows, though traditional motel rooms are offered at a lower price, and all rooms have little conveniences like microwaves and refrigerators. **Pros:** Hanksville's only motel; open year-round; located next to famed Stan's Burger Shak. **Cons:** books up months in advance during busy times; many rooms are older and haven't been updated; Hanksville has few amenities. [$] *Rooms from: $149* ✉ *90 Hwy. 95, Hanksville* ☎ *435/542–3238* 🌐 *www.dukesslickrock.com* 🛏 *23 rooms* 🍴 *No Meals.*

Activities

RIVER FLOAT TRIPS

Although nowhere near as popular a destination as other nearby waterways, the Dirty Devil River, a tributary of the Colorado, offers a chance to explore unpeopled wilderness but requires a substantial amount of planning. Often only deep enough to float unobstructed during late winter and spring (often only from February through April), the river can also be run in the early summer—as long as you drag your boat through the shallow spots. The most popular put-in is just a few miles outside of Hanksville, at the end of 650 East Road (Landfill Road).

It can take anywhere from 7 to 14 days to float the 80 miles to the take-out in Hite, depending on how many day trips up various tributaries you choose along the way. Boats can be rented at shops in Moab, including NAVTEC, though some companies won't allow their gear to travel that far. For any float down the Dirty Devil, it's imperative you carry all the food, water, and gear you need for the entire trip, as you'll be far from any town. Always make sure to contact the Bureau of Land Management office in Hanksville (see Visitor Information above) for up-to-date conditions and advice before heading out.

Backcountry Packraft Rentals

RAFTING | With no boat rentals in Hanksville, this rent-by-mail company, which is based out of Montana, could be a convenient option for your trip. It specializes in packrafts—small, lightweight rafts meant to fit into backpacks—that can be shipped anywhere in the United States. Paddles, personal flotation devices, helmets, and other gear can also be rented. When your float is over, you simply send all your rented gear back. ☎ *406/272–6468* 🌐 *www.backcountrypackrafts.com.*

Monticello

53 miles south of Moab via U.S. 191.

Monticello, the seat of San Juan County, is a mostly Mormon community. This quiet town has seen some growth in recent years, mostly in the form of new motels made necessary by a steady stream of tourists venturing south from Moab, but it still offers very few dining or shopping opportunities. Nevertheless, with several inexpensive lodging choices, it's a more convenient alternative to Moab for those visiting the Needles District of Canyonlands National Park. At 7,000 feet, Monticello provides a cool respite from the summer heat of the desert, and it's at the doorstep of the Abajo Mountains. To access the highest point in the range, 11,360-foot Abajo Peak, take a road that branches off the graded, 22-mile Blue Mountain Loop (Forest Service Road 105, which begins in Monticello).

ESSENTIALS
VISITOR INFORMATION Monticello Utah Welcome Center. ⊠ *216 S. Main St., Monticello* ☎ *435/587–3401.*

Sights

★ Bears Ears National Monument
INDIGENOUS SIGHT | FAMILY | Named for its striking pair of massive buttes, Bears Ears National Monument stretches across more than a million acres of land sacred to several Native American tribes. Countless archaeological sites and artifacts dot this remote landscape, including cliff dwellings, petroglyphs, pictographs, and a prehistoric road system. The scenery is awe-inspiring, too, with remote canyons, vast grasslands, and the kind of towering red-rock formations southern Utah is famous for. Opportunities abound here to hike, rock climb, river raft, and embark on scenic drives, and visitor information is available at both the U.S. Bureau of Land Management and U.S. Forest Service offices in Monticello. Because of the long history that surrounds you in Bears Ears, being especially respectful of your surroundings is a must. In Bluff, the **Bears Ears Education Center** offers further guidance on how to explore such a culturally important area.

While entering the monument is free, permits and passes are required in the Shash Jáa Special Recreation Management Area and the Cedar Mesa Special Recreation Management Area. Depending on the time of year, these can be purchased at trailheads or at ⊕ www.recreation.gov. The hike to **Moon House,** an Ancestral Puebloan dwelling, is so popular that only 20 hikers are allowed per day

and a separate permit is required. ⊠ *BLM Monticello Field Office, 365 N. Main St., Monticello* ☎ *435/587–1510 BLM Cedar Mesa permit desk, 435/587–1500 BLM Monticello Field Office, 435/587–2041 U.S. Forest Service Monticello Ranger District Office* ⊕ *www.blm.gov* ⓈFree.

Hotels

Inn at the Canyons
$$ | HOTEL | FAMILY | One of the largest properties in Monticello, which is just under an hour from the Needles District Visitor Center, this is also one of the comfiest, with a heated indoor pool and a hot tub that's just what the doctor ordered for soaking adventure-weary bodies, and the rates are significantly cheaper than almost anything in Moab. **Pros:** close to Needles District of Canyonlands; year-round indoor pool and hot tub; pets allowed on request with a pet fee. **Cons:** not in walking distance of many restaurants or sites; in a sleepy town with not many amenities; rates higher than many other properties in town. Ⓢ *Rooms from: $159* ⊠ *533 N. Main St., Monticello* ☎ *435/587–2458* ⊕ *www. monticellocanyonlandsinn.com* ↪ *43 rooms* Ⓞ*Free Breakfast.*

Activities

GOATreks
ADVENTURE TOURS | FAMILY | What could make exploring Southeastern Utah's expansive, red-rock scenery even more magical? Goats. This fun tour company offers guided half- and one-day hikes assisted by friendly pack goats who love to be petted. Created by a husband-and-wife team of trained naturalists, GOATreks explores some of the best lesser-known areas around Bears Ears National Monument and Moab, with photo opportunities few people get. The pair are happy to help you customize your trip, tailoring it to your ability and what kind of terrain you hope to experience.

Snacks are provided for half-day hikes, while full-day jaunts include lunch—and yes, the goats carry the food in their little customized packs. When you book a tour, you'll be given a meeting point. ☎ 231/649–2100 ⊕ www.goatreks.com 🖃 From $75 for a ½-day hike.

Blanding

19 miles south of Monticello, 126 miles south of Green River.

For nearly the first 20 years of its history, this small town near the base of the Abajo and Henry Mountains was known as Grayson. This changed when wealthy Thomas Bicknell offered a huge library of books to any town willing to take his name. In the end, another town got the name, and Blanding was honored with Bicknell's wife's maiden name, as well as a share of the book bounty.

The town itself is not a big draw, but it's a pleasant and peaceful place to stroll and stop over between adventures. As the biggest town in San Juan County and the gateway to several national monuments, state parks, and two Native American reservations, it remains vital in its own way.

GETTING HERE AND AROUND
The town is about 90 minutes from Moab traveling south on U.S. 191.

VISITOR INFORMATION
CONTACTS Blanding Visitor Center. ☒ 12 N. Grayson Pkwy., Blanding ☎ 435/678–3662 ⊕ www.blanding-ut.gov.

Sights

The Dinosaur Museum
HISTORY MUSEUM | FAMILY | Life-size dino replicas in dramatic poses will delight kids. The small museum also features many skeletons, fossils, and footprints— and reportedly the world's largest collection of movie posters starring Godzilla and other monsters dating back to the early days of film. ☒ 754 S. 200 W, Blanding ☎ 435/678–3454 ⊕ www. dinosaur-museum.org 🖃 $6 ⊗ Closed Nov.–mid-Apr.

★ Edge of the Cedars State Park Museum
HISTORY MUSEUM | FAMILY | Behind what is one of the nation's foremost museums dedicated to the Ancestral Puebloan culture, an interpretive trail leads to a village that they once inhabited. Portions have been partially excavated, and visitors can climb down a ladder into a 1,000-year-old ceremonial room called a kiva. The museum displays a variety of pots, baskets, spear points, and other rare artifacts. There's even a sash made from the colorful feathers of a scarlet macaw, a bird native to Mexico or Central America, which proves the vast distances indigenous trade routes spanned. ☒ 660 W. 400 N, Blanding ☎ 435/678–2238 ⊕ stateparks.utah.gov 🖃 $5 ⊗ Closed Sun. in Dec.–Feb.

Hovenweep National Monument
INDIGENOUS SIGHT | The best place in southeast Utah to see ancient tower ruins dotting the scenic cliffs, if you're headed south from Canyonlands and have an interest in Ancestral Puebloan culture, a visit to this monument is a must. Park rangers strongly advise following printed maps and signs from U.S. 191 near Blanding, Utah, or County Road G from Cortez, Colorado; GPS is not reliable here. Once you arrive, you'll find unusual tower structures (which may have been used for astronomical observation) and ancient dwellings. ☒ Hovenweep Rd. ☎ 970/562–4282 ⊕ www.nps. gov/hove.

Newspaper Rock State Historic Monument
INDIGENOUS SIGHT | FAMILY | One of the West's most famous rock-art sites, about 15 miles west of U.S. 191, this site contains Native American designs engraved on the rock over the course of 2,000 years. Early pioneers and explorers to the region named the site Newspaper Rock

because they believed the rock, crowded with drawings, constituted a written language with which early people communicated. Archaeologists now agree that the petroglyphs do not represent language. ✉ *Hwy. 211, Blanding.*

🍴 Restaurants

Homestead Steak House
$$ | **STEAKHOUSE** | The only full-service restaurant serving dinner in town, this very casual eatery specializes in authentic Navajo fry bread, used in a variety of massive, delicious dishes. Often busy, people also come here for a full range of steak house staples, fish dishes, and the only salad bar around. **Known for:** Navajo tacos; beef short ribs; homemade desserts. [$] *Average main: $20* ✉ *121 E. Center St.* ☎ *435/678–3456* 🌐 *www.homesteadsteakhouseut.com* 🕒 *Closed Jan.–early Feb. Closed Sun. No lunch Sat.*

Patio Diner
$ | **BURGER** | **FAMILY** | A former drive-in for generations, this casual spot leans into its retro roots, with robin's-egg–blue booths and checkerboard floors—and the best burgers, shakes, and fries in town. This is also the perfect place to try Utah's famous fry sauce, made from ketchup, mayonnaise, and a few other ingredients too secret to name. **Known for:** golden-brown onion rings; big, made-to-order burgers and other sandwiches; Oreo shakes and other ice-cream treats. [$] *Average main: $9* ✉ *95 N. Grayson Pkwy., Blanding* ☎ *435/678–2177* 🌐 *www.patiodiner.com* 🕒 *Closed Sun.*

🛏 Hotels

Stone Lizard Lodge
$$ | **HOTEL** | This rustic yet classy spot stands out from Blanding's mix of chain hotels and motor lodges with its serene garden area and individually decorated rooms, all with local art on the walls and Navajo-style rugs on the hardwood floors. **Pros:** one of the most comfortable lodgings around; hearty continental breakfast, with several hot items, chia pudding, and homemade cinnamon rolls; calming garden area with shaded spots to sit and lounge. **Cons:** due to its age, some rooms are small; more expensive than most other lodgings in the area; only a limited number of pet-friendly rooms (and only dogs are allowed). [$] *Rooms from: $144* ✉ *88 W. Center St., Blanding* ☎ *435/678–3323* 🌐 *www.stonelizardlodge.com* 🛏 *17 rooms* 🍴 *Free Breakfast.*

Natural Bridges National Monument

41 miles west of Blanding.

The scenery and rock formations found in this national monument must be seen to be believed.

👁 Sights

Natural Bridges National Monument
NATIONAL PARK | **FAMILY** | Stunning natural bridges, ancient Native American ruins, and magnificent scenery throughout make Natural Bridges National Monument a must-see if you have time to make the trip. Sipapu is one of the largest natural bridges in the world, spanning 268 feet and standing 220 feet tall. You can take in the Sipapu, Owachomo, and Kachina Bridges via an 8.6-mile round-trip hike that meanders around and under them. A 13-site primitive campground is an optimal spot for stargazing. The national monument is 40 miles from Blanding. ✉ *Hwy. 275, off Hwy. 95, Natural Bridges National Monument* ☎ *435/692–1234* 🌐 *www.nps.gov/nabr* 🎟 *$20 per vehicle.*

Natural Bridges National Monument preserves several natural bridges made from eroded sandstone, including beautiful Owachomo.

Bluff

25 miles south of Blanding via U.S. 191.

Bluff is a small but unexpectedly cool town that's built a reputation for quality lodging and restaurants, plus many fun annual events. Like Moab, it doesn't have a palpable Mormon feel, and it remains a mini–melting pot of Navajos, river rats, hippies, and old-time Utahans. The remote spot is a respite from the much busier Moab area, and in keeping with that, the cell service is spotty at best.

Settled in 1880, Bluff is one of southeastern Utah's oldest towns. Mormon pioneers from the original Hole in the Rock journey built a ranching empire that made the town, at one time, the richest per capita in the state. Although this early period of affluence passed, several historic Victorian-style homes remain. Pick up the free brochure "Historic Bluff by Bicycle and on Foot" at any business in town. Most of the original homes from the 1880 town-site of Bluff City are part of the Bluff Historic District. In a dozen or so blocks, there are 42 historic structures, most built between about 1890 and 1905. Also downtown, the re-created cabins at **Bluff Fort** offer an immersive look into the area's pioneer history.

GETTING HERE AND AROUND

Bluff is just under two hours from Moab south on U.S. 191.

FESTIVALS

Bear Dance

CULTURAL FESTIVALS | FAMILY | Every September you can see traditional Ute ceremonial dances at the Bear Dance. The dance takes place during a four-day celebration held Labor Day weekend on the Ute Reservation. The Ute Mountain powwow and dance represent the end of summer and the impending hibernation of the bear. ⊠ *Beaver La., White Mesa* ☏ *435/678–3621.*

Bluff Arts Festival

ARTS FESTIVALS | A growing local artist community shows off its talent during this annual festival in mid-October. Each year features a different theme and touts four days of artist receptions, lectures, and workshops, along with the Bluff Film Festival. ⊠ *Bluff* ☎ *435/672–2253* ⊕ *www.bluffartsfestival.org* 🖾 *Free.*

Bluff International Balloon Festival

FESTIVALS | **FAMILY** | Colorful hot-air balloons—some from as far away as England—take to the skies over the Valley of the Gods and the town of Bluff during this mid-January festival, held during the Martin Luther King Jr. holiday weekend. Attend the "glow in" if weather allows, and see balloons illuminated against the night sky by the flame from the propane heaters that fill them with hot air. Bring warm clothing and expect crisp, clear weather. ⊠ *Bluff* ☎ *435/672–2341* ⊕ *www.bluffutah.org* 🖾 *Free.*

Sights

Bears Ears Education Center

VISITOR CENTER | **FAMILY** | For any visit to Bears Ears National Monument, this is as important a stop as the BLM office in Monticello. Run by the nonprofit Bears Ears Partnership, this is not an official visitor center for the park, but it does focus on teaching visitors how to explore Bears Ears respectfully. It's also a great place to pick up maps for your trip, and do peruse the gift shop and bookstore. Indigenous pottery shards are on display, as are more modern pieces by indigenous artisans showcasing the kind of work Native people created in the area thousands of years ago. The visitor center typically has a seasonal closure in summer and winter, though the dates change depending on visitation. The Partnership's thorough website also has plenty of up-to-date information for your journey. ⊠ *567 W. Main St., Bluff* ☎ *435/672–2402* ⊕ *bearsearspartnership.org* 🖾 *Free* ⊙ *Closed Tues. and Wed. and Jan. and Feb. and July and Aug.*

★ Bluff Fort

HISTORIC SIGHT | **FAMILY** | With grounds almost a full city block in size, this very kid-friendly restored fort is a must-see, transporting you back to the 1880s and into the lives of the Mormon pioneers who settled in Bluff. Wander in and out of tiny re-created cabins (plus one original), each representing the experience of a founding family. Their descendants even helped build and decorate the cabins with family artifacts and photos, displayed alongside written histories. Children can try their hand at roping toy steers or buy some of the house-made candy at the little kitchen, which also sells soft-serve ice cream and other snacks.

A reconstructed co-op store anchors the fort and doubles as a visitor center, displaying photos and a video that tell more of the area's past. There you can also buy crafts handmade by the fort's many friendly volunteers. Dressed in historical garb, they're happy to go into even more detail with you about the history of this place and the stunning area that surrounds it. Though the grounds are open daily, the store closes on Sunday. ⊠ *550 Black Locust Ave., Bluff* ☎ *435/672–9995* ⊕ *www.hirf.org* 🖾 *Free* ⊙ *Store closed Sun.*

Four Corners Monument

OTHER ATTRACTION | **FAMILY** | The Navajo Nation manages this landmark about 65 miles southeast of Bluff and 6 miles north of Teec Nos Pos, Arizona. Primarily a photo-op spot, you'll also find Navajo and Ute artisans selling authentic jewelry and crafts, as well as traditional foods. It's the only place in the United States where four states meet at one single point. Surveyors now believe the monument—a stone and metal marker sitting at the intersection of Colorado, Arizona, Utah, and New Mexico—is roughly 1,800 feet east of the correct spot. The small entry fee of $8 per person is cash-only, so be sure to get money prior to heading out. ⊠ *Four Corners Monument Rd., off U.S. 160, Bluff* 🖾 *$8.*

Sand Island Recreation Area
INDIGENOUS SIGHT | Three miles southwest of Bluff you'll find a large panel of Ancestral Puebloan rock art. The panel includes several large images of Kokopelli, the mischief-maker from Puebloan lore. ✉ *U.S. 191, Bluff* ☎ *435/587–1500 Monticello BLM office.*

★ **Valley of the Gods**
SCENIC DRIVE | A red fairyland of slender spires and buttes, the Valley of the Gods is a smaller version of Monument Valley. Approximately 15 miles west of Bluff, you can take a pretty drive through this relatively unvisited area on 17-mile-long Valley of the Gods Road, which begins on U.S. 163 and ends on Highway 261. **TIP→ The road is unpaved but should be drivable as long as it's dry.** ✉ *Mexican Hat* ☎ *435/587–1500* 🌐 *www.bluffutah.org.*

🍴 Restaurants

Comb Ridge Eat + Drink
$$ | **AMERICAN** | One of the best restaurants in the area, this eclectic spot is housed in a false-fronted wooden building that looks straight of an old cowboy movie. The menu includes burgers, sandwiches, pastas, and salads—often with creative flares and fun names. **Known for:** signature pork poutine; fish-and-chips; craft beer and local wine. [$] *Average main: $17* ✉ *409 Main. St., Bluff* ☎ *435/487–8441* 🌐 *www.combridgeeatanddrink.com* ⏲ *Closed Sun. and Mon.*

Twin Rocks Cafe
$$ | **SOUTHWESTERN** | This diner, nestled under two striking rock spires on the edge of town, serves up some of the best fry bread around—especially good as a side with the hearty, Southwestern-inspired breakfasts and big Navajo tacos. The menu also features delicious steaks, sandwiches, and nachos, plus a selection of beer, which is not always available in small-town Utah. **Known for:** Navajo fry bread and other Native-inspired dishes; delicious and filling breakfasts; locally crafted jewelry and weavings in the trading post. [$] *Average main: $21* ✉ *913 E. Navajo Twins Dr., Bluff* ☎ *435/672–2341* 🌐 *www.facebook.com/twinrockscafe.*

🛏 Hotels

★ **Bluff Dwellings Resort & Spa**
$$ | **HOTEL** | Built right up next to the red-rock cliffs, this boutique hotel makes you feel like you're in the wilderness, even though you're on the edge of town and surrounded by luxurious amenities. **Pros:** inspired by indigenous design, beautiful inside and out; on-site spa offers plenty of services to pamper you; the most luxurious lodging in the area. **Cons:** breakfast not included; no elevator; hefty pet fee. [$] *Rooms from: $200* ✉ *2625 S. Hwy. 191, Bluff* ☎ *435/672–2477* 🌐 *www.bluffdwellings.com* 🛏 *56 rooms* 🍴 *No Meals.*

Desert Rose Resort & Cabins
$$ | **HOTEL** | A local fixture for decades, this centrally located hotel exudes rustic elegance, with a huge, two-story wooden front porch, several smartly furnished cabins, and a series of larger suites set around a courtyard. **Pros:** large bathrooms; in-house restaurant; pool and hot tub. **Cons:** no pets allowed; spendy for the area; a long drive from many attractions. [$] *Rooms from: $199* ✉ *701 W. Main St., Bluff* ☎ *435/672–2303* 🌐 *www.desertroseinn.com* 🛏 *53 rooms* 🍴 *No Meals.*

Recapture Lodge
$ | **HOTEL** | **FAMILY** | Maybe the best deal in all southeastern Utah, this family-operated inn sits right on the river, with clean, basic rooms and a pool that's a godsend on blisteringly hot days. **Pros:** shady grounds with riverside chairs and walking trails; pool and hot tub; pets and horses welcome. **Cons:** fills up quickly during the busy season; older property with small rooms and basic amenities; pool not close to rooms. [$] *Rooms from: $110* ✉ *250 E. Main St., Bluff* ☎ *435/672–2281* 🌐 *www.recapturelodge.*

Where the West Was Filmed

Without Hollywood—and a little help from Harry Goulding—Monument Valley might have remained a quiet, hidden enclave of the Navajo Nation. But Goulding urged John Ford to help bring the beauty of Monument Valley to the attention of the American public. Ford began in 1938 with his classic movie *Stagecoach*, and the film notoriety never ended. Ford subsequently filmed *My Darling Clementine* and *She Wore a Yellow Ribbon* here during the 1940s. Then came *The Searchers*, *Sergeant Rutledge*, and *Cheyenne Autumn*. And those were just the John Ford westerns. *Billy the Kid*, *Kit Carson*, *Fort Apache*, *How the West Was Won*, and Disney's Academy Award-winning *The Living Desert* were also filmed there.

While the popularity of westerns has waned, Monument Valley is still frequently seen as a backdrop for automobile and other commercials.

Dozens of films have been shot in the area, including a few classics (and nonclassics): *2001: A Space Odyssey*, *Easy Rider*, *The Moviemakers*, *National Lampoon's Vacation*, *Back to the Future Part III*, *Forrest Gump*, *Pontiac Moon*, *Waiting to Exhale*, and *The Lone Ranger*.

While many people associate Monument Valley with filmmaking or as a home to the Navajo Nation, others cannot think about the area without remembering Harry Goulding and his wife, Mike, who established the trading post there in 1923. The Gouldings, who were fluent in the Navajo language, offered crucial trading services to the Navajos for more than half a century. Today Goulding's Trading Post is on the National Register of Historic Places and still provides lodging, meals, and other services to tourists who visit the area.

---

com ☉ *Closed Dec.–Feb.* ⤴ *25 rooms* ¶○¶ *Free Breakfast.*

Activities

RIVER EXPEDITIONS
Wild River Expeditions
BOATING | FAMILY | The San Juan River is one of the prettiest floats in the region, and this reliable outfitter can take you on one- to seven-day trips. They are known for educational adventures that emphasize the geology, natural history, and archaeological wonders of the area. ✉ *2625 S. U.S. 191, Bluff* ☎ *435/672–2244* ⊕ *www.riversandruins.com* ✉ *From $199.*

Mexican Hat

20 miles southwest of Bluff.

The sleepy town of Mexican Hat lies on the north bank of the San Juan River. Named for a nearby rock formation, which you can't miss on the way into town, this is a jumping-off point for two geological wonders: the Goosenecks and Monument Valley. The latter, stretching south into Arizona, is home to generations of Navajo farmers and is very recognizable as the backdrop for many old westerns. About a half-hour from Monument Valley, Mexican Hat offers cheaper accommodations than those inside the tribal park.

GETTING HERE AND AROUND
From Bluff, go south on U.S. 191 for about 4½ miles to the intersection of U.S. 191 and U.S. 163. Take U.S. 163 into Mexican Hat.

 # Sights

Goosenecks State Park
STATE/PROVINCIAL PARK | FAMILY | Stare down the spectacular, 1,000-foot cliffs, and you can see how this remote park got its name: the San Juan River's serpentine course resembles the necks of geese. Geologists also say this is the best example of an "entrenched meander" in the world, including rock 300 million years old. The nighttime skies here are legendary, and in 2021 Goosenecks officially became an International Dark Sky Park, a recognition from the International Dark Sky Association. Camping sites are all first-come, first-served. You'll find the park 8 miles northwest of Mexican Hat off Highway 261. ✉ *Hwy. 316, Mexican Hat* ☎ *435/678–3348* ⊕ *stateparks.utah.gov/* 💲 *$8 per vehicle.*

Moki Dugway
SCENIC DRIVE | Northwest of the Valley of the Gods, Highway 261 takes you to the Moki Dugway, a graded road that was bulldozed out of a cliff during the uranium boom. It's been improved since it was originally built, but its steep grade and tight switchbacks still provide thrills sufficient for most drivers. From the top of the cliff you're rewarded with outrageous views south over the Navajo Reservation with Monument Valley visible more than 20 miles away. This drive is not recommended for vehicles more than 28 feet in length or weighing more than 10,000 pounds. ✉ *Hwy. 261, 9 miles north of Hwy. 163, Mexican Hat.*

★ Monument Valley Navajo Tribal Park
INDIGENOUS SIGHT | FAMILY | For the most breathtaking (and recognizable) views of the iconic West, this is the place. The soaring red buttes, eroded mesas, deep canyons, and naturally sculpted rock formations found here are an easy 21-mile drive south of Mexican Hat on U.S. 163 across Navajo land. Monument Valley is a small part of the more-than-7-million acre Navajo Reservation and is sacred to the Navajo Nation, or Diné (pronounced din-*eh,* which means "the people"), as they refer to themselves. For generations, the Navajo have grown crops and herded sheep in Monument Valley, considered to be one of the most scenic and mesmerizing destinations in the Navajo Nation. Director John Ford made this fantasy land of buttes, towering rock formations, and mesas popular when he filmed *Stagecoach* here in 1938.

The 90,000-acre Monument Valley Navajo Tribal Park lies within Monument Valley. A 17-mile self-guided driving tour on a dirt road (there's only one road, so you can't get lost) passes the memorable Mittens and Totem Pole formations, among others. Drive slowly, and be sure to walk (15 minutes round-trip) from North Window around the end of Cly Butte for the views. Call ahead for road conditions in winter. The Monument Valley visitor center has a small crafts shop and exhibits devoted to ancient and modern Native American history. Most of the independent guided tours here use enclosed vans and you will usually be approached in the parking lot; you can find about a dozen approved Navajo Native American guides in the center. They will escort you to places you are not allowed to visit on your own. This surreal landscape constantly changes with the rising and setting sun.

✉ *Visitor center, off U.S. 163, 21 miles south of Mexican Hat, Monument Valley* ☎ *435/727–5870 park visitor center, 928/871–6647 Navajo Parks & Recreation Dept.* ⊕ *www.navajonationparks.org* 💲 *$8 per person.*

Muley Point Overlook
SCENIC DRIVE | Five miles beyond the Moki Dugway turnoff on Highway 263 brings you to the Muley Point Overlook, which

has a panoramic view of the Goose-necks of the San Juan River, the Valley of the Gods, and Monument Valley. It's also 1,000 feet higher in elevation than the Goosenecks overlook farther south. ⊠ *Muley Point Rd., Mexican Hat.*

Hotels

Goulding's Lodge

$$ | HOTEL | With spectacular views of Monument Valley from each room's private balcony, this historic lodge often serves as a base for film crews in the area—and has for years, as cinema greats John Wayne and John Ford used to stay here. **Pros:** stunning views; one of the only lodgings in the park; dark skies and quiet nights. **Cons:** it's miles from anything in any direction; prices fluctuate wildly; you pay a high price for the unique setting. $ *Rooms from: $145* ⊠ *Off U.S. 163, Monument Valley* ⊹ *22 miles south-west of Mexican Hat* ☎ *435/727–3231* ⊕ *www.gouldings.com* ⤳ *151 rooms* ⏺ *No Meals.*

San Juan Inn

$$ | HOTEL | This peaceful spot is a well-known launching point for white-water runners on the San Juan, a river that's famed as the setting of many of Tony Hillerman's Jim Chee mystery novels. **Pros:** the peaceful setting with lovely views of the San Juan River; only 20 miles from Monument Valley; trading post and restaurant on site. **Cons:** aging rooms; spotty Wi-Fi; there's not much to do besides watch the river roll by (but that may be just what you're looking for). $ *Rooms from: $138* ⊠ *U.S. 163, Mexican Hat* ☎ *435/683–2220* ⊕ *www.sanjuaninn.net* ⊗ *Closed Dec.–mid-Feb.* ⤳ *37 rooms* ⏺ *No Meals.*

The View Hotel

$$$ | HOTEL | Aptly named, the hotel is all about the vista—prices increase the higher the floor, and almost every room looks out to the Navajo Tribal Park's famous "Mittens." The rooms are fairly simple, though the Navajo sand paintings, authentic rugs, and traditional bedspreads make for nice touches. **Pros:** wonderful views from private decks; the only hotel actually inside the tribal park; for budget travelers, some rooms without views are available at a steep discount. **Cons:** simple rooms for the price; Wi-Fi and cell reception are spotty; restaurant could be better. $ *Rooms from: $239* ⊠ *Monument Valley Navajo Tribal Park, Indian Hwy. 42* ⊹ *Off U.S. 163, 25 miles southwest of Mexican Hat* ☎ *435/727–5555* ⊕ *monumentvalleyview. com* ⤳ *96 rooms* ⏺ *No Meals.*

Lake Powell

97 miles west of Blanding via Hwy. 95 and Hwy. 276.

The placid waters of Lake Powell allow you to depart the landed lifestyle and float away on your own houseboat. With 96 major side canyons spread across 186 miles, you can spend months exploring more than 2,000 miles of shoreline. Every water sport imaginable awaits, from waterskiing to fishing. On the Arizona side, the small community of Page offers plenty of hotels, restaurants, and shops for restocking vital supplies. The nearby Wahweap Marina, is a major hub for services and a fleet of houseboats, watercraft rentals, powerboats, pontoon boats, kayaks, water toys, and boat tours. On the Utah side, Bullfrog Marina offers houseboat and watercraft rentals. Other services can be found at Halls Crossing Marina, but because of the water levels the boat launch ramp there is not operational.

Due to an ongoing drought across the West, Lake Powell's water levels have dropped to historic lows in recent years, and you should take that into consideration before any trip.

Stunning Lake Powell is worth the journey.

GETTING HERE AND AROUND

Getting here can be your biggest challenge, so it's best to plan ahead whenever possible. Contour Airlines serves Page, Arizona, from Phoenix. To get to Bullfrog, Utah, it's a 2½-hour drive from Canyonlands Regional Airport in Moab (served by Delta and United) and 3½ hours from the Grand Junction Regional Airport in neighboring Colorado.

Many people visit Lake Powell as part of grand drives across the southwestern United States. Bullfrog, Utah, is about 300 miles from Salt Lake City via I–15 to I–70 to U.S. 95 south. Take I–70 from Colorado and the east. Take U.S. 191 from either Wyoming or Arizona. Most roads are well-maintained two-lane highways, though snow can be a factor in winter. Be sure your car is in good working order as there are long stretches of empty road, and top off the gas tank whenever possible.

 Sights

Lake Powell

BODY OF WATER | FAMILY | With a shoreline longer than America's Pacific coast, Lake Powell is the heart of the huge 1.25-millon-acre Glen Canyon National Recreation Area. Created by the Glen Canyon Dam—a 710-foot wall of concrete in the Colorado River—Lake Powell took 17 years to fill. The second-largest man-made lake in the nation, it extends through terrain so rugged that it was the last major area of the country to be mapped. Red cliffs ring the lake and twist off into 96 major canyons and countless inlets with huge, red-sandstone buttes randomly jutting from the sapphire waters.

The most popular thing to do at Lake Powell is to rent a houseboat and chug leisurely across the lake, exploring coves and inlets. Like many tourist spots in the region, the lake's busiest times are in the summer, with peak visitation on holiday weekends. Book far in advance for those dates. It's also important to check with the National Park Service for current water levels, closures, and other weather-related conditions.

Southwest of Bullfrog, Rainbow Bridge National Monument is the largest natural bridge in the world, and its 290-foot-high, 275-foot-wide span is a breathtaking sight. Unfortunately, accessing this wonder is difficult. You can either hike a 14-mile trail from the Navajo Nation or boat in, though the National Park Service had to pull its dock back from the water in 2021 due to low water levels and damage from storms, with no estimate for restoring its original location. Small boats and vessels still have access to the shoreline but getting to the trail requires wading through water and mud. No special permit is needed to boat into the monument, but hiking in from the Navajo Nation requires a permit issued by the Navajo Nation Parks and Recreation Department (🌐 www.navajonationparks.org). The main visitor center for Lake Powell is Arizona's Wahweap Marina, with a campground, general store, restaurants, swimming pools, boat docks, and houseboat rentals. ✉ *Bullfrog visitor center, Hwy. 276* ☎ *435/684–7420* 🌐 *www.lakepowell.com.*

Hotels

★ Amangiri

$$$$ | RESORT | One of just five U.S. properties operated by the famously luxurious Aman resort company (three are big-city hotels), this ultraplush and ultraexpensive 34-suite compound lies just a few miles north of Lake Powell on a 900-acre plot of rugged high desert, soaring red rock cliffs, and jagged mesas. **Pros:** stunning accommodations inside and out; rates include meals, group hikes, and wellness classes; world-class restaurant and spa, with meals and wellness classes included. **Cons:** many times more expensive than most accommodations in the area; extremely remote; though all-inclusive, alcohol drinks and spa treatments are extra. [$] *Rooms from: $2800* ✉ *1 Kayenta Rd., Canyon Point* ✣ *15 miles northwest of Page, off U.S. 89* ☎ *435/675–3999, 877/695–3999 reservations* 🌐 *www.aman.com* 🛏 *34 suites* 🍴 *All-Inclusive.*

Defiance House Lodge

$$ | HOTEL | At the Bullfrog Marina, this cliff-top lodge has comfortable and clean rooms anyone can appreciate, but the real draw is the view of the lake. **Pros:** beautiful lakefront setting; adjacent restaurant; pets allowed for nightly fee. **Cons:** very remote; no general store for miles; aging rooms. [$] *Rooms from: $150* ☎ *435/684–2233, 888/896–3829* 🌐 *www.lakepowell.com* 🛏 *48 rooms* 🍴 *No Meals.*

Dreamkatchers Lake Powell Bed and Breakfast

$$ | B&B/INN | This sleek, contemporary Southwestern-style home sits on a bluff just a few miles northwest of Lake Powell and 15 miles from Page. **Pros:** peaceful and secluded location perfect for stargazing; delicious breakfasts; friendly host. **Cons:** often booked months in advance; few services in the remote surrounding area; pets not allowed. [$] *Rooms from: $200* ✉ *1055 S. American Way, Big Water* ☎ *435/675–5828* 🌐 *www.dreamkatchers-lakepowell.com* 🕒 *Closed mid-Nov.–mid-Mar.* 🛏 *3 rooms* 🍴 *Free Breakfast.*

Activities

Lake Powell Resorts & Marinas

BOATING | Boating and fishing are the major sports at Lake Powell. Conveniently, all powerboat rentals and tours are conducted by this company. Daylong tours (departing from Wahweap Marina near Page, Arizona) go to Rainbow Bridge or Antelope Canyon. There's also a tour that goes into some of the more interesting canyons and a dinner cruise. The company rents houseboats for anyone looking to make their stay here last. ✉ *Bullfrog Marina, Hwy. 276, Lake Powell* ☎ *800/528–6154* 🌐 *www.lakepowell.com* 🎟 *Tours start at $48.*

Photo Credits

Front Cover: Steve Greenwood / Alamy Stock Photo [**Description:** In this vertical shot the late-afternoon sun lights up The Castle formation in Capitol Reef National Park Utah]. **Back cover, from left to right:** Byelikova/Dreamstime. johnnya123/ iStock-523155758. FashionStock.com/Shutterstock. **Spine:** Kanonsky/ iStockphoto. **Interior, from left to right:** David Pettit/Visit Utah (1), Larry C. Price/Visit Utah (2-3). **Chapter 1: Experience Utah:** Sandra Salvas/Visit Utah (6-7). Courtesy of Deer Valley Resort (8-9). Utah Office of Tourism (9). Maridav / Shutterstock (9). Utah Office of Tourism/Steve Greenwood (10). Courtesy of Natural History Museum of Utah (10). Johnnya123/ Dreamstime (10). North2south/Dreamstime (11). ImageBROKER / Alamy (12). Dndavis/Dreamstime (12). Gestalt Imagery/Shutterstock (12). Jakub Zajic/Dreamstime (12). Austen Diamond Photography/Visit Salt Lake (13). Slrcrazy/Dreamstime (13). AustralianCamera/Shutterstock (13). Lucky-photographer/ Shutterstock (13). Ian Dagnall / Alamy (14). Keith/Shutterstock (14). Michael Runkel Utah / Alamy (14). Douglas Pulsipher/Visit Salt Lake City (15). Greg Gard / Alamy (15). Bettie Grace Miner (18). Courtesy_Alta's Rustler Lodge (18). Mike Tittel (18). St. Regis/Deer Valley (19). Eric Schramm Photography/Solitude Mountain Resort (19). Matt Morgan/Visit Utah (20). Tristanbnz/Dreamstime (20). Larry C. Price/Visit Utah (20). Galyna Andrushko / Alamy (21). Rob Maille/Shutterstock (21). Trevor Hooper Photo.com/Courtesy Of HighWest Distillery (22). Bill Coker Photography/Courtesy of Red Iguana (23). **Chapter 3: Salt Lake City:** f11photo/Shutterstock (45). Nagel Photography/Shutterstock (54). Chris Curtis/Shutterstock (59). Matthew Thomas Allen/Shutterstock (79). Walencienne (88). Kristi Blokhin/Shutterstock (97). **Chapter 4: Park City and the Southern Wasatch:** Johnnya123/iStockphoto (101). Sean Pavone/iStockphoto (108). Johnnya123/iStockphoto (121). Johnny Adolphson/Shutterstock (129). Glacieli Borges Hendler/Shutterstock (133). Robert Crum/Shutterstock (141). **Chapter 5: Northern Utah:** Guy In Utah/Shutterstock (143). Ritu Manoj Jethani/Shutterstock (151). Ritu Manoj Jethani/ Shutterstock (154). Guy In Utah/Shutterstock (158). Layne V. Naylor/ Shutterstock (162). EQRoy/Shutterstock (168). **Chapter 6: Dinosaurland and Eastern Utah:** Jnerad/Shutterstock (173). Zack Frank/ Shutterstock (183). Galyna Andrushko/Shutterstock (186). Luc Novovitch / Alamy Stock Photo (189). Claudia Johnson/Shutterstock (192). **Chapter 7: Capitol Reef National Park:** JeniFoto/Shutterstock (199). Edmund Lowe Photography/ Shutterstock (205). Chris Blashill/Shutterstock (208). **Chapter 8: Zion National Park:** Checubus/Shutterstock (213). Bjul/Shutterstock (222). **Chapter 9: Bryce Canyon National Park:** Lorcel/Shutterstock (227). Humorousking207/Dreamstime (237). **Chapter 10: Southwestern Utah:** Harry Beugelink/ Shutterstock (239). Tristanbnz/iStockphoto (251). kojihirano/iStockphoto (264). Will Sylwester/Shutterstock (270). Smaks K/Shutterstock (281). **Chapter 11: Arches National Park:** Colin D. Young/Shutterstock (285). Checubus/Shutterstock (291). **Chapter 12: Canyonlands National Park:** Edwin Verin/shutterstock (297). Alex Grichenko/Dreamstime (306). **Chapter 13: Moab and Southeastern Utah:** Dmitry Pichugin/Shutterstock (309). Abbie Warnock-Matthews/ Shutterstock (328). Inc/Shutterstock (335). Johnny Adolphson/Shutterstock (341). **About Our Writers:** All photos are courtesy of the writers.

*Every effort has been made to trace the copyright holders, and we apologize in advance for any accidental errors. We would be happy to apply the corrections in the following edition of this publication.

Notes

Fodor's UTAH

Publisher: Stephen Horowitz, *General Manager*

Editorial: Douglas Stallings, *Editorial Director;* Jill Fergus, Amanda Sadlowski, *Senior Editors;* Brian Eschrich, Alexis Kelly, *Editors;* Angelique Kennedy-Chavannes, *Assistant Editor*

Design: Tina Malaney, *Director of Design and Production;* Jessica Gonzalez, *Senior Designer;* Erin Caceres, *Graphic Design Associate*

Production: Jennifer DePrima, *Editorial Production Manager;* Elyse Rozelle, *Senior Production Editor;* Monica White, *Production Editor*

Maps: Rebecca Baer, *Senior Map Editor;* Mark Stroud (Moon Street Cartography), David Lindroth, *Cartographers*

Photography: Viviane Teles, *Senior Photo Editor;* Namrata Aggarwal, Neha Gupta, Payal Gupta, Ashok Kumar, *Photo Editors;* Eddie Aldrete, *Photo Production Intern;* Kadeem McPherson, *Photo Production Associate Intern*

Business and Operations: Chuck Hoover, *Chief Marketing Officer;* Robert Ames, *Group General Manager*

Public Relations and Marketing: Joe Ewaskiw, *Senior Director of Communications and Public Relations*

Fodors.com: Jeremy Tarr, *Editorial Director;* Rachael Levitt, *Managing Editor*

Technology: Jon Atkinson, *Director of Technology;* Rudresh Teotia, *Associate Director of Technology;* Alison Lieu, *Project Manager*

Writers: Andrew Collins, Stina Sieg, Tessa Woolf

Editor: Douglas Stallings

Production Editor: Jennifer DePrima

8th Edition

ISBN 978-1-64097-570-5

ISSN 1547–870X

All details in this book are based on information supplied to us at press time. Always confirm information when it matters, especially if you're making a detour to visit a specific place. Fodor's expressly disclaims any liability, loss, or risk, personal or otherwise, that is incurred as a consequence of the use of any of the contents of this book.

SPECIAL SALES

This book is available at special discounts for bulk purchases for sales promotions or premiums. For more information, e-mail SpecialMarkets@fodors.com.

PRINTED IN CHINA

10 9 8 7 6 5 4 3 2 1

About Our Writers

Former Fodor's staff editor **Andrew Collins** is based in both Mexico City and a small village in New Hampshire's Lake Sunapee region, but he spends much of his time traveling throughout the United States. He updated the Experience, Salt Lake City, Capitol Reef National Park, Bryce Canyon National Park, Zion National Park, and Southwestern Utah chapters. A longtime contributor to more than 200 Fodor's guidebooks, including *Pacific Northwest, Utah, Santa Fe, Inside Mexico City,* and *New England,* he's also written for dozens of mainstream and LGBTQ+ publications—*Travel + Leisure, New Mexico Magazine, AAA Living, The Advocate,* and *Canadian Traveller* among them. Additionally, Collins teaches travel writing and food writing for New York City's Gotham Writers Workshop. You can find more of his work at *AndrewsTraveling.com* and follow him on Instagram *@TravelAndrew.*

Stina Sieg has been in love with the desert ever since she moved to New Mexico in a vintage trailer at the age of 22. She's worked for newspapers and radio stations across the Southwest—including in Moab, Utah—and now cools her heels just over the Colorado border in Grand Junction, where she's the Western Slope reporter for Colorado Public Radio. For this edition, she updated the Dinosaurland and Eastern Utah, Arches National Park, Canyonlands National Park, and Moab and Southeastern Utah chapters.

Tessa Woolf is a freelance writer and editor based in Salt Lake City, Utah. Her work has appeared in the pages of *Park City Magazine, Salt Lake Magazine, Utah Style & Design, Portland Monthly, Aspen Sojourner,* and more. When she's not hitting the road to explore her beloved home state, she's catching a flight to visit destinations near and far. She updated the Park City and the Southern Wasatch and the Northern Utah chapters for this edition.